TASC

Test Assessing Secondary Completion™

for
dummies®
A Wiley Brand

by Stuart Donnelly, PhD
with Nicole Hersey
Ron Olson
Kathy Peno, PhD
Shannon Reed
Connie Sergent, MEd

for
dummies®
A Wiley Brand

TASC Test Assessing Secondary Completion™ For Dummies®

Published by: **John Wiley & Sons, Inc.**, 111 River Street, Hoboken, NJ 07030-5774, www.wiley.com

Copyright © 2016 by John Wiley & Sons, Inc., Hoboken, New Jersey

Published simultaneously in Canada

For general information on our other products and services, please contact our Customer Care Department within the U.S. at 877-762-2974, outside the U.S. at 317-572-3993, or fax 317-572-4002. For technical support, please visit https://hub.wiley.com/community/support/dummies.

Wiley publishes in a variety of print and electronic formats and by print-on-demand. Some material included with standard print versions of this book may not be included in e-books or in print-on-demand. If this book refers to media such as a CD or DVD that is not included in the version you purchased, you may download this material at http://booksupport.wiley.com. For more information about Wiley products, visit www.wiley.com.

Library of Congress Control Number: 2016947157

ISBN 978-1-118-96643-3 (pbk); ISBN 978-1-118-96645-7 (ebk); ISBN 978-1-118-96644-0 (ebk)

Manufactured in the United States of America

10 9 8 7 6 5 4 3 2 1

Contents at a Glance

Table of Contents

Introduction

Congratulations! You've just made two very smart decisions. First, you've decided to pursue your high-school equivalency, which is one of the smartest decisions you'll ever make, and second, by purchasing this book, you've decided to get the expert help you may need to achieve your goal.

Now that you've decided to get your high-school equivalency, you have several options open to you. First, you can always go back to your old high school and finish off your diploma the old-fashioned way. But I'm guessing that probably doesn't sound very appealing to you right now. After all, who wants to sit in a classroom full of teenagers who are all nudging each other and asking, "Ew! What's that *old* person doing here?" Besides, you would probably have to quit your job to attend classes every day, and even worse, that old history teacher whose classes you flunked will probably still be there (after all, who else is going to hire him?!). So let's assume that this first option isn't for you.

Your second option would be to attend night school. The problem with this option is that the courses you may need to graduate are likely to be spread out throughout the year, and the timing of each course may clash with your work schedule. It could take forever to finish — but on the bright side, at least you wouldn't be getting the stink-eye from a bunch of snarky teens (and your old history teacher!). But let's assume that this second option isn't your cup of tea either.

Don't despair — luckily, *TASC For Dummies* presents you with a third option that I think you're going to like a whole lot better. It goes something like this: Take the TASC test and earn your high-school diploma in the shortest time possible, without ever having to share a classroom with other people.

If that sounds more like it, then keep on reading — you've come to the right place!

About This Book

TASC For Dummies is an essential study tool — consider it your instruction manual for succeeding on the new TASC test. We explain everything you need to know before test day — what subject areas are tested, how long the exam is, what the test format is, how to register, how the test is scored, and so on.

Just as important, we walk you through how the new TASC test has changed to conform with Common Core State Standards and why it has replaced the GED exam in many states. Some of the question formats have changed as well, so to help you step up your game, this book includes in-depth analysis and samples of each type of question that can appear on the new TASC. These include constructive-response questions, evidence-based selected response questions, drag-and-drop questions, multiple-select response questions, and so forth.

This book also contains an in-depth subject review for each of the five subject areas: Language Arts Reading, Language Arts Writing, Mathematics, Social Studies, and Science, along with useful tips to help you understand the main concepts of each topic.

To give you an idea of how ready you are to take the new TASC, we also include two full-length practice tests in the book. These practice tests have been designed to simulate a TASC exam and are as close to the real thing as you can get. Try taking each part of the test under exam conditions to get a good idea of how you'll do on the real exam.

After taking each test, go through the answers and explanations so you can determine which subject areas you still need to work on. Then head back to the appropriate in-depth subject review chapter to brush up on those topics or concepts that you haven't yet mastered.

Foolish Assumptions

In writing this book, we assume several things about you, the reader, including the following:

» You are serious about achieving your high-school equivalency and want to pass the TASC with minimum effort and maximum efficiency.

» You've made getting your TASC a priority in your life because you want to advance in the workplace or move on to college.

» You're willing to give up some free time and activities to prepare properly for the TASC.

» You have sufficient English language skills to handle the test. (*Note:* The TASC is also available in Spanish.)

» You've already checked that the state you live in currently offers the TASC as a high-school equivalency test.

» You've already checked to make sure that you meet your state's requirements regarding age, residency, and the length of time since leaving school that make you eligible to take the TASC exam. (Double-check with your local TASC test administrator to find out your state's requirements.)

» You want a fun and friendly guide that will help you to stay on track to achieve your goal.

Icons Used in This Book

Icons are those cute little pictures that appear in the margins of this book. They indicate why you should pay special attention to the accompanying text. Here's how to decode them:

TIP

This icon points out helpful hints about strategy — what the strong test-takers already know and the rookies want to find out.

WARNING

This icon identifies the traps that the TASC-writers are hoping you fall into as you take the test. Take note of these warnings so you know what to do (and what not to do) as you move from question to question on the real TASC.

REMEMBER

When you see this icon, be sure to file away the information that accompanies it. The material will come in handy as you prepare for (and take) the new TASC.

EXAMPLE

This icon identifies questions that resemble those on the actual TASC. Be sure to read the answer explanations that always follow the questions.

Beyond the Book

In addition to the book content, you can find valuable free material online. We provide you with a Cheat Sheet that addresses important things you need to know and consider when getting ready for the TASC test. You can access this material by going to www.dummies.com and searching for "TASC Test Assessing Secondary Completion For Dummies Cheat Sheet" in the Search box.

Where to Go from Here

Some people like to read books from beginning to end. Others prefer to read only the specific information they need to know now. Either way, we've arranged the book into eight parts, which will make it easy for you to find exactly what you're looking for.

The chapters in Part 1 start off with an overview of the TASC test and how to register for the exam. For those of you who feel unsure about how best to prepare for a standardized test like the TASC, we also provide you with a wealth of study tips that will help to get you on the right path. We also review the different types of questions and how you can prepare for those subjects.

The chapters in Parts 2, 3, 4, 5, and 6 go into detail about each of the test sections. In each of those parts, you find information on the number of questions and the time permitted for that section.

When you're ready to dive into full-length practice tests that mimic the real TASC test, check out the chapters in Part 7. Be sure to check your answers with the detailed answer explanations we provide for each test section (but be sure to wait until *after* you take the practice tests to look at the answers!).

The chapters in Part 8 provide you with our top ten tips that will help you to maximize your score on the TASC and calm those pre-test jitters leading up to the morning of test day. We even include some advice on what to do right before the test starts to stay focused and relaxed.

No matter what you do next, start by doing something simple: Keep calm and carry on, and score big on the TASC.

1

Getting Started with the TASC

IN THIS PART . . .

Understand the differences between the TASC and GED.

Review the different sections and question formats of the TASC.

Improve your study skills.

Explore strategies to enhance your chances for success.

Chapter 1

Making Sense of the TASC

In this chapter, we explore the differences between the TASC test and the GED and why many states have chosen the TASC as their high-school equivalency exam. Because the TASC is aligned to the Common Core State Standards, it's important for you to know what those are. Next, we discuss the topics and format of each of the subject areas covered on the TASC. Lastly, we explore how you'll be scored in each of the different areas and what scores you need to get your TASC diploma.

Why the TASC and Not the GED?

In many states, such as New York, West Virginia, and Indiana, the TASC has replaced the GED completely. Students living in those states who are pursuing their high-school equivalency can no longer take the GED exam — they must take the TASC instead. It's worth double-checking which high-school equivalency options your state permits. Some states only offer the GED, others only offer the TASC, and others give students a choice between the GED and the TASC. Either way, it's good to keep in mind that not all high-school equivalency exams are created equal.

Two of the most noticeable differences between the TASC and GED tests are the cost and the format flexibility. The price of the TASC is more reasonable and affordable than that of the GED, and the exam is also available as a paper-and-pencil test as well as online. If English isn't your native language, you also have the option of taking the Spanish version of the TASC. There are also large-print, Braille, and audio versions of the TASC available for those students with special needs.

Another advantage that the TASC has over the GED exam is that the TASC is gradually being aligned to the Common Core State Standards. This will help you stay competitive for both career and college opportunities by showing that your abilities and knowledge in each subject are of the right standard to help you succeed.

Lastly, the types of scores you receive from taking the TASC are both College and Career Readiness (CCR) scores and passing scores. Earning a satisfactory CCR score shows how well-prepared you are and that you can compete with any American high school graduate!

Getting Up to Speed with Common Core

The Common Core State Standards provide a consistent, clear understanding of what students are expected to learn so teachers and parents know what they need to do to help them. The Standards are designed to be robust and relevant to the real world, reflecting the knowledge and skills that our young people need for success in college and careers. With American students fully prepared for the future, our communities will be best positioned to compete successfully in the global economy.

—Common Core State Standards Initiative

Today's students need to be better prepared than ever to handle the increasing demands of colleges and industry. Previously, each state in America used to have its own academic curriculum. This meant that it was virtually impossible to compare students from different states because the curriculum and standards for graduating high school varied greatly from state to state. But all that changed recently with the release of the Common Core State Standards (CCSS), which establish clear, consistent guidelines for what every student needs to know in math and English language arts (ELA) from kindergarten through 12th grade.

The Common Core State Standards were drafted by leading experts and teachers throughout the country and are designed to ensure that all students will be ready for success after high school. By focusing on developing critical-thinking, problem-solving, and analytical skills, the Common Core helps prepare students for today's freshman-level college courses, workforce training programs, and entry-level careers.

Currently, CCSS are available in ELA and mathematics, with strands devoted to the other content areas such as social studies and science. Forty-two states so far have voluntarily adopted the CCSS and are moving forward with their full implementation. Teachers in those states now have a way to measure all students' progress throughout the school year to ensure that they're on the right path to success in their academic careers.

REMEMBER

The CCSS have a greater focus on rigor and knowing a topic in depth. This means at each successive grade level, a topic is looked at again in a more detailed way. When educators and policy makers discuss *rigor*, they mean that there are now higher goals for all students. In addition, there's a greater emphasis on using evidence in all subject areas. Analyzing and using nonfiction texts are common practices in high schools today as well. In mathematics and science, there's a greater focus on solving real-world problems, methods of solving or experimenting in different situations, and the use of models.

In other words, the TASC exam just became a little bit tougher to pass! But the good news is that the new format will better prepare you for the challenging world of work or college.

TIP

To register for the TASC, visit http://www.tasctest.com and follow the instructions.

Exploring the New TASC Exam

The TASC exam measures high-school equivalency and college and career readiness in five subject areas: Language Arts–Reading, Language Arts–Writing, Mathematics, Social Studies, and Science. The entire test lasts about seven hours, with each section having its own time limits.

Subject sections

This section breaks down what each of the TASC subtests covers, what kind of questions you can expect, and how long you have to complete each subtest. With the advance of new technology, the question format for the test may change and become more interactive over time.

Language Arts–Reading

The Language Arts–Reading test includes multiple-choice, constructed-response, and technology-enhanced questions that test the student's ability to understand the information presented in excerpts from novels, short stories, poetry, plays, newspapers, magazines, and business or legal text passages. The test includes both literary (30 percent) and informational (70 percent) texts. The time limit for this section is 75 minutes, and the test consists of 50 questions.

Language Arts–Writing

The Language Arts–Writing test is separated into two parts: multiple-choice questions and an essay question. Students are expected to answer 50 multiple-choice, technology-enhanced, and constructed-response questions, in which they must identify grammar, spelling, and other mechanical writing errors and demonstrate their ability to make corrections to each sentence. The test has both passage-based items and stand-alone or discrete questions. The time limit for this first part is 60 minutes.

Students are also expected to write an essay that either states and supports a claim or provides information about a particular topic of interest. Essays are scored based on the following criteria: clear and strategic organization, clarity of expression, complete development of ideas, sentence structure, punctuation, grammar, word choice, and spelling. For the essay prompt, you have 45 minutes to construct a response to a passage, excerpt, or multiple selections.

Mathematics

The Mathematics section has five main fields: numbers and quantity (13 percent), algebra (26 percent), functions (26 percent), geometry (23 percent), and statistics and probability (12 percent). Most questions are word problems and involve real-life situations or require students to interpret information presented in diagrams, charts, graphs, and tables. Students are given a math summary sheet of formulas to use during the test. Be sure to become familiar with what formulas are on the sheet and which ones you need to remember. The question styles found in this section are multiple choice (40 questions) and gridded response (12 questions).

Section 1 of the Mathematics test allows the use of a calculator and has a time limit of 50 minutes. Section 2 does *not* permit the use of a calculator and has a time limit of 55 minutes.

Social Studies

The Social Studies exam tests students on five fields: U.S. history (25 percent), world history (15 percent), civics and government (25 percent), geography (15 percent), and economics (20 percent). The Social Studies test gauges students' understanding of the basic principles in each of those areas and tests their ability to interpret information presented in passages, illustrations, graphs, and charts. You have 75 minutes to complete the 47 multiple-choice, technology-enhanced, and constructed-response questions.

Science

The Science test focuses on multiple-choice questions pulled from three main fields: physical science (36 percent), life science (36 percent), and earth and space science (28 percent). Each discipline is subdivided into several core ideas. Questions may require the student to recall knowledge, apply knowledge and skills, or reason. The number of test questions per core idea depends on the number of performance expectations within that core idea (usually about two to five questions). You have 85 minutes to complete the 47 multiple-choice questions.

New question formats

Since 2015, the TASC has begun to feature a variety of new question formats. Because the TASC is now offered as a computer-based test, there are now more options available for online questions and responses. In this section, we list some of the new formats you can expect to see.

TIP

You can also find interactive demonstrations of these new formats on the website: `http://www.tasctest.com`.

Constructed response

A constructed-response item is a short-answer question. Instead of choosing from four multiple-choice answers, you have to come up with your own answer.

Multiple-select response

This type of question is just like the familiar multiple-choice questions that you're probably already used to, but with one big difference — instead of having a single correct answer, there is more than one possible answer, so you have to make sure you read the instructions carefully and select *all* the correct answers.

Evidence-based select response

You may see this format on the Language Arts–Reading test. In the first part, Part A, you read and analyze a text and then choose a conclusion from four multiple-choice options. In the second part, Part B, you choose evidence from the text to support your conclusion in Part A. The second part may be in multiple-choice format or it may be a multiple-select response.

Drag and drop

In this format, on the computer version of the test, you drag and drop the correct responses to complete the blanks or empty boxes in the question stem. In the print edition of this book, you simply draw lines to match answers to these spaces.

TASC at a glance

Table 1-1 summarizes the TASC test and gives the breakdown by approximate number of items and time for each section.

TABLE 1-1 Breakdown of TASC Sections

Subject	Topics	Time in Minutes (English Version)	Time in Minutes (Spanish Version)	Number of Questions
Language Arts–Reading	Information reading & language Literary reading & language	75	80	50
Language Arts–Writing	Language Writing	105	110	50 One essay
Mathematics	Numbers & quantity Algebra Functions Geometry Statistics & probability	50 (calculator) 55 (no calculator)	55 (calculator) 60 (no calculator)	40 12 gridded responses
Social Studies	U.S. history World history Civics & government Geography Economics	75	80	47
Science	Physical science Life science Earth & space science	85	90	47

Scoring: How Do You Measure Up?

Probably the one question that is most important to you is how will you be graded? Each of the multiple-choice and gridded-response questions is worth 1 point. You don't get points off for selecting the wrong answer, so make sure to answer *every* question. Multiple-response questions may be scored differently because they may have more than one correct answer. In reading questions with a Part A and Part B, you must successfully answer Part B to get credit for the question as a whole.

Your essay will be read by two readers who will each score it from 0 to 4. If both scores match or are within a point of each other, then the scores are added together and that is your essay score (out of 8 possible points). For example, if the readers score your essay as a 2 and a 3, then your essay score will be 5. On the other hand, if the two scores differ by more than a point, then a third reader will be asked to score your essay as well. For example, if the two original readers score your essay as a 2 and a 4, that's a 2-point difference, so a third reader will be brought in to read your essay. The sum of the two scores out of the three which are closest together will then be used for your overall score.

The total of all your earned points is your raw score for each section. Your raw score is then put into a mathematical algorithm to compute your scaled score. You'll receive this score (the scaled score) on your score report for each of the five areas. If you earn passing scores on all five sections, then you'll have passed the entire TASC test. The overall score is the average of the five separate subject areas. Passing scores for the subject areas are:

» Language Arts–Reading: 500

» Language Arts–Writing: 500 and at least a 2 out of 8 on the essay

» Mathematics: 500

» Social Studies: 500

» Science: 500

Besides your passing scores, you'll also receive a College and Career Readiness (CCR) score in each of the five areas. This score is used to gauge how likely a person is to succeed in college courses. If you meet or exceed the CCR passing score, then it indicates that you're likely to earn a C or better in college courses in that content area.

Chapter 2

Getting Prepped

In this chapter, we explore the different topics, techniques, and strategies that will help you sharpen your test-taking abilities as you prepare for the rigors of the new TASC exam. Before you begin studying, you need to set up a reasonable, achievable study plan (and then stick to it!), so we kick off the chapter by discussing the things to keep in mind when you're putting your study schedule together. Next, we explore how to sharpen your study skills and focus your attention on the task at hand. After all, there's no use spending hours staring at your textbooks if, at the end of the day, you can't remember anything you've just read. The good news is that studying is a skill that you can learn, so in this chapter we explore the best ways to make all that precious study time count.

Knowing how to use your time wisely also comes in handy during the test itself, so we explore various time management strategies to help you make the most of the limited time available to you. We then discuss some simple test-taking strategies to help you maximize your score and avoid the common mistakes that many students make. Some students find taking a standardized test like the TASC to be extremely nerve-racking, so we conclude the chapter by discussing the best ways to hold it all together on the big day so you're able to achieve the sort of score on the TASC that reflects your full potential.

Honing Your Study Skills

Before you begin studying for the different subject areas, look at the list of topics found in the introduction of each section of this book. Identify the topics you need to focus on and those that you already feel comfortable with. This helps you organize a study plan to use your time wisely. For some topics you may only need a quick review, while for others you may need to reread and study them in depth to get a full understanding of the main concepts. Also, make sure that your study goals are realistic, and try to add a little flexibility into your schedule so that if you start to fall behind in your studies, you don't have to abandon your study plan altogether.

TIP

When it comes to studying for a multiple-subject test like the TASC, you want to become as comfortable as possible with the important vocabulary terms used in each section. Knowing the correct jargon helps you when it comes to reading questions and spotting potential answers. You also want to become familiar with the math formulas sheet that you're given at the front of the Mathematics subtest. Make sure you know which formula to use for each type of question and also which formulae are not given to you during the test. These are the ones you need to memorize.

This book has two complete practice tests that have been designed to simulate the real TASC exam. The time limit and the number of questions you're expected to answer are listed in the directions on the front page of each of the five sections of the test. Take each part of the test under exam conditions to get a good idea of how you'll do on the real exam. This will help you learn how to pace yourself during the real thing, and you'll experience what it feels like to take a full-length test. Taking practice exams is also the best way to become familiar with how the TASC presents the material for each subject and the different question formats that you're likely to see. It's up to you how you use the practice tests. You can use one as a pre-test and one as a post-test or you can use both as practice tests after you've studied.

The Secret to Time Management

Because each section of the TASC exam has a time limit, you want to be conscious of how much time has passed as you're taking the test. One way to manage your time effectively is by simply wearing a watch. Testing centers may not always have a clock available, and you want to be able to see how much time you have left for each section. If you're taking the computer version of the test, depending on the computer interface, there may be a countdown clock feature. You can also minimize the on-screen clock if you don't want to see it ticking down in front of you the whole time.

TIP

Another way to manage your time is to skip questions you're really not sure about. Doing so allows you to focus on those questions that you can actually answer rather than wasting time on the ones that you can't. If you get stuck on a question, skip it and move on to the next. You can always come back to it at the end if you have any time left. In fact, make sure that you do leave enough time to come back to those questions you skipped. Because you don't get points off for wrong answers on the TASC, be sure to answer *all* questions.

Also make sure that you arrive at the testing center with plenty of time to spare. The last thing you want to do is arrive late (in a panic) and waste precious time searching for the correct room (or even the correct building!). Even if you finish the test before the time is up, don't leave early. Instead, use every second available to go back and check your answers and fill in any questions that you left blank.

REMEMBER

Strong test-takers arrive at the testing center early and always stay to the very end of the test.

Test-Taking Strategies

When it comes to taking a multiple-choice test, one of the most effective strategies you have at your disposal is to eliminate unlikely choices. Any choices that you can get rid of because you deem them implausible or unrealistic to the problem at hand will increase your odds of selecting the correct answer. For example, if you have four choices (A, B, C, and D) and you know the answer can't be A or D, then you now have a 50 percent chance of selecting the correct answer instead of the 25 percent chance you had before you eliminated two of the options.

TIP

If the question stem provides you with additional information such as charts, pictures, or tables, make sure you look at these carefully before selecting your answer. This additional information has been provided to you for a reason, so don't ignore it!

Another important strategy is to answer every question. Unlike some other standardized assessments, you don't get points off for wrong answers on the TASC. If you guess on a multiple-choice question that you don't know the answer to, there's a chance you may guess correctly. But if you leave it blank, there's a zero percent chance that you'll get a point from that question.

Depending on the question you're trying to answer, certain techniques can help you understand the problem. These strategies include drawing a picture, making a list, or constructing an outline. In the Math section, for example, if you're trying to solve a problem on perimeters, it may be helpful to draw the shape the problem is describing. On the Science subtest, if a question involves an element or atom, it may be helpful to draw a diagram of the nucleus and rings. An example in the Social Studies section may be that you need to construct a timeline to help you visualize the sequence of events in a passage. And making an outline is useful for the essay question because it helps you organize your thought process and ensures that you don't go off on a tangent or miss part of the prompt.

WARNING

You must stay on topic when writing your essay. Essays that don't answer the question will earn zero points, no matter how well written they are.

For further tips on test-taking strategies, check out Chapter 27. This chapter is packed with strategies that strong test-takers adopt to maximize their chances of success on the TASC exam. It also points out the common mistakes to avoid on test day and how to sharpen your skills to achieve the score you deserve on the TASC.

The Big Day(s): Test Prep Wheaties

The first thing you can do to increase your chances of being successful on test day is to get a good night's sleep. You should be well rested so you can think clearly and do your best work, so try to go to bed early the night before your test. Your brain needs fuel as well as sleep, so make sure to eat a good breakfast to provide you with the energy you'll need to focus on the test. Try not to eat right before your test to avoid grogginess, and try to avoid high-sugar food, such as cookies, and high-carb meals. Instead, eat what foods you know work best for you, or try nuts, fruits, or yogurt, which will help sustain you throughout the test.

REMEMBER

Don't look at material right before your test. Cramming won't help — in fact, it will just stress you out. Develop a study plan that allows you to spread out the work you need to cover well in advance so you can relax the day before the test.

For each section of the test, be watchful of your time. As discussed before, we suggest that you wear a watch in case your testing center doesn't have a clock. Using your time wisely to complete all the possible questions is one of the most important strategies you can use to be successful.

When you're completing a paper-based test, be careful how you place the marks on your answer sheet. Because your answer sheet will be going through a reader, make sure there are no stray marks and that you erase clearly. Also be sure that you're filling in your answer for the right corresponding question. If you skip a question, be sure you also skip the space on your answer sheet so that your answers still line up.

Lastly, if you're one of those students who gets nervous when taking a standardized test, check out Chapter 28. This chapter is crammed with useful tips that should help you stay positive and keep that anxiety at bay.

2

Language Arts: Reading

Chapter 3

Reading to Find Central Themes and Main Ideas

This chapter gets you started with strategies for reading for comprehension. Before you begin really examining text for themes and main ideas, get yourself in the right frame of mind for reading with comprehension as the main goal. The first part of this chapter helps you get into the proper mindset. Then you explore ways to find authors' themes and the main ideas of their work. This is an important step to ensure that you get the most out of what you read and that you're able to respond correctly to questions on the TASC, which is grounded in the Common Core Standards.

TIP

For more information on the Common Core Standards for reading, visit http://www.corestandards.org.

Additionally, this chapter provides you an opportunity to look at text for other clues about the author's intended meaning, such as topic sentences and details that support the author's main points. You'll see that even though you may be unfamiliar with the content of an author's work, you can search for clues to its meaning.

Learning how to identify the main idea by looking for topic sentences and further identifying themes and supporting details, especially major details, increases your reading comprehension and your reading enjoyment.

Grasping Main Ideas and Themes

You always have a reason for reading. It may be for pleasure, or to complete an assignment for school or work, or to understand your favorite author's ideas. The same is true for the author. He or she has a reason for writing — a theme and main ideas to convey. Consequently, the first skill you need to sharpen is that of recognizing the theme or main idea of the text. So what's the difference between a main idea and a theme? Think of it this way: The *main idea* of a paragraph or segment of text is a major idea expressed in that portion only. The *theme* is an idea that continues throughout the text; it can be considered to be the moral of the story.

Preparing to find the gist of a text

Before you begin your search for themes and main ideas, here's an important tip to start the reading process in the most efficient way. As a reader, you need to prepare your brain to discover the theme or main idea — that is, warm up your thinking ability before you take on the task. What can you do? Ask yourself these questions:

>> If the piece has a title, does it give you a clue about the theme or main idea?

>> Do you know anything about the topic?

>> What do you expect to learn from reading this piece?

>> What does the graphic information (pictures, tables, graphs) tell you about the theme or main idea?

As you answer these questions, you're beginning to get the gist or meaning of the text. After you know the gist, you can begin to identify the main idea and the theme(s) of the piece.

Identifying the topic sentence

Another strategy to help you identify the main idea is to look for a topic sentence. This sentence usually tells you what a paragraph is about and, therefore, may contain the main idea. For example:

Small dogs make wonderful companions for the elderly. They are easy to walk, they are loving, they like to sit on their masters' laps, and they don't eat a lot of food. They are very loyal to the person who feeds and cares for them. Often, they will warn an elderly person if someone is at the door and make the person feel safer in his own home.

To find the topic sentence, ask yourself, "What is this paragraph about?"

If you said the first sentence, "Small dogs make wonderful companions for the elderly," you are correct. Can you see that this topic sentence provides you with the main idea of the paragraph?

Discovering themes

Now that you've mastered finding the main idea, you can begin to look further into your reading for themes. The theme can be a message the author is trying to get across. You may have heard of the "moral of the story." That's the theme the author wants to convey. For example:

Stephen told his mother he was going to stay at his friend John's house for the night. Instead, he went to visit his friend in college in the next state over. While he was driving to his friend's dorm on campus, he was stopped by a police officer for speeding. The officer told Stephen that he was going to have to contact his parents because he was a minor. Stephen's first thought was, "Boy, am I in trouble now!"

What would you say is the message or theme the author is trying to convey?

Is it that you shouldn't drive too fast? That you shouldn't visit a friend in another state? Would you say that the theme might be that you shouldn't lie? Right! The theme here is that lying is the wrong thing to do.

Distinguishing between themes and main ideas

Now that you understand the difference between the theme and the main ideas of a passage, read the excerpt below from Martin Luther King's famous speech (August 28, 1963). Can you find the theme that runs throughout the passage? What are the main ideas of each paragraph? Actively look for them as you read.

> I have a dream that one day this nation will rise up and live out the true meaning of its creed: We hold these truths to be self-evident; that all men are created equal.
>
> I have a dream that one day on the red hills of Georgia the sons of former slaves and the sons of former slave owners will be able to sit down together at the table of brotherhood.
>
> I have a dream that one day even the state of Mississippi, a state sweltering with the heat of injustice, sweltering with the heat of oppression, will be transformed into an oasis of freedom and justice.
>
> I have a dream that my four little children will one day live in a nation where they will not be judged by the color of their skin but by the content of their character. I have a dream today.
>
> I have a dream that one day down in Alabama, with its vicious racists, with its governor having his lips dripping with the words of interposition and nullification, that one day right down in Alabama little black boys and black girls will be able to join hands with little white boys and white girls as sisters and brothers.

The theme expressed throughout the passage is Martin Luther King's dream of racial equality. This is the moral of the speech. The main ideas that support this theme include that all men are created equal (first paragraph), slaves and slave owners will overcome their differences (second paragraph), Mississippi and Alabama will overcome their racist ways (third paragraph and last paragraph, respectively), and that children should not be judged by the color of their skin (fourth paragraph). See how the main ideas in each paragraph support the overall theme or moral of the entire passage.

Now take a look at a much more recent article on the current employment picture.

How Long Will You Keep Your Job?

In the 1950s, workers stayed in their jobs for many years; today we have a very different employment picture. Now, workers tend to keep their jobs for about four and a half years. But that statistic does not account for millennials, those born between 1977 and 1997. Some surveys show that millennials expect to change jobs about every three years. Do the math! These folks can expect to have more than 15 jobs over their lifetimes.

Which sentence holds the main idea in this paragraph? If you said, "In the 1950s, workers stayed in their jobs for many years; today we have a very different employment picture," you are correct. Can you identify the theme? The theme is concerned with how long people keep their jobs today compared to in the past. Note how the title of the passage neatly sums up the entire theme of the passage.

Always look for clues in the title of the passage that may help you to determine the theme.

TIP

All forms of writing contain themes and main ideas. Read the following poem, "An April Day," by Henry Wadsworth Longfellow.

When the warm sun, that brings
Seed-time and harvest, has returned again,
'T is sweet to visit the still wood, where springs
The first flower of the plain.

I love the season well,
When forest glades are teeming with bright forms,
Nor dark and many-folded clouds foretell
The coming-on of storms.

From the earth's loosened mould
The sapling draws its sustenance, and thrives;
Though stricken to the heart with winter's cold,
The drooping tree revives.

The softly-warbled song
Comes from the pleasant woods, and colored wings
Glance quick in the bright sun, that moves along
The forest openings.

When the bright sunset fills
The silver woods with light, the green slope throws
Its shadows in the hollows of the hills,
And wide the upland glows.

And when the eve is born,
In the blue lake the sky, o'er-reaching far,
Is hollowed out and the moon dips her horn,
And twinkles many a star.

Inverted in the tide
Stand the gray rocks, and trembling shadows throw,
And the fair trees look over, side by side,
And see themselves below.

Sweet April! Many a thought
Is wedded unto thee, as hearts are wed;
Nor shall they fail, till, to its autumn brought,
Life's golden fruit is shed.

Can you see the theme of this poem? Look at the following statements. Remember that you're looking for the overall idea that continues throughout the poem. Does one of them look like the theme for this poem?

1. A softly warbled song is heard.

2. The bright sun can be seen in the trees.

3. Cold winter has passed; April brings beautiful spring.

If you chose 3, you're right. Sentences 1 and 2 are ideas that lead you to the theme: spring renewal.

Here's a challenge: For this example, switch your mind from beautiful flowers to an essay on diet and health.

Diet and Health

We're concerned these days about how diet affects our health. We know from scientific studies that eating too much junk food can lead to diabetes, obesity, and other health problems later in life. This is especially a problem for those who don't have access to fresh vegetables and other healthy foods. One solution for dealing with this problem is to provide health education for children of all ages so that they begin to think about eating healthier from a young age.

Providing health education is appropriate since it can address the major causes of obesity and other health issues. It can show the link between knowing about nutrition and developing good eating habits. For example, when children learn in school about the food pyramid, they begin to understand what is most important to include in their diets. People who do not know about the food pyramid are less likely to make healthy food choices.

Better health education can also address how making poor food choices can have a negative impact on health. It can help people understand that, although fast food is inexpensive, quick, and easy, it can have major long-term negative effects on a person's well-being. Many fast foods are high in salt and fat, which can lead to high cholesterol and heart disease.

Although it might not be the only answer to the problem, providing better health education to children of all ages may be a solution to many of the problems people have with their health as a result of poor diet. Having the knowledge they need to make better dietary choices will lead to healthier children and adults. When people know how to make healthier choices, they will eat better and may very well have a positive effect on the health of those around them.

Can you identify the theme of this essay? If you said that providing health education to students can help them make healthier diet choices, you are correct. Can you identify the topic sentence? If you said, "We're concerned these days about how diet affects our health," you would be correct. Can you identify the main ideas? These include: Knowledge of the food pyramid leads to healthier diet choices, fast food can be unhealthy, and an unhealthy diet can lead to serious illnesses later in life.

Filling in the Details

Another important skill that you should develop to help you read for comprehension is to be able to identify the key supporting details and ideas in what you're reading. These details and ideas provide support for the main idea and themes. In other words, they help explain the main idea. These details may be examples, descriptions, evidence, statistics, or facts.

For example, read this excerpt from *The Calling of Katie Makanya*, by Margaret McCord (Wiley):

The town around the railroad station was ugly but the location was worse than any place Katie had ever known. Here the iron houses, streaked with rust, seemed to push their way into the road. Broken windows were patched with scraps of wood and stuffed with rags. Few people wandered about in the heat of the day, though Katie heard a mumble of voices behind the walls, the whimpering of children, a quick burst of laughter. Occasionally from an open door a shrill voice called out a greeting to Charlotte, who waved and hurried on as if she did not notice the stink of urine, garbage, and stale smoke.

What is the main idea of this paragraph? If you said the passage describes the poverty of the neighborhood you are correct. What are the supporting details that the author provides? She describes the details of the poverty: the rusty iron houses, the stink of urine and garbage, and the broken windows. How do these details help you when reading this paragraph? They make the passage more interesting and help the reader to get a clearer picture of what the neighborhood is like.

Try another example:

The weather in Florida is very hot most of the year. In January and February, the average temperature is 75 degrees but rises to 78 degrees in March and April. In May and June, Floridians usually experience temperatures in the mid-80s, with increasing humidity at this time. However, once July rolls around, average temperatures can climb into the 90s and stay that way through September. October brings some relief, with less humidity and cooler temperatures, mainly in the low 80s. In November and December, those living in or visiting Florida can expect beautiful weather, with temperatures in the low to mid-70s on average. Overall, Florida is one of the hottest states in the U.S.

What is the main idea? Florida's weather is hot, right? What supporting details does the author provide? The author gives details about the average temperatures throughout the year as well as the level of humidity that you can expect to experience there. What would this passage be like if the author only provided the first and last sentence? Pretty boring, right? Can you see how important supporting details are to your reading comprehension?

Finding details in expository writing

Expository writing serves to inform or explain the author's subject to a reader. As you can imagine, supporting details are very important in this kind of writing. If you were to read a passage that was supposed to explain a concept to you and it lacked detail, it would be very difficult to understand.

For example:

So, you want to learn how to fly a kite? Well, you've come to the right place. First, get a kite. Next, fly it.

What is wrong with this paragraph? The topic sentence implies that you'll find instructions on kite flying, but the paragraph lacks supporting details.

Let's try this again:

So, you want to learn how to fly a kite? Well, you've come to the right place. First, get a kite that has string and a tail in its package. Kites come in all sizes and shapes, so you should have no trouble finding one that you like. Next, look at the picture to determine where to place the tail on the kite. The tail is important to keep your kite in the air . . .

As you can see from this short passage, the author has provided important details to help you understand kite flying.

Now read this passage from *Photography For Dummies*, by Russell Hart (Wiley):

If you've ever had to figure out where to stick batteries in your child's latest electronic acquisition, then loading batteries in your point-and-shoot shouldn't be a challenge. Turn off your camera when you install them; the camera may go crazy opening and closing its lens. (Some cameras turn themselves off after you install new batteries, so you have to turn them back on to shoot.)

With big point-and-shoot models, you typically open a latched cover on the bottom to install batteries. More compact models have a battery compartment under a door or flap that is incorporated into the side or grip of the camera. You may have to pry open such doors with a coin.

More annoying are covers on the bottom that you open by loosening a screw. (You need a coin for this type, too.) And most annoying are battery covers that aren't hinged and come off completely when you unscrew them. If you have one of these, don't change batteries while standing over a sewer grate, in a field of tall grass, or on a pier.

Whether loading four AAs or a single lithium, make sure that the batteries are correctly oriented as you insert them. You'll find a diagram and/or plus and minus markings, usually within the compartment or on the inside of the door.

Think about the details that the author supplies in this passage. How do they help you understand the main idea he is trying to get across? What might the passage be like without those supporting details? Imagine if the author had simply said, "To load batteries into your camera, simply open up your camera and put the batteries in." Without the supporting details you may be left with a lot of questions. How do you open up the camera? Does the camera need to be switched off first? Which way do the batteries go in? What type of batteries should you use? The supporting details help to fill in the blanks and make the text more interesting and useful.

Distinguishing between major and minor details

Not all supporting details are created equal. There are major and minor details that authors use to convey their messages. Both types of details can be important to a story to describe something so that a reader can comprehend what the author is talking about. However, major details offer insight into the story's meaning.

Example #1: Susan's dress was bright blue. She wore it on Tuesdays.

The color of Susan's dress is a minor detail here.

Example #2: Susan chose a blue dress to wear to her daughter's wedding to match the bridesmaids' dresses.

Here, the color of Susan's dress is a major detail because it offers insight into what the author is talking about.

Read the following passage and see if you can identify the major details and the minor details:

Mabel was the only child of Bob and Alice. She was the love of their life. When Bob came home from work, he found Mabel asleep in her crib. He had worked late again and missed putting his little sweetheart to bed. He didn't like missing these important times with her — giving her a bath, feeding her, shaking her rattle and watching her laugh. But most of all he missed rocking her to sleep. He kissed his finger and placed it on her forehead. Her skin was pale and smooth like silk. "I'll try to make it home early tomorrow night, my little love."

List the major details. List the minor details. What would happen to the story if the author left out the major details? What would happen to the story if the author left out the minor details?

If the author left out the minor details, the story may not be as interesting, but you'd still be able to understand what the author was trying to get across. Focusing on the major details when reading can help improve your comprehension.

Chapter 4

Analyzing the Structure of Text

In this chapter, we take a look at how authors structure their texts. To understand written text, it's helpful to get a grip on how the individual parts of text, such as sentences, paragraphs, and chapters, are best organized. To do so, first we examine two components: argument and structure. Then, we explore the idea of sequence of events in text — an author's way of helping the reader understand the order in which events occur. We also look at some of the tools that writers use to get their point of view and purpose across to readers.

Lastly, we cover how to determine the meaning of words. We examine the context of each phrase and how an author uses figurative language to convey meaning in a text. To do so, we look for clues in surrounding words and in the meaning of the passage.

Investigating the Structure of Text

A writer organizes text using sentences, paragraphs, and chapters to create his or her written work. The structure of the text, or how it's organized, can help you understand what you're reading. Here we look at two components: argument and structure.

Argument

You've heard the term *argument*, and it may bring to mind a negative connotation. For example, when two people are arguing, they may be mad at each other, and the conversation that ensues may become rather heated and unconstructive. However, in written text, the term *argument* often has nothing to do with negativity. It refers to a claim or statement the author is making and wants to provide evidence of. The evidence is necessary to support the claim, along with the reasoning behind it. An author will very often provide a counterargument to acknowledge that differing viewpoints exist. Here's an example of an argument that provides a claim and evidence to support the claim:

> The number one problem facing the United States today is obesity. Statistics show that 65 percent of U.S. adults are overweight or obese. The top three causes of death in the United States are heart disease, cancer, and stroke. Obesity has been determined to be the leading cause of the top three diseases causing death.

Can you determine what the claim is here? If you said, "The number one problem facing the United States today is obesity," you're correct. That's what the author is claiming to be true. But what good is the claim without supporting evidence? Would you believe this claim? Maybe not. So the author helps you become more comfortable with the claim by providing evidence: "The top three causes of death in the United States are heart disease, cancer, and stroke. Obesity has been determined to be the leading cause of the top three diseases causing death." Perhaps now you feel that there's some weight behind the claim. The author has made the claim much more compelling by providing supporting evidence.

Structure

When you understand how an author has structured a text, it's much easier to understand the text itself. The structure of a text can provide clues to help you understand its meaning. Text can be organized as follows:

- ›› Compare/contrast
- ›› Cause/effect
- ›› Problem/solution
- ›› Sequence of events

Compare/contrast

When an author uses this organizational structure, she provides both similarities and differences between at least two people, places, or things. For example:

> There are so many different types of melons, but my favorites are watermelon and cantaloupe. A watermelon is much bigger than a cantaloupe and its flesh is red in color, whereas a cantaloupe's flesh is the color of coral. Both, however, have a delicious, juicy, satisfying taste, best enjoyed on a hot summer day.

The author *compares* the two melons through the taste and texture of their flesh and *contrasts* them by discussing their differences in size and color. The power of comparing and contrasting by an author is that it helps you, the reader, make connections between the two items under discussion. It helps you derive an immediate picture of both items without having to spend too much time reading about each one individually.

Cause/effect

By using cause and effect in their text, writers provide the reasons for an action or event and also the result of the action or event — or, more simply put, the why and the what of an action or event.

TIP

You often find clue words like *if*, *then*, *because*, *since*, and *so* in text that's organized using cause and effect.

For example:

> Jay woke early on Friday morning *because* he had a long list of things to do before school. He had decided to make a list the night before. *If* he hadn't made a list, he would have forgotten everything! He had agreed to walk the next-door neighbor's dog *because* he thought his neighbor was really cute and might want to ask her for a date. Jay had put that first on his list. He would have to take Bailey for a short walk *so* he wouldn't be late for school. Next on the list was to pack a lunch *because* he had a math quiz and wouldn't have time to go out for food. The last thing on Jay's list was to put gas in his car. *Then,* if he got stuck in traffic, he wouldn't have a problem. He had thought of everything!

Notice that the italicized clues point to the fact that this author organized his text using cause/effect. Can you identify which statements represent cause and which represent effect?

Problem/solution

In this type of text organization, an author identifies a problem as well as a solution. For example:

> Research shows that teen pregnancy is on the rise. Last year, about 20 percent of teenagers became pregnant before they graduated from high school. This is up from 10 percent five years ago. Teen pregnancies make it very difficult for young mothers to finish school, work toward a career, and become independent. They may have to give up their dreams until their child is older. Fortunately, most teen pregnancies can be easily prevented by using birth control; however, birth control is not 100 percent effective. The most effective way to prevent teen pregnancies is through abstinence, which is 100 percent effective.

As you can see in this passage, the author identifies a problem — teen pregnancy is on the rise — and, therefore, it's "very difficult for young mothers to finish school, work toward a career, and become independent." The author also poses solutions — using birth control, although "birth control is not 100 percent effective. The most effective way to prevent teen pregnancies is through abstinence, which is 100 percent effective."

Sequence of events

Why is it important to understand the sequence of events? It provides a sense of order and helps a reader understand what the author is trying to get across. It's so important to be sure you understand sequence that we include several different examples here. First, take a look at this recipe:

One-pot pasta

Serves 4

Ingredients:

10 oz. ditalini pasta

1/2 cup sliced kalamata olives

5 cups water

2 tsp. kosher salt

1 tsp. fresh ground black pepper

1 tbsp. tomato paste

Red pepper flakes to taste

2 cups fresh arugula

Grated Parmesan cheese

Having a list of ingredients tells you something. You know what you need to have on hand or purchase to make this dish. It looks like it could be an interesting dish, but there's something missing. The directions! How would you know what to do with these ingredients? Let's try again.

Directions:

First, put the water into a 5-qt. Dutch oven and bring to a boil. Once it boils, add the salt, pepper, pasta, olives, and tomato paste. Then, cover and simmer over medium-low heat for 10 minutes, or until all water is absorbed. Turn off the heat, stir the mixture, and then add the red pepper flakes and arugula. Separate into four bowls and top with cheese and a drizzle of olive oil.

What do you notice about the directions? They not only tell you *what* to do, they tell you *when* to do it. Imagine if the directions didn't give you information about sequence; you might add the ingredients at the wrong times and end up with a mess! As you can see here, the author of the directions provided order so you would know what to do and when.

TIP

Now that we've established *why* sequence is important, let's look for the clues in text that help you understand the sequence of events. Look for words or phrases in the recipe directions that help you understand sequence. For example, *first, then, once . . .* these words all provide clues as to the sequence of adding and manipulating the ingredients.

Here's another piece of text to review for issues of sequence:

You think you may want to run for office in your home state. You call the state administration office and they refer you to a website for information. When you get to the website, this is what you see:

–Develop a multimedia strategy	–Put together a campaign team	–Research your opponent
–Research issues in the town	–Develop your message	–Develop a plan for raising money
–Put together a campaign slogan	–Connect with your party's leaders	–Meet with potential contributors
–Figure out a budget	–Collect the required number of signatures	–Write letters to the editors of local and state newspapers
–Have your signatures checked by the town	–Prepare for debates	–Organize volunteers

There's a lot of very helpful information here. Maybe you see things that you never thought of, but how do you know where to start? Do you read from left to right and then to the next row? Do you read down by column and then go to the next? The author neglected to provide a sequence of events, making it nearly impossible to figure out in which order you should do these things. A better approach would have been:

Instructions for Potential Candidates:

The following will provide you with what you need to do to prepare to run for office. There are three basic categories of actions you need to take: Background, Developing a Team, and Marketing Yourself.

In the **Background** category you should <u>first</u> research the issues in the town and then do some research on your opponent and his or her stand on the issues. <u>When you are finished</u>, you should be able to develop your message that you want to use throughout your campaign.

<u>Next</u>, in the **Developing a Team** category, you should put together a campaign team to help you in your bid for office. This group can then help you organize volunteers. Choose people whom you can trust, who can give you the time you need, and who share your commitment to the issues.

<u>Once that is complete</u>, you are ready to move on to the **Marketing Yourself** category. . . .

While this passage doesn't list all the strategies in the previous chart, it gives you an idea of the order of the steps you should take to begin running for office. The underlined words provide clues as to the sequence of events.

Here's a passage from history that provides other examples of clues to the sequence of events the author is describing. Read the passage and underline the clues that you see:

Mr. Vice President, Mr. Speaker, Members of the Senate, and of the House of Representatives:

Yesterday, December 7th, 1941 — a date which will live in infamy — the United States of America was suddenly and deliberately attacked by naval and air forces of the Empire of Japan.

The United States was at peace with that nation and, at the solicitation of Japan, was still in conversation with its government and its emperor looking toward the maintenance of peace in the Pacific.

Indeed, one hour after Japanese air squadrons had commenced bombing in the American island of Oahu, the Japanese ambassador to the United States and his colleague delivered to our Secretary of State a formal reply to a recent American message. And while this reply stated that it seemed useless to continue the existing diplomatic negotiations, it contained no threat or hint of war or of armed attack.

It will be recorded that the distance of Hawaii from Japan makes it obvious that the attack was deliberately planned many days or even weeks ago. During the intervening time, the Japanese government has deliberately sought to deceive the United States by false statements and expressions of hope for continued peace.

The attack yesterday on the Hawaiian Islands has caused severe damage to American naval and military forces. I regret to tell you that very many American lives have been lost. In addition, American ships have been reported torpedoed on the high seas between San Francisco and Honolulu.

Yesterday, the Japanese government also launched an attack against Malaya.

Last night, Japanese forces attacked Hong Kong.

Last night, Japanese forces attacked Guam.

Last night, Japanese forces attacked the Philippine Islands.

Last night, the Japanese attacked Wake Island.

And this morning, the Japanese attacked Midway Island.

Japan has, therefore, undertaken a surprise offensive extending throughout the Pacific area. The facts of yesterday and today speak for themselves. The people of the United States have already formed their opinions and well understand the implications to the very life and safety of our nation.

The author provides sequence using words and phrases like "yesterday," "today," "last night," "one hour after," "during the intervening time," and "this morning" — all of which provide the reader with an idea of the sequential order of events. Without the use of these terms, understanding how the events unfolded would be difficult.

Assessing Point of View and Purpose

Understanding an author's attitude about a topic and her reason for writing the text can help a reader decipher the text's meaning. Two key ideas are the author's point of view and the author's purpose. To get across her point of view, an author often uses a particular literary device.

Literary devices

The author's point of view represents her attitude toward the subject she is writing about. An author can indicate her point of view by using several literary devices, including sarcasm, satire, irony, and understatement. This section explores these literary devices.

Sarcasm

You tend to know *sarcasm* when you see it or hear it. It may be best to explain sarcasm by using examples:

> One day I wrapped my hair in a towel after washing it and my husband remarked, "Wow, I love that look!"

Do you see why this is sarcasm? Here's another:

> A man comes to breakfast after working all night. He is unshaven, his hair is disheveled, and his eyes are red and squinted from the sunlight.
>
> His wife takes one look at him and says, "Well, now, don't you look just bright and shiny this morning!"

Now that you've seen two examples, how would you describe sarcasm?

Satire

Writers use *satire* to expose and criticize foolishness and corruption of an individual or a society. To do this, they often use exaggeration, humor, irony (see the next section), or ridicule. A writer may use fictional characters (who represent real people) to expose and criticize their corruption.

For example, here's an excerpt from Mark Twain's *The Adventures of Huckleberry Finn*:

> "There warn't anybody at the church, except maybe a hog or two, for there warn't any lock on the door, and hogs likes a puncheon floor in summer-time because it's cool. If you notice, most folks don't go to church only when they've got to; but a hog is different."

As you can see, Twain is using a hog to criticize people who only go to church when they have to.

Irony

"This chair is as comfortable as sitting on nails" is an example of irony. Writers use *irony* to say one thing but mean another. Irony conveys meaning by using the opposite of what is meant. It can be confusing, but very effective, if the author connects to something readers are familiar with. In the chair example, while you most likely have never sat on nails before, you get the idea as to just how uncomfortable the chair really is. If the author had written, "That's an uncomfortable chair," it wouldn't have the same strength. By comparing the chair to sitting on nails, the reader realizes that it's an extremely uncomfortable chair.

In other uses, irony can be situational as well, if the actual result appears to be the opposite of what is expected. For an example, read this summary of a sequence of events that takes place in Shakespeare's *Hamlet:*

> Hamlet, thinking his father is hiding behind the curtain runs his sword through him, only to learn that it is the father of the woman he was about to marry. Thus, finally finding the courage to act, his action is grossly misdirected and he kills an innocent who would have been his father-in-law; a man of whom he is most fond.

Can you see the irony here?

Understatement

You may have made a statement and heard someone say to you, "That's an understatement!" What did the person mean by that? Well, an *understatement* is a figure of speech that intentionally makes something seem less important than it really is. Writers use understatement to cultivate other figures of speech, such as irony and sarcasm, by reducing how severe a situation is so that a different response is expected by readers.

For example, in J. D. Salinger's *The Catcher in the Rye,* Holden Caulfield says, "I have to have this operation. It isn't very serious. I have this tiny little tumor on the brain."

Obviously, a tumor on the brain *is* serious, but Salinger is using understatement to play down its severity. Another example would be if you won $10 million in the lottery and, when asked how you felt about it, you said, "It feels pretty good." Someone hearing that reply may think that was a huge understatement!

Purpose

It seems obvious that an author would have a purpose for his writing, but it's helpful for you to know what that is. The most common purposes include to persuade, to inform, and to entertain. Of course, an author can have more than one purpose in mind in his writing.

Here's an example with all three types represented:

> Thank you all so much for joining us today and supporting the scholarship fundraiser. This scholarship fund will support countless students who may never be able to attend college without it. Your help may change the life of a young person who may go on to do important work in his or her chosen field. To date, we have collected $100,000, but we still have a long way to go to reach our goal of $500,000. Please do whatever you can to help today. Besides, there's a pickpocket in the audience if you don't!

Can you find the sentences that represent each purpose? This passage informs you of the purpose of the fundraiser, how much money it has raised and still needs to raise, and what the result of your help may be. Then it tries to persuade you to give money, and it adds a bit of entertainment at the end.

Determining the Meaning of Words

When you learn to analyze words and phrases in text, understanding an author's intentions will be easier. Authors provide clues that help you determine the meaning that they're trying to convey. Here we look for clues in surrounding words and in the meaning of the passage.

Interpreting words and phrases in context

When you're unsure of the meaning an author is trying to convey because you're unsure of the meaning of a word or word(s), it can help to look at the words next to the ones you're unsure of to find meaning. In other words, look at the *context* of the words to try to find meaning. Here's an example:

> Although not done with their game, the baseball team needed to <u>curtail</u> the game because it was getting dark and there were no lights on the field.

You may know what the word *curtail* means, but if you don't, what words in the sentence could help you figure it out? First you can use the words "baseball team" to get a sense of what's going on, and then you can look at "not done," "dark," and "no lights" to figure out that *curtail* means to stop or end early.

Now try to figure out what the underlined phrase means in context:

> We went to the diner yesterday, and Joe was really <u>stuck in the weeds</u>! People were lined up outside, and his cashier and his other server called in sick. He was handling the whole place by himself! I've never seen him so stressed out. He was running around like mad, calling orders into the kitchen, checking people out, and serving food. People were complaining, and Joe looked like he would scream!

Although you may not have ever heard the phrase *stuck in the weeds*, can you figure out its meaning by looking at the words around it? Words and phrases like "people were lined up outside," "his cashier and his other server called in sick," and "handling the whole place by himself" give you a sense of what *stuck in the weeds* means. Right?

Getting to know parts of speech

A *part of speech* is a grammatical category that speaks to its use in a sentence. A part of speech may be an individual word or more than one word (noun, noun phrase). A single word may function as different parts of speech in different sentences. Table 4-1 shows the different parts of speech you need to be familiar with as well as their function.

TABLE 4-1 **Parts of Speech**

Part of Speech	Function in a Sentence	Examples
Noun	Person, place, thing, or idea	Girl, house, car, happiness
Pronoun	Substitute for a noun	He, them, mine, she, few
Verb	Conveys action or state of being	Run, jump, is, be
Adverb	Modifier of a verb, adjective, or other adverb; answers the questions "how," "in what way," "where," "when," and "to what extent"	Loudly, yesterday, often
Adjective	Describes nouns or pronouns	*Green* house, *brave* few
Preposition	Usually precedes a noun or pronoun to show its relationship to other words	Above, near, underneath
Conjunction	Connects parts of a sentence	A good mnemonic is FANBOYS: <u>F</u>or, <u>A</u>nd, <u>N</u>or, <u>B</u>ut, <u>O</u>r, <u>Y</u>et, <u>S</u>o
Interjection	Conveys emotion or sentiment	Hooray! Cheers! Wow!

In the following passage, *underline* the nouns and verbs first, and then read it again and *circle* the pronouns, adverbs, and adjectives. Give it another look for prepositions, conjunctions, and interjections and *place a square* around those. Now look at all your markings and you'll realize how important parts of speech are to the text!

At the annual county fair, there are cows and horses to be seen, as well as beautiful birds and dogs jumping through hoops. Besides the animals, you can eat delicious food that smells so good, you can't resist. There is a man doing tricks, and he is very good at them. He made a cow disappear! Wow! I have never seen that before! I thought maybe we would find it nearby, but it was not here nor there! I could have stayed all day, but my parents got tired.

Understanding Figurative Language

Sometimes an author uses language in a different, less direct way to get her meaning across. This is called *figurative language.* Examples of figurative language include metaphors, similes, personification, and hyperbole.

Metaphors

A *metaphor* compares two things that are different but have similarities. Metaphors don't use the word "like" or "as" to make the comparison though, as in a simile (see the next section).

>> That girl has a <u>heart of gold</u>.

>> She was fairly certain that <u>life was a bowl of cherries</u>.

>> My son's <u>room is a disaster area</u>.

>> His <u>cotton candy words</u> left her feeling sour.

>> Jen went to the grocery store with an <u>army of children</u>.

>> <u>Waves of spam</u> emails inundated his inbox.

Similes

A *simile* is a comparison between two things using the word "like" or "as" to make the comparison.

>> When he kissed her, it felt <u>like butter</u> melting on her lips.

>> Joe's jaw dropped <u>like a hammer</u> when he heard the news.

>> "Food?" Jesse cried, popping out of his seat <u>like a toaster strudel</u>.

>> From the window of the plane, the cars below looked <u>like ants</u>.

>> Sara manipulated the people in her life <u>as though they were puppets</u> on a string.

Personification

Personification is used when an author gives human characteristics to an object or an idea. By doing so, the author makes the object or idea do something that is usually done only by humans. This gives readers a frame of reference for something that may be familiar to them already.

>> Barbara was so tired, she could hear her bed calling her name.

>> The flame of the candle danced in the wind.

>> It was so hot, my flowers were begging for water!

>> The angry storm pounded against my windows.

>> Manhattan has been called the city that never sleeps.

Hyperbole

Hyperbole is the use of exaggeration to emphasize or provide effect. Here are some examples.

>> It's been ages since I saw you.

>> That lady is as old as the hills.

>> Your suitcase weighs a ton!

>> I've got a million things on my plate!

Using Academic and Domain-Specific Words and Phrases

If you find yourself reading academic articles, essays, or other text, you may find that the words used are very specific to the academic arena or a particular field of study.

Academic words

In academic writing, authors use words that more formally describe something relatively simple. For example, researchers have discovered instead of researchers have found. The use of an academic word doesn't change the meaning, but it sounds more formal when read.

Domain-specific words

Domain-specific words are found in a particular field of study and may not be heard or seen in everyday language. For example:

The math teacher was skilled in both pedagogy and andragogy, which was appropriate for her position teaching K–12 students and nontraditional aged college students.

In this sentence, while you may not know what the terms *pedagogy* and *andragogy* mean, you can get the idea from the words around those domain-specific words.

REMEMBER

Using context is often important when reading text that contains both academic and domain-specific words. When you don't understand a word or phrase, look at the words around them to help you determine meaning.

Analyzing Two or More Texts

You may be asked to look at two texts on the TASC and examine them to determine the similar or different approaches the authors took in their writing. Here we consider strategies for examining two or more texts that are similar in either theme or topic. You can start by examining the elements of the text you're reading to determine the author's approach.

Using rhetorical features

Rhetorical features represent the style and structure of an author's work that make it unique. Table 4-2 lists some of the most common rhetorical features.

TABLE 4-2 **Rhetorical Features**

Feature	Definition	Example
Alliteration	The initial consonant sounds are repeated	Lee's lizard likes leaping lions
Assonance	The use of words that have similar vowel sounds near one another	Rise high in the bright sky
Onomatopoela	Words that sound like the sound they are describing	Whiz, whee, pop
Analogy	Compares different things that are similar	His humor is as dry as dust!
Anaphora	Repeated word or phrase	"What we need in the United States is not division. What we need in the United States is not hatred. What we need in the United States is not . . ." (Robert F. Kennedy, 1968)

Linking features in two or more texts

TIP

To find similarities and differences between two or more texts, you can ground your search in the authors' points of view, the themes of the texts, and/or the content of the texts. A helpful strategy is to use a *Venn diagram* to make note of the similarities and differences in points of view, themes, and content. Figure 4-1 gives an example.

FIGURE 4-1: A Venn diagram comparing the themes of *The Lion King* and *Romeo and Juliet*.

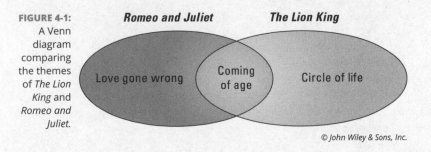

© John Wiley & Sons, Inc.

If you were asked to examine *Romeo and Juliet* by William Shakespeare and *The Lion King* by Don Ferguson for themes that are similar and different, you could place the themes for each in a Venn diagram and it may look like this. You could say the major theme of *Romeo and Juliet* is love gone wrong, and the major theme of *The Lion King* is the circle of life, but that they both share the theme of coming of age. Using a Venn diagram is an easy way to think about what is similar and different about these two works.

Linking through point of view

You can compare two or more texts by looking at them based on each author's point of view. (See the earlier section, "Assessing Point of View and Purpose," if you need a refresher on point of view.) Here's an example of reading two texts for different or similar points of view.

PASSAGE I

Young people today face an unprecedented amount of peer pressure regarding the clothing they wear to school. If a student cannot afford to wear a popular brand of sneakers or buy the latest fashion accessories, he or she runs the risk of feeling inadequate and being rejected by those students from more affluent households. Mandatory school uniforms would solve this problem since this would level the playing field for rich and poor students alike who would all be dressed the same.

PASSAGE II

Today's high school students should be free to choose what clothes they wear at school. Clothes are an important mode of expression, and students should have the right to display their own individuality. This can often be done without spending a lot of money. For example, in the 1970s, during the height of the punk rock era, the latest fashion trends involved wearing old ripped T-shirts and second-hand jeans. Entire outfits could be obtained for just a few dollars at the local thrift store. Compare that to the cost of today's school uniforms!

Linking through theme

We first visited *theme* in Chapter 3 if you need a refresher before moving on here. In that chapter, we looked at determining the theme of a work.

When comparing the themes of two passages, draw a Venn diagram and list the different themes in the outer parts of the circles. Then list the theme(s) the passages share in common in the center of the diagram between the two circles.

Linking through content

Another way to analyze text is by looking for similarities and differences in the content of the text. Again, read the two passages and analyze the text for content. Then, place the similarities and differences in a Venn diagram.

3 Language Arts: Writing

IN THIS PART . . .

Understand parts of speech.

Learn to avoid common grammatical errors.

Master the mechanics of writing.

Prepare for the TASC essay.

Chapter 5
The Basics of Writing

Language construction skills are the main focus of the TASC's Writing subtest. Being able to put words together clearly and concisely is something most people do naturally when speaking; learning to do so in writing is an important ability for high school graduates to master.

In this chapter, we help you understand the building blocks of writing in the parts of speech. Then we cover how to construct sentences from those building blocks. Finally, we look at how to make your writing more specific by using descriptive words and phrases.

The Parts of Speech

"Words, words, words," Hamlet said in despair, and he's right: They can be overwhelming. But words in sentences have functions, which, if you can identify them, can go a long way toward helping you understand how they work. While the TASC doesn't ask you to identify them by task, it does ask you to combine and rewrite sentences for better clarity. This is much easier to do when you understand the role of each of the words in a sentence. You also need to be able to write clearly and effectively in the essay section. So, let's get started learning the building blocks you'll need — we call them the parts of speech!

Nouns and pronouns

Nouns are:

» People (men, women, children, girls, boys, humans, guy, jerk, nurse)

» Places (house, store, building, field, farm, city, barracks)

>> Things (a cup, a spoon, a car, a penguin)

>> Ideas (love, hope, peace, charity, intelligence)

Each of these categories has thousands of examples, so we're only giving a few for each. A helpful way to think about nouns is to know that they're usually the *subject* of the sentence: the person, thing, or idea that's taking the action. Sometimes, nouns are also the *object* of the sentence, or the receiver of the action. Here's an example:

The dog bit the girl.

Do you see the two nouns in this sentence? Both *dog* and *girl*. Here, *dog* happens to be the subject, and *girl* the object (the action is done to her — poor thing!).

Pronouns are words that can stand in for nouns, often replacing names or places. You use them all the time, and it's a good thing, too. If pronouns didn't exist, you'd have to repeat yourself constantly. Here's what we mean. Take the sentence:

John said, "I can't find the light switch. It's got to be near me, though."

The pronouns there include *I*, *it*, and *me*. Without them, the sentence would have to read:

John said, "John can't find the light switch. The light switch has got to be near John, though."

Awful, right? Thank goodness for pronouns!

Pronouns include:

>> I, me, my, mine

>> You, yours

>> They, their, theirs

>> He, him, his

>> She, her, hers

>> It, its

>> This, that, these, those

REMEMBER

Whenever a noun (a person, place, thing, or idea) is replaced by another word, the replacement is a pronoun. In Chapter 6, we look at how pronouns can be misused and discuss ways to keep from doing so in your writing.

WHAT ARE PROPER NOUNS?

A *proper* noun sounds so, well, proper, but really, it's just a catch-all term for any specifically named noun. If *country* is the noun, then *United States* is a proper noun. *Girl* is a noun, but *Gracie* is a proper noun. *Tea* is a noun, but *Earl Grey Tea* is a proper noun. See how it works? Proper nouns are almost always capitalized, which we cover in Chapter 7.

Verbs

Verbs work with nouns to carry the weight of sentences. In fact, in some ways they're even more important than nouns because without a verb, you don't have a sentence! Verbs tell readers what is happening in the sentence, by describing either the action or the state of being that is happening. Verbs also indicate the *tense* of the writing. While there are many different verb tenses, for the sake of our sanity, we'll consider only three of them, which is all you need to know for the TASC.

Present tense is when the verbs refer to something that is happening in the present. For example, all of the following are in present tense:

>> I am walking.

>> She is present.

>> He bikes to work.

Past tense refers to something that happened in the past. Check out the following three sentences, all of which are in the past tense:

>> I was walking.

>> She was present.

>> He biked to work.

Future tense is, you guessed it, for something that will happen. Here are three examples:

>> I will walk.

>> She will be present.

>> He will bike to work.

The following sections cover the two kinds of verbs that you need to know. You can use both kinds in past, present, and future tense.

Action verbs

If someone or something is doing something in a sentence, that's the *action verb*. Action verbs are easy to spot in verbs that sound active, such as *biking, swimming,* or *batting.* But action verbs also include everything from bodily functions (*breathing*) to emotional responses (*crying*). Words are action verbs even when the action they refer to is internal, such as *thinking* or *feeling.*

State of being verbs

In contrast to action verbs, *state of being verbs* simply explain what someone or something *is.* The most common state of being verb is "to be." It's so common that sometimes you may not even realize that it's in a sentence or that it's the verb! You can see a breakdown of the tenses of the verb "to be" in Table 5-1.

TABLE 5-1 The Various Forms of the Most Common State of Being Verb, "To Be"

Subject	"To Be" in the Past Tense	"To Be" in the Present Tense	"To Be" in the Future Tense
I	Was	Am	Will be
You	Were	Are	Will be
He/She/It	Was	Is	Will be
We	Were	Are	Will be
They	Were	Are	Will be

Although "to be" is the most common state of being verb, there are other, less-common state of being verbs, including "to exist" and "to appear." The TASC doesn't ask you to sort verbs into action and state of being, but you should be able to identify the verb in a sentence. For example, the test may ask you to make sure the verb is in the correct tense for the rest of the sentence. To do that, you need to figure out which word is the verb. If it's not immediately clear because it's not an action verb, ask yourself, "Is there a state of being verb, like one of the forms of *to be*, in this sentence?" Spoiler alert: There usually is!

Adjectives and adverbs

Now we move to the not-entirely-necessary parts of a sentence. Sentences almost always have to have nouns and verbs. In contrast, adjectives and adverbs are common but not vital. Think of adjectives and adverbs as adding color to sentences. They tell readers *how* something is happening. While adjectives and adverbs often do such similar work that they can be practically interchangeable, each has a distinctive role to play in a sentence.

Adjectives describe nouns

An *adjective* describes (or, as people sometimes say, *modifies*) a noun. You can use adjectives with nouns, proper nouns, and pronouns. They state what kind, what color, which one, or how many. For example, if the noun is *ice cream*, adjectives can tell you:

>> What kind? (chocolate-chip ice cream, vanilla ice cream)

>> What color? (pink ice cream, minty-green ice cream)

>> Which one? (my ice cream, that ice cream)

>> How many? (five ice creams, some of the ice cream)

Adjectives can also be used in the adjective form of proper nouns, by the way. "What kind of ice cream?" could be answered, "Ben & Jerry's Ice Cream."

And, as mentioned, adjectives can modify pronouns. This is a bit like spotting a blue moon: It doesn't happen very often. But you may occasionally see a sentence such as, "It is a red one." The adjective is *red* (telling what color) and it's modifying *one*, a pronoun standing in for something else.

Adverbs describe verbs

An *adverb* does very similar work as an adjective, but it modifies a verb. However — and this is tricky! — adverbs can also modify adjectives and other adverbs. Let's look at their usual function first, though, before we get too crazy. For the verb *ran*, adverbs can tell you:

>> Where? (ran home, ran south)

>> When? (ran yesterday, ran earlier)

>> How? (ran quickly, ran happily)

>> In what manner? (ran barefoot)

>> To what extent? (ran faster, ran fastest)

It's common to think of adverbs as always ending in −*ly*, and as you can see from the previous examples, some adverbs do. But be careful! Not all adverbs end in −*ly*!

TIP

Instead of identifying adverbs by looking for the −*ly* ending, find them by locating the verb, adjectives, and other adverbs and then by checking to see whether any words modify them. Those are almost always the adverbs.

As we mentioned, adverbs can modify adjectives and other adverbs (but an adjective can't modify an adverb). Adverbs modify adjectives to tell to what extent a quality is true. For example, take a look at this sentence:

She was a very fast runner.

The adjective *fast* tells you what kind of runner she was. The adverb *very* tells you to what extent she was fast. *Very*, *really*, and *quite* are all adverbs that are most often used to modify adjectives to tell readers to what extent those adjectives are true.

Adverbs work in the same way when modifying other adverbs, telling readers to what extent something is true. For example:

He ran really slowly.

The adverb *really* modifies the adverb *slowly* to tell you the extent of the slowness.

If the nouns and verbs of a sentence are the meat and potatoes in the pot roast, so to speak, the adjectives and adverbs are the spices: They make the information clearer, more engaging, and more specific. Are they completely necessary? No. But most people wouldn't want to read much of anything that didn't have them!

Conjunctions and interjections

There are several other parts of speech beyond nouns, verbs, adjectives, and adverbs. They're a quirky lot, to be sure, taking care of various tasks within sentence structure. The good news is that after you understand the work that each kind does, you'll be able to spot them in a sentence with no difficulty at all.

Locating conjunctions

Conjunctions do the job of hooking up words and phrases and clauses. Conjunctions are the great communicators of the parts of speech: They want to bring pieces of sentences together and make their relationship clear, showing how two or more ideas are connected.

The most common conjunctions (and the only ones you'll need to know on the TASC) are:

>> And

>> But

>> For

>> Or

>> Nor

>> So

>> Yet

In grammatically correct writing — the kind you'll surely see on the test! — these words always and only do the work of conjunctions. If you see one of them, you'll know it's a conjunction. Here are a few examples of sentences with conjunctions:

He was late for work, *but* he stopped for coffee.

Sue was the last to leave, *and* she turned out the lights.

I love that band, *yet* their new album isn't my favorite.

Hey! What do interjections do?

Interjections are also a pretty simple concept in the parts of speech. They are words or phrases that demonstrate extremes in emotions or indicate warnings and commands. The heading of this section is a great example: "Hey!" is the interjection there. Interjections are rarely found without an exclamation point; any that appear on the test will have that mark of punctuation. Coming up with a comprehensive list of interjections could take hours and also be a lot of fun. Just to get you started, here are a few of our favorites:

>> Help!

>> Stop!

>> Wow!

>> Whoa!

>> Holy cabooses!

>> Great day in the morning!

>> Now!

REMEMBER

The most important thing to remember about interjections on the TASC is that even though they may look like incomplete sentences, they're not. In some cases, they're verbs, like "Stop!" which means that they're complete, just short. But even a sentence such as "Wow!" is acceptable without a subject or a verb because it's an interjection.

Building Sentences

Now that we've reviewed the basic parts of speech, it's time to build sentences with them. In the rest of the chapter, we take the parts of speech that you've just reviewed and show you how to put them together as sentences to convey meaning and tone.

It's important to remember that all sentences must have a subject and a verb but that sometimes the subject is implied. For example:

>> Go!

>> Stop!

>> Hey!

These are all valid sentences. The subject (always a noun) of the sentence is implied to be *you* because the sentence is really saying:

>> You go!

>> You stop!

>> Hey, you!

With that in mind, now we look at the two other key parts of sentences, subjects and objects.

Subjects and objects of sentences

With a few exceptions, all sentences in the English language have what's called a *subject* and an *object.* Don't worry if you can't remember which is which immediately. They are ideas that are important to understand but that don't actually come up in conversation that often. The *subject* of a sentence is almost always a noun or pronoun. It's the part of the sentence that shows who or what is taking the action. Take a look at the following examples, in which the subject is underlined:

>> <u>I</u> ran.

>> <u>The dog</u> was loud.

>> <u>Cynthia</u> won the role.

While almost all sentences have a *subject,* not every sentence has an *object,* which receives the action of the subject. Here are three more examples, in which we've underlined the object this time:

>> Corey studies <u>grammar</u>.

>> Modesty ran <u>the laps</u>.

>> She won <u>the role</u>.

TIP

To find the object, it's helpful to ask yourself the question implied by the sentence. So, what does Corey study? *Grammar.* What does Modesty run? *The laps.* What did she win? *The role.*

Notice that both sets of sentences are perfectly correct. You can see that the sentences that have objects give more complete information, but the lack of an object is not a flaw in a sentence.

Notice, too, that the subject and object in a sentence are always nouns. A verb, adjective, adverb, conjunction, interjection, or preposition can't be the subject or object. Only a person, place, thing, or idea can; however, the subject or object can be a pronoun, noun, or proper noun. Here are two examples:

He ate the chili dog. (*He* is a pronoun and the subject; *chili dog* is a noun and the object.)

Wei loves her cat, Buster. *(Wei* is a proper noun and the subject; *her cat, Buster* is a proper noun and the object.)

REMEMBER

When you're looking at sentences on the TASC and trying to decide what needs to be fixed within them, the best way to start is to identify the subject of the sentence. Who or what is the main actor in the sentence?

Adding verbs to sentences

After you identify the subject in a sentence, you need to find the verb to show the state of action or being. Look for the word that explains what the subject of the sentence is doing (or being). Here are three examples:

>> Dennis <u>lost</u> his keys.

>> Patrice <u>called</u> for backup.

>> John <u>is</u> exhausted.

The verbs are easy to spot here, right? Even without the underlining, you could pick out *lost, called,* and *is.* That's good! You should be able to pick out the action words or those that describe states of being.

REMEMBER

Remember that action verbs show what someone or something is doing, while state of being verbs tell the reader about someone's or something's existence. If you're having trouble finding the verb in a sentence, it's probably a state of being verb. Look for words like *am, is, was,* and *were.*

TIP

You may feel a twinge of concern right now because you know that matching subject and verbs in the correct tense and number can be quite tricky. You're right! We've dedicated the first two sections of Chapter 6 to these topics. The TASC asks many questions about both verb tense and verb agreement, so be sure to read that chapter!

Adding Descriptive Words and Phrases

Sentences can exist with just a subject and a verb, of course, but sophisticated writing includes descriptive words, such as adjectives and adverbs, as well as phrases and clauses. Phrases and clauses, in particular, can be a bit confusing if you're not familiar with them. Read on for a review of descriptive words, phrases, and clauses.

Descriptive words add color

Take a look at this sentence:

I like food.

While the point of the sentence is clear, it's not very interesting. There's so much still unknown. You don't know what kind of food this person likes, or how much the person likes to eat, or anything else, really. This is a perfect example of a sentence that needs some descriptive words, such as adjectives or adverbs, to make it more interesting and revealing. You could change it with some adjectives, like this:

>> I like spicy food.

>> I like blue food.

>> I like gluten-free food.

Each has a different meaning and makes the sentence more precise and interesting. You can also add adverbs:

>> I really like food.

>> I quite like food.

>> I slavishly like food.

Each of these examples does a better job showing how much the subject likes food. And, of course, you can add both adjectives and adverbs for a much more revealing sentence:

I absolutely like Italian food.

See how much better that sentence is? While adjectives and adverbs shouldn't be the subject or object of a sentence, you most certainly can and should use them to add clarity and interest to sentences.

Adding phrases and clauses

Along with descriptive words, phrases and clauses are very helpful for adding color and meaning to sentences. They're also one of the areas of grammar that you're sure to find mistakes in on the TASC. Before you can spot those mistakes, though, you need to review what phrases and clauses are.

A *phrase* is a group of related words used as a single part of speech. Phrases don't contain the subject or verb of a sentence. There are several kinds of phrases:

>> **Prepositional phrases** begin with a preposition and end with a noun or pronoun.

>> **Gerund phrases** contain the *–ing* form of a verb.

>> **Infinitive phrases** contain the *to* form of a verb.

>> **Participial phrases** contain the *–ing* or *–ed* form of a verb.

>> **Appositive phrases** contain a noun or pronoun and explain another noun or pronoun.

REMEMBER

It's easy to get confused about the different types of phrases that are used in the English language. Just remember that on the TASC, you don't need to diagram a sentence or explain how it works. Instead, focus on being able to recognize a well-written sentence and on being able to fix sentences that aren't well-written. Working with phrases and clauses is part of that.

Prepositional phrases

Prepositional phrases are the most common form of phrases found on the TASC. You'll recognize them right away, even if the term isn't familiar to you. They are groups of words like:

>> Next to the house

>> Beyond the grave

>> After the short summer

>> Like you

A sentence with a prepositional phrase may look like this:

She was glad to see that the house *around the corner* still stood.

Gerund phrases

A *gerund phrase* uses a verb as a noun, like these:

>> Your test taking

>> Driving a car

>> Responding as asked

A sentence with a gerund phrase may look like this:

Elio's *learning to skateboard* was the result of many hours of begging to try.

Infinitive phrases

Infinitive phrases can act as nouns, adjectives, or adverbs. They're easy to spot because they always use the word *to*, although not as a preposition (that would make the phrase prepositional, not infinitive). Here are a few examples of infinitive phrases:

>> Needs to sleep

>> A year to remember

>> Happy to assist

A sentence with an infinitive phrase may look like this:

Natalia needs *to eat* something before bed.

Participial phrases

Another very common phrase is the *participial phrase,* which acts as an adjective. Here are a few examples of participial phrases:

>> Singing happily

>> Collecting her thoughts

>> Keeping a secret

A sentence with a participial phrase may look like this:

Muttering angrily, Josh tried to fix his terrible haircut.

Appositive phrases

Appositive phrases provide more information about a noun in a sentence. Often, but not always, they explain more about the subject or object of a sentence. They're easiest to understand through example sentences:

>> Mr. Crowe, *the winner of the yearly salesmanship award,* was surrounded by admirers.

>> I gave the papers to Takeysha, *the case worker who had asked for them.*

As you can tell by now, phrases add a great deal of color and information to sentences. They can make perfectly acceptable sentences go awry, alas, but in Chapter 6, we help you understand the rules about where to place phrases. For now, it's enough for you to understand what they are and the work that they can do in a sentence.

Clauses

Clauses are similar to phrases in that they're groups of words used in sentences. However, there's a major difference between clauses and phrases. Clauses contain a subject and a verb, and they're used as all or part of a sentence. There are two kinds of clauses: *independent* and *dependent* (or *subordinate*) clauses.

An *independent clause* contains a subject and a verb and expresses a complete thought. It can stand on its own. If you're thinking, "Wait, that sounds like a sentence," you're right! *Independent clauses* are sentences.

On the other hand, *dependent clauses,* often called *subordinate clauses,* can't stand on their own, even though they have a subject and a verb. They don't express a complete thought and can't stand alone as a sentence. They're usually used as adjectives or adverbs.

TIP

You can usually spot subordinate clauses by how they begin, with words such as:

>> After

>> Although

>> As if

>> Because

>> Before

>> If

>> Since

>> That

>> Unless

>> Until

>> Which

- » While
- » Who/whom
- » Whose

Those aren't the only words that begin subordinate clauses, but they're the most common. Here are a couple of examples of sentences with subordinate clauses, just so you can begin to look for them:

> *Before you get upset,* let me explain what happened.

Here, you can see that the clause *Before you get upset* contains a subject *(you)* and a verb *(get upset)* but that the clause can't stand on its own and make sense.

> I'm allowed to borrow Gordon's snowshoes, *if I'm willing to walk his dog.*

Again, the clause is easy to spot — *if I'm willing to walk his dog* — and you can see that there's a subject *(I'm)* and a verb *(willing)* in it. But the group of words can't stand on its own, so it must be a subordinate clause.

The addition of phrases and clauses gives writers the opportunity to add so much more meaning and nuance to sentences than is possible without them. But they also add more traps to sentences, and the TASC is eager to try to catch you in them. In the next chapter, we consider the mistakes that are often found on the test.

Chapter 6

Avoiding Grammatical Errors

English grammar can be a minefield, but there are guidelines for how to use words correctly. In this chapter, we review some of the basics of correct writing. We look principally at agreement — that is, making sure that your singular subjects have singular verbs and your plural subjects have plural verbs — as well as where to drop phrases and clauses into your sentences. We also spend a bit of time on constructing parallel sentences and using active verbs instead of passive ones. Finally, we round out the chapter by discussing the grammatical issues that occur when using pronouns as the subject or object of a sentence.

By the time you've finished reading this chapter, you'll have had a good review of how to use these key ideas in grammar on the TASC. This isn't a chapter about grammar theory but a quick and dirty guide to getting words right!

Subject and Verb Agreement

One of the keys to clarity in English is to make sure that your subject and verb agree. If your subject is *singular* (referring to one person, place, thing, or idea), then your verb must match. The same is true if your subject is *plural*, meaning more than one.

Singular verbs go with singular subjects, plural verbs with plural subjects. Here are a few singular subject/verb examples:

>> I walk. (Not I *walks.*)

>> She sings. (Not she *sing.*)

>> Pedro listens. (Not Pedro *listen.*)

And here are a few plural subject/verb examples:

>> They respond. (Not they *responds.*)

>> Sheila and Dave insist. (Not Sheila and Dave *insists.*)

>> We forgive. (Not we *forgives.*)

Does an "s" always mean plural?

You may have heard the advice to look for an −s at the end of the subject and to make sure the verb is plural if you see one. The problem is that not all plural subjects end in −s, and not all subjects that end in −s are plural. Take a look at the following words:

>> Diabetes

>> News

>> Politics

These are all fairly common words that end in −s but are not plural. You should use a singular verb with them, as in this example:

Maria's diabetes *is* getting better with diet and exercise.

There are also words that don't end in −s but are plural, such as:

>> Children

>> Men

>> Women

As you can see, these words are fairly common, so it's important to know how to use them correctly. Even though they don't end in −s, they are plural, so you need to use a plural verb with them, as in this example:

The women *were* the last to board the rescue boat.

WARNING

Well-meaning people will tell you that you need only look at the end of the subject for an −s to figure out whether the sentence's verb should be singular or plural. Don't fall for this trap. It's not that simple! Read the entire sentence to be sure you understand what the subject is first.

SINGULAR GROUPS

It's important to remember that a subject can be singular even if it appears to refer to more than one person. In a sentence that uses the subject *the audience*, for example, it can seem as though the subject must be plural. After all, isn't an audience more than one person? Usually, yes. But *the audience* is still singular because it refers to one group. You would write, *The audience loves the show.* After all, it would sound odd to write or say, *The audience love the show.*

Tricky agreement cases

Sometimes it's quite difficult to figure out whether the subject of your sentence is singular or plural. The good news is that what sounds right is right almost all the time, so you should concentrate on reading sentences on the TASC carefully — perhaps even mouthing them — so that you can find the mistakes.

Groups of people in pronouns

First we look at words that, when used as a subject, are always paired with a singular verb, even though they sometimes indicate more than one person:

>> Anybody/anyone/anything

>> Everybody/everyone/everything

>> Nobody/no one/nothing

>> Somebody/someone/something

Remember, words like *group*, *audience*, and *crowd* almost always also receive a singular verb.

You know that if you see one of the words in the preceding list as the subject, you must use a singular verb:

>> Everything *is* different now.

>> No one *wants* to leave yet.

>> The crowd *was* interested in the ringmaster's spiel.

When *each* is followed by two or more singular subjects joined with the word *and*, the subject remains singular. You should use a singular verb, as in the following:

Each child and teacher *walks* on-stage for his or her award.

REMEMBER

Finding the subject in a sentence is the key to being able to figure out the correct verb to use, whether singular or plural. If you get confused about a sentence on the TASC, stop and make sure you've found the correct subject before you continue working with it.

Verbs of time, weight, volume, and money

When your sentence has a subject that involves time, weight, volume, or money, the verb will always be singular. Here are a few examples of what we mean:

>> Three months *is* a long time to wait.

>> Five hours *goes* by in a flash.

>> Three pounds of chocolate *was* all she could afford for the cake.

>> Five dollars *is* the price, and I won't change it.

You get the idea. What sounds right is almost always right. You wouldn't say, "Five dollars are the price," naturally.

The introductory "it"

It is always singular (just like in this sentence!). Thus:

> ❯❯ It is time to go.
>
> ❯❯ It was the last time I saw him.
>
> ❯❯ It will be a struggle to find a parking spot.

Subjects joined by "and"

Whenever two or more subjects are joined by *and*, the verb should be plural. Think of it this way: Linking up two or more nouns with *and* makes them plural. Thus:

> ❯❯ Susan, Faith, and David *are* going to the show.
>
> ❯❯ Purple and green *are* my favorite colors.

Plural pronouns

A handful of pronouns are always plural:

> ❯❯ Both
>
> ❯❯ Few
>
> ❯❯ Many
>
> ❯❯ Several

When you encounter them as the subject of a sentence, you should always use a plural verb, as in these examples:

> ❯❯ Many *were* called, but few were chosen.
>
> ❯❯ Both doctors *are* well-qualified.

You need a plural verb (really!)

As the heading suggests, when using *you* as a subject, the verb is always plural, even if the *you* in question is just one person. Therefore, both of the following are correct:

> ❯❯ You *are* the first person to arrive.
>
> ❯❯ You *were* able to go to Disneyland, class!

REMEMBER

One of the oddities of the English language is that it has no plural form of *you.* You use the same word whether you mean one person or a group of people. That's one of the reasons why many areas of the country have their own special term for "a group of you," such as y'all, yinz, and youse! You won't see those terms on the test, though!

Plural nouns

Of course, you know that some nouns are plural and some singular and that the verb should match. But we want to take a moment to point out that some nouns are always plural. We can't list them all, but just a few should get you thinking clearly about which ones we mean:

>> Glasses

>> Pants

>> Scissors

You get the idea. You always use a plural verb with these plural nouns, like this:

>> My pants *are* red.

>> The new sunglasses *were* exactly what Andrew wanted.

Generic references

You probably do this naturally, but remember that whenever you encounter what we call a *generic reference*, you want to use a plural verb. So, what is a generic reference? Great question! Phrases like this:

>> The British

>> The old

>> The young

Here's an example sentence:

The young *are* the nation's largest consumers of downloaded media.

Ignoring phrases for subject-verb agreement

It's not unusual for a phrase to be inserted into a sentence between the subject and the verb. There's nothing wrong with that, but you must be aware that you're matching the verb to the subject and not to a noun in the phrase. Take a look at this incorrect example:

The class, along with its teachers, depart at noon.

WARNING

If you're not paying attention, this sentence can look correct — after all, *teachers* is plural, and so is *depart*. Whoops! Nope, this sentence contains a phrase — *along with its teachers* — but the subject, *class*, is singular. This is a very common error, so remind yourself to be alert for it.

The correct version of the above example is:

The class, along with its teachers, *departs* at noon.

Here's another example. See if you can choose the correct verb:

The man, together with his children, *is/are* waiting for the train.

Same issue here: While *children* is plural, they aren't the subject. *The man* is, making the correct verb choice *is*.

However, this type of sentence can also be plural:

The women, together with their children, *is/are* waiting for the train.

As you can see, *women* is plural, so the subject is plural, and the verb should be too: in this case, *are*.

Here and there

We've shown you quite a few sentences that flow logically: subject, verb, sometimes an object. But there are plenty of sentences in the English language that aren't so conveniently written, such as this one itself. When encountering *here* or *there* in a sentence, you need to pay careful attention: They aren't the subject. The sentence will be set up so that you have *here* or *there*, then the verb, and *then* the subject. You need to match the verb to the first subject that comes after it. So:

>> There were trees and a pond in the garden. *(Were* matches *trees.)*

>> Here is the map with the directions I promised. *(Is* matches *the map.)*

Don't get tricked by this type of sentence!

Pronouns that change

Just as there are pronouns that are always plural, and those that are always singular, some pronouns can change. The most common are:

>> All

>> Any

>> Either/neither

>> More

>> Most

>> None

>> Some

These words are often followed by clarifying prepositional phrases that tell you whether you should treat them as plural or singular. Here's an example:

>> All the money *was* collected. (Here, *money* takes a singular verb, so *all* does too.)

>> All the students *were* present. (Here, *students* take a plural verb, so *all* does too.)

In the case of *either* and *neither*, you have to look at the subject closer to the verb to decide whether to use a plural or singular verb. The following examples should show what we mean:

>> Either one girl or both boys *run* for student council. (The closest subject is *boys,* so choose the plural form of the verb.)

>> Neither Casey's brothers nor her sister *was* able to go to the show. (The closest subject is *her sister,* so choose the singular form of the verb.)

Matching Pronouns and Antecedents

This section covers another common grammatical error: that of failing to match a pronoun and its antecedent. To understand the error, you need to know what an *antecedent* is because it's one of those words that only English teachers ever use. An *antecedent* is the noun the pronoun is referring to from earlier in the text. For example, look at this sentence:

Johnny saw his mom and her sister leave his house.

This sentence has three pronouns: *his, her,* and *his* again. The antecedents the pronouns refer to are Johnny, Johnny's mom, and Johnny again. This sentence uses antecedents correctly, but mistakes can often happen. Read on to find out how to spot them.

Pronouns refer to nouns

Obviously, you want to match pronouns to their antecedents. Here's an example that is clearly incorrect (unless we're talking about a girl who happens to have a male name!):

Samuel's career was *her* greatest accomplishment.

But things get trickier. You must match pronouns not only based on gender but also based on whether they're plural or singular:

>> Samuel's career was *his* greatest accomplishment.

>> Susan and Samuel felt that the house they owned was *their* greatest investment.

Be particularly careful to avoid substituting *their* instead of *his, her,* or *his or her,* as in this sentence:

Anyone who wants to do well on the TASC should have a copy of this book in *their* bookcase.

This should be:

Anyone who wants to do well on the TASC should have a copy of this book in *his or her* bookcase.

Another common mistake to avoid is using *they* instead of *he, she,* or *he or she,* as in this sentence:

If Susan or Samuel was concerned, *they* should have asked for more information.

This should be:

If Susan or Samuel was concerned, *he or she* should have asked for more information.

Pronouns refer to noun phrases

A *noun phrase* is a noun and the group of words that distinguishes it, usually adjectives or adjectival phrases. Here are a few noun phrases:

>> The large gray dog

>> Aunt Nedra's dog

>> The last dog to appear

In all these, the main noun is *dog,* and the rest of the phrase describes the main noun.

When you're using pronouns with noun phrases, be certain to choose the pronoun that best fits the subject noun in the phrase. Don't get confused and use pronouns that refer to any other nouns in the phrase. For example, if the phrase is *Aunt Nedra's knitting,* you don't want to write *We couldn't find Aunt Nedra's knitting, although we looked for her everywhere.*

A closer reading of the sentence reveals that *it* is the best fit for *knitting,* the main word in the noun phrase.

Placing Descriptive Words and Phrases

It's important to put descriptive words, such as adjectives and adverbs, and descriptive phrases next to the words they describe. If you aren't careful about that, you can end up confusing the meaning of the sentence. Here's an example of a badly placed phrase:

Running the trail through the woods, the sight of the mountains was glorious to Avery.

The phrase *running the trail through the woods* should modify *Avery*, but because of the way it's placed in the sentence, it seems to be telling readers that the *sight of the mountains* was running the trail. You can do better!

Placing descriptive words

Place adjectives and other descriptive words next to the nouns they describe.

The old black cat howled at the blue moon when it appeared on a hot August night.

If you move any of the adjectives in this sentence, your meaning will become confused!

The old cat black howled at it when on a hot August night the moon which was blue appeared.

See? What a mess!

Besides the confusion caused by letting descriptive words wander away from their nouns, doing so also tends to stretch out sentences far beyond what they really need to be. Look at this sentence:

The cat, which was orange and a tabby as well as shy, spat at the woman, who was rough in handling her.

TIP

Conciseness in writing is of value on the TASC, so you want to find ways to clearly express the thoughts of a sentence without lengthening it. The following sentence conveys the same information as the preceding sentence, but in fewer words:

The shy, orange tabby cat spat at the woman who handled it roughly.

Placing descriptive phrases

As we mention in the introduction to this section, descriptive phrases also need to be right next to the words they describe. This is a little trickier to remember to do. Sometimes when you draft an essay, it's easier to just write the words as they fall. That's fine, so long as you go back to fix them later. Look at the previous example:

Running the trail through the woods, the sight of the mountains was glorious to Avery.

You have a couple of choices. You can move the phrase to be closer to the noun (*Avery*) that it's describing:

The sight of the mountains was glorious to Avery running the trail through the woods.

Or you can reword the phrase at the beginning so that it becomes a clause and the body of the sentence so that the subject is clearer:

As she ran the trail through the woods, Avery thought the sight of the mountains was glorious.

Parallel Construction

The name of this section makes it sound as if it wandered over from the math chapters, but there is, indeed, parallel construction in grammar, too. What this concept means is that you want to be sure that all elements of your sentence match one another (or are *parallel*) and that your sentences use the fewest words possible to get your entire idea across.

Creating balanced sentences

Take a look at this sentence:

> The president outlined three ideas for her next term: balancing the budget, reducing spending, and a new relationship with Europe.

Because of the way people are used to speaking, this doesn't sound that bad, right? And it isn't horrible, but it's also not balanced or parallel. To balance this sentence, all three phrases in the list (*balancing the budget, reducing spending, and a new relationship with Europe*) need to match. Right now, the first two open with a verb and the last one is a noun. See? Not parallel. You could change this to:

> The president outlined three ideas for her next term: balancing the budget, reducing spending, and *creating* a new relationship with Europe.

This example is parallel because all the phrases begin with verbs. You can fix it up in other ways, too, if you prefer, such as making all the phrases in the list nouns.

Parallelism is also important in shorter sentences:

> He likes to swim and jogging.

You see the problem, right? It should be:

> He likes swimming and jogging *or* He likes to swim and jog.

Mistakes in parallel construction are most common in sentences that have three or more phrases, often in a list, as in the first example in this section. Keep a sharp eye out for them on the test. You can almost be sure that there will be a mistake in parallelism there.

Eliminating unnecessary words

Parallelism also means eliminating words that your sentences just don't need. This is a common idea in good writing, but here we mean that you should avoid bulking up your sentences with non-parallel constructions. Take a look at this example:

Xiomara admires people with intelligence and who have good character.

It's much simpler to make the sentence parallel and write:

Xiomara admires people with intelligence and good character.

TIP

That is a word that's very often used when it's not really needed. For example, in the sentence *Which is the car that the girl wanted to buy?* you can easily take it out: *Which is the car the girl wanted to buy?* When you're having trouble eliminating an answer choice that may be correct, check for the word *that.* It often (but not always) indicates wordiness.

Using Verbs Consistently

Using verbs correctly in sentences can be challenging. This is especially true as sentences grow longer and more complex with phrases and clauses, and even more so as you move beyond sentences to paragraphs. But nothing makes your writing seem less sophisticated than improper verb tense. This section tells you how to use verbs consistently.

Consistent verbs in sentences

No matter how long a sentence is, your verbs must remain in the same tense throughout. If the beginning of your sentence is in past tense, you almost always want the rest of the sentence in past tense, too. Here's an example of a sentence that needs to be fixed:

After learning the alphabet, Nancy will have moved on to learning numbers.

The problem here is that the first part of the sentence is in present tense, but the second part is in future perfect tense. This is better:

After learning the alphabet, Nancy *will move on* to learning numbers.

Take a look at another example:

Josh listened to the podcast and tells his friends about it.

There's something off here, too: The subject begins in past tense and then the sentence moves to present tense. This is better:

Josh listened to the podcast and *told* his friends about it.

The good news is that on the TASC, questions about this type of mistake are often very broad and easy to spot. Just be sure you read the entire sentence before making your choice.

Consistent verbs in paragraphs

It's easy, when writing at length, to let your verb tense drift. Perhaps you begin writing in present tense but suddenly drift into past tense. Obviously, rereading and revising your work will catch this problem. On the TASC, make sure the paragraphs you're given don't do something like this:

> Cows were highly prized during the famine in the late 1800s. Because people were starving and cows did not provide an immediate solution to that problem, they are a good source of milk and, eventually, meat. People do not realize how little cows consume compared to animals similar in size.

Do you see where the verb tense changes? This paragraph about cows in the 1800s starts out in past tense (*were, were, did not*) and then switches in the second sentence to being about cows today (*are, do not realize, consume*).

Choosing Active Verbs

We've already discussed how some verbs are *active*; that is, they show action of some kind, like *running, jumping, singing,* or *yelling.* There are also verbs that show *states of being: am, is, was, were,* and so on. Another word for state of being verbs is *passive.* Here, we want to encourage you to avoid passive verbs.

When you write sentences in the active form they are often clearer and more concise than those you write using passive verbs. Take a look at this sentence:

> A decision was made to postpone the game.

On its own, this sentence isn't terrible, but in a paragraph, it's dull to read and also takes up much more space than really needed. Worst of all, it's difficult to follow because the passive verb eliminates crucial information. Here's the same sentence written in an active tone:

> The coach decided to postpone the game.

Much clearer. Even though the second sentence is about the same length as the original example, it conveys more information (like *who* postponed the game) and it's more concise. Active verbs get you to that sweet spot in writing.

Pronouns: A Case of Their Own

Just in case you thought we were done with pronouns: nope! As helpful to English as they are, pronouns also present problems. One of the biggest grammatical issues they bring up is the question of how to use them as the subject or object of a sentence.

Choosing subject pronouns

Pronouns can be the *subject* (person or thing performing the action) in a sentence. That can lead to questions. For example, which is correct?

>> She and I went to the store.

>> Her and I went to the store.

>> She and me went to the store.

>> Her and me went to the store.

You've probably heard people say all these examples. You may even have thought that they all sounded reasonably okay. Perhaps in speech, yes, but in writing, there's a correct way to use these pronouns as subjects.

The best way to figure this out is to hide one of the pronouns in the subject and try the alternatives. So, which sounds better?

Her went to the store *or* She went to the store.

She, of course. Next round:

I went to the store *or* Me went to the store.

I, clearly. So the sentence should read:

She and I went to the store.

Sure, complicated reasons exist for why that's correct, but isn't it easier just to know how to figure out which you should use?

Choosing object pronouns

Pronouns can be the *object* (or receiver of the action) in a sentence, too. That can also lead to questions. For example, which is correct?

>> Tito asked her and him.

>> Tito asked she and him.

>> Tito asked her and he.

>> Tito asked she and he.

You always want to use the object form of the pronoun, which is simpler than it seems. Again, as in choosing the subject pronouns, cover one of the pronouns and figure out which would be correct:

>> Tito asked she *or* Tito asked her.

>> Tito asked he *or* Tito asked him.

Clearly, the sentence should read, *Tito asked her and him.*

It's easy to confuse *who* and *whom*, especially because people love to lecture you about which to use. Just remember that *who* is the subject form of the pronoun, and *whom* is the object form. Thus: *Who is going to the store with us?* and *She asked whom to go with us?* are correct.

Chapter 7

The Mechanics of Writing

The TASC tests you on your ability to write clearly and correctly and to find errors in sentences and paragraphs presented on the test. In this chapter, we review some of the most important aspects of grammar: the rules for capitalizing words, the different ways of punctuating a sentence, and words that are often misspelled. Knowing this information will go a long way toward improving your score on the TASC!

Capitalization

Understanding when you should capitalize a word and when you should leave it uncapitalized has confused almost everyone. The good news is that there are clear guidelines for capitalization. Memorize them, and you'll be set for the TASC, which won't give you a grammatical problem unless it has a clear answer.

Capitalization for clarity

It's helpful to remember that you capitalize words to make their importance clear to readers. That's why the words at the beginning of a sentence are capitalized, for example — to alert readers that a new thought is beginning. For the same reason, you capitalize almost all proper nouns, so as to make them stand out from the rest of the writing. Capitalization is also used to show respect (for leaders, religions, and countries, for example).

Sometimes, test-takers worry that they'll be given a "trick" question about capitalization, such as a sentence that involves an author (like ee cummings or bell hooks) who chose not to capitalize his or her name. But don't worry! The TASC won't ask you something that specialized.

A (baker's) dozen reasons to capitalize

Here are the 13 most common reasons to capitalize a word:

>> At the beginning of a sentence: She is the leader. Michigan is nearby.

>> Proper names of all types: This is Montgomery's receipt. Barry asked Rachel and Mindy to join him in Aruba.

>> Adjective forms of proper nouns: I recognize this Californian wine. Meredith sang a Russian song.

>> The titles of high-ranking leaders: The Pope met with the Queen.

>> All country names and adjectives derived from countries, even in common usage: Do they sell a lot of French fries in the United States?

>> Religions and the texts that they hold sacred: I read the Bible and Asa read the Koran. Is she Jewish?

>> Territories, including directional territories: Bill traveled to the South for his presentation. *Note:* Directions alone are not capitalized, as in "She ran north after hearing the explosion."

>> Titles of people and all parts of their names: Larry Mullen Jr., Dr. Molly Jenkins, Colonel Michael Meyer.

>> Names of mountain ranges and bodies of water: The Sierra Madres were visible outside the window. We drove until we saw Lake Erie.

>> Street addresses (all parts!): We live at 115 Briarwood Lane, Portland, Maine. ***Note:*** State and city names are always capitalized in any context.

>> Titles, although the shorter, less important words should not be capitalized: We read *Our Town*. My favorite album is *The Dark Side of the Moon*.

>> The pronoun "I": Blair asked me if I would mind replying.

>> The days of the week and the months of the year: Tuesday, Saturday, February, May.

Punctuation

The rules for punctuation are fairly simple, especially for the TASC. But errors in punctuation are common on the TASC, so you need to know how to correct them. Here are the basic forms of punctuation and when to use them:

>> The period (.) is used at the end of any sentence that doesn't ask a question or show strong emotion. Remember that periods break up a run-on sentence that's trying to express two different thoughts at once: I saw John. He was running late.

>> The question mark (?) is used at the end of any sentence that asks a question: Did you see John? Was he running late?

>> The exclamation point (!) is used at the end of any sentence that shows strong emotion: *John's running very late!* Exclamation points are used sparingly and may not even be on the TASC.

>> The comma (,) has a variety of uses. For the TASC, remember that a comma is used to separate things into lists: I took the pasta, meatballs, and sauce. A comma is also used in addresses: *We live in Johnstown, Pennsylvania.* Commas may also be used to separate clauses and phrases in a sentence (*Before she arrived, Matilda's sister called the restaurant.*) or in a sentence that joins two independent clauses into one sentence (*Bobby forgot his fiddle, but he joined in the singing.*). Also, use a comma to separate adjectives that describe different elements of the noun they're modifying: *I found this large, gray, vintage mixer in the basement.*

>> The colon (:) has several uses, but on the TASC, it's most likely used to introduce a list: *I sent Tracey the list of what we needed: glue, stickers, glitter, and a wreath form.*

>> The semicolon (;) is most commonly used to link together two independent clauses that are expressing one ongoing thought: *This is Pedro's chair; he just left for a moment.*

>> Quotation marks (" ") are used to designate some titles: We read the poem *"Stopping by Woods on a Snowy Evening"* today. They're also used to make clear someone's precise words: *"This isn't what I ordered," Mei Lang protested.*

>> Parentheses [( )] on the TASC are usually used to show that the information within them is not necessary but perhaps of interest: *This is the last football we purchased (because David said we were out of funds to buy any more).*

Spelling

If you find spelling correctly frustrating, know that you're not alone. Spelling errors are frequent and can trip up the most dedicated TASC test-taker. That said, bad spelling is a relatively easy problem to solve. All it takes is some mental effort and time to memorize how to spell words correctly. In this section, we give you our four best rules for spelling words correctly, and then we close the chapter with a list of the most commonly misspelled words.

Four good rules for better spelling

If you have trouble with spelling, remember the following rules.

Put "i" before "e"

You've probably heard this rule before: Use "i" before "e" except after "c." It's not foolproof, because English is a tricky language with many aberrations in spelling, but this rule is right most of the time. For example, *believe*, *piece*, and *receive* all follow it. Some notable exceptions are *weird*, *height*, and *foreign*.

Double the final consonant

When adding –*ing* to a word that ends in a consonant, you almost always double the consonant when a single vowel precedes it. For example, *stop* becomes *stopping*, and *occur* becomes *occurring*.

Change –y to –i

When you add a suffix (such as making the word plural) to a word that ends in –*y*, change that –*y* to an –*i*. For example, *party* becomes *parties*. This rule doesn't apply when the suffix you're adding begins with –*i* (for example, –*ing*). Thus, *try* becomes *trying*.

Drop the –e

When you're adding a suffix to a word that ends in –e, drop the –e, unless the suffix begins with a consonant (such as –ly). For example, *hope* becomes *hoping*, but *entire* becomes *entirely*.

Commonly misspelled words

Let's face it: The way words are spelled in the English language isn't very consistent. The rules are broken as often as they're kept. So sometimes it's best just to memorize the words whose spelling can give you the most trouble. Here's a list to get you started:

absence	device	library
address	disastrous	license
advice	ecstasy	maintenance
all right	embarrass	mathematics
arctic	exercise	mediocre
beginning	fascinate	millennium
believe	February	miniature
bicycle	fiery	miscellaneous
broccoli	fluorescent	mischievous
bureau	foreign	misspell
calendar	government	mysterious
camaraderie	grateful	necessary
ceiling	guarantee	neighbor
cemetery	harass	nuclear
changeable	height	occasion
conscientious	humorous	occurrence
conscious	independent	odyssey
decease	jealous	piece
deceive	jewelry	pigeon
definite	ketchup	playwright
descent	knowledge	precede
desperate	leisure	prejudice

privilege

pumpkin

raspberry

receive

rhythm

sacrilegious

science

scissors

separate

sincerely

special

thorough

through

truly

until

Wednesday

weird

you're (short for "you are")

Chapter 8

Choosing Effective Language

Not only do you need to know the rules of grammar to succeed on the TASC, but you should also be familiar with how to make your words effective as well as comprehensible. In this chapter, we look at how to choose the best words for your writing, whether for the essay (which we cover in greater depth in Chapter 9) or in evaluating sentences provided on the TASC for you to revise. We also discuss similar words — including homonyms, homographs, and homophones — that are often misused and list some of the more common ones found on the TASC exam.

Many ideas in the English language can be expressed in more than one way. Part of what the TASC is testing you on is to see whether you understand which words are not just technically correct but are appropriate for your audience. This means, in part, that you understand that casual slang like "gotta" and "Ummm, no" don't have a place in formal written English. It also means you should be able to differentiate between similar words.

Homing in on Homonyms, Homographs, and Homophones

The terms homonyms, homographs, and homophones represent words that can be tricky to figure out the meaning of when reading. The best approach to gaining an understanding of them is to look at clues in the context of the sentence, as we discuss in Chapter 4. This section defines what each of these terms actually means and then takes a look at a few examples.

Homonyms

Homonyms are words with multiple meanings; they sound the same when pronounced and often have the same spellings but have different meanings. The English language has thousands of homonyms; here are a few examples just to get you started:

Bat: Stuart failed to hit the vampire *bat* (animal) with his baseball *bat* (sports equipment).

Bear: A polar *bear* (large furry mammal) can *bear* (tolerate) very cold temperatures.

Down: John was feeling *down* (depressed) after failing to reach the top of the climbing rope so he climbed *down* (descended) and went home.

Fair: Janet said that it wasn't *fair* (justified) that she was not allowed to go to the county *fair* (event).

Left: The car *left* (departed) the parking lot and turned *left* (opposite of right) at the corner.

Right: The driver was *right* (correct) to turn *right* (opposite of left) at the traffic light.

Homographs

Homographs are words with different pronunciations and meanings but are spelled the same. Some examples are:

Bass: type of fish *or* low, deep voice

Bow: type of knot *or* to incline

Close: nearby *or* to shut

Desert: to abandon *or* arid, sandy area of land

Does: female deers *or* third person singular form of the verb "do"

Lead: to show the way *or* heavy metallic element

Moped: to act sad (past tense) *or* a bike with a motor

Produce: to create *or* fresh fruits and vegetables

Refuse: to reject *or* waste, garbage

Row: to move a boat with an oar *or* an argument

Tear: to rip *or* a drop of water from the eye

Wind: to turn *or* moving air

Wound: turned *or* an injury

Homophones

Homophones are words that sound the same but have different meanings and often different spellings. Because they sound the same, homophones are often confused for each other. There are literally hundreds of homophones, but luckily, the TASC tends to focus on the more common ones listed here:

Allowed/Aloud:

Allowed refers to something that is permitted: The dog was *allowed* to go for a walk each evening.

Aloud means to say something out loud: Reading *aloud* can help you concentrate on the meaning of the sentence.

Bear/Bare:

Bear can be used as a noun to describe a large furry mammal: The *bear* woke up after a long hibernation. *Bear* can also be used as a verb to describe supporting a heavy load: The wheels can hardly *bear* the weight of the fully loaded cart.

Bare is an adjective that describes a person or body part without clothing: My *bare* hand was burned by the hot pan.

Brake/Break:

Brake can be a verb describing the action of slowing something down: The car was going too fast to *brake* in time. *Brake* can also be a noun describing a device that slows something down: The car's *brakes* need replacing.

Break can be a verb that means to smash into pieces: If you drop your computer you will *break* it. *Break* can also be a noun meaning a short recess: I will take a *break* after typing the next chapter.

Buy/By/Bye:

Buy is used when purchasing an item: Jeff wanted to *buy* the car.

By is used as a preposition to indicate location: The coat rack is *by* the door.

Bye is short for goodbye: "Bye," said Jill, as she left the building.

Compliment/Complement:

A *compliment* is an expression of praise: Mrs. Jones was happy to receive so many *compliments* about her new hairstyle.

To complement means to enhance or complete something: Vanilla ice cream *complements* apple pie perfectly.

Hear/Here:

Hear is a verb that indicates listening: We can *hear* the bells ringing.

Here indicates location: You can park your car *here*.

It's/Its:

It's is a contraction used in place of *it is*: *It's* time to go.

Its is the possessive form meaning belonging to it: The cat licked *its* tail.

Principal/Principle:

Principal is a noun that describes either the head of a school or company, or a sum of money: The school's *principal* invested a large *principal* in her retirement scheme.

Principle is a noun that describes a basic truth or moral: The *principle* of the story was clear to all who read it.

Sail/Sale:

Sail is a part of a boat made out of fabric: The boat's *sail* was bright yellow. It can also be used as a verb as in this sentence: I want to *sail* to the island.

Sale refers to a reduced priced shopping event: The jeans were on *sale* for only $20!

Tail/Tale:

Tail is a noun that describes the rear end of some animals: The fish flicked its *tail*.

Tale refers to a story: The *tale* about the three goats and the troll is my favorite!

Their/There/They're:

Their is the possessive form and means belonging to them: Jeff wanted to see *their* new car.

There is used to indicate location: The shopping mall is over *there*.

They're is a contraction meaning *they are: They're* going to be late!

Two/Too/To:

Two is a number: Stuart wants *two* slices of cake.

Too is a synonym for also: We are coming *too. Too* can also express more than a desired amount: You are driving *too* fast!

To can be used as a preposition: We are going *to* the show. *To* is also the infinitive part of a verb: I want *to* help.

Weather/Whether:

Weather is a noun that describes the conditions outside: The *weather* is beautiful and sunny today. It can also be used as a verb as in this sentence: We should *weather* the storm in that cave over there.

Whether is a conjunction and refers to particular choices: I can't decide *whether* to try the pork or the fish first.

Witch/Which:

Witch is a noun meaning a woman thought to have magical powers: The *witch* wore a black cloak and pointed hat.

Which refers to selecting a particular thing: *Which* drink is mine?

You're/Your:

You're is a contraction used in place of *you are: You're* the first to arrive.

Your is the possessive form meaning belonging to you: *Your* hat is awesome!

When you come across these words when reading, looking at them in context will help you understand their meaning. For example:

In school we <u>read</u> a book about a little <u>red</u> hen. The hen's name was Sadie, and her best friend was a tiny mouse named Jack. Jack had a very long <u>tail</u> and loved to <u>sail</u>. Here is the <u>tale</u> of Sadie and Jack.

As you can see, the context of this short passage helps you determine the meaning of the homophones in the story.

Because homonyms and homophones sound the same, they're easy to miss when you're reading, but they're very common errors. The TASC will likely contain at least one question with homonyms or homophones. If you're prepared to look for them, you'll easily find the mistakes and earn points!

Dealing with Other Common Incorrectly Used Words

Making appropriate word choices also means that you understand the difference between easily confused words. Here's a list of commonly confused pairs, with their brief definitions, to help you. Because there are so many, we're focusing on words that are not homonyms.

Accept/Except: To *accept* is to agree to. To *except* is to leave out.

Advise/Advice: To *advise* is to give *advice.*

Affect/Effect: *Affect* is a verb, meaning to change something, while *effect* is usually a noun, meaning the result of an action.

Allusion/Illusion: An *allusion* is a subtle reference; an *illusion* is a deceptive view or idea.

Amused/Bemused: To be *amused* is to find something funny; a *bemused* person is confused.

Biannual/Biennial: A *biannual* event happens twice every year; a *biennial* event once every two years.

Climactic/Climatic: *Climactic* refers to the climax of a story, whereas *climatic* refers to the climate.

Collaborate/Corroborate: To *collaborate* is to work together, but to *corroborate* is to support someone's story.

Connote/Denote: *Connote* suggests a meaning, but *denote* is when something directly means another idea. ("Home" *connotes* "warmth," but "bayside cottage" *denotes* "home.")

Deduction/Induction: In a *deduction,* a general principle is derived from a specific set of examples. In an *induction,* a general principle yields information about specific subjects.

Elicit/Illicit: To *elicit* means to draw out, whereas *illicit* means *illegal* or *immoral.*

Farther/Further: *Farther* is about distance, but *further* refers to "in addition" or "more."

Figuratively/Literally: *Figuratively* is about metaphorical speech, and *literally* is about realistic or exact speech. It's best to try to avoid using *literally,* which has become overused.

Foreword/Forward: The *foreword* is the introduction to a text, while we move *forward.*

Historic/Historical: When something is *historic,* it is memorable; *historical* refers to any event in history.

e.g./i.e.: *e.g.* means *for example,* whereas *i.e.* means "that is to say. . . ."

Incredible/Incredulous: Something *incredible* can't be believed, but someone *incredulous* is skeptical.

Kind of/Sort of: Although common, these phrases should be avoided in formal writing. Be specific.

Later/Latter: *Later,* of course, means further on in time, whereas *latter* means the second of two choices.

Liable/Libel: When someone is *liable,* he is culpable. *Libel* is a legal term for defamation.

Loose/Lose: When something is *loose,* it is not tight. You *lose* a game or a necklace.

Passed/Past: You *passed* the turn already. History is what happened in the *past.*

Penultimate/Ultimate: *Penultimate* is the next-to-the-last, whereas *ultimate* is the best or last.

Real/Really: *Real* is used colloquially in some parts of the country as a substitute for *really* but is not correct in written English.

Supposedly/Supposably: *Supposably* is a real word, but it's rarely used correctly and shouldn't be substituted for *supposedly.*

REMEMBER

Learning this list of easily confused words that appear often on the TASC exam will go a long way toward helping you make the correct word selections and boost your score!

Paying Attention to Syntax

Syntax means the way words are put together in a sentence. It matters whether you write *Here's the old coat Mom gave away* or *Mom, here's the old coat gave away.* That's a silly example, but the order of words matters. On the TASC, you'll be asked to find the best syntax in some questions.

The following are rules for good syntax on the TASC:

» Write strong, clear sentences in the simplest style you can.

» Try to avoid complicated use of phrases and clauses.

» Be wary of using big words in an effort to prove your intelligence.

» Place adjectives as close as you can to the nouns they describe.

» Place adverbs as close as you can to the verbs (or adjectives or adverbs) they describe.

» If you speak another language besides English, make sure you don't confuse correct word placement in that language with how it works best in English.

» On TASC writing questions, take the time to break up and reorder a sentence until you get the best syntax.

» Avoid sentence fragments.

Chapter 9

Writing the TASC Essay

The second part of the TASC Writing subtest asks you to write an essay based on one or two reading passages provided for you. The reading passages are different from those provided for grammar or reading-related questions on other sections of the test. Generally, the essay prompt defines whether you need to write an argumentative or explanatory/informative essay. In this chapter, we help you develop a strategy for approaching both types of essays on the TASC. The most important thing to remember is that although the thought of writing an essay may frighten you, the TASC essay is supposed to be imperfect and not especially creative, as the test-graders know you don't have much time. A very standard, even boring, essay will do the job well here.

REMEMBER

An argumentative essay puts forth the case for something, usually some sort of fairly benign argument. You won't be asked to explain your views on abortion, for example. An informative or explanatory essay just asks you to put forth the information requested in a coherent way, but you don't need to take sides.

Plan First, Write Later

Because the essay is about halfway through the TASC, it's easy to panic and decide to just start writing. We understand the instinct, but we want to encourage you not to rush into writing. You'll likely still have quite a bit of time to write, and you'll receive a much higher score if your essay is thoughtfully planned and makes good sense.

It's also worth noting that the instructions for the essay suggest that you "plan for your essay." They go on to say, "Think about the quotes or examples you want to use. Think about how you will introduce your topic and what the main topic will be for each paragraph." From these instructions, it's clear that the test-makers and scorers are expecting a well-organized essay!

Take notes

The most important thing you can do to make your essay successful is to thoroughly read both the question being posed (in other words, the topic you are to write about) *and* the passages you're given to help support your topic. Make note of helpful phrases and sentences from the passages, especially when you find something that seems to exactly match up with the question you're being asked. If you're asked to write an argumentative essay, take particular pains to pull out words or phrases that you can use in making your argument. You should be alert for moments when the author is more extreme (using words like "always" or "never," for example) in order to build a nuanced argument.

Organize your notes

It's important to form a thesis after you've read the passage(s) thoroughly. What is the answer you're posing to the question asked in the essay prompt? Write it down in a clearly articulated way. Now, it's time to form an outline that supports your main idea, or thesis.

The TASC essay prompt doesn't suggest a specific length for your essay. While many test-takers think that a five-paragraph essay is the standard, we feel that it's more important that your essay be on point, well-crafted, and carefully organized. If that means writing a good three-paragraph essay instead of a mediocre five-paragraph essay, that's okay. Look over your notes to see how many points you can make to support your thesis. If you have two of them, plan on writing an introductory paragraph, two supporting paragraphs, and a conclusion. For three points, write three supporting paragraphs. Just one is fine, too, and unless you're a very fast writer, you probably don't want more than five paragraphs.

The introduction should — you guessed it! — introduce and explain your thesis and then refer to the points you'll be making to support your thesis. If you're going to use a specific quote from the passages, note that on your outline. Next, on your outline, figure out which supporting idea goes in each of the included paragraphs, and make a note of which quotes you'll use to support each one. Finally, your conclusion is the last paragraph in the outline. You can simply restate your argument if you like or use something more memorable: an anecdote from your own life, perhaps, or a quote from another source that supports your argument.

Write a first draft

With your outline complete, go ahead and write your first draft. You want to do this carefully, of course, but keep an eye on the time. It's better to have a few dropped words or minor grammatical errors than it is to turn in an unfinished essay. The goal is to keep your essay strong throughout, but readers are human and will be most impressed by a compelling first paragraph and more prone to forgive you if the rest of the essay is weaker.

Reread and revise

If you have time, definitely reread your essay. Although you may feel silly doing it, we strongly advise reading your work to yourself (not out loud, obviously). You'll catch errors that you would have read right past otherwise. Look for obvious errors, change words that you don't know how to spell, and make sure your quotes are correct and your logic is airtight. Don't sign off on the essay until you're sure you're satisfied or you're out of time.

Organizing the Explanatory Essay

While explanatory essays can seem simpler than argumentative essays, you do need to figure out how to organize your information in a way that makes logical sense. After you decide on your thesis and before you begin outlining, choose an organizing tool. We suggest presenting information *chronologically* (ordered in time, from oldest to newest) or using a *cause-and-effect structure* (meaning that you show something happening and then what the result of that is).

Whichever organizing method you choose, make sure it helps you clarify the relationships among the ideas and concepts in your essay. It's not helpful to try to impose a false order on a topic that doesn't really fit. For example, if you're asked to write about how authors organize information to make a point, a chronological structure most likely won't work well.

Arranging the Argumentative Essay

Organizing the argumentative essay is pretty straightforward. Just be sure that the essay prompt really is asking you to build an argument. Look for phrases like "show how" or "prove that."

Make an assertion

REMEMBER

It's important that your thesis (or assertion) be very clear in an argumentative essay. You may feel that both sides of an argument have merit (or even that the argument isn't really a matter of opinion). Nonetheless, you must choose *one* side of it to argue and argue it strongly. This isn't the time to be fair, which will only confuse your logic and make your essay seem weak. So don't just make a thesis — assert an opinion! If you're unsure which side of the argument to take, write down as many pros and cons as you can and see which option you can find more support for.

EXAMPLE

Try listing the pros and cons for the following essay prompt:

Should all public schools require their students to wear uniforms? Write an argumentative essay supporting either side of the debate in which you argue for or against mandatory school uniforms in all public schools.

Pros (in support of mandatory uniforms):

1.

2.

3.

Cons (against mandatory uniforms):

1.

2.

3.

Whichever side you found easier to fill in is probably the side of the argument that you should take.

Cite evidence

An argument needs support in a way that an informational essay, which simply reports the facts, does not. You need to pick and choose facts, opinions, and quotes to best support your argument as the evidence in each supporting paragraph. Again, be discerning. Choose support for *your* argument, not just the first facts you find. Your list of pros and cons should help you determine the main points that you can use to support your overall opinion.

EXAMPLE

For example, imagine that you had listed the following pros for the earlier essay prompt:

Pros (in support of mandatory uniforms):

1. Uniforms reduce peer pressure and teasing for students who may not be able to afford the latest fashionable clothing.

2. Uniforms help set a higher standard of behavior among students.

3. Uniforms help students identify with one another because they feel part of a larger group (the school).

Now, you would scan the supporting passages for facts, quotes, and supporting evidence for each of the points you've listed.

Draw a conclusion

Your essay should prove your argument, and it's not a bad idea to go on to draw a conclusion. Think of it this way: If A is your argument, then write a conclusion that shows that if A is true, then B, C, and D are also true. Being able to do so shows that your argument has legs.

Revise Again

We can't say it too often: Revise your essay for as long as you can until the writing section's time is called. You'll be amazed at how many mistakes you spot and by how you can refine your argument or information. It's grueling, sure, but remember — if you do it right, you only have to take the TASC once!

Mathematics

4

Chapter 10
Numbers & Quantity

I n this chapter, we explore the different topics that can be categorized as numbers and quantity. Though there are numbers all around us, they can be sorted in different ways and used in all sorts of problems.

First we discuss exponents and radicals, what they're used for, and their similarities and differences. Then we investigate different number systems or classifications of numbers. We put it all together when we use order of operations and convert units of measurement.

Exponents and Radicals

We'll let you in on a little secret: Mathematicians are lazy and don't like to write a lot if they don't have to. They'd rather not have to write $2 \cdot 2 \cdot 2 \cdot 2 \cdot 2 \cdot 2 \cdot 2$. So they came up with a shorthand for repeated multiplication, called *exponents*. To write the preceding multiplication problem, you can use an exponent to show how many "2s" are being multiplied. Thus, $2 \cdot 2 \cdot 2 \cdot 2 \cdot 2 \cdot 2 \cdot 2 = 2^7$.

Just like with other branches of mathematics, there are terms to remember when dealing with exponents. First, the number that's being repeatedly multiplied is called the *base*. The number that represents the number of times the base is being multiplied is called the *exponent* or *power*; these two terms are used interchangeably.

Exponent rules

REMEMBER

Exponents are used for repeated multiplication: $x \cdot x \cdot x \cdot x = x^4$. If there's not an explicit exponent written, then it's to the first power: $x = x^1$.

Mathematicians over the years discovered patterns when performing operations with numbers written with exponents. They were able to form general rules about these operations, shown in Table 10-1.

TABLE 10-1 **Exponent Rules**

Name of Rule	The Rule	What It Means	Example
Zero exponent rule	$x^0 = 1$	Any number raised to the zero power is equal to 1	$(576)^0 = 1$
Product rule	$x^m \cdot x^n = x^{m+n}$	When multiplying numbers with the same base, add the exponents	$(x^3y^2) \cdot (x^5y) = x^{3+5}y^{2+1}$ $= x^8y^3$
Power rule	$(x^a)^b = x^{ab}$	When raising a power to a power (inside/outside exponents), multiply the exponents	$(x^3)^5 = x^{3 \cdot 5} = x^{15}$
Quotient rule	$\dfrac{x^m}{x^n} = x^{m-n}$	When dividing numbers with the same base, subtract the exponent of the denominator from the exponent of the numerator	$\dfrac{x^8y^5}{x^2y^2} = x^{8-2}y^{5-2}$ $= x^6y^3$
Negative exponent rule 1	$x^{-a} = \dfrac{1}{x^a}$	A negative exponent in the numerator indicates that part of the term belongs in the denominator	$3x^{-5} = \dfrac{3}{x^5}$
Negative exponent rule 2	$\dfrac{1}{x^{-b}} = x^b$	A negative exponent in the denominator indicates that part of the term belongs in the numerator	$\dfrac{4}{x^4y^{-2}} = \dfrac{4y^2}{x^4}$
Negative exponent rule 3	$\left(\dfrac{x}{y}\right)^{-a} = \left(\dfrac{y}{x}\right)^a$	When raising an entire quotient to a negative exponent, you can "flip" the fraction (use the reciprocal)	$\left(\dfrac{3}{2}\right)^{-2} = \left(\dfrac{2}{3}\right)^2$
Distribution rule 1	$(xy)^a = x^ay^a$	When raising an entire product to a power, distribute the exponent to each part of the product	$(2x)^2 = 2^2x^2 = 4x^2$
Distribution rule 2	$\left(\dfrac{x}{y}\right)^b = \dfrac{x^b}{y^b}$	When raising an entire quotient to a power, distribute the exponent to each part of the quotient	$\left(\dfrac{2}{3}\right)^3 = \dfrac{2^3}{3^3} = \dfrac{8}{27}$

WARNING

Never distribute over addition or subtraction! For example, $(x+y)^2 \neq x^2 + y^2$; it really means $(x+y)^2 = (x+y)(x+y)$.

Notice that if you forget what a rule is, then you can write out what the exponents mean and use that instead. For instance, $\dfrac{x^5}{x^8} = \dfrac{x \cdot x \cdot x \cdot x \cdot x}{x \cdot x \cdot x \cdot x \cdot x \cdot x \cdot x \cdot x} = \dfrac{1}{x \cdot x \cdot x} = \dfrac{1}{x^3}$.

In addition, you can combine exponent rules and use them together. For example, $\left(\dfrac{3x^2}{2x^{-2}}\right)^{-2}$. There are many ways to approach this problem. You could simplify the inside part first, which is what I would suggest.

$$\left(\frac{3x^2}{2x^{-2}}\right)^{-2} = \left(\frac{3x^{2--2}}{2}\right)^{-2} = \left(\frac{3x^4}{2}\right)^{-2}$$

You can then use either distribution rule 2 or negative exponent rule 3. This example uses negative exponent rule 3:

$$\left(\frac{3x^4}{2}\right)^{-2} = \left(\frac{2}{3x^4}\right)^2$$

Now you can distribute the outside exponent into the quotient, using both the distribution rule and the power rule:

$$\left(\frac{2}{3x^4}\right)^2 = \frac{2^2}{3^2x^{4 \cdot 2}} = \frac{4}{9x^8}$$

So your final answer is $\left(\dfrac{3x^2}{2x^{-2}}\right)^{-2} = \dfrac{4}{9x^8}$.

Simplifying radicals and rational exponents

Mathematical operations always have opposites: addition and subtraction, multiplication and division. You can think of radicals as the "opposite" operation of applying exponents. The symbol $\sqrt{}$ is called a *radical* or *root*. Unless otherwise indicated, you're looking for the $+\sqrt{}$ or principal root when it's an even *index* (the number outside the $\sqrt{}$). Otherwise, you must consider both the positive and negative versions:

$$\sqrt{x^2} = |x| = \pm x \qquad \sqrt[3]{x^3} = x \qquad \sqrt[6]{x^6} = |x| = \pm x \qquad \sqrt[9]{x^9} = x$$

Note that if the index of the radical is not explicitly written, then you assume it's the square root, so the index is 2.

It's important to remember perfect squares. You should probably know up to 12 at least, if not 15.

$$1^2 = 1 \qquad 2^2 = 4 \qquad 3^2 = 9 \qquad 4^2 = 16 \qquad 5^2 = 25 \qquad 6^2 = 36$$
$$7^2 = 49 \qquad 8^2 = 64 \qquad 9^2 = 81 \qquad 10^2 = 100 \qquad 11^2 = 121 \qquad 12^2 = 144$$

To simplify a radical expression:

1. Make a factor tree (go to the *primes,* meaning you can't break the number down anymore).

2. Find pairs (square root), triples (cubed root), and so on.

3. Write pairs outside the radical (write only once) and leave everything else inside (think of the pairs as friends going out to play).

4. Find the products of what you "pulled out" and left behind.

Take this example: $\sqrt{75}$

So $\sqrt{75} = \sqrt{(5)(5)(3)} = 5\sqrt{3}$

Here's another example: $\sqrt{98x^4y^7}$

So $\sqrt{98x^4y^7} = \sqrt{(7)(7)(2)(x^2)(x^2)(y^3)(y^3)y} = 7x^2y^3\sqrt{2y}$

There's another way of representing radicals using rational exponents. We discuss what constitutes a rational number later in this chapter, but for the purpose of this discussion, it's important to know that these exponents are written as fractions. For instance, you can rewrite the square root to the 1/2 power. You can then use the exponent rules discussed earlier to simplify the expressions, as in this example:

$$\sqrt{16x^4y^8} = (16x^4y^8)^{\frac{1}{2}} = 16^{\frac{1}{2}}(x^4)^{\frac{1}{2}}(y^8)^{\frac{1}{2}} = 4x^2y^4$$

Estimating radicals

When calculating the root of a non-perfect square, cube, and so on, the resulting number is a non-terminating, non-repeating decimal, also known as an *irrational number,* which we discuss later in this chapter. It's important to be able to estimate the value of these radicals. When doing this estimation, you can use either the nearest perfect square method or a calculator.

Nearest perfect square method

Estimate which perfect square is closest — both smaller and larger than the number given. Then approximate the decimal in between based on the closeness. Check out this example:

$$\sqrt{50} \rightarrow \sqrt{49} < \sqrt{50} < \sqrt{64}$$
$$7 < \sqrt{50} < 8$$
$$\sqrt{50} \approx 7.1 \text{ (actually it's 7.071 ...)}$$

Here's another example:

$$\sqrt{40} \rightarrow \sqrt{36} < \sqrt{40} < \sqrt{49}$$
$$6 < \sqrt{40} < 7$$
$$\sqrt{40} \approx 6.5 \text{ (actually it's 6.324 ...)}$$

Calculator method

Plug the value into a calculator to get the decimal approximation. Remember that the memory of a calculator doesn't allow for a completely accurate approximation; calculators tend to round the answer to the last digit available on the display.

Examining the Real Number System

Almost all the numbers you deal with on a daily basis can be classified as *real numbers*. Within this classification, there are more categories that build on each other with the addition of different types of numbers. All real numbers can be classified as either rational or irrational. Further, there are subsets of the rational numbers that have distinct characteristics, starting with the natural numbers.

Natural numbers

The *natural numbers* are commonly referred to as the *counting numbers*. When you learned to count in kindergarten, they started you at the number 1. So the natural numbers start at 1 and proceed from there as if you were counting.

Natural numbers = {1, 2, 3, 4, . . .}

Whole numbers

The *whole numbers* are a set that includes *all* the natural numbers and another element, zero. Instead of starting at 1, like with the natural numbers, this sets starts at 0 and counts up from there.

Whole numbers = {0, 1, 2, 3, . . .}

Integers

The integers include both positive and negative versions of *all* the whole numbers. This set doesn't have a fixed starting point because it stretches from negative infinity to positive infinity. Think of this as a number line, with each tick mark being an integer, as shown in Figure 10-1.

Integers = {... −3, −2, −1, 0, 1, 2, 3, ...}

© John Wiley & Sons, Inc.

Rational numbers

Some people may try to generalize that all rational numbers are fractions. This isn't entirely true. A *rational number* is any number that can be written as an integer divided by an integer. So this includes traditional fractions, any terminating decimal, any repeating decimal, and any square root of a perfect square.

Some examples of rational numbers are $\frac{3}{4}$, 0.8, $0.\overline{78}$, $\sqrt{9}$.

In addition, all integers, whole numbers, and natural numbers can be represented as a fraction:

$$6 = \frac{6}{1}, \quad 0 = \frac{0}{1}, \quad -8 = \frac{-8}{1}$$

Rational numbers = {$\frac{p}{q}$, where p and q are both integers}

Irrational numbers

Rational numbers can be expressed as an integer divided by an integer; *irrational numbers*, on the other hand, are the set of numbers that can't be expressed in that form.

REMEMBER

A fairly common way to identify irrational numbers is by examining the numbers in decimal form. Irrational numbers are non-terminating, non-repeating decimals. This means the decimal representation doesn't end, nor is there a distinguishable pattern to the digits in the decimal.

Some of the most common irrational numbers are the square roots of non-perfect squares. In addition, there are very famous irrational numbers, such as π and e. If you were to type any of these cases into a calculator, it would appear as though they terminate. But you're smarter than a calculator and know that the calculator's memory space (and display space) is limited.

Figure 10-2 illustrates how each of the classifications of numbers can be nested inside another. This means that to get the next layer out, new elements are added to create a larger set.

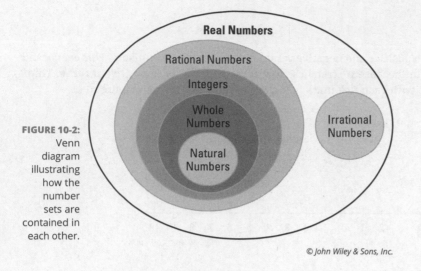

FIGURE 10-2: Venn diagram illustrating how the number sets are contained in each other.

© John Wiley & Sons, Inc.

Complex Numbers

While most of the time you deal with real numbers, on occasion you'll run into *complex numbers*. The first time most people encounter complex numbers is in algebra, when they find out that it's possible to take the square root of negative numbers. The important thing to remember here is that $\sqrt{-1} = i$. This means, for example, that $\sqrt{-9} = 3i$.

Complex numbers aren't just numbers that occur when taking the square root of negative numbers, though. They include any number that can be represented in the form $a + bi$, where a is the real part and bi is the imaginary part. This means any real number is a complex number when $b = 0$. Using this definition, Figure 10-3 expands the previous Venn diagram to show how complex numbers are the intersection of real numbers and imaginary numbers. We discuss the intersection of sets in more detail in Chapter 14.

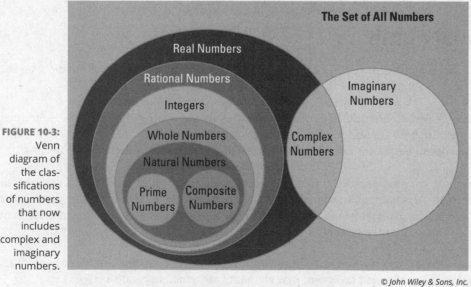

FIGURE 10-3: Venn diagram of the classifications of numbers that now includes complex and imaginary numbers.

© John Wiley & Sons, Inc.

Because complex numbers are still numbers, you can perform arithmetic operations with them, such as adding, subtracting, multiplying, and dividing.

When you add or subtract two complex numbers, you combine (add or subtract) the real parts together and the complex parts together.

Example: $(4+2i)+(5+8i)=(4+5)+(2+8)i=9+10i$

Example: $(9+5i)-(11-2i)=(9-11)+(5--2)i=-2+7i$

When multiplying two complex numbers, treat them more like polynomials than traditional numbers. This means you have to do double distribution. We like the box method the best because it keeps you organized and helps prevent losing terms. To perform multiplication using the box method, separate out each term of the complex number either along the side or on top of the box. To fill in each inside the box, multiply the column header by the row header. Lastly, you need to combine like terms (the two terms that have i in them).

$i^1=i \quad i^2=-1 \quad i^3=-i \quad i^4=1$

EXAMPLE

Take a look at this example shown in Figure 10-4: $(2+3i)(4-5i)$

FIGURE 10-4:
The box method can be used to make multiplying complex numbers easy.

	2	+3i
4	8	+12i
-5i	-10i	-15i² = -15-1 = +15

© John Wiley & Sons, Inc.

Thus $(2+3i)(4-5i)=8+12i-10i+15=23+2i$

Dividing two complex numbers would look like this:

$$\frac{a+di}{c+di}$$

To perform this division problem, you multiply both the top and the bottom of the quotient by the *complex conjugate* of the denominator. The complex conjugate of the denominator looks like the original denominator but with the opposite sign, so you would multiply the original question by: $\frac{c-di}{c-di}$ This results in a rational denominator.

Try working through this example: $(4+2i)\div(5+3i)$

$$(4+2i)\div(5+3i)=\frac{4+2i}{5+3i}$$

$$\frac{4+2i}{5+3i}\cdot\frac{5-3i}{5-3i}$$

Multiply as if they are regular fractions:

$$\frac{(4+2i)(5-3i)}{(5+3i)(5-3i)}$$

Now multiply these two complex numbers:

$$\frac{20-12i+10i-6i^2}{25-15i+15i-9i^2}$$

Simplify and you get this solution:

$$\frac{26 - 2i}{34} = \frac{13 - i}{17}$$

This tells you that the real number part of the answer is $\frac{13}{17}$ and the imaginary part is $\frac{-1}{17}i$.

Comparing Quantities

Many times you're asked to put amounts in order or to convert from one unit to another. To compare numbers, you must get them all into the same form. For example, if you're given two fractions and a decimal, then you should rewrite them all as either fractions or decimals. Similarly, when converting between different units, you either need to use a known relationship or be given one by the problem.

Different forms

Numbers come in all shapes, sizes, and forms, such as fractions, decimals, percentages, and roots. When asked to compare numbers or put a set of numbers in a certain order, it's easiest to do when they're all in the same form. Usually the easiest form to use is decimal form, especially when using a calculator.

Converting fractions to decimals

To convert a fraction to a decimal, divide the numerator by the denominator. The quotient could result in a terminating, repeating, or non-terminating, non-repeating decimal.

To represent repeating decimals, put a bar over the digits that repeat.

For example, $\frac{1}{3} = 0.3333333\ldots = 0.\overline{3}$

Here's another example: $\frac{19}{99} = 0.19191919\ldots = 0.\overline{19}$

Converting decimals to fractions

Sometimes, when comparing numbers, you may want to convert them all to fractions. You should only do this if most of the numbers are in fraction form to begin with because, to compare fractions, you must have *least common denominators (LCDs)*. So if you decide to convert decimals to fractions, you must first decide whether the decimals are terminating or repeating.

If the decimal is *terminating*, meaning it ends, you put the given digits over a power of 10. If there are two digits, you put them over 10^2 and then simplify if possible. Check out this example:

$$0.35 = \frac{35}{10^2} = \frac{35}{100} = \frac{7}{20}$$

You can always check your work by dividing numerator by denominator to make sure you get the same decimal you started with. Here's another conversion example, this one with three digits:

$$7.101 = 7\frac{101}{10^3} = 7\frac{101}{1000}$$

If the decimal is *repeating,* put the given repeating digits over 9s (depends on the number of digits that repeat). If there's one digit that repeats, then it goes over one 9; if there are two digits that repeat, they go over two 9s, so 99. Then simplify if possible. For example:

$$0.\overline{6} = \frac{6}{9} = \frac{2}{3}$$

Here's another example:

$$5.\overline{23} = 5\frac{23}{99}$$

Converting percentages to decimals

To convert a percentage to a decimal, you must consider how you got that percentage in the first place. Percentage literally means per 100, so to go from a percent to a decimal, you move the decimal two places to the left. Mathematically this means you're dividing by 100. Take at look at these examples:

$$87\% = \frac{87}{100} = .87$$

$$1,225\% = \frac{1,225}{100} = 12.25$$

$$1.2\% = \frac{1.2}{100} = 0.012$$

REMEMBER

If a question asks you to put a list of numbers in a specific order, note whether the question indicates *descending* order (largest to smallest) or *ascending* order (smallest to largest). Similarly, when ordering numbers that are negative, think about how they would look on a number line. The smaller numbers are to the left, which means the "more negative" a number is, the smaller it is.

For example, −7 is "smaller" than −3.

Units of measure (dimensional analysis)

When converting between different units of measure, it's important to keep track of the relationships between measurements. For instance, it's common knowledge that there are 12 inches in 1 foot, which is called a *unit factor.* Unit factors are made up of two measurements that describe the same thing. You can use this fact when translating one rate or measurement.

For example, if you're told that a piece of string measures a certain number of inches and you want to know how long that is in terms of feet, you can convert it using dimensional analysis. To set up the problem, you start with what you're given. Then you multiple by a ratio, in this case a unit factor, that contains both units of measure. At times you'll need to use multiple ratios to obtain the desired unit of measurement. The key to dimensional analysis is in the placement of your units — units need to be placed in opposite parts of a fraction for them to be "canceled."

Here's an example involving unit factors where multiple ratios are needed. Imagine that a car is traveling 20 miles per hour (mph) but you need to know how many inches per minute the car is going. This requires knowledge of three unit factors: 1 foot is 12 inches, 5,280 feet is 1 mile, and 60 minutes is 1 hour. Again, start with what you know and then place your converting ratios strategically based on where the units will cancel. Then multiply what's left in the numerator and denominator like regular fractions. Don't forget to simplify at the end.

You don't always use unit factors to convert between measurements. Sometimes you'll be told the relationship between two quantities of measurement, such as miles per gallon in a car. Another example is in scale or model drawings. These depictions represent something that's either too large or too small to draw at a normal size, such as a house or plant cell. The process for dimensional analysis stays the same, but it's important to read the questions carefully to pick out the units of conversion and to figure out what the question is asking you to measure.

Take a look at the example in Figure 10-5: In the scale drawing of the room layout, 1 inch represents 5 feet. What is the perimeter and area of the actual room?

FIGURE 10-5:
A scale drawing allows us to calculate the perimeter and area of the actual room.

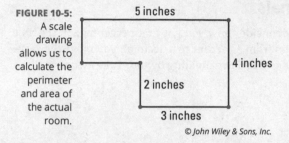

© John Wiley & Sons, Inc.

For this problem, you can either convert all the sides of the shape to feet first and then find the perimeter or find the perimeter in inches and then convert it to feet. We suggest always converting your units first.

Looking at the shape (and Figure 10-6), you can see that the perimeter would be the same as a 5-inch-by-4-inch rectangle if you "popped out that inside corner."

FIGURE 10-6:
The perimeter of the original rectangle can be used to determine the perimeter of the room.

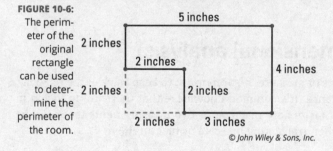

© John Wiley & Sons, Inc.

This means the lengths of the sides are:

$$5 \text{ inches} \times \frac{5 \text{ feet}}{1 \text{ inch}} = 25 \text{ feet}$$

$$4 \text{ inches} \times \frac{5 \text{ feet}}{1 \text{ inch}} = 20 \text{ feet}$$

This means the perimeter of the actual room is $25 + 20 + 25 + 20 = 90$ feet.

The area is a little different. You can see that the area of the original room is the 25-feet-by-20-feet rectangle minus the little extra rectangle that is 10 feet by 10 feet (found by converting the length and width of 2 inches into feet using the scale factor). So the area of the room is $(25 \times 20) - (10 \times 10) = 500 - 100 = 400 \text{ ft}^2$.

REMEMBER

Area is always measured in square units, perimeter is measured in linear units, and volume is measured in cubic units.

Using Order of Operations

If you ask someone off the street what the *order of operations* is, you may or may not get an answer. But we bet most people would remember what PEMDAS is. What people don't realize is that the PEMDAS acronym is used to help remember the order of operations. So what does PEMDAS stand for, and we're not talking about "Please Excuse My Dear Aunt Sally," which is just another mnemonic to help with remembering?

REMEMBER

PEMDAS stands for:

>> P: Parentheses (or other grouping symbols)

>> E: Exponents (or roots)

>> M or D: Multiplication or Division (left to right)

>> A or S: Addition or Subtraction (left to right)

WARNING

Make sure that you perform multiplication/division and addition/subtraction operations from left to right. If you don't, you may get a wrong answer. So even though the M comes before D in PEMDAS, if division shows up first when reading from left to right, then you should divide first, even if there's multiplication after it.

For example, in the problem $24 \div 3 \times 2^2 + 5$, you get an entirely different answer if you're not careful about reading left to right.

Done correctly:

$$24 \div 3 \times 2^2 + 5$$
$$24 \div 3 \times 4 + 5$$
$$8 \times 4 + 5$$
$$32 + 5$$
$$37$$

Done incorrectly:

$$24 \div 3 \times 4 + 5$$
$$24 \div 12 + 5$$
$$2 + 5$$
$$7$$

In the "done incorrectly" example, multiplication was done before division, which led to an incorrect answer.

In this next example, you would consider the radical as a grouping symbol, which means everything underneath it must be simplified first. This means that the order of operations must be followed within the order of operations.

$$\sqrt{4 + 2(7) - 2} + 2^3 - 16 \div 4$$
$$= \sqrt{4 + 14 - 2} + 2^3 - 16 \div 4$$
$$= \sqrt{16} + 2^3 - 16 \div 4$$
$$= 4 + 2^3 - 16 \div 4$$
$$= 4 + 8 - 16 \div 4$$
$$= 4 + 8 - 4$$
$$= 8$$

Chapter 11
Algebra

I n this chapter, we explore the different topics that can be categorized as *algebra*. This branch of mathematics is concerned with solving equations, isolating certain variables, and representing functions in graphical forms. To solve equations effectively, it's important to have a good understanding of the order of operations and the relationship between opposite operations.

First we discuss how to solve equations and inequalities of different forms. Then we explore properties of equations and operations performed on polynomials. Lastly, we graph different types of functions, including linear, quadratic, and exponential functions.

Algebraic Properties and Rules

There are certain basic properties that apply to all real numbers (if you're not sure what numbers qualify as real, refer to Chapter 10). Understanding these properties will help you in solving algebraic problems, such as equations, systems, or polynomials. In addition, combinations of these properties can be used to simplify equations or inequalities. The most fundamental properties used in algebra are identities, inverses, associative, and commutative properties. A summary of these properties can be found in Table 11-1.

In addition to the properties presented in this section, it's also important to recall the exponent rules discussed in Chapter 10. Refer to Table 10-1 if you need a refresher on these different rules.

Multiplication can be denoted by $\times$, $\cdot$, or numbers placed next to each other in parentheses. For example: $2 \times 3 = 2 \cdot 3 = (2)(3)$.

TABLE 11-1 Algebraic Properties

Name of Property	Explanation	Symbolic Representation	Example
Additive identity	You can add 0 to any real number and the resulting sum is that original number.	$a+0=a$	$5+0=5$
Additive inverse	You can add any real number and its "opposite" signed number and the resulting sum is 0.	$a+(-a)=0$	$4+(-4)=0$
Multiplicative identity	You can multiply any real number by 1 and the resulting product is that original number.	$a\times1=a$	$3\times1=3$
Multiplicative inverse	You can multiply any real number and its reciprocal and the resulting product is 1.	$a\times\frac{1}{a}=1$	$3\times\frac{1}{3}=1$
Commutative property Of addition Of multiplication	The order in which you add or multiply numbers does not matter.	$a+b=b+a$ $cd=dc$	$2+7=7+2$ $9\times3=3\times9$
Associative property Of addition Of multiplication	The groupings of numbers can be rearranged when you add or multiply and your answer will be the same.	$(a+b)+c=a+(b+c)$ $(de)f=d(ef)$	$(2+4)+3=2+(4+3)$ $(4\times5)\times6=4\times(5\times6)$

Like terms

In algebraic expressions and equations, you may be able to combine like terms to simplify what you're given. *Like terms* are terms of an expression that have the same variable and exponent composition; coefficients of like terms don't need to be the same. For example, $3xy$ and $8xy$ are like terms, but $3x$ and $8x^2$ aren't because the exponents don't match. To combine like terms, you add or subtract the coefficients of each term, depending on the signs. The following example shows how you would combine like terms in an expression:

$$5xy^2 - 3xy^2 = (5-3)xy^2 = 2xy^2$$

Distributive property

The *distributive property* allows you to multiply each part of a sum and then add them instead of adding before multiplying. Symbolically, this is shown as $a(b+c)=ab+ac$ or $(b+c)a=ba+ca$. These are equivalent expressions because you can apply the commutative property of multiplication and get the same answer. The following example illustrates this property.

Using the distributive property:

$3(2+4)$

$=3\times2+3\times4$

$=6+12$

$=18$

Following order of operations:

$3(2+4)$

$=3(6)$

$=18$

The preceding examples' use of the distributive property may seem unnecessary, but when there are variables involved, its use is essential. The following example illustrates how to use this property with a variable expression:

$$5(x-2)$$
$$=5x-5\times2$$
$$=5x-10$$

Solving Equations

Solving equations is a fundamental skill in mathematics and is used in many different situations. The main focus of solving equations or inequalities is to isolate certain variables or a combination of variables. Recall that a *variable* is a symbol, usually a letter, used to represent an unknown or changeable quantity.

Multistep equations

To solve an equation, you must:

1. **Be sure both sides of the equation are simplified; if they're not, simplify before proceeding.**

2. **If there are variables on both sides of the equal sign, move terms with the variables to the same side.**

3. **Move terms without variables, constant terms, to the opposite side so variables are on one side and constants are on the other.**

4. **If there's a coefficient on the term with the variable, multiply or divide to fully isolate the variable.**

REMEMBER

Division can be written as $\div a$ or $\frac{}{a}$. For example: $4\div2=\frac{4}{2}$.

In the following examples, notice how the steps are similar to reversing the order of operations: doing subtraction or addition first, then multiplying or dividing.

Example 1

$$2x+3=9$$
$$-3-3$$
$$\frac{2x}{2}=\frac{6}{2}$$
$$x=3$$

TIP

Be sure to check your answer by substituting your answer back into the original equation:

$$2(3)+3=9$$
$$6+3=9$$
$$9=9\,\sqrt{}$$

Example 2

$$3(x + 2) = 4x + 3x - 2$$
$$3x + 6 = 7x - 2$$
$$\underline{-3x \quad\quad -3x}$$
$$6 = 4x - 2$$
$$\underline{+2 \quad\quad +2}$$
$$\frac{8}{4} = \frac{4x}{4}$$
$$2 = x$$

Check:

$$3(2 + 2) = 4(2) + 3(2) - 2$$
$$3(4) = 8 + 6 - 2$$
$$12 = 14 - 2$$
$$12 = 12 \checkmark$$

Example 3

$$\frac{2x}{3} - 4 = 10$$
$$\underline{\quad +4 \quad +4}$$
$$\frac{2x}{3} = 14$$

You can solve this in two ways: You can multiply by 3 and then divide by 2 in two separate steps, or you can multiply by the reciprocal of $\frac{2}{3}$.

$$\frac{3}{2} \cdot \frac{2x}{3} = 14 \cdot \frac{3}{2}$$
$$x = 21$$

Check:

$$\frac{2(21)}{3} - 4 = 10$$
$$\frac{42}{3} - 4 = 10$$
$$14 - 4 = 10$$
$$10 = 10 \checkmark$$

REMEMBER

Not all equations have such a nice, neat answer. Some equations will result in a contradiction, which means there's no solution, denoted as $\emptyset$. On the other hand, equations could produce a true statement where the variable is eliminated. In this case, there's an infinite number of solutions, which we denote as "all real numbers."

Example 4

$$3(x + 2) = 3x - 7$$
$$3x + 6 = 3x - 7$$
$$\underline{-3x \quad\quad -3x}$$
$$6 = -7$$

Because this is false, the equation has no solution.

Example 5

$$5x + 6 - 7 = 4(x + 2) + x - 9$$
$$5x - 1 = 4x + 8 + x - 9$$
$$5x - 1 = 5x - 1$$
$$\underline{-5x \qquad -5x}$$
$$-1 = -1$$

Because this is true, the answer is all real numbers.

Equations with radicals or exponents

Not all equations are *linear*, meaning they have an exponent of 1; some common types that you may encounter are equations with exponents or radicals. Recall from Chapter 10 that exponents and radicals can be thought of as opposite operations. For example, $\sqrt[3]{x^3} = x$.

With these you follow the same steps as solving multi-step equations, but you must "undo" the exponent or radical to fully isolate the variable.

Example 1

$$x^3 - 5 = 3$$
$$\underline{+5 \ +5}$$
$$x^3 = 8$$
$$\sqrt[3]{x^3} = \sqrt[3]{8}$$
$$x = 2$$

Not all answers will simplify to an integer. You may have to simplify your answer or use a calculator to estimate it in decimal form.

Don't forget to check your answer(s):

$$x^3 - 5 = 3$$
$$(2)^3 - 5 = 3$$
$$8 - 5 = 3$$
$$3 = 3 \ \checkmark$$

Example 2

$$\sqrt{4x + 1} + 3 = 8 \quad \text{(you have to isolate the radical first)}$$
$$\underline{\qquad -3 \ -3}$$
$$\sqrt{4x + 1} = 5$$
$$(\sqrt{4x + 1})^2 = 5^2 \quad \text{(to undo the radical, square both sides)}$$
$$4x + 1 = 25$$
$$\underline{\quad -1 \ -1}$$
$$4x = 24$$
$$\frac{4x}{4} = \frac{24}{4}$$
$$x = 6$$

Check:

$$\sqrt{4(6)+1}+3=8$$
$$\sqrt{24+1}+3=8$$
$$\sqrt{25}+3=8$$
$$5+3=8$$
$$8=8\,\checkmark$$

Quadratics

A *quadratic* is a specific type of polynomial equation that is of the form $ax^2+bx+c=0$. To solve an equation in this form, there are different techniques that you can use. For simplicity purposes, we focus on two main methods: solving through factoring and solving through the quadratic formula.

Solving through factoring

Follow these steps to solve by factoring:

1. Be sure the equation is in standard form (all terms are on one side of the equal sign, the equation equals 0, and the terms are in descending order).

2. Identify *a, b,* and *c*.

3. Find the factors of *ac* that add together to give *b*.

4. Put each of these factors over *a* (the leading coefficient) and simplify if possible.

5. Set up two parentheses with the variable plus the simplified factors.

6. If the factors are in fraction form, move the denominator to be the coefficient of *x*.

7. Using the zero product property (which states that anything multiplied by zero equals zero), set each parenthesis equal to 0.

8. Solve each of the resulting equations.

9. You can also check your answers through substitution.

REMEMBER

It's important to note that not all quadratics are factorable. This doesn't mean there's no solution for the quadratic equation. It means that there may not be rational number answers, and your solution may have a radical or imaginary number as part of it.

EXAMPLE 1

$$x^2+5x+6=0$$
$$a=1 \quad b=5 \quad c=6$$

×ac (1)(6) = 6	+b +5
1·6	1 + 6 = 7
2·3	2 + 3 = 5 √

This means the two factors that multiply together to give 6 and add together to give 5 are 2 and 3.

$$(x + \tfrac{2}{1})(x + \tfrac{3}{1}) = 0$$
$$(x + 2)(x + 3) = 0$$
$$x + 2 = 0 \quad x + 3 = 0$$
$$x = -2 \quad\quad x = -3$$

This means the two solutions to this quadratic are –2 and –3.

EXAMPLE 2

$$6x^2 + x - 2 = 0$$
$$a = 6 \quad b = 1 \quad c = -2$$

×ac	+b
$(6)(-2) = -12$	+1
$-2 \cdot 6$	$-2 + 6 = 4$
$-3 \cdot 4$	$-3 + 4 = 1\sqrt{}$

This means the two factors that multiply together to give –12 and add together to give 1 are –3 and 4.

$$(x - \tfrac{3}{6})(x + \tfrac{4}{6}) = 0$$
$$(x - \tfrac{1}{2})(x + \tfrac{2}{3}) = 0$$
$$(2x - 1)(3x + 2) = 0$$
$$2x - 1 = 0 \quad 3x + 2 = 0$$
$$x = \tfrac{1}{2} \quad\quad x = -\tfrac{2}{3}$$

This means the two solutions to this quadratic are $\tfrac{1}{2}$ and $-\tfrac{2}{3}$.

Solving through the quadratic formula

You can use the *quadratic formula* to solve quadratic equations and provide a solution for all quadratics.

The quadratic formula is: $x = \dfrac{-b \pm \sqrt{b^2 - 4ac}}{2a}$. This will provide two solutions (notice the + and – signs in front of the radical). This formula may also give you answers that are irrational or complex (numbers that contain an imaginary part).

To solve using the quadratic formula:

1. Be sure the equation is in standard form (all terms are on one side of the equal sign, the equation equals 0, and the terms are in descending order).

2. Identify a, b, and c.

3. Substitute these values into the quadratic formula.

4. Simplify the resulting equation (be sure to follow order of operations).

EXAMPLE 1

$$6x^2 + x - 2 = 0$$
$$a = 6 \quad b = 1 \quad c = -2$$
$$x = \frac{-b \pm \sqrt{b^2 - 4ac}}{2a}$$
$$x = \frac{-1 \pm \sqrt{1^2 - 4(6)(-2)}}{2(6)}$$
$$x = \frac{-1 \pm \sqrt{1 - (-48)}}{12}$$
$$x = \frac{-1 \pm \sqrt{49}}{12}$$
$$x = \frac{-1 \pm 7}{12}$$
$$x = \frac{-1 + 7}{12} \quad x = \frac{-1 - 7}{12}$$
$$x = \frac{6}{12} \quad x = \frac{-8}{12}$$
$$x = \frac{1}{2} \quad x = \frac{-2}{3}$$

EXAMPLE 2

$$x^2 - 10x + 34 = 0$$
$$a = 1 \quad b = -10 \quad c = 34$$
$$x = \frac{-b \pm \sqrt{b^2 - 4ac}}{2a}$$
$$x = \frac{-(-10) \pm \sqrt{(-10)^2 - 4(1)(34)}}{2(1)}$$
$$x = \frac{10 \pm \sqrt{100 - 136}}{2}$$
$$x = \frac{10 \pm \sqrt{-36}}{2}$$
$$x = \frac{10 \pm 6i}{2}$$
$$x = \frac{10}{2} \pm \frac{6i}{2}$$
$$x = 5 + 3i \quad x = 5 - 3i$$

Inequalities

In addition to equations, you may also encounter *inequalities*. There are five symbols that can be classified as inequalities:

- ≫ $\neq$ (does not equal)
- ≫ $>$ (greater than)
- ≫ $<$ (less than)
- ≫ $\geq$ (greater than or equal to)
- ≫ $\leq$ (less than or equal to)

REMEMBER

Solving an inequality involves following the same steps you use for solving an equation except for one crucial detail: When you multiply or divide by a negative number, you must flip the inequality symbol. Just like with equations, you can still check your answers by substituting them back into the original.

REMEMBER

It's important to note that $<$ or $>$ results in an open circle ($\bigcirc$) on a number line because that value is not included as a solution; $\leq$ or $\geq$ results in a closed circle ($\bullet$).

The following examples illustrate some of the different types of inequality problems that you may encounter.

Example 1: Linear inequality

$$4x - 9 > 3$$
$$+9 \ +9$$
$$4x > 12$$
$$\frac{4x}{4} > \frac{12}{4}$$
$$x > 3$$

Check: You want to pick a value in the solution set. Because your answer is $x > 3$, you have to pick a value greater than 3. For this example, we use 5.

$$4(5) - 9 > 3$$
$$20 - 9 > 3$$
$$11 > 3 \ \sqrt{}$$

Example 2: Linear inequality with negative coefficient

$$5 - 2x \leq 7$$
$$-5 -5$$
$$-2x \leq 2$$
$$\frac{-2x}{-2} \geq \frac{2}{-2}$$
$$x \geq -1$$

Check:

$$5 - 2(0) \leq 7$$
$$5 - 0 \leq 7$$
$$5 \leq 7 \ \sqrt{}$$

Example 3: Does not equal

$$4x - 5 \neq -3$$
$$+5 \ +5$$
$$4x \neq 2$$
$$\frac{4x}{4} \neq \frac{2}{4}$$
$$x \neq \frac{1}{2}$$

Check: For this type of problem, you can pick any number except $\frac{1}{2}$. So for this example, you can pick 1 to check your solution.

$$4(1) - 5 \neq -3$$
$$4 - 5 \neq -3$$
$$-1 \neq -3 \,\sqrt{}$$

Example 4: Quadratic inequality

To solve a quadratic inequality, you must first get one side equal to zero. Then, factor each side and solve for the zeros of the quadratic. Lastly, set up a number line to check the different regions and determine which region or regions are your solution.

$$2x^2 - 5x + 4 < 2$$
$$\qquad\qquad -2 - 2$$
$$2x^2 - 5x + 2 < 0$$
$$a = 2 \;\; b = -5 \;\; c = 2$$

$\times ac$	$+b$
$(2)(2) = 4$	-5
$-1 \cdot -4$	$-1 + (-4) = -5$

$$(x - \tfrac{1}{2})(x - \tfrac{4}{2}) = 0$$
$$(x - \tfrac{1}{2})(x - 2) = 0$$
$$(2x - 1)(x - 2) = 0$$
$$2x - 1 = 0 \quad x - 2 = 0$$
$$x = \tfrac{1}{2} \qquad x = 2$$

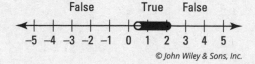

You now must check the three resulting regions.

$$x = 0$$
$$2(0)^2 - 5(0) + 4 < 2$$
$$2(0) - 5(0) + 4 < 2$$
$$0 - 0 + 4 < 2$$
$$4 < 2 \;\; \text{False}$$

$$x = 1$$
$$2(1)^2 - 5(1) + 4 < 2$$
$$2(1) - 5(1) + 4 < 2$$
$$2 - 5 + 4 < 2$$
$$1 < 2 \;\; \text{True}$$

False   True False

$$x = 3$$
$$2(3)^2 - 5(3) + 4 < 2$$
$$2(9) - 5(3) + 4 < 2$$
$$18 - 15 + 4 < 2$$
$$7 < 2 \text{ False}$$

This means the solution to this quadratic inequality is $\frac{1}{2} < x < 2$.

Example 5: Rational inequality

Just like a rational number is two integers being divided, a *rational expression* is two polynomials being divided. To solve a rational inequality problem:

1. **Get one side equal to 0.**

2. **Simplify one side as much as possible.**

   This may involve finding a lowest common denominator and combining like terms.

3. **Find the values that make the denominator equal to 0.**

   These are restrictions on the domain and will be needed when determining the solution set.

4. **Solve for when the numerator equals 0 to determine other critical values.**

5. **Set up a number line to check the different regions and determine which region or regions are your solution (similar to Example 4).**

Here's a sample problem:

$$\frac{3x - 5}{x + 2} \le 1$$
$$-1 \quad -1$$
$$\frac{3x - 5}{x + 2} - 1 \le 0$$
$$\frac{3x - 5}{x + 2} - \frac{x + 2}{x + 2} \le 0$$
$$\frac{3x - 5 - (x + 2)}{x + 2} \le 0$$
$$\frac{3x - 5 - x - 2}{x + 2} \le 0$$
$$\frac{2x - 7}{x + 2} \le 0$$

So the denominator is $x + 2$, and the value of x that results in a value of zero is $x = -2$.

Now for the numerator:

$$2x - 7 = 0$$
$$2x = 7$$
$$x = \frac{7}{2} \text{ or } 3.5$$

© John Wiley & Sons, Inc.

There's still the potential of 3.5 to be included in the solution set because the inequality symbol is $\le$. On the other hand, -2 can't be included because the denominator can never equal 0.

Pick test points from each region:

$$x = -4$$

$$\frac{3(-4) - 5}{(-4) + 2} \leq 1$$

$$\frac{-12 - 5}{-4 + 2} \leq 1$$

$$\frac{-17}{-2} \leq 1$$

$$8.5 \leq 1 \text{ False}$$

$$x = 0$$

$$\frac{3(0) - 5}{(0) + 2} \leq 1$$

$$\frac{-5}{2} \leq 1$$

$$-2.5 \leq 1 \text{ True}$$

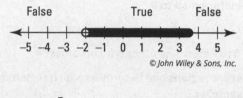

© John Wiley & Sons, Inc.

$$x = 5$$

$$\frac{3(5) - 5}{(5) + 2} \leq 1$$

$$\frac{15 - 5}{5 + 2} \leq 1$$

$$\frac{10}{7} \leq 1$$

$$1.428\ldots \leq 1 \text{ False}$$

So the solution for this inequality is $-2 < x \leq 3.5$.

Isolating a particular variable(s)

Not all equations are in single variables. There are common formulas that you may need to rearrange to find a certain variable or combination of variables.

EXAMPLE

The following examples illustrate how to isolate a particular variable given an equation or formula.

Example 1: $F = ma$, solve for m

In this example, the formula is how force is calculated: Force equals mass times acceleration. As indicated, you're solving for mass, m.

$$F = ma$$

To isolate m, notice that it's being multiplied by a.

This means you must divide by a on both sides.

$$\frac{F}{a} = \frac{ma}{a}$$

$$\frac{F}{a} = m$$

Example 2: $V = \frac{1}{3}\pi r^2 h$, solve for r.

This formula is used to calculate the volume of a cone given its height and radius. As indicated, you're solving for the radius, r.

$$V = \frac{1}{3}\pi r^2 h$$

First, multiply by 3 to "get rid of" the fraction.

$$3 \cdot V = 3 \cdot (\frac{1}{3}\pi r^2 h)$$

$$3V = \pi r^2 h$$

Don't be scared of π; it's just a number that can be divided.

Divide both sides by πh.

$$\frac{3V}{\pi h} = \frac{\pi r^2 h}{\pi h}$$

$$\frac{3V}{\pi h} = r^2$$

Lastly, take the square root of both sides to isolate r.

$$\sqrt{\frac{3V}{\pi h}} = r$$

Example 3: $4x(y + 5) = 2xy + 8$, solve for xy.

Because you're looking for xy, you need to simplify both sides and get any terms with xy onto the same side.

$$4x(y + 5) = 2xy + 8$$

Distribute $4x$.

$$4xy + 20x = 2xy + 8$$
$$-2xy \qquad\quad -2xy$$
$$2xy + 20x = 8$$
$$\quad -20x \quad -20x$$
$$2xy = 8 - 20x$$

Notice that xy is on one side, and all that's left is to divide by 2.

$$\frac{2xy}{2} = \frac{8 - 20x}{2}$$

$$xy = 4 - 10x$$

This means that the solution to this problem is $4 - 10x$.

Systems of equations

A *system of equations* is a set of equations in the same variables. The rule of thumb is that for every variable, you need that number of equations to solve for each variable. This means that if there are two variables, you need two equations in those variables to solve for both of them. There are three methods to solve a system of equations: substitution, elimination, and graphing. We discuss the first two in this section; we discuss graphing later in the chapter.

The solution to a system of two equations is an ordered pair or pairs that satisfy all equations involved. Similar to regular equations, there are different scenarios that produce different types of solutions. Table 11-2 illustrates the different types of solutions and what they mean.

TABLE 11-2 Types of Solutions

Classification	What It Means	How Solution Is Written
Consistent & independent	The system has exactly one unique solution.	(x, y)
Inconsistent	There is no solution to the system of equations.	No solution, $\varnothing$
Dependent	The equation actually represents the same thing. This means there are infinite solutions.	Represents the solution to either equation provided

Substitution method

To solve a system of two variables using the substitution method:

1. **Solve one or both equations for one of the variables.**

2. **Substitute what one variable equals into the other equation.**

3. **Solve the resulting equation for that one variable.**

4. **Substitute the found value back into either original equation to solve for the second value.**

You can also use this method to solve more than two variables, but it may require a bit more algebra because there will be more equations involved.

EXAMPLE 1

$$y = 2x + 5$$
$$3x - 4y = 10$$

Because the first equation is already solved for y, you substitute what y equals into the second equation.

$$y = 2x + 5$$
$$3x - 4y = 10$$

$$3x - 4(2x + 5) = 10$$
$$3x - 8x - 20 = 10$$
$$-5x - 20 = 10$$
$$+20 +20$$
$$-5x = 30$$
$$\frac{-5x}{-5} = \frac{30}{-5}$$
$$x = -6$$

Now that you have a value for x, you can substitute it into either of the original equations.

$$x = -6$$
$$x = 2x + 5$$
$$x = 2(-6) + 5$$
$$x = -12 + 5$$
$$x = -7$$

So the solution to the system is $(-6, -7)$. You can check this solution by substituting both values into both original equations.

EXAMPLE 2

$$2x - 4y = 6$$
$$x - 3 = 2y$$

Because neither of these equations is solved for one variable, you must do that first. Because the second equation is almost completely solved for x, that one is easier to use.

$$x - 3 = 2y$$
$$+3 \quad +3$$
$$x = 2y + 3$$

Now you can substitute what x equals into the first equation.

$$2x - 4y = 6$$
$$x = 2y + 3$$

$$2(2y + 3) - 4y = 6$$
$$4y + 6 - 4y = 6$$
$$6 = 6$$

This means that there are infinite solutions to satisfy this system.

Elimination method

To solve a system with two variables using the elimination method:

1. **Rewrite both equations so their variables are in the same order.**

2. **One pair of variables must have the same coefficients but with opposite signs.**

   For example, if one equation has $2x$, then the other equation needs to have $-2x$. If there isn't an existing pair of coefficients that meet this requirement, you must multiply or divide one or both equations.

3. **Add the equations together; the pair identified in Step 2 should cancel.**

4. **Solve the produced equation for the remaining variable.**

5. **Substitute the value obtained in Step 4 back into one of the original equations.**

6. **Solve for the other variable.**

EXAMPLE 1

$$2x - 3y = 7$$
$$3x + 3y = 8$$

Notice how the y's fit the requirement in Step 2. Add the two equations together.

$$2x - 3y = 7$$
$$+(3x + 3y = 8)$$
$$5x = 15$$
$$\frac{5x}{5} = \frac{15}{5}$$
$$x = 3$$

Now that you have a value for x, you can substitute it back into either of the original equations.

$$2(3) - 3y = 7$$
$$6 - 3y = 7$$
$$\underline{-6 \qquad -6}$$
$$-3y = 1$$
$$\frac{-3y}{-3} = \frac{1}{-3}$$
$$y = -\frac{1}{3}$$

The solution to the system is $(3, -\frac{1}{3})$.

EXAMPLE 2

$$4x = 6y + 7$$
$$6x - 9y = 10$$

For this system, you need to rearrange the equations so they're in the same order.

$$4x - 6y = 7$$
$$6x - 9y = 10$$

Now you just have to pick which variables you would like to eliminate. You need to multiply the top equation by 3 and the bottom equation by −2 for the x's to cancel.

$$(4x - 6y = 7) \cdot 3$$
$$\underline{(6x - 9y = 10) \cdot -2}$$
$$12x - 18y = 21$$
$$-12x + 18y = -20$$

If you add the equations together, both variables end up canceling:

$$0 = 1$$

This means there's no solution to this system of equations.

Arithmetic with Polynomials

A *polynomial* is an algebraic expression composed of multiple terms with non-negative integer exponents. Polynomials can be classified by the number of terms:

>> One term: Monomial

>> Two terms: Binomial

>> Three terms: Trinomial

>> Four or more terms: Polynomial

To determine the degree of a given polynomial, you must determine the degree of each term by adding the exponents of the variables together. The greatest term degree is the degree of the polynomial. In addition, the coefficient of the term with the highest degree is the *leading coefficient* of the polynomial. The mathematical convention is to write polynomials with terms in decreasing order. See Table 11-3 for examples of classification and identifying the leading coefficients and degrees.

TABLE 11-3 Classifying Polynomials

Example	Classification	Leading Coefficient	Degree
$5xy^4$	Monomial	5	5
$-3n^{1/2} + 4n$	Not a polynomial; has a rational exponent		
$-5x^3 + 6x^2 + 2x + 9$	Polynomial	-5	3
$4x^3y^4 + 2x^2y^2$	Binomial	4	7
$3t^2 - 5t + 2$	Trinomial	3	2
$\dfrac{7}{x^2} + 3x^3 = 7x^{-2} + 3x^3$	Not a polynomial; has a negative exponent		

Adding and subtracting

When it comes to adding and subtracting polynomials, the process boils down to combining like terms. The only thing to be careful of is the signs of the coefficients. There are two main methods of adding or subtracting polynomials: horizontally and vertically.

Horizontal method

With the horizontal method of adding or subtracting, you must distribute the sign to the second polynomial and then combine like terms. It may be helpful to underline or highlight like terms to track which you are combining.

EXAMPLE 1

$$\left(3x^2 + 4x - 5\right) + \left(2x^2 - 7x + 3\right)$$
$$= 3x^2 + 4x - 5 + 2x^2 - 7x + 3$$
$$= 5x^2 - 3x - 2$$

EXAMPLE 2

$$\left(5x^2 - 2x + 1\right) - \left(3x^2 - 4x + 5\right)$$
$$= 5x^2 - 2x + 1 - 3x^2 + 4x - 5$$
$$= 2x^2 + 2x - 4$$

Notice in this example that because this is a subtraction problem, the signs of the second polynomial needed to be switched. Then you can proceed with combining like terms.

Vertical method

With the vertical method of adding and subtracting polynomials, you line up the like terms, just like you line up the place value digits in a normal addition problem. Again, you have to distribute any subtraction signs to the second polynomial.

EXAMPLE 1

$$(3x^2 + 4x - 5) + (2x^2 - 7x + 3)$$

$$\begin{array}{r} 3x^2 + 4x - 5 \\ +2x^2 - 7x + 3 \\ \hline 5x^2 - 3x - 2 \end{array}$$

EXAMPLE 2

$$(5x^2 - 2x + 1) - (3x^2 - 4x + 5)$$

$$5x^2 - 2x + 1$$
$$\underline{-(3x^2 - 4x + 5)}$$

After distributing the subtraction sign, you get

$$5x^2 - 2x + 1$$
$$-3x^2 + 4x - 5$$
$$2x^2 + 2x - 4$$

Multiplying

Multiplying polynomials requires a strong understanding of the distributive property and exponent rules. When multiplying the individual terms of each polynomial, you multiply the coefficients and add the exponents (using the product rule of exponents). Similar to adding and subtracting polynomials, there are two main methods of multiplying: distribution and the box method. The box method is highly recommended because it helps to keep you organized.

Distribution

With the distribution method, you must multiply each term of one polynomial with each term of the other polynomial. There's an acronym commonly used with this technique when used with a binomial times a binomial: FOIL. This acronym tells you the order in which to multiply the different terms: First, Outer, Inner, Last.

WARNING

You can only use FOIL when you're multiplying two binomials.

EXAMPLE 1: MONOMIAL BY TRINOMIAL

$$3x\left(2x^2 - 4x + 5\right)$$
$$6x^{1+2} - 12x^{1+1} + 15x$$
$$6x^3 - 12x^2 + 15x$$

EXAMPLE 2: BINOMIAL BY BINOMIAL

$$\left(4x - 3\right)\left(2x + 5\right)$$
$$8x^{1+1} + 20x - 6x - 15$$
$$8x^2 + 14x - 15$$

Box method

The *box method* is similar in structure to a Punnett square used in biology. The dimension of the box depends on the number of terms in each polynomial. To fill in the center of the box, you multiply by the row and column headings. You can then combine like terms and get your products.

EXAMPLE 1: MONOMIAL BY TRINOMIAL

$3x(2x^2 - 4x + 5)$

So the dimension of the box will be 1 by 3.

	$2x^2$	$-4x$	$+5$
$3x$	$6x^3$	$-12x^2$	$+15x$

So the product is $6x^3 - 12x^2 + 15x$.

EXAMPLE 2: BINOMIAL BY BINOMIAL

$(4x - 3)(2x + 5)$

	$2x$	$+5$
$4x$	$8x^2$	$+20x$
-3	$-6x$	-15

Notice how the terms in the diagonal are like terms.

$8x^2 + 20x - 6x - 15$

$8x^2 + 14x - 15$

EXAMPLE 3: TRINOMIAL BY TRINOMIAL

$(2x^2 - 4x + 3)(3x^2 - 2x - 5)$

	$3x^2$	$-2x$	-5
$2x^2$	$6x^4$	$-4x^3$	$-10x^2$
$-4x$	$-12x^3$	$+8x^2$	$+20x$
$+3$	$+9x^2$	$-6x$	-15

$= 6x^4 - 16x^3 + 7x^2 + 14x - 15$

Graphing

Graphs are a visual representation of mathematical relationships. While many people think of a graph as a line, this is only one type — a continuous, linear graph. A graph can also be a discrete series of points, which are disjointed and not connected. Graphs aren't limited to just straight lines but can also represent curves or regions associated with different types of functions or relations. In this section, we explore how to graph different functions, what types of functions can be represented in tables or graphs, and different properties of functions.

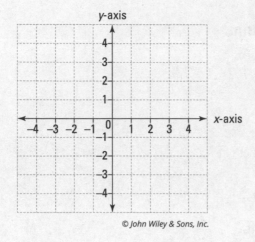

© John Wiley & Sons, Inc.

Linear

A *linear function* represents a relationship between two variables in which one variable influences the other. Usually, *x* is considered to be the independent variable and *y* to be the dependent variable (*x* influences *y*). The independent variable (*x*) runs horizontally, while the dependent variable (*y*) runs vertically. The minimum number of points you need to construct a line is two.

The common difference of the points that describes both the steepness and direction of the line is called the *slope*. This is also referred to as the *ratio* of the rate of change in the dependent variable to the rate of change in the independent variable. The letter associated with slope is *m*; if *m* is positive, then the line rises to the right, and if *m* is negative, then the line falls to the right. To determine the slope of a line, you need two points: (x_1, y_1) and (x_2, y_2). Then substitute into the formula:

$$\text{slope} = m = \frac{y_2 - y_1}{x_2 - x_1}.$$

Example 1

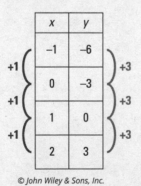

© John Wiley & Sons, Inc.

So the ratio of the common difference is $\frac{+3}{+1} = \frac{+3}{+1} = \frac{+3}{+1}$. That means this relationship is linear, and in fact, the slope of the graph is +3.

You can also see this by using the formula; just pick two of the points in the table: $m = \frac{0 - -3}{1 - 0} = \frac{0 + 3}{1 - 0} = \frac{3}{1} = 3$

Try to use points with 0 as one of the coordinates.

TIP

Example 2

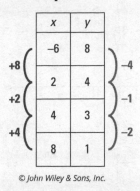

© John Wiley & Sons, Inc.

So you first check the ratio of the differences: $\frac{-4}{+8} = \frac{-1}{+2} = \frac{-2}{+4} = \frac{-1}{+2} = -\frac{1}{2}$. This means the slope of this linear function is $-\frac{1}{2}$, which you can also verify by using the formula: $m = \frac{4-8}{2--6} = \frac{4-8}{2+6} = \frac{-4}{8} = \frac{-1}{2}$.

In terms of a graph, the slope makes a staircase for the line to rest on. To graph a linear function given a table of points, plot the points in the table and connect them. The next section shows you how to graph given a formula for a linear function.

Slope-intercept form

Slope-intercept is the most commonly used formula to represent a linear function. Just as the name implies, this formula tells you the slope (*m*) of the line as well as the *y*-intercept (*b*). Recall that the *y*-intercept is the point at which the graph crosses the *y*-axis.

REMEMBER

Slope-intercept form: $y = mx + b$ (*m* is the slope and *b* is the *y*-intercept)

To graph a linear function in slope–intercept form:

1. **Plot the *y*-intercept on the *y*-axis.**

2. **Use the slope to find the next point (go up/down depending on the numerator, and then left/right depending on the denominator).**

   - If the slope is positive, go up and right (or down and left).
   - If the slope is negative, go down and right (or up and left).

3. **Plot at least two or three points using Step 2 and then connect the points.**

EXAMPLE

Here's an example:

$$y = \frac{-2}{3}x + 4$$

The *y*-intercept is 4 and the slope is $\frac{-2}{3}$.

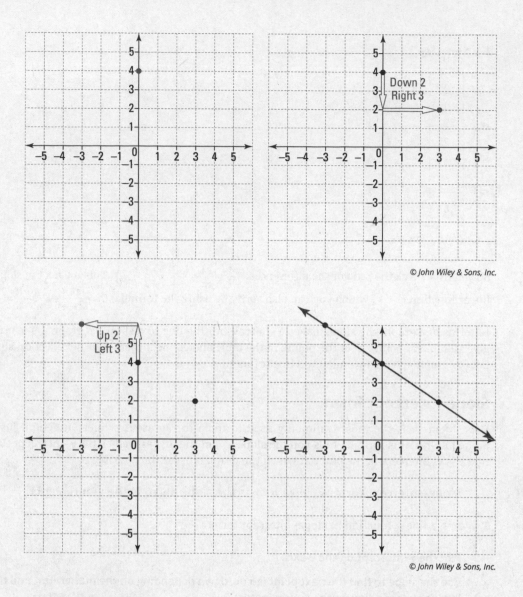

© John Wiley & Sons, Inc.

© John Wiley & Sons, Inc.

Point-slope form

A linear function in *point-slope form* looks like this: $y - y_1 = m(x - x_1)$, where m is still the slope and (x_1, y_1) is a point on the line.

Graphing in point-slope form is very similar to graphing in slope-intercept form:

1. Plot the given point (x_1, y_1).

2. Use the slope to find additional points.

3. Connect the points.

Standard form

Standard form for a linear functions is $Ax + By = C$, where A, B, and C are integers and A is positive. This means there can't be fractions or decimals as the coefficients.

To graph given a function in standard form:

1. **Find the *x*-intercept by substituting 0 in for *y* and solve** (*x*-intercept, 0).

2. **Find the *y*-intercept by substituting 0 in for *x* and solve** (0, *y*-intercept).

3. **Plot the two points found in Steps 1 and 2 and connect.**

EXAMPLE

Try this example:

$$2x - 3y = 6$$

x-intercept:

$$2x - 3(0) = 6$$
$$2x - 0 = 6$$
$$2x = 6$$
$$\frac{2x}{2} = \frac{6}{2}$$
$$x = 3$$
$$(3, 0)$$

y-intercept:

$$2(0) - 3y = 6$$
$$0 - 3y = 6$$
$$-3y = 6$$
$$\frac{-3y}{-3} = \frac{6}{-3}$$
$$y = -2$$
$$(0, -2)$$

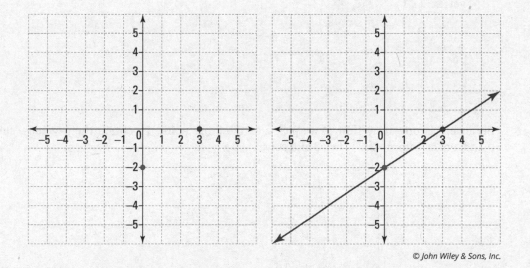

Quadratics

A *quadratic function* is a polynomial in which the highest degree is two. The shape of the graph representing the quadratic function is called a *parabola*, which is a U shape. The equation of a quadratic function comes in two main forms: standard and vertex. Both forms provide valuable information when it comes to graphing. In both cases, you can create a table, select values for the independent variable (*x*), and substitute in and solve for the values of the dependent variable (*y*). Similar to how it takes two points to construct a line, you need a minimum of three points to make a parabola.

Standard form

The standard form of a quadratic function is $y = ax^2 + bx + c$.

To graph a quadratic function in standard form:

1. Determine the axis of symmetry $x = \frac{-b}{2a}$ (this is also the *x*-coordinate of the vertex).

2. Substitute the value obtained in Step 1 back into the original formula to determine the *y*-coordinate of the vertex.

3. Pick two points that are equidistant from the *x*-coordinate of the vertex.

4. Substitute these values into the original formula (these resulting *y*-coordinates should be the same if the *x*-coordinates are the same distance away).

Try to pick when *x* = 0 as one of the values because doing so simplifies the algebra.

5. Plot the three points (vertex and two points from Step 4) on the coordinate plane.

6. Connect the points you plotted in a smooth curve (careful, you don't want to make the graph pointy or V-shaped).

Here's an example:

$$y = 2x^2 - 4x + 3$$
$$a = 2 \quad b = -4 \quad c = 3$$
$$aos = \frac{-b}{2a} = \frac{-(-4)}{2(2)} = \frac{4}{4} = 1$$

y coordinate
$$y = 2(1)^2 - 4(1) + 3$$
$$y = 2(1) - 4 + 3$$
$$y = 1$$

vertex: $(1, 1)$

x	y
0	3
1	1
2	3

Because 0 is one away from 1, we pick 2 as the other point. To obtain the *y*-values, substitute 0 and 2 back into $y = 2x^2 - 4x + 3$ and solve.

Vertex form

Similar to how the different forms of a linear equation provide different types of information, the *vertex form* of a quadratic provides specific information about a quadratic function. Specifically, this form explicitly states the vertex of the quadratic function.

The vertex form of a quadratic function is $y = a(x - h)^2 + k$, where $(h,\ k)$ is the vertex.

This form allows you to "skip" Steps 1 and 2 from graphing in standard form. So to graph from vertex form:

1. Identify the vertex $(h,\ k)$ — be careful of the signs!

2. Pick two points equidistant from the *x*-coordinate *(h)*.

3. Substitute values in and find the corresponding *y*-coordinates.

4. Plot points and connect with a smooth curve.

EXAMPLE

Try this example:

$$y = -\frac{1}{3}(x + 3)^2 + 2$$

So the vertex is $(-3,\ 2)$.

x	y
–6	–1
–3	2
0	–1

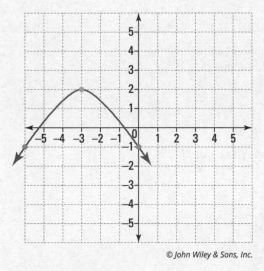

Inequalities

Graphing inequalities that are in two variables is very similar to graphing a regular function. The differences are that the line will either be dashed (if < or >) or solid (if ≤ or ≥) and that you need to pick a test point to determine which region will be shaded.

Here are the steps for graphing inequalities:

1. **Graph the function as if it were an equal sign.**

2. **Determine the type of line needed (dashed or solid): dashed if < or >; solid if ≤ or ≥.**

3. **Pick a test point; try to use the origin (0, 0) if possible.**

WARNING

The test point *can't* be part of the graph already (it can't be on the line).

4. **Substitute the test point into the original inequality.**

If inequality stays true, shade to include the test point.

If inequality becomes false, shade to exclude the test point.

Here's an example:

$$y < 2x - 3$$

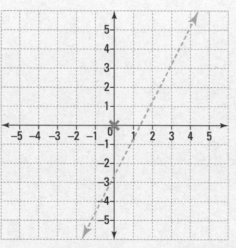

© John Wiley & Sons, Inc.

Now you pick a test point (0, 0) (marked by the X).

$$0 < 2(0) - 3$$
$$0 < 0 - 3$$
$$0 < -3$$

Because this is false, shade to not include the point.

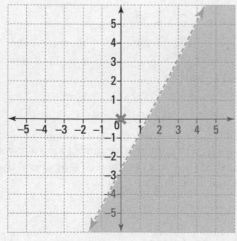

© John Wiley & Sons, Inc.

The solution to the inequality is the graph that shows the shaded region. If you want to check whether you picked the correct region, pick a point in the shaded area, substitute it, and make sure the inequality holds true. Also, these graphs aren't limited to linear inequality; they can include quadratic inequalities as well, and you would use the same process.

Systems

As stated earlier, graphing systems of equations is another method to solve for the solution. Graphically, the solution to a system of equations is the point or points where the lines or curves intersect. This means to solve a system of equations (linear, quadratic, and so on) by graphing:

1. Graph each function independently but on the same coordinate plane.

2. Look for the point/points where the functions intersect.

3. Test the points you identified by substituting them into all original equations.

While this step is optional, it's highly recommended because graphs can be drawn inaccurately if generated by hand.

Example 1

$$y = 2x - 1$$
$$y = -3x + 4$$

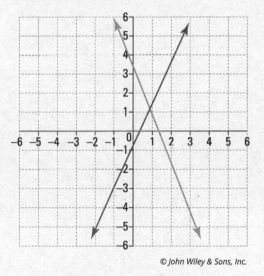

This means the solution to this system of equations is the point (1, 1).

Example 2

$$y = -\frac{1}{2}x + 2$$
$$y = -\frac{1}{2}x - 3$$

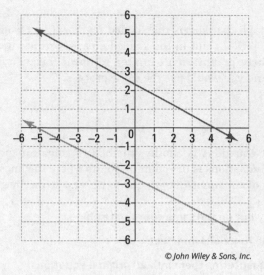

© John Wiley & Sons, Inc.

Because these lines will never intersect (these lines are *parallel*, a topic discussed in Chapter 13), there is no solution to this system of equations.

Systems of inequalities can also be solved in the same manner. You would graph each inequality as normal and look for the intersection of the shaded regions.

Chapter 12

Measurement Functions

n this chapter, we explore the different methods of representing functions, including tables, graphs, and mappings. *Functions* describe relationships between two or more variables, and this relationship can take on different forms. While functions can take on an infinite number of forms, there are four main categories that we explore in this chapter: linear, quadratic, exponential, and logarithmic. In addition, we investigate how the inverse of a function is determined and what it means. Lastly, we graph different types of functions, including linear, quadratic, and exponentials.

It's important to note that a function is a specific type of relation. A *relation* takes elements from one set and connects them to another set. For example, think of your birthday. This date is associated not only with you but also with everyone else born on that day. This is an example of a relation relating all the possible dates to all the possible people in the world. The set that you start with is called the *domain,* and the set that you end up with is called the *range.*

A function is a specific type of relation in which exactly one element of the domain is related to the range. This means that all functions are relations, but not all relations are functions. Sometimes, a relation can be a function if there's a restriction on the domain that forces the relation to fulfill the requirements of a function.

Methods of Representing Functions

The main methods of representing a function are in an equation, a table, a graph, or a mapping. Each type of representation has its pros and cons, but all can be used to represent the same function. This is an important point because you could be given an equation, for example, but a table would benefit you more. You can create a table given the equation.

Function notation

In the past few chapters, you've seen equations written as "$y =$". However, the common practice of mathematicians is to represent a function as "$f(x)$". This means that the equation you're given represents a function that you can evaluate at different points by substituting in values of x. Examples of functions written in function notation are:

$$f(x) = 2x - 5, f(x) = 3x^2 + 2x + 7, f(x) = -2, f(x) = 3^x + 2$$

Note: Other letters can be used besides "f" to represent a function. Other common ones are "g" and "h."

Tables

You can use a table to represent the relationship between two variables. More specifically, a table can illustrate a function. You can determine if a relation is a function through a table if each of the independent variables (usually x) is paired with one unique value of the dependent variable (usually y or $f(x)$). If the same independent value shows up multiple times in the table, then the same dependent value must be paired with it each time. It's important to note that the same dependent value can be used multiple times without compromising the classification of function. The pairs of numbers given in the table can also be represented as ordered pairs, which can be used in graphs or mappings.

x	y
1	3
2	5
3	3
5	−3

The preceding table represents a function because none of the independent values (x) is repeated, and each has only one corresponding dependent value (y). Each row in the table describes an ordered pair; for example, an x of value 1 corresponds to a y of value 3, so that's the ordered pair (1, 3). The whole table gives you the set of ordered pairs shown here:

{(1, 3), (2, 5), (3, 3), (5, −3)}

The next table does *not* represent a function. The x column has two values that are 7, and they correspond to two different values for y.

x	y
7	−10
1	−20
7	−30
−3	−50

When a single input (x) can produce multiple outputs (y's), the relation is not a function.

REMEMBER

Graphs

Given a graph of a relation, you can use the *vertical line test* to determine whether it's a function. If you can roll your pen or pencil across the graph from left to right (or from right to left) without it hitting the line in more than one place, then the graph is a function. On the other hand, if there's a place where a vertical line could be drawn that hits the graph in more than one place, then the graph doesn't show a function. Later in this chapter, we discuss how to determine what type of function is being shown through the different graph shapes. In addition, we discuss a test similar to the vertical line test that's used to determine whether a function (represented in graphical form) has an inverse. In the graphs shown in Figure 12-1, see whether you can determine which show a function as opposed to a relation.

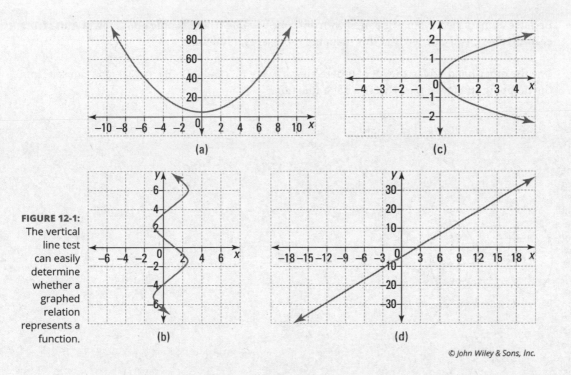

FIGURE 12-1: The vertical line test can easily determine whether a graphed relation represents a function.

© John Wiley & Sons, Inc.

In this case, graphs a and d represent functions, but graphs b and c do not. This is because in graphs b and c you can draw a vertical line that intersects each graph in more than one location.

Mappings

A *mapping* takes the set of independent values and shows which dependent values are paired with them. Similar to tables, mappings represent ordered pairs, and if a value from the independent set is paired with more than one value in the dependent set, then the mapping doesn't represent a function. For a mapping to show a function, each independent value must have only one arrow coming from it. Usually mappings are constructed when given a set of ordered pairs and use arrows to show the connections between them.

For example, if you have the set of ordered pairs {(−1, 3), (2, 0), (5, 9), (7, −2)}, then you can show it as a mapping, as depicted in Figure 12-2.

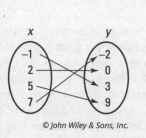

© John Wiley & Sons, Inc.

Because each of the x-values is paired with only one y-value (there is only one arrow coming from each x-value), you can see that this mapping represents a function.

One the other hand, given the set of ordered pairs {(0, −7), (1, 4), (2, 8), (1, 3)}, you can see from the mapping in Figure 12-3 that it's not a function.

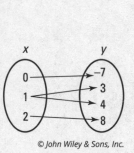

© John Wiley & Sons, Inc.

REMEMBER

It's important to note that, just like in a table, the dependent values of a mapping can be paired with more than one independent value. This means a dependent value can be on the receiving end of more than one arrow and the mapping still shows a function, as long as only one arrow emanates from each independent value.

Interpreting Functions

After you determine that a relation is a function, you can then look at the type of behavior going on and its critical values. The behavior you're looking for is whether the relationship causes the function to be increasing, decreasing, or constant. In addition, the behavior allows you to determine the domain and the range of the variables. The critical values in this case could be the maximum or minimum values or where the graph intersects the axes.

If a function is neither increasing nor decreasing, then it's considered a *constant*. The graph takes on a plateau effect or a flat line. It's also important to note that at the maximum or minimum points (the bumps in the graph), it's neither increasing nor decreasing. These are considered *critical points*, where the graph is changing direction from increasing to decreasing, or vice versa.

Increasing

When looking at the behavior of a function, you can either look at the end behavior — what happens as the graph extends to infinity — or look more closely at what's going on in the middle. In both cases, you can observe whether the relationship between the variables is increasing. This means that as one value increases, the other value increases. If looking at this function graphically, then the increasing portion(s) will be rising to the right.

The graph in Figure 12-4 illustrates a function that is increasing overall.

FIGURE 12-4: This function exhibits increasing behavior because an increase in the *x*-values causes an increase in the *y*-values.

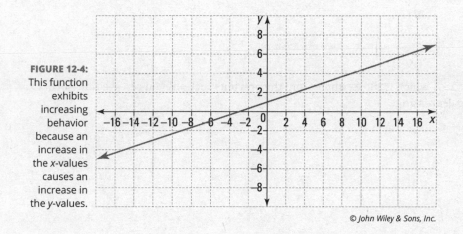

© John Wiley & Sons, Inc.

On the other hand, notice that only portions of the graph in Figure 12-5 are increasing.

FIGURE 12-5: This function exhibits increasing behavior for *x*-values between −1.8 and −0.4 and for *x*-values greater than 1.6.

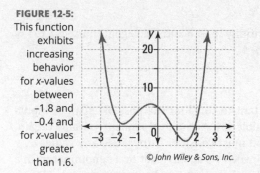

© John Wiley & Sons, Inc.

In this case, the increasing portions are from about −1.8 to −0.4 and then again from about 1.6 to infinity. This example shows how a function can increase within the domain and in its end behavior.

Decreasing

Instead of increasing, a function could be decreasing. To classify as decreasing, as the independent variable increases, the dependent variable decreases. Graphically, this means that the graph will be falling to the right. Similar to the way a function can be increasing overall or only in certain sections, a function can also be decreasing in the same manner.

The function in Figure 12-6 is always decreasing, no matter where you look.

FIGURE 12-6: This function exhibits decreasing behavior because an increase in the *x*-values causes a decrease in the *y*-values.

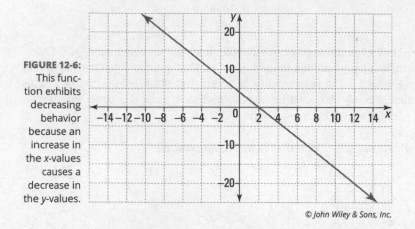

© John Wiley & Sons, Inc.

Looking at Figure 12-7, which is the example from the previous section, you can see that portions of the function are decreasing.

FIGURE 12-7: This function exhibits decreasing behavior for *x*-values between –0.4 and 1.6 and for *x*-values less than –1.8.

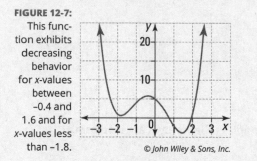

© John Wiley & Sons, Inc.

In this case, the function is decreasing from negative infinity to –1.8 and then again from –0.4 to 1.6.

Domain and range

When it comes to interpreting functions, it's important to consider the possible span of inputs and outputs. The *domain* of a function is all the possible values the independent variable (again, usually x) can take on. To determine the domain, you must consider if there are any values of x that are not possible — for example, if the function involves a square root or a denominator. In a similar way, the *range* of a function is all the possible values that the dependent variable (again, usually y) can take on.

When writing what the domain of a function is, you usually use interval notation. This shows the span of numbers that the independent value can take on.

- » To include a value, use a bracket: [or].

- » To not include a value, use parentheses: (or).

- » If using infinity as one of the end bounds, use parentheses because infinity is not an actual number that you can put your finger on.

For example, if there are no restrictions, then you can say the domain is all real numbers or $(-\infty, \infty)$.

In another example, if you have the function $f(x) = x^2 + 3$, you can interpret the domain and range in a couple of different ways. The first way would be to construct a table to test the function's behavior (see the following table). Another way would be to graph the function to give a visual representation of it (see Figure 12-8). From looking at the function, you can see that the domain is all real numbers because there are no restrictions needed to be placed on x.

x	f(x)
–10	103
–1	4
0	3
1	4
103	18

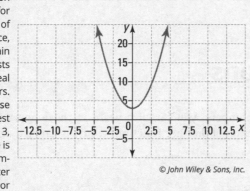

Both representations show that the range of this function is not all real numbers in this case. From the table and the graph, you can see that the lowest value of the outputs will be 3. As for the highest value of the outputs, you can see that the function will extend forever upward. This means the range is $[3, \infty)$.

Intercepts

Another important facet of interpreting functions is looking at the different intercepts. An *intercept* is where a function intersects one of the axes, and intercepts are named for the axis they cross. For instance, the x-intercept is when the graph crosses the x-axis. This definition looks at a function from a graphical perspective. The other way to understand this is that intercepts occur when the other variable takes on the value of 0.

Finding intercepts in a table means looking for the ordered pairs that have 0 as one of their coordinates. When given an equation, substitute 0 for the other variable and solve for the resulting intercept.

For example, if the function is expressed as $y = 2x - 4$, you can find the x-intercept by substituting 0 for y. You can also find the y-intercept by substituting 0 for x.

x-intercept:

$$0 = 2x - 4$$
$$+4 \quad +4$$
$$\frac{4}{2} = \frac{2x}{2}$$
$$2 = x$$

This means the x-intercept is $(2, 0)$.

y-intercept:

$$y = 2(0) - 4$$
$$y = 0 - 4$$
$$y = -4$$

Thus the y-intercept is $(0, -4)$.

REMEMBER

Intercepts can tell you important information, particularly when the function is given in the context of a word problem. For example, they can tell you the starting or ending points or the initial conditions of an event.

Operations with Functions

Just like adding and subtracting regular numbers, you can also perform these operations with functions. In addition, you can take a function of another function, which is called a *composition of functions.*

Addition and subtraction

When adding and subtracting functions, follow these steps:

1. **Evaluate each function at the value of *x* given.**

2. **Rewrite the equation but substitute what the functions are equal to.**

3. **Simplify the resulting expression (similar to adding and subtracting polynomials).**

For example: $f(x) = 2x^2 + 3x + 6$ and $g(x) = 9x - 10$

$$(f + g)(x) = f(x) + g(x) = (2x^2 + 3x + 6) + (9x - 10)$$
$$= 2x^2 + 3x + 6 + 9x - 10 = 2x^2 + 12x - 4$$

$$(f - g)(x) = f(x) - g(x) = (2x^2 + 3x + 6) - (9x - 10)$$
$$= 2x^2 + 3x + 6 - 9x + 10 = 2x^2 - 6x + 16$$

Composition

The *composition of functions* occurs when a function is applied to the results of another function. The notation is $(f \circ g)$, read as "f of g," and this can be rewritten as $f(g(x))$. This means the variable in the outer function gets replaced by the equation of the inner function.

For example: $f(x) = 3x - 2$ and $g(x) = x^2 - 5$, find $(f \circ g)$ and $(g \circ f)$

$$(f \circ g) = f(g(x))$$
$$= 3(x^2 - 5) - 2$$
$$= 3x^2 - 15 - 2$$
$$= 3x^2 - 17$$

$$(g \circ f) = g(f(x))$$
$$= (3x - 2)^2 - 5$$
$$= 9x^2 - 12x + 4 - 5$$
$$= 9x^2 - 12x - 1$$

You can also find $(f \circ f)$ or $(g \circ g)$ using the same process.

If you're given a value for x:

1. Evaluate the inner function at the value.

2. Evaluate the outer function at the resulting value from the previous step.

For example, given $f(x) = 7 - 3x$ and $g(x) = 2x + 3$, find $(f \circ g)(2)$.

$$(f \circ g)(2) = f(g(2))$$
$$g(2) = 2(2) + 3$$
$$= 4 + 3$$
$$= 7$$
$$f(7) = 7 - 3(7)$$
$$= 7 - 21$$
$$= -14$$
$$\text{So: } (f \circ g)(2) = -14$$

Identifying Functions Given a Graph or Table

Each function type has a general form that the graph takes on and an identifiable pattern in a table. Knowing these general rules helps you identify what type of function you're dealing with, and you can use this information to determine an equation for the function.

Linear

A *linear function* is a function of one or two variables in which all the variables have a maximum power of 1. Some examples of linear functions are:

$$y = 2x - 5, \ y = \frac{2x}{5} + 7, \ y = 5x, \ y = -2, \ x = 7$$

When looking at a table to determine if a function is linear:

1. Find the differences between the *x*-values.

2. Find the differences between the *y*-values.

3. Find the ratio of all the differences: $\dfrac{\text{difference of } y}{\text{difference of } x}$.

4. If the ratios found in Step 3 are constant, then it's linear.

For example, determine whether the following tables represent a linear function:

x	y
–1	–5
0	1
1	7
2	13

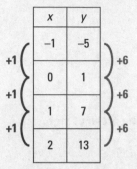

© John Wiley & Sons, Inc.

$$\frac{+6}{+1} = \frac{+6}{+1} = \frac{+6}{+1}$$
True

x	y
–2	–4
0	0
3	6
7	14

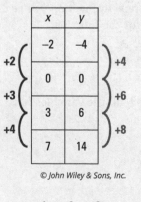

© John Wiley & Sons, Inc.

$$\frac{+4}{+2} = \frac{+6}{+3} = \frac{+8}{+4}$$
True

x	y
–1	–2
0	–6
1	–10
4	–14

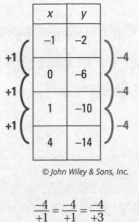

© John Wiley & Sons, Inc.

$$\frac{-4}{+1} = \frac{-4}{+1} = \frac{-4}{+3}$$

False

So the first two tables represent linear functions but the third one does not.

The common difference that we calculated to check whether the function is linear is called the *slope* of the line. This tells you the "steepness" of the line and whether it's increasing, decreasing, or constant. Other ways to refer to the slope are the "change in *y* over the change in *x*" or the "rise over run."

REMEMBER

The general formula used to calculate the slope when given two points (x_1, y_1) and (x_2, y_2) is

$$\text{slope} = m = \frac{y_2 - y_1}{x_2 - x_1}$$

REMEMBER

There are many ways to write an equation of a linear function, but here we use the most common: *slope-intercept form*. In this form, you use the slope of the line *(m)* and the *y*-intercept *(b)*:

$$y = mx + b$$

To write an equation from a table:

1. **Find the common difference (the slope).**

2. **Determine the *y*-intercept of the line.**

This may be explicitly given in the table when the *x*-value is 0. If not, pick an ordered pair to substitute into the formula and solve for *b*.

3. **Write the equation of the line using the values for *m* and *b* identified from Steps 1 and 2.**

For example, look at this table:

x	y
–1	–5
1	7
2	13
4	25

Checking the common difference, you see that this is indeed a linear function with a slope of 6.

Now you need to find the y-intercept. So, using the formula $y = mx + b$, the slope, and one of the ordered pairs from the table — say $(1, 7)$ — you can solve for the y-intercept:

$$y = mx + b$$
$$7 = 6(1) + b$$
$$7 = 6 + b$$
$$\underline{-6 \quad -6}$$
$$1 = b$$

This means that the equation of the linear function represented by this table is $y = 6x + 1$.

You can test this by substituting another x-coordinate from the table to see whether the appropriate y-coordinate is produced.

To determine whether a graph represents a linear function, look at the shape. Just as the name indicates, you look to see whether the graph makes a straight line that extends forever in both directions.

To determine the equation for a linear function given a graph:

1. **Pick two ordered pairs on the line (try to pick ones with whole number coordinates).**

2. **Calculate the slope by using the formula.**

3. **Identify the y-intercept (if shown on the graph).**

   If not, follow the same procedure as when given a table: Pick a coordinate and use the equation of the line to calculate b.

4. **Write the equation using the slope and y-intercept from Steps 2 and 3.**

Quadratic

Recall from Chapter 11 that a *quadratic equation* is a second-degree polynomial that produces a U-shaped graph called a *parabola*. To identify a quadratic function from a graph, you look for the U-shape.

To determine whether a table represents a quadratic function:

1. **Find the differences between the x-coordinates.**

2. **Find the differences between the y-coordinates.**

3. **Find the differences between the differences found in Step 2 (second-level differences).**

4. **Find the ratio of the difference from Step 3 and Step 1:**

<u>Second level-differences</u>
    Difference of x's

    If the ratios are equal, then the table represents a quadratic function.

For example:

x	y
−2	3
−1	0
0	−1
1	0

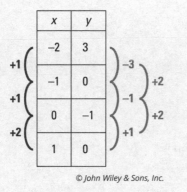

© John Wiley & Sons, Inc.

Because the second difference is constant, this table shows a second difference.

To write an equation of a quadratic function given a table:

1. **Identify the *y*-intercept (this occurs when *x* = 0).**

    This is the value of c in the standard form of a quadratic: $y = ax^2 + bx + c$.

2. **Pick an ordered pair and substitute the values for *x* and *y*.**

3. **Simplify as much as possible.**

4. **Repeat Steps 2 and 3.**

5. **This now produces a system of equations that you can use to solve for *a* and *b*.**

6. **After you identify *a, b,* and *c,* substitute these values into the standard form of a quadratic.**

Using the preceding table for an example:

y-intercept : $(0, -1)$ so $c = -1$

$$y = ax^2 + bx + c \text{ (using the } c \text{ value)}$$
$$y = ax^2 + bx - 1$$

Using the ordered pairs $(-1, 0)$ and $(1, 0)$, you get:

$$0 = a(-1)^2 + b(-1) - 1 \text{ and } 0 = a(1)^2 + b(1) - 1$$
$$0 = a - b - 1 \qquad \text{and } 0 = a + b - 1$$

Using the system, you can solve:

$$0 = a - b - 1$$
$$+ \ 0 = a + b - 1$$
$$0 = 2a - 2$$
$$ +2 \quad +2$$
$$2 = 2a$$
$$1 = a$$

Using either of the equations, substitute a back in:

$$0 = 1 - b - 1$$
$$0 = -b$$
$$0 = b$$

This means that the equation of the quadratic function is:

$$y = (1)x^2 + (0)x - 1 = y = x^2 - 1$$

Just like with a linear function, you can choose a different coordinate and substitute the value of x into the equation to see whether the corresponding y-value is produced.

Exponential

An *exponential function* is when the independent variable is in the exponent of a constant. The base of the function must be greater than 0 and not equal to 1. Some examples of exponential functions are:

$$y = 2^x, \ y = 3^{x-4} + 2, \ y = (\tfrac{2}{5})^{3x} - 7, \ y = e^x$$

REMEMBER

One of the most common bases used is the mathematical constant e. This constant is approximately equal to 2.71828. Similar to the number π, this is an irrational number and is used in many different areas of mathematics.

WARNING

Not all functions with an exponent are exponential — only when the exponent is a variable.

The graph of an exponential function rises rapidly to the right if the base is a whole number, as shown in Figure 12-9.

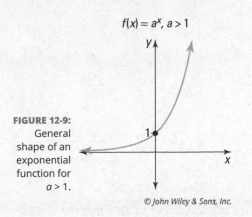

$f(x) = a^x, a > 1$

FIGURE 12-9:
General
shape of an
exponential
function for
$a > 1$.

© John Wiley & Sons, Inc.

If the base of the exponential function is a fraction, then the graph falls rapidly to the right, as shown in Figure 12-10.

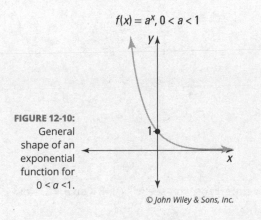

$f(x) = a^x, 0 < a < 1$

FIGURE 12-10:
General
shape of an
exponential
function for
$0 < a < 1$.

© John Wiley & Sons, Inc.

Looking for these general shapes when given a graph will indicate whether the graph represents an exponential function.

If you're given a table, to determine whether the function is exponential, check if there's a common multiple difference, meaning you can multiply each of the y-values by a number to get to the next y-value. This indicates that the function is exponential and, in fact, that that number is your base.

To write an equation for an exponential function:

1. Find the common multiple difference (this is your base, *b*).

2. Find your *y*-intercept — this is the coefficient of your exponential function *(a)*.

3. Substitute your values for *a* and *b* into the general form of an exponential: $y = a \cdot b^x$.

For example:

x	y
–1	3/2
0	3
1	6
2	12

First find whether there's a common multiple difference. It's important to note that the *x*-values are evenly spaced, which allows the common multiple to be identifiable.

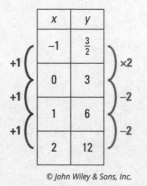

© John Wiley & Sons, Inc.

You now know that your base is 2. Looking for your *y*-intercept, you see it's (0, 3), so $a = 3$. Now substitute these values into $y = a \cdot b^x$:

$$y = a \cdot b^x$$
$$y = 3 \cdot 2^x$$

Logarithmic

A *logarithmic function* is the inverse of an exponential function. This means:

$$y = \log_b x \Leftrightarrow b^y = x$$

As with exponential functions, you can use the base of *e*. When this is the case, it produces a *natural log*, and instead of writing $\log_e(x)$, you write $\ln(x)$.

The general form of these graphs takes on the shapes shown in Figures 12-11 and 12-12.

FIGURE 12-11: General shape of a logarithmic function for *a* > 1.

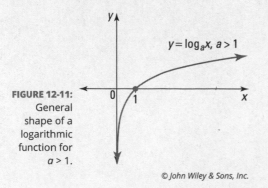

© John Wiley & Sons, Inc.

When given a table, to determine whether it represents a logarithmic function, the process is very similar to determining whether it's exponential. However, instead of looking for a multiple difference in the y-values, look for a common multiple difference in the x-values. Again, there needs to be even spacing between the y-values for the multiple difference to be shown.

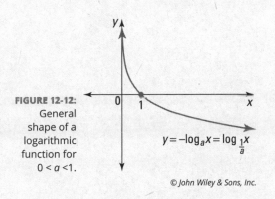

FIGURE 12-12: General shape of a logarithmic function for $0 < a < 1$.

$$y = -\log_a x = \log_{\frac{1}{a}} x$$

© John Wiley & Sons, Inc.

Chapter 13

Geometry

I n this chapter, we explore the different topics that can be categorized as *geometry.* This branch of mathematics came about because people wanted to understand and measure the world around them. First we discuss the properties of different lines that you find in shapes of all sizes and designs. Then we focus on polygons and circles and discuss ways of measuring their perimeters, areas, and volumes. We then discuss congruent and similar shapes, as well as different ways of transforming objects. We wrap up the chapter by investigating the three major trigonometric functions, which aren't as scary as the name suggests.

Terms to Remember

Geometry, like other branches of mathematics, has its own vocabulary and terminology that can sometimes be intimidating. The following list has some important definitions, terms, and notations to remember, beginning with the three important concepts — points, lines, and planes — that are the fundamental building blocks of geometry. These elements are depicted in Figure 13-1.

REMEMBER

>> A *point*, denoted by a capital letter (point *C*), has no dimension and marks a specific location in space.

>> A *line,* denoted by a script lowercase letter or identified by two points on the line (line *l* or $\overline{AB}$), is a series of points extending infinitely in both directions. You only need two points to define a line, and a line is only one-dimensional.

>> A *plane* is a collection of lines — a flat, two-dimensional space that extends infinitely in both directions. So, a plane is formed by three points and is denoted by a capital script letter, plane *M*.

» A *polygon* is a planar figure (flat or two-dimensional) and has straight sides that form a closed shape. Literally translated from Greek, *poly* means "many" and *-gon* means "angle."

» A *segment* is a part of a line named by its endpoints, $\overline{RT}$.

» A *ray* is a part of a line that has one fixed endpoint and extends forever in the one direction, $\overrightarrow{VW}$.

» If two lines or segments *intersect,* that means they have a common point of intersection where the lines "cross."

» The term *vertex* is used to describe the point of intersection of rays or segments or corners of geometric shapes.

» An *angle* is the amount of turn between two lines, usually rays, that share a point, the vertex.

» *Complementary* angles sum to 90 degrees.

» *Supplementary* angles sum to 180 degrees.

» *Bisect* means to divide into two equal parts. The *bisector* of an angle divides that angle into two equal angles, and the bisector of a line divides that line into two equal lengths.

» *Congruent* means equal in size and shape. Hence, congruent sides or segments have the same length, and congruent angles have the same measure.

FIGURE 13-1:
Plane *P* contains line *BC* (or *n*), ray *BD*, line segment *AC*, vertex *B*, and intersection point *A*.

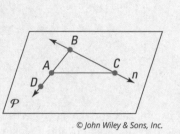

© John Wiley & Sons, Inc.

Parallel versus Perpendicular Lines

From the previous chapters, you have a good understanding of the slope and what graphs of linear functions look like. Just as a reminder, the *slope* measures the "steepness" of a line, or the ratio of its rise over its run. In both nature and man-made structures, there are lines that have certain mathematical relationships.

Parallel lines

Parallel lines, or segments, have one of the most interesting relationships. Lines that are *parallel* will never intersect, no matter how long they are. The reason these lines or segments never cross is that they have the same slope; this means that they're pointed in the same direction. The symbolic notation for parallel is ||, showing two lines that never intersect. The symbol looks like railroad tracks since they never intersect.

The lines represented by the equations $y = \frac{1}{2}x + 5$ and $y = \frac{1}{2}x - 3$ are parallel because their slopes are the same, $m = \frac{1}{2}$.

REMEMBER

If you're given one line and need to find a line parallel to it that passes through a given point, you:

1. **Determine the slope of the given line.**

2. **Using either point-slope form or slope-intercept form, substitute in the slope *(m)* and the given points *(x, y)*.**

For example, say you're asked to find an equation for the line parallel to $y = -3x + 4$ that passes through the point $(1, 5)$.

$y = -3x + 4$ tells you that the slope of the new line will also be -3.

Using slope-intercept form, use substitution: $5 = -3(1) + b$ (remember that b is the y-intercept).

Now you can solve for b:

$$5 = -3(1) + b$$
$$5 = -3 + b$$
$$\underline{+3 \quad +3}$$
$$8 = b$$

This means that an equation of the line parallel to $y = -3x + 4$ is $y = -3x + 8$. Notice how the lines have the same slope but different y-intercepts.

Perpendicular lines

All lines that aren't parallel but that are on the same plane will eventually intersect. *Perpendicular* lines or segments take this fact and put an interesting twist on it. Lines that are perpendicular intersect at exactly one point *and* they intersect at a right angle. The symbolic notation of perpendicular is $\perp$, which shows two lines meeting at a right angle. The symbol looks like an upside-down capital T.

The slope of the lines is important in determining if the lines are perpendicular. Perpendicular lines have negative reciprocals of each other. For instance, if one line is represented by the equation $y = \frac{2}{5}x - 4$, then a line that is perpendicular to it will have a slope of $-\frac{5}{2}$. So if you're given one line and need to find a line perpendicular to it that passes through a given point, it's just like the parallel example in the preceding section *except* the slope is not the same but is the negative reciprocal.

Polygons

A *polygon* is a two-dimensional shape that consists of three or more straight lines that are joined to form a closed figure. The TASC tends to focus on two particular types of polygons: triangles (three sides) and quadrilaterals (four sides), so we begin by exploring each of these in more detail.

Triangles

One of the most recognizable shapes in geometry is a *triangle*, which is defined as a three-sided polygon. A triangle has three sides made up of line segments and three angles that sum to 180 degrees.

Types of triangles

Triangles are classified based on the lengths of the sides or on the size of the angles:

>> An *equilateral* triangle has three equal sides and three equal angles (each equal to 60 degrees).

>> An *isosceles* triangle has two equal sides and two equal angles. The angle in between the congruent sides has a different measure, while the base angles are the equal ones.

>> A *scalene* triangle has sides of three different lengths and three different-sized angles.

REMEMBER

One of the most important types of triangles is a *right* triangle (either an isosceles or scalene triangle), which has exactly one right angle. Because it's a special triangle, the sides have specific names: The sides that form the right angle are called the *legs*, and the side opposite the right angle (the longest side) is called the *hypotenuse.*

The Pythagorean theorem

The sides of a right triangle have a special relationship, and by knowing two of them, you can use the Pythagorean theorem to find the length of the third side. This theorem says that the sum of the squares of the legs equals the square of the hypotenuse (see Figure 13-2).

FIGURE 13-2:
You can use the Pythagorean theorem to find the length of a missing side of a right triangle if you know the other two sides.

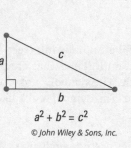

$$a^2 + b^2 = c^2$$

© John Wiley & Sons, Inc.

REMEMBER

Remember that you can only use the Pythagorean theorem for right triangles and that c represents the longest side (the hypotenuse).

Quadrilaterals

Add a side to a triangle and you have a geometric figure known as a *quadrilateral,* which literally translates to "four sides." In all quadrilaterals, the four angles sum to 360 degrees. Though any four-sided polygon is a quadrilateral, there are specific properties that allow us to further classify them. Figure 13-3 illustrates the many quadrilaterals.

Parallelograms

Parallelograms are quadrilaterals that have two pairs of opposite sides that are both parallel and congruent. In addition, opposite angles in a parallelogram are congruent, and their diagonals bisect each other. So, given a quadrilateral, you can determine if it's a parallelogram by determining if any of these properties apply to that figure. In the case of the sides, you need one pair of opposite sides that is both parallel and congruent or two pairs that are either parallel *or* congruent. If you show that both pairs of opposite angles are congruent, then you know the quadrilateral is a parallelogram, just like if you show that the diagonals bisect each other.

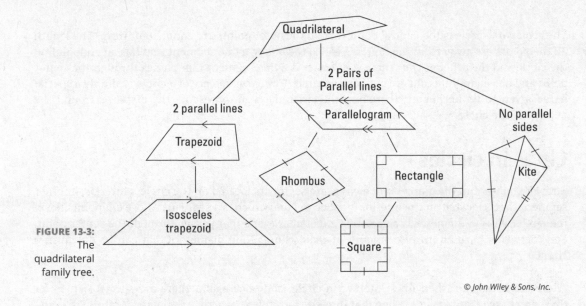

FIGURE 13-3:
The quadrilateral family tree.

Rectangles

Classification of quadrilaterals doesn't end with parallelograms; in fact, it has only begun! If a parallelogram has right angles, then you actually have a *rectangle* on your hands. Similarly, if the two diagonals of a parallelogram are congruent, then that figure is also a rectangle.

Rhombuses

On the other hand, if you have a parallelogram with no right angles but all four sides are congruent, then the parallelogram can be more specifically called a *rhombus.* In addition, the diagonals of a rhombus are congruent and they bisect opposite angles. Rectangles and rhombuses have all the properties of parallelograms but add their own twist.

Squares

Combining the properties of parallelograms, rectangles, and rhombuses results in the *square.* A square has four congruent sides that are equal in length and four congruent angles that are each 90 degrees.

Trapezoids

If a quadrilateral only has one pair of opposite sides that are parallel, then that shape can be classified as a *trapezoid.* Those parallel sides are called the *bases,* and the non-parallel sides are called *legs.* If the legs of the trapezoid are congruent, then that trapezoid is called an *isosceles trapezoid,* like a cut-off isosceles triangle. The base angles of an isosceles trapezoid are congruent.

Circles

A *circle* is a planar figure that is the set of points equidistant from a center point. A circle is always 360 degrees. One way to remember this is to think of extreme sports like snowboarding. When someone does a "360," that means the person makes one full revolution.

REMEMBER

The *center* of a circle is the central point that all the outer points are equidistant from. The length all the points are away from the center is called the *radius*, a line segment that has an endpoint on the circle and the other at the center. A *diameter* is a line segment that passes through the center point and has endpoints that are both on the circle. The *circumference* of a circle is simply a special name given to its perimeter; therefore, the circumference represents the distance around the outside of the circle.

Lines in circles

Both the radius and the diameter of a circle are segments located on the circle's interior. Another segment that's located on the interior is called a *chord*, which is a segment whose endpoints lie on the circle. Thus, a diameter is a specific type of chord, one that passes through the center point. Fun fact: There are an infinite amount of radii, chords, and diameters that can be drawn in a circle.

There are occasions when lines intersect a circle, and once again, there are special names for these lines (see Figure 13-4). A line that intersects a circle at exactly two points, a "through-and-through," is called a *secant*. The segment inside the circle that results from a secant is then a chord. A line that intersects a circle at exactly one point, a "hit-and-run," is called a *tangent* line.

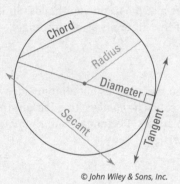

FIGURE 13-4: Important lines in circles.

© John Wiley & Sons, Inc.

Arcs

An *arc* of a circle is a portion of the outside of the circle (see Figure 13-5). The shortest arc between the points named is called the *minor arc*, and the rest of the circle is called the *major arc*. Like line segments, arcs are named by their endpoints. So when naming the major arc, you must indicate that by including an extra point to indicate orientation; otherwise, an arc is assumed to be the shortest one. Usually when measuring arcs, we talk about them in degrees, just like we do for angles. In fact, there's an interesting relationship between the measure of an arc and the angles that intercept it.

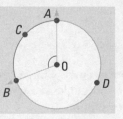

FIGURE 13-5: Naming arcs in circles: Minor arc is $\overset{\frown}{ACB}$ and major arc is $\overset{\frown}{ADB}$.

© John Wiley & Sons, Inc.

Angles in circles

When you start combining lines in circles, you get resulting angles. If two radii form an angle, it's called the *central angle.* The arc intercepted by a central angle has the same degree measure as that angle. An *inscribed angle* is an angle formed by two chords in a circle that have a common endpoint. The arc intercepted by an inscribed angle is twice the measure of that angle.

TIP

The measure of the intercepted arc angle is *twice* that of the inscribed angle (see Figure 13-6).

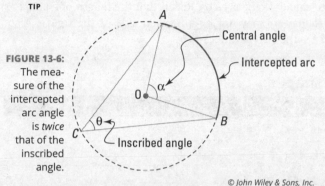

FIGURE 13-6:
The measure of the intercepted arc angle is *twice* that of the inscribed angle.

© John Wiley & Sons, Inc.

An arc that's intercepted by a diameter is actually a *semicircle,* meaning it's half a circle and measures 180 degrees. Similarly, if an inscribed angle intercepts a diameter or semicircle, then that angle is right.

Perimeters, Areas, and Volumes

Geometry was invented (or discovered!) to help us make sense of the world around us. You often need to take measurements to determine how big or small an object is, so in this section, we discuss several different metrics, including perimeter, area, and volume, that help you compare different shapes.

Perimeter

The *perimeter* of a geometric figure measures the distance around a shape. If you're given the lengths of all the exterior sides (or if you can deduce them), you simply add them all up. If you're given coordinates of the vertices of a planar figure, then you need to determine the lengths of the sides. Sometimes you can do this by observation, but other times you need to use the distance formula to calculate the lengths. For instance, if you know the vertices of a shape are $(0,2),(4,2),(0,6),$ and $(4,6)$ and you do a sketch of this figure by plotting the points on the coordinate plane, you'll see that this shape is a square and that you can count the lengths of the four sides, $s = 4$. This means the perimeter is $P = 4 + 4 + 4 + 4 = 16$ units.

At other times, the lengths can't be determined accurately through observation, so it becomes necessary to use the distance formula. The distance between two points (x_1, y_1) and (x_2, y_2) is given by the formula: distance $= \sqrt{(x_2 - x_1)^2 + (y_2 - y_1)^2}$.

Area

One of the most discussed concepts in geometry is *area*, which measures the amount of two-dimensional space contained within a figure. In more common terminology, this is the amount of coverage (amount of squares) used to cover a shape. Because there are two dimensions, the units for area are always squared: in^2, ft^2, and so on.

There are particular formulas that can be used to calculate the area of common shapes. Check out Table 13-1 for specifics. If the shape is not common or is an irregular shape, you may need to break it up into shapes you know how to calculate the area of. Recall that the height of a shape is always measured at a right angle, so it may or may not be an actual side of the figure. Also, remember that the bases of a trapezoid are the two parallel sides.

TABLE 13-1 **Area Formulas for Common Shapes**

Shape	Formula for Area	Notation
Rectangle (or square)	length × width	*lw* or *bh*
Parallelogram	base × height	*bh*
Trapezoid	$\frac{1}{2} \times \text{height} \times (\text{base}_1 + \text{base}_2)$	$\frac{h(b_1 + b_2)}{2}$
Triangle	$\frac{1}{2} \times \text{base} \times \text{height}$	$\frac{bh}{2}$
Circle	$\pi \times \text{radius}^2$	πr^2

Volume

Just like area is concerned with the amount of coverage of a two-dimensional shape, *volume* measures the amount of space inside a three-dimensional figure. For instance, how much soda does a can hold? Because there are three dimensions now, the units for volume are always cubed: in^3, ft^3, and so on.

Prisms

One of the most common 3-D figures is a *prism* — a three-dimensional shape that has two bases that are parallel and have the same size and shape. To calculate the volume of a prism, you just multiply the area of the base by the height (or the length) of the prism. For example, in the triangular prism in Figure 13-7, the area of the triangular base is $\frac{bh}{2}$, so now you multiply this area by the "height of the prism," which in this case is its length.

Volume of triangular prism = area of cross-section × length

$$= \frac{1}{2} \times b \times h \times l$$

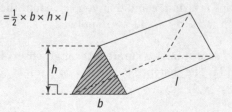

FIGURE 13-7:
Finding the volume of a triangular-based prism.

Note that a *cylinder* is just a circular-based prism, so to find the volume of a cylinder you simply multiply the area of the base (πr^2) by the height of the cylinder. Hence:

Volume of a cylinder = $\pi r^2 h$

Pyramids

Similarly, the process to calculate the volume of any *pyramid*, a figure that has one base and triangular sides that meet at a point, is the same no matter what shape the base is. Once again, you need to calculate the area of the base and multiply it by the height, just like for a prism. However, this time you must divide this product by 3 (or multiply by $\frac{1}{3}$). This shows the relationship between a prism and pyramid that have the same shape base and same height: It takes three pyramids to fill a prism.

Note that a *cone* is simply a circular-based pyramid, so the volume of a cone is simply:

Volume of a cone = $\frac{1}{3}\pi r^2 h$

REMEMBER

Cylinders and *cones* are just circular prisms and circular pyramids given special names since they don't have edges.

Spheres

A *sphere* is a 3-dimensional circle — like a ball. It is the set of all points that are equidistant from a single point in space. The distance from the center of the ball to its surface is the radius of the sphere. You calculate the volume of a *sphere* by the formula $\frac{4}{3}\pi r^3$.

Similar versus Congruent Polygons

You may notice shapes you encounter in everyday life that look the same but are different sizes. You're actually noticing figures that mathematicians would classify as similar figures: shapes that have corresponding congruent angles and ratios between the corresponding sides that are equal. When talking about the proportion between the sides, the term that is commonly used is *scale factor*, which shows the relationship between the lengths.

Similar polygons

When proving that polygons are similar, you must check that all corresponding angles are congruent *and* that all corresponding sides have the same proportion. If one rectangle has sides with lengths of 4 and 12 and the other rectangle has sides with lengths of 6 and 18, then you can check the proportion: $\frac{4}{6} = \frac{12}{18}$? When solving a proportion, you need to cross-multiply to see if the quantities are equal: $4 \times 18 = 6 \times 12$, so $72 = 72$. Another way to proceed is to rewrite the ratios in lowest terms, $\frac{2}{3}$ in this case, which also gives you your scale factor. Note that the symbolic notation for similar polygons is "~" and it's read as "similar to."

Congruent polygons

Not only are there polygons that are similar, but there are also those that are congruent. This means that all corresponding sides and angles are congruent (the same size); it's as though the original figure was duplicated and renamed. One thing to be careful of with figures is that the corresponding sides or angles may not be in the same "location" on the other figure. The symbolic way to represent congruence is "≅". Notice in Figure 13-8 how $\triangle ABC \cong \triangle DEF$ even though it looks like $\triangle DEF$ is turned. In both the similar polygon and congruent polygon cases, the order of the names is crucial; it tells the pairings. For instance, in $\triangle ABC \cong \triangle DEF$, you know that $\angle B \cong \angle E$ because they're both the middle letter in the names. You also know that $\overline{AC} \cong \overline{DF}$ because they're the first and last letter of the names.

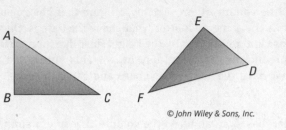
So, by knowing polygons are congruent, you can find missing side lengths or angles by matching them to their corresponding parts.

Proving congruent triangles

While all polygons can have a congruent counterpart, when it comes to triangles, we are particularly interested in proving that two triangles are indeed congruent. Triangles have always fascinated mathematicians, maybe because they have the fewest sides that form a closed figure. Earlier we talked about the different types of triangles, and when proving a pair of triangles is congruent, there are three ways:

TIP

>> Side-angle-side (SAS): This means that if you can prove two pairs of corresponding sides are congruent and that their included angle is congruent, then you have enough information to conclude that the two triangles are congruent. The important thing to notice here is that it *must* be the included angle, as in the angle between the two sides is the one you're concerned with.

One way to remember this is that there is no swearing in math, so you can't have angle-side-side (or side-side-angle).

>> Another way to prove two triangles are congruent is using angle-side-angle (ASA). In this case, you need two pairs of corresponding angles to be congruent, along with their shared side.

>> Triangles congruent using side-side-side (SSS).

Unfortunately, angle–angle–angle (AAA) doesn't help prove that the triangles are congruent because there are no restrictions on the lengths of the sides. So, you need at least one side to prove that the triangles are congruent.

Transformations

Figures can be displayed on a coordinate plane where their vertices are given as a set of coordinates. These shapes can be moved around the plane, which results in a transformation of the shape. There are four types of mathematical transformations, three of which are rigid transformations and the last which is not. In a rigid transformation, the size of the shape is maintained, which means the length of the sides, angles, perimeter, and area is consistent (resulting in congruent shapes). The three types of rigid transformations are translations, rotations, and reflections. The general notation for all transformations is adding " ' " to the letters, called a *prime*. So if the point *A* is transformed, its counterpart would be called *A'*, pronounced "*A* prime." This notation shows the original figure (*A*) and its image (*A* prime) formed after the transformation. Lastly, the different types of transformations can be combined, such as having a reflection and a rotation applied to one figure.

Translations

A *translation* moves the original figure to a different location in the coordinate plane. The orientation of the shape stays the same, so it's not twisted or turned. The notation for a translation is $T_{a,b}(x,y) = (x+a, y+b)$, where $T_{a,b}(x,y)$ is your transformation function, and all the coordinates (x,y) are moved *a* units left or right and *b* units up or down, depending on the sign. For example, $T_{-6,2}(x,y) = (x-6, y+2)$ shifts the coordinates 6 units to the left and 2 units up (see Figure 13-9).

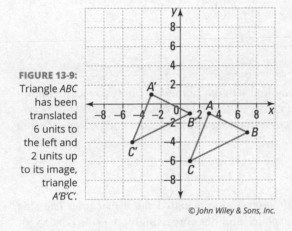

FIGURE 13-9:
Triangle *ABC* has been translated 6 units to the left and 2 units up to its image, triangle *A'B'C'*.

© *John Wiley & Sons, Inc.*

Rotations

If you were to rotate something, what does that mean? You most likely thought of twisting something or turning an object. You would be correct. However, in mathematics, you don't just randomly turn something; it's described by an angle and the orientation of the turn. For example, say that you're rotating an object 90 degrees counterclockwise about the origin (see Figure 13-10). This tells you that you're turning the coordinate plane "one quarter twist" to the right.

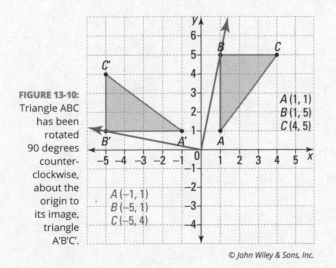

FIGURE 13-10:
Triangle ABC has been rotated 90 degrees counter-clockwise, about the origin to its image, triangle *A'B'C'*.

© *John Wiley & Sons, Inc.*

Reflections

Most likely, you see a reflection every day when you look in the mirror. It looks like you but it's just reversed — your right is its left and the mirror serves as the line of symmetry. The same principle applies in mathematics — when a figure is reflected over a line, the line is like the "mirror" that you could fold the paper on and have the shapes line up perfectly. Common lines to reflect a figure over are the x-axis (whose equation is: $y = 0$), y-axis (whose equation is: $x = 0$), and the line $y = x$.

Dilations

Dilations are a non-rigid transformation that can be applied to figures. This transformation is a stretch or shrink of the shape by a certain factor. Sometimes the factor will be the same, resulting in a stretch/shrink of the same amount in both directions, producing a similar figure. Other times the shape is distorted in one direction and not the other. The notation is similar to the notation for translations: $(x', y') = T(x, y) = (ax, by)$. So if the dilation is $T(x, y) = (5x, 5y)$, then the point $(1, 2)$ is transformed to be $(5, 10)$, showing a stretch of factor 5.

Trigonometry

Trigonometry can be one of the most intimidating topics in mathematics, but if you just remember a few key steps, you'll be fine. Literally translated, trigonometry means "the measure of triangles," so it's the study of the relationships between the sides and angles of triangles, specifically right triangles.

SOH-CAH-TOA

REMEMBER

With right triangles, you already know that the longest side is called the *hypotenuse.* The side opposite from an angle of interest is called the *opposite,* and not surprisingly, the side next to (or adjacent to) the angle is called the *adjacent.* There are three fundamental trigonometric functions involved here: *sine* (sin), *cosine* (cos), and *tangent* (tan). These functions are defined as the ratios of two sides of the triangle: Sine is the ratio of the opposite side to the hypotenuse, cosine is the ratio of the adjacent side to the hypotenuse, and tangent is the ratio of the opposite side to the adjacent side. As illustrated in Figure 13-11, there is a mnemonic to help remember this relationship: SOH-CAH-TOA (for example, CAH means cosine is calculated from the adjacent and the hypotenuse).

$$\sin A = \frac{\text{opp}}{\text{hyp}} \quad \cos A = \frac{\text{adj}}{\text{hyp}} \quad \tan A = \frac{\text{opp}}{\text{adj}}$$

FIGURE 13-11: SOH-CAH-TOA helps you remember the ratios associated with each trig function.

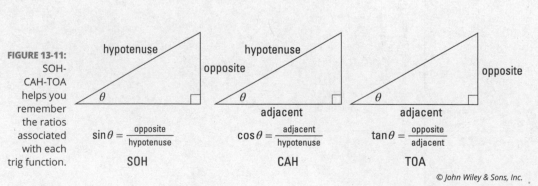

© John Wiley & Sons, Inc.

Using trigonometric functions to find missing sides

You can use trigonometry to find the missing sides of a triangle if you're given at least one angle and one side. In the triangle in Figure 13-12, the measure of angle A is 30 degrees and the hypotenuse is of length 4. Find the lengths of sides X and Y.

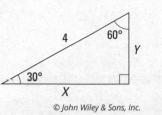

© John Wiley & Sons, Inc.

To find side Y, you know the hypotenuse and you're seeking the length of the side opposite of the 30 degree angle, so you use sine:

$$\sin\theta = \frac{\text{opposite}}{\text{hypotenuse}}$$

$$\sin 30 = \frac{Y}{4}$$

$$0.5 = \frac{Y}{4}$$

$$0.5(4) = Y$$

$$Y = 2$$

To find the length of X (the side adjacent to the 30 degree angle), you use cosine, as shown here:

$$\cos\theta = \frac{\text{adjacent}}{\text{hypotenuse}}$$

$$\cos 30 = \frac{X}{4}$$

$$0.87 = \frac{X}{4}$$

$$0.87(4) = X$$

$$X = 3.5$$

Using trigonometric functions to find missing angles

To find missing angles, you need to use inverse trigonometric functions ($\sin^{-1}$, $\cos^{-1}$, $\tan^{-1}$).

TIP

To find inverse trigonometric functions, press the second button on your calculator first before pressing the trig function button (this tells the calculator that you're looking for an angle rather than a side).

For example, find the measure of angle A in Figure 13-13.

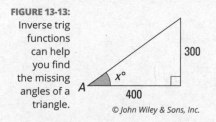

© John Wiley & Sons, Inc.

Because you know the length of the sides adjacent to and opposite from angle A in the triangle in Figure 13-13, you can use the tangent of angle A. After you calculate the value of the opposite divided by the adjacent (300/400 = 0.75), you can find angle A by applying the inverse tangent (tan⁻¹) to your answer:

$$\tan\theta = \frac{\text{opposite}}{\text{adjacent}}$$

$$\tan A = \frac{300}{400}$$

$$\tan A = 0.75$$

$$A = \tan^{-1}(0.75) \text{ (use calculator to find } \tan^{-1}0.75)$$

$$A = 36.9°$$

Chapter 14

Statistics and Probability

"May the odds always be in your favor." This blessing applies to both taking the TASC and life in general.

In this chapter, we explore the different methods of representing data, including bar graphs, pie charts, and scatter plots. Central tendencies give you information about data sets and provide a method for discussing their behavior. When looking at sets, you can observe what happens between two or more sets by considering their unions, intersections, and complements. Finally, we round out the chapter by applying knowledge of sets to determine the probability of independent and dependent events.

Data Representations

Different types of graphs and charts provide visual representations of data sets. Each type of representation has its strengths and weaknesses and should be used in different situations. In addition, you can gather information about the original data from looking at these representations.

Bar graphs and histograms

A *bar graph* is useful when comparing quantities between different groups or to track large changes over time. A *histogram* is a special type of bar graph in which data is shown as frequencies within given ranges. You can look at the frequency of the data using these representations.

To construct a bar graph:

1. Determine the frequencies of each group.

2. On your graph, along the bottom axis (*x*-axis), mark your categories; on the vertical axis, place tally marks for your frequencies (you'll want to determine an appropriate scale for these numbers).

3. Construct vertical bars for each category as tall as the corresponding frequency.

4. Be sure to label your axis and title your graph.

Note: You can also switch the direction by putting the categories along the vertical axis and frequencies along the horizontal axis. This will result in horizontal bars instead of vertical ones.

Figure 14-1 is an example of a bar graph that shows how many students in a class have birthdays in each month. You can clearly see from this data representation that June has the most birthdays, while August has the fewest.

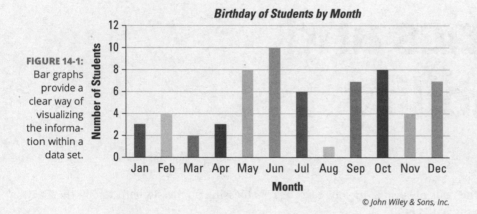

FIGURE 14-1: Bar graphs provide a clear way of visualizing the information within a data set.

© John Wiley & Sons, Inc.

To construct a histogram:

1. Look at the range of data and determine how long you want each range to be.

2. Determine the different ranges.

3. Tally the frequencies of occurrence in each of the different ranges.

4. Along your vertical axis, place tally marks for your frequencies.

5. Along your horizontal axis, mark the lower bound of each range and then the highest value so that each range is complete.

6. Construct bars as tall as the corresponding frequency in each range.

Figure 14-2 is an example of a histogram showing how many students scored within certain ranges. You can see that the highest frequency of scores occurred between a 60 and an 80.

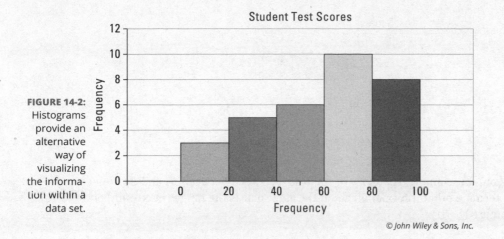

FIGURE 14-2:
Histograms provide an alternative way of visualizing the information within a data set.

© John Wiley & Sons, Inc.

Box-and-whisker plot

A *box-and-whisker plot* is useful in showing the extreme values and medians of a data set. (We discuss what a median is in the later "Central Tendencies" section.)

To construct a box-and-whisker plot:

1. **Put the data in order from least to greatest.**

2. **Identify the minimum, maximum, and middle value (Q2).**

   If there are two middle values (from an even number of data points), add the two together and divide by 2. (**Note:** Box-and-whisker plots divide data into groups of 25%, so the Q stands for *quartile.*)

3. **Using the median (the middle number from Step 2) as a halfway point, find the median of the lower half (Q1) and the upper half (Q3) separately.**

4. **Draw a number line long enough to accommodate the data's span and include appropriate tally marks.**

5. **Above the number line, mark the five important points (Q1, Q2, Q3, max, min) found in Steps 2 and 3.**

6. **Use the three middle points (Q1, Q2, and Q3) to construct the box.**

7. **The min to Q1 is one whisker, and Q3 to the max is the other.**

EXAMPLE

Construct a box-and-whisker plot from this set of test scores: 45, 72, 50, 94, 80, 76, 90, 88, 79.

First, put the numbers in order: 45, 50, 72, 76, 79, 80, 88, 90, 94. Then figure out your important values:

Min: 45	Max: 94	Median (Q2): 79
Lower half: 45, 50, 72, 76	Q1: 61	
Upper half: 80, 88, 90, 94	Q3: 89	

Using these values, you can construct the box-and-whisker plot shown in Figure 14-3.

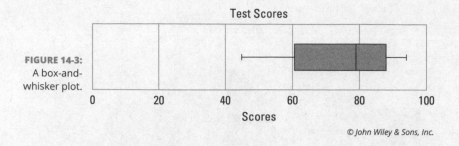

FIGURE 14-3:
A box-and-whisker plot.

© John Wiley & Sons, Inc.

This tells you, for example, that 50% of the test scores fell between 61 and 89. You can use this chart to determine other information about the data such as the range (max−min) and the interquartile range (Q3−Q1).

Circle graph/pie chart

A *circle graph (pie chart)* shows the percent or fractions of data and is useful when comparing parts to the whole.

To construct a circle graph:

1. Determine the percentage of each category, if not given. $\dfrac{\text{Frequency}}{\text{Total}}$

2. Use the percentages to calculate the central angles for the circle and construct the wedges.

EXAMPLE

Construct a circle graph from the following data (see Figure 14-4).

Favorite Color	Votes
Blue	12
Red	16
Green	9
Yellow	3

Calculating the percentages:

Favorite Color	Votes	Percent
Blue	12	$\dfrac{12}{40} = 30\%$
Red	16	$\dfrac{16}{40} = 40\%$
Green	9	$\dfrac{9}{40} = 22.5\%$
Yellow	3	$\dfrac{3}{40} = 7.5\%$

When given a circle graph, you can use the percentages to calculate information about a group. For example, if you're given the circle graph above and told that there are 500 total students, you can calculate how many students chose either red or blue as their favorite color.

Favorite Color Choices

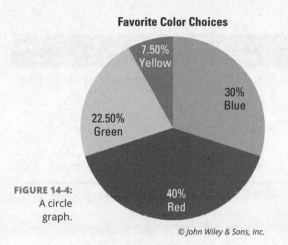

FIGURE 14-4:
A circle graph.

© John Wiley & Sons, Inc.

You know that the total percentage of students who chose either red or blue is 70%. This means you can multiply 500 by 70%:

$$500(0.7) = 350$$

So 350 students chose either red or blue as their favorite color.

Scatter plot

A *scatter plot* shows the relationship between two variables. When looking at a scatter plot, you look at the *correlation*, which gauges the strength of the relationship and the direction. This means a correlation can be strong or weak and can be positive, negative, or neither. Depending on the strength of the correlation, you can infer a trend in the relationship. Figure 14-5 illustrates some examples of scatter plots and the types of correlations that can appear. Notice how when there is a correlation, the points tend to line up in one direction.

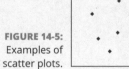

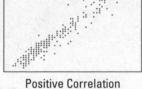

FIGURE 14-5:
Examples of scatter plots.

No Correlation   Negative Correlation   Positive Correlation

© John Wiley & Sons, Inc.

A common example of a scatter plot is the relationship between people's shoe sizes and their IQs. When a large data collection is analyzed, you see that there's no correlation. If there were one, you could make a statement like "People with bigger shoe sizes are smarter." However, there's a wide range of IQs and shoe size combinations, and you can't gauge a person's intelligence based on his or her shoe size (no correlation).

Central Tendencies

Given a set of data, you can use different measures of *central tendencies* (mean, median, and mode) to describe trends in the data. The different central tendencies show the middle number in specific ways. Each is useful in its own way, as shown in Table 14-1.

TABLE 14-1 **Central Tendencies**

Measure of Central Tendency	Pros	Cons
Mean	Includes all data points	Affected by extreme points (outliers), which skews the data sets
Median	Not affected by extreme points (outliers)	Only focuses on the middle of the data
Mode	Easy, no calculation required	Sometimes there is no mode (or many different ones); hard to repeat with different samples

Mean

The *mean* is one of the most commonly used measures of central tendency and is commonly called the *average* or the *arithmetic mean*.

To calculate the mean of a data set:

1. **Find the sum of all the data points (add all the points together).**

2. **Divide the sum from Step 1 by the number of data points.**

EXAMPLE

Find the mean of the following test scores: 45, 72, 50, 94, 80, 76, 90, 88, and 79.

$$45 + 72 + 50 + 94 + 80 + 76 + 90 + 88 + 79 = 674$$

$$\frac{674}{9} = 74.9$$

This means that the average score on this test is 74.9.

EXAMPLE

You can also use the average to determine a missing data point. For example, if Sam's grade is based on 4 test scores and he scored a 78, 92, and 80 on the first 3 exams and wants an average of 87, what does he need to get on the fourth test? Using the formula you get:

$$\frac{78 + 92 + 80 + x}{4} = 87$$

$$\frac{250 + x}{4} = 87$$

$$250 + x = 348$$

$$x = 98$$

This means that Sam needs to score a 98 on his last test to get an average of 87.

Median

The *median* of a data set is the middle number of the distribution.

To find the median:

1. **Put the numbers in order from least to greatest.**

2. **Find the middle number (usually by crossing off numbers from each end).**

- If there's an odd number of data points, then there will be one middle number.
- If there's an even number of data points, then there will be two middle numbers, so you average them.

EXAMPLE

Find the median of the data set 1, 2, 6, 1, 7, 9, 2, 3, 5, 5.

Putting the numbers in order you get: 1, 1, 2, 2, 3, 5, 5, 6, 7, 9.

1, 1, 2, 2, 3, 5, 5, 6, 7, 9

Because you have two middle numbers, you have to calculate their average:

$$\frac{3+5}{2} = \frac{8}{2} = 4$$

This means the median of this data set is 4.

REMEMBER

Notice how the median doesn't necessarily have to be one of the data points in the set.

Mode

The *mode* of a data set is the number or numbers that occur the most frequently. One way to remember mode is that this measure of central tendency is the only one that starts with *m-o*, which could stand for "most often."

To find the mode:

1. **Put the numbers in order from least to greatest (not required, but makes identifying the mode easier).**

2. **Find the number(s) that occurs most often in the list.**

REMEMBER

There can be more than one mode if there are two or more data points that occur the same number of times. There can also be no mode if all the data points occur the same number of times.

Find the mode of 2, 3, 7, 9, 2, 5, 7, 6.

EXAMPLE

Put the numbers in order from least to greatest: 2, 2, 3, 5, 6, 7, 7, 9.

The modes are 2 and 7 because they each occur twice in the data set.

Range

Though it's not a measure of central tendency, the *range* provides information about the span of the data set and is usually provided in conjunction with one of the other measures. You find the range by subtracting the lowest extreme point (minimum) from the highest extreme point (maximum).

Using the previous example, calculate the range of this data set: 2, 2, 3, 5, 6, 7, 7, 9.

Range = 9 − 2 = 7

REMEMBER

You can see that without knowing any of the measures of central tendency, the range only tells you that all the data points are within 7 units of one another. However, this could mean that the minimum is 92 and the maximum is 99 instead of 2 and 9. This is why a middle measure is useful to give context to the range.

Sample Space

In mathematics, a *sample space* is the set of all possible values that an experiment could produce. For example, the sample space of a coin toss is {heads, tails} because those are the only two outcomes a coin toss could have. Another example is if you're looking at the word *math* and want to know the probability of picking one of the letters at random. The sample space in this case is {m, a, t, h} because those are the only letters in the word. It's important to define your sample space before you start looking at the probability or operations with sets.

Some of the most common situations for which you need to know sample spaces are using a coin, dice, or deck of cards. If you recall, a deck of cards has 52 cards — 4 suits with 13 cards in each suit. So, a sample space of suits would be {diamonds, hearts, clubs, spades}. However, you would use a different sample space if you were looking for all the face cards in a deck, for example.

Sets

In mathematics, a *set* is a collection of elements. An *element* is any object contained in a set, which could be numbers, shapes, equations, and so on. Some examples of sets are the set of all even numbers, the set of all numbers divisible by 5, the set of all geometric figures that have 4 sides, and so on. When naming a set, you use a capital letter, and two sets are equal if and only if they contain all the same elements.

When writing a set, use curly brackets, { }, and separate each distinct element by a comma. If there's a pattern to the elements, for example the set of all even numbers, you would write it as {0, 2, 4, 6, . . .}; there needs to be enough elements shown to indicate the pattern.

Another way to write a set is using *set builder notation,* where there's an explicit formula or condition that dictates membership of its elements. For example, you can represent the set containing all positive numbers by either of the following notations:

$$\{x \mid x > 0\} \text{ or } \{x : x > 0\}$$

In both cases, the ":" and "|" mean "such that" only numbers greater than 0 are included in the set.

The rest of this section describes how to perform various operations with sets.

Union

When dealing with two or more sets, you can perform operations with them. The *union* of sets is when the elements of one set are combined with the elements of another set, essentially adding the two sets together. This means that an element in the union can be contained in one or both sets, as shown in Figure 14-6. The shaded region shows all the elements contained in the union of sets A and B (denoted as $A \cup B$). The notation of a union uses the $\cup$ symbol, called a *cup.*

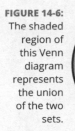

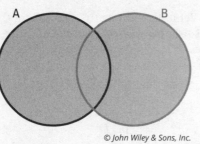
Figures 14-7 and 14-8 depict a couple of examples.

EXAMPLE

Example 1:

$A = \{2, 4, 6\}$ and $B = \{3, 5, 7\}$

$A \cup B = \{2, 3, 4, 5, 6, 7\}$

FIGURE 14-7:
The union
of two sets
includes all
elements
that appear
in either or
both sets.

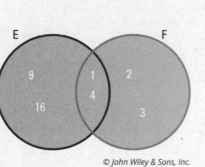

© John Wiley & Sons, Inc.

EXAMPLE

Example 2:

$E = \{1, 4, 9, 16\}$ and $F = \{1, 2, 3, 4\}$

$E \cup F = \{1, 2, 3, 4, 9, 16\}$

FIGURE 14-8:
Elements
that appear
in both sets
are listed
only once in
the union.

© John Wiley & Sons, Inc.

REMEMBER

Notice how, in Example 2, the two elements that are in both sets (1 and 4) are represented only once in the union. Though the Venn diagrams aren't necessary to solve these problems in these two simple cases, they help demonstrate why the solutions are written in this way.

Intersection

Another operation that can be performed with sets is an intersection. The *intersection* represents what elements the two sets have in common (the elements found in both sets). Figure 14-9 illustrates the intersection of two sets using a Venn diagram as the part where the two circles overlap. The notation for the intersection of sets uses the ∩ symbol, called a *cap*.

FIGURE 14-9:
The shaded region of this Venn diagram represents the intersection of the two sets.

© John Wiley & Sons, Inc.

If there are no elements in common between the sets, then there are no elements in the intersection and it is denoted as ∅.

Check out Figures 14-10 and 14-11 for a couple of examples.

EXAMPLE

Example 1:

$A = \{2, 4, 6\}$ and $B = \{2, 4, 8\}$

$A \cap B = \{2, 4\}$

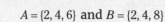

FIGURE 14-10:
The intersection of two sets includes all elements that appear in both sets.

© John Wiley & Sons, Inc.

EXAMPLE

Example 2:

$E = \{-3, 0, 3\}$ and $F = \{5, 6, 7\}$

$E \cap F = \varnothing$

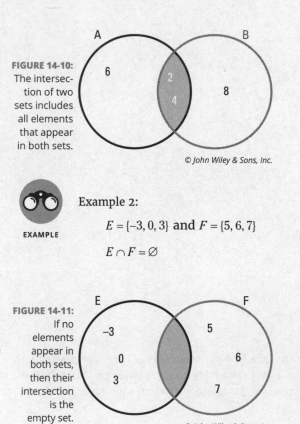

FIGURE 14-11:
If no elements appear in both sets, then their intersection is the empty set.

© John Wiley & Sons, Inc.

Complement

The *complement* of a set are the elements not contained within that set, as shown in Figure 14-12. This operation is similar to the operation of subtraction, where you subtract the elements of the second set from the elements of the first. Notation for the complement is A^c or A'. The universal set, U, is the larger set from which you take elements to create other, smaller sets. For example, you could say the universal set is the set of all natural numbers and that set A contains the integers between −5 and 5.

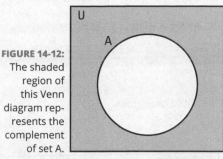

FIGURE 14-12: The shaded region of this Venn diagram represents the complement of set A.

© John Wiley & Sons, Inc.

If you're given two sets, A and B, then you can look at the *relative complement* between them. The relative complement of A in B are all the elements in B that are not in the intersection of A and B $(A \cap B)$, as shown in Figure 14-13. This can be denoted as $B - A$ or $B \setminus A$.

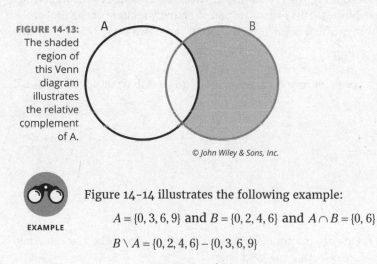

FIGURE 14-13: The shaded region of this Venn diagram illustrates the relative complement of A.

© John Wiley & Sons, Inc.

EXAMPLE

Figure 14-14 illustrates the following example:

$A = \{0, 3, 6, 9\}$ and $B = \{0, 2, 4, 6\}$ and $A \cap B = \{0, 6\}$

$B \setminus A = \{0, 2, 4, 6\} - \{0, 3, 6, 9\}$

Because 0 and 6 are in the intersection, $B \setminus A = \{2, 4\}$.

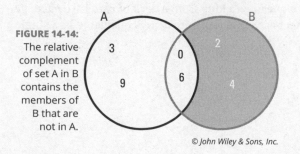

FIGURE 14-14: The relative complement of set A in B contains the members of B that are not in A.

© John Wiley & Sons, Inc.

Probability

Probability measures how likely an event is to occur. When looking at probability, you can consider the experimental probability or the theoretical probability of an event. The *experimental probability* is the probability based on test results where an experiment is repeated and the results are observed. If an experiment is performed enough times, then the results will approach the *theoretical probability* of the event. The theoretical probability is based on calculations and formulas.

The probability of an event is determined by the number of ways the event can occur divided by the total number of possible outcomes:

$$P(event) = \frac{\text{\# of favorable outcomes}}{\text{total \# of possible outcomes}}$$

What's the probability of rolling a 4 on a die?

$P(4) = \frac{1}{6}$ because there is only one way to roll a 4 out of 6 possible outcomes.

EXAMPLE

What's the probability of picking a 2 from a deck of cards?

$P(2) = \frac{4}{52} = \frac{1}{13}$ because there are 4 possible 2s in a deck of 52 cards.

EXAMPLE

Independent events

Independent events are two events in which the outcome of one event doesn't affect the outcome of the other event. When you're calculating the probability of two independent events occurring, you multiply their individual probabilities. This is because you're actually looking at the probability of events A and B both happening, which is the intersection of these two sets.

$$P(A \text{ and } B) = P(A \cap B) = P(A)P(B)$$

What is the probability of rolling an even number on a die and selecting a club from a deck of cards?

EXAMPLE

$P(\text{even and club})$

$= P(\text{even})P(\text{club})$

$= \frac{3}{6} \cdot \frac{13}{52}$

$= \frac{1}{2} \cdot \frac{1}{4}$

$= \frac{1}{8}$

Other examples of independent events are multiple coin tosses, multiple dice rolls, and selecting an object and then replacing it before selecting the next object.

If you're looking for the probability of mutually exclusive events occurring, then you add the individual probability. For example, selecting a queen or a king from a deck of cards are *mutually exclusive* events because these events don't affect each other and are being considered in a single occurrence. The probability in this case is:

$P(A \text{ or } B) = P(A \cup B) = P(A) + P(B)$

$P(\text{queen or king})$

$= P(\text{queen}) + P(\text{king})$

$= \frac{4}{52} + \frac{4}{52}$

$= \frac{1}{13} + \frac{1}{13}$

$= \frac{2}{13}$

If the events aren't mutually exclusive, then you still add the probabilities of the individual events together but subtract the probability of both occurring.

$$P(A \text{ or } B) = P(A) + P(B) - P(A \text{ and } B)$$

What is the probability of rolling a multiple of 3 or an even number on a die?

$$P(\text{even or multiple of 3}) = P(\text{even}) + P(\text{multiple of 3}) - P(\text{even multiples of 3})$$

EXAMPLE

The even possibilities are 2, 4, and 6. The multiples of 3 are 3 and 6. The even multiple of 3 is 6.

$$= \frac{3}{6} + \frac{2}{6} - \frac{1}{6}$$
$$= \frac{4}{6}$$
$$= \frac{2}{3}$$

Dependent events

When the outcome of one event affects the outcome of another event, then they are *dependent events*. One common example is when an object is selected but not replaced before the next object is selected. When this occurs, you must reduce the total of possible outcomes and, in some cases, the number of ways the event could occur.

A jar contains 5 blue, 3 red, and 7 green marbles. What is the probability of selecting two blue marbles in a row if the first marble is not replaced?

EXAMPLE

The first event, that the first marble is blue, is a simple independent probability in which there are 5 to choose from out of 15 total.

$$P(\text{1st marble is blue}) = \frac{5}{15} = \frac{1}{3}$$

However, for the second event of another blue marble being selected, both the number of blue marbles and the total number of marbles in the jar have been reduced by 1.

$$P(\text{2nd marble is blue}) = \frac{5-1}{15-1} = \frac{4}{14} = \frac{2}{7}$$

Now you multiply the probability of these two events:

$$P(\text{blue, blue}) = \frac{1}{3} \cdot \frac{2}{7} = \frac{2}{21}$$

This means there is a 2 in 21 chance of selecting two blue marbles in a row.

Conditional probability

Another type of dependent probability is *conditional probability*, which calculates the probability of one event given the occurrence of another event. The notation for conditional probability is $P(B \mid A)$, which indicates the probability of B occurring given that A has already occurred.

$$P(B \mid A) = \frac{P(A \cap B)}{P(A)}$$

You reduce the sample space for the set of A because you're now concerned with B occurring inside of A. Using a Venn diagram, as shown in Figure 14-15, can help you visualize this situation. You can see that if you're already in region A, you can use the intersection of the two sets to find the probability of B then occurring.

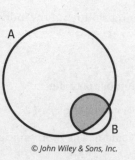

© John Wiley & Sons, Inc.

EXAMPLE

A rather unreliable test for a certain disease gives positive results in 65% of all cases for people who take the test (whether they actually have the disease or not). However, the probability that you test positive and actually have the disease is only 15% due to false positives. What is the probability of having the disease given that you have already tested positive?

$$P(\text{having disease} \mid \text{tested positive}) = \frac{P(\text{testing positive and having disease})}{P(\text{testing positive})}$$

$$= \frac{.15}{.65}$$

$$= .23077$$

This means there is only about a 23% chance of you actually having the disease even if you have already tested positive.

5

Social Studies

Chapter 15

U.S. History

F reedom. It's the primary driving force behind the foundation of this nation and the driving force that maintains the quality of our lives in this country. Freedom has taken many paths and faced many challenges from the first time explorers and settlers set foot on this continent. Our country has been and continues to be shaped by the concept of freedom.

Although the information presented in this chapter is helpful, it should trigger areas that you need to study in a bit more depth before taking the TASC exam. Approximately 25 percent of the Social Studies section of the TASC exam will cover U.S. history questions, and another 25 percent will cover government and civics. So, with 50 percent of this section focusing on these two areas, it would be to your advantage to take time to study and review this material carefully. Use the tips in this chapter to review major points and practice skills.

Preparing for the U.S. History Section of the TASC

It will be useful for you to "think like a historian" when considering the various themes in U.S. history and to view them through a set of "lenses":

>> **Long-term/short-term causes:** What makes things tick? Understand why something happened the way it did and connect the dots over a period of time.

>> **Chronology:** How to see things in order; consider how and why things began to change and try to understand the time period in which the changes took place.

>> **Seeing change over time:** Identify an area of change and ask yourself why change occurred and why it was significant.

>> **Using evidence:** See yourself as a crime scene investigator (CSI agent) — examine and compare evidence, and interpret artifacts, to gain a better overall understanding.

>> **Compare and contrast:** Why did things happen the way they did? What were the similarities to past events? What were the differences?

By using your set of "lenses," you will begin to understand the historical landscape in front of you. Consider these themes when you think about the major events that happened in the timeline of U.S. history. There will be approximately 12 questions about U.S. history on the Social Studies portion of the TASC exam. The majority of these questions will focus on events from the Civil War and Reconstruction eras; the 1930s into the modern era — World War II, Cold War, Vietnam, and civil rights; and events since the 1970s. There will be some information that will also appear from earlier times in U.S. history: settlement of the colonies, the Revolutionary War period, pre-Civil War era, the Gilded Age, and the Progressive Era. While you don't need to know a great deal of specific details, you should understand some of the broad themes and events that took place so that you can make connections with the challenges of freedom in U.S. history.

The style of questions on the TASC exam is changing, however — some things just never stay the same. Most, if not all, of the 47 questions on the new TASC exam will be *stimulus-based,* meaning that you'll see some sort of primary source, such as a photograph (that says a thousand words), a political cartoon (they can be funny yet serious at the same time), a chart or graph (pie charts, bar graphs), or excerpts from letters, journals, or news reports. The questions will either be stand-alone questions or grouped with other questions from the same stimulus. To prepare for primary source analysis, you need to practice interpreting documents. So in addition to knowing the facts, you need to understand how to work with the factual data and understand why it's important.

TIP

You can find primary document analysis worksheets at the National Archives and the Library of Congress. If you want practice with analyzing sources, you can find documents at websites like Digital History (http://www.digitalhistory.uh.edu/). A little work on your part will help you understand primary sources so that you're not surprised by content on the TASC exam. You need to be familiar with how to work with and understand a variety of types of primary documents.

REMEMBER

In the realm of social studies, history, government, geography, and economics are often intertwined. As you're reviewing for the U.S. history portion of the TASC exam, don't forget to examine historical maps in various time periods so that you can recognize and analyze changes to the expansion and growth of the country.

So, as you prepare for this exam, keep in mind two things: content knowledge (all that "stuff" and big ideas) as well as skills (a lot of how-to's — reading carefully and critically, knowing how to interpret a primary source, and using it to answer test questions).

The Long and Winding Road to Independence

Although the time period of 1607 to 1776 is a low priority era for a question on the TASC exam, it would be helpful to understand the basics of this period so that you're not caught off guard. This period witnessed several monumental changes and challenges for the colonists in this new land. How did a group of people who at the beginning considered themselves loyal subjects of the British crown struggle with the concepts of identity (who am I?) and unity (working together) over nearly a 170-year period to strike out and declare independence?

Morphing from being a loyal British subject to "I am an American"

On a hot summer day in Independence Hall in Philadelphia, Pennsylvania, 56 men (soon to be labeled traitors by the British crown) inked their names on a new document saying that they "mutually pledge to each other our lives, our fortunes, and our sacred honor" by proclaiming the formation of the new nation of the United States of America. The Declaration of Independence set forth their calculated reasoning of protected rights and the proper role of government. Change is not easy, and breaking up can indeed be "hard to do." This is one of the challenges of freedom.

The colonists embarked on new challenges in the colonies as they developed unique ways of life and trade with each other and Great Britain. Because of the nearly 4,000 miles that separated the colonists from the mother country of Great Britain, the colonists developed a sense of independence through "salutary neglect" because Britain did not micromanage their affairs. Labor systems of indentured servitude and slavery emerged as the colonies grew crops, produced goods, supplied natural resources, and traded with Britain and other countries.

After the French and Indian War, Britain began to change its ideas on how it viewed the colonists. After the Treaty of Paris of 1763, the Proclamation Line of 1763 began to limit or "fence in" the colonists and placed them under the intense scrutiny of the king and Parliament. To pay off the debt of the French and Indian War that Britain had incurred, a variety of taxes (Stamp Act, Sugar Act, Tea Act, and others) were enacted to have the colonists pay for their share of the war. Many colonists felt harassed by the new tight British control, and Britain in turn began to question colonial loyalty.

The road to rebellion: "Breaking up is hard to do"

In a short span of 13 years, the colonies began to see themselves as indeed "separate" from Great Britain and also began to slowly come together as a group of colonies with shared ideals. Although not all colonists favored separation, actions were in place to make it a "point of no return" by the summer of 1776.

Parliament began enacting a series of taxes — taxes about which the colonists had no representation or voice, so they began taking action into their own hands. The Sons and Daughters of Liberty began a series of boycotts and protests. Boston became a hotbed of activity in March of 1770 after British troops known as *lobsterbacks* (or *redcoats*) opened fire on peacefully protesting colonists, killing five of them, in a pivotal event called the Boston Massacre. Then in December 1773, a protest tea party of sorts occurred when nearly 700,000 pounds of British tea was dumped into the Boston Harbor.

It was as if the colonists were now set on a road of no return with the closing of Boston Harbor and the colonial appeals to Parliament falling on deaf ears. April 1775 witnessed a "shot heard 'round the world" when British soldiers and colonial minutemen exchanged shots at Lexington and Concord. War was on, and attempts at reconciliation between the two parties were to no avail.

In January of 1776, a recent British immigrant named Thomas Paine argued in a lengthy pamphlet that it simply made "common sense" to sever economic and political ties with Great Britain and to make the world anew based on one major principle: liberty. That idea rang a bell when after 17 days of intense labor, Thomas Jefferson submitted his work for a formal declaration on June 28, and six days later it was signed, released to the public, and read aloud. The king was attacked as a tyrant, and reasons were set forth declaring that the colonies be "free and independent states" based on the reasoning of the guarantee of the basic rights of life, liberty, and the pursuit of happiness. Now a war ensued between Britain and the newly created "United States of America."

Governing the New Nation: "Who Is in Charge?"

The Revolutionary War was fought and finally won by the Americans with their final victory over the British with the British surrender at Yorktown in October 1781. The landscape of North America was changed with the British removed from the region and the former colonial region now extended beyond the Appalachian Mountains to the Mississippi River.

Now that the former colonists had finally gained their independence after a hard-fought war, it was time to forge a new identity and establish a form of government for the new nation. Fears from British rule would soon shape how the new country would govern themselves. The big question would be how to protect their new sense of freedom. (Turn to Chapter 17 for details on the Articles of Confederation and the Constitution.)

Developing an Identity Crisis

The first five decades of the 1800s would be a time when America was growing — economically, politically, socially, and geographically. Events would unfold prior to the Civil War that would shape and challenge the concept of freedom in the country on a variety of fronts.

The politics of a race enslaved

The decision not to deal with the problem of slavery during the discussion of the Constitution would prove to be a defining issue all the way to the outbreak of the Civil War in April 1861. This would prove to be one of the greatest challenges to freedom. During the debate in the Constitutional Convention in 1787, Northerners denounced slavery as a "cruel war against human nature." But to secure Southern votes for ratification, the only thing the Constitution said about slavery was that the slave trade would end in 1808 and that for purposes of population for representation in the House of Representatives, slaves could be counted as three-fifths of a person (three-fifths compromise), helping the South with their representation in the House of Representatives.

Northerners and Southerners continued their disagreements on the legitimacy of the institution of slavery. Abolitionists in the North led the charge in promoting the idea that slavery should be abolished and that the federal government could make laws in their favor for the good of the public according to the "elastic clause," or necessary and proper clause of the Constitution. Southerners, on the other hand, used the 10th Amendment with the argument of "states' rights" — that if an issue was not specifically stated in the Constitution, it was left up to the states to determine the matter. So, it all narrowed down to an interpretation of the Constitution — and both sides felt they were right!

Then a series of compromises were used as a "band-aid" approach to deal with the issue of slavery. By using the Missouri Compromise line in 1820, slavery was not allowed north of the Missouri Compromise line, but states south of the line could continue with the institution of slavery. And for every new state in the North, a new state was added in the South to keep the representative balance equal in the Senate. Furthermore, Southerners used the tactic of the "gag rule" in 1832 to attempt to limit discussion of slavery in Congress. Then the argument of slavery continued with the concept of popular sovereignty in the late 1840s. As new territories were added to the Union, they were encouraged to decide on the issue of slavery themselves. Then the Compromise of 1850 abolished the equal state admissions status and enforced a Fugitive Slave Act to capture and return runaway slaves. Once again, it failed to adequately deal with the heart of the issue of slavery. This led to continued deep divisions within the country that were evidenced in a divisive presidential election in 1860 (the election of Abraham Lincoln), the formation of the Confederacy, and war breaking out at Fort Sumter on April 12, 1861. Now freedom would face its most important challenge to date.

TIP

Create a timeline of events — 10 to 12 events from 1789 to 1861 that pertain to the issue of slavery. Chronology is an important skill to develop. You can place significant events and people on this timeline.

Women's rights and the abolition movement

Women and their growing involvement in society would present another challenge to the U.S. interpretation of freedom. Which groups of people were covered by the concept of freedom and which groups were omitted from this discussion? From Abigail Adams's correspondence with her husband John with her admonition of "remember the ladies" to Elizabeth Cady Stanton and Lucretia Mott and their "Declaration of Sentiments" issued at the Seneca Falls convention in 1848, women were determined to keep their goal of women's rights in the public discussion. Women, both Northerners and Southerners, black and white, played a predominant role in the area of women's rights and the abolitionist movement. During the period of antebellum reform (prior to the Civil War), women were involved in other areas of reform such as temperance (banning alcohol), prison reform, education, writing, and fashion. But the impending crisis of the Civil War would put most of their efforts on hold. Women were successful in their part of the 13th Amendment abolishing slavery after the Civil War, but they lost the battle of voting rights when all men regardless of color gained the right to vote with the 15th Amendment. They would begin to claim their right to vote with the equality clause of the 14th Amendment. After western states followed Wyoming's lead granting women the right to vote in the years after Reconstruction, the battle would continue in the first part of the 20th century. Participation in the war effort in World War I, protests, marches, and jail time became part of the strategy for women, who finally gained the right to vote with the 19th Amendment in 1920.

TIP

Because the topic of women's rights is quite prevalent in U.S. history, it would be a good idea to make a chart with three brackets and list women and their focus of rights to compare across three time periods — 1776–1861, 1880s–1920, and 1920–present. The skill of "change over time" would be great to apply to this topic. After you've applied the skill to this topic, use that same skill with other time periods in U.S. history. This is a great way to "train your brain" to look for patterns of *similarity and change* and then to ask yourself why things change or stay the same. Remember the old adage — history repeats itself!

Westward ho!

Expansion westward also shaped the identity of the nation. The challenge of a free people was the acquisition of land for the growth of the country. The purchase of the Louisiana Territory followed by the exploration of new land by Lewis and Clark continued the growth of the nation in the 19th century. The addition of the state of Texas, the additional territory gained after the Mexican-American War (stirred on by the concept of *manifest destiny* — that it was "ordained by God" that we move west), and the addition of new states and territories fueled the debate of the expansion of slavery. The gold rush in California in 1849 fueled dramatic growth, leading to the addition of California as a state in 1850. The Oregon and California trails lured people westward. California's admission to the Union as a slave state ended the Missouri Compromise plan of admitting a slave state and free state to keep the balance of free and slave states in Congress. This would be one of the triggers that led to the Civil War in 1861.

After the Civil War ended in 1865, the expansion of the country was advanced by the construction of the transcontinental railroad. The Central and Union Pacific Railroad companies worked to join East and West on May 10, 1869, at Promontory Point, Utah. The country continued to pursue the addition of more territory — the purchase of Alaska in 1869, the addition of the territory of Hawaii in 1892, and the islands of Guam, Puerto Rico, and the Philippines following the end of the Spanish-American War in December 1898. Growth and territorial expansion added to the concept of freedom (unless you happened to be Native American!) and also opened up new challenges to that freedom.

TIP

Once again it would be a good geographical skill to study various maps of U.S. growth and expansion during the 1800s. Things to look for: geographical features, territorial boundaries, and states added to the Union. Ask yourself how the country was challenged and changed with the expansion of territorial lines.

Tearing Apart and Rebuilding

As the country expanded with the addition of new states and territories, the debate of slavery and popular sovereignty became the overriding issue in the years leading up to the Civil War. The country was torn apart during the four-year struggle of North-South, Union-Confederacy in the Civil War. Freedom faced a bloody challenge.

The institution of slavery

Because the Founding Fathers in 1776 felt it wise at the time to avoid addressing the issue of slavery (several of them actually owned slaves themselves!), it set the stage for a major watershed moment in the nation's history when over 620,000 lives were lost, large parts of land were destroyed, and the economic survival of the nation was challenged by war. The issue of slavery was the root cause of the Civil War. Constitutional interpretations of how to make laws, the challenge of enforcing laws, and the growth and rapid increase of sectionalism continued to deeply divide the nation. Harriet Beecher Stowe added to the climate of fear and distrust with the publication of her novel *Uncle Tom's Cabin* in 1852, detailing gruesome horrors of slavery. Northerners were shocked and Southerners outraged by this book.

The Supreme Court entered the fray in 1857 with the ruling in the Dred Scott case in which the case was overturned because slaves were considered to be property rather than citizens, and therefore, they couldn't find help in the court of law. The institution of slavery was tearing the nation apart. The South laid down the gauntlet by presenting the challenge of "no one dare make war on cotton because cotton is king!" The crisis at Harper's Ferry in 1859 ignited by an attempted slave uprising by John Brown (and his execution), and finally the election of Republican candidate Lincoln in 1860, brought the nation to the brink of war. Compromise was over. Eleven Southern states led by South Carolina seceded from the U.S. and formed the Confederate States of America, and war was all but inevitable. The opening shots were fired on April 4, 1861, at Ft. Sumter.

A nation divided

President Lincoln led the Union in the four years of Civil War, and his counterpart Jefferson Davis led the states of the Confederacy. Blue versus gray. Brother versus brother. North versus South. Lincoln sought to preserve the Union at all costs. He felt the Confederacy had no legal right to leave the Union. The Confederacy was bent on preserving its institution of slavery. After Lincoln issued the Emancipation Proclamation aimed at freeing slaves in January 1863, the focus of war now included ending slavery.

During the war, the North maintained economic, geographic, social, and military advantages. They would use these advantages to eventually force a surrender of the South in April 1865. Before the end of the war, numerous battles would be fought, with every battle exacting large casualties on both sides. The turning point of the war would be the Battle of Gettysburg in early July 1863. The bloodiest battle of the war saw enormous casualties of dead and wounded on both sides. Lincoln delivered his famous Gettysburg Address in November 1863 dedicating the military cemetery and promising a "new birth of freedom" for the nation he sought to preserve.

After four long years of conflict, General Robert E. Lee surrendered to General Ulysses S. Grant at Appomattox Courthouse. The war was finally over. Plans were in place to bring the Confederate states back into the Union. Those plans were changed and left in doubt on April 14, 1865, when an assassin's bullet at Ford's Theater ended Lincoln's life.

Effects of the war:

>> Four million slaves gained their freedom.

>> Several thousand African Americans fought for the Union during the war and made up 10 percent of the fighting force.

>> Women were involved in the war with their work as nurses, government workers, factory workers, volunteers, and spies.

>> The cotton economy of the South was in ruins.

>> The North had the economic advantage with business and railroad transportation.

>> The 13th, 14th, and 15th Amendments were added to the Constitution.

TIP

Just a quick note about major wars and test questions — what do you need to know? Although students want to study various intricacies about battles, strategies, and statistics, it's more important to study the long-term and short-term causes that led up to the war and the short-term and long-term effects of the end of the war. Think of these as "bookends" to the war. Although the stuff in the middle is interesting, focus more on the bookends of the conflict.

To rebuild or not rebuild

Prior to the end of the Civil War, Lincoln had already begun to put a lenient plan in place to restore the Southern states to the Union. He planned to "bind up the nation's wounds," but this plan was challenged by the Radical Republicans and Democrat President Johnson following the death of Lincoln in April 1865. Would Congress or the president dictate terms of reconstruction? The challenge remained — rebuild Southern society or punish them harshly for their actions in the war?

The Radical Republicans quickly began working on Civil Rights legislation to secure civil rights for the nearly 4 million freed slaves. The Freedmen's Bureau sought to build schools and hospitals in the South, as well as provide economic support to the former slaves. The Civil Rights Acts of 1866 and 1875 attempted to guarantee rights for African Americans, but they were quickly undermined by Southern actions.

In the midst of this struggle, Republicans in Congress impeached President Johnson for a violation of the Tenure of Office Act when he tried to remove a Lincoln appointee from office. Beneath the surface, Republicans wanted Johnson removed because they opposed his actions of reconstruction legislation. Despite the fact of 11 charges against the president, the Senate failed to remove him from office by one vote.

Reaction to reconstruction legislation in the South was swift. The KKK was formed to intimidate African Americans and keep them from voting. Black Codes and Jim Crow laws created a segregated society in the South by various discriminatory policies. Sharecropping was started to keep African Americans tied to the land by working the land for landowners. Later in 1896, the *Plessy v. Ferguson* case upheld the policy of segregation, claiming that separate schools, water fountains, parks, businesses, and so forth could be established on the basis of "separate but equal." This was another attempt at limiting equality for African Americans in the South.

After 12 years of attempting to rebuild Southern society, the Republicans retreated in 1877. This left the Democrat Party back in control of Southern states. African Americans' rights were severely limited, leaving them virtually as second-class citizens living in fear of a white-dominated society. So 4 years of war and 12 years of rebuilding Southern society left things largely in favor of the white society in the South. It would not be until the modern civil rights movement in the 1950s and 1960s and new legislation that the victory of the Civil War would finally be in place.

Growth, Challenges, and Reform

During the period of the Gilded Age during the last quarter century in the 1800s, the era of big business dramatically changed the economic standing of the United States. Businesses grew, vertical and horizontal integration in business helped monopolies to form, rising immigration rates in the U.S. fueled the need for cheap labor, and businessmen sought to consolidate business practices and increase their wealth and power. Men like John Rockefeller (Standard Oil), Andrew Carnegie (steel industry), J. P. Morgan (finance), and Jay Gould and Cornelius Vanderbilt (railroads) shaped the business practices of the day. As the men of business continued their practices, government began to challenge their power. Laissez-faire politics stressed the desire for minimal government intervention while allowing businesses to regulate themselves.

Many of the abuses brought about in the Gilded Age would be challenged by a large and diverse group of reformers during the Progressive Era during the first part of the 20th century. Men and women and African-American leaders would challenge reform areas such as workplace safety, child labor, meatpacking plant abuses, women in the workplace, trade unions, wages paid to workers, conservation, and settlement houses. The diverse group of reformers were successful in bringing about changes that benefited society and attempted to rein in abusive practices. But once again, an era of reform would be sidelined by war.

The later part of the 19th century and early 20th century saw a dramatic wave of immigrants coming to America. Millions saw the U.S. as a land of opportunity. Immigrants from Asia (China, Japan, and Korea) entered the mainland often through Angel Island in San Francisco. Many of these new immigrants found jobs out West working in gold mines, building railroads, and working in agricultural areas. Fears of job loss and immigration growth led to the first law targeting a specific group of people from entering the country. The Chinese Exclusion Act of 1882 targeted Chinese immigrants and later would be expanded to limit other Asian immigrants from entering the country. Immigrants from Eastern and Southern Europe fled government and religious persecution as well as economic struggles and sought a new life in America. Many of them saw the Statue of Liberty in the New York Harbor as their first glimpse of freedom. The first decade of the new century saw an average of nearly a million immigrants per year coming to America. Immigrants often were exploited as cheap labor in the workplace, and many chose to live in immigrant sections of large cities like New York and Chicago. They added a new dynamic to the U.S. population. World War I slowed down immigration, and growing fears of immigrants led to the formation of a new law in 1924 establishing quotas to limit immigration from Southern and Eastern Europe.

TIP

Do some quick research and reading about the era of immigration from 1880 to 1920 and record a list of eight to ten items: countries of origin, numbers of immigrants coming to America, places of destination, and ethnic groups represented. Then do some quick research and reading about immigration trends from 1964 to the present and record a list of eight to ten items to compare/contrast with the other chart on immigration.

Making the World Safe for Democracy

At the same time America experienced economic growth and challenges at home, America began an involvement in foreign affairs. Since the Farewell Address of George Washington in 1796, America had been urged to be friends with other nations and trade with them but warned not to become entangled in their struggles. So, for the most part the U.S. stayed out of foreign entanglements.

In 1898, President McKinley declared war on Spain when it was believed that Spain had attacked the U.S. by blowing up the USS *Maine* in the harbor in Havana. After a quick and decisive war with the final skirmish being won by Teddy Roosevelt and the Rough Riders as they fought on San Juan Hill, the war treaty was signed in December, further limiting Spain's influence by granting the U.S. the Philippines in the Pacific, Puerto Rico in the Caribbean, and the U.S. influencing affairs in Cuba. At the same time, Hawaii was made an official U.S. territory, and a naval base was established at Pearl Harbor.

In 1914, the same year that the U.S.-built Panama Canal opened for trade, war broke out in Europe. An assassin's bullet that killed the Archduke Franz Ferdinand in Sarajevo triggered the involvement of the major powers of Europe in what became known as the "Great War." It was widely believed that the Great War would be over by Christmas of 1914 but instead it became a long, drawn-out struggle that would not end until an armistice was established at the eleventh hour on November 11, 1918. The U.S. attempted to avoid being drawn into the struggle, but events in January 1917 changed that. After the German Zimmerman Telegram (which proposed a German alliance with Mexico against the U.S.) was intercepted by Britain and after Germany resumed unrestricted submarine warfare, the U.S. was finally drawn into the conflict when President Wilson declared war (with the permission of Congress) to "make the world safe for democracy" in April 1917.

Wilson not only planned to involve the country in the war in Europe but also sought to reshape the nation's foreign policy. At the end of the war, Wilson negotiated the Treaty of Versailles with the major intent of creating a League of Nations to keep world peace. Member nations could reach out to the league for support when threatened by outside forces. The member nations would be bound to assist with military force. This meant that the U.S. could be drawn into a conflict without approval of Congress. This also represented a huge shift from George Washington's Farewell Address, which had urged the U.S. not to become involved in foreign entanglements. The Democratic President Wilson sought to have the country become a major player in world affairs, but this was challenged by Republicans in Congress who didn't agree with his views. Despite the work and change for foreign policy, the treaty was not ratified by the U.S., and we never joined the League of Nations. This began a time of retreat from foreign affairs involvement for the U.S.; this inward-looking approach of isolationism continued for the next two decades.

Recklessness to Despair

The Roaring Twenties was a raucous decade in which the country retreated from the horrors of war and sought out a variety of pleasure-seeking venues. Fashion, jazz, bootleg liquor, cars, and consumerism dominated life. But the party atmosphere came to a crashing halt with the Stock Market Crash of October 1929. The years of purchasing goods on credit as well as buying stock on margin and wild speculation on the stock market led to enormous bank failures and business failures following the crash. Within a matter of weeks the nation plunged into what became known as the Great Depression. The next 12 years would see sharp rises in unemployment (reaching a peak of 24 million in 1932), tremendous loss of wealth in the stock market, a dramatic downturn in business output, and a steep decline in the gross national product.

The Great Depression became one of the most defining points in the history of the nation. President Herbert Hoover was blamed for the beginning of the crisis yet he still failed to begin focusing the federal government to address the needs of people and businesses. President Hoover's "hope is just around the corner" slogan failed to appease the American public. As various cardboard shantytowns sprung up in the outskirts of large cities, they quickly were nicknamed "Hoovervilles." As the crisis worsened, the presidential election of 1932 saw a new Democratic candidate, Franklin Delano Roosevelt, offering a "new deal" for the American people. What was needed was action to address a wide range of needs. FDR promised to do this, and the public put their trust in him, leading to his landslide election victory of 1932.

FDR began the first 100 days of his new term in office by setting his plans in motion. Over the next several months, various aspects of his New Deal plan were put in place. Banking practices and stock market operations saw new government regulations. An "alphabet soup" of new programs was enacted to deal with the crisis:

>> **AAA (Agriculture Administration Act):** Focused on managing aid to farmers and crop regulations

>> **CCC (Civilian Conservation Corps):** Promoted environmental conservation and helped put young people to work

>> **PWA and WPA (Public Works Administration and the Works Progress Administration):** Put people to work with a wide range of internal improvement projects

>> **FDIC (Federal Deposit Insurance Corporation):** Focused on banking regulations

On top of this was a drought in the midwestern United States that coincided with crop failures, causing the region to be referred to as the "Dust Bowl." Dust storms ravaged the region as crops died and huge areas of topsoil were blown away in various storms, and daylight turned to night as dust chocked the region. As farmers lost their homes and crops, thousands of these "Okies" fled the region in search of hope and jobs in California.

FDR's New Deal program signaled a big change for the federal government. It brought involvement of the federal government policies that would support state government and the public at large. FDR communicated his work to the public with a variety of "fireside chats" in which he used radio programs to reach out to people. To begin to instill a sense of hope in people, FDR began his first inaugural address with the phrase, "the only thing we have to fear is fear itself." First Lady Eleanor Roosevelt later involved herself in communicating the president's message to the American public by traveling around the country, as well as speaking out on policies during her own radio program. People around the country began to feel connected to the president as he worked to solve the country's problems. The policies began to get the country out of the damaging effects of the Depression, but it would not be until the involvement of the U.S. in World War II after the attack at Pearl Harbor on December 7, 1941, that the U.S. would finally pull out of the Depression. By 1945, the Great Depression was finally over, and the economy roared back as a new era of prosperity was ushered in.

Power Struggle on the World Stage

The nation would face a grave challenge to its freedom on an early Sunday morning on December 7, 1941, when Japan attacked the naval base at Pearl Harbor. At the end of the two-hour surprise attack, America's Navy in the Pacific had been severely crippled and over 2,400 people killed. FDR quickly responded the following day with congressional approval to declare war on Japan, citing the attack would be a "date which will live in infamy." Three days later the U.S. also became involved in the war in Europe, which had been raging since September 1939. By this time, Hitler controlled vast parts of Europe as Great Britain remained to challenge his conquest. FDR worked with British Prime Minister Winston Churchill and Russian Leader Vladimir Stalin to lead attacks on Germany.

The U.S. worked with its allies to create strategies in the Pacific that would eventually end in the defeat of Germany and Japan. The Battle of Midway in 1942 proved to be a turning point of the war in the Pacific that would eventually lead to the dropping of two atomic bombs on the cities of Hiroshima and Nagasaki on August 6 and 9 in 1945, bringing an end to the war in the Pacific on V-J Day, August 15, with the surrender of Japan.

On the European front, battle strategies and bombing raids would lead to the D-Day invasion of Normandy, France, on June 6, 1944. Despite the large loss of life on the Allies' side, this began the end of Hitler's dominance in Europe as the Allied Forces in the West and East put the squeeze on Germany, resulting in V-E Day in Europe on May 8, 1945, with the surrender of Germany.

The war also brought new challenges on the home front:

>> Images of Rosie the Riveter popularized the participation of women in the workplace. As men left to fight in the war, millions of women took up jobs in factories across the country helping with the war effort by building tanks, planes, weapons, and other items necessary to wage war. Thousands of women also participated in active roles in women's auxiliary groups of the armed services.

>> The Tuskegee Airmen was formed from African-American air pilots in Tuskegee, Alabama. Their valiant efforts led them to various victories and citations as one of the most decorated air groups in World War II.

>> Over 120,000 Japanese-Americans in Executive Order 9066 faced over four years of internment in ten camps across the interior of the U.S. beginning in the spring of 1942 in response to fears after the attack at Pearl Harbor.

>> The Army also saw participation of Japanese-American soldiers in the 100th and 442nd Army groups as they fought valiantly for the U.S. and became one of the most widely decorated groups of American soldiers in the European theater of the war.

Cold War Flash Points

Freedom would now face a new challenge. In 1945, the U.S. had transformed itself into one of the world's superpowers with the development of the atomic bomb. Its stance on foreign affairs would be drastically changed, and isolation was no longer possible. That standing would be quickly challenged as distrust between former allies in World War II — the U.S. and Russia — created a climate of fear. In the summer of 1949, Russia conducted its first nuclear test of its bomb, built in large part on secrets stolen from the United States Manhattan Project. So, not only did the U.S. have to work to rebuild the economies of various countries in Europe with the Marshall Plan and help rebuild the economy of Japan, but it also faced a new threat from Russia, resulting in a new war — the Cold War — in which democracy and communism would challenge each other. The addition of China as a communist nation in 1949 widened the challenge of the spread of communism and how to best deal with it.

(*Note:* Communist challenges in Europe after World War II are covered in Chapter 16.)

TIP

It's time again to think about maps and geography. Locate maps by doing a web search so that you know how to locate countries and flashpoints in the Cold War.

Building bombs and more

Following the Russian test of a nuclear weapon, the U.S. and Russia began a tremendous nuclear weapon buildup. In addition to the buildup of troops, planes, and submarines, it included a weapons stockpile, with both nations detonating their own H-bombs by 1953 and then the U.S. detonating a thermonuclear device at the Bikini Atoll in 1954. Since that time, nine other nations have developed nuclear weapons and have conducted a wide range of their own tests.

This new arms race spread to space, with the Russian launch of its satellite Sputnik in October 1957. Over the next decade, Russia and the U.S. competed to see who could put the first man in space and eventually land a man on the moon. The U.S. took the lead in the space race on July 20, 1969, when Neil Armstrong landed on the moon and took "one small step for man; one giant leap for mankind."

Crisis in Korea

The Cold War took another turn in Asia with the invasion of South Korea (a new ally of the U.S.) on June 25, 1950, by the communist forces in North Korea led by Kim Il Sung. The recently created United Nations responded to South Korea's appeal for help leading to the invasion of UN forces at Inchon in September 1950. The UN forces and South Korean troops managed to push back the communist North Korean and Chinese troops to the border of China by the winter of 1950. But the "see-saw" part of the war ended with troops on both sides fighting the next two years of the war along the demilitarized zone of the 38th parallel. An armistice was agreed upon in July 1953, but no formal peace treaty was ever signed by North and South Korea. Even today, North Korea remains defiant in its approach toward the U.S., and its border with South Korea along the 38th parallel remains the most heavily fortified border in the world.

Challenge in Vietnam

In the mid-1950s, the country of Vietnam was divided into a communist north and democratic south. Russia and China supported the north, while the U.S. threw its support to the south. An election to reunite Vietnam failed. Fears of communist tensions in the region led to the formation of the "domino theory," that if one nation in Asia fell to communism, others were sure to follow. After the assassination of John F. Kennedy in November 1963, the U.S. became drawn into conflict in the region.

August 1964 brought that conflict to a head in the waters off the coast of North Vietnam, when two American warships were attacked. President Lyndon Johnson urged Congress to pass the Gulf of Tonkin Resolution giving the president authority to send in troops and attack in retaliation.

U.S. involvement in Vietnam continued to escalate over the next three years. Soldiers were drafted and sent to fight. By 1968, the U.S. had nearly 500,000 troops in the region. During the early part of the war, LBJ kept reassuring the American public that we were winning the war, and he complied with General William Westmoreland's requests for more soldiers and firepower.

The watershed year of 1968 changed this. The Tet Offensive at the end of January witnessed the North Vietnamese surprise attack on several outposts in the south. The U.S. and South Vietnamese were caught off guard. Even though the U.S. forces retaliated and pushed the North Vietnamese soldiers back, the war had become unwinnable in the hearts and minds of the American public. War protests mounted back home, and violence erupted in the civil rights movement with the assassination of Martin Luther King in April. LBJ decided not to run for reelection. Nixon ran on the Republican ticket with a "secret plan to end the war" and was elected president in 1968 and again in 1972. The U.S. withdrew its troops and pulled out of Vietnam in 1973. South Vietnam finally surrendered to North Vietnam two years later.

The Modern Era

The time period from the 1960s to the present has been marked by various political and social changes at home as well as abroad. Assassinations, presidents misleading the public, civil rights challenges, threats to world peace, economic challenges, the suppression of women's rights, and terrorism have dominated the news at various times. Each of these events has challenged our freedom and our response to life in this modern era.

TIP

This area is broad and covers nearly 60 years of history. It is a low-emphasis portion of the TASC exam, but you still need to be aware of some of the major points during this time frame. It would be wise to once again utilize some outside sources and create a timeline of significant events from roughly 1968 to 2008. See if you can pick out any patterns of "history repeating itself."

Securing the dream

The Civil Rights Movement gained momentum following the 1954 landmark ruling of the *Brown v. Board of Education* Supreme Court case which stated that "separate is not equal," thus overturning the separate but equal ruling in the *Plessy v. Ferguson* case 58 years earlier. Events that followed ended with African Americans finally gaining civil rights with the Civil Rights Act of 1964, which prohibited segregation in places of public accommodation and segregation on the basis of race or color. The 24th Amendment outlawed the poll tax that had created a barrier to voting. The Voting Rights Act of 1965 secured the right of African Americans to simply register and vote without any stipulations. But to get to this point, various walks, sit-ins, protests, and violence occurred with the goal of securing freedom:

>> **Montgomery Bus Boycott:** Rosa Parks's refusal to give up her seat on the bus led to an 11-month boycott of the bus system led by MLK. The Supreme Court stated segregation on the bus system was illegal.

>> **Freedom Rides:** May 1961 saw a series of bus trips across interstate lines protesting segregation in the South, resulting in violence that was reported by the media.

>> **Children's March:** May of 1963 resulted in the arrest of over 5,000 African-American students and children by Sheriff Bull Connor. The media coverage of this caused JFK to propose civil rights legislation. (He was assassinated in November 1963, and it would be up to LBJ to continue that legislation.)

>> **March on Washington:** In August 1963, MLK spoke to a crowd of over 250,000 people in front of the Lincoln Memorial with his "I Have a Dream" speech.

>> **Bombing at 16th Street Baptist Church:** Four little girls were killed in a bombing attack on Sunday, September 15, 1963.

>> **Selma:** In 1965, MLK pressured President Johnson for voting rights legislation after the march from Selma to Montgomery in March. On August 6, LBJ signed the Voting Rights Act, securing the right for African Americans to register to vote without restrictions.

>> **Watts riots in Los Angeles:** Six days after the signing of the Voting Rights Act, race riots broke out in Los Angeles.

Locate a copy of two of MLK's speeches and use a primary document analysis worksheet to break apart the speech and look for items that relate to the Civil Rights Movement.

TIP

Challenges at home and abroad

The latter part of the 20th century and the beginning of the 21st century have been marked by growth, decline, threats, and victories that have once again challenged our freedoms. Watergate resulted in the resignation of President Nixon in 1974 before he could be impeached for his role in the cover-up of the break-in at the Democratic national headquarters.

The last part of the decade of the 1970s saw economic challenges with OPEC and our dependence on foreign oil. President Jimmy Carter was challenged by the takeover of the U.S. embassy in Tehran, Iran in 1979.

President Ronald Reagan openly challenged the "evil empire" of Russia and began negotiations with Mikhail Gorbachev that would eventually lead to the end of the Cold War in 1991. President George H. W. Bush led a UN coalition of forces in the invasion of Iraq in the Persian Gulf War. President Bill Clinton worked with a Republican Congress to reform welfare and other issues, yet he was caught up in an impeachment scandal about Monica Lewinsky and obstruction of justice before being acquitted by the Senate, which allowed him to serve out his full second term as president.

President George W. Bush had his presidency transformed by the tragic events of 9/11 when the Twin Towers and the Pentagon were the focus of terrorists attacks (as well as the plane taken over by terrorists aiming for the White House which was taken down by passengers over Pennsylvania). The resulting war on terrorism would consume the rest of his presidency. He invaded Iraq (a country unrelated to the 9/11 attacks) after convincing the American public that Iraqi leader Saddam Hussein possessed "weapons of mass destruction" (he did not). After Hurricane Katrina in 2005, Bush saw his image tarnished due to his slow response to this weather disaster.

President Barack Obama became the first African-American president elected in 2008. During his presidency, Obama managed the slow but steady recovery of the economic collapse left over by his predecessor and achieved the passage of healthcare reform known as "Obamacare." He also continued to deal with the war on terrorism, including killing Osama Bin Laden (the architect of the 9/11 attacks). Obama's presidency was marked by constant challenges to his programs and proposals by Republicans and the Tea Party in Congress.

Chapter 16

World History

World history is the study of the past — an attempt to understand why major global events happened the way they did so you can learn from them and apply the lessons they teach you to your understanding of the complex world you live in today. Shakespeare said it best with his quote "all the world's a stage." You should familiarize with a broad scope of events from the time of the ancient civilizations of Greece, Rome, China, and India; major religions in the world; migrations and settlements of people around the globe; political and philosophical ideas that have shaped lives around the world; and, of course, the impact of wars and terrorist acts. It may seem a bit daunting, but keep in mind that you don't need to know a lot of specific details (every battle in the war, casualty counts, every major world leader, and so on), but you should do some reading and studying to at least familiarize yourself with trends and events over a broad spectrum of time — that's why it's called "world history." Don't forget the "story" behind it all.

In this chapter, as you prepare for the Social Studies TASC examination, we guide you through a broad overview of events, places, and people that have had an impact on world history. There will be approximately seven questions about world history on this portion of the exam. The majority of these questions will focus on events in the 19th and 20th centuries, but there may be questions from earlier time periods. You can't memorize over 4,000 years of history. Instead, you need to think like a historian by looking for the main points, trends, and ideas.

Impact of Early Civilizations

From the time of the early river civilizations of China, India, the Middle East, and Egypt all the way to the empires of Greece and Rome, the world was an exciting place. Interactions within a region and interactions between regions provide a dynamic picture of the story of humankind. To gain a broad understanding of different early cultures, consider the following civilizations to guide your study:

>> The river civilizations in Egypt, Mesopotamia, India, and China

>> The Phoenicians, ancient Israel, Assyria, and Babylonia

>> The Greek and Roman empires

TIP

Time for a web search: Locate a map of each of the civilizations listed here, as well as the Silk Road. Look at various geographical features — rivers, mountains, bodies of water, cities, and neighboring countries. Ask yourself what made each civilization's location unique.

Location, location, location

Yes, as stated by the old adage of real estate, location does matter. The four ancient river civilizations marked their places as complex societies developed in each region, and they were all tied to the rivers for their development. Geographic barriers and very long distances separated these civilizations. Crops, floods, droughts, transportation, and trade shaped life in each area. Beginning around 3100 BCE and continuing for nearly 3,000 years, Egypt's civilization thrived mainly on a 10-mile-wide strip of land irrigated by the Nile River. The subcontinent of India was the home of the civilization along the Indus River that spanned a little over 700 years, beginning around 2600 BCE. Mesopotamia along the Tigris and Euphrates rivers was the home of several cities, with a vast trade network beginning around 3300 BCE. And China's ancient civilization began along the Yangtze and Yellow rivers, isolated geographically from the other societies.

Trade and economic development

Coins, items for trade, and bartering were central parts of the complex economic structure in ancient societies. China developed four ancient inventions — gunpowder, paper, movable type, and the compass, along with silk and spices that defined its culture and intrigued outsiders. Among other things the Chinese worked on were shipbuilding and suspension bridges. A network of trade routes known as the *Silk Road*, stretching over 4,000 miles, linked China to the Fertile Crescent in the Middle East and made it possible to trade unique goods and ideas to each region.

Written language

The use of a written language helped preserve the history of ancient cultures. Language also helped with trade and the formation of arts and literature.

>> Sumerian cuneiform, the earliest form of writing, involved pictographs and wedge-shaped strokes and symbols marked on clay tablets.

>> Egyptian hieroglyphics used symbols to represent various concepts, sounds, or objects.

>> The Phoenicians developed an alphabet that utilized symbols for sounds.

>> China developed a very complex system of thousands of symbols that represented words and ideas.

Religion

Religion played a significant role in unifying many of the ancient civilizations. Polytheism in Egypt, with its array of gods and goddesses, held a major focus on the afterlife. Hinduism and Buddhism emerged from the culture in ancient India. Hinduism is a complex religion focusing on the ultimate goal of reaching a union with a form of Brahman through a series of reincarnations. Buddhism began around the early 500s BCE and was based on the life and teaching of Buddha, which stresses living a moral life, karma, and meditation, with the final goal of reaching nirvana. Confucianism took root in China around 550 BCE and stressed harmony and duties and responsibilities to family and government. The Hebrews (Israelites) created a monotheistic religion based on the belief of one all-knowing and all-powerful god. History, moral standards of behavior, and faith were central to their religious practices, as recorded in the Torah.

Social classes

The river civilizations all had complex social hierarchal systems in place, where ruling families, priests, and government officials ranked at the top while farmers, tradesmen, and slaves were at the bottom. Slave labor provided a substantial workforce in many societies. Farmers made up one of the largest classes of people and faced many challenges. A complex caste system in India was created to classify people into social groups with little or no mobility between castes. These classifications centered around power struggle and authority.

Natural resources

Use of metals by the various civilizations helped them wage war and create farming tools, ritual vessels, horse-drawn chariots, and coins for trade. Bronze was one of the earliest metals used, but it was replaced with iron (a stronger metal), used for weapons and farming instruments.

Development of government and city-states

Pharaohs in Egypt created a series of dynasties that lasted for over 31 centuries beginning around 3100 BCE. Mummification and the pyramids were testimonies to the pharaohs' belief in the after-life. Dynastic rule in China, with the mandate of heaven (the divine right to rule), stretched from around 1766 BCE to the modern era, ending with the last dynasty in 1911 CE.

Empires

The Greeks and Romans built two of the largest empires in the world. The rise, dominance, and fall of these empires left a lasting legacy of influence in the world.

Greece

The Ancient Greek empire lasted from 800 BC to 146 BC.

>> Main city-states of Sparta and Athens

>> Sparta was a warrior society; Athens developed a democracy, giving people a say in their government

>> Both societies stressed education — in Sparta, military training and sporting contests

>> Polytheistic religion

>> New standards in architecture, literature, drama, study of history

>> Philosophy, morality, ethics debated by Socrates, Plato, Aristotle

>> Persian Empire under Alexander the Great stretched from Greece to India; fell into disarray after his death

>> Spread Greek culture

>> Advances in education, medicine, philosophy

Rome

The Roman Republic lasted from 509 BCE to 14 CE. The Roman Empire existed from 14 CE to 476 CE.

» Republic form of government (elected officials)

» Education stressed for boys and girls

» Larger role for women

» Polytheistic worship of gods (many borrowed from Greek culture)

» Law, history, education, philosophy, architecture, science, math

» Rise of Christianity based on the teachings of Jesus, spread throughout the empire by disciples. The teachings included God's love and loving your neighbor. They also stressed justice, morality, service, and forgiveness. The Apostle Paul was extremely influential in spreading Christianity throughout Italy, Greece, and Asia Minor. Christianity eventually became the official religion of the empire in 313 CE.

» In 313, Constantine divided the Roman Empire with a new capital of the eastern part of the empire in Constantinople in Asia Minor. Rome remained the capital of the western portion of the Roman Empire.

» Military attacks by outsiders, and economic, political, and social problems led to the fall of the western portion of the Roman Empire to Germanic nomadic invaders (Visigoths and Vandals) in 476, while the empire in the east lasted for another thousand years.

In the Dark

Most of the Western world entered a time known as the *Middle Ages*, which witnessed a dramatic decline politically, socially, and economically in Europe and then a slow march of growth that set the stage for an explosive reformation of society. The early part of this *Medieval* period, also known as the *Dark Ages*, kept Europe isolated from China, India, and the Middle East. Trade and education declined, and political divisions separated vast parts of Europe. Things would gradually change, and forces were at work to transform society and reach out to the wider world.

Another world religion takes hold

The birth and spread of Islam began with the birth of its prophet Muhammad in 570. Their holy book is the Quran, and adherents practice the five pillars of Islam: faith, prayer five times a day, charity to the poor, fasting during the month of Ramadan, and the *hajj*, or pilgrimage to Mecca. Islam united the Arabs, and their influence spread in the Middle East, across Northern Africa, and in Spain. Muslim influence in Spain would last nearly 800 years until they were expelled in 1492.

Transformation of Europe

After the Germanic tribes — the Visigoths, Vandals, Saxons, and Franks — invaded the Romans, small kingdoms were created in Western Europe. These small kingdoms would take hold until nation-states were formed years later.

» Europe would be threatened by the spread of Islam.

» Charlemagne's rule unified parts of France, Germany, and Italy in 768 by using religion and government.

>> The Vikings, Angles, and Saxons invaded and eventually settled in England. The Vikings spread their culture in England, northern France, and parts of Russia in addition to establishing a short-lived colony in North America around 1,000.

>> *Feudalism* involved a system in which lords ruled the surrounding land to create *fiefs* (or estates), with castles built for defense. Rival lords would use warfare as a way to train knights for defense. Serfs were bound to the land around the estate or manor.

The power of the church

The Roman Catholic Church became firmly established and dominated virtually every aspect of daily life during medieval times. The Pope became the official spokesman of the church (from Rome), and local priests performed mass (in Latin) with local parishioners. Some men and women withdrew from daily life and secluded themselves in monasteries to live out their religious lives of work and religious study including prayers, musical chants, and copying sacred scriptures. After the 1100s, several communities in northern Europe built elaborate cathedrals as monuments to their religious influence. The power of the church would grow and become virtually unchallenged until the early 1400s.

Nation-states take root

Beginning around 1100, as the population began to grow, towns and cities began to expand, and trade routes were established.

Monarchial powers began to take hold, and nation-states began to form governments. As the nation-state evolved in Britain, the Magna Carta was signed in 1215, giving nobles and eventually citizens in England rights protected by the government. It also established Parliament as a way to limit the power and authority of the king. As nation-states were established in England, France, Spain, and Italy, the power of the governments would also be challenged by the power and authority of the church. The new regions sought to solidify their power within their territories, setting the stage for future conflicts.

The Holy Roman Empire came into being under the rule of Duke Otto I, who was crowned emperor by the Pope in 962. This region would be dominated by the power of the church and the Pope. Power struggles within the region of Germany and Italy reduced them to scattered feudal states and, unlike the other nation-states, they would not become unified as nation-states until the mid-1800s.

The world outside of Europe

As the world outside of Western Europe flourished with growing cultures in China, India, and western Africa, Europe began to emerge from nearly 500 years of isolation from the rest of the world. News arrived asking Pope Urban to send help to the Holy Land of Jerusalem to fight back incursions by the Muslim Turks in the region. After the appeal in 1096, thousands of knights and commoners began the long pilgrimage to fight in the Holy Land. There was a series of four crusades and clashes over the next 200 years. In addition to the religious warfare among Muslims, Christians, and Jews, people in Europe became enamored by exotic goods not available in Europe.

Following the Crusades, Marco Polo left Venice in 1271 and ventured to China, where he lived for 17 years. He wrote about his adventures under the Mongol emperor Kublai Khan. The stories of his time in China excited people in Europe. They also became interested in new products from China, including gunpowder, paper, silk, and spices. The worldview of Europe continued to expand.

TIP Time again for another internet map search: Locate maps of the Crusades, Marco Polo's travel to China, and the Black Death. This geographical skill will help you understand the importance of location and where in the world things are happening.

Meanwhile, education, art, and literature began to flourish once again in medieval Europe. Science, math, architecture, philosophy, and literary works enlightened people's curiosity and learning. These new ideas would lead to remarkable changes in Europe in the coming years.

Rats

As trade began to flourish from China and parts of Asia with Europe, they became vulnerable to the spread of the *Black Death,* or *bubonic plague.* Around 1347, flea-infested rats on trade ships spread the disease from Italy to Spain, France, England, and the rest of Europe; 1 in 3 people died from this disease over nearly a century — nearly 70 million deaths. The disease was also prevalent in China and the Middle East, killing millions in its wake. As the population began to rebound, social and economic upheaval became the new norm as Europe struggled to recover over the next century.

In the midst of the challenges of plague, crop failures, and economic turmoil, England and France fought a series of battles from the 1330s to the 1450s that is known as the *Hundred Years War.* As a result of the series of "wars," intense nationalism began to take root, and the governments of France and England poured vast resources into new weapons and armies. They also began to look to other regions for trade and territory. The world was beginning to change again.

Rebirth, Renewal, Revolutions

A *renaissance,* or literally a "rebirth," took hold in Italy and spread across Western Europe in the early 1300s and began to radically transform society over the next 200 years. This ushered in the modern era and became one of the most remarkable watershed events that changed the world. Education, the arts, technology, religion, and trade dominated this period. Classical learning from ancient Greece and Rome combined with natural curiosity fueled this change and focused on humanism to understand the world.

» Johann Gutenberg's invention of the printing press in 1455 sparked an educational resurgence by allowing books to be printed quickly and cheaply, allowing them to be read by the masses. The first book he printed was a copy of the Bible. As books became readily available, education grew as people learned to read and gain access to a wide range of knowledge, from religion to law to architecture to the world at large.

» Shakespeare, Cervantes, and others contributed greatly to the literary works of the time.

» Leonardo da Vinci, Michelangelo, Raphael, and Rembrandt transformed the world of art with paintings, statues, and inventions that were demonstrations of the human spirit.

» Martin Luther sparked controversy within the church when in 1517 he nailed his 95 Theses to a church door in which he openly challenged the teachings of the Catholic Church, including the sale of *indulgences* (pardons for sins). This bold action led to a split within the Catholic Church and became known as the *Protestant Reformation,* with two main religious groups — Roman Catholics and Protestants.

» Religious debates began to span across Europe. Luther made the claim that "the just shall live by faith." John Calvin promoted what became known as *Calvinism* with the doctrine of *predestination* (that God chooses who will be saved). Both Luther and Calvin stressed the reading of the Bible as the source of truth.

>> Henry VIII broke with the Roman Catholic Church when it denied his divorce from Catherine of Aragon so he could marry Anne Boleyn. He began the Church of England with the king as the head of the church.

>> Scientific knowledge took a great leap with the studies of Copernicus, Galileo, and Newton. Many of their theories and discoveries where unsuccessfully challenged by the church. The church was horrified to learn that the Earth was not the center of the universe and that scientific laws governed the rule of the universe. Knowledge gained through astronomy, mathematics, chemistry, and physics helped scientists understand the world around them.

Trade routes from earlier time periods had been used to carry not only goods but also intellectual ideas between various regions. With the renewal of learning and curiosity in Europe, a resurgence in exploration was about to take place and catapult the world at large into the modern era. Trade routes were established, discoveries were made, trade of goods increased, and colonization efforts were established.

>> At first, Portugal and Spain would take the lead in European exploration. Later, England and France would also become involved in exploration and colonization.

>> China's Zheng He explored parts of land and territories in the Pacific region in the early 1400s with his seven explorations. Due to a change in leadership within China, his discoveries and accomplishments were largely forgotten as China focused inward, and European nations would take the lead in exploration and discoveries.

>> Explorations around Africa at the Cape of Good Hope in search of a shortcut to the Indies for trade led to numerous voyages from Portugal and Spain (Vasco da Gama, Christopher Columbus, Ferdinand Magellan). Soon after, the slave trade raised its ugly head, and by the 1800s it had resulted in the largest forced migration in world history, amounting to over 12 million slaves forced to leave the continent of Africa to be transported to the New World.

>> The Columbian Exchange connected the Old World of Europe to that of the New World in the Americas. New crops such as corn, sweet potatoes, peppers, cocoa, squash, and vanilla, along with gold and silver from the New World, were introduced to Europe, while domesticated animals, slaves, wheat, barley, bananas, grapes, coffee, and sugar cane were brought over from European trade. The European explorers also introduced devastating diseases — small pox, measles, and influenza — to the native populations in the Americas so that, within a century of contact, nearly 90 percent of the native population in many areas had been wiped out by these new diseases, to which they had no immunity.

>> Another big change in the world of exploration occurred when England defeated the Spanish Armada in 1588, ushering in a period of dominance by Great Britain in trade, colonization, and power in the world for the next 300 years.

>> Spain and Portugal took the lead, followed by England and France, with a series of conquests and settlements in the New World. Trade, territorial conquest, greed, and religion played major roles in the colonization of the New World.

Do a web search about the Middle Passage and the triangular trade routes. Locate a map and historical drawings. How did the trade and routes impact the world economically and socially?

The Enlightenment, beginning in the early 1700s, ushered in the *Age of Reason* — using natural laws and the power of reason to shape economic, social, and political thought.

>> Thomas Hobbes and John Locke promoted the concept of a *social contract* — that the role of government was to protect the natural rights of its citizens. Locke's philosophies would encourage numerous conflicts across Europe and the Americas over the next two centuries. Montesquieu and Jean-Jacques Rousseau promoted ideas of government power.

>> During the Glorious Revolution, the English Bill of Rights was introduced in 1689 in Parliament, further limiting the power of the monarch, increasing the power of Parliament, and promoting the rights of citizens. This influenced other nations seeking rights for their citizens.

>> The 13 colonies in America declared their independence from the British crown on July 4, 1776, citing the rights of the citizens to "life, liberty and the pursuit of happiness" and listing 27 abuses of power by the king in denying those rights.

>> This was followed by the French Revolution in 1789, in which citizens in France rebelled against the absolute rule of the monarch and the abusive government in favor of basic rights and changes to how the government ruled the nation. Heads literally rolled during the revolution with the introduction of the guillotine as a tool against traitors.

>> Following the Reign of Terror, Napoleon rose to power for 15 years, until 1815. He would terrorize France and Europe until he was stopped by extreme winter conditions during his invasion of Russia and finally defeated at Waterloo in 1815 by British and Prussian forces.

Great Britain transformed the world yet again during the Industrial Revolution beginning in the late 1700s with the introduction of machinery that could easily handle the work normally done by hand by hundreds of men. Tools and machines would help advance trade and the need for natural resources and labor. Despite challenges by the working poor and terrible working conditions, a global market economy began to take hold. Britain would lead the world for over a century as it dominated world trade and the world economy. This was followed by the rise of the United States to economic dominance, and by 1900, over one-third of world goods were being produced in America. *Laissez-faire* economics (promoted by Adam Smith in *The Wealth of Nations* in 1776) came to dominate the relationship between government and business, with a "hands-off" approach to government regulation, allowing for the explosive growth of big businesses in Britain and then the U.S. Advances in steel production and transportation (especially railroads) propelled economic growth, and new markets for trade around the globe were established.

Philosophical Challenges

Beginning around mid-century in the 1800s, various "isms" began to take hold in Europe that would set the stage for radical transformations in the 20th century. Forces that had been at work in Britain, France, and the U.S. had begun to spread across Europe.

>> Karl Marx and Friedrich Engels published *The Communist Manifesto* in 1848, promoting communism as a type of socialism in which a "classless society" would be created that would take care of the evils of the problems in the workplace and social divisions in society. This would challenge free-market capitalism in which businesses competed for production and traded for profit.

>> Germany, and then Russia and independence movements in Asia, Africa, and Latin America, would look to Marxism as a means to solve social and political ills and spark revolution. By the end of the 20th century, many nations around the world embraced democratic ideals and capitalism as a means of economic growth and survival.

>> During the later part of the 1800s, *nationalism* began to take hold in various regions of Europe. This excessive ethnic pride in one's country laid the groundwork for serious conflicts in the 20th century as nations fought wars for economic, political, and geographic dominance.

>> Militarism witnessed the excessive buildup of weapons, armies, and battleships in preparation for war. Britain and Germany led the charge in this "arms race" that became a major factor in the outbreak of World War I.

>> *Imperialism* was yet another destructive force that led European nations to stake territorial claims in Africa and Asia that would help European nations advance their trade and political dominance. This would sow the seeds of numerous rebellions by conquered nations in the mid-20th century. The old adage was indeed true: "land equals power." India became the crown jewel of the British Empire, while nearly the entire continent of Africa was carved out by the major nations of Europe. China also became a target of imperialism and free trade with Russia, the U.S., and major countries in Europe.

>> Alliances were also made across Europe. These sometimes secret alliances divided Europe into two camps — the *Triple Alliance* (Central powers) of Germany, Italy, and Austria-Hungary and the *Triple Entente* (Allied powers) of Great Britain, France, and Russia. Germany also had an alliance pact with the Ottoman Empire. It set the stage for conflict erupting in 1914.

The World at War Again and Again

Several different crises had been brewing across the continent of Europe for decades prior to the outbreak of the Great War in 1914. After the French loss to the Prussians in 1871 resulted in the loss of territory from France in the Alsace–Lorraine region (rich in coal and iron ore deposits), a motive of revenge was in place. The Balkan Peninsula became the focal point or the "powder keg" of Europe. It only took the Serbian terrorist act of Gavrilo Princip of the Black Hand organization to ignite the flames when he assassinated Austrian Archduke Ferdinand and his pregnant wife Sophie on June 28, 1914, while they were on a goodwill trip to Sarajevo. When the terms of the ultimatum were ignored by Serbia, war broke out on July 28, and within a week, all six major powers of Europe were involved in open conflict. What was thought to be a short war that would be over by Christmas erupted into a four–year conflict that would dramatically change Europe and set the stage for another world conflict only two decades later.

TIP

Time for another web search: Locate a map of Europe in 1914 and in 1918 and compare the territorial changes prior to World War I and immediately following it. What new countries were created after the end of the war?

The Great War

The world was now at war. After the utter failure of the Schlieffen Plan of Germany to quickly defeat the French on the western front and then move rapidly and defeat the Russians on the eastern front, the war became divided between two fronts, and this would prove disastrous for Germany.

>> The Western Front became the focal point for most of the war, with trench warfare being waged on a 600-mile strip of land between France and Germany.

>> The Eastern Front posed a threat for Germany, forcing a split of troops and resources to fight a two-front war. This came to an abrupt end on the eastern front when Russia secretly pulled out of the war and signed a pact with Germany in March 1918 (this was after the Russian Revolution in November 1917).

>> New weapons of warfare were introduced, making this war even more deadly. German submarines, mustard and chlorine gases (and the introduction of the gas mask), tanks, airplanes, machine guns, and German zeppelins contributed a new dynamic to deadly warfare.

>> By Christmas of 1914, the war remained largely one of a huge stalemate. Each side would gain and lose territory as causality rates increased. The sinking of the *Lusitania* in 1915 and the Zimmerman Telegram in 1917, along with the Germans resuming unrestricted submarine warfare, finally saw the U.S. entry into the war with President Woodrow Wilson's challenge of "making the world safe for democracy."

>> This helped turn the tide of the war, with an armistice being signed at the 11th hour on November 11, 1918. Fighting finally ceased.

>> Leaders from the U.S., Britain, France, Italy, and other nations met to create the Treaty of Versailles, formally ending the war with total blame being placed on Germany. The League of Nations was formed as a peace organization (with the goal of preventing another global crisis), but after the U.S. Senate refused to ratify the treaty, the stage was set for yet another major conflict.

World War II: Here we go again

In the two decades following the end of World War I, Great Britain, France, and the U.S. pursued policies of isolationism and appeasement. As the decade of the 1920 came to an end, the Great Depression began in late 1929 and soon came to impact various regions around the globe. While the world dealt with the devastating economic effects of the Great Depression, this allowed for dramatic changes in leadership, with Vladimir Lenin and Joseph Stalin gaining control in communist Russia, Benito Mussolini creating a fascist government in Italy, Adolph Hitler gaining power and creating a Nazi state in Germany in 1932, and Emperor Hirohito solidifying power in Japan. Failure to confront these opposing forces would set the stage for the outbreak of yet another global conflict.

>> Japan began this conflict with the conquest of Manchuria in 1932 and the brutal invasion of Nanking in China in 1937. Within five years Japan controlled 25 percent of China as well as outposts in the Pacific (and set its eyes on Pearl Harbor in December 1941).

>> Alliances were yet again in place, with the *Axis powers* of Germany, Italy, and Japan and the *Allied powers* of Britain, France, and Russia (and later the U.S. at the end of 1941).

>> Compromise failed. Giving in to the demands of Hitler from 1936 to 1939 allowed him to exert his new military might by claiming more territory in Europe and planning for his blitzkrieg invasion of Poland in September 1939. All these actions openly violated the Treaty of Versailles, so Great Britain declared war on Germany, and the world was in turmoil yet again.

>> Hitler marched across mainland Europe so that by the summer of 1941, Great Britain was the only power in Europe challenging Hitler. In August 1941, Hitler made a grave mistake by opening yet again a two-front war by invading Russia. After the Siege of Leningrad ended in the winter of 1944, the Russians forced Germany to retreat.

>> Japan forced the entry of the U.S. into the war with its attack on Pearl Harbor on December 7, 1941. Now the war had two major fronts — the war in Europe and northern Africa and the war in the Pacific.

>> One of the greatest tragedies to emerge from World War II was the *Holocaust,* in which Hitler carried out his plan of genocide to systematically kill 6 million (over 75 percent) of the Jews in Europe with the use of exterminations at various concentration camps in Eastern Europe. These horrors would not be fully disclosed until the end of the war.

>> June 6, 1944 (D-Day), witnessed the Allied invasion at Normandy, which began the major push to drive Hitler's forces back. After Hitler's suicide in late April 1945, Germany surrendered on May 8, and V-E Day was celebrated.

>> Fighting continued in the Pacific and culminated with President Truman issuing the order to drop newly developed atomic bombs on Hiroshima and Nagasaki on August 6 and 9, resulting in the deaths of hundreds of thousands of Japanese and the destruction of the two cities. V-J Day was on August 15, with Japan's formal surrender on September 1, 1945. The war to end all wars was finally over.

A New World Order

Before the end of World War II, delegates from 50 nations gathered in San Francisco to create the United Nations in April 1945 with the goal of promoting world peace. Member nations had representation in the General Assembly, and the Security Council had five permanent members (the U.S., Britain, France, China, and the USSR) and ten other members on a rotating basis. The council could utilize economic sanctions and deploy peacekeeping troops to deal with disputes. World peace would be tested at various times since the inception of the UN, with conflicts surrounding the spread of communism and later terrorism making headline news.

The *Cold War* began right at the end of World War II as a clash between democracy and the spread of communism took center stage. The U.S. became the leading superpower with its atomic weapons in 1945. This was soon followed in 1949 with the USSR becoming the other superpower with the testing of its own atomic device in September 1949 over Siberia. These two nations would embark on a nearly 40-year quest of building up their nuclear arsenals, pushing the world ever closer to the brink of nuclear war until the fall of communism in the USSR on December 31, 1991.

Western Europe was in shambles at the end of World War II. As the war drew to a close, Russia claimed territory in Eastern Europe and transformed the region into communist satellite countries. Former Prime Minister Winston Churchill proclaimed in March 1946 that an "iron curtain" had descended upon the continent of Europe, dividing communist East from the free West. Germany and its capital Berlin were divided into East and West, and in 1961, the Berlin Wall was erected with 27 miles of barbed wire and concrete physically dividing East and West. The wall would stand as this symbol until its fall in November 1989, when democratic reforms swept across Eastern Europe. U.S. leaders beginning in 1961 challenged the communist leaders in Russia to "tear down" the wall. East Germany would also collapse as East and West Germany reunited in 1990. Prior to 1989, Eastern Europe witnessed several challenges to communist rule in Hungary, Poland, Yugoslavia, and Romania.

The U.S. proclaimed the *Truman Doctrine* in 1946 as a means of containing the spread of communism and limiting it to regions already in communist control. This would be challenged throughout the Cold War era.

The U.S. economic plan to rebuild the economies of Western Europe, the *Marshall Plan*, became a success story as the nations of Western Europe received assistance to rebuild after the ravages of World War II. The allied Berlin airlift began in June 1948 when Stalin closed off the city of Berlin. For more than a year, the U.S.-led Allied forces began an airlift of all goods into West Berlin. Russia eventually relented and the blockade was ended, but it also escalated tensions between East and West.

In 1949, a new military alliance, *NATO* (North Atlantic Treaty Organization), was formed with the U.S. and ten other nations to combat the advances of communist Russia. The Soviet Union responded to this with the formation of its own alliance group, the *Warsaw Pact*, composed of Russia and its Eastern European countries. When the USSR dissolved in 1991, the Warsaw Pact also collapsed. And now some of the former members of the Warsaw Pact are NATO members.

Conflicts surrounding communism spread throughout Asia. In October 1949, China became a communist nation under the rule of Chairman Mao. Then in June 1950, Kim Il Sung, the communist leader of North Korea, invaded and nearly defeated South Korea (a new ally of the U.S. after the end of World War II). The newly formed UN responded to pleas for help, and 16 nations sent in troops to aid South Korea. The conflict stopped with the signing of an armistice in July 1953, but the war has yet to be formally resolved. To this day North Korea blames the U.S. for the invasion of South Korea, and the leaders of the Kim family still pose a threat on the Korean Peninsula and in the neighboring region.

Challenges in the Middle East ignited yet again with the formation of the modern nation of Israel in 1949. Several clashes over territory have occurred and are still ongoing as the Palestinians and others challenge Israel's right to exist.

In 1960, five oil-producing nations in the Middle East forged a new organization, *OPEC* (Organization of the Petroleum Exporting Countries), to regulate the supply of oil and control oil prices on the world market. Today, the 12-member organization is still wielding its influence on the world economy, with various changes in production and price controls. As the world's thirst for oil continues, OPEC remains a major player in the world's economy.

In 1972, U.S. President Nixon stunned the world with his famous trip to China in which he formally opened up relations between the two nations. The two nations since then have been involved in various economic and political endeavors. Nixon also reached out to the USSR with his visit three months later to talk to the communist leader Leonid Brezhnev. This trip began talks of arms limitations between the two superpowers.

Over the next nearly 20 years, the arms race would escalate in the early 1980s when U.S. President Ronald Reagan referred to the USSR as the "evil empire," and both nations pursued a dangerous policy of nuclear arms buildup. Then, after the nuclear mishap with a meltdown at a nuclear power plant in Chernobyl in the Ukraine in 1986, Reagan and the new leader Mikhail Gorbachev began a series of summit meetings that led to the end of the Cold War in 1991.

While the U.S. dealt mainly with the war in Vietnam from 1964 to 1973, Eastern Europe was the scene of violent protests and skirmishes, with communist Russia exerting its influence in the communist countries created in Eastern Europe following the end of World War II.

Democratic reform began to take a foothold in Europe and in other parts of the world when, in September 1980, communist Poland pushed for the creation of the trade union Solidarity. This would lead to the formation of a democratic Poland with the election of its president, Lech Walesa. June 1989 saw a challenge to communist rule in China with the protest by college students at Tiananmen Square. "Tank Man" became the iconic photo of one man's challenge to communist rule in China. This peaceful protest ended brutally as the communist government reclaimed the square, killing hundreds of unarmed protesters and enforcing its power and push back against democratic reform. Democratic reform took hold in communist countries in Eastern Europe, which demanding democratic changes. The Berlin Wall, which separated communist East Germany from democratic West Germany, collapsed on the evening of November 9, 1989 when students climbed the wall and began breaking up this symbol of division. Communism ended its 74-year reign in Russia at the end of 1991. Russia dissolved into a confederacy, with the eventual breakup of all 15 territories to become independent nations. South Africa also witnessed democratic reform with the release of Nelson Mandela in 1990 after serving 27 years of a life sentence for his opposition to apartheid. Four years later he would be elected president of the new South Africa, creating a reformed democratic nation and ending over 200 years of segregation and Apartheid.

In 1990, Iraqi leader Saddam Hussein invaded the oil-producing country of Kuwait, resulting in a swift response from the U.S. and a coalition of UN countries that prevented further Iraqi aggression. January 1991 saw the UN coalition beginning a six-week bombing of Iraq, leading to Operation Desert Storm in February. Within 100 hours of the attack, with patriot missiles and the use of the stealth bomber, Hussein was forced out of Kuwait, but he was not forced out of power in Iraq. Then, 12 years later, U.S. forces invaded Iraq after convincing the American public that Hussein had *WMDs* (weapons of mass destruction) and ended Hussein's rule in Iraq. No WMDs were ever found, and Hussein's death in 2006 left behind a power vacuum that quickly led to the rise of ISIS and the destabilization of the entire region.

The rise of Al Qaeda, with its leader Osama Bin Laden, threatened world peace with their series of attacks beginning in 1993 with the garage bombing at the World Trade Center in New York City, two embassy attacks in Kenya and Tanzania, and the attack on the USS *Cole* in 2000. September 11, 2001, witnessed the horror of terror with the attack in the U.S. and destruction of the Twin Towers of the World Trade Center. Bin Laden was finally brought to justice in May 2011 when President Barack Obama ordered Special Forces to track him down and put him out of his misery.

Chapter 17

Civics and Government

"We the People." The U.S. Constitution begins with those three simple words. And the power of the American government lies right there — in the *people*. It's up to the people — indeed, it's their civic duty — to understand, participate in, challenge, and protect their government. In this chapter of civics/government, as you prepare for the TASC examination, we guide you through a broad overview of documents, powers of the government, challenges to the government, and the safeguards in place to preserve the government. It will be useful for you to consider one of your civic duties in understanding your government by first studying foundational documents that affect the lives of the citizens of this civilized nation.

TIP

There will be approximately 12 questions about civics/government on the Social Studies portion of the TASC exam. These questions deal with your knowledge of foundational documents (the Declaration of Independence, the Articles of Confederation, and the Constitution), concepts of liberty, separation of powers in the government, and the responsibility of you, "Joe Public," actively participating in your government. Because when all is said and done, it's up to *you* to make this grand experiment of democracy keep working. While you won't need to know a great deal of specific details, you should understand some of the broad themes and events over time that have kept this country working.

Making the Foundational Puzzle Pieces Work

Thomas Jefferson set out to define clearly the reasons that impelled the 13 colonies to separate from the royal authority and governance of the king and Parliament of Great Britain — not only separate but also assume the power and equal station as a clearly defined nation among others. That was pretty radical thinking for that time — for a colony to tell the mother country to simply take a hike. There was a price to be paid. As the ink dried after the 56 men signed the Declaration of Independence, they were all considered to be traitors in the eyes of Britain, and, of course, you know the penalty for treason — death. But this did not dissuade the Founding Fathers. They were intent on creating a country based on the founding ideals of rights and freedoms.

Jefferson and others were very well educated and based their ideas of a government protecting the rights of its citizens, and of governing in a just manner, from historical events:

>> **The Romans:** Elected officials who represent the people; an elected body of officials making laws and working with the government leadership

>> **The Magna Carta:** Equality of people under the law, responsibility of leaders to govern fairly, and the participation of people in their government

>> **British Parliament:** A two-house legislative body voted upon by the people

>> **The Enlightenment:** Philosophical leaders promoting ideas of equality, the rule of law, liberty and the rights of people, separation of powers within the government, and the relationship between government and the individual (see John Locke, Montesquieu, Jean-Jacque Rousseau, John Stuart Mill)

Piece one: Declaring independence

Independence Hall in Philadelphia, Pennsylvania, was the site on July 4, 1776, when 56 men boldly inked their names on a new document proclaiming the formation of the new nation of the United States of America. Jefferson took the lead in the committee of five men selected by the Continental Congress to draft a formal declaration in a little over two weeks. The document was presented to the congress, where John Hancock led the charge by being the first to sign — with a large signature so that King George III could literally "read it without his glasses!" (That's why your signature is often referred to as your "John Hancock.")

TIP

Take time to read a copy of the Declaration of Independence. YouTube has videos of people reading it in presentations. Do both — read and listen. Use a document analysis sheet or simply annotate the document looking for significant details that would define this new nation.

Jefferson put forth a convincing argument about the proper role of government in the Declaration of Independence. He began with the bold statement that "all men are created equal" and that they are "endowed by their creator with certain unalienable rights." By defining the role of government as one of "protecting rights" — life, liberty, and the pursuit of happiness — and by giving a warning when the government fails in its paramount duty, he was attempting to unify a varied group of people by laying out aspirations and principles of rules.

TIP

Create a timeline of the equality phrase used by Jefferson. At first it was "all men" are created equal, and that has now broadened to include men regardless of color, women, Native Americans, and 18-year-olds. How has this changed since the original document in 1776?

Jefferson opened by questioning when is the time to break away from the mother country and form your own country. That is not an easy task. He clearly states that the role of government is to protect people's basic rights because the people give the government the power to do just that. But when the government fails to do its job, something must be done. He goes on to state that the reasons to "alter or abolish it" must be well thought out and that it may be better to stay in the current condition. But, after sound reasoning, if it makes sense to make a break, he says to list those reasons and go for it. By attacking the king 27 times with a laundry list of "he has . . ."

statements, people could clearly see that their rights were being abridged. So when their repeated pleas to the king fell on deaf ears, they were left with no other viable option than to make a clean break and declare their independence. Jefferson also spoke of the necessity of the new union to stay together by supporting each other in this new venture: "We mutually pledge to each other our Lives, our Fortunes and our sacred Honor."

Another reason the Declaration of Independence is such a watershed document is that it has been used to influence people around the globe:

>> The people involved in the French Revolution

>> Women suffragists working for the right to vote in America

>> Countries in Eastern Europe in 1989 with the fall of communist rule

>> The creation of a new South Africa and the election of Nelson Mandela as its new president in 1994

Piece two: Protecting independence

Freedom plays a huge role in defining people as their government rules them. Liberty gives people control over their lives and a choice in how to safeguard that liberty. Now that people have gained their freedom, they need to institute a government that will protect them and promote their livelihood. That's a tall order. How much power do you give a government, and what does that look like? What role does a federal government play in ruling states, and what role do the states play in governing the people?

The ultimate question here is who has the power. To set out a plan of governance, the newly founded states adopted the Articles of Confederation in 1777, and it was adopted by all the states in 1781. Out of a fear of a strong centralized government (and nightmares about King George III's harsh rule over the colonies), most of the power of the new government was granted to the states. There was a weak federal government with no chief executive and no federal court system. What was created was simply a firm league of friendship. It was a single-house legislative branch with all states having one equal vote. The problem was that the smaller, less populous states had just as much say as the more populous states. The central government had to ask for donations and help from the states. The central government had no power to tax and could not regulate actions between states. Nearly all acts had to be passed unanimously, and there was no way to enforce the laws that were passed. Each state retained the ultimate authority in its actions with the central government. Now wait a minute — is this the way to really run a country, with everyone calling the shots? It was as if the 13 states were in a big boat, and each one was rowing its oar as it saw fit. If this carried on for long, it was doomed for disaster.

Piece three: Hitting the reset button

It's time for more reading. Locate a copy of the U.S. Constitution, either online or in a study book. Take the time to read it. You may want to print a copy and annotate it to help you gain an understanding of the various parts of the document.

When an armed insurrection in 1787 threatened the stability of the new government, it was time to reconsider the role of the central government and state governments in maintaining the rule of law and protecting the rights of citizens. How do citizens live together in a civil society with a government structured to secure and protect the rights of its citizens?

After the failed attempt in 1786 by farmers in western Massachusetts to lead an armed uprising over taxes and government seizure of land of those who could not pay their taxes, it was time to consider how to best represent the rule of law in the newly formed United States. If no action was taken, the union would soon unravel.

So, in May 1787, 55 state delegates attended the Constitutional Convention in Philadelphia to address the failures of the Articles of Confederation. George Washington was chosen to preside over this group. At first, the delegates were tasked with examining ways in which to amend the Articles of Confederation. They soon came to the conclusion that a change was in order and that there was no way to fix the doomed document.

Right from the beginning, the Founding Fathers sought to define the role of government and maintain the unity of the country with five propositions:

>> To establish *justice* (the rule of law)

>> To ensure *domestic tranquility* (peace at home)

>> To provide for the *common defense* (to protect us at home and abroad)

>> To promote the *general welfare* (helping out people at home)

>> To secure the *blessings of liberty* (to celebrate our independence and freedoms)

The delegates then set about the task of designing a new concept of rule of government for the United States. After various forms of debate, they agreed upon a new design for power for the central government. The power of the federal government would be divided among three separate branches of government. Each would have its unique role in governing as well as establishing checks and balances for each branch.

>> There would be an executive (the president) to preside over the *executive branch* of the federal government.

>> The *legislative branch* would be divided into two houses — a Senate with equal representation from each state and a House of Representatives with representation based on a state's population.

>> The *judicial branch* would be established to interpret the rule of law with the Supreme Court and a series of lower federal courts.

After three months of work and debate, the delegation voted on the new constitution. It was then sent out to the states, where debates raged between two political groups — the *Federalists* (who supported a much-needed strong federal government with distinct powers to govern) and the *Anti-Federalists* (who maintained their support of states' rights over that of the federal government). The debate waged on for nearly two years. Finally, in 1789, the necessary nine votes for ratification were in, and the Constitution was formally adopted as the new form of governance for the United States.

The Balance of Power

The Founding Fathers thought it best to divide the power of the federal government into three separate groups. Each group would have distinct power itself, and each group could challenge the power of the other two groups. It may sound a bit confusing when you look at the "power struggle," but in the end it does make sense and has actually worked for over 200 years!

A tree with three branches

The division of power has been divided into three separate groups, each with its own set of responsibilities. This system of checks and balances was established with the purpose of one group not having more power than the other two. Over the past 200 years, there has been a growth in power and influence of each of the three branches of government. This continues to happen even today.

Executive branch

The power of the executive branch is vested in the President of the United States, who also acts as head of state and commander-in-chief of the armed forces. The following lists some of the requirements and responsibilities of the President:

>> Qualifications: Minimum age 35, U.S. natural-born citizen, lived in U.S. for the last 14 years

>> Duties: Enforces the laws as commander-in-chief, negotiates treaties with foreign nations, grants pardons, makes appointments to the federal courts and cabinet officials and other department positions, sets a policy agenda for Congress, addresses the nation each year in a State of the Union address

>> Has veto power to override actions of Congress

>> After the 25th Amendment, the president is subject to a two-term limit of office (four years each term)

Legislative branch

The legislative branch is made up of the two houses of Congress—the Senate and the House of Representatives. The following lists some of the requirements and responsibilities of the legislative branch:

>> Representative qualifications: Minimum age 25, U.S. citizen for at least seven years, lives in the state that he or she represents

>> Duties: Retains the "power of the purse" in that bills dealing with revenue originate in the House of Representatives, helps make laws, grants the president the right to declare war

>> For a bill to become law, must pass both houses of Congress and get a presidential signature

>> Serves a two-year term with no term limits

>> With a two-thirds vote of Congress can override a presidential veto

>> Representation in the states is re-apportioned every ten years so that the current 435 members are established based on the population of the states (larger states get more representatives and less populated states have fewer representatives)

>> Senate qualifications: Minimum age 30, U.S. citizen for nine years, lives in the state he or she represents, each state is granted two senators (equal balance among the states, with the current 100 senators)

>> Duties: Can impeach and remove the president or other federal officials with impeachment trials held in the Senate, helps make laws, grants the president the right to declare war

>> With a two-thirds vote of Congress can override a presidential veto

>> Serves six-year terms with no term limits (one-third of the Senate is up for reelection every two years so that there is stability)

TIP

Do you know the senators and representatives in your state? Do a Google search for a current Electoral College map to see the total number of representatives in your state and then search for the names of the representatives in your state — that's an easy list if you live in Wyoming but a bit complicated if you live in California.

Judicial branch

The judicial branch is comprised of the Supreme Court and other federal courts. Members of the Supreme Court have the following requirements and responsibilities:

>> Qualifications: Nominated by the president and approved by the Senate (the usual number is nine justices and currently is a mix of men and women serving on the court)

>> Duties: Interprets the laws passed by Congress and signed into law, can declare presidential actions and those of Congress unconstitutional

>> Can declare a law unconstitutional, making it null and void

>> Serves lifetime appointments (presidential appointees can be used to create a lasting legacy of a president; after a president leaves office, his appointees to the courts remain)

The election process

The Senate and House of Representative candidates are elected by popular vote in each state.

TIP

Locate the 2016 copy of the current Electoral College map. Make a list of eight to ten strategies you would use to plan a presidential campaign. Why are those strategies important?

In the case of electing the president, popular votes within each state are used to determine the number of electoral votes each state awards to the winning candidate. In nearly every state it's a winner take all — a winning presidential candidate with the majority of popular votes is awarded all the electoral votes within that state. There are a total of 538 votes in the Electoral College. A winning candidate needs 270 electoral votes to win the presidential election. Here's how that's broken down:

>> 100 for the senators

>> 435 for the 435 members of the House of Representatives

>> 3 votes for the District of Columbia

>> The number of electoral votes in your state equals the number of representatives within your state — two for the two senators, plus the number of representatives your state has in the House of Representatives based on population. More populous states (California, Texas, and Florida) have more Electoral College votes than less populous states (Wyoming, Alaska, and Montana).

>> States with larger Electoral College votes play a huge role in presidential campaigns and elections, but *swing states* (that often change which party they vote for) can also be crucial to the final outcome.

Federalism and the division of power

The foundation of this nation was based on a power struggle. Power is important to rule, but the big questions remain — who has power, how much power do they have, and how is that power distributed? You can see this actively at work in your government today. Power is divided among federal, state, and local governments.

At times that has seemed to be an easy task, but as it has played out in day-to-day politics, it has become a struggle of sorts. As the federal government begins to claim more authority, it runs into conflicts with state governments. Dual and cooperative concepts of federalism deal with the concepts of shared powers and cooperation to collaborate on policy matters. The 10th Amendment states that what is not specifically delegated as a power or action of the federal government becomes a "states' rights" issue. Arguments over this power have led the federal government to use the "elastic clause" of Article 1 of the Constitution giving the federal government broad powers to enact laws and measures for the good of the people. The states often counter that argument with the states' rights measure of strictly interpreting from the Constitution that if a measure isn't mentioned in the Constitution, then it remains an issue for the state to decide on.

Regarding the powers of the federal government, certain constitutional powers include

>> Levy and collect taxes

>> Declare war

>> Make laws necessary and proper for the country

>> Establish an army and navy for defense

>> Coin money

>> Regulate interstate trade (between the states)

Regarding the powers of the state governments, certain powers include

>> Levy and collect taxes

>> Establish criteria for voting and elections

>> Control intra-state trade (trade within a state)

>> Honor actions of other states

>> Issue various licenses (including business and marriage)

>> Transportation

Regarding the powers of local governments, certain powers include

>> School boards

>> City councils

>> Mayors

>> Transportation and safety

>> City and county responsibilities

And just how does this work?

Just to give you a broad, quick example of this power struggle and balance between federal and state governments, look briefly at these two issues.

Highway funding:

>> Tax money from the sale of gasoline goes to the federal and state governments for the management of the infrastructure of highways and bridges.

>> Now, if the federal government wants to establish a legal drinking age of 21 or set a DWI limit of .08, it can suggest this to the states, but it can also withhold federal dollars for highway programs until states comply with the "suggested" federal guidelines.

>> So, the states are forced to comply with the federal regulations for their funding.

Education:

>> States have the ability to establish education policies and guidelines within their state.

>> Local government establishes school boards to govern policy in their locales.

>> The federal government has begun funding educational programs and increasing stipulations for that funding. Funding for math and science programs, special education, Title IX, and No Child Left Behind policies come with strings attached. To qualify for funding, educational policies in the state must comply with federal guidelines to receive monies and not face sanctions or lose federal funding.

Making a Change

When the government was created with the ratification of the Constitution in 1789, the functions of that new government were not entirely set in stone. The Constitution is kind of like a living document in that it can change and adapt over time. Those changes are grounded in the guidelines of the Constitution and have grown to broaden and protect the rights of the citizens of the nation.

TIP

Go back to your copy of the Constitution and read the list of 27 amendments. Why are these changes significant? How have they expanded and protected the rights of the people?

Amending the Constitution

Part of the ratification process of adopting the Constitution included a *Bill of Rights* — ten amendments to the Constitution that specifically add protections for the people to the Constitution. It was important that these rights were guaranteed in writing and not just based on common law (as was the case with certain rights in Britain). Since 1789, 17 additional amendments have been added. There have been hundreds of proposals for change, but for now there are only 27 formal "changes" to the Constitution.

Here are the amendments in the Bill of Rights:

>> **Amendment 1:** Five basic freedoms: freedom of speech, freedom of religion, freedom of the press (media), right to petition (challenge) the government, and the right to assemble (gather together in groups)

>> **Amendment 2:** The right to bear arms

>> **Amendment 3:** No quartering (housing) of troops in your home

>> **Amendment 4:** The right against unreasonable search and seizure of your property and establishes the rule of the issue of a warrant for searches

>> **Amendment 5:** Establishes the due process of law, your right not to testify against yourself, and once innocent you can't be tried for the same crime twice

>> **Amendment 6:** You're granted a speedy trial by a jury of your peers, you have the right to know the nature of the accusation(s) against you and the evidence in the case, and your right of legal counsel in presenting your case

>> **Amendment 7:** If the property value of the case is in excess of $20, you get a trial by jury

>> **Amendment 8:** No excessive bail or cruel or unusual punishments to be used against you

>> **Amendment 9:** Just because a "right" is not included in the written Constitution does not imply that you don't have that right

>> **Amendment 10:** If a power is not specifically granted to the federal government, then that right is reserved to the states and the people

We discuss other amendments in the next section.

"I'm just a bill . . ."

So how does a bill become a law? It's not an easy or quick process. There are various hoops to jump through to actually get a bill signed into law. Because of the checks and balances section of the Constitution, each branch of government has a distinct role in bills becoming laws (or not).

The road to becoming a law:

1. **The president can suggest a piece of legislation in his agenda.**

2. **Either house in Congress can take up the president's suggestion and turn it into a bill or propose their own piece of legislation.**

3. **A committee will decide if it comes up for approval in one house and then sends it to the other house for approval.**

4. **If both houses approve the bill, then it goes to the president for a signature.**

5. **The president can then either sign it into law or veto it.**

6. **It a veto is given, then it's up to each house to try to override it by a two-thirds majority vote (this is tough to do and doesn't happen that often!).**

7. **When a bill becomes law, the process isn't entirely over. The Supreme Court can rule a law unconstitutional, and it's thrown out.**

The supreme challenge

The Supreme Court is the highest court of law in the country. Its rulings on various court cases can set precedents for decades. When a court case reaches the highest court in the land, it is researched and debated. If the justices decide to hear the challenge and rule on it, big changes and challenges occur. Rulings can range from unanimous rulings (all the justices are in agreement) to split decisions (generally 6 to 3 or 5 to 4 — these happen when the court is divided along lines of conservative and liberal points of view). Over the past 200 years, the court has heard various cases with major impacts on our society:

>> *Marbury v. Madison* (1803): Judicial review (giving the court the right to overturn a law)

>> *Dred Scott v. Sandford* (1857): Not allowing a slave to sue in a court of law because slaves were not citizens at that time and therefore had no basic rights

>> *Plessy v. Ferguson* (1896): A case allowing for segregation on the basis of separate but equal

>> *Brown v. Board of Education* (1954): Overturning the Plessy case decades later on the basis that separate is not equal

>> *Gideon v. Wainwright* (1963): Establishing the right of a defendant to legal counsel even if he or she can't afford it

>> *Miranda v. Arizona* (1966): Establishing the precedent of your "Miranda rights" to have your rights stated out loud to you upon an arrest

>> *New York Times Co. v. United States* (1971): Upholding the right of *The New York Times* newspaper's first amendment right to publish an article about the U.S. government's deception to the American public about the war in Vietnam

>> *Roe v. Wade* (1973): The right of a woman for an abortion on demand

>> *U.S. v. Nixon* (1974): Ruling that the president could not cite executive privilege in refusing to turn over tapes in the Watergate investigation

>> *Texas v. Johnson* (1989): Upholding Johnson's right of free speech to burn an American flag

>> *National Federation of Independent Businesses v. Sebelius* (2012): Ruling upholding the Patient Protection and Affordable Care Act ("Obamacare") with a split decision ruling in favor of the government taxing people for not having healthcare and the expansion of Medicaid in some states to help people get medical coverage (this case has faced several challenges in Congress)

TIP

Google one or two of these court cases and look at the major point in the case and the majority and minority ruling in the case. Ask yourself, "What makes this case important?" and "What citizen rights are being addressed?"

The Rights and Responsibilities of the Citizen

You have an enormous civic duty in this country. Your right to vote is a privilege and a right that should not be underestimated. Just a few votes decided the 1960 election of Democrat John F. Kennedy and Republican Richard Nixon, and the same thing happened again in 2000 between Democrat Al Gore and Republican George W. Bush, when just a few hundred votes in a recount separated the two candidates (with the Supreme Court ultimately throwing out the recount and deciding that Bush won the election). Your votes do matter. It can be a landslide election or a close nail-biter. In the end, what counts is that you voted! So how do you exercise this right?

Becoming an American citizen

The first part of being able to participate in elections is to be aware of your citizenship status. The 14th Amendment provided a definition of citizenship as that of anyone born in the United States (or U.S. territory). It also granted citizenship to the 4 million former slaves after the Civil War. That's huge. Being born here in America gives *you* citizenship, and that means you have the right to vote. That also means that if you are born here and your parents aren't legal citizens, you are still granted citizenship on the merit of you being born here. That's also huge!

Now if you've immigrated to this country, there's still a way for you to gain citizenship through the naturalization process. If you have lived in the U.S. for five years or have lived here for three years while married to a U.S. citizen, you're eligible to apply for citizenship by

» Filing an application

» Living here for five years or three years if married to an American citizen

» Learning English and learning about U.S. history and government in preparation for the citizenship test

» Taking the citizenship test

Understanding the right to vote

We're citizens and we get to exercise our rights to vote. America has seen many changes and challenges to this right to vote. At first, that right was limited to white male landowners. In the early 1800s, the landowning stipulation was eased, but voting was still limited to white males. Women, African Americans, and Native Americans were all ignored. Changes to who could vote over time have broadened the electorate and voter participation. The changing demographics in America will continue to shape the political landscape with African Americans, Hispanics, Asians, and women changing the face of politics. Although citizens have the right to vote, issues, candidates, voter ID requirements, and voter apathy impact voter turnout on Election Day.

» **The 15th Amendment** in 1870 granted the right to all men regardless of color the right to vote. This gave the former male slaves the right to vote. This was challenged by the formation of the KKK and Jim Crow laws aimed at restricting African Americans from voting. Poll taxes and literacy tests also deterred African Americans from voting. The presidential election of 2008 was a watershed election when America elected its first African-American president — Barack Obama.

» **The 19th Amendment** in 1920 gave women the right to vote. Women had long been fighting for this right. Now that women are allowed to vote, statistics show that in some instances, more women than men are voting in certain national elections. Today, many women are also serving in Congress. Many states also have female governors. Because of women's increased participation in politics, there's an increased likelihood that the U.S. could have a female president in the not-so-distant future.

» **The 24th Amendment** in 1964 eliminated the poll tax in voting. No longer could people be forced to pay a tax in order to cast a ballot.

» **The 26th Amendment** in 1972 gave 18-year-olds the right to vote. Because the average age of the American soldiers in the Vietnam War was 19 yet the voting age was 21, young men could be drafted, go fight in a war, and even die but couldn't vote. That finally changed.

» **The Voting Rights Act** in 1965 removed all barriers to being able to register to vote. The march from Selma to Montgomery in March 1965 highlighted this long-overlooked action. President Lyndon Johnson took action by signing the act into law in August 1965.

Understanding other rights and civil liberties

The roles of the federal government have evolved dramatically since the ratification of the Constitution in 1789. Over the past several decades, we have come to expect much more out of our government. We want our rights protected. We have come to expect our government to focus on the needs and protection of the individual. As recently illustrated, the Supreme Court and amendments to the Constitution have addressed many of those issues. The 14th Amendment plays an increasing role as the "due process" clause is applied, in that all the laws are supposed to apply equally to everyone.

Civil liberties and civil rights play an increasing role of citizens in our society. We have taken a stance that we want action taken at the federal level. Issues get complicated, and often people and political candidates and leaders are at odds with how to best address issues. Sometimes there is a consensus on the actions that need to be taken to address a particular issue, but recently, opinion has become more polarized on a whole range of different issues:

>> Religious freedom and tolerance

>> What is protected speech, and how far can you go with freedom of speech?

>> What words and actions can be said and seen on television?

>> Can music be labeled for offensive lyrics?

>> Gun control laws — is there a need for increased legislation in light of acts of violence with weapons?

>> Search and seizure by police

>> Legalization of marijuana — should this be a state or federal issue?

>> Same-sex marriage

>> Immigration and the current debate of legal and illegal immigrants

>> The women's rights movement long fought for equality and the right to vote

>> African Americans have struggled for basic civil rights following the end of the Civil War, and many of those rights were not totally upheld until the Civil Rights Act of 1964 and the Voting Rights Act of 1965 (doing the basic math, it took almost a century for these rights to be upheld after the end of the Civil War)

TIP

Time for a bit of research again. Select two of these issues and do a quick web search. Create your chart and look for arguments on both sides of the issue and the outcome of actions taken. Can you see any trends?

Party, Party, Party

Political parties have long been a mainstay of American politics since George Washington's first term in office. Although times have changed and various issues have taken hold of the public's interests, the U.S. political system is basically a two-party system with various smaller parties springing up from time to time. The modern Democratic Party has been around since the late 1820s, and the modern Republican Party has been around since the early 1850s. Other labels include conservative, moderate, and liberal, as well as right and left to identify candidates and voters. Issues and candidates continue to impact public opinion and voter participation in elections.

Here are some voter characteristics:

>> **Age:** In recent elections, older voters tend to turn out in larger numbers due to their previous participation and knowledge of issues. Medicare and Social Security are two main issues that impact older voters. Younger voters tend not to participate in large numbers in elections because they don't relate to many of the issues. But groups like Rock the Vote have been working to get younger voters active in voting, and they did exactly that in 2008 when Obama was elected.

>> **Education level:** Typically, the higher a person's education level, the greater likelihood of voter participation. Also, higher education levels impact a person's party allegiance to a particular party.

>> **Issues:** African Americans as a block of voters have been voting heavily democratic since 1936. Women as a block of voters tend to vote for a candidate based on issues that tend to impact women — education, healthcare, child care, and jobs. Minority groups — Hispanics and Asians — tend to vote on issues of family values, jobs, education, and healthcare. The issues of Social Security, Medicare, welfare, abortion, immigration, and affirmative action also influence voters.

>> **Third-party influences:** Although no third-party candidates have won a presidential election, they have had major impacts on presidential elections. They can draw the focus away from a candidate when a party "splits," thus allowing the other opposing party to gain traction. Third-party groups can be regional or be based on ideological party beliefs from the major party. At various times in American politics, third-party groups have formed mainly over social, civil, and economic issues. Recently, third-party groups continue various ways to get their message out to the public.

- Ross Perot had a major impact in the 1992 election when he ran on the United We Stand America ticket. Although he didn't win any Electoral College votes, he managed to take over 19 million popular votes, and that had a major impact on George H. W. Bush's reelection, allowing Bill Clinton to win the election with less than 50 percent of the popular vote.

- The Tea Party since 2010 has been an ultra-conservative group of Republicans who are not content with the way the Republican Party has focused on issues. They have been accused of taking over the Republican Party by focusing on very conservative viewpoints and challenging not only the Democrat Party as being too liberal but also the Republican Party establishment itself. Their refusal to compromise on any issue has led to much of the gridlock that has paralyzed Congress in the past few years.

Political parties serve as a way to attract and influence people and to present a particular point of view on popular topics in society. Political parties relate government to the individual citizen. There has also been a rise in the government being divided on leadership and political parties, with one party controlling the presidency and either one or both houses of Congress being controlled by the opposing party. This makes compromise on issues challenging, as both sides try to get their message across.

The Republican Party today tends to

>> Be more conservative

>> Favor reduced levels of taxation and spending

>> Favor smaller government and fewer government regulations

>> Be composed of upper-income Americans

>> Be more composed of white males, with fewer minorities and women

>> Have differing opinions on social programs

The Democrat Party today tends to

>> Be more liberal

>> Favor tax increases and spending on social programs

>> Favor bigger government and more government regulation

>> Be composed of many lower-income groups, minorities, and women

>> Want the government to address social needs with various programs

TIP

Do a web search on three different presidential election results since 1992. Examine the electoral and popular vote. Study the election map and look for trends of party strengths across the different regions of the country. Make a chart to compare and contrast results.

A foreign crisis such as a terrorist attack or involvement in a war (Vietnam, Persian Gulf, Iraq, Afghanistan) can define a presidency and for a time unite the country. A domestic crisis such as the Great Depression, the Great Recession, Civil Rights protests, inflation, Watergate, and the impeachment of a president can also define a presidency and either unite the country or divide it over how issues are addressed.

Getting the Message Out

The first amendment rights of freedom of speech and freedom of the press are alive and well in today's political climate. Back in the day, speeches and rallies were mainstays of political campaigns. Then debates entered in as a way for candidates to get their message out to the public. Newspapers have long been used by candidates to get their messages out. Editors of newspapers and magazines have used their platforms to editorialize about campaigns, candidates, and issues and have used political cartoons to focus the public's attention on the matters at hand.

The 20th and 21st centuries have witnessed even more changes in the media and its attempts to get the public to focus on candidates and issues. Franklin Roosevelt used the radio with his "fireside chats" during the Great Depression as he rolled out his New Deal programs in dealing with the economic effects of the Depression. The public responded greatly by listening to him speak as if he was specifically talking to them personally. The radio and newsreels became popular methods of communicating a particular message to the public.

The advent of television has added another dimension to campaign strategies. Kennedy and Nixon capitalized on this with the first televised presidential debates. Radio was one thing — you just heard the voices. Now with television, you could "see" the candidates. Although Nixon won the debate on the radio, the televised debate had Kennedy the winner, appearing more youthful and energetic than a tired looking Nixon. Since then, televised debates during a presidential election (as well as races at the state level) are very much in place. In addition, advertising during campaigns is now another mainstay of elections, with millions of dollars being spent during the election year as the airwaves are bombarded with ads, many of which are attack ads that can be negative in their approach. All of this is used to sway public opinion and garner votes on Election Day.

Public opinion polls are utilized to get a daily or weekly snapshot of how the public thinks the candidates or issues are being addressed.

The Internet has opened up another nearly instant way of getting news and communicating your message to the American public. News agencies on the Internet now post constant updates with news items during a campaign. Texting, Facebook, and Twitter have also changed the political landscape. Not only can candidates communicate their message, but the public can become more engaged by communicating with their friends and the candidates themselves.

Campaign donations continue to be a paramount focus in campaigns. More and more money is being spent on campaigns by PACs (political action committees) and by individuals. Just as an example, the two main presidential candidates in the 2012 election (Obama and Mitt Romney) raised over a billion dollars for their campaigns. That's a lot of money — and that was only for the presidential race. Many contested senate and representative races have also witnessed a dramatic increase in campaign donations and spending.

America on the World Stage

America attempted for a little over 100 years after George Washington's Farewell Address in 1796 not to become entangled in foreign conflicts. Events of the 20th century changed that. Wars, treaties, armistice agreements, the formation of the United Nations, the development of atomic weapons, and the U.S. becoming a superpower after World War II have greatly altered our role in the world. Isolation was no longer a viable option. We are now a major world leader, which involves the president as well as Congress, the expansion of our military, intelligence agencies, diplomacy, and economic measures.

Since 1945, the U.S. has become increasingly intertwined with actions of other countries:

>> The formation of the United Nations in 1945 (and our permanent seat on the Security Council)

>> Cold War threats of communist challenges to democracy in East Asia and Eastern Europe (China becoming communist in 1949, the Berlin Wall in 1961, and the collapse of the wall and communism in several Eastern European countries in 1989)

>> Wars and conflicts around the globe (Korean War, Vietnam War, Persian Gulf War, the wars in Iraq and Afghanistan)

>> Treaty negotiations with other countries

>> Human rights issues around the world

>> OPEC and our dependence on oil from the Middle East

>> The increasing threats of terrorism since Al-Qaeda in the late 1990s and the terrorist attacks on September 11, 2001

>> Economic growth and challenges with our major trading partners continue to shape our relations with leaders and countries around the world (trading partners in Europe as well as the importance of trade with China and Japan in Asia)

During these challenges, the American people increasingly look to their president for leadership and guidance. He is a communicator, commander in chief, and diplomat. He also uses his cabinet and advisors for guidance. The secretary of state has increasingly played a vital role with our communication and diplomacy with other nations. Congress also plays its role by either support-ing actions of the president or calling them into question. In addition, the public can support the policies of the president, call them into question, or persuade him to address needs and concerns that may need attention. As we attempt to retain the founding ideals of our nation, we are also faced with our increasing role in the affairs of the world. This remains one of the great challenges facing our nation in the 21st century.

Chapter 18

Geography

Geography is the study of the physical features of the Earth and its atmosphere and how those features affect human activities, including the distribution of populations, resources, land use, and industries. What makes a place unique? How have things changed over time? How have past interactions impacted the world we live in today? What forces are at work shaping our world today? How will all this impact our future? In this chapter, as you prepare for the Social Studies section of the TASC examination, we guide you through a broad overview of a variety of themes related to the study of geography. This portion of the exam will have approximately seven questions about geography.

Understanding Maps

One of the major tools we use to determine location is maps. If you're traveling to a new city or going on vacation, what process do you use to get there? Do you know the basics of reading a map? Even if you rely on GPS, Google maps, or the maps app on your smartphone, you still need skills in map reading. You can't just let the "voice app" guide your steps. You need to be in control!

Your world in spatial terms

Knowing your place — that unique location — is important to understand. First of all, you need to grasp the basics of your locale — city, state, region, country. Start with the simple things first. What makes the location of your city important?

» What are the characteristics of the population? How large is the population, and how diverse is it — what ethnic groups, age groups, and education levels are represented?

» Do you live in an urban, suburban, or rural environment? Huge metropolitan area or small town? Coastal or inland? What are the transportation, manufacturing, and trade/commerce characteristics?

> » How fast is your city growing? Is the growth slow or do you live in a boomtown, and how are the job opportunities?
>
> » What region of the state is your city located in? What makes that unique? What challenges does that present?
>
> » What challenges are happening within your country, the neighboring countries, and that region of the world in general?

As you can see, what you may have thought was a simple answer about the location of your residence is actually quite complicated. When you add in the layers of characteristics and challenges, you begin to see the uniqueness and complexities of the location where you live.

Map it out

Maps are used to represent a variety of physical and political features that can help you further understand places in the world:

> » **Historical maps:** These maps are from different time periods and are used to represent various political challenges and changes largely as a result of war, colonization, or conquest. You can find individual maps or use a historical atlas, which contains a variety of maps over various time periods.
>
> » **Physical maps:** These record land features that are unique to a region — mountains, rivers, deserts, elevation levels, coastal locations, and other terrain features. Weather patterns and climate are impacted by the physical characteristics of an area. The physical features of an area have a great influence on lifestyle in that area.
>
> » **Political maps:** These show how states/provinces are established within a country. They also show country divisions on a particular continent. There's often a great deal of change in certain regions over time with political boundaries — for example, the breakup of the former Soviet Union into 15 separate countries, or the way country boundaries on the continent of Africa continue to change over time. When examining political maps, be sure to consider the time period of the map — wars, colonization efforts, a split in a country, and territorial acquisitions greatly determine political boundaries at that time and place in history.
>
> » **Special purpose maps:** These maps are used to illustrate a wide range of characteristics: population distribution, outcomes of political elections, ethnic or religious groups in a region, natural resources, climate, land usage, urban and rural areas, manufacturing, trade, and so on. These maps add levels of understanding of an area.

Latitude and longitude

When you are trying to locate a place on a world map, it is often useful to know its latitude and longitude. As you can see in Figure 18-1, the *latitude* of a location refers to its position above or below the equator. The equator is an imaginary line on the Earth's surface that divides the globe into the Northern Hemisphere and the Southern Hemisphere. Lines of latitude run parallel to the equator (which has a latitude of zero). The North Pole is located at positive 90 degree latitude (or 90 degrees N) and the South Pole located at negative 90 degrees latitude (or 90 degrees S). Hence, locations in the Northern Hemisphere have positive latitudes (between 0 and 90 degrees) whereas places located in the Southern Hemisphere have negative latitudes (between 0 and −90 degrees).

The *longitude* tells you how far east or west a location is compared to a reference line called the Prime Meridian (which runs from the North Pole to the South Pole through Greenwich, England). Positive values of longitude (between 0 and 180 degrees) refer to location east of the Prime Meridian where as negative values (between 0 and −180 degrees) are west of the line.

Longitude and Latitude

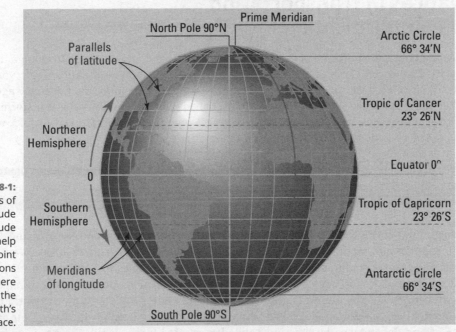

Prime Meridian

North Pole 90°N

Parallels of latitude

Arctic Circle 66° 34'N

Tropic of Cancer 23° 26'N

Northern Hemisphere

Equator 0°

0

Southern Hemisphere

Tropic of Capricorn 23° 26'S

Meridians of longitude

Antarctic Circle 66° 34'S

South Pole 90°S

© John Wiley & Sons, Inc.

FIGURE 18-1: Lines of longitude and latitude can help to pinpoint locations anywhere on the Earth's surface.

REMEMBER

When reading a map, you need to understand the concepts of latitude, longitude, and directions (north, south, east, and west).

TIP

Try the following exercises to get some practice using maps:

>> Do a web search to locate a physical map of the state and country you reside in. Make a chart of at least five physical features in your state and country — what makes these features important?

>> Do a web search to locate three different special purpose maps — a population distribution map (current), an outcome of a presidential election in the United States, and a natural resources map. Make a chart of at least five characteristics that you notice on each map.

>> Do a web search to locate three different historical maps over broad ranges of time. Make a chart and list five observations you can make about each map. How do the historical maps compare with a current political map of the same region?

Places and Regions

How do people determine where they live? Places around the world are characterized by both physical and human characteristics. This decision is often based primarily on the need for survival — the availability of food, water, and shelter. The ability to raise livestock and apply farming methods, the availability of natural resources, and prospects for trade are secondary factors. Political factors that help shape the region and apply barriers for protection are also important in the decision of where to live.

Advances in transportation and communication

Advancements in transportation and technology have changed and continue to change the world we live in. Zheng He, Christopher Columbus, and other explorers set sail on epic voyages to "discover" distant places and open them up for settlement and exploitation. Covered wagons, and then railroad transportation in the United States, Canada, Europe, and Russia, transformed individual lives and places by allowing people to travel much faster. What used to take weeks or months to travel could now be accomplished in a matter of days.

Advances in communication from runners between cities and riders on horseback to the telegraph allowed people to transmit messages over broad distances, making the world seem ever smaller and more connected.

At the beginning of the 20th century, the inventions of the automobile and the airplane dramatically altered lives around the world. Urban areas around the globe have grown by leaps and bounds as traffic and transportation shape lives in cities from Los Angeles to London, from Mumbai to Hong Kong, from Paris to Tokyo. We are now very dependent on various modes of transportation. This is all complicated by oil availability and prices. As more people around the world own and drive automobiles, the demand for oil has dramatically increased, as has the rate of air pollution. The use of and dependence on the automobile has created traffic jams, the need for increased efficiency, and challenges for traffic flow and the infrastructure of roads and bridges. And now subways, bus transportation, and light rail are adding transportation options for city dwellers. Commercial airlines transport thousands of people from country to country in a matter of hours. But air travel also has brought its own set of problems: air pollution, crowded air space, and the need for efficiency.

After the launch of Sputnik by the Russians in 1957, satellites, rockets, space shuttles, and space stations added new dimensions to travel and technology. The International Space Station is currently a huge undertaking by the United States, Canada, Japan, Russia, and the European Space Agency. The Russians and Americans at one time had a "monopoly" on space travel, but China is currently challenging their dominance with its recent landing of a probe on the surface of the moon and its goal within the next decade or so of attempting a manned lunar mission.

And finally, satellite communication continues to transform our lives. Cellphone technology and the Internet have dramatically shaped the world we live in. Communication and information are literally at our fingertips. Our lives in the world have become increasingly intertwined with and dependent on communication and the "information superhighway" as we live our lives in different regions of the globe.

Natural resources and consequences

Another aspect of the study of geography is to examine the impact of natural resources around the world. Population growth, expansion of manufacturing and industry, the need for land for housing and agriculture and water to meet the needs of Earth's growing population (more than 7 billion people!), the increasing use of fossil fuel (a nonrenewable source), air pollution, water pollution, and deforestation all present serious challenges ahead.

>> **Forests:** Although over 30 percent of the Earth's land surface is still covered by forests, deforestation is an ongoing problem, with huge areas of forested land being cleared to provide land for agriculture and housing for our growing population. Serious long-term consequences as a result of the continual loss of forested land include the loss of habitat for animals and climate change due to the loss of the natural beneficial effects trees have on the composition of the atmosphere.

- » **Metals and minerals:** Diamonds and gold are examples of two very valuable natural resources. Over 20 countries around the globe are involved in gold mining. Russia, India, Brazil, and several countries in Africa are currently the world leaders in diamond mining. The economies of regions involved in diamond and gold mining are often directly related to these natural resources, making those economies susceptible to changes in global prices. Mining can also cause problems such as pollution, and conflict often arises as regions fight over the control of these precious resources.

- » **Oil, coal, and natural gas:** Although the use of oil, coal, and gas has helped to drive the growth in the global economy, the increased use of these nonrenewable fossil fuels is beginning to have a serious impact on the world around us, including air pollution, climate change, and major oil spills.

People and places

An intriguing aspect of geography is the intertwined relationship between people and places. The physical characteristics of a particular place help to determine its suitability for settlement and transport — will it make a good port city, can we establish trade routes among cities and regions to connect isolated areas, can we make use of bridges to span rivers or dams to control flooding or generate hydroelectric power? As the populations of cities continue to grow and resources become equally shared, adequate housing becomes a serious issue, with slums arising in many places around the world.

- » **Bridges:** Bridges have long been important to connect areas for the purposes of trade and travel. Famous bridges around the world include the Golden Gate Bridge in San Francisco and the Akashi Kaikyo Bridge in Kobe, Japan. But bridges are not without their challenges — they need constant maintenance to ensure that they're safe and not in any danger of collapsing.

- » **Dams:** The Three Gorges Dam project on the Yangtze River in China became fully operational in July 2012. It is the largest hydroelectric dam in the world. It is not only able to control flooding and aid in shipping along the river but also capable of producing 12 percent of the electrical power in China. It is helping to curb some of the emissions of burning coal for power. The project was not without controversy, as over a million people were displaced from villages as the project was being developed.

- » **Port cities:** Either natural or man-made harbors provide regions with a valuable asset for trade and transportation. The U.S. ports of New York City, Boston, Los Angeles, San Francisco, Seattle, and Pearl Harbor are vital for trade and travel, and many have been the site of significant historical incidents — the Boston Tea Party, the gold rushes in California and Alaska, the 9/11 attack on the World Trade Center, and of course the infamous Japanese bombing at Pearl Harbor on December 7, 1941.

- » **Suburbs and slums:** As populations have swelled in large metropolitan areas such as Manila in the Philippines, New Delhi and Mumbai in India, Johannesburg in South Africa, Mexico City, and Sao Paolo and Rio de Janeiro in Brazil, population growth has created a divided society with the poorest of society forced to live in deplorable conditions while others live in the better regions of the city or the suburbs, distancing themselves from the abject poverty. Governments are tasked with how to combat these problems.

- » **Trade routes:** For over 16 centuries, the trade route, named the Silk Road, connected China, India, the Middle East, and Eastern Europe. Goods and culture were exchanged on this trade route, allowing the spread of Buddhism, silk, gunpowder, spices, paper, jade, pearls, and other unique goods and cultural traditions. Today, the Panama Canal is vitally important to global trade.

Formation of regions

Wars, conquests, colonialism, and the desire for freedom can have major impacts on each region. Territory can be won, lost, and challenged. Political and ethnic divisions can divide a region. Change may take place over a long period of time or it may happen virtually overnight. Borders can quickly change, forcing people to adapt to new realities. For example, take a look at the following changes that helped shape much of the world over the last few centuries:

>> Slaves from the continent of Africa became part of the largest forced migration in history, as over 12 million slaves were forcibly removed from Africa and transported to various locations in the New World from the 1500s to the early 1800s.

>> In 1917, many Jewish people fled persecution as the communists asserted their power in Russia. Then in World War II, as a result of the Holocaust, over 6 million Jewish people were exterminated in German concentration camps.

>> Native Americans in the southern portion of the United States were forced off their ancestral lands and made to relocate to desolated areas during the Trail of Tears march in the 1830s.

>> After the end of the Civil War in the United States in 1865, thousands of freed slaves migrated from the South to locales in the North, especially to cities like Chicago, Philadelphia, and New York.

>> Millions of Europeans fled conditions in southern and eastern Europe and migrated in huge numbers from the 1880s until World War I in 1914. The average rate of immigration in the United States was nearly 1 million per year during the first decade of the 20th century.

>> World War I caused many changes to the political geography of Europe. A simple comparison of a map of Europe in 1914 with the new map redrawn after 1919 reflects the formation of new countries in central and eastern Europe.

>> Today in the United States, immigration is a hot-button political issue as the government and states struggle to deal with over 11 million illegal immigrants, mostly from Mexico and Central America.

Change and Mother Nature

Time proves that, indeed, nothing remains the same. Physical changes and the human dynamic are often intertwined. Earthquakes, floods, droughts, tsunamis, volcanic eruptions, and hurricanes can alter landscapes and life in an instant. Lives are lost, homes and businesses are destroyed, and the physical landscape is dramatically altered when a natural disaster occurs. Then the human equation comes into play with the decision to either rebuild life in a region or abandon the area completely.

>> December 26, 2004, saw the third largest earthquake recorded as a 9.1 magnitude earthquake occurred, resulting also in a tsunami in Indonesia that caused catastrophic damage in the region. In addition to the damage caused by the earthquake and resulting flooding from the tsunami, over a quarter of a million lives were lost.

>> Hurricane Katrina in late August 2005 formed in the Gulf of Mexico as a category 5 storm and hit the mainland, impacting New Orleans and nearby coastal regions. Nearly 2,000 lives were lost and billions of dollars in damage to property resulted from this storm. This was one of the worst catastrophes to occur in the United States, and the situation was made worse by the government's inadequate response to the disaster. Even today, years later, parts of the affected area are still suffering from the storm's after effects.

» March 2011 saw a massive earthquake strike off the coast of Japan in the Sendai area north of Tokyo. The mammoth quake caused a tsunami, which killed over 15,000 people, caused extensive property damage, and severely damaged nuclear power plants in the Fukushima region. This has resulted in parts of the region being abandoned and people being forced to relocate.

» Volcanic eruptions in Washington State at Mount St. Helens (May 1980), Iceland (with several active volcanoes recently), and the state of Hawaii have had devastating impacts on lives and the environment. Volcanic eruptions in Iceland have impacted air travel in Europe, with volcanic ash threatening the safety of air travel in the area from time to time.

Human Interactions with the Environment

Our environment is fascinating and complex. We depend on our environment for energy, fresh air, agricultural production, and the availability of fresh water. Human interactions around the globe are dependent on favorable living conditions, but at the same time we are witnessing changes to our environment brought about by these very same human interactions.

Environmental damage

The following are just a few of the major environmental challenges that humans currently face:

» **Air pollution:** People in big cities around the globe (Los Angeles, Beijing, Mexico City, London, Paris, New Delhi, Shanghai, Tokyo, and others) have seen their daily lives dramatically impacted by rising levels of pollution due to the increasing use of fossil fuels (petroleum, natural gas, and coal). For instance, the smog in Beijing can be so bad that on certain days people wear masks, schools and businesses close, and people are urged to stay indoors and refrain from driving.

» **Climate change and global warming:** Global temperatures are rising due to the rapid increase in the level of carbon dioxide present in the atmosphere during the last 100 years. As energy consumption rises on a global scale and more fossil fuels are consumed each year, the problems will only get worse. Melting ice pack in the Arctic and Antarctica will continue to pose threats to coastal cities as ocean levels rise. Rising temperatures are also impacting weather patterns around the world as extreme storms and conditions occur more frequently. Increased droughts, powerful hurricanes, increased snowfall, torrential rains, and heat waves are all exacerbated by changes in the global climate.

» **Water system pollution:** Rivers, lakes, and coastal cities continue to be compromised by chemicals and waste that are being dumped into the water. Fish and wildlife are dying off, waterborne diseases threaten populations, and clean water resources are declining. If conditions don't change and measures enacted to protect water resources aren't successful, lives around the globe will face an uncertain future.

In addition to these big-picture issues, individual accidents and mistakes by humans can have a huge impact on local environments. Here are just a few examples:

» The fragile environment of Prince William Sound off the coast of Alaska was the site of a tragic environmental accident in March 1989 when the oil tanker *Exxon Valdez* ran aground, and thousands of barrels of oil were spilled into the sound. It was the second largest oil spill in U.S. history and one of the leading environmental disasters in history, as wildlife and the waters suffered the devastating impact of this man-made disaster.

>> In April 2010 another devastating oil spill occurred — the BP oil spill in the Gulf of Mexico that created another man-made disaster as thousands of barrels of oil gushed from an underwater oil rig pipeline. The resulting disaster affected life along the Gulf Coast from Texas to Florida (with Louisiana taking the brunt of the impact).

>> A disaster of another type occurred at the Chernobyl nuclear power plant in Ukraine in April 1986. This was the site of the worst nuclear disaster in history as an explosion at the power plant resulted in the release of deadly radioactive material. The Soviet Union remained tight-lipped for 24 hours about the event, but world outrage forced the Soviet Union to report on the incident as neighboring countries began detecting high levels of radiation and used maps to trace it back to the Chernobyl plant. This event challenged Soviet leader Mikhail Gorbachev's new goals for the Soviet Union: *glasnost* (openness) and *perestroika* (restructuring).

Technology and communications

Technological advancements, especially in the past 150 years, have dramatically impacted life around the globe. The Industrial Revolution ushered in the use of machines to aid in manufacturing goods and helped make Great Britain the world leader in manufacturing of goods at that time. Today, China, the United States, and Japan are the global manufacturing leaders and account for almost 50 percent of all goods manufactured around the world.

Economic conditions continue to influence where people live and work. Large industrial areas in China have seen explosive population growth as urban areas that provide jobs in manufacturing. This is also true in other major manufacturing areas around the world. People are attracted to areas for work and relocate there, causing increased demands for housing, food, fuel, water, and so forth.

Communications have progressed dramatically since the invention of the telephone in the late 1800s. That single invention has transformed our world and connected us in ways that were previously unimaginable. A simple phone call allows us to talk to a person living across the globe. World leaders can instantly communicate in times of crisis to avert calamities. The invention of the Internet has also opened up communication via email, and cellphones have added texting and instant messaging. We can access news and information instantly via our computers and cellphones. Our world has now become very connected to and dependent on these new technologies.

Political unrest

Political factors continue to influence people around the globe today. Political insurgents in parts of Africa have killed thousands and forced others to relocate for political reasons as countless battles continue to be fought among various religious groups. Rwanda has been the site of the atrocities of genocide, with over three-quarters of a million people killed since the mid-1990s, and the extremist Muslim group Boko Haram is threatening the lives of thousands of people in Nigeria, Chad, and Cameroon today.

The rise of ISIS and other extreme Islamic terrorist groups also threatens stability in the Middle East. The civil war in Syria has killed more than 250,000 Syrians during five years of armed conflict, and more than 11 million others have been forced from their homes as forces loyal to President Bashar al-Assad and those opposed to his rule battle each other — as well as jihadist militants from the so-called Islamic State.

Wars and conflicts around the world continue to threaten cooperation and world stability. The greatest challenge we face in the 21st century is how to understand the past, relate to our history, and work together to chart plans for peace. This involves a deep understanding of geography, history, religion, politics, the environment, places, and people.

Chapter 19

Economics

Economics is the social science that deals with the production, distribution, and consumption of goods and services, and the transfer of wealth among groups of people and individuals. In the past, long before money was invented, people simply swapped their own goods and services for those produced by others. This was known as the *barter system*. But economics has come a long way since then; it now involves allocating resources to provide goods and services to satisfy the demands of consumers.

Economists often use technical jargon that can be a bit confusing at first, so to get you started, we kick off the chapter by describing the key terms and principles you're expected to know for the TASC exam. Then, after you have your footing, we dive straight into the vibrant world of micro-economics, which deals with the market behavior of individual consumers and attempts to understand the decision-making process of small firms and households. Then we look at macroeconomics, which deals with the overall economy and how local, state, and national governments make financial decisions that can affect your daily life. After discussing the role that government plays in the national economy, we round out the chapter by exploring the relationship between international trade and foreign policy.

TIP Expect to see about 9 questions about economics on the TASC exam.

Basic Economic Principles

Your daily life is controlled by various economic forces, some of which are within your control and some of which are not. The better informed you are as a consumer about monetary situations, the more control you'll have over your financial life — and the better you'll score on this section of the TASC exam. So before delving into the exciting world of micro- and macroeconomics, there are a few basic economic terms and principles that you need to know.

Key terms

Here are the main basic economic terms and definitions that you'll be expected to know for the Economics section of the TASC exam.

Capital

In economics, *capital* describes everything that a company makes an investment in to produce income. For example, a company that produces cellphones may make capital investments that include technology, patents, factory equipment, raw materials, and factory buildings. The company will then hire workers who provide the necessary labor to transform this capital investment into *consumer goods* (in this case, the cellphones) that the company will then try to sell for a profit. If the company is successful at making a profit, it has added *value* to the original capital investment. Note that many companies add value by providing intangible *services* (such as consulting) rather than building physical objects.

Cost-benefit analysis

You don't get anything for nothing, as the saying goes, so before a company or individual decides to make capital investments, a *cost-benefit analysis* should be performed to determine whether the *benefits* (what is to be gained) outweigh the *cost* (what needs to be invested). For example, when you decided to study for the TASC exam, you probably performed a cost-benefit analysis without even realizing it. You probably weighed the money, time, and effort needed to study for the exam (all part of the cost) against the potential opportunities that may be available to you after you pass the TASC (the benefits). Companies do the same thing when evaluating their potential investments.

Supply and demand

Supply tells you how many items are available. *Demand* tells you how many consumers want to buy that item. The *law of supply and demand* states that when the supply is bigger than the demand, the price goes down, but when the demand is bigger than the supply, the price goes up.

You've probably seen the law of supply and demand in action many times without even realizing it. For example, when the iPhone 5 was first released, the demand for the phone was greater than the supply (which explains why you saw long lines of people outside the Apple store trying to get their hands on one before they sold out) and so the price was high. But a year or so later, people were not as interested in buying the old iPhone 5 (particularly because the new iPhone 6 was due to be released in a few months), so at that point the supply was greater than the demand, which caused the price to come down. This example also explains why companies like Apple continually innovate and improve their existing products so they can release new models that help keep the demand (and the prices) high.

Boycotts

The law of supply and demand can be put to good use when attempting to force a company to change its unethical business practices. If a company does something that you consider to be unethical, you can make a personal decision to *boycott* (not buy) its products or service. When a large enough group of individuals join the boycott, this can be very effective because it puts financial pressure on the company. Not only does the company lose revenue due to the sudden decrease in sales, but also the decrease in demand forces it to lower its prices, making it even harder for the company to make a profit. If the boycott is successful, the company will usually back down and change its behavior to try to win back customers and increase the demand for its products again.

An example of a successful boycott happened in 2005 when clothing manufacturer Abercrombie & Fitch was forced to discontinue a line of T-shirts that contained offensive sexist slogans. The boycott was started by a group of teenage girls who were appalled by the company's lack of good judgment. News of the boycott quickly spread, and the story was reported on national television. The company realized that it was in danger of losing a lot of customers (think money!), so it quickly withdrew the product before more damage was done.

Types of markets

After goods and services have been produced, they need to be distributed so they can reach the *consumer* (the person buying them). This is achieved via the *market system*, which consists of established networks and routines where buyers and seller interact with each other to negotiate prices and compete for the best deals available. *Retail* markets sell products directly to the consumer (the end user), whereas *wholesale* markets sell products to a *middleman* who doesn't use the product himself but instead, sells it to the end consumer at a profit.

Free-market economy

A *free-market economy* is a market system in which the law of supply and demand sets the prices for most goods and services with little or no government control or restrictions. The United States operates under a free-market system, but even so, there are some government restrictions and laws that still apply. For example, the sale of tobacco and alcohol is strictly controlled by government agencies such as the Food and Drug Administration (FDA), and laws exist to prevent monopolies from forming. See "The Role of Government in the National Economy" later in the chapter for more details on how the government is involved in the economy.

Monopolies

A *monopoly* is a market structure that occurs when there is a single seller selling a unique product in the market. Monopolies aren't good news for the end consumer because a single seller has no competition and can set the price as high as he or she wishes. Hence, the U.S. government has laws to try to prevent monopolies from occurring.

Microeconomics

Microeconomics deals with how individuals make economic decisions on a personal, household, or single business level. It focuses on the supply and demand of goods and services and the allocation of scarce resources. Your household budget is a good example of microeconomics in action. Your household budget can help you determine what you can afford and what you may have to put aside on your wish list. Personal economics relies on making smart decisions about money — and earning more than you spend! Many people make the mistake of not setting themselves a *balanced budget* (one in which your income is equal to or greater than your expenses) and sticking to it. If you end up spending more than you earn, you'll end up in *debt*.

Making a budget

Your salary is a key component to consider when making your household budget. It determines your earning power and what you have available to spend on essentials and nonessential items. Hence, when you get your paycheck, you need to *budget* how much you can afford to spend on each of your essential household expenses: rent (or mortgage payment), food, transport, insurance, utilities, healthcare, and so on.

After you've taken care of your *needs,* any money that's left over is your *discretionary income,* which you can use for your *wants* — nonessential items such as going to the movies or saving for a vacation. Knowing how much discretionary income you have each month helps you prioritize which of these nonessential luxuries you can afford and which will have to wait until later. Can you afford to go out to dinner and a movie or do you need to stay home and "Netflix and chill"?

WARNING

Inflation can also affect discretionary spending. *Inflation* occurs when the price of goods and services increases faster than your salary does, so your dollar doesn't stretch as far as it used to. When prices go up, you have to make some tough economic choices. Do you need to curb your discretionary spending so that you can afford to buy the basics? How do you save money on transportation? What about that vacation? During an extended time of inflation, you as a consumer need to make wise choices.

TIP

Also, don't forget to put some money aside each month so that you have savings for your "rainy day" emergency fund. Most financial advisors recommend having an emergency fund equivalent to three to six months of your current salary. Having an emergency fund available can be a life-saver, particularly if you lose your job suddenly or can't work due to illness. Your emergency fund should be separate from any money that you're saving for big-ticket items like the down payment on a car or a house.

REMEMBER

Hence, household budgets are your friend. A budget is one of the best financial tools at your disposal that will help you keep your personal finances healthy so you can stay out of debt.

Debt and bankruptcy

Paying off a debt is not quite as simple as paying off the principal amount of money that you've borrowed. You also have to pay interest. *Interest* is the fee that lenders make you pay for the privilege of borrowing money from them. It is usually expressed as an annual percentage rate. There are two main types of interest that apply to loans: simple interest and compound interest. *Simple interest* charges you a fee equal to a percentage of the amount of money you borrowed, whereas *compound interest* charges you a fee equal to a percentage of the amount borrowed plus any interest that you still owe.

Interest continues to grow over time and can end up being many times bigger than the original amount of money you borrowed in the first place. This is particularly true with credit card debt because credit cards have compound interest rates that are usually very high, and there are additional fees if you miss a monthly payment. Many people who don't stick to a budget find themselves slipping into debt, and in extreme cases, their debt grows so large that they can't ever hope to pay it off. In this situation, the person is forced to declare *bankruptcy.*

WARNING

Bankruptcy offers an individual protection from debt collectors, but it comes at a steep cost. Declaring bankruptcy affects your *credit score,* which can seriously affect your ability to borrow money in the future, making it very difficult to get a mortgage or a loan for a new car. Also, you can't declare bankruptcy to avoid paying off your student loans or taxes. Uncle Sam (the U.S. government) is going to get his money no matter what!

Macroeconomics

Macroeconomics looks at the "big picture" of a variety of trends impacting the overall economy and how decisions made by local, state, and national governments can ultimately affect your daily life. Small businesses and larger corporations form the major part of a market-based economy.

As you'll see in this section, wages, prices, and unemployment are all crucial factors that can affect the health and growth of the national economy.

The U.S. economic system

A *capitalist* economy is one in which individuals own and control all companies and industries, and the natural competition of the free market sets wages and prices. The United States has a capitalist economy. A *socialist* economy is one in which the government owns all companies and industries, and wages and prices are artificially fixed. North Korea and Cuba have socialist economies. A *mixed economy* is a combination of these two systems. In a mixed economy, the government owns and operates some industries, whereas others are owned by private individuals. Most western European countries have mixed economies.

In the United States, the economy can be classified as *laissez-faire capitalism*, which is based on the ideas of Adam Smith, an 18th-century economist, who believed that when individuals are free to act in their own best economic interests, society as a whole does better. In the United States, you're free to make your own decisions about how to spend or save most of your income (after taxes have been taken out). You have the freedom to accept employment offers from whomever you choose, become an entrepreneur and start your own business, or go back to school to get the training and qualifications that you may need to reach your career goals.

The United States has a free-market economy, so the law of supply and demand sets the prices for most products and services, with little government control or restrictions. Companies compete with each other for customers. Small startup companies have an incentive to grow and expand their capacity to make more profit, and this has played an important role in the development of our economy.

The banking sector plays an important role in making funds available to companies that want to expand or make other capital investments. Companies can also raise capital by *going public* on the stock exchange. This allows investors to purchase *shares of stock,* which represent a partial ownership of the company. Investing in a stock can be risky, however, because the stock's value usually depends on the success of the business. However, the potential *return* on the investment is often much higher than those offered by savings accounts or government bonds.

The free enterprise system sparks healthy competition among companies. This leads them to develop technological innovations that have helped drive economic growth in the United States. But even a strong economy can be unpredictable, and a variety of factors can slow or even stop growth. The economy tends to move through a *cycle* with identifiable phases (expansion, peak, depression, recession, recovery), but the strength and length of the cycle and its phases can vary greatly. And that's where the U.S. government comes in.

Wages, labor, and unemployment

A worker's total compensation for a job he or she performs is the combined value of *wages* and other benefits. Other benefits can include health insurance, paid vacation time, company car, retirement contributions, or even shares in the company. Many workers are paid on an hourly basis, which means they only get paid for the number of hours they actually work. Others are paid on a *piecework* basis — that is, for each piece of work they complete. If the number of hours worked or the number of items completed varies significantly from week to week, a worker's take-home pay can fluctuate greatly.

Most workers sign individual contracts with their employers that clearly state what duties they're expected to perform and what compensation the company will give. However, workers in certain industries (such as teaching, manufacturing, steel, and so on) are members of *labor unions* that negotiate contracts for better wages and working conditions on behalf of their members via the power of *collective bargaining.* Unions can be very powerful because they can call a *strike* if the company refuses to meet their demands. When workers walk off the job, the factory sits idle, and the company earns no profits. A company that fails to earn a profit or ends up making a loss or *deficit* can wind up in bankruptcy pretty quickly, so there's a big incentive for company executives to sit down with labor union leaders and reach a compromise that everyone can live with.

As you read earlier, *inflation* affects prices. When prices become too high, consumers often cut back on their discretionary spending because they can't afford to buy luxury items. Due to the law of supply and demand, this has a direct impact on the economy because the fall in demand for these luxury products may force companies to lay off workers or cut back production.

Unemployment figures refer to the percentage of workers who are actively seeking work but who don't currently have a job. This number doesn't include people who are too young, too old, or too ill to join the workforce — your 87-year-old grandmother, for example, is not unemployed! If you become unemployed, you'll suddenly be earning less money (assuming you're eligible for unemployment benefits), and this impacts your ability to spend. Major technological changes can sometimes cause workers to lose their jobs. For example, rapid changes in the home computing industry caused the collapse of the typewriter manufacturing industry. After all, why buy a typewriter when you already have a computer with a keyboard and printer?

REMEMBER

Unemployment figures have a major impact on the national economy, and there's a strong correlation between wages and unemployment. When wages are high, people spend more because they have more discretionary income available. When people spend more, demand goes up, which causes prices to rise. In this situation, unemployment will be low and the economy strong. But the reverse is also true: When wages stay stagnant or begin to fall, spending goes down, which causes prices to fall and unemployment to rise. These are the signs of a weak economy. If the national unemployment figures continue to rise for the overall economy, then growth is stalled and even more unemployment can occur.

REMEMBER

Bad economies can be classified as recessions or depressions. A *recession* is an economic *slowdown* where wages, prices, and employment fall slowly over time. A *depression* is more serious because it refers to a sudden economic *crash.* During a depression, wages, prices, and employment fall rapidly.

The Role of Government in the National Economy

Even thought the United States has a free-market economy, the U.S. government still has a major role to play in managing the national economy and maintaining the conditions necessary for the free-market system to operate effectively. It does this by setting interest rates and tax rates, and sometimes by passing laws that set restrictions on certain business practices. It is the federal government's responsibility to promote the general health of the nation, so the government will often step in and take over those functions that the free-market system tends to ignore.

The federal government is the world's largest employer, paying the salaries of over 3 million workers, and it consists of many specialized agencies whose responsibilities include regulating commerce, enforcing safety standards, building and maintaining infrastructure, providing funding for scientific research and education, and maintaining the nation's parks and nature preserves. The federal government also provides a safety net — Medicare, Medicaid, and Social Security — to help low-income families or retirees make ends meet.

Consumers need to be protected from unsafe products, so the government created an agency called the *Food and Drug Administration* (FDA) to ensure that all food products and medicines meet safety standards. Another government agency called the *Federal Trade Commission* (FTC) protects consumers from fraudulent business practices by checking the validity of advertising claims and the labels on packaged items.

Workers also need to be protected from exploitation and dangerous working conditions, particularly in hazardous industries, so the government created the *Occupational Safety and Health Administration* (OSHA) to protect the safety of workers on the job. There are strict laws regarding child labor and safe working conditions. Companies that violate these laws can be prosecuted or even shut down.

The U.S. dollar is the most stable and trusted currency in the world, and it's the federal government's job to keep it that way. The government does this by controlling the *U.S. Mint*, which makes coins and prints paper money. The role of the *Federal Reserve System* is to control interest rates and manage the total amount of money available in the private banking system that can be used for capital investments.

A healthy economy also needs a strong infrastructure, so the federal government also builds and maintains bridges, tunnels, interstate highways, ports, and dams, all of which are necessary to support economic activities.

As you can see, the U.S. government is responsible for steering the economy and keeping it on the right path. But like any other large organization, the government needs to have sources of income *(revenue)* to pay for its expenses. Both the federal and state governments raise revenue from two main sources: taxes and bonds.

Taxes

Here are a few of the taxes that most U.S. citizens have to contend with:

>> **Income tax:** These federal and state taxes are the first ones to be deducted from your paycheck and represent the percentage of individual or business income paid to the government. There's no way around federal taxes (unless you can afford to hire a team of accountants), but there are a few states that don't have any state income tax.

>> **Sales tax:** This is a small percentage added to the price of an item or a service. You see this right away with almost every purchase you make — most items have sales tax attached to them. Some states exempt certain food items at grocery stores from taxes, but pretty much everything else is taxed, unless you live in a state (like Oregon) that has no sales tax.

>> **Property tax:** These taxes are assessed on property and land that individuals own. Money raised from property taxes help local municipalities fund things like education, fire and police protection, and other local needs.

>> **Social Security and Medicare:** Also known as *FICA* taxes (Federal Insurance Contributions Act), this tax comes out of your paycheck and is also matched by your employer (you each pay a little under 8 percent). This contribution goes to fund benefits for retirees, disabled people, and children whose parents are deceased, as well as providing insurance benefits for retirees.

Bonds

When you buy a *savings bond,* you're essentially lending money to the U.S. government. The bond (which is a piece of paper) has a face value marked on it equal to the amount you paid for the bond on the date you purchased it. In the future, when you decide to sell the bond, you'll get the *face value* back, along with any interest that the money has earned since you purchased the bond. The longer you keep the bond, the more it will be worth when you sell it. For example, if your grand-mother gave you a $100 savings bond when you were born, it could be worth thousands of dollars by the time you need to sell it to pay for going to college. Bonds are thought to be a much safer investment than stocks, but the interest rate you receive may not be as high as the returns given by the stock market.

After the government has collected these sources of revenue, it announces the U.S. government budget, which determines how much will be spent on the military and how much will go to each of the government agencies. If there's a budget surplus, then the government may decide to reduce taxes or expand its services. If there's a budget deficit, the government may decide to raise more money by raising taxes, selling bonds, or borrowing money, or it may simply decide to reduce expenses by cutting back on some of the services it provides.

As you can see, the government has a very large and direct impact on the national economy.

International Trade and Foreign Policy

International trade involves the import and export of goods between different countries. *Imports* are goods that are purchased from a foreign country, whereas *exports* are goods that are sold to a foreign country. For example, the United States imports rice from China but exports cars made by General Motors to countries all around the world.

Due to their different climates and geographical locations, each country has its own unique col-lection of natural resources available to it. Countries must trade with others to gain the resources that they can't provide for themselves. For example, Great Britain has large reserves of natural gas and oil but doesn't have the right climate to grow rice. India has plenty of rice but not enough petroleum; hence, Great Britain can trade its surplus petroleum to India in exchange for India's surplus rice.

REMEMBER

But countries also need to be conscious about trade imbalances. If you export more than you import, you have a *trade surplus.* The opposite is also true: If you import more than you export, you have a *trade deficit.* The struggle, then, is to find the right balance of trade. Cheap foreign prod-ucts, lower labor and production costs abroad, outsourcing of jobs, and trade tariffs can compli-cate matters even further.

A country's *gross domestic product* (GDP) is the total value of the goods and services that the country produces in one year. The size of the GDP helps determine the relative strength of each country's economy. The top four economies — the United States, China, Japan, and Germany — compete to secure their standings in the world economy; hence, the connection between interna-tional trade and foreign policy is easy to see. Countries want to protect their investments in the products they produce when trading with other countries. To protect local markets, countries often impose a *tariff* (a tax on imported goods) to help protect the price of local goods. Competi-tion in the marketplace is fierce!

The *General Agreement on Tariffs and Trade* (GATT, 1948) and the *World Trade Organization* (WTO, 1995) work to establish fair tariffs, expand trade, negotiate trade agreements, and solve trade disputes between member nations. As the world economy expands, countries continue to be closely intertwined in a global economy. Many countries in Europe have worked together to create the *European Union* (EU) as a trade organization to compete in the world marketplace. The *North American Free Trade Agreement* (NAFTA, 1994) created a free-trade zone among Canada, the United States, and Mexico. Several nations in Asia are also working together to create competition and promote the growth of Asian economies (as many of the world's fastest-growing economies are in Asia).

When nations are at war or have major disagreements between them, one country may establish an *embargo* against the other by refusing to export or import any goods to or from that country. For example, due to political differences between the two countries, the United States established an embargo against Cuba in the early 1960s, but recent negotiations between the two nations are easing those restrictions.

Just as embargo restrictions can change over time with the U.S. and Cuba, the U.S. still maintains and adds restrictions against the ruling Kim family of North Korea due to various human rights violations and blatant violations of U.N. sanctions on missile and nuclear technologies. Political upheavals around the globe today challenge trade agreements and call into question the need to support oppressed people. Skirmishes and various activities in Eastern Europe, the Middle East, and parts of Africa call into question levels of economic intervention.

6 Science

IN THIS PART . . .

Examine the structure of atoms and other concepts of physical science.

Review the major topics of life science.

Explore earth and space science.

Chapter 20

Physical Science

P hysics and chemistry are two closely related sciences that help you understand the physical world around you. Everything that has mass and takes up space is made from *matter*. Matter is all around you. Everything you can see, taste, smell, or touch is made of matter (including you), so it's important that you understand the structure and properties of matter and how you interact with it.

In this chapter, we start off by exploring the building blocks of matter (atoms) and how two or more atoms can join together to form molecules. We then take a look at the different phases that matter can exist in (solids, liquids, or gases) before delving into the explosive world of chemical reactions. Then we explore the work of one of the world's most famous physicists, Sir Isaac Newton, whose three laws of motion and work on gravitational forces helped man walk on the moon almost 300 years later. Finally, we round out the chapter by describing how the movement of atomic charges can produce electricity and magnetism.

TIP

There will be about 18 questions about the physical sciences on the Science section of the TASC exam. You may also be asked to interpret data presented in graphs, charts, or tables.

The Structure of Atoms

All matter is made up of atoms. An *atom* is the smallest particle of an element that retains the properties of that element. For example, an atom of gold is the smallest amount of gold that can exist. If you tried to divide an atom of gold any further, it would no longer be gold.

Atoms themselves consist of three main subatomic particles called *protons, neutrons,* and *electrons.* Electrons have a negative charge, protons have a positive charge, and neutrons are neutral. Together, protons and neutrons form the *nucleus* of the atom, which contains most of the atom's mass. Electrons are negatively charged particles that are much smaller than protons and neutrons (for the TASC exam you can assume that electrons have zero mass). Electrons orbit around the nucleus of the atom in distinct energy levels called *shells.* The electrons in the outer shell are known as *valence electrons.* Valence electrons are involved in chemical reactions, and the number of valence electrons determines how reactive a particular element is. Because atoms are electrically neutral, they must contain the same number of electrons and protons so that the negative charge from the electrons is canceled out by the positive charge from the same number of protons.

The number of protons is known as the *atomic number,* and this determines the identity of an element. For example, look at Figure 20-1, the model of a carbon atom. Carbon's nucleus contains six protons. If the nucleus had seven protons instead, it would no longer be carbon — it would be nitrogen. So any atom containing six protons will always be carbon. Because atoms are electrically neutral, carbon must also contain six electrons to cancel out the charge from the six protons. Carbon atoms also contain six neutrons. The *atomic mass* of an atom is simply the sum of the number of protons and neutrons. Hence, an atom of carbon has an atomic mass of 12 (six protons plus six neutrons).

FIGURE 20-1:
The nucleus of a carbon atom contains six protons and six neutrons. Carbon also has six electrons, which orbit around the nucleus in distinct energy levels or shells.

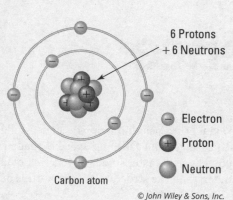

6 Protons + 6 Neutrons

− Electron
+ Proton
Neutron

Carbon atom

Neutrons are important when considering isotopes. An *isotope* of an element consists of two atoms with the same number of protons but with different numbers of neutrons. Have you ever heard of *carbon dating?* We're not taking carbon out to dinner and a movie, but using an isotope of carbon to determine how old an artifact may be. Carbon-14 is a common isotope that's used in carbon dating.

How many protons are found in carbon-14? A trick question, we know. Remember, carbon always has six protons. If it doesn't, it's no longer carbon. So the real question is, how many neutrons does carbon-14 have? If you said eight, you are correct. Ding! Ding! Ding!

REMEMBER

Isotopes of an element consist of two atoms with the same number of protons but different numbers of neutrons. An isotope of an element has the same atomic number but a different atomic mass.

Radioactivity decay: Nuclear fission and fusion

Because like charges repel, the positively charged protons in a nucleus are all trying to get away from each other, but a strong nuclear force holds them all together. Without the strong nuclear force, all atoms except hydrogen would be unstable, and their particles would fly off in all directions.

Many heavier elements tend to have unstable nuclei because the strong nuclear forces can't cope with holding together so many positively charged protons. Uranium, for example, has 92 protons. These unstable nuclei tend to be radioactive and emit smaller particles such as alpha or beta particles (and energy) to transform into different, more stable elements. This process of splitting a nucleus into two or more smaller pieces is known as *nuclear fission*.

Alpha particles are made up of two protons and two neutrons. So when an atom emits an alpha particle, it becomes a different smaller and more stable element. Uranium (U), for example, undergoes a decay series in which alpha particles are emitted. The start of this decay series is shown here:

$$^{238}_{92}U \rightarrow {}^{234}_{90}Th + {}^{4}_{2}\alpha$$

Uranium loses two protons and two neutrons when it emits an alpha particle; therefore, the atomic number (number of protons) goes down by two, and the atomic mass (number of protons plus neutrons) goes down by four. This changes uranium into a different element, thorium (Th).

A *beta particle* is a fast-moving electron, so it has a negative charge and a mass close to zero. When a radioactive element emits a beta particle, its atomic number goes up by one, and the mass number stays the same.

For example, an atom of lead (Pb) changes into an atom of bismuth (Bi) by emitting a beta particle:

$$^{214}_{82}Pb \rightarrow {}^{214}_{83}Bi + {}^{0}_{-1}e$$

Nuclear fusion occurs when two smaller nuclei fuse together to form a larger, more stable nucleus. Energy is released in the process. Nuclear fusion reactions occur in every star cluster of the universe. Closer to home, this process also keeps everything on Earth alive. It is how the sun produces its energy.

But nuclear fission and fusion reactions also have a darker side — these are the same reactions used in atomic bombs and thermonuclear weapons. Atomic bombs use fission reactions to split larger nuclei, such as enriched uranium or plutonium, into smaller fragments, releasing energy. Some of these fragments can smash into other uranium or plutonium atoms, causing a chain reaction to occur, where more and more energy is released. Although devastating when used in weapons, nuclear fission reactions can be controlled and used to generate electricity in nuclear power stations.

Thermonuclear weapons, also known as *hydrogen bombs* (or H-bombs), are even more devastating than atomic bombs. Hydrogen bombs use nuclear fusion reactions to combine hydrogen nuclei together, releasing vast amounts of energy. But getting the hydrogen atoms close enough to each other to fuse isn't easy (remember that all nuclei are positively charged, and like charges repel). In fact, thermonuclear weapons use atomic bombs (fission reactions) as their detonators just to get the fusion reaction started!

The periodic table

About 150 years ago, a Russian scientist named Mendeleev organized the known elements into a simple table. It turns out that this table is a pretty remarkable thing. It really does a great job of representing properties of matter, reactivity of elements, sizes of nuclei, radioactivity, and so on. Bottom line: The periodic table is your friend. Nowadays, it gets updated on occasion with newly discovered elements, so check out the most recent version with a simple online search.

The rows of the periodic table are called the *periods.* Hydrogen starts Row 1 (Period 1), and then lithium starts Row 2 (Period 2), and so on. Elements in the same period have the same number of electron shells, or *energy levels.* Period 1 has one energy level, Period 2 has two energy levels, and so on.

The columns of the periodic table are called *groups.* The groups are separated into Group A and Group B. Here's the awesome thing about the periodic table: Of the Group A elements, you can see which elements are likely to react with each other and what type of bonds they're likely to form. All this reactivity business is based on the number of electrons in the outermost energy level (the valence electrons) and the fact that all atoms like to have their outermost energy level filled. The first shell is full when it has two electrons, and the second shell is full when it has eight electrons.

REMEMBER

The periodic table makes it easy to determine how many valence electrons each element in Group A has (don't worry about Group B for the TASC exam). All elements in Group 1A have one valence electron. All elements in Group 2A have two valence electrons. Group 3A has three, Group 4A has four, Group 5A has five, Group 6A has six, Group 7A has seven, and Group 8A has eight valence electrons. Pretty simple, huh?

Each group has its own distinct properties. For example, Group 1A elements are highly reactive. They are some busy elements! On the other hand, Group 8A elements have full outer shells and are therefore completely unreactive.

Remember our carbon atom? It has six electrons, with two electrons in the first energy level and four electrons in the outer energy level. So what group do you think it would be in? If you said Group 4A, you're correct! All elements in Group 4A have four valence electrons.

It's also important to notice the sections of the periodic table. The elements on the left-hand side are metals, and the elements on the right-hand side are nonmetals. They're separated by a zigzag-looking line. Along this line are the *metalloids.* They're called metalloids because, you guessed it, they have the characteristics of both metals and nonmetals. So if you were asked about helium, the gas in balloons, you would look for it on the side of the periodic table where all the gases are — to the right of the zigzag line.

Bonds and the States of Matter

The basis of all matter is the bonding of atoms into molecules. *Molecules* consist of two or more atoms joined together by *bonds.* If the atoms are identical, then the molecules represent an element. For example, two hydrogen atoms can bond together to form a hydrogen molecule. If the atoms are different, then the molecule represents a *compound.* For example, one atom of oxygen can bond to two atoms of hydrogen to produce one molecule of water (now you know why water is also known as H_2O).

Bonds

We mention earlier that the number of valence electrons in an atom helps you to determine how that element will react (or bond) with other atoms. All atoms like to have full outer energy levels and hence, they will try to bond to other atoms to achieve just that. For the TASC exam, you need to be familiar with the two main types of chemical bonds:

>> Ionic bonds

>> Covalent bonds

Ionic bonds

Ionic bonds form between metals and nonmetals and involve the *transfer* of electrons from one atom to another to form charged atoms known as *ions*. The atom that loses valence electrons becomes a positively charged ion (called a *cation*), whereas the atom that gains additional valence electrons becomes a negatively charged ion (called an *anion*). These oppositely charged ions now attract each other to form strong ionic bonds.

For example, sodium (Na) is in Group 1A and therefore contains one valence electron in its outer shell. It must lose this electron to gain a full outer shell. Chlorine (Cl) is in Group 7A and therefore already has seven valence electrons. Chlorine needs an additional electron to gain a full outer shell of eight electrons. Hence, sodium and chlorine react together to form a new ionic compound, *sodium chloride* (also known as salt), as shown in Figure 20-2.

FIGURE 20-2:
Ionic bonding: A sodium atom gives away its valence electron to a chlorine atom to form an ionic bond and produce a compound called *sodium chloride* (salt).

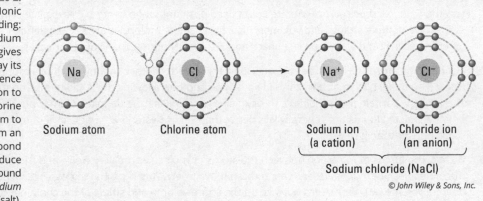

Sodium atom   Chlorine atom   Sodium ion (a cation)   Chloride ion (an anion)

Sodium chloride (NaCl)

© John Wiley & Sons, Inc.

Covalent bonds

Covalent bonds form between nonmetals and involve the *sharing* of valence electrons. Nonmetals are on the right-hand side of the periodic table, so they have four or more valence electrons (except for hydrogen, which has only one valence electron). Carbon, for example, is in Group 4A and contains four valence electrons. Carbon is unlikely to lose all those valence electrons because the positively charged protons hold them in pretty tightly, so instead, carbon shares its electrons with other atoms to form covalent bonds (see Figure 20-3).

FIGURE 20-3:
Covalent bonding: A carbon atom sharing its valence electrons with four hydrogen atoms to form covalent bonds and produce a compound called *methane* (natural gas).

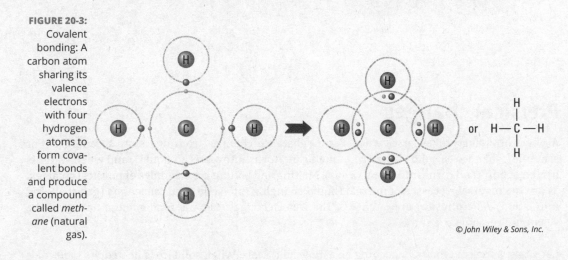

© John Wiley & Sons, Inc.

In fact, carbon's ability to form multiple covalent bonds with many different elements (including itself) is one of the reasons that all life on Earth is carbon-based. All the important molecules that make up your body have a regular arrangement of chains of carbon atoms.

REMEMBER

Atoms bond with each other to achieve full valence shells. The first shell can hold two electrons; the second shell can hold eight electrons. Ionic bonds involve the *transfer* of electrons between atoms to form ions, whereas covalent bonds involve the *sharing* of electrons between atoms.

States of matter

Under normal conditions, matter here on Earth exists in one of three distinct states, illustrated in Figure 20-4:

>> **Solids:** The atoms or molecules are unable to move freely because they're bonded tightly together. Hence, they can only vibrate about fixed positions when heated. This explains why solids have definite shapes and volumes. Also, because the molecules are packed tightly together, solids tend to take up less space and are usually denser than liquids or gases.

>> **Liquids:** The atoms or molecules are only loosely bonded together so they can move more freely. The molecules in a liquid can slide over one another, allowing the liquid to take up the shape of the container that holds it. This explains why liquids have definite volumes but no definite shape. Liquids are generally less dense than solids (water is a notable exception) but much denser than gases.

>> **Gases:** The forces of attraction between the atoms or molecules are very weak, and therefore, the molecules are much farther apart and can move freely. This explains why gases have no definite volume or shape. A gas will take up the entire volume and shape of the container that holds it. Gases have much smaller densities than either liquids or solids.

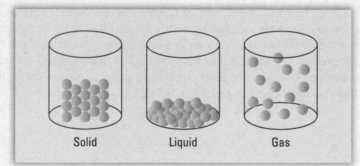

FIGURE 20-4: The arrangement of molecules in solids, liquids, and gases.

© *John Wiley & Sons, Inc.*

Physical changes

A physical change takes place whenever a substance changes from one state to another. For example, when ice (a solid) is heated, it melts and turns into water (a liquid), and when water is heated, it boils and turns into steam (a gas). Melting and boiling are examples of physical changes, as are the reverse processes of *freezing* (liquid changing into solid) and *condensing* (gas changing into liquid). The physical appearance of the water changes, but the fundamental nature of the substance remains the same.

Let's take a look at what's happening on a molecular scale. When solid ice is heated, its molecules become energized and begin to vibrate more and more as the temperature of the ice begins to rise.

When the temperature reaches the melting point of water (0°C), some of the bonds begin to break, and the molecules slide over each other as the ice starts to melt. Because the molecules are no longer held as tightly together, the liquid water can now flow and take up the shape of its container. If you continue to add heat, the water molecules will start to move faster and faster, causing the temperature of the water to rise. When the temperature reaches the boiling point of water (100°C), some of the molecules are moving so fast that they manage to escape the container as water vapor and can move about freely as the water turns into steam (a gas).

Chemical Reactions

Chemical reactions involve the transformation of one set of chemicals (the *reactants*) into another set of chemicals (the *products*). The products of a chemical reaction often have very different properties than those of the original reactants. For example, pH is a property that measures how acidic or basic a substance is. A *neutral* substance has a pH equal to 7, whereas an *acid* has a pH less than 7, and a *base* has a pH greater than 7. Now consider the popular volcano reaction between baking soda and vinegar. Baking soda is a base and vinegar is an acid. When you mix an acid and a base (the reactants), you get the products water (which is neutral) and a salt. The reaction transforms the reactants into two completely different substances.

Here's a list of ways to tell whether a chemical change has occurred:

>> A temperature change occurs.

>> A color change occurs.

>> A solid is formed.

>> A gas is released.

Reactions that give off energy are called *exothermic* reactions. For example, burning fossil fuels gives off heat. Reactions that absorb energy are called *endothermic* reactions. For example, during *photosynthesis* (the reaction that occurs in plants), sunlight energy is absorbed and used to convert carbon dioxide and water into food and oxygen.

REMEMBER

The *law of conservation of mass* states that matter can't be created or destroyed. This also holds true for chemical reactions — the number of atoms of each element at the beginning of the reaction must remain the same at the end of the reaction. Remembering this fact can help you balance chemical equations. For example, consider the combustion of natural gas (methane). When methane is burned in the presence of oxygen, it produces carbon dioxide and water. If you have a natural gas heater at your house or apartment, this is what is going on in that closet. The following unbalanced equation lists the reactants and the products for this reaction:

Reactants   Products
$$CH_4 + O_2 \rightarrow CO_2 + H_2O$$

Now apply the law of conservation of mass to see whether this equation is balanced. The number of carbon atoms on each side of the equation matches (one C atom on each side), but the number of hydrogen atoms doesn't match (there are four H's on the reactant side but only two H's on the product side). Because the number of hydrogen atoms doesn't match, this equation is not yet balanced.

To balance the equation, you need to add *coefficients* — big numbers in front of the formula that refer to everything in the compound. You can't change the little numbers (the subscripts). They tell you how many atoms are in that compound.

To balance the number of H atoms, you can start off by adding the coefficient 2 to the H_2O, which then gives you $2H_2O$, which is 2 x 2 = 4 hydrogen atoms and 2 x 1 = 2 oxygen atoms. The equation now looks like this:

$$CH_4 + O_2 \rightarrow CO_2 + 2H_2O$$

The number of carbon atoms and hydrogen atoms are now balanced, but the number of oxygen atoms is still off (two oxygen atoms before, compared to four oxygen atoms after). Try adding the coefficient 2 to O_2 to get $2O_2$, which gives you 2 x 2 = 4 oxygen atoms. The equation now looks like this:

$$CH_4 + 2O_2 \rightarrow CO_2 + 2H_2O$$

Because the numbers of carbon atoms, hydrogen atoms, and oxygen atoms on the reactants side match those on the products side, the equation is now balanced, and the law of conservation of mass has been satisfied.

Forces

A *force* is a push or a pull on an object as a result of its interaction with another object. Some forces, like the gravitational force, control big things like holding planets in orbit around the sun, whereas other forces, such as the strong nuclear force, control very small things like holding subatomic particles together in an atom's nucleus. The main forces that the TASC tends to focus on are described in the following sections.

Gravitational force

Gravitational force is a force of attraction that acts between all objects that have mass. The bigger the mass of the objects, the bigger the gravitational force. Also, the farther away the objects are, the weaker the force of attraction between them. When one of the objects is very large, like the Earth, its gravitational force attracts other smaller objects (like us) to it. The gravitational force acting on an object at the Earth's surface is also called the *weight* of the object. English physicist Sir Isaac Newton came up with a universal law of gravitation to determine the size of the gravitational force:

$$F = \frac{Gm_1m_2}{r^2}$$

In this equation, F is the force due to gravity, G is the gravitational constant, m_1 is the mass of object one, m_2 is the mass of object two, and r is the distance between the centers of the two objects.

Electrostatic force

Electrostatic forces act between charged particles. These forces can be either attractive or repulsive (like charges repel; unlike charges attract). The bigger the charge on the objects, the bigger the electrostatic force. Also, the farther away the objects are, the weaker the force between them. French scientist Charles Coulomb came up with the following formula to determine the size of the electrostatic force:

$$F = \frac{kq_1q_2}{r^2}$$

In this equation, F is the electrostatic force, k is a constant, q_1 is the charge of object one, q_2 is the charge of object two, and r is the distance between the centers of the two objects.

Frictional force

Frictional force is a resistive force that's created whenever two surfaces move or try to move across each other. Friction always opposes the attempted motion and depends on the texture of the two surfaces that are trying to slide over each other and the normal reaction force of the object.

Strong nuclear force

Strong nuclear forces hold the protons and neutrons together in a nucleus.

Newton's Three Laws of Motion

Sir Isaac Newton was one of the greatest scientists the world has ever known. You may be familiar with the story of an apple falling on Newton's head as he sat under a tree and how this event inspired him to discover his universal law of gravitation. But Newton did a lot more than providing a soft landing for apples! When he realized that the math that had been discovered up until that time was not advanced enough to handle his theories about gravity, he didn't just give up; instead, he invented a whole new branch of mathematics called *calculus.* (He was also one of the greatest mathematicians in the world!) Newton also invented the reflecting telescope and discovered how white light is made up of all the colors of the rainbow.

REMEMBER

But his crowning achievement is probably his three laws of motion listed here:

>> **Law of inertia:** Every object stays in its state of rest or uniform motion in a straight line unless acted on by an unbalanced force.

>> **Law of acceleration:** The unbalanced force acting on an object is equal to the object's mass times its acceleration, $F = ma$.

>> **Law of action and reaction:** For every action, there is an equal and opposite reaction.

Newton's first law of motion

Consider a book resting on a table. The book will stay where it is (in a state of rest) because there are no unbalanced forces acting on it. The weight of pushing down on the table is balanced out by the normal reaction force of the table pushing up on the book, so the net force acting on the book is zero. This is an example of Newton's first law of motion, where the object is stationary.

Now consider a car traveling along a straight, flat highway at a constant speed. The car will continue to move in a straight line and at the same speed because there are no unbalanced forces acting on it. The driving force of the engine is balanced out by the air resistance and frictional forces, so once again, the net force is zero. This is another example of Newton's first law of motion, but in this case the object is moving with constant velocity.

How does this relate to inertia, and what is inertia anyway? *Inertia* is the tendency of an object to resist a change in its motion. Do you wear your seat belt? Hopefully you do because seat belts are designed to protect you from your own inertia. Imagine you're in your car traveling at 60 miles per hour — you and the car are both moving at that same speed. If you gently apply the brakes, the car slows down gradually, and you slow down too. The friction of your body against the seat helps you slow down with the car. But if the car were to crash into a wall, the car would stop suddenly, but your body's inertia would keep you moving forward (at 60 mph!), straight through the windshield and head first into the wall! This is why you need to wear a seat belt.

Newton's second law of motion

Consider the previous example of the book resting on the table. If you were to now give the book a push, it would begin to accelerate and move away from you across the table. You would have caused the book to change its state of motion (from rest to moving) because you would have just applied an unbalanced force to it. This is an example of Newton's second law of motion because the unbalanced force made the book accelerate (change its velocity).

Consider the example of the car traveling along a straight, flat highway at a constant speed. If you were to now press harder on the accelerator, the car would *accelerate* (speed up) because there would now be an unbalanced force acting on the car in its direction of motion. Similarly, if you were to slam on the brakes instead, the car would *decelerate* (slow down) because there would now be an unbalanced force acting on the car against its direction of motion.

TIP

REMEMBER

When dealing with Newton's second law *(F = ma)*, remember that the F is the unbalanced force (net force).

If you know the mass of an object and the size of the forces acting on it, you can use Newton's second law to calculate the object's acceleration. For example, if a box of mass 10 kg is subjected to a force of 50 N, what is the box's acceleration? Simply plug the numbers into the equation:

$$F = ma$$
$$50 = 10(a)$$
$$\frac{50}{10} = a$$
$$a = 5\text{m/s}^2$$

Newton's third law of motion

Let's consider our book sitting on the table once more. The book's weight pushes down on the table, but the table also pushes back on the book with an equal but opposite force. This is called the *normal reaction force*. You can also experience this force yourself. If you slap the table with the palm of your hand, it hurts. That's because although you're exerting a force on the table, the table is also exerting a reaction force on your hand. That's Newton's third law of motion in action (or should we say *reaction*!).

Momentum

The *momentum* of an object is calculated as *p = mv*, where *p* is the momentum (measured in kg/m/s), *m* is the mass (measured in kg), and *v* is the velocity of the moving object (measured in m/s). If you know the mass of an object and its velocity, you can calculate its momentum. Because momentum depends on velocity and mass, both must be considered when comparing the momentum of different objects. For example, which would you rather get hit by, a train whose mass is 10,000 kg moving at 5 m/s or a bicycle whose mass is 10 kg moving at 5 m/s? Even though they're both traveling at the same speed, the train has a much larger momentum (50,000 kg/m/s) compared to that of the bicycle (50 kg/m/s) because the train has a much larger mass.

Or consider this example: Which would you rather get hit by, a bullet whose mass is 0.01 kg traveling at 5 m/s or an identical bullet traveling at 500 m/s? Even though they both have the same mass, the first bullet has a much smaller momentum (0.05 kg/m/s) compared to that of the second bullet (5 kg/m/s) because the first bullet is traveling much slower.

REMEMBER

Objects that are moving in the forward direction have positive momentum. Objects moving backward have negative momentum. Objects that are at rest (stationary) have zero momentum because their velocity is zero.

REMEMBER

The *conservation of momentum* states that when two objects collide, the total momentum before the collision must equal the total momentum after the collision. This can be seen whenever two billiard balls collide and one ball gives its momentum to the other, or when a gun recoils after a bullet is fired. In each case, the total momentum is conserved.

Energy

There are lots of different types of energy — chemical, gravitational, mechanical, nuclear, electrical, heat, light, motion, and sound. No matter which type of energy you're talking about, energy is measured in *joules* (J). But just what exactly is energy? *Energy* is defined as the ability to do work. When work is done, energy is transformed from one type to another. The two forms of energy that you'll encounter most on the TASC exam are kinetic energy and potential energy.

Kinetic energy

Kinetic energy (KE) is the energy that an object has due to its motion. The kinetic energy of an object of mass m, moving at velocity v, is given by this formula:

$$KE = \frac{1}{2}mv^2$$

For example, what is the kinetic energy of a 4 kg object moving at a velocity of 10 m/s?

$$KE = \frac{1}{2}4(10)^2$$
$$KE = 2(100)$$
$$KE = 200J$$

Potential energy

Potential energy (PE) is the energy that an object has stored within it due to its position. The gravitational potential energy of an object of mass m, at a height h above the ground, with acceleration due to gravity (g), is given by this formula:

$$PE = mgh$$

For example, what is the potential energy of a 4 kg object positioned 3 m above the ground? (Note that g = 10 m/s/s/ at the Earth's surface.)

$$PE = 4(10)(3)$$
$$PE = 120J$$

Conservation of energy

The *conservation of energy* states that energy is always conserved. Energy can't be created or destroyed; it can only be converted from one form to another.

Mechanical energy

Mechanical energy is the sum of the kinetic and potential energy that an object has while moving. Consider a pendulum bob swinging, as shown in Figure 20-5.

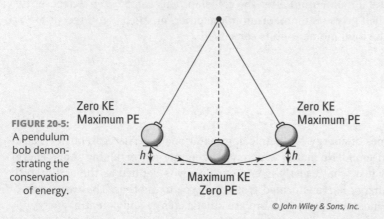

FIGURE 20-5: A pendulum bob demonstrating the conservation of energy.

Zero KE
Maximum PE

Zero KE
Maximum PE

h

h

Maximum KE
Zero PE

© John Wiley & Sons, Inc.

At the top of the swing, the bob has maximum potential energy because the ball is at the highest point above the ground. The bob is momentarily at rest ($v = 0$) here, so it has zero kinetic energy at the top of the swing. As the bob begins to fall, its potential energy is converted into kinetic energy, which reaches a maximum value at the bottom of the swing (the bob is moving fastest here). The potential energy at the bottom is at a minimum because the bob is at its lowest point above the ground. So all the potential energy that the bob possessed at the top has been converted into kinetic energy at the bottom. As the pendulum bob rises, the kinetic energy is converted back into potential energy again, and the process repeats itself. The total mechanical energy of the pendulum remains the same, as expected by the conservation of energy.

Another example of conservation of energy is the conversion of chemical energy stored in your body into mechanical energy. As you eat, your body converts the chemical energy stored in the food to energy that allows you to read and understand all the science coming at you. Some of that energy is transferred to the movement of your heart cells keeping your heart beating, some to the movement of your hands allowing you to turn the pages of this book, and some to your brain firing your brain cells. Remember how all your teachers used to tell you to eat a good breakfast before school? Make sure you eat something healthy before you go take this test!

Heat transfer

Heat energy is also known as *thermal energy.* Heat always flows from hot objects to cooler objects, but it's important not to confuse heat and temperature. The *temperature* of an object is the average kinetic energy of the molecules within the object. The hotter the object, the faster its molecules move. Thermal energy (heat) therefore flows from the object with the higher temperature to the object with the lower temperature.

Heat energy is transferred in one of three ways:

» **Conduction:** This form of heat transfer takes place when two solid objects that are at different temperatures are placed in physical contact with each other. Heat energy flows from the hotter object to the cooler object, but the objects themselves don't move.

» **Convection:** This form of heat transfer takes place in fluids and is due to the movement of the fluid itself.

» **Radiation:** This form of heat transfer (also called *thermal radiation*) occurs in the form of electromagnetic waves. Thermal radiation can pass from a hot object to a cooler object that isn't even touching it. For example, heat energy from the sun reaches you via electromagnetic waves, which demonstrates that thermal radiation can pass through a vacuum. Lucky for you, Earth dweller!

Figure 20-6 shows an example of the three types of heat transfer.

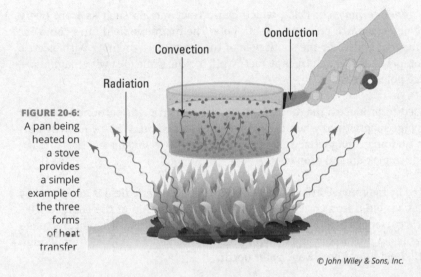

FIGURE 20-6: A pan being heated on a stove provides a simple example of the three forms of heat transfer

© John Wiley & Sons, Inc.

The pan sitting on the stove in Figure 20-6 is in contact with the burner, so the pan gets hot via conduction. Similarly, the handle of the pan is in physical contact with the hotter body of the pan, so the handle also gains heat via conduction. Convection is also occurring in this example. As the pan is heated, the water at the bottom of the pan gets hotter and becomes less dense. These warmer molecules rise to the surface of the liquid and cause the colder, denser liquid at the top of the pan to sink. This flow of water produces *convection currents* that transfer heat throughout the water. Heat is also being transferred by thermal radiation in Figure 20-6. For example, if you were to stand a few feet away from the stove, you would still be able to feel the heat coming from it, even though you wouldn't be touching the pan.

Electricity

As you may recall from the earlier discussion on atoms, when an atom loses electrons, it becomes a positively charged ion (a *cation*), whereas if it gains electrons, it becomes a negatively charged ion (an *anion*). This can also happen on a larger scale. If two objects made from different materials are rubbed together, friction can cause one object to pull electrons away from the other, so both objects become oppositely charged. This is an example of creating *static electricity*.

A fun way of experiencing static electricity is to try the following trick. Next time you're wearing sneakers, rub your feet on a woolen carpet for a few minutes. Then touch the back of your friend's neck. A small spark of electricity will shoot out of your fingers and zap your friend. (This can be a lot of fun, particularly if you sneak up on your friend!)

In this case, the rubber soles of your sneakers pull electrons away from the carpet and store the negative charge on your body. Rubber is an *insulator,* so the electrons can't flow back to the carpet through your sneakers. But your friend's sweaty neck is a relatively good *conductor,* which allows the electrons to flow into him. The flow of electrons is called *electricity,* or an *electric current.*

REMEMBER

Conductors allow electricity to pass through them easily, whereas insulators do not. Semiconductors conduct electricity under certain conditions but act like insulators under other conditions.

Magnetism

Magnetic materials can generate *magnetic fields,* which can attract metals such as iron. Every magnet has two separate poles: a north pole and a south pole. The magnetic field lines come out of the north pole of the magnet and enter the south pole of the magnet. Remember with electric charges how like charges repel and unlike charges attract? Well, it's the same idea with magnets — like poles repel and unlike poles attract.

Electricity can also be used to produce a magnet. If you wrap an electric wire around a piece of metal, the metal will become magnetized when the current is switched on. When you switch off the current, the metal is no longer magnetized. This is known as an *electromagnet.* Electromagnets are used in junkyards to pick up and drop cars.

Magnetic fields are created by moving electric charges. The Earth's magnetic field is generated by the spinning of the planet's molten iron core. As the core spins, the motion of the charged particles generates an electric current, which produces the Earth's magnetic field. The Earth's magnetic field also has two poles, a north pole and a south pole. If you hold a compass, it will align with the Earth's magnetic field lines and always point north.

Finally, a moving magnet can generate electricity. If you pass a magnet through a coil of wire, the wire will begin to generate an electric current. When the magnet stops moving, the current will also stop. This is how power stations generate the electricity you use in your home. The power plant uses the energy stored in fossil fuels to spin a giant turbine that contains magnets. The motion of the magnets as the turbine spins generates an electric current. Electrical energy can then be used to power devices such as light bulbs, electric heaters, or an electric motor, which convert the electrical energy into light energy, heat energy, or kinetic energy, respectively. These are all examples of the conservation of energy.

Chapter 21

Life Science

Matter is classified as living (alive), nonliving (was never alive), or dead (used to be alive but now isn't). In this chapter, we focus on living matter, so it makes sense to begin by discussing the building blocks of life — cells. After noting the similarities and differences between plant and animal cells, we then explore how cells obtain the energy they need to survive. Then we compare the two types of cell division (mitosis and meiosis) and see how organisms pass on their traits during reproduction to the next generation. After that we explore the structures of living things and discover what makes all life on Earth so similar and yet so very different. Next up is the circle of life as we consider how energy is transferred among the different members of an ecosystem. This life science chapter wouldn't be complete without a discussion of how biological evolution and natural selection have led to the enormous level of biodiversity on the planet.

Expect to see about 17 questions about life science on the TASC exam. In addition to testing your basic understanding of each topic, these questions may expect you to interpret information represented in diagrams, tables, graphs, and charts.

Cells: The Building Blocks of Life

The basic unit of life is the *cell.* Simple organisms such as bacteria, which consist of a single cell, are known as *unicellular organisms.* More complex life forms (like you) contain trillions of cells and are known as *multicellular organisms.* Everything in your body consists of cells, so it's important to know what cells are made of and what makes them tick.

Cell structure

The specialized structures inside the cell are called *organelles.* Both plant and animal cells contain three main structures: the cell membrane, the cytoplasm, and the nucleus. Figure 21-1 shows the similarities and differences between plant and animal cells.

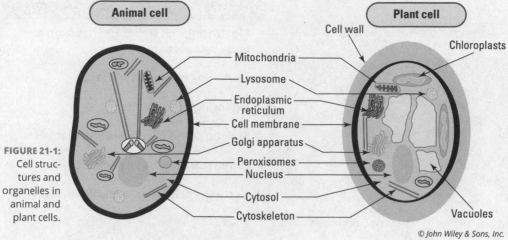

FIGURE 21-1: Cell structures and organelles in animal and plant cells.

© John Wiley & Sons, Inc.

Cells may not seem exciting at first glance, but there's actually a lot going on inside them. Cells contain different types of organelles that help them keep the organism alive by moving materials from cell to cell, producing proteins, using and storing energy, replicating DNA, and reproducing themselves. Here's a list of organelles that are found in both plant and animal cells, along with their main functions.

» **Cell membrane:** A protective membrane that selectively allows material in and out of the cell.

» **Cytoplasm:** The liquid inside the cell where all the organelles are found.

» **Nucleus:** The brain of the cell and where all the genetic material (DNA) for reproduction is stored.

» **Mitochondria:** The powerhouse of the cell. This is where cells obtain energy from food by way of cellular respiration.

» **Lysosomes:** Where waste material is broken down inside the cell.

» **Golgi apparatus/Golgi body:** Where proteins and lipids for the cell are packaged.

» **Endoplasmic reticulum:** The cell's highway system. Cell material is transported along the endoplasmic reticulum.

» **Ribosomes:** Where proteins for the cell are made.

» **Chromosomes:** Found inside the nucleus. This is the genetic material, the DNA, the instructions for life.

Notice in Figure 21–1 that plant cells also have a few additional organelles that animal cells don't possess. These include a cell wall, vacuoles, and chloroplasts. The main function of these plant cell organelles are:

» **Cell wall:** A thick, sturdy outer covering of plant cells. This surrounds the cell membrane and gives plants their support.

» **Vacuoles:** Large sacs filled with water that help support the plant.

» **Chloroplasts:** This is where photosynthesis takes place (see "Photosynthesis and Respiration" later in the chapter).

Whether organisms are multicellular or unicellular, all life forms need food, energy, water, a way to dispose of waste, and an environment in which to live. Inside the cell, many chemical reactions take place to keep the organism functioning and able to carry on its life processes.

Human body systems

Humans and other animals have highly organized body systems. You have red blood cells, muscle cells, skin cells, and the ever-important brain cells. Each of those cells is different based on the job it does for you. For multicelled organisms, cells make up *tissues*, different tissues make up *organs*, and different organs make up *organ systems*, which in turn make up the entire *organism*.

Atoms → Molecules → Organelles → Cells → Tissues → Organs → Organ Systems → Organism

All the cells that make up the organs of body systems must function together to keep the organism healthy and alive. There is communication throughout the organism that seeks *homeostasis* — the balance of the internal workings of the organism with its external environment.

Table 21-1 lists the 12 systems of the human body with their functions and their organs.

TABLE 21-1 **Systems of the Human Body**

System	Function	Organs
Circulatory	Transports blood through the body	Heart, veins, arteries
Digestive	Digestion and absorption of nutrients	Mouth, esophagus, stomach, intestines, gallbladder, liver, colon
Endocrine	Regulates hormones	Glands
Excretory	Filters and removes waste from the body	Kidneys, bladder, ureter, urethra
Immune	Identifies and fights foreign substances such as diseases	Spleen, white blood cells
Integumentary	Protects the interior of the body	Skin
Lymphatic	Cleans and filters the blood	Lymph nodes
Muscular	Movement and support of the body	Muscles and connective tissue
Nervous	Responds to stimuli, records and sends information, regulates homeostasis	Brain, spinal cord, nerves
Reproductive	Reproduction and, in females, gestation	Uterus, ovaries, testes, penis
Respiratory	Gas exchange — O_2 and CO_2	Trachea, lungs, bronchi, alveoli
Skeletal	Support and movement of the body	Bones

Photosynthesis and Respiration

Plants are awesome. They provide us with food and oxygen. If you like to eat and breathe, you've got to love plants! Even if you hate vegetables, there's a cow or chicken out there that got its energy from eating plants. But where do plants get their food and energy from? Plants are *autotrophs*, which means that they create their own food. Plant cells possess *chloroplasts*, and it is within these tiny organelles that an amazing chemical reaction called *photosynthesis* takes place.

REMEMBER

In photosynthesis, carbon dioxide and water are combined using the energy from the sun to produce a sugar called *glucose*. Oxygen gas is also given off as a waste product — lucky for us air breathers. The balanced chemical equation for the reaction looks like this:

$$6CO_2 + 6H_2O + Sunlight \rightarrow C_6H_{12}O_6 + 6O_2$$

Photosynthesis captures the energy from sunlight and stores it within the bonds of the glucose molecule, which can then be converted into starch for later use.

Photosynthesis happens in plant cells, so plants are autotrophs. Animals, on the other hand, can't produce their own food (because animal cells don't contain chloroplasts), so they must rely on eating plants or other animals to survive. Organisms that can't produce their own food are called *heterotrophs*.

TIP

You can use prefixes and root words of long scientific words to dissect their meaning. The prefix "auto" means *self,* while the prefix "hetero" means *different.* The root word "troph" refers to feeding.

When an animal eats a plant, the animal takes in the sugars and starches that were produced by the plant during photosynthesis. The animal's digestive system converts these sugars back into glucose, which then enters the cells of the animal's body.

The process by which heterotrophs (including you) get energy is called *cellular respiration* and takes place in the mitochondria. When you breathe in, oxygen from the air enters your lungs and is passed on to your cells, where it's used to break down glucose molecules via *aerobic respiration.*

The equation for aerobic cellular respiration should look familiar — it's the reverse reaction of photosynthesis. Oxygen is used to break down the glucose molecule and release the energy stored within its bonds. This also produces carbon dioxide and water.

$$C_6H_{12}O_6 + 6O_2 \rightarrow 6CO_2 + 6H_2O + \text{Energy}$$

Some bacteria live in environments that don't have any oxygen, but they can still respire and survive. They are called *anaerobic bacteria.* But humans need oxygen to live. You can go for days without food or water, but if you stop breathing, you'll die within a few minutes because your cells won't be able to perform aerobic respiration and produce the energy they need to survive.

Ecosystem Dynamics

An *ecosystem* is a community of plants and animals that interact with each other in a particular environment. In an ecosystem, energy resources and food flow from producers to consumers. Ecosystems have an organized structure similar to cells. Just as the cell is the basic unit of a tissue, an organism is the basic unit of an ecosystem. A group of the same organisms, a *species*, makes up a population. Different populations form communities, which all exist together in an ecosystem. All the ecosystems on Earth make up the *biosphere.*

Numerous interactions take place between all living creatures, the *biotic factors,* and their physical environment, the *abiotic factors.* Imagine a desert where there's very little rain but a whole lot of sunshine. The rain and sunshine are the abiotic factors that determine what life forms can exist there. The availability of water is one of the major factors that determines the types of plants that can survive in an ecosystem. The types of plants that are present will in turn determine what types of animals can also survive there.

For example, ducks need ponds, lakes, or marshes. They make their homes along the sheltered edges of the water, and they eat grasses, algae, and other plants, as well as what they catch swimming by in the water. If they live in an environment where their lake or pond freezes, they migrate south to another lake or pond. The availability of liquid water, an abiotic factor, is essential for survival of ducks.

REMEMBER

All organisms in an ecosystem must obtain energy to stay alive. We classify feeding relationships based on where the energy for an organism comes from. Because plants produce the food in an ecosystem, they're classified as the *producers*. Animals that eat the plants or other animals are the *consumers* in an ecosystem. *Herbivores* eat only plants, so they're considered first-level consumers. Animals that eat animals that eat plants are second-level consumers. If they eat only meat, they're *carnivores*, and if they eat both plants and animals, they're *omnivores*. Herbivores, omnivores, and carnivores are all consumers.

There's another very important group of organisms that can't be left out, the *decomposers*. These are the fungi or bacteria that get their energy from dead or decomposing matter. It may sound disgusting, but if it wasn't for decomposers, we would all be up to our necks in the piles of waste left over from hundreds of years of animals and plants. Decomposers are also important for recycling nutrients back into the ground.

Food chains and food webs

Food chains are used to represent the flow of energy in an ecosystem. Can you classify the organisms based on the feeding relationships in the following food chain?

Phytoplankton → Dragonfly → Frog → Snake

The phytoplankton is the producer. The dragonfly, the frog, and the snake are all consumers. The dragonfly is a first-level consumer, the frog is a second-level consumer, and, if you want to be specific, the snake is a *tertiary* — or third-level — consumer. The dragonfly is a herbivore. The snake is a carnivore. After the snake has died and its body decomposes, its body will provide food and energy for the decomposers, such as fungi and bacteria.

An expanded food chain is called a *food web* (see Figure 21-2). It's important to notice that the arrows in a food chain or a food web go in the direction of the energy flow, or rather to the organism that's doing the eating. For example, in the food web in Figure 21-2, the arrow from the dragonfly to the salamander means the salamander eats the dragonfly.

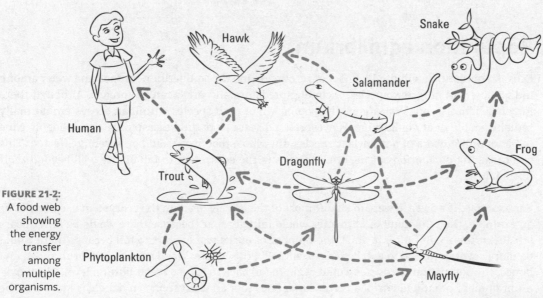

FIGURE 21-2: A food web showing the energy transfer among multiple organisms.

© John Wiley & Sons, Inc.

When the concept of energy transfer comes up, you have to think about energy efficiencies. Every time there's a transfer of energy, some of that energy is lost in the form of heat. Consider the energy pyramid shown in Figure 21-3. The bottom of the pyramid contains the largest number of organisms. These plants are the producers because they derive their energy from the sun. When a herbivore eats a producer, approximately 90 percent of the energy stored in the plant is lost as heat and is not transferred to the animal that eats it. So, for example, a whole lot of algae is needed to make for a healthy population of ducks. The coyotes that eat the ducks get even less of that initial energy because approximately 90 percent of the energy stored in the duck will also be lost as heat rather than being transferred to the coyotes. Hungry grizzly bears that eat coyotes will get even less energy, because again, 90 percent of the energy is lost as heat as you go from one food source to the next in the food chain. So you can see that eating meat is a very inefficient way of using the energy that plants have captured from the sun. For this reason, as you move up the food chain/web, the number of individuals in the populations decreases.

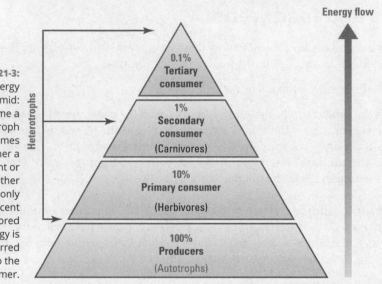

FIGURE 21-3: An energy pyramid: Each time a heterotroph consumes either a plant or another animal, only 10 percent of the stored energy is transferred to the consumer.

© John Wiley & Sons, Inc.

Population equilibrium

Ecosystems contain a limited number of resources, and the competition for food and water among individuals and different species, including predators and prey, can be intense. Although there may be slight seasonal variations, the population of each species within an ecosystem normally remains stable or at equilibrium. However, if a disease or natural disaster were to suddenly wipe out a lot of members of a particular species, the whole food web would be severely affected. This can cause the populations of the other species in the ecosystem to fall or rise well beyond their normal level.

For example, if a disease were to kill off most of the grizzly bears in the ecosystem used earlier as an example, then the number of coyotes would initially soar (because there would be fewer bears left to eat them). But after a while, the number of ducks would start to fall because there would be more coyotes around to eat them. So eventually, the coyotes' food supply would run short, and hence, the population of coyotes would begin to fall back to its usual equilibrium level. The maximum number of individuals of a particular species that an ecosystem can handle is known as the *carrying capacity.* When this is reached, the population will stabilize or begin to drop because there won't be enough food, or water, or shelter, or maybe even mates to go around.

Reproduction: Mitosis and Meiosis

By definition, if something is alive it reproduces. When you were just a gleam in your father's eye, half of your genetic material was in a sperm cell belonging to your father. The other half of your genetic material came from an egg cell belonging to your mother. From those two cells came the multicelled organism you are today. This type of reproduction is *sexual reproduction*. It requires two specialized sex cells or two sets of genetic material.

Single-celled organisms, and some multicellular organisms, reproduce on their own by just dividing one cell into two. This is called *asexual reproduction*. Either way, from old cells come new cells.

Mitosis

Individual cells can replicate. This doesn't have anything to do with sexual reproduction, just growing and making new cells. You weren't born the size you are now. What if your lungs were the size they are now in the little baby body you once were? You would have never learned to walk. Many cells have been created and replaced just to get you to the size you are now. The process that produces replicated cells is *mitosis*.

The nucleus of a cell contains all the genetic material, wound up in strands called *chromosomes*. This is *DNA*, the double helix molecule discovered by the scientists James Watson and Francis Crick — with a lot of help from another scientist named Rosalind Franklin. The DNA molecule unwinds and makes copies of itself. The chromosomes are copied. *Genes* are located on the chromosomes. Human cells have 46 chromosomes. Some ferns have over 1,000 chromosomes. (Remember, we said plants have been around for a very long time.) Whether it be a plant cell or an animal cell, cell replication follows the stages of the cell cycle and mitosis, as shown in Figure 21-4.

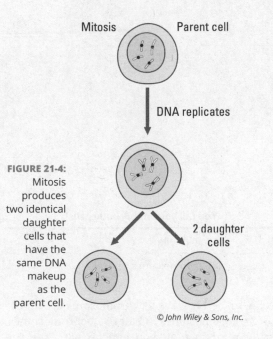

Mitosis   Parent cell

DNA replicates

FIGURE 21-4: Mitosis produces two identical daughter cells that have the same DNA makeup as the parent cell.

2 daughter cells

© *John Wiley & Sons, Inc.*

In asexual reproduction, the daughter cells have the same genetic information as the parent cells. This doesn't really allow for much variation. If you're an amoeba, unless you have some sort of genetic mutation, you are an exact replica of your amoeba parent.

Meiosis

Sexual reproduction is important to the survival of a species because it allows for a mix-up of genetic material, which can sometimes lead to beneficial traits. Look at the massive amount of diversity in dogs. Big dogs, little dogs, brown, black, spotted, freckled, long-haired, short-haired . . . the list could go on and on. After many years of keeping and breeding dogs, we have a great amount of variation in the appearance and nature of dogs.

REMEMBER

The process by which sexual reproduction produces sex cells, or *gametes,* is called *meiosis.* It sounds a bit like mitosis and is similar to mitosis, but be careful — it has a whole different result. In meiosis, instead of ending up with two cells, each with a complete set of identical DNA, you end up with four specialized sex cells, each containing half of the DNA. There's an extra cell division in there. Meiosis results in *haploid* cells, or cells with half of the genetic material. Regular body cells are referred to as *diploid* cells, or cells with the full amount of the genetic material. Figure 21-5 shows meiosis. Pay attention to the extra division and the resulting number of daughter cells. This is what makes meiosis unique and very special.

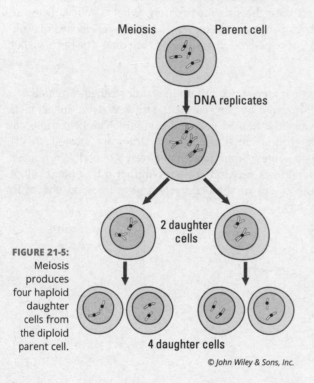

FIGURE 21-5: Meiosis produces four haploid daughter cells from the diploid parent cell.

© *John Wiley & Sons, Inc.*

Let's look at how meiosis led to you:

Mom (egg)	Dad (sperm)	You (all your many body cells)
Haploid cell	Haploid cell	Diploid cells
23 chromosomes	23 chromosomes	46 chromosomes

In order for your mom's egg cell and your dad's sperm cell to have 23 chromosomes each, the extra division in meiosis divides the normal set of 46 chromosomes in half to 23 chromosomes. When these specialized sex cells combine during reproduction, you end up with the full 46 chromosomes again (half from your mom and half from your dad). You could not have survived if you were only haploid.

Plants are very different from animals in many ways, but they can also mix genetic material via sexual reproduction. That's what all that "birds and bees" business is about. A bee visits a flower and gets pollen on its legs. Pollen is the male sex cell for plants. The bee flies to another flower and, when it lands, some of the pollen falls off its legs, into the opening of the flower. Inside the flower is an egg cell. The two haploid cells come together, and a diploid seed is formed.

Traits and Inheritance

The study of traits and inheritance really started with an Austrian monk named Gregor Mendel, who also happened to be a pretty serious gardener. He noticed he could select traits in his pea plants. He had tall plants and short plants. The thinking during the mid-19th century, when Mendel was alive, was that by crossing a tall plant with a short plant you'd get a medium-sized plant. After all, tall people who married short people frequently had children who were of medium height. But Mendel discovered that this was not the case with the pea plants. The offspring from tall and short plants were always either tall or short, but none were medium. He also found that the pea pods would be either wrinkled or smooth. No plants had pods that were in between. Mendel called these inherited characteristics *traits.* He didn't really know anything about genes or DNA or chromosomes, but after much experimentation, he did figure out a lot about how inheritance works and how to pollinate his plants and select them for particular traits.

After many years of experimentation and crossbreeding pea plants, Mendel published his work and became very important in science as the father of modern genetics. He established the number one rule of inheritance, which is that genes come in pairs that are inherited as single units, one from each parent.

What is the likelihood that a particular trait from the parents is passed on to their offspring? For example, if a father has blue eyes and a mother has brown eyes, what is the chance that their child will have blue eyes? A *Punnett square* can help you answer this question, but first there are two terms you need to know — genotype and phenotype. The *genotype* represents which two genes are present, whereas the *phenotype* is the physical expression of those genes — in this case, what color the child's eyes are.

The trait for brown eyes is the *dominant trait,* whereas having blue eyes is the *recessive trait.* An uppercase letter is used to represent the dominant trait, which will always be expressed if it appears at all in the genotype. The recessive trait will only be expressed if both genes show the recessive trait. Weirdly enough, the same letter is used for the recessive trait but lowercase.

In the eye color example, "B" is used to represent the dominant gene for brown eyes, and "b" is used to represent the recessive gene for blue eyes. Because the blue eyes trait is recessive, the father's genotype must be *homogeneous* (two similar genes) — in this case "bb." But because the trait for brown eyes is dominant, the brown-eyed mother could be either homogenous ("BB") or *heterogeneous* (two different genes) — "Bb" in this case. Here's a summary:

Father:	genotype = bb	phenotype = blue eyes
Mother:	genotype = BB (homogeneous) or Bb (heterogeneous)	phenotype = brown eyes (due to the presence of at least one dominant B gene)

The Punnett square for each of these possibilities is shown in Figure 21-6.

FIGURE 21-6:
Punnett
squares
showing the
probability
of blue-eyed
offspring
from a
blue-eyed
father and
a hetero-
geneous
brown-eyed
mother
or from a
blue-eyed
father and
a homo-
geneous
brown-eyed
mother.

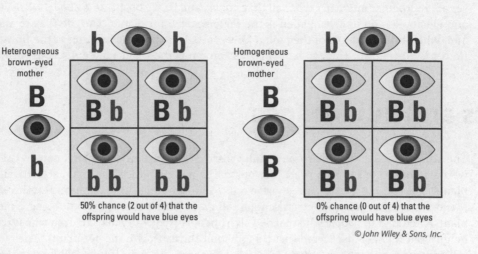

50% chance (2 out of 4) that the offspring would have blue eyes

0% chance (0 out of 4) that the offspring would have blue eyes

© John Wiley & Sons, Inc.

Genes can also be used to determine the sex of an offspring. In humans, the genotype for a female is XX, and for male it's XY. Two letters are used to represent the two sets of genetic material. The phenotype of XX is all the characteristics that define a female body, and the phenotype of XY is all the characteristics that define a male body.

Biological Evolution and Natural Selection

Rain forests are known for their extreme biodiversity. There are so many different types of plants and animals that it's almost impossible to count them all. But where did this great variety of different species come from? Why do some varieties thrive while others decline or become extinct? The answer lies in biological evolution and natural selection.

Common ancestry

Believe it or not, all the different species of plants and animals on Earth developed from a common ancestor. The relationship among different species can be represented by an evolutionary tree such as the one in Figure 21-7, which shows which species are the most closely related to humans.

FIGURE 21-7:
An evolu-
tionary tree
showing
some of
humans'
common
ancestors.

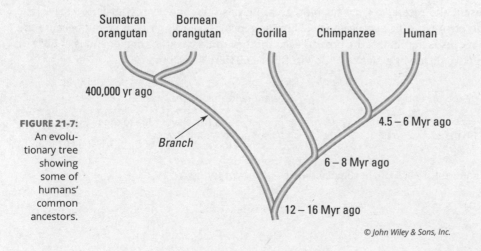

© John Wiley & Sons, Inc.

If you start off with the branch that represents humans and follow it back through time about 5 million years ago, you come to the branch that leads off to chimpanzees. Chimpanzees are humans' closest ancestors — their DNA is 98.4 percent identical to human DNA! If you continue going back further in time down the main branch to approximately 7 million years ago, you come to the branch that leads to the gorillas. Gorillas are therefore a more distant relative of humans than are chimpanzees (although gorilla DNA is still 97.7 percent identical to human DNA). From the evolutionary tree diagram, you can see that gorillas are common ancestors to both chimpanzees and humans.

Because all organisms on Earth have a common ancestry, a large percentage of their DNA is identical to that of other related species. It's not too surprising, therefore, that many different animals have similar anatomical structures. An example of these homologous structures is shown in Figure 21-8.

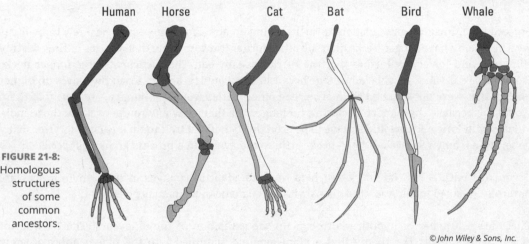

FIGURE 21-8: Homologous structures of some common ancestors.

© John Wiley & Sons, Inc.

Have you ever looked at a picture of an early fetus in the womb and thought, "Wow, it doesn't even look human"? It turns out that a lot of different animal species, including humans, start out looking the same as the embryos from other species as they develop in the womb, in a shell, or in an egg. This again provides evidence of our common ancestry.

Fossils

Fossils are the remains of animals or plants that died long ago. You can learn a lot about what life was like in the ancient past and how different organisms evolved by studying fossils. But how do you know how old these fossils are? Remember in Chapter 20 when you looked at decay series of radioactive elements? Well, scientists use the half-lives of various isotopes to determine the age of the rock that a fossil was found in.

Fossils can also be dated based on the depth of the layer of rock they appear in. For example, the walls of the Grand Canyon are made from layers of sedimentary rock that formed on top of each other over millions of years. Therefore, you know the rocks at the bottom of the canyon and any fossils you find there are older than the fossils you may find nearer the top. The earliest fossils in the lower layers are single-celled plant or algae fossils. The higher layers have fossils from many different types of aquatic creatures, and then higher up you start to see land plants, insects, amphibians, and then reptiles in the fossil record that spans over millions of years. Dinosaurs appeared after reptiles and before birds. Birds, grasses, and flowers all appear in the fossil record around the same time. The last group to appear in the fossil record is humans. It's generally accepted that life originated in the ocean, and all life can trace its ancestry back to those early life forms. Scientists believe that of all the species on Earth that have ever existed, 99 percent of them are now extinct. For over a billion years our planet has seen life begin, adapt, and evolve — or become extinct. The great diversity on Earth now is the result.

Natural selection

You already know that life on Earth is derived from a common ancestor and that over millions of years, numerous different species evolved into the great variety of organisms alive today. But how did this process of evolution occur? The answer to this question was discovered by the English scientist Charles Darwin, who identified *natural selection* as the mechanism that underlies evolution. Natural selection is also known as "survival of the fittest" because it allows organisms that are the best "fit" for the ecosystem they live in to thrive and pass on their beneficial traits to their offspring.

For example, imagine a population of turtles living on an island. There may be a few individuals who happen to have longer necks than the other turtles. Now imagine that a series of fires destroy the grass and low-lying bushes that the turtles usually eat. The turtles with the longer necks would have a distinct survival advantage because they would be able to reach the leaves on higher bushes that were not touched by the fire. The other turtles would go hungry, and many of them would die because their short-neck trait no longer fits their new environment. Only those individuals with long necks would survive to pass on this beneficial trait to their offspring. Over many generations, a new species of long-neck turtle would evolve in a process known as *speciation*.

REMEMBER

Organisms with beneficial traits that help them to adapt to changes in their environment are naturally selected to survive. Organisms with less beneficial traits may go extinct.

There are a number of hypotheses to explain the extinction of the dinosaurs. There's a lot of evidence to support the theory that a giant asteroid slammed into the planet approximately 65 million years ago and played a major role in their demise. One thing for sure though is that if dinosaurs still roamed the surface of Earth today, you would not have to worry about taking the TASC test.

Chapter 22

Earth and Space Science

Ever since our prehistoric ancestors first looked up at the night sky and gazed upon the heavens in wonder, humans have sought the answers to some of life's most interesting questions: What are the stars made of? What holds them together? How old is the universe? Where did the universe come from? How big is the universe? Where is Earth's place in the cosmos?

For centuries, the answers to these important questions were limited to the various imaginative and often conflicting explanations offered by mythology, superstition, or religion. Recently, however, scientists have begun to develop the tools and mathematical models needed to gain a much deeper understanding of the universe than ever before. This chapter presents the scientific answers to many of these cosmological questions and explores the evidence that allows scientists to gain knowledge about objects that are so far away and events that happened so long ago. Then, after exploring the solar system, we return back to Earth to examine the planet's structure, systems, and natural resources. Finally, we round out the chapter by discussing the negative impact that humans are having on our fragile planet and present possible solutions that may slow down or even reverse these effects.

TIP

Expect to see about 13 questions about earth and space science on the TASC exam. You will be tested not only on your fundamental knowledge of each topic but also on your ability to analyze and interpret scientific data presented in graphs, charts, and tables.

Earth's Place in the Universe

Earth may seem like a pretty big place, but in the grand scheme of things it's merely a drop in the cosmic ocean. The universe is truly enormous, and the distances between the objects in space are often so large that they are difficult to put into context. To help us handle these huge distances we use a special unit of measurement called a *light year* to describe them. As its name suggests, a light year is equal to the distance that light travels in one year. Light is the fastest thing in the universe and moves at a speed of 300,000 km per second through space, so in one year a beam of light can travel an astounding 10 trillion km!

TIP

Thinking in terms of light years makes cosmological distances easier to manage. For example, the nearest star is 40 trillion km away from Earth. But if you think in terms of light years, this same distance becomes 4 light years (since 40 trillion divided by 10 trillion equals 4). Not only is this number much easier to manage, but it also makes sense because the light from that star takes four years to reach us.

Some of the stars you see in the night sky are so far away from Earth that the light from them has taken millions of years to reach you. So what you are really seeing is what those stars looked like millions of years ago. You are actually seeing into the past. In fact, some of those stars may no longer even exist; they may have exploded out of existence thousands of years ago but because the light from those explosions hasn't had time to reach Earth yet, the stars still appear to be there.

If an advanced race of aliens, living on a planet 70 million light years away, were able to look at the Earth through a powerful telescope, they would not see our planet as it is today; instead, they would see dinosaurs roaming the Earth. That's because the light from the dinosaurs that lived here 70 million years ago would have only just begun to arrive at the aliens' distant planet.

When scientists look through very powerful telescopes, such as the Hubble telescope, they are able to see very distant galaxies. The light from these galaxies has taken billions of years to reach Earth so scientists can witness what these galaxies looked like billions of years ago. Studying the ancient light from these distant galaxies has helped scientists to formulate and test their theories about the origin of the universe.

Stars and the building blocks of life

At first glance, the universe may seem to consist of nothing but empty space, but this void is not quite as empty as it appears to be. There are actually countless astronomical objects of various shapes and sizes dispersed throughout space. There are several important types of astronomical objects (also known as *celestial bodies*); stars are one type, planets are another.

Stars are enormous luminous balls of plasma (hot ionized gas) and consist mostly of hydrogen and a little helium. The center of a star is incredibly dense because of the strong gravitational forces there that compress the hydrogen atoms at the star's core so tightly together that they transform into helium atoms in a process known as *nuclear fusion.* Nuclear fusion also produces electromagnetic energy, which is released by the star in the form of light and heat. This makes the star shine and prevents it from collapsing in on itself. Stars can also provide light and warmth to the planets that orbit around them. The sun is the closest star to Earth; without the light and warmth generated by the sun's nuclear fusion reactions, life on our planet would simply not exist.

Over millions of years, as stars age, they begin to run out of the hydrogen atoms needed to fuel their nuclear fusion reactions. At that point, stars begin to consume helium atoms instead, fusing them together to form heavier elements like carbon. At the end of the star's life cycle, the dying star releases these heavier materials back out into space, sometimes in a giant explosion called a *supernova.* Supernovas produce larger atoms such as iron or nickel, and these heavier elements eventually become the building blocks for new astronomical objects such as planets and satellites.

But because all life on Earth depends on the sun (which is a star) and all stars are destined to die, you may be wondering if you need to start panicking yet. Well, there's some good news and some bad news. First, the bad news. As the sun ages and consumes all its hydrogen, it will slowly turn into a red giant star, which will expand to many times its original size. That will begin to make conditions here on Earth very uncomfortable. Surface temperatures will start to rise and eventually become so hot that the oceans will evaporate, leaving the planet too dry and barren to support life. The red giant star will continue to expand until it engulfs the inner planets, including Earth. Our fragile planet will not survive its brief encounter with the solar surface and will rapidly disintegrate in a spectacular fiery death. Pretty scary stuff, huh?

But before you reach for your extra strength sunscreen, here's the good news. The Earth still has about 5 billion years to go before it is completely destroyed by the sun, and our planet should still be able to support life for another billion years or so. That means that mankind still has plenty of time to develop the technologies needed for interstellar space travel, which will allow the human race to migrate to other habitable planets in distant solar systems. And look on the bright side: The death of one star often gives rise to the birth of another; in fact, that's how our own solar system came into creation.

The solar system and beyond

Scientists estimate that about 4.6 billion years ago, a huge supernova exploded near a gigantic cloud of gas left over from the birth of the universe. The shockwave from this explosion caused the cloud to begin rotating around its center, and the forces of gravity caused the hydrogen atoms at the center of the cloud to compress into a denser region, leading to the formation of a single star (our sun). As the cloud continued to spin around this newly formed star, the material within the gas cloud began to separate into distinct bands due to their different masses. Particles within each band began to collide and stick together, forming larger clumps of material which, over millions of years, grew into enormous balls of hot matter. This led to the formation of the planets that orbit the sun, including the Earth, and that's how the solar system was born (see Figure 22-1).

Just think about it. You and everyone you know are all made from the same celestial building blocks ejected by the explosive death of a distant star billions of years ago. Talk about the ultimate recycling plan!

FIGURE 22-1: Our solar system consists of a star (the sun) and all the objects that orbit around it, including the eight planets and their satellites (moons), asteroids, and comets.

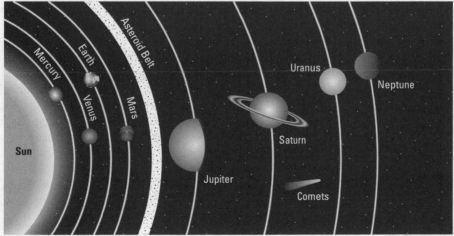

© John Wiley & Sons, Inc.

The four planets closest to the sun are Mercury, Venus, Earth, and Mars, in that order. These inner planets are known as *terrestrial planets* because they have solid rocky surfaces and consist mainly of heavier materials such as metals and minerals. The four planets farthest from the sun are Jupiter, Saturn, Uranus, and Neptune, respectively. These outer planets are known as *giants* because they are much bigger than the terrestrial planets and consist mainly of lighter elements including hydrogen, helium, carbon, and oxygen. Jupiter and Saturn are gas giants, whereas Uranus and Neptune are ice giants.

REMEMBER

What happened to Pluto? Isn't Pluto also a planet? Well, not anymore. Pluto was recently reclassified as a *dwarf planet* so it's no longer counted as a real planet. Sorry Pluto!

There are many other astronomical objects in our solar system that are also not regarded as planets. The moon, for example, is a satellite. A *satellite* is a spherical object that orbits around a planet (planets orbit around a star). Planets can have more than one moon. Our nearest neighbor, Mars, has 2 moons, whereas both Saturn and Jupiter have over 60 each. There are also hundreds of thousands of *asteroids* (airless rocky worlds) in our solar system. Asteroids orbit around the sun but are considered too small to be classified as planets. Most of them are gathered into the main *asteroid belt,* a thick, donut-shaped ring between the orbits of Mars and Jupiter.

The sun is much bigger than any of the planets (more than one million Earths could fit inside the sun!), but the sun is still considered to be an average sized star. Because stars are so large, they have huge forces of gravity and tend to attract other celestial bodies to them, including other stars. Because of this, stars are held together and travel in large groups called *galaxies.* Our sun is just one of the 200 billion stars that belong to a spiral-shaped galaxy called the *Milky Way.*

Galaxies also attract each other and are bound together by gravity into larger groups called *clusters.* The Hubble telescope has discovered over 100 billion galaxies in the universe so far. So when you stop to think about it, you are standing on a tiny planet, orbiting around a medium-sized star that is just one out of the 200 billion stars that make up the Milky Way, which itself is just one out of the 100 billion galaxies that are spread out across our vast and expanding universe. Makes you feel rather small, doesn't it?

The Origin of the Universe and the Big Bang Theory

So where did the universe come from? How did it all begin? You've probably heard of the expression "going out with a bang!" Well, the birth of the universe is the ultimate example of "coming in with a bang," a very big bang to be precise. Scientists have calculated that the universe came into existence about 14 billion years ago.

At that time, all the matter and energy that exists today was packed together into an infinitely dense, infinitely hot, and infinitely small point called a *singularity.* Scientists don't know where this singularity came from, but they do know that before it existed, nothing else existed. There was no matter, no energy, no time, no space. Singularities are extremely unstable, so a fraction of a second after it appeared, the singularity began to expand rapidly (creating both time and space) in what scientists now refer to as the *Big Bang theory.*

REMEMBER

Because both time and space were created at the moment of the Big Bang, it makes no sense to ask, "What happened before the creation of the universe?" There simply was no before!

Over the next 300,000 years or so, as the newly formed universe continued to expand, it cooled enough to allow some of the first atoms of hydrogen and helium to be be created. Gravity caused these lighter elements to attract each other and collect into large clouds of matter in a process known as *accretion.* Over billions of years, the enormous gravitational fields at the centers of these balls of matter caused the hydrogen atoms there to begin to fuse together, giving rise to the first generation of stars and galaxies.

How can scientists know what happened so long ago and so far away? How can you be sure that the Big Bang theory is actually right? Luckily, there happens to be a lot of evidence that scientists can point to in order to support their claims.

TIP

When studying for the TASC exam, it's more important to remember the supporting evidence for the Big Bang theory, along with the related terms and definitions, than it is to understand every detail of the theory itself.

Supporting evidence of the Big Bang theory includes:

>> Spectral analysis of starlight showing the relative abundance of hydrogen and helium in the universe as predicted by the theory

>> The Doppler effect and redshift of starlight showing that all galaxies are moving away from each other in every direction (like the fragments from a huge explosion)

>> Cosmic microwave background radiation showing the existence of the ancient light left over from the Big Bang

Spectral analysis of starlight

Scientists need to have access to useful data whenever they're trying to test their theories and develop knowledge of their surroundings. Therefore, to learn more about the stars, scientists must analyze the only information that is able to travel through space to reach us here on Earth — the electromagnetic radiation (or light) produced by the stars' nuclear fusion reactions. Electromagnetic radiation travels through space at the speed of light in the form of transverse waves, which oscillate at right angles to the direction of motion (see Figure 22-2).

FIGURE 22-2: Transverse waves oscillate perpendicular to the direction of motion.

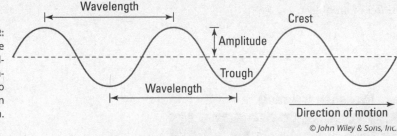

© John Wiley & Sons, Inc.

REMEMBER

The highest point on a transverse wave is called a *crest.* The lowest point on the wave is called a *trough.* The distance between two adjacent pairs of crests or troughs is called the *wavelength.* The number of waves (or cycles) passing by each second is called the *frequency.*

The visible light that humans are able to see is only a small part of the entire electromagnetic spectrum, which includes gamma rays, X-rays, ultraviolet light, visible light, infrared light, microwaves, and radio waves (see Figure 22-3). Each type of electromagnetic wave has its own range of wavelengths and frequencies; gamma rays have the shortest wavelengths (or highest frequencies), while radio waves have the longest wavelengths (or smallest frequencies).

FIGURE 22-3:
The electro-
magnetic
spectrum
consists
of several
different
types of
electromag-
netic waves.
Visible light
accounts
for only a
small part
of the entire
spectrum.

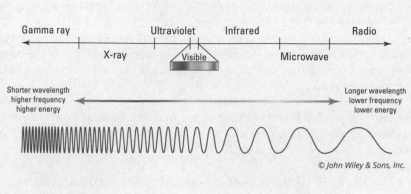

© John Wiley & Sons, Inc.

White light consists of all the colors of the rainbow including red, orange, yellow, green, blue, indigo, and violet. Each color has its own distinct range of frequencies and wavelengths; violet light has larger frequencies and smaller wavelengths compared with red light, which has smaller frequencies and larger wavelengths.

When light shines on the surface of an object, some of the colors are reflected by the object's surface, whereas other colors are absorbed and pass into the object. The frequencies of light that bounce off the object's surface determine its color because these are the only colors that manage to reach our eyes. For example, a red hat appears red because the hat reflects more of the red light and absorbs more of the other colors. A blue sweater would reflect more blue light, which is why it appears blue.

Hot solid objects emit light with a continuous spectrum of wavelengths. Hot gases, on the other hand, only emit certain wavelengths of light, which appear as distinct lines of color corresponding to those wavelengths. The emission spectrum belonging to each element is unique and provides a "fingerprint" that helps scientists to recognize the presence of that element.

Hot objects consisting of plasma (like stars), which are surrounded by clouds of gas, emit near-continuous spectra that contain dark bands or absorption lines corresponding to the emission spectra of the surrounding gases. By analyzing the emission spectrum of a star and comparing these dark absorption bands to the emission spectra of each element, it is possible to determine what elements the gas surrounding the star contains (see Figure 22-4). This is known as the *chemical composition* of an object.

FIGURE 22-4:
The near-
continuous
emission
spectra of
the sun con-
tains dark
absorption
lines that
correspond
to the
emission
spectra of
hydrogen.
This shows
that the sun
contains
hydrogen.

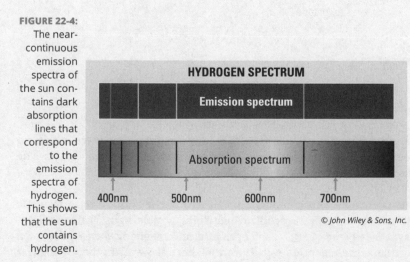

© John Wiley & Sons, Inc.

REMEMBER

The Big Bang theory predicts that the earliest matter in the universe consisted almost entirely of the lightest elements — hydrogen and helium. Spectral analysis of the emission spectra of the sun and other stars has confirmed that hydrogen and helium account for 98 percent of the total matter in the universe. This validates the relative abundance of these lighter elements as predicted by the Big Bang theory.

Doppler effect, red shift, and the expanding universe

When a moving object emits a wave, the relative motion between the source and an observer affects the frequency and wavelength of the detected wave. As the object moves forward, the waves in front of it tend to bunch up in the direction of the motion, making the wavelength shorter in front of the source. This causes the frequency of the waves to increase when the source is coming toward you. At the same time, the waves behind the moving object become stretched out, making the wavelength longer behind the source. This causes the frequency of the waves to decrease as the object moves away from you. This shift in frequency is known as the *Doppler effect*, and it occurs in all types of waves whenever there is relative motion between the source and the observer (see Figure 22-5).

FIGURE 22-5:
The Doppler effect causes an increase in frequency when the source of the waves is approaching an observer and a decrease in frequency when the source is moving away from the observer.

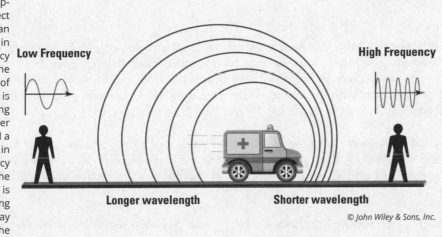

Low Frequency

High Frequency

Longer wavelength   Shorter wavelength

© John Wiley & Sons, Inc.

TIP

You can experience the Doppler effect yourself whenever an ambulance or firetruck passes you by. As the siren approaches, you hear a higher-pitched sound. But as the siren passes you by, you hear a sudden drop in the pitch (or frequency) of the sound as the source moves away from you.

The Doppler effect can be also be observed in light waves emitted from moving objects such as stars. The direction of the shift in frequency of the light depends on the star's direction of motion. If the star is moving toward Earth, the starlight will experience an increase in frequency and its color will shift toward the blue end of the spectrum (because blue light has a higher frequency than red light). This is known as the *blue shift*. Similarly, if a star is moving away from Earth, the starlight will experience a decrease in frequency and will shift toward the red end of the spectrum (because red light has a lower frequency than blue light). This is known as the *red shift*.

The sun provides scientists with a useful reference point with which to compare the light from other stars. We know that the sun contains both hydrogen and helium because there are black lines in its emission spectrum where hydrogen and helium have absorbed those frequencies of light. When scientists look at the emission spectrum of a distant galaxy, those same black lines are still present but they have been shifted toward the red end of the spectrum (see Figure 22-6). This shows that the galaxy is moving away from Earth.

FIGURE 22-6:
Comparing the emission spectra from the sun and a distant star. The black absorption lines present in the emission spectrum of the distant star have been redshifted, showing that the star is moving away from Earth.

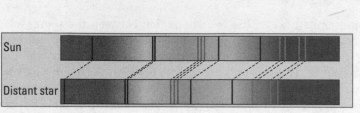

© John Wiley & Sons, Inc.

Whenever scientists study the emission spectrum from any distant galaxy, the light from that galaxy is always redshifted, showing that all the galaxies are moving away from each other. Hence, in the past, every galaxy must have originated from the same common point, which corresponds perfectly with the initial sudden expansion of the universe as proposed by the Big Bang theory.

TIP

Imagine that each galaxy has been drawn on the surface of a rubber balloon. Now imagine that the balloon is expanding. Each galaxy appears to be moving away from all the others, so the light from any galaxy (including our own) will appear redshifted when viewed from any of the other galaxies.

By measuring how far the light from distant galaxies has been redshifted, scientists can determine how fast the galaxies are moving. Cosmologists already know how far apart the galaxies are, so they can use the speed given by the red shift to calculate how long ago the galaxies began moving apart (when the Big Bang occurred). This allows us to predict the age of the universe, which is estimated to be approximately 14 billion years old. Who would have thought that you could discover so much by simply staring up at the stars?

Detection of cosmic microwave background radiation

The Big Bang theory also predicts that shortly after the universe began, conditions were so hot that atoms were unable to form. Instead, for the first 300,000 years or so, the universe consisted of a cloudy mixture of protons and electrons that blocked the light and prevented it from traveling through space. Eventually, as things started to cool, the first atoms of hydrogen began to appear, and the clouds of elementary particles slowly cleared, allowing the first rays of light to begin their journey through the expanding universe. This ancient light, called *cosmic microwave background (CMB) radiation*, is the oldest perceivable light in the universe and has been traveling through space for so long that it has become redshifted to microwave frequencies.

CMB radiation was first detected in the 1960s and has the exact properties predicted by the Big Bang theory; it has the same intensity in every direction and is not being emitted from any astronomical object in space.

Earth's Structure and Systems

A famous donkey once said that ogres are like onions because they have layers, but did you know that the Earth itself is also a bit like an onion? That's right, the Earth has layers: the inner core, the outer core, the lower mantle, the upper mantle, the lithosphere, and the crust. Each of these layers has its own distinct properties.

Earth's structure

The Earth is separated into several layers, each with its own distinct properties. You can see the breakdown of the layers in Figure 22-7.

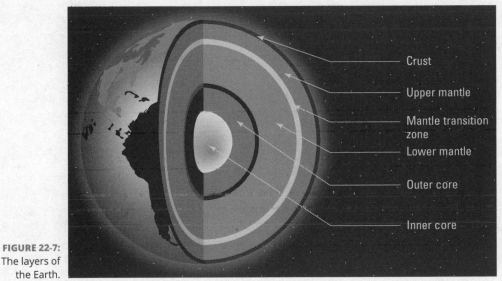

Crust

Upper mantle

Mantle transition zone

Lower mantle

Outer core

Inner core

© John Wiley & Sons, Inc.

FIGURE 22-7:
The layers of the Earth.

The Earth's inner core is as hot as the surface of the sun and consists of minerals and heavier elements (mostly iron and a little nickel). But despite these incredibly hot conditions, Earth's inner core remains solid. So why doesn't the iron at the inner core melt? This is because of the extreme pressure from the weight of the surrounding layers, which prevents the iron in the inner core from changing state no matter how high the temperature becomes.

TIP

This same principle explains why most of the water in a pressure cooker remains liquid even though the temperature may rise to well above water's usual boiling point. The high pressure in the pan prevents most of the water from changing state.

Surrounding the Earth's solid inner core is the liquid outer core. The outer core also consists mostly of iron and is also extremely hot, but because the pressure there is not as great as in the inner core, the outer core is able to melt and become liquid. The molten metal of the outer core flows slowly and is responsible for generating Earth's magnetic field.

Above the iron core lies Earth's thickest layer, called the *mantle.* The mantle is 1,800 miles thick and accounts for 85 percent of the planet's entire volume. The mantle consists of rocky material and is separated into two layers: the solid lower mantle and the molten upper mantle. The lower mantle surrounds Earth's core and consists of solid rock because the high pressure there prevents the rock from melting. The outer mantle consists of molten rocks that are able to flow in huge convection currents below Earth's surface. *Convection currents* occur whenever the bottom of a liquid is exposed to heat, causing the heated parts of the liquid to become less dense and rise. This upward movement forces the cooler, denser parts of the liquid to sink until they too become exposed to the heat, which makes them rise, and the process repeats itself.

The convection currents in the upper molten mantle have a huge effect on the *lithosphere,* which rests on the denser upper mantle rather like ice floating on the surface of a lake. The lithosphere is only about 60 miles thick and consists of the cooler, rigid parts of the upper mantle and the Earth's *crust,* a thin rigid layer of rock that provides the planet with a solid outer surface. More than three-quarters of Earth's rocky surface is covered with water forming the oceans, with the remaining dry land forming the continents. Scientists have recently discovered that all Earth's continents were, at one time, joined together into a single landmass called *Pangaea* (see Figure 22-8). This super continent began to break up 175 million years ago and slowly drift apart to form the separate continents we see today.

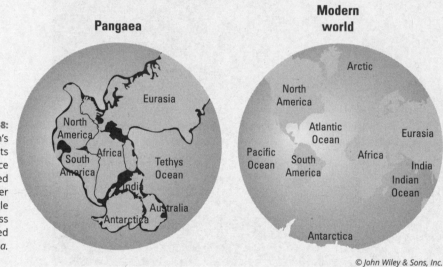

FIGURE 22-8:
Earth's continents were once joined together into a single landmass called *Pangaea.*

© *John Wiley & Sons, Inc.*

REMEMBER

The evidence supporting the Pangaea theory becomes clear when you look at the map of Earth's continents. Notice how each of the continents appears to fit together like the pieces of a huge jigsaw puzzle. For example, the west coast of Africa seems to fit perfectly with the east coast of South America. But that isn't the only evidence that supports the theory. Recently, paleontologists have discovered matching mineral deposits and fossils from identical species of land animals at corresponding locations along both coasts. These findings could only be explained if the two continents were once joined together along these two coastlines. But if all the continents were once joined together into one giant landmass, what caused them to separate?

Plate tectonics

Earth's lithosphere consists of separate continent-sized pieces of solid crust known as *tectonic plates,* which float on the denser but more fluid mantle below. Some plates are covered by the oceans, but others remain above sea level forming the continents. The mantle's fluidity allows the tectonic plates to move relative to each other, and over time, convection currents within the mantle have caused the continents to separate in a process known as *continental drift.* For example, the North American and European plates are currently moving apart at a rate of approximately 3 centimeters per year. Scientists have used this drift rate, combined with the current distances between the continents, to estimate that the pieces of Pangaea began to separate approximately 175 million years ago.

The movement of the plates produces several other natural phenomena depending on the direction of motion (see Figure 22-9). Plates that are moving together have *convergent boundaries.* Plates that are drifting apart have *divergent boundaries.* Plates that slide sideways over each other have *transform boundaries.* Each of these relative motions affects the Earth's crust in different ways, as do the types of boundaries that appear between the two moving plates.

FIGURE 22-9: Continental plate convergence forms mountain ranges. Oceanic plate convergence forms deep ocean trenches, volcanoes, and island arcs.

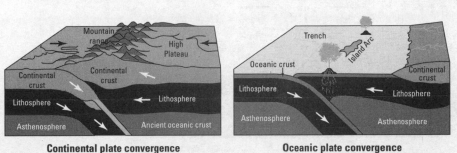

Continental plate convergence   **Oceanic plate convergence**

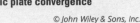

When convergent boundaries occur between two continental plates that are colliding head on, the crust at the point of the collision becomes compressed and is thrust upwards, creating mountain ranges like the Andes or the Himalayas. When convergent boundaries occur between two oceanic plates (or an oceanic plate and a continental plate), one of the plates is forced down below the other, forming a deep trench in the ocean floor. This process is called *subduction.* The immense heat of the mantle turns the lower plate into molten rock called *magma.* Magma often forces its way back to the Earth's surface by forming a tube up through the crust creating a volcano. Eventually, as the pressure inside the volcano builds up, the volcano erupts, releasing molten rock that rises to the surface, where is it called *lava.*

Divergent boundaries occur when two plates move apart, creating a space between them in a process known as *rifting* (see Figure 22-10). This space becomes filled with molten rock thrust up from the mantle, which cools and solidifies to form new crust. Underwater mountain ranges known as *mid-ocean ridges* are created by rifting.

Transform boundaries (also known as *faults*) occur when two plates move sideways against each other (see Figure 22-11). The plate boundaries are not smooth, and they occasionally become locked together as they attempt to pass each other. This causes the pressure to build up until finally the two plates manage to thrust past each other in a jerky motion that causes the Earth's surface to shake. This sudden release of vibrational energy is known as an *earthquake.*

Earth's systems and cycles

The Earth is divided into several different but interconnected systems called *spheres:* the lithosphere (the rocks), the hydrosphere (the water), the atmosphere (the air), and the biosphere (life). As mentioned previously, the *lithosphere* consists of the upper, cooler parts of the mantle, along with the crust that forms the tectonic plates. The *hydrosphere* consists of all the water found on Earth's surface, including the oceans, rivers, and lakes. Above the Earth's surface is the *atmosphere,* which contains the layer of gas that surrounds our planet. The *biosphere* consists of all the living organisms found on Earth. The water cycle, carbon cycle, and rock cycle demonstrate how Earth's systems interact with each other and cause considerable changes to the surface of the planet.

FIGURE 22-10:
Divergent boundaries occur when plates move away from each other, allowing magma from the mantle to rise up and solidify to form new crust. Divergent boundaries form mid-ocean ridges.

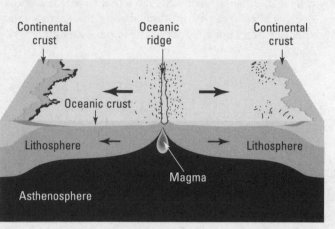

© John Wiley & Sons, Inc.

FIGURE 22-11:
Transform boundaries occur when two plates slide sideways over each other. The San Andreas fault is an example of a transform boundary with a lot of earthquake activity.

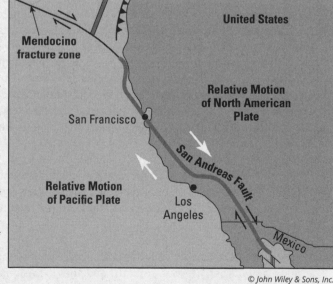

© John Wiley & Sons, Inc.

Water cycle

The *water cycle* describes how the heat from the sun causes water from the surface of the oceans to evaporate into the atmosphere (see Figure 22-12). As the warm water vapor rises, it begins to cool and condense into tiny droplets, forming clouds that can be blown long distances by high atmospheric winds. Changes in atmospheric conditions eventually cause these tiny droplets to converge into larger drops that fall out of the clouds in the form of precipitation (rain, snow, hail, sleet, and so on) and return to Earth's surface. Some precipitation falls in the very cold region of the Earth, where it remains trapped as snow or glacial ice, but most precipitation collects in rivers or streams and eventually finds its way back to the oceans, where it will evaporate once more, restarting the cycle. This cycle of water into and out of Earth's atmosphere plays a significant role in our planet's weather patterns and is essential in providing the supply of fresh water that most animals and plants need to survive.

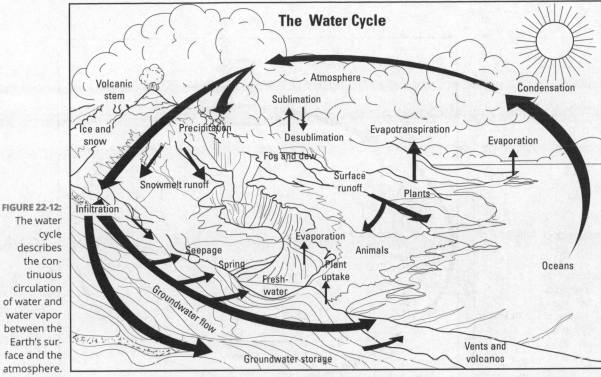

FIGURE 22-12: The water cycle describes the continuous circulation of water and water vapor between the Earth's surface and the atmosphere.

© John Wiley & Sons, Inc.

Carbon cycle

The *carbon cycle* describes the circulation and transformation of carbon between living things and the environment as it moves through Earth's different systems (see Figure 22-13). Carbon is an essential element because it is present in all living things like plants and animals (and humans) and also in nonliving things like soil, petroleum, and rocks. Carbon compounds can exist as solids (such as coal), as liquids (such as crude oil), or as gases (such as carbon dioxide).

When carbon dioxide is present in the atmosphere in just the right amount, it helps to regulate Earth's climate by trapping enough of the heat from the sun to keep the planet warm enough to support life. The amount of carbon on the planet is fixed, but the amount present in the atmosphere or the biosphere is dynamic as carbon changes form and moves between living and nonliving things. Carbon sources release carbon into the atmosphere, whereas carbon sinks remove carbon from the atmosphere and store it in plants, animals, rocks, and water.

REMEMBER

Carbon is removed from the atmosphere by plants during photosynthesis, which take in carbon dioxide and convert it into solid carbohydrates that become part of the physical structure of the plants. Plants are then eaten by animals, and these carbon-based compounds become part of the animals' bodies. Some of this carbon is released back to the atmosphere during respiration, when the animals breathe out carbon dioxide. The rest is released to the soil during excretion or when the animals die. These carbon compounds then either decompose to produce carbon dioxide (which is released back into the atmosphere) or form stable carbon sinks such as fossil fuels that can remain trapped in the soil for long periods of time. Eventually, even these carbon atoms find their way back to the atmosphere when fossil fuels, such as coal or petroleum, are burned to produce heat and carbon dioxide.

It's amazing to think that the carbon atoms in your body were probably once part of a tree or a cow. And who knows where they will end up next?

The Carbon Cycle

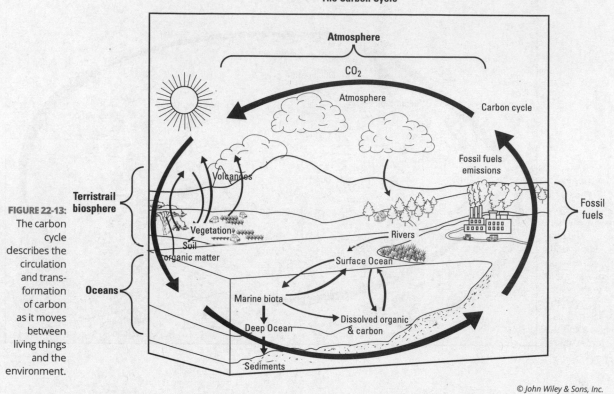

FIGURE 22-13: The carbon cycle describes the circulation and transformation of carbon as it moves between living things and the environment.

Rock cycle

At first glance, the rocks that make up the Earth's crust appear to be steady, permanent objects, so you may not expect them to change much over time. However, rocks also pass through their own endless cycle of destruction and renewal, continually changing from one form to another. There are three main types of rocks: igneous rocks, sedimentary rocks, and metamorphic rocks.

All three types of rocks began as molten rock or magma within the mantle beneath the Earth's surface. *Igneous rocks* are formed when molten rock rises and begins to cool and crystalize. This can happen during violent volcanic eruptions, when magma is ejected above the ground and released as lava. Igneous rocks such as granite can also form below the ground when magma rises and cools slowly but remains below the Earth's surface.

Over thousands of years, weathering gradually breaks down all three types of rocks by the action of the wind and precipitation into tiny pieces of sand or gravel known as *sediment.* This sediment gets washed away and is deposited into layers that, over time, become so thick that they begin to exert enormous pressure on the layers below. These lower layers become compressed and slowly change their crystals and textures to form *sedimentary rocks* such as limestone or shale. As the layers of rock become deeper, the pressure from above becomes even more extreme, and the heat from Earth's mantle causes the rocks to transform into *metamorphic rocks* such as slate or marble.

The rock cycle (see Figure 22-14) shows that each type of rock continually changes into the other types. So it appears that being "as steady as a rock" is not quite as steady as you may have imagined it to be!

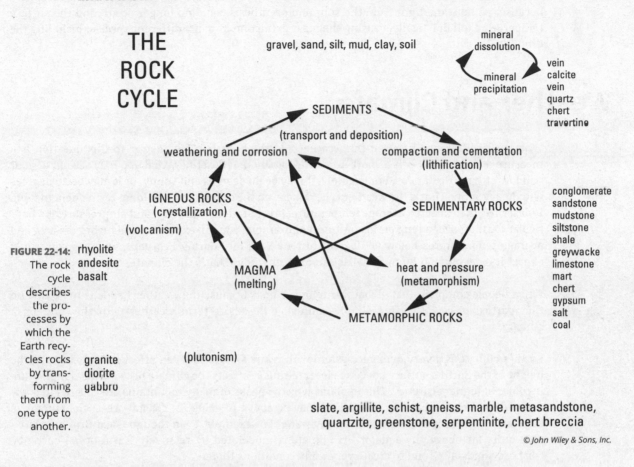

THE ROCK CYCLE

gravel, sand, silt, mud, clay, soil

mineral dissolution
mineral precipitation

vein calcite
vein quartz
chert
travertine

SEDIMENTS
(transport and deposition)

weathering and corrosion

compaction and cementation (lithification)

IGNEOUS ROCKS (crystallization)

(volcanism)

SEDIMENTARY ROCKS

conglomerate
sandstone
mudstone
siltstone
shale
greywacke
limestone
mart
chert
gypsum
salt
coal

MAGMA (melting)

heat and pressure (metamorphism)

METAMORPHIC ROCKS

(plutonism)

FIGURE 22-14: The rock cycle describes the processes by which the Earth recycles rocks by transforming them from one type to another.

rhyolite
andesite
basalt

granite
diorite
gabbro

slate, argillite, schist, gneiss, marble, metasandstone, quartzite, greenstone, serpentinite, chert breccia

© John Wiley & Sons, Inc.

Dynamic systems and positive feedback

Earth's systems are *dynamic*, which means that they can adapt and respond to changes in any of the other systems. Sometimes, an initial change in one system can lead to responses from the other systems that amplify the initial change in the first system. This is known as *positive feedback*. An example of positive feedback among Earth's systems began about 3 billion years ago. At that time, the atmosphere contained virtually no oxygen and hence, the biosphere was limited to *anaerobic* bacteria (that don't need oxygen) living in the oceans. These simple life forms eventually evolved and developed the ability to turn sunlight and carbon dioxide into food via photosynthesis. Photosynthesis also produces oxygen, which was released into the air, gradually changing the composition of the atmosphere. This allowed *aerobic* life forms (that need oxygen) to develop, including plants and simple land animals.

Earth's surface at that time consisted mainly of bare rock and sand, but as these simple plants and land animals died and decomposed, they began to contribute a layer of organic matter in the form of soil, which, in turn, made it easier for more complex species of plants and animals to survive. The proliferation of new plants released even more oxygen into the air, amplifying the the initial change to the composition of the atmosphere making it even easier for more complex life forms to survive.

As this example shows, changes in Earth's biosphere led to significant changes in each of the other systems, which responded in ways that amplified the initial changes in the biosphere.

Although this process happened over millions of years, occasionally very rapid changes can occur. For example, about 65 million years ago, an asteroid collided with the Earth, sending huge dust clouds into the air, blocking out the sunlight. This had a devastating effect on Earth's biosphere because, without the light from the sun, photosynthesis could no longer occur, and the surface temperature fell drastically, causing the mass extinction of many different species, including the dinosaurs.

Weather and Climate

What's the difference between the weather and the climate? The answer to this question is a measure of time. *Weather* is a short-term phenomenon. It describes what you may see out of your window on a particular day. For example, it may be 80 degrees and sunny, or it may be 20 degrees with heavy snow. That's the weather. The *climate*, on the other hand, is a long-term phenomenon. It describes the expected average temperature, precipitation, humidity, and air pressure at a particular location over a long period of time. For example, you can expect several inches of snow and average temperatures below 30 degrees in New York City during February, whereas you would expect it to be hot and humid in Mississippi during July. That's the climate.

TIP

When people complain that global warming is a hoax because the weather happens to be cold on that particular day, they are simply confusing the short-term weather with the long-term climate.

Earth's climate is a very dynamic system with many factors that can affect it. For example, the height of the Earth's surface above sea level (altitude) affects the climate because the temperature is cooler at higher altitudes. This explains why the peaks of many mountains are covered in snow even when the temperature at sea level may be above freezing. In coastal areas, the climate is affected by the temperature of the nearby water. For example, even though Great Britain is situated quite far above the equator, its climate is moderated by relatively warm ocean currents. Onshore winds also tend to create very rainy conditions there.

However, the biggest factor affecting the climate is the sun. Without the light and warmth that our planet receives from the sun, the climate would be drastically different, and life on Earth would simply not exist, so it's important to understand exactly how the sun affects our climate.

The sun's effect on climate

The amount of sunlight shining on the Earth's surface significantly affects the climate at that location. The Earth is a sphere, so the curvature of its surface enables more sunlight to be concentrated directly on the middle of the planet rather than at the poles. This is rather like shining a torch onto an object from directly above compared to shining it from an angle, as shown in Figure 22-15. Hence, the average temperatures at the equator are usually much higher than those at the North or South poles.

The Earth rotates about its own axis every 24 hours, causing a regular variation in the amount of sunlight reaching the surface at each location. Day occurs when the Earth's surface at a particular location is facing toward the sun. Night occurs when that part of the Earth's surface is facing away from the sun. Not surprisingly, the average temperatures during the day are usually warmer than those during the night.

a. Shining a torch at an angle spreads out the light rays over a larger surface area than shining it from directly above. b. Similarly, the sun's rays are focused on a smaller surface area at the equator than at other regions of the Earth, making the equator warmer than elsewhere on Earth.

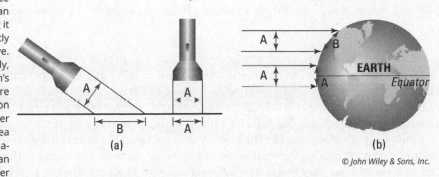

(a)

(b)

© John Wiley & Sons, Inc.

Earth's tilt and the seasons

REMEMBER

Every location on Earth also experiences *seasons*, or regular changes in climate throughout the year. The seasons — spring, summer, fall, and winter — are due to the tilt in the Earth's axis of rotation, which causes each region to experience varying amounts of sunlight during particular times of the year as the Earth orbits the sun (see Figure 22-16). The top half of the planet is called the Northern Hemisphere, and the bottom half is called the Southern Hemisphere. When the sun is shining directly on one hemisphere, it experiences summer. At the same time, the other hemisphere, which is receiving less sunlight, experiences winter. As the Earth orbits the sun, the tilt in the Earth's axis causes a gradual switch in which hemisphere receives the most sunlight, and the seasons move from one extreme to the other.

FIGURE 22-16:
The seasons are due to the tilt of the Earth, which always points in the same direction as the Earth orbits around the sun, exposing each hemisphere to different amounts of sunlight throughout the year.

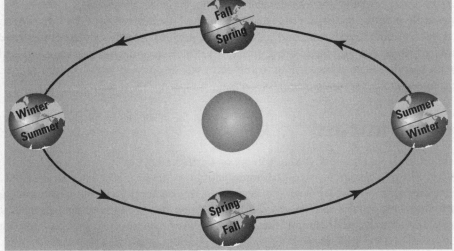

© John Wiley & Sons, Inc.

Carbon dioxide and global warming

Carbon dioxide plays an important role in the carbon cycle and by nature of the carbon atom bonds, helps to keep some of the sun's energy in the lower atmosphere. This is known as the natural *Greenhouse Effect,* and it keeps the planet warm and allows life on Earth to exist.

Without enough greenhouse gases such as Carbon Dioxide in the atmosphere, the Earth would be a very cold and barren place. But larger amounts of carbon dioxide is a problem for life as we know it.

If the amount of carbon dioxide in the atmosphere were to significantly rise, larger amounts of the sun's energy would be kept in the lower atmosphere causing global temperatures to rise. A large rise in surface temperatures would cause melting of Earth's ice sheets and ice caps. Not only does this melting lead to sea level rise but it also has a positive feedback effect that further contributes to warming. It works like this: Ice reflects sunlight so when ice is no longer present, more of the sun's energy is absorbed by the ground or the ocean. This warms the ground or ocean causing more ice to melt making for more warming. Another problem associated with melting of ice on land is under the ice caps the frozen soil contains vast amounts of stored carbon dioxide and methane. Methane is another important greenhouse gas. As the frozen soil thaws, carbon dioxide and methane are released into the air, adding to the trapping of the sun's energy in the atmosphere and adding to the rise in surface temperatures.

Natural Resources and Human Impact

Throughout history, humans have relied on the Earth's natural resources (fresh water, food, wood, fossil fuels, and so on) to survive. The hydrosphere and water cycle provide sources of fresh water in the form of rivers, lakes, and groundwater. The biosphere and the carbon cycle provide food in the form of plants and animals, as well as wood for cooking, building, and heating.

Our ancestors were nomadic, constantly moving from one area to another as they used the available resources at their current location. But around 7,500 year ago, things began to change when humans invented agriculture. Rather than relying on hunting and gathering, humans learned to manage their food supply by growing crops and raising livestock, allowing them to settle in one area. The earliest civilizations arose near rivers, which provided their populations with fertile soil and fresh water for drinking and irrigating crops.

More recently, during the Industrial Revolution, humans developed the tools needed for the large-scale manufacturing of products. This sparked the beginning of the huge demand for fossil fuels such as coal, petroleum, and natural gas needed to provide the enormous energy requirements of these new manufacturing processes. These recent changes have allowed the global human population to grow rapidly to the point where our activities are now starting to have a measurable impact on our planet's systems.

Human impact

There are now over 7 billion humans living on Earth, and our ever-growing population consumes a lot of natural resources. Recent human activities have caused deforestation, pollution, and global warming, which are having a negative effect on Earth's systems. Humans are currently destroying vast areas of rain forest every year to provide space for settlements and farmland. The forests are the planet's lungs; they remove excess amounts of carbon dioxide from the atmosphere and release oxygen that animals (including humans) need to survive. Rain forests are also home to hundreds of thousands of different species of plants and animals that may become extinct because of the loss of habitat as the forests are destroyed. This will have a devastating impact on the biosphere and greatly reduce the diversity of life on Earth.

Cities produce a lot of waste and industrial pollution, which reduces the quality of the water and air. Beijing, for example, is often surrounded by thick clouds of smog, and the air quality is now so poor that many residents wear surgical masks whenever they go outside. Man-made plastics don't *biodegrade* (break down) as easily as natural materials, so when we throw these items away, they often end up polluting our freshwater resources and oceans.

Climate change

The most serious impact that humans are currently having on the planet, however, is *global warming* or *climate change.* Before the Industrial Revolution, the amount of carbon dioxide in the atmosphere was relatively stable, as maintained by the carbon cycle. But over the past century, the large-scale consumption of fossil fuels has led to a measurable increase in the amount of carbon dioxide present in the atmosphere. Over this same period, average global temperatures have gone up, the ice caps, ice sheets, and glaciers have shrunk, and sea levels across the planet have begun to rise. These trends are likely to continue unless we can find alternative sources of energy that reduce our reliance on fossil fuels.

REMEMBER

So who cares if the Earth becomes a little warmer? Isn't that a good thing? Well, not according to the experts. Scientists predict that global warming will have a severe impact on humans. Global crop failures and livestock shortages could become common as violent storms and flooding or severe droughts and the spread of infectious diseases destroy crops and kill animals. The loss of arable land due to shifting climate patterns and rising sea levels will also make agriculture more difficult to sustain. Many scientists believe that we are already starting to experience the early effects of global warming today, so it's clearly in humanity's best interest to begin addressing these problems now before it is too late.

Combating global warming

REMEMBER

So what can we do to reduce the negative impact that climate change may have on our fragile planet? It is largely agreed upon that the easiest and most significant way to conserve any resource, such as energy, is to increase efficiency. In this same line of thinking, because excess carbon dioxide is one of the main causes of global warming, we need to reduce our dependence on fossil fuels and develop alternative sources of renewable energy that don't produce carbon dioxide when burned. These include solar energy (from the sun), wind energy, and geothermal energy.

Hybrid and electric cars reduce the consumption of petroleum, but these cars are currently expensive and make up only a small fraction of all the vehicles currently on the roads. However, as new technologies are developed, alternatively powered vehicles and mass transit systems may begin to significantly reduce the amount of carbon dioxide released into the atmosphere each year. Lastly, but perhaps most importantly, deforestation and destruction of the rain forests must be slowed or stopped. We can alleviate the loss of rain forest lands by using less, recycling paper and wood products, and encouraging sustainable farming practices and urbanization.

This may all seem like a lot of work, but the careful management of our natural resources is the only way to ensure that they will still be available to us in the future. We all share the same small planet, so it's everyone's responsibility to look after it.

7

Practice Tests

Chapter 23

Practice Test 1

Taking a practice exam is the best way to test how well you know each subject area and is the key to improving your TASC scores, so this chapter contains the first of two complete practice tests that have been designed to simulate the real TASC exam. The entire test lasts about seven hours, with each section having its own time limits. The time limit and the number of questions you're expected to answer are listed in the directions on the front page of each of the five sections of the test. This information has also been summarized for you in Table 23-1 shown below.

TABLE 23-1 Breakdown of TASC Sections

Subject	Time in Minutes	Number of Questions
Language Arts–Reading	75	50 multiple choice questions
Language Arts–Writing	105	50 multiple choice questions plus one essay
Mathematics	50 (calculator section) 55 (no calculator section)	40 multiple choice questions and 12 gridded responses
Social Studies	75	47 multiple choice questions
Science	85	47 multiple choice questions

Try taking each part of the practice test in this chapter under exam conditions to get a good idea of how you'll do on the real exam. This will help you learn how to pace yourself during the real thing, and you'll experience what it feels like to take a full-length test.

REMEMBER

Skip questions you're really not sure about so you can focus on those questions that you can easily answer rather than wasting time on the ones that you can't. If you get stuck on a question, skip it and move on to the next. You can always come back to it at the end if you have any time left.

TIP

Because you don't get points off for wrong answers on the TASC, be sure to answer *all* questions. There is simply no excuse for leaving questions blank on the TASC exam.

WARNING

When writing your essay you must stay on topic. Essays that don't answer the question will earn zero points, no matter how well written they are.

For further tips on test-taking strategies, check out Chapter 27. This chapter is packed with strategies that strong test-takers adopt to maximize their chances of success on the TASC exam. It also points out the common mistakes to avoid on test day and how to sharpen your skills to achieve the score you deserve on the TASC.

Answer Sheet

TIP

When you're completing a paper-based test like this one, be careful how you place the marks on your answer grid. Make sure there are no stray marks and that you erase clearly. Also be sure that you're filling in your answer for the right corresponding question. If you skip a question, be sure you also skip the space on your answer sheet so that your answers still line up.

Section 1: Language Arts – Reading

1. Ⓐ Ⓑ Ⓒ Ⓓ	11. Ⓐ Ⓑ Ⓒ Ⓓ	21. Ⓐ Ⓑ Ⓒ Ⓓ	31. Ⓐ Ⓑ Ⓒ Ⓓ	41. Ⓐ Ⓑ Ⓒ Ⓓ
2. Ⓐ Ⓑ Ⓒ Ⓓ	12. Ⓐ Ⓑ Ⓒ Ⓓ	22. Ⓐ Ⓑ Ⓒ Ⓓ	32. Ⓐ Ⓑ Ⓒ Ⓓ	42. Ⓐ Ⓑ Ⓒ Ⓓ
3. Ⓐ Ⓑ Ⓒ Ⓓ	13. Ⓐ Ⓑ Ⓒ Ⓓ	23. Ⓐ Ⓑ Ⓒ Ⓓ	33. Ⓐ Ⓑ Ⓒ Ⓓ	43. Ⓐ Ⓑ Ⓒ Ⓓ
4. Ⓐ Ⓑ Ⓒ Ⓓ	14. Ⓐ Ⓑ Ⓒ Ⓓ	24. Ⓐ Ⓑ Ⓒ Ⓓ	34. Ⓐ Ⓑ Ⓒ Ⓓ	44. Ⓐ Ⓑ Ⓒ Ⓓ
5. Ⓐ Ⓑ Ⓒ Ⓓ	15. Ⓐ Ⓑ Ⓒ Ⓓ	25. Ⓐ Ⓑ Ⓒ Ⓓ	35. Ⓐ Ⓑ Ⓒ Ⓓ	45. Ⓐ Ⓑ Ⓒ Ⓓ
6. Ⓐ Ⓑ Ⓒ Ⓓ	16. Ⓐ Ⓑ Ⓒ Ⓓ	26. Ⓐ Ⓑ Ⓒ Ⓓ	36. Ⓐ Ⓑ Ⓒ Ⓓ	46. Ⓐ Ⓑ Ⓒ Ⓓ
7. Ⓐ Ⓑ Ⓒ Ⓓ	17. Ⓐ Ⓑ Ⓒ Ⓓ	27. Ⓐ Ⓑ Ⓒ Ⓓ	37. Ⓐ Ⓑ Ⓒ Ⓓ	47. Ⓐ Ⓑ Ⓒ Ⓓ
8. Ⓐ Ⓑ Ⓒ Ⓓ	18. Ⓐ Ⓑ Ⓒ Ⓓ	28. Ⓐ Ⓑ Ⓒ Ⓓ	38. Ⓐ Ⓑ Ⓒ Ⓓ	48. Ⓐ Ⓑ Ⓒ Ⓓ
9. Ⓐ Ⓑ Ⓒ Ⓓ	19. Ⓐ Ⓑ Ⓒ Ⓓ	29. Ⓐ Ⓑ Ⓒ Ⓓ	39. Ⓐ Ⓑ Ⓒ Ⓓ	49. Ⓐ Ⓑ Ⓒ Ⓓ
10. Ⓐ Ⓑ Ⓒ Ⓓ	20. Ⓐ Ⓑ Ⓒ Ⓓ	30. Ⓐ Ⓑ Ⓒ Ⓓ	40. Ⓐ Ⓑ Ⓒ Ⓓ	50. Ⓐ Ⓑ Ⓒ Ⓓ

Section 2: Language Arts – Writing

1. Ⓐ Ⓑ Ⓒ Ⓓ	11. Ⓐ Ⓑ Ⓒ Ⓓ	21. Ⓐ Ⓑ Ⓒ Ⓓ	31. Ⓐ Ⓑ Ⓒ Ⓓ	41. Ⓐ Ⓑ Ⓒ Ⓓ
2. Ⓐ Ⓑ Ⓒ Ⓓ	12. Ⓐ Ⓑ Ⓒ Ⓓ	22. Ⓐ Ⓑ Ⓒ Ⓓ	32. Ⓐ Ⓑ Ⓒ Ⓓ	42. Ⓐ Ⓑ Ⓒ Ⓓ
3. Ⓐ Ⓑ Ⓒ Ⓓ	13. Ⓐ Ⓑ Ⓒ Ⓓ	23. Ⓐ Ⓑ Ⓒ Ⓓ	33. Ⓐ Ⓑ Ⓒ Ⓓ	43. Ⓐ Ⓑ Ⓒ Ⓓ
4. Ⓐ Ⓑ Ⓒ Ⓓ	14. Ⓐ Ⓑ Ⓒ Ⓓ	24. Ⓐ Ⓑ Ⓒ Ⓓ	34. Ⓐ Ⓑ Ⓒ Ⓓ	44. Ⓐ Ⓑ Ⓒ Ⓓ
5. Ⓐ Ⓑ Ⓒ Ⓓ	15. Ⓐ Ⓑ Ⓒ Ⓓ	25. Ⓐ Ⓑ Ⓒ Ⓓ	35. Ⓐ Ⓑ Ⓒ Ⓓ	45. Ⓐ Ⓑ Ⓒ Ⓓ
6. Ⓐ Ⓑ Ⓒ Ⓓ	16. Ⓐ Ⓑ Ⓒ Ⓓ	26. Ⓐ Ⓑ Ⓒ Ⓓ	36. Ⓐ Ⓑ Ⓒ Ⓓ	46. Ⓐ Ⓑ Ⓒ Ⓓ
7. Ⓐ Ⓑ Ⓒ Ⓓ	17. Ⓐ Ⓑ Ⓒ Ⓓ	27. Ⓐ Ⓑ Ⓒ Ⓓ	37. Ⓐ Ⓑ Ⓒ Ⓓ	47. Ⓐ Ⓑ Ⓒ Ⓓ
8. Ⓐ Ⓑ Ⓒ Ⓓ	18. Ⓐ Ⓑ Ⓒ Ⓓ	28. Ⓐ Ⓑ Ⓒ Ⓓ	38. Ⓐ Ⓑ Ⓒ Ⓓ	48. Ⓐ Ⓑ Ⓒ Ⓓ
9. Ⓐ Ⓑ Ⓒ Ⓓ	19. Ⓐ Ⓑ Ⓒ Ⓓ	29. Ⓐ Ⓑ Ⓒ Ⓓ	39. Ⓐ Ⓑ Ⓒ Ⓓ	49. Ⓐ Ⓑ Ⓒ Ⓓ
10. Ⓐ Ⓑ Ⓒ Ⓓ	20. Ⓐ Ⓑ Ⓒ Ⓓ	30. Ⓐ Ⓑ Ⓒ Ⓓ	40. Ⓐ Ⓑ Ⓒ Ⓓ	50. Ⓐ Ⓑ Ⓒ Ⓓ

Section 3: Mathematics

1. Ⓐ Ⓑ Ⓒ Ⓓ	12. Ⓐ Ⓑ Ⓒ Ⓓ	23. Ⓐ Ⓑ Ⓒ Ⓓ	34. Ⓐ Ⓑ Ⓒ Ⓓ	45. Ⓐ Ⓑ Ⓒ Ⓓ
2. Ⓐ Ⓑ Ⓒ Ⓓ	13. Ⓐ Ⓑ Ⓒ Ⓓ	24. Ⓐ Ⓑ Ⓒ Ⓓ	35. _____	46. Ⓐ Ⓑ Ⓒ Ⓓ
3. Ⓐ Ⓑ Ⓒ Ⓓ	14. Ⓐ Ⓑ Ⓒ Ⓓ	25. Ⓐ Ⓑ Ⓒ Ⓓ	36. Ⓐ Ⓑ Ⓒ Ⓓ	47. Ⓐ Ⓑ Ⓒ Ⓓ
4. Ⓐ Ⓑ Ⓒ Ⓓ	15. _____	26. Ⓐ Ⓑ Ⓒ Ⓓ	37. Ⓐ Ⓑ Ⓒ Ⓓ	48. _____
5. Ⓐ Ⓑ Ⓒ Ⓓ	16. Ⓐ Ⓑ Ⓒ Ⓓ	27. Ⓐ Ⓑ Ⓒ Ⓓ	38. Ⓐ Ⓑ Ⓒ Ⓓ	49. Ⓐ Ⓑ Ⓒ Ⓓ
6. Ⓐ Ⓑ Ⓒ Ⓓ	17. _____	28. _____	39. _____	50. Ⓐ Ⓑ Ⓒ Ⓓ
7. _____	18. Ⓐ Ⓑ Ⓒ Ⓓ	29. Ⓐ Ⓑ Ⓒ Ⓓ	40. Ⓐ Ⓑ Ⓒ Ⓓ	51. _____
8. Ⓐ Ⓑ Ⓒ Ⓓ	19. Ⓐ Ⓑ Ⓒ Ⓓ	30. Ⓐ Ⓑ Ⓒ Ⓓ	41. Ⓐ Ⓑ Ⓒ Ⓓ	52. Ⓐ Ⓑ Ⓒ Ⓓ
9. Ⓐ Ⓑ Ⓒ Ⓓ	20. Ⓐ Ⓑ Ⓒ Ⓓ	31. Ⓐ Ⓑ Ⓒ Ⓓ	42. Ⓐ Ⓑ Ⓒ Ⓓ	
10. Ⓐ Ⓑ Ⓒ Ⓓ	21. _____	32. Ⓐ Ⓑ Ⓒ Ⓓ	43. _____	
11. _____	22. Ⓐ Ⓑ Ⓒ Ⓓ	33. Ⓐ Ⓑ Ⓒ Ⓓ	44. Ⓐ Ⓑ Ⓒ Ⓓ	

Section 4: Social Studies

1. Ⓐ Ⓑ Ⓒ Ⓓ	11. Ⓐ Ⓑ Ⓒ Ⓓ	21. Ⓐ Ⓑ Ⓒ Ⓓ	31. Ⓐ Ⓑ Ⓒ Ⓓ	41. Ⓐ Ⓑ Ⓒ Ⓓ
2. Ⓐ Ⓑ Ⓒ Ⓓ	12. Ⓐ Ⓑ Ⓒ Ⓓ	22. Ⓐ Ⓑ Ⓒ Ⓓ	32. Ⓐ Ⓑ Ⓒ Ⓓ	42. Ⓐ Ⓑ Ⓒ Ⓓ
3. Ⓐ Ⓑ Ⓒ Ⓓ	13. Ⓐ Ⓑ Ⓒ Ⓓ	23. Ⓐ Ⓑ Ⓒ Ⓓ	33. Ⓐ Ⓑ Ⓒ Ⓓ	43. Ⓐ Ⓑ Ⓒ Ⓓ
4. Ⓐ Ⓑ Ⓒ Ⓓ	14. Ⓐ Ⓑ Ⓒ Ⓓ	24. Ⓐ Ⓑ Ⓒ Ⓓ	34. Ⓐ Ⓑ Ⓒ Ⓓ	44. Ⓐ Ⓑ Ⓒ Ⓓ
5. Ⓐ Ⓑ Ⓒ Ⓓ	15. Ⓐ Ⓑ Ⓒ Ⓓ	25. Ⓐ Ⓑ Ⓒ Ⓓ	35. Ⓐ Ⓑ Ⓒ Ⓓ	45. Ⓐ Ⓑ Ⓒ Ⓓ
6. Ⓐ Ⓑ Ⓒ Ⓓ	16. Ⓐ Ⓑ Ⓒ Ⓓ	26. Ⓐ Ⓑ Ⓒ Ⓓ	36. Ⓐ Ⓑ Ⓒ Ⓓ	46. Ⓐ Ⓑ Ⓒ Ⓓ
7. Ⓐ Ⓑ Ⓒ Ⓓ	17. Ⓐ Ⓑ Ⓒ Ⓓ	27. Ⓐ Ⓑ Ⓒ Ⓓ	37. Ⓐ Ⓑ Ⓒ Ⓓ	47. Ⓐ Ⓑ Ⓒ Ⓓ
8. Ⓐ Ⓑ Ⓒ Ⓓ	18. Ⓐ Ⓑ Ⓒ Ⓓ	28. Ⓐ Ⓑ Ⓒ Ⓓ	38. Ⓐ Ⓑ Ⓒ Ⓓ	
9. Ⓐ Ⓑ Ⓒ Ⓓ	19. Ⓐ Ⓑ Ⓒ Ⓓ	29. Ⓐ Ⓑ Ⓒ Ⓓ	39. Ⓐ Ⓑ Ⓒ Ⓓ	
10. Ⓐ Ⓑ Ⓒ Ⓓ	20. Ⓐ Ⓑ Ⓒ Ⓓ	30. Ⓐ Ⓑ Ⓒ Ⓓ	40. Ⓐ Ⓑ Ⓒ Ⓓ	

Section 5: Science

1. Ⓐ Ⓑ Ⓒ Ⓓ	11. Ⓐ Ⓑ Ⓒ Ⓓ	21. Ⓐ Ⓑ Ⓒ Ⓓ	31. Ⓐ Ⓑ Ⓒ Ⓓ	41. Ⓐ Ⓑ Ⓒ Ⓓ
2. Ⓐ Ⓑ Ⓒ Ⓓ	12. Ⓐ Ⓑ Ⓒ Ⓓ	22. Ⓐ Ⓑ Ⓒ Ⓓ	32. Ⓐ Ⓑ Ⓒ Ⓓ	42. Ⓐ Ⓑ Ⓒ Ⓓ
3. Ⓐ Ⓑ Ⓒ Ⓓ	13. Ⓐ Ⓑ Ⓒ Ⓓ	23. Ⓐ Ⓑ Ⓒ Ⓓ	33. Ⓐ Ⓑ Ⓒ Ⓓ	43. Ⓐ Ⓑ Ⓒ Ⓓ
4. Ⓐ Ⓑ Ⓒ Ⓓ	14. Ⓐ Ⓑ Ⓒ Ⓓ	24. Ⓐ Ⓑ Ⓒ Ⓓ	34. Ⓐ Ⓑ Ⓒ Ⓓ	44. Ⓐ Ⓑ Ⓒ Ⓓ
5. Ⓐ Ⓑ Ⓒ Ⓓ	15. Ⓐ Ⓑ Ⓒ Ⓓ	25. Ⓐ Ⓑ Ⓒ Ⓓ	35. Ⓐ Ⓑ Ⓒ Ⓓ	45. Ⓐ Ⓑ Ⓒ Ⓓ
6. Ⓐ Ⓑ Ⓒ Ⓓ	16. Ⓐ Ⓑ Ⓒ Ⓓ	26. Ⓐ Ⓑ Ⓒ Ⓓ	36. Ⓐ Ⓑ Ⓒ Ⓓ	46. Ⓐ Ⓑ Ⓒ Ⓓ
7. Ⓐ Ⓑ Ⓒ Ⓓ	17. Ⓐ Ⓑ Ⓒ Ⓓ	27. Ⓐ Ⓑ Ⓒ Ⓓ	37. Ⓐ Ⓑ Ⓒ Ⓓ	47. Ⓐ Ⓑ Ⓒ Ⓓ
8. Ⓐ Ⓑ Ⓒ Ⓓ	18. Ⓐ Ⓑ Ⓒ Ⓓ	28. Ⓐ Ⓑ Ⓒ Ⓓ	38. Ⓐ Ⓑ Ⓒ Ⓓ	
9. Ⓐ Ⓑ Ⓒ Ⓓ	19. Ⓐ Ⓑ Ⓒ Ⓓ	29. Ⓐ Ⓑ Ⓒ Ⓓ	39. Ⓐ Ⓑ Ⓒ Ⓓ	
10. Ⓐ Ⓑ Ⓒ Ⓓ	20. Ⓐ Ⓑ Ⓒ Ⓓ	30. Ⓐ Ⓑ Ⓒ Ⓓ	40. Ⓐ Ⓑ Ⓒ Ⓓ	

Section 1: Language Arts – Reading

TIME: 75 minutes for 50 questions

DIRECTIONS: This section tests your knowledge of reading comprehension. Pick the best answer(s) for each question and then mark the space on your answer sheet that corresponds to the question number and the letter indicating your choice.

Read this passage and then answer the questions that follow.

From **A Christmas Carol,** *by Charles Dickens*

Scrooge never painted out Old Marley's name. There it stood, years afterwards, above the warehouse door: Scrooge and Marley. The firm was known as Scrooge and Marley. Sometimes people new to the business called Scrooge Scrooge, and sometimes Marley, but he answered to both names: it was all the same to him.

Oh! But he was a tight-fisted hand at the grind-stone, Scrooge! a squeezing, wrenching, grasping, scraping, clutching, covetous, old sinner! Hard and sharp as flint, from which no steel had ever struck out generous fire; secret, and self-contained, and solitary as an oyster. The cold within him froze his old features, nipped his pointed nose, shriveled his cheek, stiffened his gait; made his eyes red, his thin lips blue and spoke out shrewdly in his grating voice. A frosty rime was on his head, and on his eyebrows, and his wiry chin. He carried his own low temperature always about with him; he iced his office in the dogdays; and didn't thaw it one degree at Christmas.

External heat and cold had little influence on Scrooge. No warmth could warm, no wintry weather chill him. No wind that blew was bitterer than he, no falling snow was more intent upon its purpose, no pelting rain less open to entreaty. Foul weather didn't know where to have him. The heaviest rain, and snow, and hail, and sleet, could boast of the advantage over him in only one respect. They often "came down" handsomely, and Scrooge never did.

Nobody ever stopped him in the street to say, with gladsome looks, "My dear Scrooge, how are you? When will you come to see me?" No beggars implored him to bestow a trifle, no children asked him what it was o'clock, no man or woman ever once in all his life inquired the way to such and such a place, of Scrooge. Even the blind men's dogs appeared to know him; and when they saw him coming on, would tug their owners into doorways and up courts; and then would wag their tails as though they said, "No eye at all is better than an evil eye, dark master!"

But what did Scrooge care? It was the very thing he liked. To edge his way along the crowded paths of life, warning all human sympathy to keep its distance, was what the knowing ones call "nuts" to Scrooge.

The door of Scrooge's counting-house was open that he might keep his eye upon his clerk, who in a dismal little cell beyond, a sort of tank, was copying letters. Scrooge had a very small fire, but the clerk's fire was so very much smaller that it looked like one coal. But he couldn't replenish it, for Scrooge kept the coal-box in his own room; and so surely as the clerk came in with the shovel, the master predicted that it would be necessary for them to part. Wherefore the clerk put on his white comforter, and tried to warm himself at the candle; in which effort, not being a man of a strong imagination, he failed.

"A merry Christmas, uncle! God save you!" cried a cheerful voice. It was the voice of Scrooge's nephew, who came upon him so quickly that this was the first intimation he had of his approach.

"Bah!" said Scrooge, "Humbug!"

He had so heated himself with rapid walking in the fog and frost, this nephew of Scrooge's, that he was all in a glow; his face was ruddy and handsome; his eyes sparkled, and his breath smoked again.

"Christmas a humbug, uncle!" said Scrooge's nephew. "You don't mean that, I am sure."

"I do," said Scrooge. "Merry Christmas! What right have you to be merry? What reason have you to be merry? You're poor enough."

"Come, then," returned the nephew gaily. "What right have you to be dismal? What reason have you to be morose? You're rich enough."

Scrooge having no better answer ready on the spur of the moment, said "Bah!" again; and followed it up with "Humbug."

"Don't be cross, uncle!" said the nephew.

"What else can I be," returned the uncle, "when I live in such a world of fools as this? Merry Christmas! Out upon merry Christmas! What's Christmas time to you but a time for paying bills without money; a time for finding yourself a year older, but not an hour richer; a time for balancing your books and having every item in 'em through a round dozen of months presented dead against you? If I could work my will," said Scrooge indignantly, "every idiot who goes about with 'Merry Christmas' on his lips, should be boiled with his own pudding, and buried with a stake of holly through his heart. He should!"

"Uncle!" pleaded the nephew.

"Nephew!" returned the uncle, sternly, "keep Christmas in your own way, and let me keep it in mine."

"Keep it!" repeated Scrooge's nephew. "But you don't keep it."

"Let me leave it alone, then," said Scrooge. "Much good may it do you! Much good it has ever done you!"

"There are many things from which I might have derived good, by which I have not profited, I dare say," returned the nephew. "Christmas among the rest. But I am sure I have always thought of Christmas time, when it has come round — apart from the veneration due to its sacred name and origin, if anything belonging to it can be apart from that — as a good time: a kind, forgiving, charitable, pleasant time: the only time I know of, in the long calendar of the year, when men and women seem by one consent to open their shut-up hearts freely, and to think of people below them as if they really were fellow-passengers to the grave, and not another race of creatures bound on other journeys. And therefore, uncle, though it has never put a scrap of gold or silver in my pocket, I believe that it *has* done me good, and *will* do me good; and I say, God bless it!"

The clerk in the tank involuntarily applauded: becoming immediately sensible of the impropriety, he poked the fire, and extinguished the last frail spark for ever.

"Let me hear another sound from *you*," said Scrooge, "and you'll keep your Christmas by losing your situation. You're quite a powerful speaker, sir," he added, turning to his nephew. "I wonder you don't go into Parliament."

1. Who was Marley?

   (A) The passage does not say.

   (B) Scrooge's employee

   (C) Scrooge's nephew

   (D) Scrooge's ex-business partner

2. The author describes Scrooge as a very cold man who keeps his feelings to himself. Which lines from the passage best support this description?

   (A) Scrooge never painted out Old Marley's name. There it stood, years afterwards, above the warehouse door: Scrooge and Marley.

   (B) Sometimes people new to the business called Scrooge Scrooge, and sometimes Marley, but he answered to both names.

   (C) "Nephew!" returned the uncle, sternly, "keep Christmas in your own way, and let me keep it in mine."

   (D) Hard and sharp as flint, from which no steel had ever struck out generous fire; secret, and self-contained, and solitary as an oyster.

3. Read this excerpt from *A Christmas Carol.*

   Even the blind men's dogs appeared to know him; and when they saw him coming on, would tug their owners into doorways and up courts; and then would wag their tails as though they said, "No eye at all is better than an evil eye, dark master!"

   What does the author imply that the dogs are thinking?

   (A) It is better to be blind like the dog's master rather than nasty like Scrooge.

   (B) Only a blind man can see pure evil.

   (C) The dogs are "turning a blind eye" to their master's evil nature.

   (D) The best eye is an evil eye.

4. Scrooge's opinions about Christmas include all the following EXCEPT:

   (A) People who celebrate Christmas are foolish.

   (B) Christmas is a time to eat unusual candies such as "humbugs."

   (C) Christmas makes him angry.

   (D) Christmas is a time to take stock of one's financial situation.

5. All the following are given in the passage as reasons why Scrooge's nephew loves and celebrates Christmas EXCEPT:

   (A) Christmas is a time to be charitable to others.

   (B) Christmas is a time to celebrate its religious origins.

   (C) Christmas has made him better off financially.

   (D) Christmas helps people to connect with others around them.

6. According to the passage, what does Scrooge's financial situation appear to be?

   (A) Scrooge is a wealthy politician.

   (B) Scrooge is the wealthy owner of his own company but he doesn't appear to like spending money.

   (C) Scrooge is a poor employee at an unsuccessful business that cannot afford to heat its offices.

   (D) The passage does not say.

7. Read this excerpt from *A Christmas Carol.*

   "Let me hear another sound from *you*," said Scrooge, "and you'll keep your Christmas by losing your situation."

   Why does Scrooge say this to the clerk?

   (A) Scrooge is offering to give his employee the day off to celebrate Christmas.

   (B) Scrooge is suggesting that the clerk should consider becoming a politician.

   (C) Scrooge is inviting the clerk to join in the conversation about Christmas.

   (D) Scrooge is annoyed that his clerk agrees with his nephew and is threatening to dismiss his employee if he says another word.

GO ON TO NEXT PAGE

8. Read this excerpt from *A Christmas Carol.*

"You're quite a powerful speaker, sir," he added, turning to his nephew. "I wonder you don't go into Parliament."

What is Scrooge's intention when he says this to his nephew?

(A) to compliment his nephew on his powerful speech

(B) to give his nephew serious career advice

(C) to be sarcastic

(D) to assure his nephew that he would vote for him if he decided to become a politician

---

Read this passage and then answer the questions that follow.

From Animal Farm, by George Orwell

Every human being held it as an article of faith that the farm would go bankrupt sooner or later, and, above all, that the windmill would be a failure. They would meet in the public-houses and prove to one another by means of diagrams that the windmill was bound to fall down, or that if it did stand up, then that it would never work. And yet, against their will, they had developed a certain respect for the efficiency with which the animals were managing their own affairs. One symptom of this was that they had begun to call Animal Farm by its proper name and ceased to pretend that it was called the Manor Farm. They had also dropped their championship of Jones, who had given up hope of getting his farm back and gone to live in another part of the county. Except through Whymper, there was as yet no contact between Animal Farm and the outside world, but there were constant rumours that Napoleon was about to enter into a definite business agreement either with Mr. Pilkington of Foxwood or with Mr. Frederick of Pinchfield — but never, it was noticed, with both simultaneously.

It was about this time that the pigs suddenly moved into the farmhouse and took up their residence there. Again the animals seemed to remember that a resolution against this had been passed in the early days, and again Squealer was able to convince them that this was not the case. It was absolutely necessary, he said, that the pigs, who were the brains of the farm, should have a quiet place to work in. It was also more suited to the dignity of the Leader (for of late he had taken to speaking of Napoleon under the title of "Leader") to live in a house than in a mere sty. Nevertheless, some of the animals were disturbed when they heard that the pigs not only took their meals in the kitchen and used the drawing-room as a recreation room, but also slept in the beds. Boxer passed it off as usual with "Napoleon is always right!", but Clover, who thought she remembered a definite ruling against beds, went to the end of the barn and tried to puzzle out the Seven Commandments which were inscribed there. Finding herself unable to read more than individual letters, she fetched Muriel.

"Muriel," she said, "read me the Fourth Commandment. Does it not say something about never sleeping in a bed?"

With some difficulty Muriel spelt it out.

"It says, 'No animal shall sleep in a bed with sheets,'" she announced finally.

Curiously enough, Clover had not remembered that the Fourth Commandment mentioned sheets; but as it was there on the wall, it must have done so. And Squealer, who happened to be passing at this moment, attended by two or three dogs, was able to put the whole matter in its proper perspective.

"You have heard then, comrades," he said, "that we pigs now sleep in the beds of the farmhouse? And why not? You did not suppose, surely, that there was ever a ruling against beds? A bed merely means a place to sleep in. A pile of straw in a stall is a bed, properly regarded. The rule was against sheets, which are a human invention. We have removed the sheets from the farmhouse beds, and sleep between blankets. And very comfortable beds they are too! But not more comfortable than we need, I can tell you, comrades, with all the brainwork we have to do nowadays. You would not rob us of our repose, would you, comrades? You would not have us too tired to carry out our duties? Surely none of you wishes to see Jones back?"

The animals reassured him on this point immediately, and no more was said about the pigs sleeping in the farmhouse beds. And when, some days afterwards, it was announced that from now on the pigs would get up an hour later in the mornings than the other animals, no complaint was made about that either.

9. What event appears to have happened in the story just before the beginning of the excerpt?

   (A) The men had decided to build a windmill.

   (B) Mr. Jones, the previous owner of Manor Farm, decided to enter into a business agreement either with Mr. Pilkington or with Mr. Frederick.

   (C) Mr. Jones changed the name of his farm to Animal Farm.

   (D) The animals had staged a rebellion and have taken over the farm.

10. How did the humans' opinions regarding Animal Farm change over time?

    (A) from concealed anger to open hostility

    (B) from respect to anger

    (C) from disdain to respect and acceptance

    (D) from acceptance to rebellion

11. Who is Napoleon?

    (A) the owner of a neighboring farm that competes with Manor Farm

    (B) a farmer who has just bought Manor Farm from Mr. Jones

    (C) the leader of pigs

    (D) an army general

12. The role that Squealer plays in Animal Farm is similar to that of

    (A) a politician trying to excuse the unethical behavior of others.

    (B) a teacher trying to clarify confusing details to his students.

    (C) a humble co-worker who does not expect any special treatment.

    (D) the leader of a corporation.

13. Squealer mentions all the following reasons to convince the animals that the pigs should now sleep in the farmhouse EXCEPT

    (A) The pigs have important work to do and need a quiet place to think.

    (B) It is beneath the dignity of the leader to sleep in a sty.

    (C) The farmhouse provides good views of the entrance of the property so the pigs could warn the other animals if Jones tries to come back.

    (D) There is no rule against doing so.

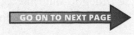

14. Read this excerpt from *Animal Farm*.

> Curiously enough, Clover had not remembered that the Fourth Commandment mentioned sheets; but as it was there on the wall, it must have done so.

What does the author imply by Clover's reaction to the Fourth Commandment?

(A) The Fourth Commandment has always mentioned sheets.

(B) The Fourth Commandment was recently changed to mention sheets without the other animals' knowledge.

(C) Clover is slowly losing her mind.

(D) Clover cannot read without her glasses.

15. What is the most likely reason why there were no complaints when it was announced that the pigs would get up an hour later in the mornings than the other animals?

(A) The other animals had been made to feel guilty about questioning the pigs' motives previously and were afraid that Jones would return if they continued to complain.

(B) The other animals felt that the pigs deserved the extra sleep due to their hard work.

(C) The other animals realized that pigs are superior animals.

(D) The other animals were afraid that the pigs would punish them.

16. What does the author imply about the pigs' behavior throughout the passage?

(A) The pigs are the most moral animals on the farm and always follow the rules.

(B) The pigs consider the other animals to be comrades and their equals.

(C) The pigs are the most hardworking animals on the farm.

(D) The pigs are not being entirely honest and are starting to behave more like humans than animals.

Read this passage and then answer the questions that follow.

From The Metamorphosis, *by Franz Kafka*

One morning, when Gregor Samsa woke from troubled dreams, he found himself transformed in his bed into a horrible vermin. He lay on his armour-like back, and if he lifted his head a little he could see his brown belly, slightly domed and divided by arches into stiff sections. The bedding was hardly able to cover it and seemed ready to slide off any moment. His many legs, pitifully thin compared with the size of the rest of him, waved about helplessly as he looked.

"What's happened to me?" he thought. It wasn't a dream. His room, a proper human room although a little too small, lay peacefully between its four familiar walls. A collection of textile samples lay spread out on the table — Samsa was a travelling salesman — and above it there hung a picture that he had recently cut out of an illustrated magazine and housed in a nice, gilded frame. It showed a lady fitted out with a fur hat and fur boa who sat upright, raising a heavy fur muff that covered the whole of her lower arm towards the viewer.

Gregor then turned to look out the window at the dull weather. Drops of rain could be heard hitting the pane, which made him feel quite sad. "How about if I sleep a little bit longer and forget all this nonsense," he thought, but that was something he was unable to do because he was used to sleeping on his right, and in his present state couldn't get into that position. However hard he threw himself onto his right, he always rolled back to where he was. He must have tried it a hundred times, shut his eyes so that he wouldn't have to look at the floundering legs, and only stopped when he began to feel a mild, dull pain there that he had never felt before.

"Oh, God," he thought, "what a strenuous career it is that I've chosen! Travelling day in and day out. Doing business like this takes much more effort than doing your own business at home, and on top of that there's the curse of travelling, worries about making train connections, bad and irregular food, contact with different people all the time so that you can never get to know anyone or become friendly with them. It can all go to Hell!" He felt a slight itch up on his belly; pushed himself slowly up on his back towards the head-board so that he could lift his head better; found where the itch was, and saw that it was covered with lots of little white spots which he didn't know what to make of; and when he tried to feel the place with one of his legs he drew it quickly back because as soon as he touched it he was overcome by a cold shudder.

He slid back into his former position. "Getting up early all the time," he thought, "it makes you stupid. You've got to get enough sleep. Other travelling salesmen live a life of luxury. For instance, whenever I go back to the guest house during the morning to copy out the contract, these gentlemen are always still sitting there eating their breakfasts. I ought to just try that with my boss; I'd get kicked out on the spot. But who knows, maybe that would be the best thing for me. If I didn't have my parents to think about I'd have given in my notice a long time ago, I'd have gone up to the boss and told him just what I think, tell him everything I would, let him know just what I feel. He'd fall right off his desk! And it's a funny sort of business to be sitting up there at your desk, talking down at your subordinates from up there, especially when you have to go right up close because the boss is hard of hearing. Well, there's still some hope; once I've got the money together to pay off my parents' debt to him — another five or six years I suppose — that's definitely what I'll do. That's when I'll make the big change. First of all though, I've got to get up, my train leaves at five."

He was still hurriedly thinking all this through, unable to decide to get out of the bed, when the clock struck quarter to seven. There was a cautious knock at the door near his head. "Gregor," somebody called — it was his mother — "it's quarter to seven. Didn't you want to go somewhere?" That gentle voice! Gregor was shocked when he heard his own voice answering, it could hardly be recognized as the voice he had had before. As if from deep inside him, there was a painful and uncontrollable squeaking mixed in with it, the words could be made out at first but then there was a sort of echo which made them unclear, leaving the hearer unsure whether he had heard properly or not. Gregor had wanted to give a full answer and explain everything, but in the circumstances contented himself with saying: "Yes, mother, yes, thank-you, I'm getting up now."

17. What is the main purpose of the passage?

  (A) to shock the reader

  (B) to show what type of person Gregor Samsa is

  (C) to introduce a main character and the background pressures that have caused his feelings of isolation

  (D) to discuss a recurring dream that the main character has when he feels happy

18. What appears to have happened to Gregor during the night?

  (A) He has turned into a giant cockroach.

  (B) He has turned into a rat.

  (C) He was sleepwalking and has now woken up in the wrong room.

  (D) He was out partying with his friends and is now feeling sick.

GO ON TO NEXT PAGE ➤

19. Where does this part of the story take place?

    (A) in Gregor's parents' house

    (B) in a hotel for vacationers

    (C) in a guest house for traveling salesmen

    (D) in Gregor's luxury mansion

20. Read this excerpt from *The Metamorphosis*.

It showed a lady fitted out with a fur hat and fur boa who sat upright, raising a heavy fur muff that covered the whole of her lower arm towards the viewer.

Who is the lady in the picture?

    (A) Gregor's mother

    (B) Gregor's wife

    (C) Gregor's daughter

    (D) an unknown lady from a magazine

21. What type of job does Gregor have?

    (A) He is a hotel inspector.

    (B) He is a traveling salesman.

    (C) He sells cars.

    (D) He is currently unemployed.

22. Read this excerpt from *The Metamorphosis*.

He'd fall right off his desk! And it's a funny sort of business to be sitting up there at your desk, talking down at your subordinates from up there, especially when you have to go right up close because the boss is hard of hearing.

What reason is implied to explain why Gregor's boss prefers to sit on his desk rather than on a chair?

    (A) He is partially deaf, and sitting on his desk helps him to hear his employees' concerns.

    (B) He likes to look down on his employees and make them feel inferior.

    (C) His office chair is broken.

    (D) His desk is extremely comfortable.

23. Why does Gregor continue working for a boss whom he clearly despises?

    (A) He enjoys traveling.

    (B) He loves his job.

    (C) He needs to pay off his parents' debt to his boss.

    (D) He is saving up to buy a car.

24. All the following factors add to the overall feeling of despair that Gregor is experiencing EXCEPT

    (A) the constant demands of his job

    (B) his relationship with his boss

    (C) financial pressure from his parents' debt

    (D) his relationship with his wife

Read this passage and then answer the questions that follow.

From The Secret Life of Dust, *by Hannah Holmes (Wiley)*

Flying diatoms don't add significantly to the airborne vegetable matter, in terms of simple tonnage. But when these glass-shelled algae do take a spin through the atmosphere, they raise interesting questions. They seem to defy the size limit for far-flying dust, for one thing. And they may sometimes fly with a purpose.

Michael Ram, a professor of physics at the University of Buffalo, has become an expert at teasing these tiny organisms out of ice cores from Antarctica and Greenland. Deep glaciers preserve thousands upon thousands of fine layers, each representing a year. And trapped in each layer is a sprinkling of fallen desert dust, Stardust, volcanic ash, pollen, insect parts — and diatoms. Ram melts a bit of ice, then puts the remaining sediment under a microscope.

The diatoms, he says, stand out due to their geometric perfection. Desert dust, under the microscope, resembles shattered rock. But diatoms often resemble delicately etched pill-boxes or broken shards of the same.

Most diatoms spend their brief lives adrift in rivers, ponds, lakes, and oceans. And when they die, their little shells sink. Ram says the ideal source of diatom dust is a shallow lake that shrinks in the dry season, exposing the sediment at its edges to the wind. Africa and the western United States are both pocked with excellent candidates.

Ram originally intended to use the diatoms he found to trace the source of the dust and diatoms in each sample: if the ice of one century was rich in North American diatoms, and the next century's ice held African diatoms, he could conclude that the prevailing wind had shifted. This might reveal something about the dynamics of climate change. But Ram's diatoms proved coy about their place of origin. Many of them look alike. Scientists with more diatom expertise are pursuing this line of inquiry.

And Ram's diatoms have caused additional head scratching. Generally, scientists don't expect things much larger than a few hundredths of a hair's width to fly long distances. But Ram has seen disks as wide as a hundred, or even two hundred, microns — that's a whopping two hairs in diameter. "These diatoms are large, but they have a large surface area, and they're light," Ram speculates in the accent that remains from his European upbringing. "They're like Frisbees. They're very aerodynamic."

The size of the diatoms may also relate to the strength of the wind that lifted them. An uncommonly strong wind can lift uncommonly large dust, as a survey of hailstone cores has suggested. Carried up into a storm cloud and then coated in ice until they fell again have been such "dusts" as small insects, birds, and at least one gopher tortoise. Perhaps a large diatom is not such a challenge.

But a third source of puzzlement is what appears to be a complete colony of diatoms that evidently dwelled smack atop the Greenland glacier about four hundred years ago. It is common for living diatoms to blow into melt pools at the edges of glaciers and there start a family. But the founder of the little clan Ram discovered apparently flew all the way to the center of the immense island before dropping into a puddle. And that pioneer was still in good enough shape to launch a modest dynasty.

25. The best title for this passage is

(A) The Life and Work of Professor Ram

(B) A Day in the Life of Diatoms

(C) Diatoms: Windborne Wonders

(D) A Scientific Study of Algae

26. According to the passage, "flying diatoms" are

(A) tiny winged insects.

(B) small pieces of glass.

(C) dead algae that is transported through the air.

(D) living or dead algae that is transported through the air.

27. Read this excerpt from *The Secret Life of Dust*.

"These diatoms are large, but they have a large surface area, and they're light," Ram speculates in the accent that remains from his European upbringing. "They're like Frisbees. They're very aerodynamic."

Why does professor Ram compare diatoms to Frisbees?

(A) to give the reader an easy-to-visualize example of a large object that can fly long distances

(B) He loves playing with Frisbees.

(C) Frisbees are about the same size as diatoms.

(D) Both Frisbees and diatoms come from Europe.

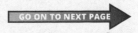GO ON TO NEXT PAGE

28. Scientists who study diatoms are seeking the answers to all the following puzzles EXCEPT:

(A) how diatoms are able to defy the size limit for far-flying dust

(B) how a single diatom could find a small puddle in the center of such a large country like Greenland

(C) where diatoms spend most of their brief lives

(D) how diatoms sometimes appear to fly with a purpose

29. Read this excerpt from *The Secret Life of Dust*.

Michael Ram, a professor of physics at the University of Buffalo, has become an expert at teasing these tiny organisms out of ice cores from Antarctica and Greenland.

The word "teasing" as it is used in the context of this paragraph can best be translated as

(A) making fun of.

(B) extracting.

(C) encasing.

(D) annoying.

30. What unusual feature of diatoms stands out when they are viewed under a microscope?

(A) their resemblance to shattered rock

(B) their bright colors

(C) they are usually covered in desert dust

(D) their geometric perfection

31. Read this excerpt from *The Secret Life of Dust*.

An uncommonly strong wind can lift uncommonly large dust, as a survey of hailstone cores has suggested. Carried up into a storm cloud and then coated in ice until they fell again have been such "dusts" as small insects, birds, and at least one gopher tortoise.

Why does the author mention the gopher tortoise?

(A) Gopher tortoises are often found covered in diatom dust.

(B) Gopher tortoises feed on the diatoms.

(C) to reinforce the theory that heavy objects can be lifted and transported by strong winds

(D) He is using the gopher tortoise as a metaphor.

Read the two passages and then answer the questions that follow. Passage I is an excerpt from The House of Science, *by Philip R. Holzinger (Wiley). It discusses the origins of the Earth. Passage II is an excerpt from* The Big Splat, or How Our Moon Came to Be, *by Dana Mackenzie (Wiley). In Passage II, the author discusses Immanuel Kant's theories on the origin and nature of the solar system.*

Passage 1

The story of our earth begins about 4.6 billion years ago — a time when the rest of the planets in our solar system were also forming. Early in its history, our planet was made up of a hodgepodge of materials, some of which were radioactive. These radioactive materials generated great quantities of heat, as did the large number of meteors that struck the earth at this time. The heat generated was sufficient to melt most of the planet, making our early earth a forbidding molten world!

Passage 2

Kant's model of the solar system began with an initial, formless cloud of gas or smoke, which contracts under the force of gravity. One might expect the cloud to simply collapse to a point, end of story. But Kant assumed that the "fine particles" in the cloud would also repel each other. (He made an incorrect analogy to the diffusion of smoke, which he thought was due to a repulsive force.) This repulsion would give them a sideways motion and allow them to take up circular orbits around the growing Sun. After many collisions between these orbiting particles [Kant thought], an overall direction of rotation would be established.

32. What does the word "hodgepodge" mean as it is used in the context of Passage 1?

    (A) a dangerous group

    (B) a confused mixture

    (C) an anomaly

    (D) a hot meal

33. According to Passage 1, what caused most of the Earth to melt?

    (A) the heat from the sun

    (B) meteors that passed by close to the Earth

    (C) the heat from radioactive elements and collision with objects from outer space

    (D) nuclear explosions

34. Why does the author of Passage 1 end the paragraph with an exclamation point?

    (A) to let the reader know that he disapproves of radioactive elements

    (B) The author was probably bored of using periods to end his sentences.

    (C) to emphasize the great difference in the conditions on Earth at that time compared to today

    (D) The author wants the reader to know he is feeling angry.

35. What does the word "analogy" mean as it is used in the context of Passage 2?

    (A) an analysis

    (B) a mistake

    (C) an assumption

    (D) a comparison

36. Both passages are primarily concerned with

    (A) the dangers of radioactive materials.

    (B) conditions on Earth long ago.

    (C) astronomy.

    (D) the origin of planets and other astronomical objects.

37. What is the main difference between Passage 1 and Passage 2?

    (A) Passage 1 focuses on how the planets became molten, whereas Passage 2 focuses on why the planets spin.

    (B) Passage 1 focuses on the dangers of radioactive particles, whereas Passage 2 focuses on their benefits.

    (C) Passage 1 includes quotes from an expert, whereas Passage 2 does not.

    (D) Passage 1 focuses on the origin of the moon, whereas Passage 2 focuses on the origin of the Earth.

Read this passage and then answer the questions that follow.

"How Must Employees Behave?" (Wiley)

It is expected that employees behave in a respectful, responsible, professional manner. Therefore, each employee must do the following:

- Wear appropriate clothing and use safety equipment where needed.

- Refrain from the use and possession of alcohol and/or illicit drugs and associated paraphernalia throughout the duration of the work day.

- Refrain from associating with those who pass, use, and are under the influence of illicit drugs and/or alcohol.

- Address all other employees and supervisors with courtesy and respect, using non-offensive language.

 GO ON TO NEXT PAGE

- Accept the authority of supervisors without argument. If you consider an action unfair, inform the Human Resources department.

- Respect the work environment of this company and conduct oneself in a manner conducive to the growth and the enhancement of our business.

- Refrain from inviting visitors to our place of work to keep the premises secure.

- Promote the dignity of all persons, regardless of gender, creed, or culture and conduct oneself with dignity.

- If the employee chooses *not* to comply:

  - On the first offense, the employee meets with his or her supervisor. A representative from Human Resources may choose to attend.

  - On the second offense, the employee meets with the Vice President of Human Resources before returning to work.

  - On the third offense, the employee is dismissed.

38. According to these rules, are employees allowed to invite friends to visit them at work?

(A) yes, the more the merrier

(B) no because of security issues

(C) only on casual Fridays

(D) The rules do not say.

39. According to these rules, what should an employee do if he believes his supervisor is treating him unfairly?

(A) Obey the supervisor without question.

(B) Start an argument with the supervisor.

(C) Ignore the supervisor's requests.

(D) Inform the Human Resources department.

40. What is the company's policy regarding sexist behavior?

(A) Employees must not wear "sexy" outfits.

(B) It will not be tolerated.

(C) It is fine as long as everyone "gets the joke."

(D) Only supervisors are allowed to be sexist.

41. What would happen to a new employee who is caught drinking a beer during lunchtime while at work?

(A) The employee would be fired immediately.

(B) The employee would be required to meet with his or her supervisor.

(C) The employee would be required to meet with the Vice President of Human Resources before returning to work.

(D) The employee would be asked to organize the office Christmas party.

42. Read this excerpt from "How Employees Must Behave."

If the employee chooses *not* to comply . . .

What is the most likely reason why the company used the word "choose" in this statement?

(A) to shift the responsibility for non-compliance back to the employee rather than the company

(B) The word "choose" was probably selected at random.

(C) to emphasize that employees must obey their supervisors without question

(D) to play "mind games" with the employees

43. All the following are likely reasons why the company has announced its policy on employee behavior EXCEPT:

(A) to ensure that employees understand what behavior is expected of them

(B) to make it harder to dismiss disruptive employees

(C) to ensure the safety of the working environment

(D) to make the working environment more pleasant for everyone

---

Read this passage and then answer the questions that follow.

From Photography For Dummies, *by Russell Hart (Wiley)*

If you've ever had to figure out where to stick batteries in your child's latest electronic acquisition, then loading batteries in your point-and-shoot shouldn't be a challenge. Turn off your camera when you install them; the camera may go crazy opening and closing its lens. (Some cameras turn themselves off after you install new batteries, so you have to turn them back on to shoot.)

With big point-and-shoot models, you typically open a latched cover on the bottom to install batteries. More compact models have a battery compartment under a door or flap that is incorporated into the side or grip of the camera. You may have to pry open such doors with a coin.

More annoying are covers on the bottom that you open by loosening a screw. (You need a coin for this type, too.) And most annoying are battery covers that aren't hinged and come off completely when you unscrew them. If you have one of these, don't change batteries while standing over a sewer grate, in a field of tall grass, or on a pier.

Whether loading four AAs or a single lithium, make sure that the batteries are correctly oriented as you insert them. You'll find a diagram and/or plus and minus markings, usually within the compartment or on the inside of the door.

If your camera doesn't turn on and the batteries are correctly installed, the batteries may have lost their punch from sitting on a shelf too long. Which is where the battery icon comes in.

If your camera has an LCD panel, an icon tells you when battery power is low.

44. What device does the passage explain how to install batteries into?

(A) an electronic device recently purchased by your child

(B) a cellphone

(C) a camera

(D) The passage does not specify.

45. What must you do first before installing the batteries?

(A) turn on the device

(B) turn off the device

(C) open and close the lens rapidly

(D) open a latched cover or concealed door

46. How do you know when you will soon need to replace the batteries?

   (A) The device is dead.

   (B) The batteries will automatically eject from the device.

   (C) A battery icon tells you when battery power is low.

   (D) The LCD panel is too bright.

47. When you are about to load new batteries into an empty device, what guidance is given regarding selecting the correct orientation of the batteries?

   (A) The LCD panel will display the correct battery orientation.

   (B) A battery icon tells you which way the batteries should be placed.

   (C) The orientation of the batteries is not important.

   (D) A diagram and/or plus and minus markings is present within the compartment or on the inside of the door.

48. Assuming that you have already loaded new batteries into the device, how do you know if you have oriented them incorrectly?

   (A) The device will not switch on.

   (B) A battery icon tells you that the batteries are oriented incorrectly.

   (C) The batteries will automatically eject from the device.

   (D) The LCD panel will be dimly lit.

49. Read this excerpt from *Photography For Dummies,* which refers to unhinged battery covers.

   If you have one of these, don't change batteries while standing over a sewer grate, in a field of tall grass, or on a pier.

   Why should precautions be taken when changing the batteries of devices that have unhinged covers?

   (A) The entire cover comes off when you unscrew them.

   (B) You may get an electric shock if you are standing near water.

   (C) Rain or dirt may get into the battery compartment.

   (D) People may be watching you.

50. Who is most likely to find the article the useful?

   (A) an amateur photographer

   (B) a professional photographer

   (C) a child who has just purchased a new cellphone

   (D) a battery manufacturer

Section 2: Language Arts – Writing

Part 1: Language

TIME: 55 minutes for 50 questions

DIRECTIONS: This section tests your ability to identify various types of errors in writing. Pick the best answer(s) for each question and then mark the space on your answer sheet that corresponds to the question number and the letter indicating your choice.

1. Which of these sentences is punctuated correctly?

   (A) Susan purchased a life insurance policy; which asked for her home address.

   (B) Since she had just read an article about the dangers of sharing too much personal information, Susan was reluctant to write her address.

   (C) Instead: she attached a note with a request to call, email, or text her for the information.

   (D) When the insurance office worker saw the note; she laughed and laughed.

2. Read this paragraph.

   Summer is the busiest time of year for American highways. From May to August, millions of Americans depart on road trips and vacations. However, gas prices rise during this time of year, making such trips even more expensive.

   Which sentence *best* concludes this paragraph?

   (A) Increasingly, Americans are concluding that using public transportation makes for a cheaper trip.

   (B) Planes are expensive to own and operate.

   (C) October is the least busy month for American highways.

   (D) Gas prices are affected by the cost of crude oil, which can vary widely.

3. Which of these sentences includes a misspelled word?

   (A) Annette felt relieved when she saw her score on the test.

   (B) Bartho was permanently certified to drive a truck.

   (C) Chan wants to get his licence too.

   (D) The road runs by the cemetery.

4. Read this sentence.

   After running the marathon, Mercedes feeling exhausted but happy.

   Which of these is the *most* accurate and effective revision to the sentence?

   (A) After running the marathon, Mercedes felt exhausted but happy.

   (B) After she ran the marathon, happy and exhausted describe how Mercedes felt.

   (C) She ran the marathon and will be feeling exhausted but happy.

   (D) After she ran the marathon, Mercedes was left to feel exhausted but happy.

5. Read this sentence.

   From below, we heard their cries for help.

   Which revision of the sentence *best* expresses the idea correctly and precisely?

   (A) We heard their cries for help and ran below.

   (B) Their cries of help from below were heard by us.

   (C) We heard their cries for help from below.

   (D) Below their cries, we heard their help.

6. Which of these sentences is punctuated correctly?

   (A) I was born in nineteen eighty-four.

   (B) I found all of the americans in the back.

   (C) Who is that guy.

   (D) Sheila was asked to fill out an I-90.

7. Read this paragraph.

They generally spend their entire lives in less than a quarter-acre of land. Voles build a system of burrows and tunnels, although they do not match the complexity of other animals and insects. Although commonly mistaken for mice, voles are a distinct animal, which is clear when their heads can be seen.

Which sentence would *best* open the paragraph to introduce the topic?

(A) Although little-understood, voles are widely believed to be the world travelers of the rodent family.

(B) If you see a vole, don't scream!

(C) Many people pass by voles every day without realizing that the little animals are underfoot.

(D) Voles are not mice.

Read this excerpt of a draft of an essay. Then answer Questions 8 and 9.

When Ada Lovelace was born in 1815, her birth was noted because of her famous father: Lord Byron. Her father separated from her mother, Anne Isabella Byron, just a month after Ada was born. He died when Ada was 8 years old. In order to guard against the mental illness Anne worried that Ada would inherit from her father, the mother encouraged the daughter to study mathematics and logic.

Chief among Ada's successes were her work on Charles Babbage's early mechanical general-purpose computer, which they called the "Analytical Engine." Notes that Ada made in developing the machine reveal what is widely believed to be an algorithm intended to be performed by the engine. This algorithm has given rise to the idea that Ada was the world's first computer programmer. This is an idea that's difficult to dispute.

8. Which sentence would be the *most* effective addition to the end of the first paragraph?

(A) Ada developed an algorithm that was necessary for computing.

(B) Among other notables born in 1815 was Elizabeth Cady Stanton.

(C) She had lost her father when she was still very young.

(D) She would go on to achieve far more than was expected by a well-born lady of her time.

9. Which revision *most* effectively combines the ideas of the last two sentences of the second paragraph?

(A) This algorithm has given rise to the idea that Ada was the world's first computer programmer, an idea that's difficult to dispute.

(B) This algorithm, which is an idea that's difficult to dispute, has given rise to the idea that Ada was the world's first computer programmer.

(C) Algorithms are undisputable, and so is the idea that Ada was the world's first computer programmer.

(D) Given that she was the world's first computer programmer, Ada's algorithm is difficult to dispute.

10. Which of these sentences contains an error or errors in capitalization?

   (A) Every Winter, the students gather for a carnival.

   (B) It's held on Main Street but stretches to north and east.

   (C) The dunking booth is the favorite for all the faculty because the school principal takes a turn!

   (D) Alumni from as far away as Brooklyn and Queens attend.

11. Read these sentences.

   Inevitably, some of the swimmers must stop racing to rehydrate, despite the time they lose in the race. Still, they know that rehydration is _____ to avoid physical collapse.

   Which word, when added in the blank, would *best* stress the importance of rehydration?

   (A) helpful

   (B) vital

   (C) optional

   (D) important

12. Read this sentence.

   Once she organized all of the new library books, the head librarian had given LaTonya a break.

   Which of these is the most correct and concise revision to the sentence?

   (A) Once she had organized all of the new library books, the head librarian had given LaTonya a break.

   (B) Once she took a break, LaTonya organized all of the new library books.

   (C) Once she was finished organizing the new library books, the head librarian gave LaTonya a break.

   (D) Once LaTonya was finished organizing the new library books, the head librarian gave her a break.

13. Which of these sentences contains a mis-spelled word?

   (A) After Andrew took a financial planning course, he was eager to draft a budget.

   (B) Most of the people we met had trans-fered their membership already.

   (C) "This is all right by me," Julia said.

   (D) She concurred at first but then decided not to agree.

14. Read this sentence.

   Maria found the television show boring, she much preferred the movie.

   What change should be made to correct the sentence's punctuation?

   (A) Change the comma to a period.

   (B) Eliminate the comma.

   (C) Change the comma to a semicolon.

   (D) Add a comma after the word "show."

15. Which of these sentences contains a gram-matical error?

   (A) Either Michael or Peter are in charge of the field trip.

   (B) Irina, Nancy, and I have arranged for tickets.

   (C) If you see Michael or Irina, give me a call.

   (D) Neither he nor she has the directions to the museum.

16. Read this sentence.

   The idea of taking a trip to Paris was presented to the club by our president, Lu Wei.

   Which of these is the *most* accurate and effec-tive revision to the sentence?

   (A) Taking a trip to Paris, as a club, was the idea presented by Lu Wei, the club president.

   (B) President Lu Wei presented the idea of taking a club trip to Paris.

   (C) President Lu Wei presented the club with the idea of taking a trip.

   (D) Club president Lu Wei presented the idea of a trip to Paris.

GO ON TO NEXT PAGE ▶

17. Read this paragraph.

The school board met to discuss the problem of underage drinking after high school football games. The problem has increased, they noted, since a 24-hour grocery story carrying beer has opened down the street from the football field. "Perhaps we can open a discussion with the store owners about the penalties for selling alcohol to minors," Sam Bonds, the board president stated.

Which sentence *best* concludes this paragraph?

(A) The board ultimately voted in favor of approaching the store amicably.

(B) Sam Bonds runs a construction business.

(C) Underage drinking is a national problem.

(D) Underage drinking is far less of an issue at high school soccer games.

Read this excerpt of a draft of a report. Then answer Questions 18–20.

Although many readers will associate the song "Respect" with Aretha Franklin's definitive version, the song was written and first recorded by Otis Redding in 1965. Franklin's version became a hit upon release in 1967. _____ the song is recognizably the same in both versions, each artist gave it a unique flavor. Redding's song is a plea that his woman return to him — he'll give her anything she wants, so long as she respects him. He sings in the voice of a hardworking man who wants to come home to the comforts he expects. The song returns repeatedly to the idea of respect, even in the verses, and has the feel of a blues song.

It's more up-tempo, jazzed to life by the backup singers' — Franklin's sisters Erma and Carolyn — repetition of "Sock it to me." Franklin's version also includes the iconic spelling of R-E-S-P-E-C-T as part of the bridge, an improvisation that propels the song to a new level.

18. Which word would *best* fit in the blank to clarify the transition between ideas?

(A) however

(B) since

(C) although

(D) perhaps

19. Which sentence would be the most effective addition to the beginning of the second paragraph?

(A) Franklin turned the song into a feminist declaration, demanding the respect she knows she deserves.

(B) Franklin's version of the song is different.

(C) Redding wrote the song.

(D) Many people don't realize just who the backup singers on Franklin's version are.

20. Where might the author add a paragraph break to better organize the text?

(A) after the first sentence

(B) after the second sentence

(C) after the third sentence

(D) after the fourth sentence

21. Read this sentence.

> I would expect Nigel surprise everyone with his insights.

Which of these is the *most* accurate and effective revision to the sentence?

(A) I would expect Nigel to surprise everyone with his insights.

(B) Nigel surprising everyone with his insights is expected.

(C) I would expect Nigel had impressed everyone with his insights.

(D) I would expect Nigel surprising everyone with his insights.

22. Which of these sentences contains a misspelled word?

(A) Francisco relieved the pitcher before the inning began.

(B) Although Francisco usually played first base, he had maintained his pitching ability.

(C) His techinque was strong and he had an exceptional curveball.

(D) While subbing in a position player was not ideal, Francisco did a brilliant job.

23. Which of these sentences is punctuated correctly?

(A) *Our Town,* is a play about the fictional town of Grover's Corner, New Hampshire.

(B) Among the major roles: the Stage Manager, Mrs. Webb, Mr. Webb and Emily.

(C) More than 30 characters appear in the play.

(D) The play is considered a "classic".

24. Which of these sentences contains an error or errors in capitalization?

(A) We traveled to the West after we heard the news.

(B) I reread *To Kill a Mockingbird* last summer.

(C) Jackson asked for recommendations for a good restaurant in Pittsburgh.

(D) This is the last time I'll take german this semester.

25. Read this paragraph.

> Johnstown, Pennsylvania is sometimes called "Flood City" because three major floods have devastated the town. The worst was in 1889, when more than 2,000 people were killed by a flood that began in the Allegheny Mountains east of the city and tore through the town. Floods in the 1930s and 1970s caused significant damage as well, although less loss of life.

Which sentence *best* concludes this paragraph?

(A) There were no floods after 1979.

(B) The nickname reflects Johnstown's characteristic humor, along with the ability to make the best of a bad situation.

(C) Baltimore, Maryland, is called "Charm City."

(D) Another important town in Pennsylvania is Harrisburg, the state capitol.

Read this excerpt of a draft of an essay. Then answer Questions 26 and 27.

While baseball is widely believed to have been invented by Abner Doubleday in the 1800s, we now know that it evolved from older bat-and-ball games. Evidence shows that it may have been developed in England.

Today, baseball is considered "as American as apple pie" as the saying goes. Also, it is called the "national pastime." Even if baseball was developed in England, it is so identified with America now that most people believe it was invented in the States. In the end, where baseball began is not as important as where it was perfected: in the United States of America.

GO ON TO NEXT PAGE

26. How could the first two sentences of the second paragraph best be combined?

(A) Today, baseball is considered to be "as American as apple pie" and the "national pastime," as the saying goes.

(B) Called the "national pastime," baseball is considered "as American as apple pie" today.

(C) As the saying goes, the "national pastime," baseball, is "as American as apple pie."

(D) The United States sees baseball as "American as apple pie" and a "national pastime" as it is called.

27. Which sentence would be the *most* effective addition to the beginning of the first paragraph?

(A) Is baseball American in origin?

(B) Baseball is a game played with a bat and a ball.

(C) Some people say basketball is the only sport truly invented in America. Is it?

(D) From the dawn of time, man has developed ways to compete.

28. Read this sentence.

The movie was much longer than we expected, and thus for that reason we canceled our dinner plans.

Which revision of the sentence *best* expresses the idea precisely and concisely?

(A) The movie was much longer than we expected, so for that reason we canceled our dinner plans.

(B) The movie was much longer than we expected, canceling our dinner plans.

(C) The movie was much longer than we expected, forcing us to cancel our dinner plans.

(D) The movie was much longer than we expected. Therefore, canceling our dinner plans.

29. Read this paragraph.

Begin by placing both the jars and the lids you intend to use in boiling water. After the jars and lids are sterilized, allow them to remain in the warm water. Remove one jar at a time, and then pour in the jelly, quickly sealing it with a lid and a canning ring. You will need to boil the jars after filling them. Consult your recipe to determine how long to do so.

Which sentence would *best* open the paragraph to introduce the topic?

(A) Canning is very dangerous and should not be attempted at home.

(B) Canning preserves food for later consumption.

(C) When canning food, begin by deciding what kind of food you wish to preserve.

(D) If you are willing to follow a careful process, at-home canning can be very rewarding.

30. Which of these sentences is punctuated incorrectly?

(A) All five-hundred people were surprised when the announcement was made.

(B) "The park will close early!" the loudspeaker crackled.

(C) They rushed to the exits at all three gates.

(D) Several people stopped to talk to the reporters gathered on the scene.

31. Read this sentence.

A cottage designed in the Arts and Crafts style, their house is next to a park.

Which of these is the *most* accurate and effective revision to the sentence to emphasize the home's location?

(A) A cottage next to a park, their house is designed in the Arts and Crafts style.

(B) Their house, a cottage designed in the Arts and Crafts style, is next to a park.

(C) The cottage is designed in the Arts and Crafts style.

(D) Nicely situated next to a park, the cottage is designed in the Arts and Crafts style.

32. Which of these sentences contains a misspelled word?

(A) It was impossible to hear Sophia over the noise of the machinery.

(B) The train tracks ran parallel to the site.

(C) The train was apparrently one of the reasons Sophia had chosen that location.

(D) After trying to be heard, though, she knew that calling for a vote would be unnecessary.

Read this excerpt from a draft of an essay. Then answer Questions 33–35.

At home, have a family tornado plan in place, which must be specific to the type of house or apartment in which you live. Every member of the family should know where they can safely shelter, _____ practice a drill to do so at least once a year.

Flying debris is the greatest danger in tornadoes, so store protective coverings in or next to your shelter space, ready to use on a few seconds' notice. When a tornado watch is issued, think about the drill and check to make sure all your safety supplies are handy. Turn on local TV or the radio and stay alert for warnings. All school administrators should have a tornado safety plan in place, with easy-to-read signs posted to direct everyone to a shelter. Schools should regularly run well-coordinated drills.

33. Which word or words would *best* fit in the blank to clarify the transition between ideas?

(A) however

(B) such as

(C) therefore

(D) except

34. Which sentence would be the *most* effective addition to the start of the first paragraph?

(A) Every home should have a plan for what to do in the case of a tornado.

(B) Do not be scared of natural weather disasters.

(C) Recent events remind us that life is precious.

(D) Debris is a real danger in the event of a tornado.

35. Where might the author add a paragraph break to better organize the text?

(A) between the first and second sentence of the second paragraph

(B) between the second and third sentence of the second paragraph

(C) between the third and fourth sentence of the second paragraph

(D) between the fourth and fifth sentence of the second paragraph

36. Which of these sentences is grammatically correct?

(A) The graduation ceremony will be two weeks away, so we are buying our robes.

(B) Once we have our robes, we will be ready for the event!

(C) In the meantime, several people from my class is not sure they will pass.

(D) The final test in Biology is being a big deal for them.

37. Read this sentence.

The restaurant is a popular spot to eat for visitors and residents in the town's main shopping district.

Which of these is the *most* accurate and effective revision to the sentence?

(A) For both visitors and residents, the restaurant in the town's main shopping district is a popular spot to eat.

(B) In the town's main shopping district, both visitors and residents meet.

(C) The restaurant in the town's main shopping district is a popular spot for residents to meet visitors.

(D) The restaurant in the town's main shopping district is a popular spot to eat visitors and residents.

38. Read this sentence.

A twenty-dollar bill in a plastic bag was found at the park by my brother and me.

Which revision of the sentence is *most* correct and concise?

(A) In a plastic bag, my brother and me found a twenty-dollar bill.

(B) My brother and I found a plastic bag at the park which had a twenty-dollar bill in it, too.

(C) In the park, a twenty-dollar bill in a plastic bag was found by my brother and I.

(D) My brother and I found a twenty-dollar bill in a plastic bag in the park.

39. Read this sentence.

Janey is an excellent speaker, she's president of the school debate team.

What change should be made to correct the sentence's punctuation?

(A) Change the comma to a semicolon.

(B) Change the comma to a period.

(C) Change the period to a question mark.

(D) Eliminate the comma.

40. Read this paragraph.

The population of Meyerdale was over 50,000 residents in 1889, and still climbing. By 1920, however, the population had dropped to 4,500. Main Street was practically deserted, and only the religious commune to the north of the town appeared lively to any visitor who happened to travel past.

Which sentence *best* concludes this paragraph?

(A) The religious commune was that of the Fervors, a sect that had all but disappeared by 1950.

(B) Meyerdale is but one example of a town decimated by the replacement of the railroad as the primary means of transit by cars.

(C) Main Street's churches remained active, although most members moved out of town.

(D) Note that the religious commune was supported by outside funding from Norway.

41. Read this sentence.

Having asked for the day off, Ming now waiting for her boss's answer.

Which of these is the *most* accurate and effective revision to the sentence?

(A) Now waiting for her boss's answer, since Ming asked for the day off.

(B) Having asked for the day off, Ming will now waiting for her boss's answer.

(C) Ming awaits her boss's answer, because she have asked for the day off.

(D) Having asked for the day off, Ming must now wait for her boss's answer.

42. Which of these sentences contains an error or errors in capitalization?

(A) Nancy is employed by Matthew's store.

(B) It is located on Maplethorpe avenue.

(C) They carry clothing from the Arsenal Apparel company, among others.

(D) They also carry a selection of produce, including Rome apples delivered daily.

43. Read this paragraph.

Irish horses were domesticated by the Gaelic tribes many millennia ago. They are small horses, with stocky legs. They are often gray in color, and are very strong, allowing their use for farm work. Irish horses are particularly found in the Galway region.

Which sentence *best* concludes this paragraph?

(A) While usually gray, Irish horses are also sometimes pale gold in color.

(B) As their ancestors did, modern Irish farmers recognize the value of these horses.

(C) Galway is in the southwest of Ireland.

(D) Irish horses are not suitable for riding.

44. Which of these sentences contains a mis-spelled word?

(A) Although he was interrupted several times, Pedro was able to finish the paper.

(B) It was his testimonial about what he achieved in school.

(C) He said that it was an honor and a privi-ledge to work with the teachers.

(D) Of course, he also made a joke at the principal's expense!

45. Read this sentence.

All Angie wanted was to ride the Ferris wheel; eat some kettle-corn, and enjoy the day at the park.

What change should be made to correct the sentence's punctuation?

(A) Change the semicolon to a comma.

(B) Add a comma after "day."

(C) Remove the comma after "kettle-corn."

(D) Eliminate the semicolon.

46. Which of these sentences is punctuated incorrectly?

(A) Julio bought three things: a beach towel, a book, and a water bottle.

(B) Robert, however, brought three bags, of stuff.

(C) Ingrid was the driver; her car could hold all of us.

(D) Last to arrive was Natalia, who is often late.

47. Read this paragraph.

The hair dryer, once an appliance found only in a hair salon, has become a necessary addi-tion to most peoples' hairstyling routine. Technology often becomes cheaper as it is _____, allowing the hair dryer to move from its status as a luxury item, only afford-able to a small business, and into the everyday home.

Which word, when added in the blank, would *best* stress how the technology is affected?

(A) revised

(B) challenged

(C) removed

(D) refined

Read this excerpt of a draft of an essay. Then answer Questions 48–50.

Growing up in the American South in the 1930s and 40s, Harper Lee was deeply affected by the racism she saw around her. _____, as a writer, Lee's work addressed the horrors of racism.

She called that novel *To Kill a Mockingbird.* It is set in the 1950s. It also shows complex relationships between the characters, both black and white.

Lee maintained for years that *Mockingbird* would be her only novel. In 2015, she published *Go Set a Watchman.* It was over 50 years since her first novel was published.

48. Which word would *best* fit in the blank to clarify the transition between ideas?

    (A) therefore

    (B) however

    (C) instead

    (D) despite

49. Which sentence would be the *most* effective addition to the start of the second paragraph?

    (A) Lee was close friends with the writer Truman Capote.

    (B) In fact, Lee's most famous work deals directly with the problem of racism.

    (C) Lee did not publish much of her work.

    (D) Gregory Peck portrayed the character of Atticus Finch in the movie version of her most famous novel.

50. How could the first two sentences of the third paragraph *best* be combined?

    (A) Lee maintained for years that *Mockingbird* would be her only novel. And then, in 2015, she published *Go Set a Watchman.*

    (B) Although Lee maintained for years that *Mockingbird* would be her only novel, she went ahead and published *Go Set a Watchman* too.

    (C) Having maintained for years that *Mockingbird* would be her only novel, Lee publishing *Go Set a Watchman.*

    (D) Although Lee maintained for years that *Mockingbird* would be her only novel, she published another novel, *Go Set a Watchman,* in 2015.

Part 2: Writing

TIME: 50 minutes

DIRECTIONS: Write an essay that addresses the argument made by the author of the following passage, "Time to Buckle Up." The article takes a strong stance on the effectiveness of seat belts. Does the author effectively support her argument? Why or why not? Weigh the claims the author makes, and then write an argumentative essay either supporting or disagreeing with the author.

Be sure to use information from the text in your argumentative essay. As you read the text, think about what details from the text you might use in your argumentative essay. You may take notes or highlight the details as you read. After reading the text, create a plan for your argumentative essay. Think about ideas, facts, definitions, details, and other information and examples you want to use. Think about how you will introduce your topic and what the main topic will be for each paragraph. Now write your argumentative essay.

Be sure to:

- Introduce your claim.

- Support your claim with logical reasoning and relevant evidence from the passage.

- Acknowledge and address alternate or opposing claims.

- Organize the reasons and evidence logically.

- Use words, phrases, and clauses to connect your ideas and to clarify the relationships among claims, counterclaims, reasons, and evidence.

- Establish and maintain a formal style.

- Provide a concluding statement or section that follows from and supports the argument presented.

"Time to Buckle Up," by Melissa Marr

The Centers for Disease Control and Prevention tells us that "motor vehicle crashes are a leading cause of death" in those aged 1 to 54. In fact, the CDC says, over 2.2 million people were treated in America's emergency rooms for injuries sustained during car accidents. Consistent use of seat belts would drastically lower both of these statistics, yet millions of adults do not buckle up. It's time for this to change!

It's a common misconception that most auto accidents happen when the driver is far away from home, driving in unfamiliar territory. In fact, the exact opposite is true. When driving close to home, many people have a false sense of ease and neglect basic elements of driving. They forget to put on a turn signal before pulling into their driveway or change lanes without checking to see who's behind them. Worst of all, they neglect to buckle their seat belts, assuming that nothing will happen if they're within five miles of home. This can lead to disaster.

One way to assure greater usage of seat belts is the passage of seat belt usage laws. The CDC shows that states that require the use of seat belts boast an 89% usage rate. That's a remarkable level of compliance! The laws achieve this by imposing significant fines and allowing police officers to place points on the driver licenses of those who are pulled over.

There are currently 33 states that lack seat belt usage laws for every seat in a vehicle. If those 33 states were to pass complete seat belt usage laws, thousands of lives would be saved. Please join me in writing to your congressperson in support of this initiative.

Section 3: Mathematics

Part 1

TIME: 50 minutes for 26 questions

DIRECTIONS: This section tests your knowledge of mathematics. Pick the best answer(s) for each question and then mark the space on your answer sheet that corresponds to the question number and the letter indicating your choice. You may use a calculator during this part of the test.

1. Marsha is determining what her gross pay at the end of the week should be. If she gets paid $10.15 per hour and works 17 hours, what would her gross pay be?

(A) $27.15

(B) $172.55

(C) $209.10

(D) $255.15

2. Solve for x: $2^x = 16$.

(A) −2

(B) 2

(C) 3

(D) 4

3. A bag contains 20 marbles. There is an equal number of marbles of each of 4 colors — blue, red, green, and yellow — in the bag. If 4 marbles are removed one at a time from the bag, with replacing, what is the probability of selecting 4 red marbles in a row?

(A) $\frac{1}{48}$

(B) $\frac{1}{256}$

(C) $\frac{1}{6,561}$

(D) $\frac{1}{11,880}$

4. Which of the following is equivalent to $\sqrt[3]{64x^6 y^2}$?

(A) $8x^2 y^2$

(B) $8x\sqrt[3]{xy^2}$

(C) $4x^2 y$

(D) $4x^2 \sqrt[3]{y^2}$

5. What is equivalent to $8^{\frac{2}{3}}$?

(A) 2

(B) 4

(C) 64

(D) 243

6. The cost of a phone plan is shown in the following graph, where the x-axis is in months and the y-axis is in dollars.

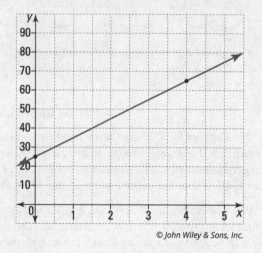

© John Wiley & Sons, Inc.

What is the initial startup fee for a new plan?

(A) $0

(B) $10

(C) $25

(D) $75

7. The circumference of a giant beach ball is 301.44 inches. Using 3.14 as π, what is its radius?

8. Simplify $3(2^0 + 5^2)$.

(A) 21

(B) 31

(C) 75

(D) 78

9. What is the transformation in the following illustration?

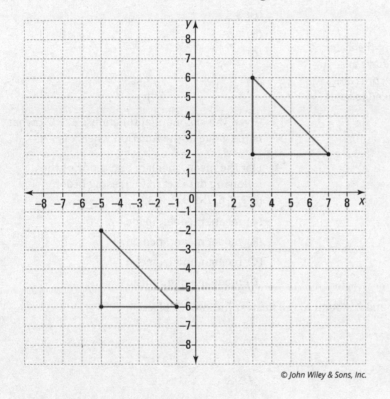

© John Wiley & Sons, Inc.

(A) rotation 180° about the origin

(B) translation down 8 units, left 8 units

(C) reflection over the x–axis

(D) reflection over the line y = x

GO ON TO NEXT PAGE

10. What is the missing value in the table?

x	y
−2	−4
−1	−1
0	2
1	?
2	8

(A) 5

(B) $\frac{1}{4}$

(C) −6

(D) 3

11. Chris's grade is calculated by taking the average of 5 test scores. If he wants to have an 87 in the class and his first 4 test scores are 90, 83, 75, and 96, what does he need to score on the last test?

12. Solve for x: $4x^2 - 6 = 19$.

(A) {−5, 5}

(B) {−2, 5}

(C) {−2.5, 2.5}

(D) {−5, 2}

13. A 2013 Honda Civic averages 32 mpg and holds approximately 13 gallons of gas. If Jake is driving from Boston, Massachusetts, to the Grand Canyon in Arizona, and the distance between the two locations is 2,219 miles, how many tanks of gas will he need?

(A) 4 tanks

(B) 5 tanks

(C) 6 tanks

(D) 7 tanks

14. Which of the following is equivalent to 35%?

(A) 3.5

(B) 0.7

(C) $\frac{7}{200}$

(D) $\frac{7}{20}$

15. Given the exponential function $f(x) = 2^x$, what is the value of the function when x is −3?

16. List the mean, median, and mode of the following data set in increasing order: {3, 7, 2, 6, 7, 4, 9, 3, 2, 3}

(A) mean, median, mode

(B) mode, mean, median

(C) median, mode, mean

(D) mode, median, mean

17. Find the distance between point A and E. Round to the nearest hundredth place.

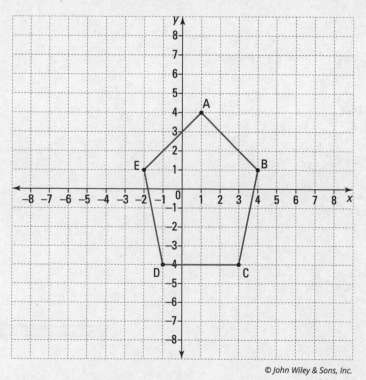

18. What is the solution to the following equation?: $2(x-3)+4x = 5(7-2x)$

(A) 4.75

(B) 2.375

(C) 3.417

(D) 2.5625

19. The two parallelograms are similar. What is the measure of x?

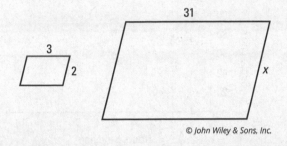

© John Wiley & Sons, Inc.

(A) 20.7

(B) 46.5

(C) 22.3

(D) 30

20. The eighth grade drama club is selling tickets to their spring play. Children's tickets cost $5 each, and adult tickets cost $7 each; the drama club made $415 through ticket sales. If they sold a total of 65 tickets, what system of equations would be used to find out how many of each ticket type was sold?

(A) $5a + 7c = 415$
 $a + c = 65$

(B) $5c + 7a = 65$
 $a + c = 415$

(C) $5a + 7c = 65$
 $a + c = 415$

(D) $5c + 7a = 415$
 $a + c = 65$

21. In Carter's wallet he has a bunch of coins with the total worth of $1.55. Suppose he has twice as many dimes as quarters and has exactly 4 nickels and no pennies. How many dimes does he have?

22. Four friends are going to the movies. They arrive just in time to get the last 4 seats that are available together in a row. How many different seating arrangements can the friends sit in?

(A) 4

(B) 10

(C) 24

(D) 68

23. Solve: $2x^2 + 3x - 9 = 0$

(A) $\{-2,\ 0\}$

(B) $\{\frac{3}{2},\ -3\}$

(C) $\{-\frac{3}{2},\ 3\}$

(D) $\{-1,\ 3\}$

24. Simplify $4\sqrt{2x^2} + 6\sqrt{2x^2}$

(A) $10\sqrt{2x^4}$

(B) $20x$

(C) $10\sqrt{2x^2}$

(D) $20x\sqrt{2}$

25. The sum of $\frac{7}{4}$ and π is _____.

(A) always a rational number

(B) sometimes a rational number

(C) always an irrational number

(D) sometimes an irrational number

26. Which of the following is listed in ascending order?

(A) $\frac{2}{5}, .6, 1\frac{2}{3}, 350\%$

(B) $.6, 350\%, \frac{2}{5}, 1\frac{2}{3}$

(C) $1\frac{2}{3}, 350\%, .6, \frac{2}{5}$

(D) $350\%, \frac{2}{5}, 1\frac{2}{3}, .6$

Part 2

TIME: 55 minutes for 26 questions

DIRECTIONS: You may NOT use a calculator during this part of the test.

27. Two parallel lines, *l* and *m*, are cut by line *n*. What is the measure of $w + z$?

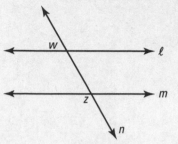

© John Wiley & Sons, Inc.

(A) 90°

(B) $2w$

(C) 180°

(D) $\frac{z}{2}$

28. What is the median of following data set?

10   3   7   4   3   5   8

29. The formula for the volume of a cone is $V = \frac{\pi r^2 h}{3}$, where *r* is the radius of the base and *h* is the height of the cone. Which formula could be used to find *h* if given *V* and *r*?

(A) $h = \frac{3V}{\pi r^2}$

(B) $h = \frac{V}{3\pi r^2}$

(C) $h = \frac{\pi r^2}{3V}$

(D) $h = \frac{3\pi r^2}{V}$

30. What statement corresponds to the relationship illustrated by the following scatter plot?

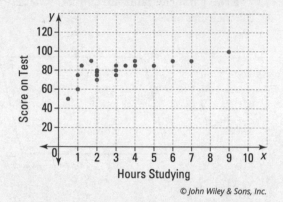

© John Wiley & Sons, Inc.

(A) The longer you study, the worse you will do on the test.

(B) The longer you study, the better you will do on the test.

(C) The amount of time studying does not affect the score on the test.

(D) Not enough information can be gathered.

31. Which line would be parallel to the line $y = -3x + 4$?

(A) $y = -3x - 2$

(B) $y = 3x + 4$

(C) $y = \frac{1}{3}x - 7$

(D) $y = -\frac{1}{3}x + 2$

32. What happens to the area of a rectangle that has both its width and length doubled?

(A) The area stays the same.

(B) The area gets multiplied by a factor of 2.

(C) The area gets divided by 2.

(D) The area gets multiplied by a factor of 4.

33. Which inequality's solution is represented by the following number line?

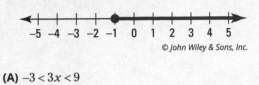

© John Wiley & Sons, Inc.

(A) $-3 < 3x < 9$

(B) $x - 5 > 4$

(C) $4x + 3 \geq -1$

(D) $3 - 2x \geq 1$

34. Which cylinder has a greater volume?

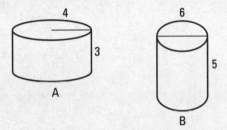

© John Wiley & Sons, Inc.

(A) Cylinder A

(B) Cylinder B

(C) Both cylinders have the same volume.

(D) Not enough information.

35. The letters of "MATHEMATICS" are all written on separate cards. What is the probability of selecting an M followed by an A if the cards are not replaced?

36. What number, when squared, is –9?

(A) 3

(B) –3

(C) $3i^2$

(D) $3i$

37. Which is equivalent to the expression $(\sqrt{2x^3 y})^2$?

(A) $2x^3 y$

(B) $4x^6 y^2$

(C) $2x^6 y^2$

(D) $\sqrt[2]{2x^3 y}$

38. What is the inverse of the function $f(x) = \frac{2}{3}x - 8$?

(A) $f^{-1}(x) = -8x + \frac{2}{3}$

(B) $f^{-1}(x) = \frac{2}{3}(x - 8)$

(C) $f^{-1}(x) = \frac{3}{2}(x + 8)$

(D) $f^{-1}(x) = -\frac{3}{2}x - 8$

39. What is the measure of $\overline{AC}$?

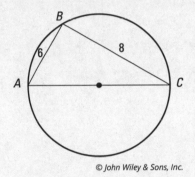

© John Wiley & Sons, Inc.

40. Based on the following graph, what is the minimum on the interval [0, 3]?

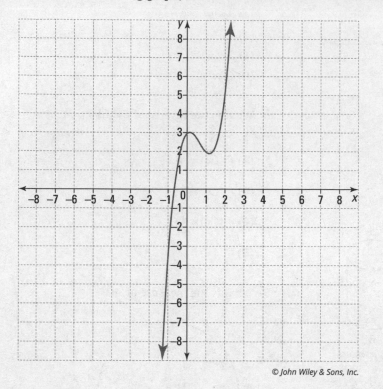

© John Wiley & Sons, Inc.

(A) (0, 3)

(B) (1.2, 2)

(C) (2, 5)

(D) (2, 1.2)

41. Which of the following is **NOT** true of all parallelograms?

(A) Opposite sides are congruent.

(B) Opposite angles are congruent.

(C) The sum of all angles is 360°.

(D) Both diagonals are congruent.

42. Which system of equations is represented by the following graph?

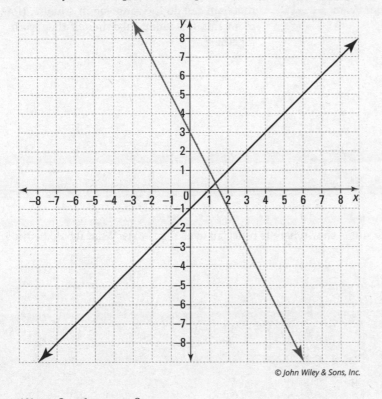

© John Wiley & Sons, Inc.

(A) $y = 2x - 1; \; y = x + 3$

(B) $y = -2x + 3; \; y = x - 1$

(C) $y = -x + 3; \; y = 2x - 1$

(D) $y = -x - 1; \; y = 2x + 3$

43. Solve for x: $3(2x - 4) = 4(x + 2) + 6$.

44. Which expression is equivalent to $(3x^4)^{-2}$?

(A) $9x^2$

(B) $-6x^{-8}$

(C) $\dfrac{9}{x^8}$

(D) $\dfrac{1}{9x^8}$

45. Lisa and Nancy were investigating the relationship of their ages. They figured out that Nancy's age is currently 4 less than twice Lisa's age. In addition, the sum of their ages is 62. How old are Lisa and Nancy?

(A) 14 and 24

(B) 30 and 56

(C) 22 and 40

(D) 10 and 16

46. David launches a model rocket from a cliff that is 30 feet high off the ground. What is the possible domain for the height of the rocket with respect to the ground?

(A) all positive real numbers and zero

(B) all real numbers

(C) all integers

(D) all integers except zero

GO ON TO NEXT PAGE

47. What is the median number of dates a college senior has attended in his or her four years while at the university?

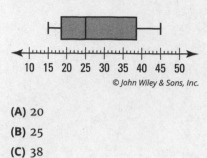

© John Wiley & Sons, Inc.

(A) 20

(B) 25

(C) 38

(D) 45

48. Suppose Jaime can cut a lawn in 2 hours and that Sam can do the same job in 4 hours. How many minutes will it take them if they work together?

49. Imagine that the graph of rectangle *ABCD* shown here is reflected over the *x*-axis. What would be the coordinate of *A'*?

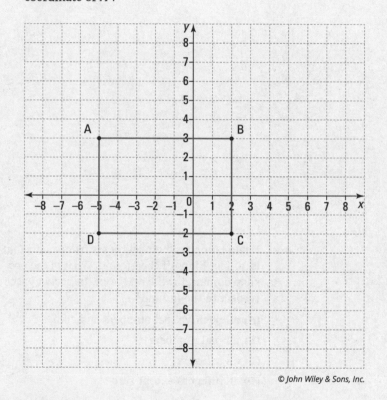

© John Wiley & Sons, Inc.

(A) $(5, 3)$

(B) $(-5, 1)$

(C) $(-5, -3)$

(D) $(2, 3)$

50. Simplify: $(2x+4)(3x-2)$

(A) $6x^2 + 8x - 8$

(B) $5x^2 + 12x - 8$

(C) $6x^2 + 16x - 8$

(D) $5x^2 + 7x + 2$

51. What is the next term in the following sequence? $1600,\ -800,\ 400,\ -200,\ \ldots$

52. Emily's garden has the same length perimeter as area. Which of the following could be the shape and dimensions of her garden?

(A) rectangle; $2\,\text{ft} \times 8\,\text{ft}$

(B) square; $2\,\text{ft} \times 2\,\text{ft}$

(C) rectangle; $3\,\text{ft} \times 7\,\text{ft}$

(D) square; $4\,\text{ft} \times 4\,\text{ft}$

DO NOT TURN THE PAGE UNTIL TOLD TO DO SO **STOP** DO NOT RETURN TO A PREVIOUS TEST

Section 4: Social Studies

TIME: 75 minutes for 47 questions

DIRECTIONS: This section tests your knowledge of social studies. Pick the best answer(s) for each question and then mark the space on your answer sheet that corresponds to the question number and the letter indicating your choice.

1. Read the following excerpt from George Washington's Farewell Address of 1796.

   The great rule of conduct for us in regard to foreign nations is in extending our commercial relations, to have with them as little political connection as possible. So far as we have already formed engagements, let them be fulfilled with perfect good faith. Here let us stop. Europe has a set of primary interests which to us have none; or a very remote relation. Hence she must be engaged in frequent controversies, the causes of which are essentially foreign to our concerns. Hence, therefore, it must be unwise in us to implicate ourselves by artificial ties in the ordinary vicissitudes of her politics, or the ordinary combinations and collisions of her friendships or enmities. Our detached and distant situation invites and enables us to pursue a different course.

   What was significant about his advice for the young nation of the United States as it related to foreign affairs?

   (A) We should eagerly pursue relationships with foreign nations to enhance our political connections with new alliances.

   (B) We should remain isolated and have as little to do with other nations as possible.

   (C) We should pursue trade with other nations but be careful about political involvement in their affairs because Europe has its own political agenda separate from ours.

   (D) We should carefully consider how our friendship with nations of Europe may affect trade or politics.

2. In 1917, women had begun protesting for suffrage outside the White House. Their target in this appeal was President Wilson. What goal were these women trying to achieve?

   (A) equal pay with men

   (B) the creation of an Equal Rights Amendment

   (C) the creation of a commission to investigate workplace abuses

   (D) the granting of the right of women to vote

3. Unemployment figures peaked in 1932–33 but remained high throughout the 1930s after the elections (1932, 1936, 1940) of FDR and the wide range of New Deal programs. What inference can you make about the data about why unemployment figures remained at an average of nearly 17% for the decade of the 1930s, declined in 1941, and remained low through 1945?

U.S. Unemployment Rate, 1930-1945

© John Wiley & Sons, Inc.

(A) An influx in spending on New Deal Programs kept unemployment high.

(B) America's involvement in World War II after December 7, 1941, brought about a steep decline in unemployment. It was the U.S. involvement in World War II that finally brought an end to the Great Depression.

(C) A gradual decrease in spending in New Deal programs stalled unemployment.

(D) The government was working on a new set of programs to bring down unemployment and it was finally beginning to work.

4. After the end of the Civil War in 1865, the Radical Republicans set the agenda for Reconstruction. Much of their work was opposed by Democrat President Johnson. What did the following pieces of legislation attempt to do for freed blacks?

Reconstruction Civil Rights Legislation

1866 Civil Rights Act	Granted citizenship to former slaves and granted them equal protection of the law
Freedmen's Bureau	Provided for the education of blacks, relief efforts for blacks, and regulation of labor
1875 Civil Rights Act	Granted blacks access to public accommodations

(A) forced them to wait ten years for any assistance

(B) granted them immediate rights and privileges

(C) granted them gradual rights and privileges

(D) attempted to grant blacks rights but they were opposed by presidential vetoes that could not be overturned

GO ON TO NEXT PAGE

5. After the Spanish-American War ended in 1898 with the victory by the United States, President Teddy Roosevelt began taking a more aggressive foreign policy approach with countries in Latin America. In an effort to extend U.S. influence in the area:

(A) The U.S. negotiated successfully with Columbia for access to build a canal across Panama.

(B) The U.S. exerted its force and growing influence in Latin America by "negotiating" with Panama to build a canal in the region.

(C) The U.S. was waiting for approval by Columbia to enter the region.

(D) The U.S. was about to adopt a wait and see attitude with involvement in Latin America.

6. In October 1963, the United States (President JFK) and the USSR (leader Nikita Khrushchev) faced a 13-day standoff from the 15th to the 28th after the United States discovered nuclear missiles in Cuba that could potentially strike almost anywhere in the continental United States. As a result of this:

(A) The USSR negotiated a treaty with the United States to keep the missiles in place without the threat of them ever being used.

(B) The United States backed down on its insistence that the missiles be removed immediately from Cuba.

(C) President JFK was able to get the Soviet Union to withdraw its missiles from Cuba while the United States agreed to remove nuclear missiles from Turkey.

(D) The standoff ended with the USSR violating the U.S. blockade of Cuba.

7. During the Cold War, the fear of the spread of communism was expressed in the U.S. policy known as the Domino Theory. What is the likely meaning of this theory as it applied to actions in Asia from 1945–1975?

(A) When China became communist in 1949, the Korean War broke out in 1950, and the U.S. entered the conflict in Vietnam in 1964, the generalized fear was that if one country fell to communism that other countries would also fall to communism.

(B) The actions of the spread of communism was only related to the Korean War between North and South Korea that ended with an armistice in 1953.

(C) The fear of the spread of communism was only related to the war in Vietnam that ended in 1975 with the victory of North Vietnam over South Vietnam.

(D) This fear was unsubstantiated when China became a communist country in 1949.

8. Read the following excerpts from Abigail Adams and John Adams in 1776.

I long to hear that you have declared an independency. And, by the way, in the new code of laws which I suppose it will be necessary for you to make, I desire you would remember the ladies and be more generous and favorable to them than your ancestors. Do not put such unlimited power into the hands of the husbands. Remember, all men would be tyrants if they could. If particular care and attention is not paid to the ladies, we are determined to foment a rebellion, and will not hold ourselves bound by any laws in which we have no voice or representation. –Abigail Adams, March 31, 1776

As to your extraordinary code of laws, I cannot but laugh. We have been told that our struggle has loosened the bonds of government everywhere; that children and apprentices were disobedient; that schools and colleges were grown turbulent; that Indians slighted their guardians, and negroes grew insolent to their masters. But your letter was the first intimation that another tribe, more numerous and powerful than all the rest, were [sic] grown discontented. –John Adams, April 14, 1776

While work was about to be done on the Declaration of Independence, Abigail Adams took the rather bold step of expressing the desire of women to gain representation in the new government. According to the excerpts, which of the following is true?

(A) John Adams took her advice to heart and assured her that changes would be made.

(B) Abigail Adams knew that women would probably need to "foment a rebellion" to achieve representation in government.

(C) John Adams was willing to think of a compromise with Abigail Adams's request.

(D) Abigail Adams was willing to seek a compromise with John Adams as work was about to be done on the Declaration of Independence.

9. During the Vietnam War, support for the war was strong in 1965 but within less than two years, the war had become unpopular at home as protests spread across the country. What would be a cause for the rise in student protest of the war? All the following would be a valid reason for protest EXCEPT:

(A) The numbers of casualties were increasing each year, and more and more troops were being sent over to fight in the war.

(B) The longer the war continued, students began protesting and showing their lack of support for President LBJ and the war effort.

(C) The students felt that they were the only ones protesting the war effort in Vietnam.

(D) More and more young people were being drafted to fight in Vietnam (with the average age of the U.S. soldier in Vietnam being 19 years old — old enough to fight in the war but not old enough to vote).

10. In 1945, why did President Truman decide to use atomic weapons against Japan?

(A) to end the war by forcing an immediate Japanese surrender

(B) to see whether the newly developed atomic weapons actually worked

(C) to convince the Germans in Europe to surrender to the allied forces

(D) to stop the Japanese army from invading the U.S.

11. During World War II, women on the U.S. home front made a significant contribution to the war effort by

(A) taking a reduction in pay so that the working men could still support their families.

(B) taking up roles in war industries filling jobs that were needed for the war effort because so many men were away fighting the war.

(C) not openly protesting the war effort.

(D) taking a reduction in work hours to allow minorities to work longer hours.

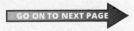
GO ON TO NEXT PAGE

12. Prior to the end of the French and Indian War being settled in 1763, the American colonists considered themselves to be loyal British subjects. From 1763 to 1776, this loyalty was challenged because of actions of Parliament and the King of England.

Road to Revolution

Sugar Act – 1764	This tax on sugar was meant to raise revenue for Britain; the colonists responded by growing protests.
Stamp Act – 1765	Most paper products had to have the official "stamp" of the British government and constituted a direct tax; the colonists responded by Patrick Henry's declaration of "no taxation without representation" and protests by the Sons and Daughters of Liberty.
Boston Massacre – 1770	Five colonists were killed by British redcoats, and the colonists were inflamed with their increasing anger against Britain.
Boston Tea Party – 1773	As a protest against the Tea Act, a group of colonists responded by throwing over 300 crates of tea into the Boston harbor.

The information in the chart reveals that:

(A) Parliament consulted with the colonists for the best way to gradually tax the American colonists.

(B) The colonists became compliant with the newly imposed taxes.

(C) The colonists took limited action to oppose British regulations.

(D) The colonists took targeted actions to oppose British regulations.

13. The 1896 *Plessy v. Ferguson* Supreme Court case resulted in the majority opinion of "separate but equal" doctrine in determining the legality of separate facilities for black and white Americans. As a result of this ruling, Jim Crow laws were

(A) gradually imposed by states that began to impose segregation rules about public facilities for blacks and whites in the South only.

(B) openly challenged in 1954 with the *Brown v. Board of Education* Supreme Court case that ruled in a unanimous decision that "separate was not equal."

(C) restricted by a ten-year moratorium on separate facilities.

(D) limited in places of accommodation where segregation could take place.

14. Which of the following concepts is not related to the American concept of liberty?

(A) freedom of speech

(B) freedom of religion

(C) the right to petition your government

(D) limits on the press (media)

15. According to the Articles of Confederation, who controlled the execution of laws in the newly formed country of the United States following the end of the Revolutionary War?

(A) the president

(B) the Congress

(C) the state governments

(D) the federal judiciary

16. Which amendment to the Constitution stated that the powers not delegated to the national government or prohibited to the states were "reserved to the states"? This also sets up the concept of "states' rights" that allowed for the argument for Southerners to maintain the institution of slavery until the end of the Civil War in 1865.

(A) 1st amendment

(B) 10th Amendment

(C) 12th Amendment

(D) 14th Amendment

17. Title IX passed in 1972 as part of Education Amendments states:

"No person in the United States shall, on the basis of sex, be excluded from participation in, be denied the benefits of, or be subjected to discrimination under any education program or activity receiving federal financial assistance."

It has been used in the area of high school and collegiate sports to

(A) allow more access for girls in sports in high school and college by allowing girls equal access to sport programs and scholarships.

(B) limit participation of girls in sports and programs.

(C) set a time frame for participation of girls in sports.

(D) set protection for men's sports programs to maintain their dominance.

18. The 2000 presidential election between Al Gore (D) and George W. Bush (R) ended up in a recount of votes in the state of Florida to decide the outcome of the election because neither candidate had enough electoral votes to win the election. The outcome of the election was finally decided in favor of Mr. Bush when the Supreme Court ordered a halt to the recount of votes in Florida.

With the Electoral College votes of 270 needed to win the election, what does the following chart suggest about the outcome of the election?

2000 Presidential Election

Al Gore – Democrat	Popular Vote – 50,999,897
	Electoral Vote – 266 (without Florida)
George W. Bush – Republican	Popular Vote – 50,456,002
	Electoral Vote – 246 (without Florida)
State of Florida	25 Electoral Votes

(A) The candidate who took the state of Florida would win the election (passing the minimum of 270 electoral votes needed).

(B) The candidate with the highest amount of votes in the popular vote would win the election.

(C) Neither candidate would have enough electoral votes to win the election.

(D) Because of the controversy of the election, a new election was planned because there was no clear winner.

GO ON TO NEXT PAGE

19. The Bill of Rights was a written guarantee of rights of the citizens of the United States and was added right after the adoption of the Constitution in 1789. The purpose of these ten Amendments was meant to

(A) continue the tradition of "common law" from Parliament in Great Britain.

(B) guarantee the rights of the people and restrict some of the power of the federal government.

(C) guarantee the power of the federal government.

(D) extend of power of the federal government over the states and the people.

20. American politics has been dominated by a two-party political system beginning with the Federalists and Anti-Federalists in 1796 to the current system with the two major parties: the Democrats and Republicans.

Third Party Political Parties

Teddy Roosevelt – "Bull Moose" or Progressive Party – 1912	Formed as a split in the Republican party and allowed the Democrat candidate Wilson to win the election
Eugene Debs – Socialist Party – 1920	Although in jail for a variety of government offenses, he gained nearly a million votes but no impact on the election
Ross Perot – Independent candidate (1992) and Reform Party candidate in 1996	Did not take any electoral votes in the 1992 election but gained nearly 19 million votes that took votes away from George H. Bush (R) and allowed Clinton (D) to win the election
Tea Party – 2008 – Sarah Palin, Rand Paul, Michelle Bachmann, Ron Paul (and others)	A conservative wing of the Republican party formed to promote the limit on the extension of the federal government and its programs

Despite the influence of the two-party system in U.S. politics, what does the information in the chart suggest about the influence of third parties in U.S. federal elections?

(A) Third-party political parties are losing their influence in American politics.

(B) Third-party political parties have had minimal influence in American politics.

(C) Third-party political parties can influence the outcomes in presidential elections (if there is a split in a major party or an independent party forms, it can take away votes in an election).

(D) Third-party political parties fail to gain grassroots support for their causes.

21. Every ten years, a census takes place to determine the population and to allow for reapportionment of the members of the House of Representatives based on population in the states. The 435 seats are divided among the states according to the most populous and least populous states. Examine the two electoral maps (1980 and 2016) and see what trend(s) are evident.

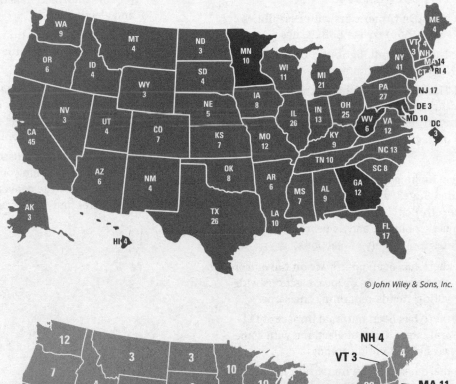

© John Wiley & Sons, Inc.

© John Wiley & Sons, Inc.

(A) States in the northeast are retaining their dominance in Electoral College votes.

(B) States in the south, southwest, and west are gaining Electoral College votes and will gain impact in the future presidential elections.

(C) States in the west are losing their importance in Electoral College votes.

(D) States in the Midwest are remaining flat with their importance in Electoral College votes.

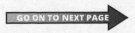

22. Which of the following civil rights issues deals with business actions and access to public accommodations?

    (A) the Equal Rights Amendment and the 1964 Civil Rights Act

    (B) The ADA (Americans with Disabilities Act – 1990) covers both issues.

    (C) The 1964 Civil Rights Act dealt with both issues of discriminatory practices.

    (D) The 1964 Civil Rights Act and the ADA (Americans with Disabilities Act – 1990) both dealt with discriminatory protections.

23. When looking at the current electorate in the United States, variables of education, income, race, ethnicity, and gender create differences of public opinion, and as people vote for candidates in a variety of elections,

    (A) there has been no impact on the outcome of federal, state, or local elections with voting trends remaining the same.

    (B) there has been minimal impact of federal, state, or local elections with some variance in voting trends.

    (C) there has been an increasing impact in federal, state, and local elections with voters expressing their votes on certain candidates and issues.

    (D) men and women have remained about the same in their voting in federal, state, and local elections.

24. What media trend has NOT been a factor in major political elections since 1960?

    (A) People rely more on mainstream news agencies than on cable news sites for reliable information about candidates and elections.

    (B) JFK/Nixon held the first televised presidential debates, and they continue to be televised today.

    (C) The Internet news agencies have had a major impact on recent elections as people rely more on online news and diversity of viewpoints of online information.

    (D) Print media and mainstream news outlets on television continue to be challenged by the convenience of online news sites and cable news.

25. Read the information in the following chart. The information on the chart best describes reasons for war for which global conflict?

    Reasons for Going to War

Secret alliances – agreements between countries for support in case of a war
Militarism – military might of weapons and armies
Imperialism – the desire for the conquest of land
Nationalism – excessive pride in one's country

    (A) Persian Gulf War

    (B) Cold War

    (C) World War I

    (D) the war in the Balkans

26. Apartheid in South Africa, a system of legalized racial segregation or "apartness," was the official state policy from 1948 to 1994. The best illustration for the ending of this policy was

(A) the election of Nelson Mandela as the first black African to be elected president of the newly organized nation of South Africa when blacks were given the right to vote for the first time in their country's 200+ year history.

(B) the establishment of a ten-year gradual change for segregation in parts of South Africa.

(C) a set of 5-year plans to end racial segregation early in the 21st century.

(D) the United Nations' temporary control of the government of South Africa for a seven-year period to allow for the adoption of a new constitution.

27. Adolph Hitler sought to blame Germany's post-World War I problems on the Jewish population. Once Kristallnacht (the "night of broken glass") began in November 1938, Hitler began his plan for the Holocaust, which

(A) was a program to relocate all the Jews out of Germany and into Poland.

(B) was a program in which he used several concentration camps to exterminate 6 million Jews (75% of the Jewish population of Europe).

(C) was a program to encourage Jewish resettlement to other countries in Europe.

(D) was a program to convert Jews into Christians.

28. The Korean War began in June 1950 when North Korea, under the leadership of Kim Il Song, crossed the 38th parallel and invaded South Korea. South Korea made an appeal to the newly formed United Nations for assistance. As a result of the request,

(A) the appeal came too late, and North Korea completed its takeover of South Korea.

(B) the appeal was put on hold for 48 hours until the Security Council could meet.

(C) the appeal was answered, and the United States and 15 other UN member nations sent troops to help South Korea push back the assault of the North Korean army for three years until an armistice was signed in July 1953 halting but not resolving the conflict.

(D) only UN nations in Europe assisted, as the U.S. was not able to offer any support.

29. The Industrial Revolution began in the mid-1700s and continued into the 1800s with Great Britain quickly taking the lead to become the number one producer of goods in the world in the 1800s. Which of the following was NOT a factor in Britain's rise to dominance in world trade until the late 1890s?

(A) stagnant population growth — laborers were in short demand

(B) Skilled laborers were abundant in Britain.

(C) The business class (entrepreneurs) in Britain had begun to accumulate capital to invest in capital ventures.

(D) Britain had a stable government that sought to support economic growth and had a large navy to protect the country as well as protect shipping and trade.

GO ON TO NEXT PAGE

30. The Cold War, which had its start at the end of World War II, was a contest between the democratic United States and communist Soviet Union. Each nation feared the other one and began to build an arsenal of nuclear weapons to oppose each other. Which of the following statements is NOT true about the early part of the Cold War.

(A) The United Nations was formed to primarily promote world peace after two devastating world wars.

(B) The United States and western European nations felt threatened by communist actions in Eastern Europe and felt they needed to form an alliance to confront those threats.

(C) NATO and the Warsaw Pact were created to work together to promote world peace.

(D) The Warsaw Pact was created as a response to the formation of NATO.

31. Why would American workers generally support tariffs being placed on foreign imports?

(A) Tariffs can promote free trade among competing nations.

(B) Tariffs can help to mend strained relationships between hostile nations.

(C) Tariffs increase the demand for American-made goods.

(D) Tariffs lower prices of American-made goods.

32. How does boycotting a company that is engaged in unethical behavior put economic pressure on the company to change its ways?

(A) The sudden increase in demand for the company's products helps to drive up the price.

(B) The sudden decrease in demand for the company's products helps to drive down the price.

(C) Workers demand higher wages.

(D) Workers go on strike, bringing production to a halt.

33. Inflation generally occurs when prices for goods and services rise while income remains stagnant. As a result of inflation, what occurs?

(A) Unemployment decreases as jobs are created.

(B) Consumers reduce their spending on nonessential items, demand goes down, and unemployment begins to rise.

(C) Shortages of goods occur, and prices decline.

(D) Government agencies and businesses generally operate on a wait-and-see prospect to see how bad inflation really is.

34. Unemployment figures during the Great Recession from 2008 to 2009 show the impact of unemployment across a wide range of groups. Study the chart and answer the following question: Which of the following is NOT supported by data from the chart?

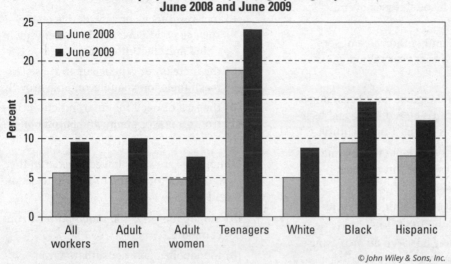

Unemployment rates by demographic group, June 2008 and June 2009

© John Wiley & Sons, Inc.

(A) Teens were relatively unaffected by unemployment.

(B) More men than women were affected by rising unemployment rates.

(C) Hispanics were impacted more than whites by rising unemployment rates.

(D) Unemployment rates for blacks were the highest among ethnic groups.

35. Which statement is true regarding stocks and bonds?

(A) They are both risk-free.

(B) They both pay a fixed interest rate.

(C) They both raise money for capital investments.

(D) Bonds are always safer than stocks.

36. All the following are true statements regarding a communist economy EXCEPT:

(A) The government makes all economic decisions.

(B) The government encourages entrepreneurs to start, own, and operate their own companies.

(C) The government controls the prices of all goods and services.

(D) The government owns all the factories and controls all industries.

37. Which of the following is an example of capital?

(A) a factory

(B) a skilled electrician

(C) a deposit of aluminum

(D) the CEO of a company

38. Which of the following is an example of essential infrastructure that supports economic activity?

(A) local sales taxes

(B) the national highway system

(C) the annual U.S. budget

(D) the public school system

39. What does a worker's total compensation consist of?

(A) wages only

(B) wages plus whatever office supplies the worker can sneak home

(C) wages and benefits

(D) unemployment benefits

GO ON TO NEXT PAGE

40. The GDP (Gross Domestic Product) of a nation is generally the total value of

   (A) goods and services produced in one year.

   (B) goods produced over a two-year period.

   (C) services offered by businesses over a one-year period.

   (D) goods produced minus the value of services offered in a one-year period.

41. As countries around the globe have becoming increasingly intertwined by economic and technological growth over the past half century,

   (A) refugee problems of people fleeing one region to seek assistance in another region have declined.

   (B) human rights issues around the world have actually begun to decline.

   (C) the global economy has seen an increasing number of countries growing more dependent on each other for economic growth.

   (D) terrorist activities have finally begun to decrease as more countries are working in cooperation with one another.

42. Why are strikes such an effective tool that workers can use to gain improvements in their wages and working conditions?

   (A) A strike allows a company to hire new workers.

   (B) The general public usually takes the side of the company in the strike.

   (C) Strikes usually shut down all production, which harms the company financially.

   (D) It's always best to "strike while the iron is hot."

43. The slave trade across the Middle Passage in the Atlantic from Africa to the New World from the mid-1500s to the mid-1800s resulted in

   (A) the largest forced migration of a group of people in world history.

   (B) only Spain and Portugal becoming involved in the slave trade business.

   (C) a minimal impact on South America in the New World.

   (D) Britain and Spain monopolizing the slave trade business.

44. As China and the United States continue their reliance upon coal and petroleum, a result of this could lead to all the following EXCEPT

   (A) increased pollution in large cities such as Beijing and Los Angeles.

   (B) increased focus on alternative energy such as wind power and solar energy in China and the United States.

   (C) the increase of reliance upon these two fossil fuels to expand economic growth.

   (D) the lack of need for environmental controls on power plants and automobiles.

45. Monopolies are not allowed to exist in the United States for all the following reasons EXCEPT:

   (A) Monopolies give too much power to one company.

   (B) Monopolies give consumers fewer choices.

   (C) Monopolies have an unfair advantage that prevents healthy competition.

   (D) Monopolies are too efficient.

46. The impact of transportation of goods with railroads, highways (semitrucks), and airplanes has resulted in

   (A) less of a reliance on infrastructural needs in large communities.

   (B) more connections with port cities to expedite transportation of goods through the country.

   (C) a decline on the impact of goods being routed through port cities.

   (D) the decline of large population centers.

47. Which of the following is the riskiest investment?

   (A) buying stock in several large established corporations

   (B) buying stock in a single startup company

   (C) buying U.S. Government savings bonds

   (D) putting your money in a savings account at the bank

DO NOT TURN THE PAGE UNTIL TOLD TO DO SO STOP **DO NOT RETURN TO A PREVIOUS TEST**

Section 5: Science

TIME: 85 minutes for 47 questions

DIRECTIONS: This section tests your knowledge of science. Pick the best answer(s) for each question and then mark the space on your answer sheet that corresponds to the question number and the letter indicating your choice.

Use the following information to help answer Questions 1–4.

In a food chain, hawks get their energy by consuming rabbits; rabbits get their energy by consuming plants. Plants produce their own food by using the energy from the sun to make glucose, as shown in the following figure:

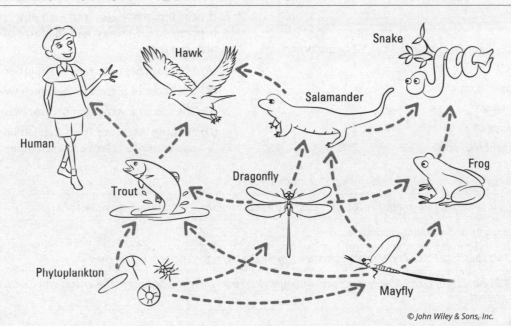

© John Wiley & Sons, Inc.

1. Which reaction is shown by the following equation?

   $$\text{Sunlight} + 6CO_2 + 6H_2O \rightarrow 6O_2 + C_6H_{12}O_6$$

   (A) cellular respiration

   (B) ATP synthesis

   (C) photoelectric effect

   (D) photosynthesis

2. Which type of chemical reaction is shown by the previous equation in question 1?

   (A) endothermic reaction

   (B) exothermic reaction

   (C) nuclear fission reaction

   (D) nuclear fusion reaction

3. The following reaction shows aerobic cellular respiration that produces energy in the cells of both the rabbit and the hawk. Which of the following shows the missing reactant?

   $$\text{Glucose} + \underline{\hspace{1cm}} \rightarrow \text{Water} + \text{Carbon dioxide} + \text{Energy}$$

   (A) sunlight

   (B) oxygen

   (C) carbon monoxide

   (D) photosynthesis

4. Which of the following correctly fills in the blanks in the right order in the following statement? The rabbit is a _____, the plant is a _____, the hawk is a _____.

(A) herbivore, producer, carnivore

(B) producer, carnivore, herbivore

(C) producer, primary consumer, secondary consumer

(D) primary consumer, secondary consumer, producer

5. Which element is the basis of all living organisms on Earth?

(A) hydrogen

(B) carbon

(C) oxygen

(D) carbon dioxide

6. Why is the light detected by the Hubble telescope from distant galaxies redshifted?

(A) It bounces off the surface of the red planet Mars before reaching us.

(B) The distant galaxies are speeding up.

(C) Greenhouse gases in the atmosphere filter out blue light so only red light remains.

(D) The distant galaxies are moving away from the Earth.

7. If two stars move closer to each other, what happens to the strength of the force of gravity between them?

(A) The stars begin to repel each other.

(B) The force of attraction becomes weaker.

(C) The force of attraction becomes stronger.

(D) Nothing. Stars are fixed in position and cannot move relative to each other.

Use the following information to help answer Questions 8–11.

A student is investigating magnetic fields and forces. She has the following equipment available to her:

Two bar magnets and a plotting compass

Circuit 1: This consists of a coil of wire attached to a light bulb. There is no battery in this circuit.

Circuit 2: This consists of a coil of wire wrapped around an iron bar. There is a battery in this circuit and a switch but no light bulb present.

8. What happens when the student moves one of the magnets into and out of Circuit 1?

(A) The light bulb lights up.

(B) The light bulb remains unlit because there is no battery to power the circuit.

(C) An electromagnet is generated.

(D) The magnet becomes demagnetized.

9. What happens when the student positions the two magnets near each other with both north poles facing each other?

(A) The magnets are unaffected by each other's presence.

(B) The magnets attract each other.

(C) The magnets repel each other.

(D) The magnets become warm due to electromagnetic radiation given off by their north poles.

10. Which direction will the plotting compass point when the student places it at the south pole of one of the bar magnets?

(A) toward the Earth's South Pole

(B) away from the Earth's South Pole

(C) toward the magnet's south pole

(D) away from the magnet's south pole

11. What happens when the student closes the switch in Circuit 2?

(A) The iron bar becomes magnetized.

(B) The light bulb lights up.

(C) Nothing because iron does not conduct electricity.

(D) The iron bar begins to melt.

12. Which of the following always stays the same when a chemical reaction takes place?

   (A) the amount of gas

   (B) the temperature

   (C) the number of molecules

   (D) the number of atoms

13. Which of the following is NOT responsible for changes in the Earth's surface?

   (A) ozone

   (B) earthquakes

   (C) volcanic eruptions

   (D) plate tectonics

14. The human body system that serves as a transport for blood and other nutrients in the blood stream is the

   (A) muscular system

   (B) digestive system

   (C) integumentary system

   (D) circulatory system

Use the following information to help answer Questions 15–17.

Polar bears have a thick layer of fat and dense, white fur that help to protect them from the freezing temperatures of the Arctic habitat where they live. Natural selection is thought to be involved in the evolution of the polar bear's thick coat of fur.

---

15. Which of the following best explains how natural selection is involved in the evolution of the polar bear's thick fur coat?

   (A) Polar bears with thick fur coats killed off all the polar bears with thinner coats.

   (B) Polar bears with thick coats preferred to mate only with other polar bears who had thick fur coats.

   (C) Polar bears with thinner coats did not survive because they were not well suited to the harsh conditions of their environment.

   (D) Polar bears with thinner coats migrated south for the winter.

16. How does the polar bear's thick fur coat help to keep the animal warm in the frigid Arctic conditions?

   (A) The white color of the fur reflects thermal radiation from the sun.

   (B) Fur traps a layer of air next to the animal's body, which keeps it warm because air is a poor conductor of heat.

   (C) The thick fur helps convection currents to direct heat from the surroundings into the animal's skin.

   (D) Fur is a good conductor of heat so the bear absorbs heat from the surroundings.

17. Why is it usually much colder in the Arctic compared to places nearer the equator?

   (A) The curvature of the Earth's surface causes the sun's rays to spread out over a larger surface area at the poles compared to at the equator.

   (B) The Arctic is farther away from the sun than most other places on Earth.

   (C) Much of the ice in the Arctic is left over from the last ice age, when the Earth was much cooler than it is today.

   (D) There is no atmosphere at the North Pole, so all the heat escapes, causing the temperature to drop.

18. In the progression of life on Earth according to the fossil record, which of the following sequences is correct?

   (A) fish, amphibians, birds, reptiles, humans

   (B) fish, amphibians, reptiles, birds, humans

   (C) fish, reptiles, amphibians, birds, humans

   (D) humans, birds, amphibians, reptiles, fish

19. A student was conducting an investigation using two liquids. Both liquids were clear and were at the same temperature, 25° Celsius. When the student combined the liquids in a large beaker, gas bubbles were produced. The student took the temperature of the beaker, which now measured 23° Celsius. Which of the following is the most likely explanation of what occurred?

(A) The mixing of the liquids produced heat.

(B) A disintegration of the first solution occurred.

(C) Evaporation occurred, causing the gas bubbles to appear.

(D) A chemical reaction took place.

20. Newton's first law (the law of inertia) states that an object at rest stays at rest and an object in motion stays in motion at the same speed in the same direction unless acted upon by an unbalanced force. Which of the following is the best example of this?

(A) applying the brakes in your car until it slows down and stops

(B) the recoil of a gun when a bullet is fired into the air

(C) When a book falls and lands on the floor, the floor pushes back on the book with an equal but opposite force.

(D) a sky diver falling at a constant speed toward the ground

Use the following diagram to help answer Questions 21–23.

When a plane flies there are several forces acting on it, as shown in the figure.

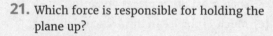

Lift

Drag ← → Thrust

Weight

© John Wiley & Sons, Inc.

21. Which force is responsible for holding the plane up?

(A) weight

(B) lift

(C) thrust

(D) drag

22. If the plane maintains a constant speed and altitude and travels in a straight line, which of the following must be true according to Newton's law of inertia?

(A) The thrust must be greater than the drag to keep the plane moving forward.

(B) The lift must be greater than the weight to keep the plane from falling to the ground.

(C) There are no unbalanced forces acting on the plane.

(D) The plane is weightless.

23. If the mass of the plane is 10,000 kg and the drag force equals 20,000 N, what will be the acceleration of the plane if the thrust of its engine equals 80,000 N?

(A) 2 m/s²

(B) 6 m/s²

(C) 8 m/s²

(D) The plane is moving at constant velocity.

24. In the hierarchy of living organisms, what is the classification from smallest to the largest?

(A) organism, organ system, organ, tissue, cell

(B) organ system, organ, tissue, cell, organism

(C) cell, tissue, organ system, organ, organism

(D) cell, tissue, organ, organ system, organism

25. In a particular ecosystem there are plants that have adapted to living in the shade of the trees and other plants that have adapted to living in bright sunlight. The intensity of the sunlight is a/an

(A) abiotic factor in the ecosystem.

(B) biotic factor in the ecosystem.

(C) time-related factor in the ecosystem.

(D) competitive factor in the ecosystem.

Use the following paragraph and diagram to help answer Questions 26–29.

A brown-eyed father and a blue-eyed mother want to calculate the probability that their child will have blue eyes. The Punnett square shown in the following figure displays the genes of the parents and the potential offspring.

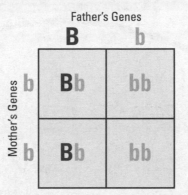

© John Wiley & Sons, Inc.

26. What is the probability that their child will have blue eyes?

(A) 0%

(B) 25%

(C) 50%

(D) 100%

27. Which of the following correctly fills in the blanks in the right order in this statement?

The trait for blue eyes is _____, and the trait for brown eyes is _____.

(A) dominant, dominant

(B) recessive, recessive

(C) dominant, recessive

(D) recessive, dominant

28. Which of the following correctly fills in the blanks in the right order in this statement?

The mother is _____ for the blue eyes, and the father is _____ for brown eyes.

(A) homozygous, heterozygous

(B) heterozygous, homozygous

(C) heterozygous, heterozygous

(D) homozygous, homozygous

29. If the parents get divorced and the mother later marries a man who also has blue eyes, what is the probability that their child will have brown eyes?

(A) 0%

(B) 25%

(C) 50%

(D) 100%

The carbon cycle describes the circulation and transformation of carbon between living things and the environment as it moves through Earth's different systems. Carbon dioxide plays an important role in the carbon cycle and helps to keep the planet warm enough to support life. However, recent human activities have caused an increase in the amount of carbon dioxide released into the atmosphere, which has led to global warming. The carbon cycle is shown in the following figure.

The Carbon Cycle

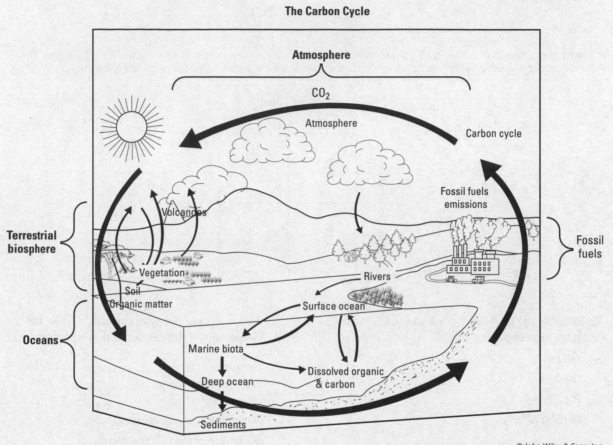

© John Wiley & Sons, Inc.

30. Which process does NOT add carbon dioxide to the atmosphere?

(A) plant respiration

(B) auto and factory emissions

(C) formation of fossil fuels

(D) animal respiration

31. When carbon dioxide in the atmosphere dissolves in rainwater, the resulting product is likely to have what impact on the environment over time?

(A) The fish will convert the carbon dioxide into glucose via photosynthesis so the lake will become sticky.

(B) The acidity level of lakes and rivers will rise, harming fish and other wildlife in the ecosystem.

(C) The water will become unsafe to drink because carbon dioxide is poisonous.

(D) There will be no impact on the environment.

32. Which human activity has led to a recent sharp increase in the amount of carbon dioxide released into the atmosphere, contributing to global warming?

(A) human respiration

(B) burying waste matter in landfills

(C) an increase in the rate of combustion of fossil fuels

(D) using renewable energy sources such as wind or solar power

33. Which of the following is a way to combat global warming?

(A) cutting down more trees in the rainforests

(B) drilling for oil offshore rather than on land

(C) banning gardeners and farmers from using greenhouses because carbon dioxide is a greenhouse gas

(D) using renewable energy sources such as wind or solar power

34. Which of the following statements describes the role of DNA in a cell?

(A) DNA is the building block for all the other molecules in the cell.

(B) DNA provides information to make proteins for the cell.

(C) DNA provides the energy that fuels the cell's activities.

(D) DNA is the material that the cell wall is constructed from.

35. A *thermostat* is a device that controls the temperature of your home. If the room is too hot, the thermostat turns on the air conditioning until it reaches the desired temperature. If the room is too cold, the thermostat turns on the heating until, once again, the desired temperature is reached. A similar negative feedback mechanism occurs within humans. The brain controls all the processes within the human body (including those that maintain the right body temperature) and tries to keep them in equilibrium. This is an example of

(A) positive feedback mechanism

(B) homeostasis in the body

(C) global warming

(D) meiosis

Use the following information to help answer Questions 36–38.

The sun produces an enormous amount of energy. Some of that energy reaches Earth in the form of sunlight and affects Earth's systems. Light travels at 300,000 km per second in the vacuum of space.

36. Which statement explains how the sun produces its energy?

(A) The sun produces energy via exothermic chemical reactions on its surface.

(B) The sun produces energy via combustion reactions on its surface.

(C) The sun produces energy via nuclear fusion reactions at its core.

(D) The sun produces energy via nuclear fission reactions at its core.

37. Which statement explains how the energy from the sun reaches the Earth?

(A) The sun's energy reaches the Earth via convection currents.

(B) The sun's energy reaches the Earth via thermal radiation in the form of electromagnetic waves.

(C) The sun's energy reaches the Earth via alpha particles given off during radiative decay.

(D) The sun's energy reaches the Earth via conduction because heat flows from the hot sun to the cooler Earth.

38. The light from the sun takes 8 minutes 20 seconds to reach us. How far away is the sun from the Earth?

(A) 1.5 million km

(B) 2.5 million km

(C) 150 million km

(D) 250 million km

39. The number of which subatomic particle determines the identity of the element?

(A) protons

(B) neutrons

(C) electrons

(D) alpha particles

40. The sum of which subatomic particles determines the atomic mass number of an atom?

(A) protons and electrons

(B) protons and neutrons

(C) protons, electrons, and neutrons

(D) electrons and neutrons

41. Which of the following correctly fills in the blanks in the right order in this statement?

An isotope of an element contains the same number of _____ but a different number of _____ within the nucleus of the atom.

(A) protons and electrons

(B) protons and neutrons

(C) neutrons and protons

(D) electrons and neutrons

Use the following information and figure to help answer Questions 42–44.

Scientists now believe that Earth's continents were once joined together into a single landmass called Pangaea. This super continent began to break up 175 million years ago and slowly drift apart in a process known as continental drift to form the separate continents we see today. This diagram shows what Pangaea is believed to have looked like and how the continents have slowly drifted apart to appear as they do today.

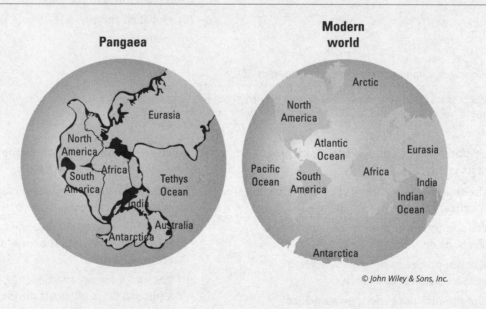

© John Wiley & Sons, Inc.

42. Which of the following statements does NOT support the Pangaea theory?

(A) The shape of the west coast of Africa seems to fit perfectly with the shape of the east coast of South America.

(B) Paleontologists have discovered matching fossils from identical species of land animals at corresponding locations along both the African and South American coasts.

(C) The Big Bang theory states that all matter in the universe expanded outward from the same point in space.

(D) Identical deposits of minerals have been found at corresponding locations along both the African and South American coasts.

43. What was the main cause of continental drift?

(A) Convection currents within the Earth's fluid mantle caused the tectonic plates floating upon the mantle to move relative to each other and separate.

(B) The meteorite that killed off the dinosaurs smashed into Pangaea 65 million years ago, causing it to split and drift apart.

(C) thermal expansion of the rock due to global warming

(D) weathering and erosion at the Earth's surface

44. Which of the following can occur when two continents drift apart from each other?

(A) the formation of a V-shaped valley

(B) the formation of a U-shaped valley

(C) the formation of an ocean ridge

(D) the formations of extreme weather including tornadoes

Use the following information and diagram to help answer Questions 45–46.

This figure shows how the sound waves from the siren of an ambulance appear to change as the ambulance moves toward or away from a stationary observer.

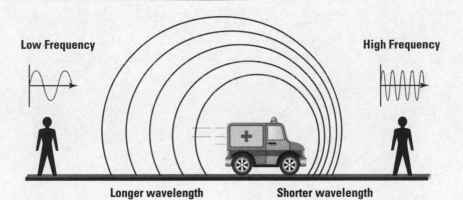

Low Frequency

High Frequency

Longer wavelength

Shorter wavelength

© John Wiley & Sons, Inc.

45. This figure shows an example of which phenomenon?

(A) Doppler effect

(B) reflection of waves

(C) constructive interference

(D) Newton's third law of motion

46. Which of the following correctly fills in the blanks in the right order in this statement?

As the ambulance moves *toward* the stationary observer, the frequency of the siren appears to _____. As the ambulance moves *away from* the stationary observer, the frequency of the siren appears to _____.

(A) decrease, increase

(B) increase, decrease

(C) become quieter, become louder

(D) appear, vanish

47. Which type of particle is emitted in the nuclear decay reaction shown here?

$$^{214}_{82}Pb \rightarrow\ ^{214}_{83}Bi +\ ^{0}_{-1}e$$

(A) an alpha particle

(B) a beta particle

(C) a gamma decay

(D) a proton

Chapter 24

Answers and Explanations for Practice Test 1

After you finish the practice test in Chapter 23, take some time to go through the answers and explanations in this chapter to find out which questions you missed and why. Even if you answered the question correctly, the explanation may offer a useful strategy that helps you improve your performance.

Answers for Section 1: Language Arts – Reading

1. **D.** You're told in the opening paragraph that the firm is called Scrooge and Marley, so Marley is Scrooge's ex-business partner.

2. **D.** The line "Hard and sharp as flint, from which no steel had ever struck out generous fire; secret, and self-contained, and solitary as an oyster" describes Scrooge as a cold, emotionally withdrawn person, so Choice (D) is correct.

3. **A.** The author implies that the dogs think it is better to be blind than to be nasty because they lead their blind masters away from Scrooge's unpleasant presence. The dogs appear to be happy with their blind masters and glad that they do not belong to someone unpleasant like Scrooge, hence Choice (A) is correct.

4. **B.** The passage clearly states Scrooge's dislike of Christmas and those who celebrate it, which rules out Choice (A). Christmas definitely makes Scrooge angry so you can rule out Choice (C). Scrooge describes Christmas as a "time for balancing your books" or taking stock of one's financial situation, so you can reject Choice (D). Although Scrooge replies "Humbug" when his nephew wishes him a Merry Christmas, this is meant as a curse (not a desire to eat humbug candies), so Choice (B) is correct.

5. C. The passage tells you that Scrooge's nephew clearly loves Christmas. He speaks passionately when defending Christmas to his uncle and mentions all the statements in Choices (A), (B), and (D) during his speech. He makes a point of saying that he loves Christmas despite the fact it has *not* made him better off financially, hence Choice (C) is correct.

6. B. The opening paragraph tells you that Scrooge owns the company, so Choice (B) is correct. Later in the passage, when his nephew is arguing with Scrooge, he replies to Scrooge, "You're rich enough," so you know that Scrooge is wealthy. Although Scrooge keeps his office poorly heated in winter, he only does so because he is a miser, making Choice (C) incorrect.

7. D. Scrooge is angry at the clerk for applauding his nephew's speech. When he says to the clerk, "and you'll keep your Christmas by losing your situation," the *situation* he is referring to is the clerk's job, hence Scrooge is threatening to fire him.

8. C. Scrooge's tone is sarcastic — he is making fun of his nephew's passionate speech, so Choice (C) is correct. He is not trying to praise his nephew or give him career advice or assure him that he would vote for him in the future, so you can reject Choices (A), (B), and (D).

9. D. The entire passage appears to be about a farm run by animals, but you're told that Jones, the previous owner, had given up hope of getting his farm back and had gone to live in another part of the county. Therefore, it appears that the animals have staged a rebellion and taken over the farm, making Choice (D) correct. Choice (A) is incorrect because it was the animals (not the men) who decided to build the windmill. Similarly, Choice (B) is incorrect because it was the animals (not Jones) who decided to enter into a business agreement with Mr. Pilkington or with Mr. Frederick. Choice (C) is wrong because the animals (not Jones) changed the name of the farm.

10. C. The opening paragraph describes how the humans were disdainful of Animal Farm at the beginning and assumed that it would fail. But as time went on they reluctantly changed their minds and started to respect the efficiency with which the animals were managing their own affairs. Hence, Choice (C) is correct.

11. C. The passage mentions that Squealer had begun speaking of Napoleon as the "leader," hence, Napoleon is the leader of pigs, making Choice (C) correct.

12. A. Throughout the passage Squealer tries to persuade the other animals that the pigs' behavior is acceptable even though it appears to be against the original rules of the farm. He is therefore acting like a politician trying to excuse the unethical behavior of others, making Choice (A) the correct answer.

13. C. Squealer uses all the reasons given in Choices (A), (B), and (D) to convince the animals that the pigs should now sleep in the farmhouse. Although he brings up the possibility that Jones might come back, this is to intimidate the animals into agreeing with him, making Choice (C) a false statement and hence, the correct answer.

14. B. Clover's reaction to the Fourth Commandment seems to imply that the commandment had been changed recently (without her knowledge) by adding in the words "with sheets" to the end of it. This rules out Choice (A). Choice (B) ties in well with the overall theme of the passage, which implies that the pigs are not really playing fairly, hence, Choice (B) is the correct answer. There is no indication that Clover is slowly losing her mind, Choice (C), or that she wears glasses, Choice (D).

15. A. Although many of the animals are beginning to suspect that something is going wrong with the pigs' behavior, Squealer had made them feel guilty and afraid that Jones could return if they continue to question their motives. Hence, Choice (A) is correct.

16. **D.** Throughout the passage the author implies that the pigs are not being entirely honest and are starting to behave more like humans than animals. Hence, Choice (D) is correct.

17. **C.** The main purpose of the passage is to introduce the main character, Gregor, and the background pressures that have caused his feelings of isolation. Hence, Choice (C) is correct. Although the reader may find the passage shocking, it is not the main intent of the author, so Choice (A) is incorrect.

18. **A.** The first few lines of the passage suggest that Gregor has turned into a giant cockroach. "His many legs, pitifully thin compared with the size of the rest of him, waved about helplessly as he looked." Hence, Choice (A) is correct.

19. **A.** This part of the story takes place in Gregor's parents' house. The room is familiar to him but is small and shabby, ruling out Choice (D). Toward the end of the passage, his mother appears outside his door, ruling out Choices (B) and (C). Hence, Choice (A) is correct.

20. **D.** The passage mentions that Gregor had recently cut the picture out of an illustrated magazine, hence, the picture is of an unknown lady from a magazine, making Choice (D) correct.

21. **B.** The passage mentions that Gregor is a traveling salesman.

22. **B.** The passage mentions that Gregor's boss prefers to sit on his desk so he can talk down at his subordinates. This implies that the boss wants to make his employees feel inferior, hence, Choice (B) is correct.

23. **C.** The passage mentions that Gregor longs to quit his job, but he can't do so until he has paid off his parents' debt to his boss, making Choice (C) the correct answer.

24. **D.** The passage mentions that all the factors in Choices (A), (B), and (C) add to Gregor's overall feeling of despair and hence, you can reject those answer choices. There is no mention of Gregor's wife or even whether he is married, so Choice (D) is a false statement making it the correct answer.

25. **C.** The passage is focused on diatoms, not professor Ram, so you can reject Choice (A). The passage states that diatoms are amazing little structures that can fly huge distances when they are taken up by the wind, so Choice (C) summarizes this nicely. Choice (B) is not bad but doesn't mention that they fly, and Choice (D) is too general — it doesn't mention diatoms at all.

26. **D.** The opening paragraph of the passage mentions that diatoms are glass-shelled algae that are transported through the air, so you can narrow your options down to either Choice (B) or Choice (D). The last paragraph discusses living diatoms, hence the correct answer must by Choice (D).

27. **A.** You are seeking an answer that explains how mentioning Frisbees can help the reader to understand why diatoms are able to fly even though they are relatively large. Choice (A) is correct because the reader can easily visualize a Frisbee, which is an example of a large object that can fly long distances. Choices (B) and (D) may be true but don't help explain why diatoms can fly. Choice (C) is untrue — Frisbees are much larger than diatoms.

28. **C.** The opening paragraph of the passage mentions that diatoms "raise interesting questions. They seem to defy the size limit for far-flying dust, for one thing. And they may sometimes fly with a purpose." Hence, Choices (A) and (D) are true statements and can therefore be

rejected. The last paragraph mentions Choice (B) so that can be rejected, which leaves you with Choice (C) as the correct answer.

29. **B.** The word "teasing" is used in the second paragraph to describe how professor Ram removes or *extracts* the diatoms from their ice core, hence, the best answer is Choice (B).

30. **D.** The third paragraph mentions that diatoms' geometric perfection makes them stand out when they are viewed under a microscope, hence, Choice (D) is correct. Choice (A) refers to desert dust particles, not diatoms. There is no mention of their color, so Choice (C) can also be rejected.

31. **C.** The excerpt focuses on giving example of heavy items that have been carried by the wind, so Choice (C) is correct.

32. **B.** The word "hodgepodge" means a confused mixture.

33. **C.** Passage 1 states that the heat from radioactive elements, as well as the heat produced during a collision with meteors, caused most of the Earth to melt, so Choice (C) is correct. Choice (B) is wrong because meteors that pass close to the Earth without colliding would not produce any heat.

34. **C.** The author of Passage 1 ends the paragraph with an exclamation point to emphasize the great difference in the conditions on Earth at that time compared to today. Hence, Choice (C) is correct. There's no indication that the author disapproves of radioactive elements or is feeling bored or angry, so you can reject Choices (A), (B), and (D).

35. **D.** The word "analogy" mean a comparison, making Choice (D) correct.

36. **D.** Based on the titles of the passages alone, you can tell that both passages are primarily concerned with the origin of planets and other astronomical objects including the moon, making Choice (D) the correct answer.

37. **A.** The main difference between the passages is that Passage 1 focuses on how the planets became molten, whereas Passage 2 focuses on why the heavenly bodies start to rotate, making Choice (A) the best answer. Passage 2 makes no mention of the benefits of radioactive materials, so you can reject Choice (B). The only quote from an expert comes in Passage 2 (not Passage 1), so Choice (C) is wrong. Passage 2 (not Passage 1) focuses on the origin of the moon, so you can reject Choice (D).

38. **B.** The rules state that employees must refrain from inviting visitors to the workplace in order to keep the premises secure, hence Choice (B) is correct.

39. **D.** The rules state that if an employee believes his supervisor is treating him unfairly, he should inform the Human Resources department, hence Choice (D) is correct.

40. **B.** The rules state that employees must not use offensive language and must respect the dignity of all persons, regardless of gender, creed, or culture, and conduct themselves with dignity. Hence sexist behavior (discrimination based on sex) will not be tolerated by anyone, making Choice (B) correct. Although Choice (A) is probably a true statement, it's not the correct answer because it doesn't describe sexist behavior.

41. **B.** Because the employee is new, you can assume that this is his first offense, so he would be required to meet with his supervisor, making Choice (B) correct. Choice (A) would only happen after the third offense (not the first), whereas Choice (C) would only happen after the second offense. Choice (D) is amusing but should be rejected.

42. **A.** The most likely reason why the company used the word "choose" is to shift the responsibility for non-compliance back to the employee rather than the company. Hence, Choice (A) is the best answer. The wording of the rules appears to have been carefully selected, making Choice (B) unlikely. The rules state that employees must accept the authority of supervisors without argument but that they can still go to the Human Resources department to complain if they are being treated unfairly, making Choice (C) wrong. There is no indication that the company is playing mind games with its employees, so you can reject Choice (D).

43. **B.** The company has probably announced its policy on employee behavior for several reasons, including to ensure that employees understand what behavior is expected of them, Choice (A); to ensure the safety of the working environment, Choice (C); and to make the working environment more pleasant for everyone, Choice (D). Hence, only Choice (B) remains as the correct answer. The rules actually make it easier for the company to fire any non-compliant employees because the employee can't argue that he was not aware of the rules.

44. **C.** The title of the passage makes it clear that the article is about photography and cameras, so Choice (C) is correct.

45. **B.** The passage states that you must turn off the camera before opening the latched cover or concealed door when installing the batteries, so Choice (B) is correct.

46. **C.** The passage states that a battery icon on the LCD tells you when battery power is low, making Choice (C) the best answer. The question stem says that you will have to replace the batteries *soon* so the device is not dead yet, making Choice (A) incorrect. Choice (B) is silly, whereas Choice (D) would suggest that the batteries have too much power rather than need replacing.

47. **D.** The passage states that a diagram and/or plus and minus markings are usually present within the compartment or on the inside of the door, making Choice (D) the best answer. The question stem tells you that the camera is empty, so the LCD and battery icon will not be on, making Choices (A), (B), and (C) incorrect.

48. **A.** If the batteries are in the wrong way, the camera will not switch on, making Choice (A) the correct answer. This also eliminates Choices (B) and (D). Choice (C) is silly and should be rejected.

49. **A.** The passage states that with unhinged covers, the entire cover comes off when you unscrew them, so you risk losing them if they fall when you're outside. Hence Choice (A) is correct.

50. **A.** The passage explains very basic features about cameras (like how to change the batteries), hence Choice (A) is the best answer. A professional photographer would already know how to change the batteries, so you can reject Choice (B).

Answers for Section 2: Language Arts – Writing

Part 1: Language

1. **B.** The story told here is silly, but don't let that distract you from looking closely at the punctuation. Choice (B) is the only correctly punctuated sentence. Choice (A) places a semicolon where no punctuation is needed. Choice (C) uses a colon where a comma would work best, and Choice (D) places a semicolon in the middle of a sentence, but it should be used for joining two independent clauses.

2. **A.** The idea here is to choose the sentence that best completes the thoughts begun in the paragraph. Choice (A) does the best job here, by bringing the paragraph to a natural conclusion. Choice (B) is off-topic, and both Choices (C) and (D) offer further information to a specific fact in the paragraph, but do not conclude the main idea presented.

3. **C.** Choice (C) contains the misspelled word "license."

4. **A.** The trick here is to find the best answer, as more than one sentence may be correct. Choice (A) is the best sentence here. Choice (B) is technically correct, but awkward, with Choice (A) expressing the same idea better. Choice (D), similarly, is not horribly wrong, but again is too awkward to be the best answer. And Choice (C) confuses verb tenses, using past tense in the first part and future tense in the second, which can't be correct.

5. **C.** You may feel that the original sentence is correct, but do note that it's not offered as an option. Out of what remains, Choice (A) is a clear sentence but is slightly different in meaning than the original. Choice (B) is awkward, and Choice (D) is gibberish — just a reshuffled sentence. That leaves Choice (C) as the best option. Note that it makes clear that the cries were coming from below, not the speakers.

6. **D.** You need to remember a few grammatical rules to get this one right. Years are always written in numerical form, so Choice (A) is wrong. Likewise, Choice (B) can't be correct because country names (including their adjective form) are always capitalized. Choice (C) is clearly a question but doesn't end with a question mark. That leaves Choice (D). Even if you don't know whether the name of the form is correctly punctuated (which it is), you know that the other three sentences are wrong, so this one must be correct.

7. **C.** Notice that this question asks you to find the best opening sentence, which is often a way of asking you to find the best thesis for a paragraph. You can eliminate Choice (D) immediately, as it is restated later in the paragraph. Choice (B) is off-topic. Choice (A) seems like a good bet, but notice how the use of the term "world traveler" directly contradicts the second sentence, which says that voles rarely leave a small parcel of land. Thus, Choice (C) is the best answer as it leads directly into the rest of the paragraph.

8. **D.** The key here is to choose the answer that is most effective. Choice (B) is interesting enough, but off-topic, and thus not effective. Choice (C) restates a prior sentence in the paragraph, and Choice (A) gives away what's coming in the next paragraph. (Remember, you can't change the other sentences!) That leaves Choice (D) as the best answer. It effectively finishes the first paragraph and leads into the next.

9. **A.** Here, the correct answer must keep the meaning of the two sentences while also linking them together more effectively. Choice (A) does the best job at that task. Choices (B) and (D) both manage to change the meaning of the sentence, by rearranging the words. Choice (C)

keeps the general meaning of the original, but mistakenly implies that algorithms are always undisputable, which can't be true.

10. **A.** It's tempting to select Choice (B), but directions are not capitalized — phrases like "the North" or "the South" are. Choice (C) contains no errors because "principal" isn't capitalized, and Choice (D) is also correct. That leaves Choice (A), which contains an error: seasons of the year are not capitalized. Thus, Choice (A) is the correct answer.

11. **B.** Here, the word that best stresses how important rehydration is must be chosen. That eliminates Choices (C) and (A), which are both too weak. Choice (D) is a good answer, but Choice (B) means "very important, even key," which makes it the stronger answer. Given the question's parameters, Choice (B) is the best choice.

12. **D.** Remember that you're asked to find the sentence that is most correct and concise. Choice (A) is technically correct, but the verbs are awkward. Choice (B) changes the order in the original sentence. Choice (C) is getting closer, but you'll note that it does not solve the problem of which "she" the first part of the sentence is referring to. That leaves Choice (D) as the best answer.

13. **B.** Choice (B) contains a spelling error: "transferred" is the correct spelling. Note that Choice (D) contains a similar word spelled correctly ("concurred"), which should alert you that one or the other is wrong.

14. **C.** Choice (C) is the best answer because the sentence is two separate independent clauses, best joined together with a semicolon. Choice (B) would make it a run-on sentence, while Choice (A) would be correct if it included the suggestion that "She" be capitalized. That leaves Choice (D), which only suggests an unnecessary comma.

15. **A.** Here, the best way to work is to eliminate the answers that are correct. Choice (B) seems to be fine. Although you might question the comma, you'll remember that the Oxford comma (after "Nancy") is acceptable. Choice (C) is also correct, as is Choice (D). There's something off about Choice (A), though: The verb should match the noun it's closest to in a compound subject. You wouldn't write "Peter are," so there's the error!

16. **B.** Choice (D) may seem like a good guess, but it changes the meaning of the sentence so that it is no longer clear that Lu Wei is presenting the trip as an idea for the club. Choice (A) is awkward, while Choice (C) doesn't include all the information in the original sentence. That leaves Choice (B), the best answer because it's both accurate and effective.

17. **A.** Choice (A) is the best answer. Choice (B) gives unnecessary information, and Choice (C) makes the topic much more broad than the rest of the paragraph. That leaves Choice (D), which is also off-topic (and would make the paragraph sound a bit prejudiced toward soccer!).

18. **C.** The blank represents a transition wherein the sentence makes it clear the song remained the same but the artists interpreted it uniquely. That makes Choice (C) the best choice because it shows that transition. The other answers show different kinds of transitions that are not appropriate to the sentence's content.

19. **A.** Here, you're looking for the introductory sentence for the third paragraph. You can eliminate Choice (D) right away because the paragraph later repeats the same information. Choice (B) restates an earlier sentence in simpler language, and Choice (C) is also information that's been presented before. Choice (A) is the best answer because it introduces the rest of the paragraph's topic.

20. **C.** The paragraph break should come after the third sentence in the first paragraph. If you know that paragraphs should have three or more sentences, you can eliminate Choices (A) and (B). A close look shows that the fourth sentence ought to be the first sentence of a second paragraph, so Choice (D) can be eliminated. That leaves Choice (C) as the correct answer.

21. **A.** Choice (A) is the best restructuring of the original sentence, which is missing the preposition "to." Choice (B) changes the word order but not effectively, and Choice (C) makes the end of the sentence past tense, which is not the original meaning. Finally, Choice (D) doesn't fix the problem of the missing "to."

22. **C.** In Choice (C), "technique" is misspelled.

23. **C.** Choice (C) is the only sentence that is punctuated correctly. Choice (A) contains an unnecessary comma, while Choice (B) uses a colon where the verb should appear. Finally, Choice (D) places the end punctuation outside of the quotation marks instead of within them, as is proper.

24. **D.** While it may seem incorrect, Choice (A) is actually right. When referring to an area instead of a direction (as in "I grew up in the South"), capitalize the word. Choice (B) is also correct because you should capitalize all the important words (and the first word) in a title. As for Choice (C), it is correct to capitalize the name of a city. You should also capitalize the adjective form of country names (as in English, French, Iranian) so Choice (D) is incorrect and the right answer.

25. **B.** Here, you must find the best conclusion, which Choice (B) surely is. Choice (A) provides unnecessary information, while Choice (C) is off-topic. Choice (D) might be the first sentence in a subsequent paragraph, but does not finish this one.

26. **B.** Combining sentences can be tricky. Choice (B) is the answer that best keeps the meaning behind the two sentences. Choice (A) is awkward with the phrase "as the saying goes" tagged on the end, too far from the saying. Choice (C) is awkward, too, sticking the subject of the sentence in the middle of two phrases. Finally, Choice (D) almost works, until that last phrase, which is awkwardly stuck on to the sentence.

27. **A.** This question requires you to look carefully at the paragraphs given and decide what thesis is correct. Choice (B) is a definition of baseball and too general for the specific topic in the draft, which is whether baseball is American in origin. Choice (C) seems better but implies that the topic of the paragraph is basketball. Choice (D) is far too general. That leaves Choice (A), which asks the question the rest of the draft seeks to answer.

28. **C.** The key here is to keep the original intent of the sentence while eliminating extra words. Choice (A) is not shorter because it simply replaces "thus for that reason" with "so for that reason." Choice (B) slightly changes the meaning by implying that the movie itself canceled their dinner plans. Choice (D) splits the sentence in two, creating a fragment. That leaves Choice (C), which keeps the meaning of the sentence but makes it read more clearly.

29. **D.** The first sentence in a paragraph is generally the thesis sentence. Thus, you need to choose the answer that best states the topic of the rest of the paragraph. It isn't about the dangers of canning nor about what canning is, so eliminate Choices (A) and (B). Choice (C) might work but also seems a little broad. Plus, Choice (C) seems very similar to the paragraph's existing first sentence. That makes Choice (D) the best option.

30. **A.** The error is in Choice (A). Five hundred does not need a hyphen. The test-makers assume you will guess Choice (B) because of the quotation marks included, but because you know the rules for quotation marks, you won't be fooled!

31. **B.** The question asks you to choose the version of the sentence that best emphasizes the home's location. That makes it easy to eliminate all the choices in which the location is in a phrase instead of the main portion of the sentence: Choices (A) and (D). You can also eliminate Choice (C) because that answer does not even mention the cottage's location. That leaves Choice (B), the best choice because the location is the main information of the sentence.

32. **C.** Choice (C) includes an incorrect spelling of the word "apparently."

33. **C.** The blank is between a general statement in the sentence and what appears to be an example that further proves the sentence. Choices (A) and (D) would each change the meaning of the sentence, so they can't be correct. Choice (B) is close, but not the best answer. Choice (C) is grammatically correct and continues the sentence's meaning correctly, making it the best choice.

34. **A.** The first sentence generally introduces the topic of the essay. In this case, there's no topic sentence, so you know you must choose the option that best provides one. Choice (B) is a little broad for an essay about tornado readiness. Choice (C) is off-topic (as well as broad). Choice (D) ties into the rest of the essay but is too specific; the remainder of the essay is not only about debris. That leaves Choice (A), an effective topic sentence.

35. **C.** You may feel that the second does not need to have a paragraph break; however, no break is not an option in the answers, so you must choose the one you think will work best. There is a natural break in Choice (C), as the topic turns from home preparedness to that of a school. That makes this the best answer.

36. **B.** Errors in verb tense are frequently featured on the TASC; looking at the verbs in each sentence is a safe bet. Remember, you want to find the sentence that does not contain errors. Here, Choice (B) is the best answer. In Choice (A), the sentence should read that the graduation ceremony "is" two weeks away. In Choice (C), there is a subject/verb disagreement, because "are" should be used with "several." In Choice (D), the correct verb is "is," not "is being."

37. **A.** You can eliminate Choice (D) quickly, as the verb is wrong. Choice (B) doesn't include enough of the information in the original sentence, while Choice (C) twists the meaning because the original does not suggest that it's a good place for residents to meet visitors. That leaves Choice (A), which does preserve the meaning of the sentence in the original form while also making it clearer.

38. **D.** Another opportunity to keep the meaning in the original sentence while making it more clear. Choice (A) leaves out the information about the park, while Choice (B) uses more words than necessary in the supporting phrases. As for Choice (C), it's pretty good until the last section, which should read "my brother and me." That makes Choice (D) the best answer.

39. **A.** The best answer is to change the comma to a semicolon, Choice (A). This will allow the joining of two independent clauses. A period could be added, but then "she's" would need to be capitalized, so the answer can't be Choice (B). There's no need for a question mark, as in Choice (C), and eliminating the comma, as in Choice (D), doesn't fix the run-on sentence.

40. **B.** Here, you must decide what sentence best sums up the information presented in the paragraph. In a sense, you're looking for the topic sentence, or what the paragraph has been building to. Choices (A) and (C) provide more information but don't end the paragraph, as at least one more sentence would be needed. Choice (D) adds more information about one aspect of the first paragraph but does not conclude it. That leaves Choice (B), the best conclusion provided.

41. **D.** The provided sentence lacks a verb, so you must find the answer that best revises that mistake. Choice (A) flips the opening phrase and the independent clause, but without correcting the grammar. Choice (B) adds in "will" but doesn't fix the sentence. Choice (C) looks good at first, but the verb is wrong, because a singular subject like "Ming" needs "has," not "have." That leaves Choice (D), which is correct.

42. **B.** Proper names, whether of clothing companies, apples, or avenues, must be capitalized. So, too, should all peoples' names. In Choice (B), "Maplethorpe Avenue" is the full name of the street, and avenue should be capitalized.

43. **B.** Notice that the question asks you to find the best conclusion for this paragraph. You can thus eliminate Choice (D), which simply provides more information about the subject. Choice (C) seems slightly off-topic, and Choice (A) repeats information and then adds a bit more, but does not conclude the paragraph. Only Choice (B) does that.

44. **C.** In Choice (C), "privilege" is misspelled.

45. **A.** The semicolon is incorrectly placed where a comma would be better. That makes Choice (A) the best answer. While Choice (C) does advise a change that can be acceptable, it does not fix the biggest problem in the sentence's punctuation. Remember that a comma in a list before "and" is optional.

46. **B.** Choice (B) contains an extra comma, between "bags" and "of stuff." The three remaining sentences are correct in their punctuation.

47. **D.** "Refined" best shows how the technology is changed. Choice (A) is not a bad choice, but Choice (D) is better because it implies that the technology is improved, not just changed.

48. **A.** Choice (A) is the best answer. The sentences are linked in that the second proves the first. The other three answer choices imply that the second sentence contradicts the first.

49. **B.** You need to find the word that best connects the two ideas. Reading the sentence will show that the connection is one of support: Because Lee grew up in the South, she wrote about racism. Thus, Choice (B) is the best answer.

50. **D.** Again, the key is finding the relationship between the two existing sentences. The first makes a statement, and the second shows how the facts contradict it. In Choice (C), however, that relationship is not clear (and there's a verb error, as well). Choice (A) is similarly unclear, seeming to demonstrate that the second novel proves the first sentence, instead of contradicting it. Choice (B) is correct in meaning but is not grammatically correct. That leaves Choice (D) as the best choice.

Part 2: Writing

The following is an example of an essay that would likely score a 4 on the TASC. It scores high because the author takes a clear stand on the opinion presented in the essay; in this case, it supports the author's logic. The essay includes solid details and facts from the text. Compare it to your own sample essay and note where you might improve.

I concur with Melissa Marr, the author of "Time to Buckle Up," that all states should have mandatory seat belt usage laws for every seat in a vehicle. The author effectively proves that such laws would save lives. It is a convincing argument.

The Centers for Disease Control and Prevention (called the CDC) provided the author with some of the statistics she quotes. For example, the CDC says that 2.2 million people enter an emergency room at a hospital every year with injuries sustained in a car crash. Also, the author shows that the CDC shows that auto accidents are a leading cause of death. Right there, you have two pieces of evidence that show that we need to make riding in cars safer.

One of the best ways to do that, according to Melissa Marr, is to wear a seat belt. Wearing a seat belt will save lives by allowing people to survive accidents. She particularly makes the point that people should wear seat belts even when driving in an area close to their homes. Too many people assume that if they feel comfortable, as they would around their own hometowns, they do not need to worry about safety. However, if people knew that they could face a big fine, they probably would remember to buckle up, even when just running an errand at home. The author says that there are 33 states that don't have such laws, and I agree that they should pass those soon.

It's true that wearing a seat belt will not result in an accident-free world. There are many other ways drivers can cause accidents, from being inattentive to operating cars that are not in good condition. However, Marr has convinced me that wearing a seat belt — and having laws that strongly encourage drivers to do so — is a good first step in saving lives.

Answers for Section 3: Mathematics

Part 1

1. **B.** To calculate gross pay, you multiply the per hour rate by the number of hours worked. This means you multiply 10.15×17 and get (B) \$172.55. Choice (A) is incorrect because you added the two values together instead of multiplying them. Choices (C) and (D) are calculator errors.

2. **D.** To check which of the answers is correct, you can substitute all the possible choices and see which holds true. If you substitute Choice (A) you get: $2^{-2} = 16$ which gives you $\frac{1}{4} = 16$. Because this is false, Choice (A) is incorrect. Following the same process, you see Choices (B) and (C) produce false statements as well. This means that the correct answer is Choice (D) because $2^4 = 16$ is true.

3. **B.** Because the probability of an independent event is calculated by the number of ways the event can occur out of the total possible number of outcomes, the probability for picking a red marble is $\frac{5}{20} = \frac{1}{4}$. If there are more than one independent event occurring, you multiply the individual probabilities. This means the probability for each red is independent of the others (because the marble is replaced) and leaves you with: $\frac{1}{4} \cdot \frac{1}{4} \cdot \frac{1}{4} \cdot \frac{1}{4} = \frac{1}{256}$, which is Choice (B).

4. **D.** To simplify a cube root, find the prime factorization and look for triples in the factors of 64: $4 \cdot 4 \cdot 4 = 64$. This means a 4 can be factored out from underneath the radical. In addition, you see that the x^6 can be made into three groups of x^2, which means x^2 can be factored out: The y's don't have enough to make a triple, so that stays under the radical. This gives you the simplified form of $4x^2 \sqrt[3]{y^2}$, which is Choice (D). Choices (A) and (B) are incorrect because the cube root of 64 is not 8. Choice (C) is incorrect because you factored out a y when you were unable to do so.

5. **B.** With rational exponents, recall that the denominator becomes the index of the radical so $\frac{1}{3} = \sqrt[3]{}$. This means you take the cube root of 8 first, $\sqrt[3]{8} = 2$, and then square it, $2^2 = 4$, which is Choice (B). Choice (A) is incorrect because you forgot to square it. Choices (C) and (D) are incorrect because you took the radical or raised it to the power incorrectly.

6. **C.** Because the initial startup fee occurs when there are no additional costs, it occurs when the line crosses the y-axis. Based on this graph, the initial fee is $25, Choice (C).

7. **48 inches.** To calculate this you must recall that circumference is $2\pi r$ or πd. This means $301.44 = (3.14)(2)(r)$ and solve the resulting equation.

8. **D.** You should notice that you must use both the order of operations and the exponent rules. Recall that anything to the 0 power is 1, so using the exponent rules you get $3(1+25) = 3(26) = 78$, which is Choice (D). Choices (A) and (C) result from applying the 0 exponent rule incorrectly.

9. **B.** Because the orientation of the shapes is the same, you can rule out Choice (A) because a rotation would change the direction of the shape. Similarly, a reflection would flip the directionality of the figure, so you can rule out Choices (C) and (D). This leaves you Choice (B), which is correct because it's almost as if you picked up the shape and moved it into its new position.

10. **A.** The answer is Choice (A) because you see the pattern in the y-column is increasing by 3 each time and $2 + 3 = 5$.

11. **91.** Find the sum of the four current test scores, which is 344. Then multiply 87 by 5 to find what the sum should be, which is 435. Now subtract 435 minus 344 and you get the test score needed to get an 87 average.

12. **C.** Because this is a quadratic equation, you can solve it in multiple ways. One method is factoring, in which you set the equation equal to 0 by subtracting 19 from both sides. This results in a difference of squares structure, where you can factor it into $(2x + 5)(2x - 5)$. Solving this requires setting each factor equal to 0, and solving the resulting equations produces Choice (C).

13. **C.** The first thing you need to calculate is the number of miles the car can do on one tank by multiplying 32 by 13, which is 416 miles. Then divide the miles of the trip by the miles in one tankful: $2219 \div 416 = 5.334$. This means the correct answer is Choice (C) because 5 tanks would not be quite enough to make it.

14. **D.** You can express 35% as both a decimal and a fraction. As a decimal it is .35, which rules out Choices (A) and (B). Recall that to write a percentage as a fraction you write the percent over 100 and simplify: $\frac{35}{100} = \frac{7}{20}$, which is Choice (D).

15. **0.125.** To find the function value at the given x-value, substitute -3 in for x and then simplify: $2^{-3} = \frac{1}{2^3} = \frac{1}{8}$ or 0.125.

16. **D.** First calculate the mean, median, and mode of the data set. The results are: mean = 4.6, median = 3.5, and mode = 3. This means the correct answer is Choice (D) because it shows them in order from smallest to largest.

17. **4.24.** To calculate the distance between the two points, first find the ordered pairs for each point: E $(-2, 1)$ and A $(1, 4)$. Now use the distance formula to calculate the length of that segment: $\sqrt{(-2-1)^2+(1-4)^2}=\sqrt{9+9}=\sqrt{18}\approx 4.2426$. Rounding to the nearest hundredth place means rounding to two decimal places, which gives you the answer of 4.24.

18. **D.** The correct answer is Choice (D). If you chose Choice (A) or (B), you did not distribute correctly, and Choice (C) was an error with combining like terms.

19. **A.** The correct answer is Choice (A). To solve this problem, you can either find the scale factor or set up a proportion: $\frac{\text{Small}}{\text{Large}}:\frac{3}{31}=\frac{2}{x}$. To solve a proportion, cross multiply and solve the resulting equation.

20. **D.** To set up a system of equations, first define your variables: a = # of adult tickets sold and c = # of child tickets sold. Because the prices of each ticket are given as well as the total proceeds, multiply each variable by its associated price: $7a$ and $5c$. This will allow you to eliminate Choices (A) and (C). The total proceeds are $415, which you find from adding $7a+5c$ together. Similarly, adding the number of each ticket sold, a and c, together will give you the total ticket sales: $a+c=65$. This reveals that the correct answer is Choice (D).

21. **6.** Because you know he has exactly 4 nickels, you can subtract 20 cents from the total: $1.55-.2=1.35$, which is the sum of quarters and nickels: $.25q+.1d$. In addition, you know that there are twice as many dimes and quarters: $d=2q$. Combining the two equations you get: $.25q+.1(2q)=1.35\to .25q+.2q=1.35\to .45q=1.35$ so $q=3$. Now that you know how many quarters there are, just double it to find how many dimes: 6.

22. **C.** The number of different ways to place 4 different items in order is simply $4!=(4)(3)(2)(1)=24$, Choice (C). Another way is to consider how many friends are left to sit in each chair. Any of the 4 friends can sit on the first seat; any of the remaining 3 friends can sit on the second seat; any of the remaining 2 friends can sit on the third seat; and there is only one friend left for the remaining seat. Multiply these results together to get Choice (C).

23. **B.** Because this is a quadratic equation, it can be solved in one of three ways: factoring, quadratic formula, or completing the square. The quadratic formula is the most efficient because it can work in every situation. This means, substituting $a=2$, $b=3$, $c=-9$ into $x=\dfrac{-b\pm\sqrt{b^2-4ac}}{2a}$ results in Choice (B).

24. **C.** When combining radicals, you first have to check that the radicands (the expression under the radical symbol) are the same. Because they are in this problem, you add the two coefficients together and leave the radicands alone, which results in Choice (C).

25. **C.** The sum of a rational number and an irrational number is always an irrational number. Because $\frac{7}{4}$ is a rational number and pi is an irrational number, their sum will always be irrational — Choice (C).

26. **A.** Comparing numbers in different forms can be difficult, so you want to rewrite them all into the same form (usually decimals is the easiest). $\frac{2}{5}=.4$, .6 is already a decimal, $1\frac{2}{3}=1.\overline{6}$, and $350\%=3.5$. Now that they're all in decimal form, you need to remember what ascending means → smallest to largest. This means the order should be .4, .6, $1.\overline{6}$, 3.5. Substituting back in the original values, you get: $\frac{2}{5}$, .6, $1\frac{2}{3}$, 350%, which is Choice (A).

Part 2

27. **C.** Using the fact that line *n* can be called a *transversal,* you see that there special types of angle relationships formed. You can see that the angles are complementary, so they sum to 180°, so Choice (C) is the correct answer.

28. **5.** To find the median of the data set, first put the numbers in order from least to greatest. After the data points are in order, look for the "middle" number by counting from each end. In this case the median is 5.

29. **A.** To isolate a particular variable, you "un-do" the operations surrounding it. The first thing to do to isolate *h* is multiply both sides by 3: $3V = \pi r^2 h$. Notice that the operations on the left side are all multiplication. This means you need to divide both sides by πr^2. This results in Choice (A) as the correct formula.

30. **B.** Because the trend line, or line of best fit, of this scatter plot has a positive slope, there is a positive relationship between the variables. This means as one increases the other increases: the longer you study, the better you will do on the test, Choice (B) is correct. For there to be no relationship, the line of best fit would be a "flat" horizontal line. For a negative relationship, the slope would be negative or "pointing down."

31. **A.** Because you're looking for a line parallel to the given line, the new equation would have the same slope: $m = -3$. Because Choice (A) is the only equation with that slope, it's the correct answer. Choice (C) represents a line perpendicular to the given line, while Choices (B) and (D) have slopes that have no specific relationship with the given slope.

32. **D.** With the length and width being doubled, you can represent it as 2*l* and 2*w*. Using these representations of the new width and length, you can calculate the area of the rectangle by multiplying them: $2l \cdot 2w = 4lw$. This means that the original area, *lw*, has been multiplied by a factor of 4, Choice (D).

33. **C.** The solution represented on the number line is $x \geq -1$, which eliminates Choices (A) and (B) because they don't have an "or equal to" part of their inequality symbols. This leaves you with two inequalities to solve and find the solutions to. Choice (D)'s solution is $x \leq 1$, which is not what is shown on the number line. Be careful with the negative signs when solving Choice (D). This leaves you with Choice (C) as the answer, which is correct.

34. **A.** The first step to solve this problem is to calculate the volume of both cylinders. Because calculators are not allowed in this section, it would be wise to just leave both volumes in terms of π. The volume formula for a cylinder is $V = \pi r^2 h$. Using the formula, you see that the volume of cylinder A is $V_A = \pi(4)^2(3) = \pi(16)(3) = 48\pi$. Be careful when calculating the volume of cylinder B because you're given the diameter, not the radius. Calculating the volume of cylinder B is $V_B = \pi(3)^2(5) = \pi(9)(5) = 45\pi$. This means that cylinder A has a greater volume, so the correct answer is Choice (A).

35. **0.0364 or 3.64%.** When calculating the probability of an event, you divide the number of ways the event can happen out of the total number of possible outcomes. In this case, the two events are dependent because the outcome of the second event is affected by the outcome of the first. In this case, the probability of selecting an M is $\frac{2}{11}$ and then the probability of selecting an A is $\frac{2}{10} = \frac{1}{5}$, 10 is the denominator because one of the M's was selected already. You now multiply the two probabilities and get $\frac{2}{55}$ or 0.0364 or 3.64%.

36. **D.** To find this answer, you can square each of the choices given to you. The only one that results in –9 is Choice (D). Another way to solve this problem is to take the square root of –9, which results in $3i$.

37. **A.** Because taking the square root and squaring an expression are opposite operations, they "undo" each other. This means $(\sqrt{2x^3y})^2 = 2x^3y$, which is Choice (A).

38. **C.** To find the inverse of a function, start by substituting y in for $f(x)$, then switch x and y. Now solve for y:

$$f(x) = \frac{2}{3}x - 8$$
$$y = \frac{2}{3}x - 8$$
$$x = \frac{2}{3}y - 8$$
$$x + 8 = \frac{2}{3}y$$

Recall at this point, you would multiply by 3 and then divide by 2 *or* multiply by the reciprocal of $\frac{2}{3}$, which is $\frac{3}{2}$. This means the correct answer is Choice (C).

39. **10.** From the diagram, you can see that $\overline{AC}$ is a diameter of the circle. This means that $\angle ABC$ intercepts a semicircle, which means that $\angle ABC$ is a right angle. Because this is a right triangle, you can solve for the missing side, the hypotenuse to be exact, by using the Pythagorean theorem. This means that $\overline{AC} = 10$.

40. **B.** Visually, you can see that the minimum occurs just a little after 1, so the x-coordinate of the ordered pair should be slightly greater than 1. Inspecting what options you're given, you can guess that the coordinate should be 1.2 because that is the only one that occurs between 1 and 2. This means Choice (B) is correct.

41. **D.** The only type of parallelograms that have congruent diagonals are rectangles, so that is the only property that does not apply to *all* parallelograms. Hence, Choice (D) is the correct answer.

42. **B.** The first thing to do is identify the y-intercepts: 3 and –1. Now find the slopes of the lines associated with each of the y-intercepts; the line with a y-intercept of 3 has a negative slope, which eliminates Choices (A) and (C). Further inspection allows you to conclude that the slope associated with 3 is –2, while the slope of the line with the y-intercept of –1 is 1. This means the equation of the two lines is $y = -2x + 3$ and $y = x - 1$, which is Choice (B).

43. **13.** When solving a multi-step equation, first simplify both sides of the equation by distributing into the parenthesis and combining like terms. Then get x's to one side and constants to the other. Lastly, divide by the coefficient of x.

$$3(2x - 4) = 4(x + 2) + 6$$
$$6x - 12 = 4x + 8 + 6$$
$$6x - 12 = 4x + 14$$
$$2x = 26$$
$$x = 13$$

44. **D.** First "take care" of the negative exponent on the outside: $\frac{1}{(3x^4)^2}$. Now distribute the outside exponent: $\frac{1}{9x^8}$; recall that you will be using the power rule on inside/outside exponents, which is Choice (D).

45. **C.** Create a system of equations by defining Nancy's age as n and Lisa's age as l. Using the information in the problem, you see that $n = 2l - 4$ and $n + l = 62$. To solve the system, substitute in the expression for n and solve.

$$(2l - 4) + l = 62$$
$$3l - 4 = 62$$
$$3l = 66$$
$$l = 22$$

Now that you know Lisa's age is 22, you can see that the answer is Choice (C).

46. **A.** Because the distance is based off the ground and not the cliff, the distance can only be positive, so Choice (A) is correct.

47. **B.** Because the median of a data set is illustrated by the center line in the box part of a box-and-whisker plot, the median of this data set is Choice (B), which is 25.

48. **80 minutes.** This type of word problem is a work problem so you first find the rate that each one can do the job: $J = \frac{1}{2}$ and $S = \frac{1}{4}$. Because they're working together, add the two rates together: $J + S = \frac{1}{2} + \frac{1}{4} = \frac{3}{4}$. Now "flip" the resulting rate to find out how long it will take them to cut this one lawn together: $\frac{3}{4}$ of an hour. Now convert this answer into minutes by multiplying by 60 to give your final answer which equals 80 minutes.

49. **C.** When reflecting an object over the x-axis, the sign of the y-coordinate changes. Because the original coordinates of A is $(-5, 3)$, the coordinates of A' is $(-5, -3)$, which is Choice (C).

50. **A.** When multiplying polynomials, look at what type of polynomials you're multiplying. In this case, because it's a binomial times a binomial, you can use the FOIL method to multiply. This results in $6x^2 + 12x - 4x - 8$, which simplifies to Choice (A), $6x^2 + 8x - 8$.

51. **100.** Because the pattern is dividing by -2 each time, the next term in the sequence is 100.

52. **D.** Calculate the area and perimeter of each of the options. Recall the perimeter is found by adding up all the sides, and the area of a rectangle/square is found by multiplying length times width. In this case, the only dimensions provided that satisfy the problem is the square with dimensions of $4\,\text{ft} \times 4\,\text{ft}$, Choice (D), because its area is $16\,\text{ft}^2$ and its perimeter is 16 ft.

Answers for Section 4: **Social Studies**

1. **C.** Washington is urging caution for us in our relationship with Europe — trade freely with them but beware of political entanglements — we don't need to get caught up in their complicated affairs.

2. **D.** The granting of the right to vote for women was their goal.

3. **B.** Despite all of FDR's efforts to curb unemployment, it was America's involvement in World War II that finally brought down the unemployment figures.

4. **B.** Granting freed blacks civil rights of voting, education, and desegregation (all of which were challenged by the KKK and Southern states opposing these rights for blacks).

5. **B.** President Teddy Roosevelt was using a corollary of the Monroe Doctrine by becoming the "policeman" of U.S. affairs and actions in Latin America.

6. **C.** The USSR removed the nuclear missiles from Cuba, and the U.S. agreed to remove its nuclear weapons from Turkey.

7. **A.** According to the Domino Theory, once one country fell to communism, all the countries in the region would fall to communism.

8. **B.** Women did indeed "foment" a rebellion over the next 144 years, until women got the right to vote in 1920.

9. **C.** The protest had begun to spread across various parts of the population and was not just limited to college students protesting the war effort.

10. **A.** President Truman used atomic weapons against the Japanese to force them to surrender. Although the atomic weapons killed thousands of people, millions of lives were actually saved (on both sides) by bringing the war to an early end.

11. **B.** Women filled jobs in the private sector and government sector as men were off fighting the war.

12. **D.** Colonists including the Sons of Liberty and Daughters of Liberty and regular colonists took targeted actions of boycotts and protests to demonstrate their dislike of the taxes imposed upon them by Parliament.

13. **B.** The ruling of "separate but equal" in the *Plessy* case (1896) was overturned 58 years later with the ruling in the *Brown* case, which concluded that "separate is not equal."

14. **D.** There is a written guarantee of "freedom of the press" (media) in the 1st Amendment in the Constitution.

15. **C.** The states controlled the power in the new government out of fear of a centralized government like Parliament and the King of England — the states wanted control of the new government.

16. **B.** The 10th Amendment sets up the concept of "states' rights" — that what is not delegated to the federal government is then delegated to the states. This also sets up the argument of the elastic clause (necessary and proper) for the federal government to make laws versus a strict interpretation of states' rights.

17. **A.** This increased the participation of girls in sports in high school and college as well as college scholarships for girls in sports.

18. **A.** The winner of the state of Florida would take the 25 electoral votes and win the election. This would be George Bush, who had fewer popular votes but won the election.

19. **B.** The Bill of Rights was meant to protect the people from the power of the federal government. It was written as a guarantee of restrictions of the federal government and protects the rights of the people.

20. **C.** Third Party candidates and their issues can have an impact on elections by a third-party candidate picking up popular votes (thus taking them away from a Democrat or Republican candidate), and they can also bring up arguments about political hot topical issues.

21. **B.** States in the south, southwest, and west have picked up a substantial number of electoral votes, and the population has shifted to more people living in those areas. The traditional stronghold of the northeast is losing electoral votes as people are relocating to warmer regions of the country.

22. **D.** The Civil Rights Act of 1964 dealt with ending discrimination in business practices, and the ADA in 1990 dealt with access to public accommodations.

23. **C.** Varying levels of education, levels of employment, race, ethnicity, and gender have all had varying degrees of impact on voter participation in recent elections.

24. **A.** People are relying less on mainstream news for political information and gaining more information on cable news and Internet news sites.

25. **C.** These reasons all point to the outbreak of World War I in Europe in August 1914.

26. **A.** Nelson Mandela was the symbol of the new South Africa. He was elected the first black president of South Africa once the black population (70 percent of the population) got the right to vote for the first time.

27. **B.** Hitler's plan of concentration camps to exterminate 6 million Jews (75 percent of the European Jewish population) by using gas chambers and torture in various camps.

28. **C.** The UN responded sending in 16 member nations (the U.S. was the major nation) to push back the North Korean advance with an armistice halting the conflict in July 1953.

29. **A.** Britain had a growing population to use in business ventures and industrialization.

30. **C.** NATO and Warsaw Pact alliance groups were formed out of opposition to each other during the Cold War.

31. **C.** Tariffs increase the demand for American-made goods by making imported foreign goods more expensive.

32. **B.** The sudden decrease in demand that comes from a boycott of a company's products helps to drive down the price, which puts economic pressure on the company, often forcing it to change its ways.

33. **B.** When inflation occurs, one of the first things to happen is that consumers reduce their spending on nonessential items, which causes the demand for those items to drop, and unemployment begins to rise.

34. **A.** According to the chart, teens were impacted the most with the highest rate of unemployment because jobs were no longer available for this segment of the population.

35. **C.** Both bonds and stocks raise money for capital expenditures. Although bonds are usually a safer investment, that isn't always the case. Both have risks associated with them.

36. **B.** Communist economies are run by the government. Private ownership is not allowed.

37. **A.** A factory is a capital resource. Aluminum deposits are an example of raw materials, the CEO is an entrepreneur, the skilled work is part of the labor force.

38. **B.** Infrastructure includes interstate highways, bridges, ports, and so on.

39. **C.** Total worker compensation consists of wages plus benefits such as healthcare, paid vacations, and so on.

40. **A.** The GDP or Gross Domestic Product is simply the total value of goods and services produced in a year in a country. More goods and services produced results in a higher GDP.

41. **C.** The world has become just a "bit smaller" as countries become intertwined in economic growth. Each country is becoming increasingly dependent upon other countries for growth and progress.

42. **C.** Strikes usually shut down all production, which harms the company financially, putting pressure on the company to give in to the workers' demands.

43. **A.** The slave trade is the largest forced migration of a people group in world history, as 12 million slaves were forced to relocate outside of Africa for places in the New World over a 300-year time frame.

44. **B.** Since the question stem tells us that both counties are continuing their reliance on fossil fuels, they are unlikely to increase their focus on alternatives such as wind power and solar energy.

45. **D.** Monopolies are not allowed in the United States because they give too much power to one company, which can set its prices as high as it likes. Monopolies are less efficient because there is no competition, making Choice (D) correct.

46. **B.** Connectivity with ports of trade are important for goods to be transported via railways, highways with semitrucks, and air traffic.

47. **B.** Nine out of ten startup companies fail, so investing in them is riskier than the other investments, even though they can give spectacular returns when successful.

Answers for Section 5: Science

1. **D.** The equation shown is photosynthesis. Plants use photosynthesis to convert carbon dioxide and water into glucose and oxygen. Choices (A) and (B) are incorrect because they represent the reverse reaction in which cells break down glucose in the presence of oxygen and convert it back into water and carbon dioxide. This produces energy and ATP. Choice (C) describes the process by which metals emit electrons when light shines on them.

2. **A.** The equation shown is photosynthesis, which requires sunlight energy. Because this reaction absorbs (takes in) energy, this is an endothermic reaction. Exothermic reactions, Choice (B), give out energy. Choices (C) and (D) are nuclear reactions, not chemical reactions.

3. **B.** The reaction that produces energy in the cells of both the rabbit and the hawk is cellular respiration. This is the reverse reaction to photosynthesis. Cellular respiration uses oxygen to break down the glucose molecule to produce carbon dioxide, water, and energy that can be stored in APT molecules for later use.

4. **A.** Plants produce their own food via photosynthesis and are therefore known as producers. The rabbit is a herbivore because it eats plants, and the hawk is a carnivore because it eats the rabbits.

5. **B.** All life on Earth is carbon-based. Note that Choice (D) is not an element — it's a compound.

6. **D.** Redshift occurs when an object emitting light is moving away from us. Choice (A) may be tempting, but there is no reason why light from distant galaxies would need to reflect from Mars's surface before reaching us. Choice (B) may or may not be true but is not the right answer because only motion toward Earth would cause a redshift. Choice (C) is also incorrect because the Hubble telescope is in orbit above Earth's atmosphere.

7. **C.** The gravitational force always attracts objects toward each other, so Choice (A) is wrong. Newton's universal law of gravitation tells us that the closer the objects are to each other, the stronger the force of attraction becomes, so Choice (B) is wrong. Stars can and do move relative to each other, so Choice (D) is false.

8. **A.** Moving magnets can generate electricity (this is how power stations work); hence the light bulb in Circuit 1 will light up as the magnet moves into and out of the coil, making Choice (B) incorrect. Choice (C) occurs when an electric current produces a magnet (not the other way around), and Choice (D) is a false statement because the magnet is unharmed.

9. **C.** Like poles repel, and unlike poles attract, so Choice (A) is incorrect. Choice (B) would occur if two unlike poles (a north and a south) were facing each other. Choice (C) is correct because the student placed two north poles (like poles) facing each other. Magnets don't give off electromagnetic radiation, so Choice (D) is false.

10. **C.** Magnetic field lines come out of the north pole of a magnet and go into the south pole. The plotting compass will align itself in the direction of these magnetic field lines, hence Choice (C) is correct.

11. **A.** When the switch is closed in Circuit 2, electricity flows through the coil, which will magnetize the iron bar, turning it into an electromagnet. There is no bulb in Circuit 2, so Choice (B) is wrong. Iron is a metal so it will conduct electricity, making Choice (C) a false statement. Iron has a very high melting point, so Choice (D) is unlikely to occur.

12. **D.** The conservation of mass states that matter is always conserved. For chemical equations this means that the number of atoms of each type of element remains the same at the end of the reaction as it was before the reaction, hence Choice (D) is correct. Choice (A) is not true because chemical reactions can produce gases. Choice (B) is incorrect because exothermic reactions give off heat, causing the temperature of the surrounding to rise, and endothermic reactions take in heat, causing the temperature of the surrounding to fall. Choice (C) is tempting but is incorrect. It is the number of *atoms* that stays the same, not the number of *molecules.*

13. **A.** Ozone is a gas present in the atmosphere that helps to protect the biosphere from harmful radiation from the sun. Because this does *not* affect the Earth's surface, Choice (A) is correct. Earthquakes and volcanic eruption do affect the surface of the Earth, making Choices (B) and (C) incorrect. Plate tectonics are responsible for causing earthquakes and volcanic eruptions, so Choice (D) is also incorrect.

14. **D.** The circulatory system transports nutrients dissolved in the blood to all the cells of the body, hence Choice (D) is correct. The muscular system is responsible for the movement of

the body itself, so Choice (A) is incorrect. Choice (B) may sound tempting because the digestive system is involved in breaking down food into nutrients, but it is not involved in transporting them through the body. Choice (C), the integumentary system, is the protective layer of the body, including the skin, hair, and nails.

15. **C.** Natural selection is the process by which individuals within a population are better adapted to their environment tend to survive and produce more offspring than those who are not well adapted. The population of bears with the thicker coats were better adapted to the cold conditions of the Arctic than the bears with thinner coats. Even if the statements in Choices (A), (B), or (D) were true (which they are probably not), they are still unrelated to natural selection.

16. **B.** The layer of air trapped by the fur is a poor conductor of heat, so it prevents the bear's body heat from escaping. Choice (A) would make the bear colder not warmer. Choices (C) and (D) don't make sense because heat flows from hot objects (the bear) to cold objects (the surroundings), not the other way around.

17. **A.** When the sun's rays hit the Earth's surface at an angle (like at the pole), the heat energy from them is spread out over a larger surface area, making it cooler there. Choices (B) and (D) are false statements. Choice (C) may or may not be true but still does not explain why the poles are colder than the equator.

18. **B.** The fossil record begins with fish, so if you thought Choice (D) was the answer, you are thinking of the question backwards. We humans are last. According to the fossil record, the shallow water ecosystems that contained amphibians began to dry up, and that is what led to the reptiles. So the amphibians had to come next after the fish. That leaves Choice (A) or Choice (B). Birds are really amazing creatures that are believed to have evolved from reptiles so the answer is Choice (B).

19. **D.** Although the two solutions were mixed, the temperature dropped, suggesting that a chemical reaction took place, making Choice (D) the correct answer and Choice (A) incorrect. There is nothing that tells you anything has disintegrated, so Choice (B) is not correct. Evaporation occurs at the surface of a liquid and therefore would not cause gas bubbles, so Choice (C) is incorrect.

20. **D.** Because the sky diver is falling at a constant speed toward the ground, there are no unbalanced forces acting on him (his weight is balanced out by the air resistance), making Choice (D) correct. Choice (A) is an example of Newton's second law because there is an unbalanced force acting on the car, which slows it down. Choice (B) is an example of the conservation of momentum, not Newton's law of inertia, and Choice (C) is an example of Newton's third law.

21. **B.** The lift force is the only force in the diagram that acts in the upward direction, making Choice (B) the correct answer. The weight acts downward, so Choice (A) is wrong. The thrust and the drag both act in the horizontal direction, so they can only speed up or slow down the plane but not hold the plane up — hence, Choices (C) and (D) are incorrect.

22. **C.** Newton's first law tells us that an object moving at constant velocity is not acted upon by an unbalanced force, so all the forces acting on the plane must cancel each other out, making Choice (C) the correct answer. If the thrust were bigger than the drag, the plane would accelerate, but the plane is moving at constant speed, so Choice (A) must be wrong. If the lift were bigger than the weight, the plane would rise, but the plane is moving at constant altitude, so Choice (B) must be wrong. The plane is not weightless because the Earth's gravitational force is still acting on the plane, making Choice (D) incorrect.

23. B. Because the thrust is now greater than the drag, there is an unbalanced force (thrust minus drag) acting on the plane, which means that we must use Newton's second law ($F = ma$) to calculate the acceleration, as shown here:

$$\text{unbalanced force} = (\text{thrust} - \text{drag}) \rightarrow 80{,}000\text{N} - 20{,}000\text{N} = 60{,}000\text{N}$$

$$F = ma$$

$$60{,}000 = 10{,}000(a)$$

$$\frac{60{,}000}{10{,}000} = a$$

$$a = 6$$

24. D. The basic unit, and smallest, of life is the cell. So because the question asks from smallest to largest, the only correct choices are the ones that start with "cell." Those are Choices (C) and (D). An organ system consists of organs that are made of tissue, so the correct answer is Choice (D).

25. A. Because you were told different plants are found in the shade than in bright sunlight, they are not competing for light because they have already adapted to the light intensity where they prefer to live, so Choice (D) is not correct. There is nothing to suggest anything about time, so Choice (C) is also incorrect. That leaves Choices (A) or (B). The prefix "bio-" means life, and the prefix "abio-" means without life. Light intensity is not a living entity so it is abiotic, making " (A) correct.

26. C. Because the trait for blue eyes is recessive, only those offspring that are homozygous "bb" for the gene will have blue eyes. From the Punnett square you can see that two out of four offspring (50 percent) are homozygous for blue eyes, making Choice (C) correct. Offspring who are heterozygous would have brown eyes because they contain a dominant brown gene "B," which is always expressed in the phenotype when present.

27. D. The trait for blue eyes is recessive, and the trait for brown eyes is dominant, hence Choice (D) is correct.

28. A. The mother has two genes for blue eyes "bb" and is therefore homozygous (same genes), whereas the father has one gene of each type "Bb" and is therefore heterozygous (different genes). Hence, Choice (A) is correct.

29. A. Both the mother and her new husband have blue eyes. The trait for blue eyes only appears when a person is homozygous "bb" for this recessive gene. There is zero possibility that their child will have brown eyes (or any color other than blue) because both parents will pass on a "b" gene to their offspring. (Neither parent has a brown gene "B" to pass on to their offspring).

30. C. From the diagram you can see that both plant respiration and animal respiration release carbon dioxide into the atmosphere, so Choices (A) and (D) must both be wrong. Choice (B) is also wrong because auto and factory emissions release carbon dioxide. The formation of fossils and fossil fuels helps to trap carbon below the Earth's surface; hence, Choice (C) is correct.

31. B. When carbon dioxide dissolves in rain water it produces carbonic acid, which contributes to acid rain; hence, Choice (B) is correct. Only plants can use photosynthesis (not fish), so Choice (A) is incorrect. Carbon dioxide is not poisonous, so Choice (C) is false. Because acid rain is harmful to the environment, Choice (D) is incorrect.

32. **C.** The relatively recent increase in the consumption of fossil fuels (which produce carbon dioxide) has caused an increase in the amount of carbon dioxide released in the atmosphere, making Choice (C) correct. Although human respiration adds carbon dioxide to the air, Choice (A) would not explain why there has been a recent increase. Burying waste in landfills traps the carbon in beneath the Earth's surface, so Choice (B) is wrong. Using renewable fuels sources would reduce the carbon dioxide emissions, not increase them, so Choice (D) is incorrect.

33. **D.** One of the causes of global warming is due to the increased emission of carbon dioxide into the atmosphere. Renewable fuels sources such as solar or wind power don't produce carbon dioxide, so this would reduce the amount of carbon dioxide released to the atmosphere, making Choice (D) correct. Cutting down trees would prevent them from removing carbon dioxide from the air during photosynthesis, so that would make the problem worse, not better, and hence, Choice (A) is wrong. It doesn't matter where we drill for fossil fuels — they still produce carbon dioxide when we burn them, so Choice (B) is wrong. Choice (C) is hilarious but incorrect!

34. **B.** DNA provides information to make proteins that the cell needs, so Choice (B) is correct. DNA is not the building block for all the other molecules in the cell; hence, Choice (A) is wrong. DNA does not provide the energy for the cell's activities, so Choice (C) is wrong. Cell walls are made from *cellulose*, not DNA, so Choice (D) is incorrect.

35. **B.** Homeostasis is the mechanism by which the body tries to maintain equilibrium (including maintaining the correct body temperature), making Choice (B) correct. The question stem tells you that this is a negative feedback mechanism, not a positive feedback mechanism; hence, Choice (A) is wrong. The question stem refers to the temperature of the body, not global temperatures, so Choice (C) is wrong. Meiosis refers to cell reproduction, which produces haploid sex cells, which has nothing to do with maintaining equilibrium, so Choice (D) is incorrect.

36. **C.** The sun produces energy via nuclear fusion reactions at its core, making Choice (C) right. The sun uses nuclear reactions, not chemical reactions (which involve valence electrons), so Choice (A) is wrong. Combustion requires oxygen, which is not present in the sun, so Choice (B) is incorrect. Nuclear fission involves splitting up larger nuclei, not fusing them together, so Choice (D) is incorrect.

37. **B.** The sun's energy reaches the Earth via thermal radiation in the form of electromagnetic waves. Thermal radiation is the only method of heat transfer that can pass through the vacuum of outer space, making Choice (B) right. Convection current can't occur in a vacuum, so Choice (A) is wrong. The sun does not give off alpha particles, so Choice (C) is incorrect. Conduction can't occur unless the two solid objects are in contact, so Choice (D) is incorrect.

38. **C.** The correct answer is calculated as follows:

    8 mins and 20 secs = 60(8) + 20 = 500 secs
    distance = speed × time
    distance = (300,000)(500) = 150,000,000 km = 150 million km

39. **A.** The number of protons determines the identity of the element, so Choice (A) is correct. This is also known as the *atomic number* of the atom.

40. **B.** The sum of the protons and neutrons determines the atomic mass number of an atom, so Choice (B) is correct.

41. **B.** An isotope of an element contains the same number of protons but a different number of neutrons within the nucleus of the atom.

42. **C.** The Big Bang theory refers to the beginning of the universe, not the breakup of Pangaea; hence, Choice (C) is your answer. All the other choices add support to the single super-continent theory.

43. **A.** Continental drift is caused by convection currents within the Earth's mantle, which makes the tectonic plates (that float on top of the mantle) separate. Hence, Choice (A) is right. The meteorite that killed off the dinosaurs smashed into Earth 65 million years ago, but Pangaea began drifting apart 175 million years ago, so Choice (B) is wrong. Choices (C) and (D) would not cause the continents to drift apart, making them incorrect.

44. **C.** When two tectonic plates drift apart, an ocean ridge forms between them, making Choice (C) right. V-shaped valleys are caused by rivers, so Choice (A) is wrong. U-shaped valleys are caused by the movement of glaciers, so Choice (B) is wrong. Extreme weather is not usually caused by the movement of tectonic plates, so Choice (D) is incorrect.

45. **A.** The Doppler effect describes how the frequency of waves emitted from a moving source appears to change when there is relative motion between the source and an observer, making Choice (A) right. The waves are not reflecting, so Choice (B) is false. The waves are not interfering with each other, so Choice (C) is false. Newton's third law of motion is not relevant here, making Choice (D) incorrect.

46. **B.** As the ambulance moves *toward* the observer, the frequency of the siren appears to *increase*, but as the ambulance moves *away from* the observer, the frequency of the siren appears to *decrease*, making Choice (B) correct. Choice (A) accidentally inverts the answers, making this incorrect. Frequency has nothing to do with loudness, so Choice (C) is wrong. The frequency does not vanish or reappear, so Choice (D) is a false statement.

47. **B.** The question stem shows a beta particle being emitted in the nuclear reaction, making Choice (B) correct.

Answer Key for Practice Test 1

Section 1: Language Arts – Reading

1. D	14. B	27. A	40. B
2. D	15. A	28. C	41. B
3. A	16. D	29. B	42. A
4. B	17. C	30. D	43. B
5. C	18. A	31. C	44. C
6. B	19. A	32. B	45. B
7. D	20. D	33. C	46. C
8. C	21. B	34. C	47. D
9. D	22. B	35. D	48. A
10. C	23. C	36. D	49. A
11. C	24. D	37. A	50. A
12. A	25. C	38. B	
13. C	26. D	39. D	

Section 2: Language Arts – Writing

1. B	14. C	27. A	40. B
2. A	15. A	28. C	41. D
3. C	16. B	29. D	42. B
4. A	17. A	30. A	43. B
5. C	18. C	31. B	44. C
6. D	19. A	32. C	45. A
7. C	20. C	33. C	46. B
8. D	21. A	34. A	47. D
9. A	22. C	35. C	48. A
10. A	23. C	36. B	49. B
11. B	24. D	37. A	50. D
12. D	25. B	38. D	
13. B	26. B	39. A	

Section 3: Mathematics

1. B	14. D	27. C	40. B
2. D	15. 0.125	28. 5	41. D
3. B	16. D	29. A	42. B
4. D	17. 4.24	30. B	43. 13
5. B	18. D	31. A	44. D
6. C	19. A	32. D	45. C
7. 48 inches	20. D	33. C	46. A
8. D	21. 6	34. A	47. B
9. B	22. C	35. 0.0364 or 3.64%	48. 80 minutes
10. A	23. B	36. D	49. C
11. 91	24. C	37. A	50. A
12. C	25. C	38. C	51. 100
13. C	26. A	39. 10	52. D

Section 4: Social Studies

1. C	13. B	25. C	37. A
2. D	14. D	26. A	38. B
3. B	15. C	27. B	39. C
4. B	16. B	28. C	40. A
5. B	17. A	29. A	41. C
6. C	18. A	30. C	42. C
7. A	19. B	31. C	43. A
8. B	20. C	32. B	44. B
9. C	21. B	33. B	45. D
10. A	22. D	34. A	46. B
11. B	23. C	35. C	47. B
12. D	24. A	36. B	

Section 5: Science

1. D	13. A	25. A	37. B
2. A	14. D	26. C	38. C
3. B	15. C	27. D	39. A
4. A	16. B	28. A	40. B
5. B	17. A	29. A	41. B
6. D	18. B	30. C	42. C
7. C	19. D	31. B	43. A
8. A	20. D	32. C	44. C
9. C	21. B	33. D	45. A
10. C	22. C	34. B	46. B
11. A	23. B	35. B	47. B
12. D	24. D	36. C	

Chapter 25

Practice Test 2

Practice makes perfect so in this chapter we have provided you with the second of two complete practice tests that have been designed to simulate the real TASC exam. The entire test lasts about seven hours, with each section having its own time limits. The time limit and the number of questions you're expected to answer are listed in the directions on the front page of each of the five sections of the test. This information has also been summarized for you in Table 25-1 shown below.

TABLE 25-1 Breakdown of TASC Sections

Subject	Time in Minutes	Number of Questions
Language Arts–Reading	75	50 multiple choice questions
Language Arts–Writing	105	50 multiple choice questions plus one essay
Mathematics	50 (calculator section) 55 (no calculator section)	40 multiple choice questions and 12 gridded responses
Social Studies	75	47 multiple choice questions
Science	85	47 multiple choice questions

Try taking each part of the practice test in this chapter under exam conditions to get a good idea of how you'll do on the real exam. This will help you learn how to pace yourself during the real thing, and you'll experience what it feels like to take a full-length test.

REMEMBER

Skip questions you're really not sure about so you can focus on those questions that you can easily answer rather than wasting time on the ones that you can't. If you get stuck on a question, skip it and move on to the next. You can always come back to it at the end if you have any time left.

TIP

Because you don't get points off for wrong answers on the TASC, be sure to answer *all* questions. There is simply no excuse for leaving questions blank on the TASC exam.

WARNING

When writing your essay you must stay on topic. Essays that don't answer the question will earn zero points, no matter how well written they are.

For further tips on test-taking strategies, check out Chapter 27. This chapter is packed with strategies that strong test-takers adopt to maximize their chances of success on the TASC exam. It also points out the common mistakes to avoid on test day and how to sharpen your skills to achieve the score you deserve on the TASC.

Answer Sheet

TIP When you're completing a paper-based test like this one, be careful how you place the marks on your answer grid. Make sure there are no stray marks and that you erase clearly. Also be sure that you're filling in your answer for the right corresponding question. If you skip a question, be sure you also skip the space on your answer sheet so that your answers still line up.

Section 1: Language Arts – Reading

1. Ⓐ Ⓑ Ⓒ Ⓓ   11. Ⓐ Ⓑ Ⓒ Ⓓ   21. Ⓐ Ⓑ Ⓒ Ⓓ   31. Ⓐ Ⓑ Ⓒ Ⓓ   41. Ⓐ Ⓑ Ⓒ Ⓓ
2. Ⓐ Ⓑ Ⓒ Ⓓ   12. Ⓐ Ⓑ Ⓒ Ⓓ   22. Ⓐ Ⓑ Ⓒ Ⓓ   32. Ⓐ Ⓑ Ⓒ Ⓓ   42. Ⓐ Ⓑ Ⓒ Ⓓ
3. Ⓐ Ⓑ Ⓒ Ⓓ   13. Ⓐ Ⓑ Ⓒ Ⓓ   23. Ⓐ Ⓑ Ⓒ Ⓓ   33. Ⓐ Ⓑ Ⓒ Ⓓ   43. Ⓐ Ⓑ Ⓒ Ⓓ
4. Ⓐ Ⓑ Ⓒ Ⓓ   14. Ⓐ Ⓑ Ⓒ Ⓓ   24. Ⓐ Ⓑ Ⓒ Ⓓ   34. Ⓐ Ⓑ Ⓒ Ⓓ   44. Ⓐ Ⓑ Ⓒ Ⓓ
5. Ⓐ Ⓑ Ⓒ Ⓓ   15. Ⓐ Ⓑ Ⓒ Ⓓ   25. Ⓐ Ⓑ Ⓒ Ⓓ   35. Ⓐ Ⓑ Ⓒ Ⓓ   45. Ⓐ Ⓑ Ⓒ Ⓓ
6. Ⓐ Ⓑ Ⓒ Ⓓ   16. Ⓐ Ⓑ Ⓒ Ⓓ   26. Ⓐ Ⓑ Ⓒ Ⓓ   36. Ⓐ Ⓑ Ⓒ Ⓓ   46. Ⓐ Ⓑ Ⓒ Ⓓ
7. Ⓐ Ⓑ Ⓒ Ⓓ   17. Ⓐ Ⓑ Ⓒ Ⓓ   27. Ⓐ Ⓑ Ⓒ Ⓓ   37. Ⓐ Ⓑ Ⓒ Ⓓ   47. Ⓐ Ⓑ Ⓒ Ⓓ
8. Ⓐ Ⓑ Ⓒ Ⓓ   18. Ⓐ Ⓑ Ⓒ Ⓓ   28. Ⓐ Ⓑ Ⓒ Ⓓ   38. Ⓐ Ⓑ Ⓒ Ⓓ   48. Ⓐ Ⓑ Ⓒ Ⓓ
9. Ⓐ Ⓑ Ⓒ Ⓓ   19. Ⓐ Ⓑ Ⓒ Ⓓ   29. Ⓐ Ⓑ Ⓒ Ⓓ   39. Ⓐ Ⓑ Ⓒ Ⓓ   49. Ⓐ Ⓑ Ⓒ Ⓓ
10. Ⓐ Ⓑ Ⓒ Ⓓ   20. Ⓐ Ⓑ Ⓒ Ⓓ   30. Ⓐ Ⓑ Ⓒ Ⓓ   40. Ⓐ Ⓑ Ⓒ Ⓓ   50. Ⓐ Ⓑ Ⓒ Ⓓ

Section 2: Language Arts – Writing

1. Ⓐ Ⓑ Ⓒ Ⓓ   11. Ⓐ Ⓑ Ⓒ Ⓓ   21. Ⓐ Ⓑ Ⓒ Ⓓ   31. Ⓐ Ⓑ Ⓒ Ⓓ   41. Ⓐ Ⓑ Ⓒ Ⓓ
2. Ⓐ Ⓑ Ⓒ Ⓓ   12. Ⓐ Ⓑ Ⓒ Ⓓ   22. Ⓐ Ⓑ Ⓒ Ⓓ   32. Ⓐ Ⓑ Ⓒ Ⓓ   42. Ⓐ Ⓑ Ⓒ Ⓓ
3. Ⓐ Ⓑ Ⓒ Ⓓ   13. Ⓐ Ⓑ Ⓒ Ⓓ   23. Ⓐ Ⓑ Ⓒ Ⓓ   33. Ⓐ Ⓑ Ⓒ Ⓓ   43. Ⓐ Ⓑ Ⓒ Ⓓ
4. Ⓐ Ⓑ Ⓒ Ⓓ   14. Ⓐ Ⓑ Ⓒ Ⓓ   24. Ⓐ Ⓑ Ⓒ Ⓓ   34. Ⓐ Ⓑ Ⓒ Ⓓ   44. Ⓐ Ⓑ Ⓒ Ⓓ
5. Ⓐ Ⓑ Ⓒ Ⓓ   15. Ⓐ Ⓑ Ⓒ Ⓓ   25. Ⓐ Ⓑ Ⓒ Ⓓ   35. Ⓐ Ⓑ Ⓒ Ⓓ   45. Ⓐ Ⓑ Ⓒ Ⓓ
6. Ⓐ Ⓑ Ⓒ Ⓓ   16. Ⓐ Ⓑ Ⓒ Ⓓ   26. Ⓐ Ⓑ Ⓒ Ⓓ   36. Ⓐ Ⓑ Ⓒ Ⓓ   46. Ⓐ Ⓑ Ⓒ Ⓓ
7. Ⓐ Ⓑ Ⓒ Ⓓ   17. Ⓐ Ⓑ Ⓒ Ⓓ   27. Ⓐ Ⓑ Ⓒ Ⓓ   37. Ⓐ Ⓑ Ⓒ Ⓓ   47. Ⓐ Ⓑ Ⓒ Ⓓ
8. Ⓐ Ⓑ Ⓒ Ⓓ   18. Ⓐ Ⓑ Ⓒ Ⓓ   28. Ⓐ Ⓑ Ⓒ Ⓓ   38. Ⓐ Ⓑ Ⓒ Ⓓ   48. Ⓐ Ⓑ Ⓒ Ⓓ
9. Ⓐ Ⓑ Ⓒ Ⓓ   19. Ⓐ Ⓑ Ⓒ Ⓓ   29. Ⓐ Ⓑ Ⓒ Ⓓ   39. Ⓐ Ⓑ Ⓒ Ⓓ   49. Ⓐ Ⓑ Ⓒ Ⓓ
10. Ⓐ Ⓑ Ⓒ Ⓓ   20. Ⓐ Ⓑ Ⓒ Ⓓ   30. Ⓐ Ⓑ Ⓒ Ⓓ   40. Ⓐ Ⓑ Ⓒ Ⓓ   50. Ⓐ Ⓑ Ⓒ Ⓓ

Section 3: Mathematics

1. Ⓐ Ⓑ Ⓒ Ⓓ   12. Ⓐ Ⓑ Ⓒ Ⓓ   23. Ⓐ Ⓑ Ⓒ Ⓓ   34. Ⓐ Ⓑ Ⓒ Ⓓ   45. Ⓐ Ⓑ Ⓒ Ⓓ
2. Ⓐ Ⓑ Ⓒ Ⓓ   13. Ⓐ Ⓑ Ⓒ Ⓓ   24. _____   35. _____   46. Ⓐ Ⓑ Ⓒ Ⓓ
3. _____   14. Ⓐ Ⓑ Ⓒ Ⓓ   25. _____   36. Ⓐ Ⓑ Ⓒ Ⓓ   47. _____
4. Ⓐ Ⓑ Ⓒ Ⓓ   15. _____   26. Ⓐ Ⓑ Ⓒ Ⓓ   37. Ⓐ Ⓑ Ⓒ Ⓓ   48. Ⓐ Ⓑ Ⓒ Ⓓ
5. Ⓐ Ⓑ Ⓒ Ⓓ   16. Ⓐ Ⓑ Ⓒ Ⓓ   27. Ⓐ Ⓑ Ⓒ Ⓓ   38. Ⓐ Ⓑ Ⓒ Ⓓ   49. Ⓐ Ⓑ Ⓒ Ⓓ
6. Ⓐ Ⓑ Ⓒ Ⓓ   17. Ⓐ Ⓑ Ⓒ Ⓓ   28. Ⓐ Ⓑ Ⓒ Ⓓ   39. Ⓐ Ⓑ Ⓒ Ⓓ   50. Ⓐ Ⓑ Ⓒ Ⓓ
7. Ⓐ Ⓑ Ⓒ Ⓓ   18. Ⓐ Ⓑ Ⓒ Ⓓ   29. Ⓐ Ⓑ Ⓒ Ⓓ   40. _____   51. _____
8. Ⓐ Ⓑ Ⓒ Ⓓ   19. Ⓐ Ⓑ Ⓒ Ⓓ   30. Ⓐ Ⓑ Ⓒ Ⓓ   41. Ⓐ Ⓑ Ⓒ Ⓓ   52. _____
9. Ⓐ Ⓑ Ⓒ Ⓓ   20. Ⓐ Ⓑ Ⓒ Ⓓ   31. _____   42. Ⓐ Ⓑ Ⓒ Ⓓ
10. Ⓐ Ⓑ Ⓒ Ⓓ   21. _____   32. Ⓐ Ⓑ Ⓒ Ⓓ   43. Ⓐ Ⓑ Ⓒ Ⓓ
11. _____   22. Ⓐ Ⓑ Ⓒ Ⓓ   33. _____   44. _____

Section 4: Social Studies

1. Ⓐ Ⓑ Ⓒ Ⓓ	11. Ⓐ Ⓑ Ⓒ Ⓓ	21. Ⓐ Ⓑ Ⓒ Ⓓ	31. Ⓐ Ⓑ Ⓒ Ⓓ	41. Ⓐ Ⓑ Ⓒ Ⓓ
2. Ⓐ Ⓑ Ⓒ Ⓓ	12. Ⓐ Ⓑ Ⓒ Ⓓ	22. Ⓐ Ⓑ Ⓒ Ⓓ	32. Ⓐ Ⓑ Ⓒ Ⓓ	42. Ⓐ Ⓑ Ⓒ Ⓓ
3. Ⓐ Ⓑ Ⓒ Ⓓ	13. Ⓐ Ⓑ Ⓒ Ⓓ	23. Ⓐ Ⓑ Ⓒ Ⓓ	33. Ⓐ Ⓑ Ⓒ Ⓓ	43. Ⓐ Ⓑ Ⓒ Ⓓ
4. Ⓐ Ⓑ Ⓒ Ⓓ	14. Ⓐ Ⓑ Ⓒ Ⓓ	24. Ⓐ Ⓑ Ⓒ Ⓓ	34. Ⓐ Ⓑ Ⓒ Ⓓ	44. Ⓐ Ⓑ Ⓒ Ⓓ
5. Ⓐ Ⓑ Ⓒ Ⓓ	15. Ⓐ Ⓑ Ⓒ Ⓓ	25. Ⓐ Ⓑ Ⓒ Ⓓ	35. Ⓐ Ⓑ Ⓒ Ⓓ	45. Ⓐ Ⓑ Ⓒ Ⓓ
6. Ⓐ Ⓑ Ⓒ Ⓓ	16. Ⓐ Ⓑ Ⓒ Ⓓ	26. Ⓐ Ⓑ Ⓒ Ⓓ	36. Ⓐ Ⓑ Ⓒ Ⓓ	46. Ⓐ Ⓑ Ⓒ Ⓓ
7. Ⓐ Ⓑ Ⓒ Ⓓ	17. Ⓐ Ⓑ Ⓒ Ⓓ	27. Ⓐ Ⓑ Ⓒ Ⓓ	37. Ⓐ Ⓑ Ⓒ Ⓓ	47. Ⓐ Ⓑ Ⓒ Ⓓ
8. Ⓐ Ⓑ Ⓒ Ⓓ	18. Ⓐ Ⓑ Ⓒ Ⓓ	28. Ⓐ Ⓑ Ⓒ Ⓓ	38. Ⓐ Ⓑ Ⓒ Ⓓ	
9. Ⓐ Ⓑ Ⓒ Ⓓ	19. Ⓐ Ⓑ Ⓒ Ⓓ	29. Ⓐ Ⓑ Ⓒ Ⓓ	39. Ⓐ Ⓑ Ⓒ Ⓓ	
10. Ⓐ Ⓑ Ⓒ Ⓓ	20. Ⓐ Ⓑ Ⓒ Ⓓ	30. Ⓐ Ⓑ Ⓒ Ⓓ	40. Ⓐ Ⓑ Ⓒ Ⓓ	

Section 5: Science

1. Ⓐ Ⓑ Ⓒ Ⓓ	11. Ⓐ Ⓑ Ⓒ Ⓓ	21. Ⓐ Ⓑ Ⓒ Ⓓ	31. Ⓐ Ⓑ Ⓒ Ⓓ	41. Ⓐ Ⓑ Ⓒ Ⓓ
2. Ⓐ Ⓑ Ⓒ Ⓓ	12. Ⓐ Ⓑ Ⓒ Ⓓ	22. Ⓐ Ⓑ Ⓒ Ⓓ	32. Ⓐ Ⓑ Ⓒ Ⓓ	42. Ⓐ Ⓑ Ⓒ Ⓓ
3. Ⓐ Ⓑ Ⓒ Ⓓ	13. Ⓐ Ⓑ Ⓒ Ⓓ	23. Ⓐ Ⓑ Ⓒ Ⓓ	33. Ⓐ Ⓑ Ⓒ Ⓓ	43. Ⓐ Ⓑ Ⓒ Ⓓ
4. Ⓐ Ⓑ Ⓒ Ⓓ	14. Ⓐ Ⓑ Ⓒ Ⓓ	24. Ⓐ Ⓑ Ⓒ Ⓓ	34. Ⓐ Ⓑ Ⓒ Ⓓ	44. Ⓐ Ⓑ Ⓒ Ⓓ
5. Ⓐ Ⓑ Ⓒ Ⓓ	15. Ⓐ Ⓑ Ⓒ Ⓓ	25. Ⓐ Ⓑ Ⓒ Ⓓ	35. Ⓐ Ⓑ Ⓒ Ⓓ	45. Ⓐ Ⓑ Ⓒ Ⓓ
6. Ⓐ Ⓑ Ⓒ Ⓓ	16. Ⓐ Ⓑ Ⓒ Ⓓ	26. Ⓐ Ⓑ Ⓒ Ⓓ	36. Ⓐ Ⓑ Ⓒ Ⓓ	46. Ⓐ Ⓑ Ⓒ Ⓓ
7. Ⓐ Ⓑ Ⓒ Ⓓ	17. Ⓐ Ⓑ Ⓒ Ⓓ	27. Ⓐ Ⓑ Ⓒ Ⓓ	37. Ⓐ Ⓑ Ⓒ Ⓓ	47. Ⓐ Ⓑ Ⓒ Ⓓ
8. Ⓐ Ⓑ Ⓒ Ⓓ	18. Ⓐ Ⓑ Ⓒ Ⓓ	28. Ⓐ Ⓑ Ⓒ Ⓓ	38. Ⓐ Ⓑ Ⓒ Ⓓ	
9. Ⓐ Ⓑ Ⓒ Ⓓ	19. Ⓐ Ⓑ Ⓒ Ⓓ	29. Ⓐ Ⓑ Ⓒ Ⓓ	39. Ⓐ Ⓑ Ⓒ Ⓓ	
10. Ⓐ Ⓑ Ⓒ Ⓓ	20. Ⓐ Ⓑ Ⓒ Ⓓ	30. Ⓐ Ⓑ Ⓒ Ⓓ	40. Ⓐ Ⓑ Ⓒ Ⓓ	

Section 1: Language Arts – Reading

TIME: 75 minutes for 50 questions

DIRECTIONS: This section tests your knowledge of reading comprehension. Pick the best answer(s) for each question and then mark the space on your answer sheet that corresponds to the question number and the letter indicating your choice.

Read these passages and then answer the questions that follow. Passage 1 is from Death Valley in '49, *by William Manly. Passage 2 is from* The Land of Little Rain, *by Mary Austin. Both passages discuss Death Valley, an area in the western United States.*

Passage 1

The moon gave us so much light that we decided we would start on our course, and get as far as we could before the hot sun came out, and so we went on slowly and carefully in the partial darkness, the only hope left to us being that our strength would hold out till we could get to the shining snow on the great mountain before us. We reached the foot of the range we were descending about sunrise. There was here a wide wash from the snow mountain, down which some water had sometime run after a big storm, and had divided into little rivulets only reaching out a little way before they had sunk into the sand.

We had no idea we could now find any water till we at least got very near the snow, and as the best way to reach it we turned up the wash although the course was nearly to the north. The course was up a gentle grade and seemed quite sandy and not easy to travel. It looked as if there was an all day walk before us, and it was quite a question if we could live long enough to make the distance. There were quite strong indications that the water had run here not so very long ago, and we could trace the course of the little streams round among little sandy islands. A little stunted brush grew here, but it was so brittle that the stems would break as easy as an icicle.

In order to not miss a possible bit of water we separated and agreed upon a general course, and that if either one found water he should fire his gun as a signal. After about a mile or so had been gone over I heard Roger's gun and went in his direction. He had found a little ice that had frozen under the clear sky. It was not thicker than window glass. After putting a piece in our mouths we gathered all we could and put it into the little quart camp kettle to melt. We gathered just a kettle full, besides what we ate as we were gathering, and kindled a little fire and melted it.

I can but think how providential it was that we started in the night, for in an hour after the sun had risen that little sheet of ice would have melted and the water sank into the sand. Having quenched our thirst we could now eat, and found that we were nearly starved also. In making this meal we used up all our little store of water, but we felt refreshed and our lives renewed so that we had better courage to go on.

Passage 2

The desert floras shame us with their cheerful adaptations to the seasonal limitations. Their whole duty is to flower and fruit, and they do it hardly, or with tropical luxuriance, as the rain admits. It is recorded in the report of the Death Valley expedition that after a year of abundant rains, on the Colorado Desert was found a specimen of Amaranthus ten feet high. A year later the same species in the same place matured in the drought at four inches. One hopes the land may breed like qualities in her human offspring, not tritely to "try," but to do. Seldom does the desert herb attain the full stature of the type. Extreme aridity and extreme altitude have the same dwarfing effect, so that we find in the high Sierras and in Death Valley related species in miniature that reach a comely growth in mean temperatures. Very fertile are the desert plants in expedients to prevent evaporation, turning their foliage edgewise toward the sun, growing silky hairs, exuding gum. The wind, which has a long sweep, harries and helps them. It rolls up dunes about the stocky stems, encompassing and protective, and above the dunes, which may be, as with the mesquite, three times as high as a man, the blossoming twigs flourish and bear fruit.

There are many areas in the desert where drinkable water lies within a few feet of the surface, indicated by the mesquite and the bunch grass (Sporobolus airoides). It is this nearness of unimagined help that makes the tragedy of desert deaths. It is related that the final break down of that hapless party that gave Death Valley its forbidding name occurred in a locality where shallow wells would have saved them. But how were they to know that? Properly equipped it is possible to go safely across that ghastly sink, yet every year it takes its toll of death, and yet men find there sun-dried mummies, of whom no trace or recollection is preserved. To underestimate one's thirst, to pass a given landmark to the right or left, to find a dry spring where one looked for running water — there is no help for any of these things.

1. Why are the travelers in Passage 1 heading toward the mountains?

    (A) They want to stand on higher ground to look for water sources in the surrounding landscape.

    (B) They plan to use the snow on the mountaintops as a source of water.

    (C) They left their canteens of water there.

    (D) They were going to the mountain village to ask for help.

2. Why did the travelers in Passage 1 decide to split up?

    (A) They had a disagreement about which way to go.

    (B) They thought that would give them a better chance of finding water.

    (C) They agreed that it would be better if they were to adopt an "every man for himself" attitude.

    (D) The passage does not say.

3. Read this excerpt from *Death Valley in 49*.

    I can but think how providential it was that we started in the night, for in an hour after the sun had risen that little sheet of ice would have melted and the water sank into the sand.

    What is the best meaning of "providential" as it is used in this excerpt?

    (A) well-planned

    (B) lucky

    (C) unfortunate

    (D) annoying

4. Which of the following statements about the narrator and his fellow travelers in Passage 1 is true?

    (A) They are competing with each other for food and water.

    (B) They are tired and thirsty from a long day's hike.

    (C) They cannot agree which way to go.

    (D) They are in danger of dying.

5. Read this excerpt from *The Land of Little Rain*.

    It is recorded in the report of the Death Valley expedition that after a year of abundant rains, on the Colorado Desert was found a specimen of Amaranthus ten feet high. A year later the same species in the same place matured in the drought at four inches. One hopes the land may breed like qualities in her human offspring, not tritely to "try," but to do.

    What point is the author trying to make in this excerpt?

    (A) She hopes that humans will learn to adapt to the changing conditions of the desert as well as plants have been able to.

    (B) She hopes to breed a race of tiny humans no taller than four inches in height.

    (C) She hopes to breed a race of giant humans ten feet tall.

    (D) She wants humans to water the desert plants during drought time.

6. Desert plants use all the following methods to prevent water loss EXCEPT

    (A) turning their foliage edgewise toward the sun

    (B) growing exceptionally large leaves

    (C) growing silky hairs

    (D) exuding gum

7. Read this excerpt from *The Land of Little Rain.*

There are many areas in the desert where drinkable water lies within a few feet of the surface, indicated by the mesquite and the bunch grass (Sporobolus airoides). It is this nearness of unimagined help that makes the tragedy of desert deaths.

Why does the author of Passage 2 describe desert deaths as a "tragedy"?

    (A) All deaths are tragedies no matter where they occur.

    (B) Many people who suffer desert deaths are turned into sun-dried mummies.

    (C) Many of the deaths occur because people are unaware of nearby water sources.

    (D) All deaths are preventable if suitable precautions are taken.

8. According to Passage 2, Death Valley got its forbidding name from

    (A) the fact that no life exists there.

    (B) the fact that people who visit the region usually die soon afterwards.

    (C) a tragic event that involved a party of travelers who died of thirst while trying to cross the desert.

    (D) The passage does not say.

9. In comparison with Passage 2, Passage 1 is

    (A) less personal.

    (B) less scientific.

    (C) less interesting.

    (D) more technical.

Read this passage and then answer the questions that follow.

From **The Calling of Katie Makanya,** *by Margaret McCord (Wiley)*

The town around the railroad station was ugly but the location was worse than any place Katie had ever known. Here the iron houses, streaked with rust, seemed to push their way into the road. Broken windows were patched with scraps of wood and stuffed with rags. Few people wandered about in the heat of the day, though Katie heard a mumble of voices behind the walls, the whimpering of children, a quick burst of laughter. Occasionally from an open door a shrill voice called out a greeting to Charlotte, who waved and hurried on as if she did not notice the stink of urine, garbage, and stale smoke.

"Is this where we live?" Katie gasped. "Everything's so — I want to vomit."

Charlotte stopped suddenly, turning to face her. "Who do you think you are, to come here and criticize? Are you too big for the rest of us?

Ma doesn't complain. She says we're lucky to find a house with a real chimney and an inside stove. Are you better than Ma?"

Perhaps she had worked too long for Mrs. Hutchinson, for after the first happiness of seeing Ma and Charlotte, Katie began to miss some of the luxuries she had taken for granted in Port Elizabeth — the long bars of yellow soap, the soft sea mist, the endless supply of water.

It was the dry season in Kimberley when she arrived. The water tank was empty. There were rivers in the distance, but it was a long way for the girls to carry water, and Ma doled it out sparingly — so much set aside for tea and coffee, a cupful each morning for their body-washing, and all the rest saved for the

GO ON TO NEXT PAGE

laundry. There was never enough water to grow vegetables except during the rainy season when the trash overflowed and the roads became rivers of slippery clay.

Ma never complained. One afternoon a boy fell on the road and cut his leg on some broken glass. Ma hurried out to him with bandages and a pan of salt water. Soon the neighbors were calling on her whenever anyone was sick or wounded. Once, when Mrs. Cele fell sick with the fever, Ma sent Katie over to her house several times a day to wipe her body down with a wet towel until her fever broke.

"You're a very good nurse," Mrs. Cele told Katie.

"That's what I want to be — a nurse," Katie told Ma when she got home.

Ma hesitated and then spoke slowly. "It takes much study to be a proper nurse. You have to know all about medicines —"

"You can teach me."

Mama shook her head. "All I know is how to wash out wounds and bandage them up. This I learned when I was a girl and watched your grandfather caring for his workers on the farm in Blinkwater. But I know nothing about sickness or medicine —"

"You can't be a proper nurse," Charlotte interrupted scornfully. "The nursing schools here are only for white girls. If you go to work in a hospital, you will just be a servant, mopping floors and cleaning up after the Europeans. If you really want to do important work, then you must study hard and become a teacher."

"I don't want to be a teacher," Katie said, feeling discouraged. She too wanted to make Pa proud, but she was having as much difficulty at her school in Kimberley as she had had in Port Elizabeth. Her head-aches were more frequent now, and by afternoon her eyes were red and swollen.

Ma took her to see a white doctor who gave her some medicine — it cost seven and sixpence — and told her not to use her eyes so much. But how could she stop using her eyes when she had to read her books?

With Charlotte's help Katie managed to pass her Standard Six examination but she did not win a scholarship to any high school. Although Pa could not hide his disappointment, Katie was secretly relieved. She knew she was not clever in her head like Charlotte. All her cleverness was in her hands. Already Ma had taught her how to use the sewing machine, and she was making Charlotte's clothes as well as her own.

"How is it you don't get headaches when you sew, only when you read?" Charlotte asked. When Katie did not answer, she added, "I think you're just lazy."

To make matters worse, Pa would not allow her to go anywhere without Charlotte. And Charlotte gave her no peace. If Katie wanted to stay home and sleep, Charlotte called her a know-nothing. If she wanted to visit her friend Martha, Charlotte would not leave them alone but listened to everything they said.

"Am I a baby to be carried around on my sister's back?" Katie grumbled.

---

10. The detailed description of the town given in the first paragraph serves primarily to show

    (A) that the town is almost deserted.

    (B) that Katie is a snob.

    (C) the poverty of the neighborhood.

    (D) that Katie does not belong there.

11. All the following are luxuries that Katie misses from Port Elizabeth EXCEPT

    (A) the soft sea mist

    (B) Mrs. Hutchinson

    (C) the endless supply of water

    (D) the long bars of yellow soap

12. Read this excerpt from *The Calling of Katie Makanya.*

"Ma doesn't complain. She says we're lucky to find a house with a real chimney and an inside stove. Are you better than Ma?"

Why does Charlotte ask Katie if she is better than Ma?

    (A) to find out the secret of Katie's superiority over her mother

    (B) to find out if Katie is actually better than Ma

    (C) to show that Ma complains too much

    (D) to show that Katie complains too much

13. How does Ma react to Katie's announcement that she wants to be a nurse?

   (A) She is delighted and offers to teach Katie everything she knows.

   (B) She is scornful.

   (C) She is cautious.

   (D) She dismisses the idea as ridiculous for a non-white girl.

14. How can the relationship between Charlotte and her sister best be characterized?

   (A) affectionate

   (B) nurturing

   (C) jealous rivals

   (D) irritable

15. Read this excerpt from *The Calling of Katie Makanya*.

   Ma took her to see a white doctor who gave her some medicine — it cost seven and sixpence — and told her not to use her eyes so much. But how could she stop using her eyes when she had to read her books?

Ma takes Katie to see a "white doctor" because?

   (A) Katie is a racist.

   (B) Katie is white.

   (C) Katie needs real medicine.

   (D) A visit to a white doctor cost seven and sixpence, which is the exact amount of money that Ma had on her.

16. All the following statements are true EXCEPT

   (A) Port Elizabeth is near the sea.

   (B) Katie is lazy.

   (C) Charlotte is a better student than Katie.

   (D) Katie is good with her hands.

17. What is the overall tone of the passage?

   (A) argumentative

   (B) realistic

   (C) nostalgic

   (D) angry

Read this passage and then answer the questions that follow.

From "Rip Van Winkle," by Washington Irving

Whoever has made a voyage up the Hudson must remember the Catskill Mountains. They are a branch of the great Appalachian family, and are seen away to the west of the river, swelling up to a noble height, and lording it over the surrounding country. Every change of season, every change of weather, indeed, every hour of the day, produces some change in the magical hues and shapes of these mountains, and they are regarded by all the goodwives, far and near, as perfect barometers.

At the foot of these fairy mountains the traveler may have seen the light smoke curling up from a village, whose shingle roofs gleam among the trees, just where the blue tints of the upland melt away into the fresh green of the nearer landscape. It is a little village of great age, having been founded by some of the Dutch colonists in the early times of the province, just about the beginning of the government of the good Peter Stuyvesant (may he rest in peace!), and there were some of the houses of the original settlers standing within a few years, built of small yellow bricks brought from Holland, having latticed windows and gable fronts, surmounted with weathercocks.

In that same village, and in one of these very houses, there lived, many years since, while the country was yet a province of Great Britain, a simple, good-natured fellow, of the name of Rip Van Winkle. He was a descendant of the Van Winkles who figured so gallantly in the chivalrous days of Peter Stuyvesant, and accompanied him to the siege of Fort Christina. He inherited, however, but little of the martial character of his ancestors. I have observed that he was a simple, good-natured man; he was, moreover, a kind neighbor and an obedient, henpecked husband.

Certain it is that he was a great favorite among all the goodwives of the village, who took his part in all family squabbles; and never failed, whenever they talked those matters over in their evening gossipings, to lay all the blame on Dame Van Winkle. The children of the village, too, would shout with joy whenever he

approached. He assisted at their sports, made their playthings, taught them to fly kites and shoot marbles, and told them long stories of ghosts, witches, and Indians. Whenever he went dodging about the village, he was surrounded by a troop of them, hanging on his skirts, clambering on his back, and playing a thousand tricks on him; and not a dog would bark at him throughout the neighborhood.

The great error in Rip's composition was a strong dislike of all kinds of profitable labor. It could not be from the want of perseverance; for he would sit on a wet rock, with a rod as long and heavy as a lance, and fish all day without a murmur, even though he should not be encouraged by a single nibble. He would carry a fowling piece on his shoulder for hours together, trudging through woods and swamps, and up hill and down dale, to shoot a few squirrels or wild pigeons. He would never refuse to assist a neighbor even in the roughest toil, and was a foremost man at all country frolics for husking Indian corn, or building stone fences; the women of the village, too, used to employ him to run their errands, and to do such little odd jobs as their less obliging husbands would not do for them. In a word, Rip was ready to attend to anybody's business but his own; but as to doing family duty, and keeping his farm in order, he found it impossible.

His children, too, were as ragged and wild as if they belonged to nobody. His son Rip promised to inherit the habits, with the old clothes, of his father. He was generally seen trooping like a colt at his mother's heels, equipped in a pair of his father's cast-off breeches, which he had much ado to hold up with one hand, as a fine lady does her train in bad weather.

Rip Van Winkle, however, was one of those happy mortals, of foolish, well-oiled dispositions, who take the world easy, eat white bread or brown, whichever can be got with least thought or trouble, and would rather starve on a penny than work for a pound. If left to himself, he would have whistled life away in perfect contentment; but his wife kept continually dinning in his ear about his idleness, his carelessness, and the ruin he was bringing on his family. Morning, noon, and night, her tongue was incessantly going, and everything he said or did was sure to produce a torrent of household eloquence. Rip had but one way of replying to all lectures of the kind, and that, by frequent use, had grown into a habit. He shrugged his shoulders, shook his head, cast up his eyes, but said nothing. This, however, always provoked a fresh volley from his wife; so that he was fain to draw off his forces, and take to the outside of the house — the only side which, in truth, belongs to a henpecked husband.

18. Who originally founded the village where Rip Van Winkle lives?

(A) Peter Stuyvesant

(B) the Van Winkles

(C) Dutch colonists

(D) the British

19. How do the wives of the village predict the weather?

(A) They use perfect barometers.

(B) The look for color changes in the shapes of the mountains.

(C) They watch the local weather channel.

(D) They never have any idea how to predict the weather.

20. Rip's usual response to his wife's requests include all the following EXCEPT

(A) shrugging his shoulders.

(B) shaking his head.

(C) promising to do them later.

(D) casting his eyes upward.

21. Read this excerpt from "Rip Van Winkle."

This, however, always provoked a fresh volley from his wife; so that he was fain to draw off his forces, and take to the outside of the house — the only side which, in truth, belongs to a henpecked husband.

What does the author mean by the phrase "the outside of the house — the only side which, in truth, belongs to a henpecked husband"?

(A) Rip can only relax when he is outside the house, away from his nagging wife.

(B) Rip keeps his chickens outside the house.

(C) Rip's wife owns the deed to the interior of the house, but Rip owns the house's exterior.

(D) Rip enjoys painting the outside of the house.

22. Whom do the village wives blame for Rip's domestic squabbles?

(A) Rip himself

(B) Rip's wife

(C) Rip's lazy son

(D) Rip's ancestors

23. What is the usual reaction of the village children whenever they see Rip approaching?

(A) They avoid him at all costs.

(B) They shout with joy.

(C) They keep a respectful distance from him.

(D) They are careful not to upset him due to his violent nature.

24. What according to the author was Rip's main character flaw?

(A) He has an unpleasant personality that causes most people to dislike him.

(B) He is lazy and avoids helping his neighbors.

(C) He has a strong dislike of all kinds of profitable labor.

(D) He gives up easily.

25. All the following are true statement regarding Rip Van Winkle EXCEPT:

(A) He was very popular.

(B) He despised doing household chores.

(C) Dogs appear to like him.

(D) He was a good father.

Read this passage and then answer the questions that follow.

From The Adventures of Tom Sawyer, *by Mark Twain*

"Tom!"

No answer.

"Tom!"

No answer.

"What's gone with that boy, I wonder? You Tom!"

No answer.

The old lady pulled her spectacles down and looked over them about the room; then she put them up and looked out under them. She seldom or never looked through them for so small a thing as a boy; they were her state pair, the pride of her heart, and were built for "style," not service — she could have seen through a pair of stove-lids just as well. She looked perplexed for a moment, and then said, not fiercely, but still loud enough for the furniture to hear:

"Well, I lay if I get hold of you I'll —"

She did not finish, for by this time she was bending down and punching under the bed with the broom, and so she needed breath to punctuate the punches with. She resurrected nothing but the cat.

"I never did see the beat of that boy!"

She went to the open door and stood in it and looked out among the tomato vines and "jimpson" weeds that constituted the garden. No Tom. So she lifted up her voice at an angle calculated for distance and shouted:

"Y-o-u-u Tom!"

There was a slight noise behind her and she turned just in time to seize a small boy by the slack of his roundabout and arrest his flight.

"There! I might 'a' thought of that closet. What you been doing in there?"

"Nothing."

"Nothing! Look at your hands. And look at your mouth. What *is* that truck?"

"I don't know, aunt."

"Well, I know. It's jam — that's what it is. Forty times I've said if you didn't let that jam alone I'd skin you. Hand me that switch."

The switch hovered in the air — the peril was desperate —

"My! Look behind you, aunt!"

The old lady whirled round, and snatched her skirts out of danger. The lad fled on the instant, scrambled up the high board-fence, and disappeared over it.

His aunt Polly stood surprised a moment, and then broke into a gentle laugh.

"Hang the boy, can't I never learn anything? Ain't he played me tricks enough like that for me to be looking out for him by this time? But old fools is the biggest fools there is. Can't learn an old dog new tricks, as the saying is. But my goodness, he never plays them alike, two days, and how is a body to know what's coming? He 'pears to know just how long he can torment me before I get my dander up, and he knows if he can make out to put me off for a minute or make me laugh, it's all down again and I can't hit him a lick. I ain't doing my duty by that boy, and that's the Lord's truth, goodness knows. Spare the rod and spile the child, as the Good Book says. I'm a laying up sin and suffering for us both, I know. He's full of the Old Scratch, but laws-a-me! he's my own dead sister's boy, poor thing, and I ain't got the heart to lash him, somehow. Every time I let him off, my conscience does hurt me so, and every time I hit him my old heart most breaks. Well-a-well, man that is born of woman is of few days and full of trouble, as the Scripture says, and I reckon it's so. He'll play hookey this evening, and I'll just be obleeged to make him work, to-morrow, to punish him. It's mighty hard to make him work Saturdays, when all the boys is having holiday, but he hates work more than he hates anything else, and I've *got* to do some of my duty by him, or I'll be the ruination of the child."

26. Why does Tom not answer his aunt when she calls him?

(A) He can't hear her.

(B) He doesn't like his aunt so he ignores her.

(C) He is hiding from his aunt because she plans to punish him.

(D) They are playing a game of hide and seek.

27. Where had Tom been hiding when Aunt Polly found him?

(A) under the bed

(B) in the garden

(C) in a closet

(D) on top of the stove

28. What evidence (if any) is there in the passage that Aunt Polly is a religious woman?

(A) There is no evidence of this in the passage.

(B) She quotes from the Bible several times.

(C) She prefers not to have to make Tom work on Saturdays.

(D) She is angry at Tom for tricking her.

29. Read this excerpt from *The Adventures of Tom Sawyer*.

The old lady pulled her spectacles down and looked over them about the room; then she put them up and looked out under them. She seldom or never looked through them for so small a thing as a boy; they were her state pair, the pride of her heart, and were built for "style," not service.

What does the author mean when he says that Aunt Polly's spectacles were built for "'style,' not service"?

(A) She wears them to look good but they don't help her to see very well.

(B) They are in need of repair.

(C) They are not designed to be worn during church services.

(D) She needs good eyesight to see through them.

30. Why does Tom live with his Aunt Polly?

(A) He is on vacation for the summer.

(B) His mother is dead.

(C) He loves spending time with his aunt.

(D) The passages does not say why.

31. Who is Old Scratch?

(A) the family dog

(B) the devil

(C) God

(D) Tom's good friend

32. Why did Mark Twain make so many grammatical errors in this dialogue?

(A) He was a terrible writer who did not understand the rules of grammar.

(B) He was attempting to be funny.

(C) The rules of grammar were different back then.

(D) He wanted to reflect the personality of the character who was speaking.

Read this passage and then answer the questions that follow.

From The War of the Worlds, by H. G. Wells

Then came the night of the first falling star. It was seen early in the morning, rushing over Winchester eastward, a line of flame high in the atmosphere. Hundreds must have seen it, and taken it for an ordinary falling star. Albin described it as leaving a greenish streak behind it that glowed for some seconds. Denning, our greatest authority on meteorites, stated that the height of its first appearance was about ninety or one hundred miles. It seemed to him that it fell to earth about one hundred miles east of him.

I was at home at that hour and writing in my study; and although my French windows face towards Ottershaw and the blind was up (for I loved in those days to look up at the night sky), I saw nothing of it. Yet this strangest of all things that ever came to earth from outer space must have fallen while I was sitting there, visible to me had I only looked up as it passed. Some of those who saw its flight say it travelled with a hissing sound. I myself heard nothing of that. Many people in Berkshire, Surrey, and Middlesex must have seen the fall of it, and, at most, have thought that another meteorite had descended. No one seems to have troubled to look for the fallen mass that night.

But very early in the morning poor Ogilvy, who had seen the shooting star and who was persuaded that a meteorite lay somewhere on the common between Horsell, Ottershaw, and Woking, rose early with the idea of finding it. Find it he did, soon after dawn, and not far from the sand pits. An enormous hole had been made by the impact of the projectile, and the sand and gravel had been flung violently in every direction over the heath, forming heaps visible a mile and a half away. The heather was on fire eastward, and a thin blue smoke rose against the dawn.

The Thing itself lay almost entirely buried in sand, amidst the scattered splinters of a fir tree it had shivered to fragments in its descent. The uncovered part had the appearance of a huge cylinder, caked over and its outline softened by a thick scaly dun-coloured incrustation. It had a diameter of about thirty yards.

GO ON TO NEXT PAGE

He approached the mass, surprised at the size and more so at the shape, since most meteorites are rounded more or less completely. It was, however, still so hot from its flight through the air as to forbid his near approach. A stirring noise within its cylinder he ascribed to the unequal cooling of its surface; for at that time it had not occurred to him that it might be hollow.

He remained standing at the edge of the pit that the Thing had made for itself, staring at its strange appearance, astonished chiefly at its unusual shape and colour, and dimly perceiving even then some evidence of design in its arrival. The early morning was wonderfully still, and the sun, just clearing the pine trees towards Weybridge, was already warm. He did not remember hearing any birds that morning, there was certainly no breeze stirring, and the only sounds were the faint movements from within the cindery cylinder. He was all alone on the common.

Then suddenly he noticed with a start that some of the grey clinker, the ashy incrustation that covered the meteorite, was falling off the circular edge of the end. It was dropping off in flakes and raining down upon the sand. A large piece suddenly came off and fell with a sharp noise that brought his heart into his mouth.

For a minute he scarcely realised what this meant, and, although the heat was excessive, he clambered down into the pit close to the bulk to see the Thing more clearly. He fancied even then that the cooling of the body might account for this, but what disturbed that idea was the fact that the ash was falling only from the end of the cylinder.

And then he perceived that, very slowly, the circular top of the cylinder was rotating on its body. It was such a gradual movement that he discovered it only through noticing that a black mark that had been near him five minutes ago was now at the other side of the circumference. Even then he scarcely understood what this indicated, until he heard a muffled grating sound and saw the black mark jerk forward an inch or so. Then the Thing came upon him in a flash. The cylinder was artificial — hollow — with an end that screwed out! Something within the cylinder was unscrewing the top!

"Good heavens!" said Ogilvy. "There's a man in it — men in it! Half roasted to death! Trying to escape!"

At once, with a quick mental leap, he linked the Thing with the flash upon Mars.

33. Who is the greatest authority on meteorites?

    (A) Albin

    (B) Ogilvy

    (C) Denning

    (D) the narrator

34. All the following are true regarding the falling object that appeared in the night sky EXCEPT:

    (A) It produced a line of flame high in the atmosphere.

    (B) It left a greenish streak behind it that glowed for several seconds.

    (C) The narrator saw it fall.

    (D) It first appeared at an altitude of approximately 100 miles above the Earth.

35. Why does the author use capital letters when describing the object as the Thing?

    (A) To emphasize that this was no ordinary object.

    (B) The author made a grammatical error.

    (C) That is the name that was printed on the outside of the cylinder.

    (D) Thing is the name of the company that manufactured the cylinder.

36. All the following factors regarding the physical appearance of the Thing made it unusual compared to other meteorites EXCEPT

    (A) its large size.

    (B) its shape.

    (C) its color.

    (D) the layer of ash coating it.

37. What disturbed Ogilvy about the ash that was falling off the Thing?

   (A) The wind was blowing the ash into his face.

   (B) The ash was still dangerously hot.

   (C) The color of the ash was unusual.

   (D) It was falling off the cylinder at only one end.

38. What did Ogilvy initially assume the stirring noise coming from the Thing was due to?

   (A) the man inside

   (B) unequal cooling of its surface

   (C) the engines

   (D) a loudspeaker inside the cylinder

39. Read this excerpt from *The War of the Worlds*.

   It was such a gradual movement that he discovered it only through noticing that a black mark that had been near him five minutes ago was now at the other side of the circumference. Even then he scarcely understood what this indicated, until he heard a muffled grating sound and saw the black mark jerk forward an inch or so.

What does the movement of the black mark indicate?

   (A) The black mark indicates how deep the Thing was buried.

   (B) The mark was moving due to the surface contracting as it cooled.

   (C) Something within the cylinder was unscrewing the top.

   (D) Someone had erased the original black mark and redrawn it at a different place.

40. What did Ogilvy eventually realize the Thing is?

   (A) a normal meteorite

   (B) an unusual meteorite

   (C) an elaborate practical joke

   (D) a spaceship from Mars

Read this passage and then answer the questions that follow.

From **The Strange Case of Dr. Jekyll and Mr. Hyde,** *by Robert Louis Stevenson*

Nearly a year later, in the month of October, 18—, London was startled by a crime of singular ferocity and rendered all the more notable by the high position of the victim. The details were few and startling. A maid servant living alone in a house not far from the river, had gone up-stairs to bed about eleven. Although a fog rolled over the city in the small hours, the early part of the night was cloudless, and the lane, which the maid's window overlooked, was brilliantly lit by the full moon. It seems she was romantically given, for she sat down upon her box, which stood immediately under the window, and fell into a dream of musing. Never (she used to say, with streaming tears, when she narrated that experience), never had she felt more at peace with all men or thought more kindly of the world. And as she so sat she became aware of an aged and beautiful gentleman with white hair, drawing near along the lane; and advancing to meet him, another and very small gentleman, to whom at first she paid less attention. When they had come within speech (which was just under the maid's eyes) the older man bowed and accosted the other with a very pretty manner of politeness.

It did not seem as if the subject of his address were of great importance; indeed, from his pointing, it sometimes appeared as if he were only inquiring his way; but the moon shone on his face as he spoke, and the girl was pleased to watch it, it seemed to breathe such an innocent and old-world kindness of disposition, yet with something high too, as of a well-founded self-content. Presently her eye wandered to the other, and she was surprised to recognise in him a certain Mr. Hyde, who had once visited her master and for whom she had conceived a dislike. He had in his hand a heavy cane, with which he was trifling; but he

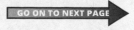

answered never a word, and seemed to listen with an ill-contained impatience. And then all of a sudden he broke out in a great flame of anger, stamping with his foot, brandishing the cane, and carrying on (as the maid described it) like a madman. The old gentleman took a step back, with the air of one very much surprised and a trifle hurt; and at that Mr. Hyde broke out of all bounds and clubbed him to the earth. And next moment, with ape-like fury, he was trampling his victim under foot and hailing down a storm of blows, under which the bones were audibly shattered and the body jumped upon the roadway. At the horror of these sights and sounds, the maid fainted.

It was two o'clock when she came to herself and called for the police. The murderer was gone long ago; but there lay his victim in the middle of the lane, incredibly mangled. The stick with which the deed had been done, although it was of some rare and very tough and heavy wood, had broken in the middle under the stress of this insensate cruelty; and one splintered half had rolled in the neighbouring gutter — the other, without doubt, had been carried away by the murderer. A purse and a gold watch were found upon the victim: but no cards or papers, except a sealed and stamped envelope, which he had been probably carrying to the post, and which bore the name and address of Mr. Utterson.

This was brought to the lawyer the next morning, before he was out of bed; and he had no sooner seen it, and been told the circumstances, than he shot out a solemn lip. "I shall say nothing till I have seen the body," said he; "this may be very serious. Have the kindness to wait while I dress." And with the same grave countenance he hurried through his breakfast and drove to the police station, whither the body had been carried. As soon as he came into the cell, he nodded.

"Yes," said he, "I recognise him. I am sorry to say that this is Sir Danvers Carew."

"Good God, sir," exclaimed the officer, "is it possible?" And the next moment his eye lighted up with professional ambition. "This will make a deal of noise," he said. "And perhaps you can help us to the man." And he briefly narrated what the maid had seen, and showed the broken stick.

Mr. Utterson had already quailed at the name of Hyde; but when the stick was laid before him, he could doubt no longer; broken and battered as it was, he recognised it for one that he had himself presented many years before to Henry Jekyll.

"Is this Mr. Hyde a person of small stature?" he inquired.

"Particularly small and particularly wicked-looking, is what the maid calls him," said the officer.

Mr. Utterson reflected; and then, raising his head, "If you will come with me in my cab," he said, "I think I can take you to his house."

41. At what time did the murder most likely take place?

(A) shortly before 11 p.m.

(B) shortly after 11 p.m.

(C) around noon

(D) just after 2:00 a.m.

42. Read this excerpt from *The Strange Case of Dr. Jekyll and Mr. Hyde.*

London was startled by a crime of singular ferocity and rendered all the more notable by the high position of the victim.

What is the meaning of the phrase "high position of the victim" as it is used in the context of the excerpt?

(A) The victim was standing on a ledge high above the ground.

(B) The victim was an important person.

(C) The victim had been taking illegal drugs.

(D) The victim was one of the highest paid maids in London.

43. What was the name of the victim?

    (A) Mr. Hyde

    (B) Dr. Jekyll

    (C) Mr. Utterson

    (D) Sir Danvers Carew

44. What can be deduced by the fact that the victim's purse and gold watch were found at the scene of the crime?

    (A) The attacker had dropped them during his escape.

    (B) The motive for the murder was probably not robbery.

    (C) The victim sold gold watches for a living.

    (D) The attacker planted them on the victim.

45. Why was the maid able to recognize Mr. Hyde?

    (A) She recognized him from a drawing that the police sketch artist made based on her description of the attacker.

    (B) Mr. Hyde is a famous doctor.

    (C) She had seen him once before when he had come to visit her master and she had taken an instant dislike to him.

    (D) It was foggy that night.

46. Why did the maid initially pay more attention to the older gentleman in the alley?

    (A) She thought he was handsome.

    (B) He was carrying a heavy cane.

    (C) He spoke in a very loud voice.

    (D) He was a very short man.

47. How did the victim die?

    (A) He was beaten with a cane and stomped to death.

    (B) He was stabbed through the heart.

    (C) He was shot.

    (D) He accidentally fell, breaking his bones in the process.

48. Read this excerpt from *The Strange Case of Dr. Jekyll and Mr. Hyde.*

    "Good God, sir," exclaimed the officer, "is it possible?" And the next moment his eye lighted up with professional ambition. "This will make a deal of noise," he said.

    Why did the officer's eye light up with professional ambition?

    (A) He realized that he could arrest Mr. Utterson.

    (B) He realized that solving the murder of such an important person would be very good for his career.

    (C) He wanted to get revenge on Mr. Hyde.

    (D) He wants Mr. Utterson to hire him.

49. What connection does the lawyer have to the murder weapon?

    (A) He has never seen it before in his life.

    (B) He gave it to Dr. Jekyll many years ago.

    (C) He gave it to Mr. Hyde many years ago.

    (D) It was stolen from him by Mr. Hyde.

50. Mr. Hyde is described as all the following EXCEPT

    (A) a person of small stature.

    (B) wicked-looking.

    (C) ill-tempered.

    (D) white-haired.

Section 2: Language Arts – Writing

Part 1: Language

TIME: 55 minutes for 50 questions

DIRECTIONS: This section tests your ability to identify various types of errors in writing. Pick the best answer(s) for each question and then mark the space on your answer sheet that corresponds to the question number and the letter indicating your choice.

1. Which of these sentences is punctuated incorrectly?

   (A) Frances made a list of what she wanted to purchase, including, both food and camping supplies.

   (B) Since she had already purchased her tent, there was no need to look in that section.

   (C) However, she eventually noticed that tents were on sale; she then went to investigate.

   (D) The tents were reasonably priced, but Frances chose to keep her old one.

2. Read this paragraph.

   Take a piece of embroidery floss about nine inches long, and use it to thread a needle. It's best to use cross-stitch fabric for this type of craft. If you look at the fabric, you'll see that the holes form squares. Bring the floss through one hole and then back down through the hole diagonal to your first stitch.

   Which sentence *best* begins this paragraph?

   (A) Make sure you create a cross by choosing the opposite hole for the next stitch.

   (B) Floss comes in many colors, so choose your favorite.

   (C) Cross-stitch is a simple form of embroidery to learn.

   (D) Crafting can be a wonderful way to relax.

3. Which of these sentences includes a misspelled word?

   (A) We bought the permits for the beach and packed the luggage.

   (B) It was incoveneint to leave early in the morning, but Luigi insisted.

   (C) Beverly slept on the ride, despite the agitation from the vehicle.

   (D) We found it inconceivable that she could sleep through the beautiful sunrise.

4. Read this sentence.

   Before getting a haircut, Luke feeling unkempt.

   Which of these is the *most* accurate and effective revision to the sentence?

   (A) Before he got a haircut, Luke feeling unkempt.

   (B) Before getting a haircut, "unkempt" is one word that would describe Luke.

   (C) Despite feeling unkempt, Luke got a haircut.

   (D) Before getting a haircut, Luke felt unkempt.

5. Read this sentence.

   Around the lake, Jessica ran three miles in the rain.

   Which revision of the sentence *best* expresses the idea correctly and precisely?

   (A) Jessica, who was around the lake, ran three miles in the rain.

   (B) Around the lake, in the rain, Jessica ran three miles.

   (C) Despite the rain, Jessica ran three miles on the path around the lake.

   (D) Jessica in the rain ran around the lake for three miles.

6. Which of these sentences is punctuated incorrectly?

(A) The menu from the 1800s was very revealing.

(B) Who knew that they had mashed-potatoes back then?

(C) There was a special cake for celebrating the Fourth of July!

(D) I wasn't interested in the Russian borscht, however.

7. Read the paragraph.

Professional bullfighters are called *toreros*, with the head *torero* known as the *matador*. Once in the arena with a bull, they perform a series of maneuvers that cause the bull to charge them. The audience expects the *toreros* to risk being trampled or gored by the bull, until, at last, the torero stabs and kills the bull, a scene that Hemingway powerfully captured in his novel.

Which sentence would *best* open the paragraph to introduce the topic?

(A) Bullfighting is a tradition in Spain that was brought to America's attention by Ernest Hemingway's novel *The Sun Also Rises*.

(B) Many people protest the cruelty of bullfighting.

(C) Several people have been critically injured, even killed, while participating in the running of the bulls.

(D) Bulls are actually quite docile animals.

Read this excerpt of a draft of an essay. Then answer Questions 8 and 9.

Cape Cod is a peninsula that extends into the Atlantic Ocean. It is the eastern-most portion of the state of Massachusetts. Many people go to Cape Cod in order to enjoy the beaches. They swim in the ocean. At some beaches, they surf.

Those interested in American history will also want to visit. It was long a noted land by Europeans exploring the region, and, in 1620, the Puritans landed at Provincetown, on the tip of the Cape to settle there.

8. Which sentence would be the *most* effective addition to the beginning of the second paragraph?

(A) Many people are surprised to learn that one can surf on Cape Cod.

(B) Cape Cod is not just a destination for relaxing on the beach.

(C) The Puritans did not land on Plymouth Rock, despite the popular myth.

(D) Captain John Smith was their leader.

9. Which revision *most* effectively combines the ideas of the last two sentences of the first paragraph?

(A) They swim and, at some beaches, surf.

(B) They surf at some beaches and swim at others.

(C) Beaches are available for swimming or surfing.

(D) Swimming at beaches and surfing at other beaches.

10. Which of these sentences contains an error or errors in capitalization?

(A) We prefer to go on a Spring cruise.

(B) The ship is docked at Fulton Street at that time of year.

(C) Traffic is not nearly so bad there as it is heading east.

(D) After a short drive in from New Jersey, we're ready to go!

11. Read these sentences.

It is true that the craft fair is not for two more weeks. However, if we want to order a banner for our booth, it is _____ that we place it today. The banner company needs two weeks to make it.

Which word, when added in the blank, would *best* stress the importance of ordering a banner today?

(A) worthwhile

(B) imperative

(C) realistic

(D) compelling

12. Read this sentence.

Anita listened to the ideas for the magazine, and on how to improve it, with more interest after she returned from her vacation.

Which of these is the most correct and concise revision to the sentence?

(A) Returning from vacation, Anita much more interested in improving the magazine.

(B) Being returned from vacation, Anita was much more interested in listening to our suggestions for improving the magazine.

(C) After she returned from vacation, Anita was much more interested in listening to our suggestions for improving the magazine.

(D) After vacation, Anita was much more interested.

13. Which of these sentences contains a misspelled word?

(A) The argument was audible to the entire room.

(B) Most of us politely pretended we could not hear it.

(C) Cindy pretended to find it humorous.

(D) I was very embarassed.

14. Read this sentence.

I really enjoy baseball, the long season, the pace of play, and the traditions it encompasses.

What change should be made to correct the sentence's punctuation?

(A) Change the comma to a period.

(B) Eliminate the comma.

(C) Change the comma to a colon.

(D) Add a comma after the word "and."

15. Which of these sentences contains a grammatical error?

(A) One of the teams is going.

(B) Betty or Nancy signed up, too.

(C) Either one of them are able to keep score.

(D) Neither one is traveling on the team bus.

16. Read this sentence.

The cat was found by our daughter's best friend in an alley on the outskirts of town.

Which of these is the *most* accurate and effective revision to the sentence?

(A) The cat, found by our daughter's best friend on the outskirts of town, is ours.

(B) Our cat was found on the outskirts of town in an alley by our daughter's best friend.

(C) In an alley on the outskirts of town, the cat was found by our daughter's best friend.

(D) Our daughter's best friend found the cat in an alley on the outskirts of town.

17. Read the paragraph.

The drama club's first meeting was on Monday. With a quorum of ten students attending, they were able to vote on their spring musical. While some were in favor of the show *Cats*, more of the club seemed to favor a newer show, such as *Suessical*. A vote was taken.

Which sentence *best* concludes this paragraph?

(A) *Suessical* will be the spring musical this school year.

(B) Several members of the club abstained from voting.

(C) Those in favor of *Cats* were extremely fervent.

(D) They also discussed the fall play.

Read this excerpt of a draft of a report. Then answer Questions 18–20.

Located in Fayette County, Pennsylvania, Fort Necessity was the site of an early battle in the French and Indian War. The fort was founded by then-British General George Washington in 1754, who ordered its immediate construction to reinforce his position. _____ before the fort was completed, battle commenced on July 3rd.

Therefore, by the end of the day, Washington agreed to terms of surrender. He later stated that had he been aware that British troops were on their way to support his position, he would not have surrendered. The terms of surrender did allow Washington to peacefully withdraw his troops. In the 21st century, Fort Necessity has found new purpose as an educational institution and National Historic Battlefield. The French and Indian War was a complicated historical event, and the people involved had many differing agendas and motivations. Fort Necessity now tries to give insight into the complex history of both the fort and the war.

18. Which word would *best* fit in the blank to clarify the transition between ideas?

(A) However

(B) Since

(C) Although

(D) Perhaps

19. Which sentence would be the most effective addition to the beginning of the second paragraph?

(A) Fort Necessity remained uncompleted.

(B) The French were clearly superior in number.

(C) Fort Necessity is not open during snowstorms.

(D) General Washington did not speak French.

20. Where might the author add a paragraph break in the second paragraph to better organize the text?

(A) after the first sentence

(B) after the second sentence

(C) after the third sentence

(D) after the fourth sentence

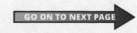 GO ON TO NEXT PAGE

21. Read this sentence.

Benji expected his dad sings to him every night.

Which of these is the *most* accurate and effective revision to the sentence?

(A) Benji expects his dad sings to him every night.

(B) Benji, expecting his dad to sing to him, every night.

(C) Benji expects his dad to sing to him every night.

(D) Benji expects to his dad sing to him every night.

22. Which of these sentences contains a misspelled word?

(A) We liked the apartment, but the large maintance fee was disappointing.

(B) We asked Magda if she could recommend another apartment complex.

(C) She gave us a reference to Matthews Estates.

(D) Luckily, they were able to accommodate us immediately.

23. Which of these sentences is punctuated correctly?

(A) The drive begins an overlook, where, you can see the Pacific Ocean.

(B) From there you drive about 13 miles to the cottages where you can stay overnight.

(C) My favorite cottage is; the Rose Garden.

(D) Make sure to tell Reynolds, the house-keeper, that you know me.

24. Which of these sentences contains an error or errors in capitalization?

(A) I asked the President of the United States for help.

(B) She invited me to the White House for dinner.

(C) I was relieved that she served french fries.

(D) I admired photos of the USS *Arizona* in the dining room.

25. Read the paragraph.

The little penguin is the smallest species of penguin, growing, on average, only 13 inches in height. Little penguins live on the coast of New Zealand and Australia. Australians call them "fairy penguins," while Kiwis (as residents of New Zealand are called) call them "little blue penguins."

Which sentence *best* concludes this paragraph?

(A) Like most seabirds, they have a long life span.

(B) Little penguins might be small, but they are beloved.

(C) Another kind of penguin is the chinstrap penguin.

(D) Although they are often confused, Australia and New Zealand are not the same landmass.

Read this excerpt of a draft of an essay. Then answer Questions 26 and 27.

The keytar is a lightweight keyboard that can be worn on a strap around the neck so that the player can hold it across his or her chest. As is implied by the name, the keytar is quite similar to the guitar. Not really the sound but how it is held.

The main benefit of a keytar is that it allows for much greater movement on the part of the player. A keyboard, usually in the form of a piano or synthesizer, is traditionally too heavy to move.

26. How could the last two sentences of the first paragraph best be combined?

(A) As is implied by the name, the keytar is quite similar to the guitar, not in the sound so much as in how it is held.

(B) As is implied by the name, the keytar is quite similar to the guitar; the sound not how it is held.

(C) How it is held is the way that a keytar is similar to a guitar, not in how it sounds.

(D) As is implied by the name "keytar," they are quite similar to the guitar, not really the sound but how it is held.

27. Which sentence would be the *most* effective addition to the end of the second paragraph?

(A) Pianos can weigh up to a ton!

(B) However, with a keytar, the player is free to move about the performance space as he wishes.

(C) Keytars are sometimes dismissed as faddish.

(D) Keytars allow for greater movement on the part of the player.

28. Read this sentence.

The sun was much brighter than we had expected, for that reason we decided to leave the beach earlier in the afternoon than we had planned.

Which revision of the sentence *best* expresses the idea precisely and concisely?

(A) The sun was brighter than we had expected, so we had planned to leave the beach earlier.

(B) We decided to leave the beach earlier in the afternoon than we had planned because of the sun.

(C) Because the sun was much brighter than we had expected, we decided to leave the beach earlier in the afternoon than planned.

(D) We had planned to stay at the beach into the afternoon, but, once we saw how hot it was because of the sun, we decided to leave the beach earlier in the afternoon.

29. Read the paragraph.

Books can be quite heavy, especially if they are hardcovers or run more than 200 pages. An e-reader is a good option, instead. Additionally, e-readers can be loaded with many titles at once, and are much easier to carry than a dozen books!

Which sentence would *best* open the paragraph to introduce the topic?

(A) Reading is a wonderful hobby.

(B) Many people find e-readers difficult to adjust to using.

(C) I read *Pride and Prejudice* on an e-reader recently, and was pleasantly surprised.

(D) Book lovers who suffer from chronic back pain may find relief by using an e-reader.

30. Which of these sentences is punctuated correctly?

(A) "The hockey game will begin as soon as the Club President arrives," Corey said.

(B) Nancy was surprised to learn that there was heavy traffic on Hansen Street.

(C) "Is that because it is a catholic feast day?" she asked.

(D) "No," Corey said. "The traffic is always bad on the parkway coming from the west."

31. Read this sentence.

Central Park located in the center of Manhattan, always lovely in the fall.

Which of these is the *most* accurate and effective revision to the sentence to emphasize the park's location?

(A) Always lovely in the fall, Central Park located in the center of Manhattan.

(B) Central Park is always lovely in the fall, and is located in the center of Manhattan.

(C) In the center of Manhattan is Central Park, which is always lovely in the fall.

(D) Always lovely in the fall, Central Park is located in the center of Manhattan.

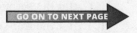 GO ON TO NEXT PAGE

32. Which of these sentences contains a misspelled word?

(A) Adil was used to the rhythym of the photocopier.

(B) Therefore, he was surprised when it ground to a halt.

(C) There was a jam in the copier's machinery.

(D) Adil had to defer finishing his work while the repairman fixed it.

Read this excerpt from a draft of an essay. Then answer Questions 33–35.

The Supreme Court of the United States is the highest federal court in the land. Established by the U.S. Constitution in 1789, it has the ultimate jurisdiction over the entire court system in the United States. _____, the Supreme Court is not obliged to hear every disputed court case that rises to appeal at its level; they can and do decline to hear appeals.

Once appointed, the justices have life tenure unless they choose to resign or retire. Many people do not realize that justices can be impeached; so far, that has never happened. Some of the more famous cases that the Supreme Court has decided are *Brown v. the Board of Education* and *Roe v. Wade*.

33. Which word or words would *best* fit in the blank to clarify the transition between ideas?

(A) therefore

(B) finally

(C) however

(D) moreover

34. Which sentence would be the *most* effective addition to the start of the second paragraph?

(A) The Court consists of nine judges appointed by the President and con-firmed by Congress, including a Chief Justice.

(B) Several justices have faced fierce ques-tioning by Congress.

(C) The Supreme Court is the lesser-known "third branch" of the government, along with Congress and the Presidency.

(D) Only one U.S. President has also been a Supreme Court Justice.

35. Where might the author add a paragraph break in the second paragraph to better organize the text?

(A) after the first sentence

(B) at the semicolon in the second sentence

(C) after the second sentence

(D) after the third sentence

36. Which of these sentences is grammatically correct?

(A) Singapore being a city I have never been.

(B) Once I have gone there, I will have visited every city in Asia.

(C) You, I suppose, is also excited to go.

(D) We will be first-time visitors together!

37. Read this sentence.

An order of French fries and a hamburger was the order placed by both Nadia and me.

Which of these is the *most* accurate and effec-tive revision to the sentence?

(A) Nadia and me each placed an order for an order of French fries and a hamburger.

(B) Nadia and I each ordered French fries and a hamburger.

(C) French fries and a hamburger were ordered by Nadia and me.

(D) Nadia ordered French fries and a hamburger, and so did me.

38. Read this sentence.

Jelani is an excellent tennis player, she has won the club trophy twice.

What change should be made to the sentence's punctuation?

(A) Change the comma to a semicolon.

(B) Remove the comma.

(C) Add a comma after "excellent."

(D) Change the comma to a period.

39. Read this sentence.

The store across from the theater at the bottom of the hill is where I suggest we meet.

Which of these is the *most* accurate and effective revision to the sentence?

(A) At the bottom of the hill across from the theater is where the store is that I suggest we meet at.

(B) I suggest we meet at the store that is across from the theater at the bottom of the hill.

(C) The theater is where we should meet: across from the store at the bottom of the hill.

(D) I suggest we meet at the theater across from the store at the bottom of the hill.

40. Read this paragraph.

The average rent in the area is $1,500 a month. This average rises to $2,000 when only the eastern-most neighborhoods in the city are considered, but drops to $1,000 when only the central and western-most neighborhoods are considered.

Which sentence *best* concludes this paragraph?

(A) Thus, it can be reasonably assumed that the wealthiest neighborhoods are in the eastern-most part of the city.

(B) There are more houses in the Colonial style in the western part of the city.

(C) The city was founded in 1927.

(D) Businesses do not pay rent in this city.

41. Read this sentence.

Having washed all the dishes, Nigel now waiting for his next assignment.

Which of these is the *most* accurate and effective revision to the sentence?

(A) Having washed all the dishes, now Nigel waiting for his next assignment.

(B) Having washed all the dishes, now Nigel awaiting his next assignment.

(C) Having washed all the dishes, here is Nigel now waiting for his next assignment.

(D) Having washed all the dishes, Nigel now waited for his next assignment.

42. Which of these sentences contains an error or errors in capitalization?

(A) Bertha lives on Mapplethorpe Row.

(B) Her house is next door to a Russian restaurant.

(C) McKinley Middle School is across the street.

(D) It's typical of cities in the west to have just one school building.

43. Read the paragraph.

A candy store on the New Jersey shore was flooded, and a batch of soft taffy was soaked in ocean water. An enterprising worker told customers that this was "saltwater taffy" and soon sold out of the batch, which was widely agreed to be delicious.

Which sentence *best* begins this paragraph?

(A) Saltwater taffy comes in many flavors.

(B) Many inventions arose from the Jersey shore.

(C) Saltwater taffy is a surprisingly apt name.

(D) From then on, the candy store added saltwater to every batch.

44. Which of these sentences contains a misspelled word?

   (A) The pronounciation of the country's name confused Carl.

   (B) He turned to Amir in desperation for help.

   (C) "Oh, that's elementary," Amir laughed.

   (D) With persistence, Carl was able to learn it.

45. Read this sentence.

   Mark was tired of being misunderstood; by his coworkers and he resolved to speak to his superior.

   What change should be made to correct the sentence's punctuation?

   (A) Change the semicolon to a comma.

   (B) Add a comma after "coworkers."

   (C) Add a period after "coworkers."

   (D) Eliminate the semicolon.

46. Which of these sentences is punctuated incorrectly?

   (A) Before we went hiking, in the woods, we packed a lunch.

   (B) Natalia put the following in her bag: trail mix, water and an apple.

   (C) Brad said he would get a hamburger at the park, as there is a small stand there.

   (D) I brought a sandwich; I had eaten earlier.

47. Read these sentences.

   Occupational therapy is the use of assessment and treatment to develop and reestablish skills needed for daily life. The word "occupational" _____ that the therapy will help the patient be able to return to a job, but, in fact, occupational therapy may involve regaining or learning skills such as brushing one's teeth or putting on shoes and socks.

   Which word, when added in the blank, would *best* show what the word "occupational" does?

   (A) insists

   (B) implies

   (C) removes

   (D) asserts

Read this excerpt of a draft of an essay. Then answer Questions 48–50.

   The Basement Tapes is an album recorded by Bob Dylan and the Band, the 16th studio album for Dylan. After the Band backed Dylan during his world tour of 1965–66, four of them moved to be near Dylan in Woodstock, New York, to collaborate with him on music and film projects. _____ they recorded more than 100 tracks together in 1967, including original compositions, contemporary covers and traditional material.

   The world tour had controversially mixed folk and rock. Dylan's new style moved away from rock. It moved from the urban sensibilities and extended narratives of his most recent albums. The new songs covered a range of genres.

48. Which word would *best* fit in the blank to clarify the transition between ideas?

(A) therefore

(B) however

(C) eventually

(D) despite

49. Which sentence would be the *most* effective addition to the start of the second paragraph?

(A) Dylan's sound was changing rapidly.

(B) The Band would go on to record on their own.

(C) Dylan never achieved the same fame again.

(D) Portions of Dylan's recent tour had been filmed.

50. How could the second and third sentences of the second paragraph *best* be combined?

(A) Dylan's new style moved away from rock, but moved from the urban sensibilities and extended narratives of his most recent albums.

(B) Moving away from rock, moving from urban sensibilities, moving from extended narratives.

(C) Dylan's new style moved away from rock as well as the urban sensibilities and extended narratives of his most recent albums.

(D) Moving away from urban sensibilities and extended narratives of his most recent albums, Dylan's new style moved away from rock.

GO ON TO NEXT PAGE

Part 2: Writing

"Against Mining in Bristol Bay," by Ron Boyer

Lake Clark National Park, part of the Bristol Bay watershed in Alaska, is a popular destination for brown bears — who come for the 1.5 million salmon swimming in the lake — and for tourists who want to see the majestic wildlife in action. Yet Lake Clark is threatened; massive deposits of copper and gold have been found in the lands adjacent to the park, and efforts to open these lands up to mining are underway. Allowing this to happen would be devastating to the wildlife in the region.

The project proposed would be the largest mine in Alaska, built in an area so remote, over 100 miles of road would need to be laid simply to access the minerals. Additionally, miles of pipeline would be needed. Can you imagine the devastation this would cause to this otherwise pristine wilderness?

The Society for the Conservation of Lake Clark National Park commissioned a study on the impact of such a mine and found that wildlife would be displaced, air quality would rapidly worsen, food and shelter for animals would be compromised, and tourism would significantly decrease. For all of these reasons and more, the society is against the mine.

While it's undeniable that such a vast reserve of copper and gold is appealing, we should not be mercenary about the project. The impact such a mine would have on the Bristol Bay watershed is significantly negative. As the great naturalist Edward Abbey said, "We need wilderness whether or not we ever set foot in it. We need a refuge even if we never go there." Lake Clark National Park is a refuge for humanity and a home to the brown bear and other animals. We must protect it.

Section 3: Mathematics

Part 1

TIME: 50 minutes for 26 questions

DIRECTIONS: This section tests your knowledge of mathematics. Pick the best answer(s) for each question and then mark the space on your answer sheet that corresponds to the question number and the letter indicating your choice. You may use a calculator during this part of the test.

1. Chicken broth is sold in both rectangular card-board cartons and large cylindrical cans. The carton has dimensions of 2 inches by 5 inches by 8 inches and costs $3.25. The can has a radius of 2 inches and a height of 10 inches and costs $2.40. Which is a better buy?

   (A) carton

   (B) can

   (C) Both containers are the same value.

   (D) not enough information

2. Which of the following is in descending order?

   (A) $\frac{3}{100}$, 5%, $\sqrt{7}$, .7

   (B) $\sqrt{7}$, $\frac{3}{100}$, .7, 5%

   (C) $\frac{3}{100}$, 5%, .7, $\sqrt{7}$

   (D) $\sqrt{7}$, .7, 5%, $\frac{3}{100}$

3. Alicia and Michelle each have a quarter, and Stefanie has a six-sided die. What is the prob-ability that both coins will land on heads and the die will show a 4 if they toss the coins and roll the die at the same time?

4. Solve for x: $3^x = \frac{1}{27}$.

   (A) −2

   (B) −3

   (C) 3

   (D) 4

5. What is the area of the shaded region? (Recall that this is commonly called a *sector.*)

   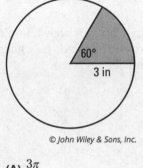

   © John Wiley & Sons, Inc.

   (A) $\frac{3\pi}{2}$

   (B) π

   (C) $\frac{3}{2}$

   (D) $\frac{2\pi}{3}$

6. $\sqrt{127}$ is between which numbers?

   (A) 8 and 9

   (B) 11 and 12

   (C) 13 and 14

   (D) 63 and 64

7. Ryan works at a coffee shop that sells an aver-age of 114 cups of coffee an hour. If one pot of coffee fills 8 cups, how many pots of coffee will the shop go through on an average day if the shop opens at 8 a.m. and closes at 6 p.m.?

   (A) 122 pots

   (B) 142 pots

   (C) 143 pots

   (D) 1,140 pots

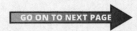
GO ON TO NEXT PAGE

8. Cory is a skateboarder and can travel at a speed of 15 miles per hour. How fast does Cory go in feet per minute?

(A) 1,320

(B) 1,750

(C) 1,820

(D) 4,752,000

9. What is equivalent to $64^{\frac{3}{2}}$?

(A) 512

(B) 327.68

(C) 16

(D) 21.3

10. The cost of a parking garage is shown in the following graph, where the x-axis is in hours and the y-axis is in dollars.

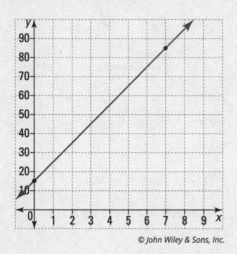

© John Wiley & Sons, Inc.

What is the cost per hour of parking in the garage?

(A) $0

(B) $10

(C) $15

(D) $25

11. The volume of a cube is 216 cubic inches. What does its total surface area equal?

12. Simplify $(2^4 + 6^2)^0$.

(A) 0

(B) 1

(C) 32

(D) 52

13. What is the missing value in the table?

x	y
−4	−9
−1	−3
0	−1
?	3
5	9

(A) 1

(B) 2

(C) 3

(D) 4

14. What is the transformation illustrated here?

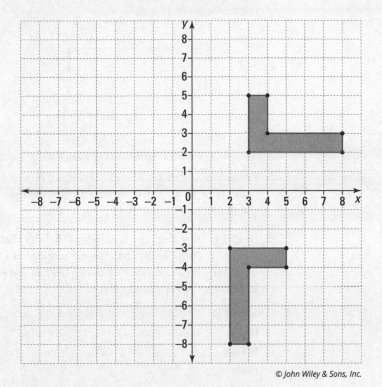

© John Wiley & Sons, Inc.

(A) rotation 90° clockwise about the origin

(B) translation down 9 units, left 1 unit

(C) reflection over the x-axis

(D) reflection over the line $y = x$

15. Kyle has played many rounds of the same video game. His scores were 97, 83, 70, 92, 83, and 85. What was the mean of his scores?

16. Solve for x: $x^2 - 10 = 6(1 + x)$.

(A) {−2, 8}

(B) {−4, 4}

(C) {−8, 2}

(D) {−16, 1}

17. In a fun-sized bag of candy there are 7 red, 6 green, 5 blue, and 3 yellow pieces. What is the probability of selecting a red piece followed by a blue piece?

(A) $\frac{5}{63}$

(B) $\frac{4}{7}$

(C) $\frac{1}{35}$

(D) $\frac{1}{12}$

18. Which of the following is equivalent to .8?

(A) $\frac{2}{25}$

(B) 8%

(C) .08%

(D) $\frac{4}{5}$

19. A picture frame has the outside dimensions of 18 in × 20 in. If Spencer is putting a mat inside the frame that is x units wide all the way around, what expression represents the area of open glass?

(A) $(18 - 2x)(20 - 2x)$

(B) $(18)(20)(2x)$

(C) $(18 - x)(20 - x)$

(D) $\frac{(18)(20)}{2x}$

GO ON TO NEXT PAGE

20. In a right triangle, the two legs measure $a = 5$ and $b = 7$. What is the measure of angle A?

(A) 11.5°

(B) 44.4°

(C) 35.5°

(D) 45.6°

21. What is the length of the line segment between $(-2, 5)$ and $(4, 2)$? Round to the nearest hundredth.

22. Solve for x: $\log_4 2x = \log_4 (x + 3)$

(A) 1

(B) 2

(C) 3

(D) 4

23. Which of the following is equivalent to 2,592?

(A) $4^3 5^2$

(B) $2^5 3^4$

(C) $2^4 3^5$

(D) $4^2 5^3$

24. The following two figures are similar. What is the measure of x?

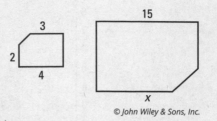

© John Wiley & Sons, Inc.

25. Sarah has 4 books she is arranging on her shelf. How many different orders can she put the books in?

26. In Lauren's wallet, she has some U.S. bills that total $52. Suppose she has the same number of ones and fives and twice as many tens as ones. How many tens does she have?

(A) 2

(B) 4

(C) 6

(D) 8

Part 2

TIME: 55 minutes for 26 questions

DIRECTIONS: You may NOT use a calculator during this part of the test.

27. Taylor gets her haircut every 3 weeks and gets her nails done every other week. If she got both her haircut and her nails done this week, how many weeks will it be until she has both done in the same week again?

(A) 3 weeks

(B) 4 weeks

(C) 5 weeks

(D) 6 weeks

28. The following graph tracks Jason's heart rate during a workout. What do you think he is doing from 40 minutes to 50 minutes?

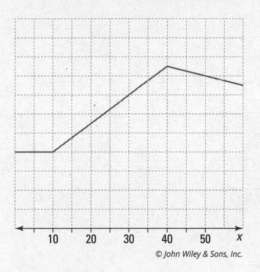

© John Wiley & Sons, Inc.

(A) running on a treadmill

(B) stretches

(C) cool down

(D) lifting weights

29. Given the equation $a = \dfrac{bc^2}{d}$, solve for c.

(A) $c = \dfrac{ad}{b}$

(B) $c = \dfrac{\sqrt{b}}{ad}$

(C) $c = \dfrac{b}{a^2 d^2}$

(D) $c = \sqrt{\dfrac{ad}{b}}$

30. What is the inverse of the function $f(x) = \sqrt{x-4}$?

(A) $f^{-1}(x) = \sqrt{x+4}$

(B) $f^{-1}(x) = (x+4)^2$

(C) $f^{-1}(x) = x^2 + 4$

(D) $f^{-1}(x) = x^2 - 4$

31. Here is a pie chart based on a survey given to 100 second-grade students. How many students chose pink as their favorite color?

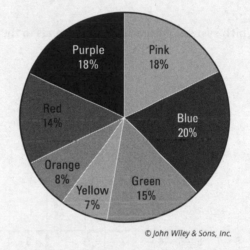

© John Wiley & Sons, Inc.

32. The equation of the line perpendicular to $y = -\dfrac{1}{2}x + 4$ is _____.

(A) $y = 2x - 5$

(B) $y = -2x + 8$

(C) $y = -\dfrac{1}{2}x + 7$

(D) $y = \dfrac{1}{2}x + 1$

33. Amy can swim 4 laps in 12 minutes. How long should she plan to practice if she needs to swim 7 laps?

34. Which number line illustrates the solution to $1 < x + 4 \le 5$?

(A)
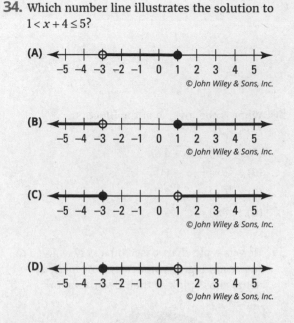
© John Wiley & Sons, Inc.

(B)
© John Wiley & Sons, Inc.

(C)
© John Wiley & Sons, Inc.

(D)
© John Wiley & Sons, Inc.

35. If both of these rectangular prisms have the same volume, what does the missing dimension have to be?

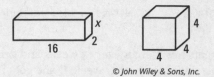
© John Wiley & Sons, Inc.

36. Which system of equations corresponds to the following graph?

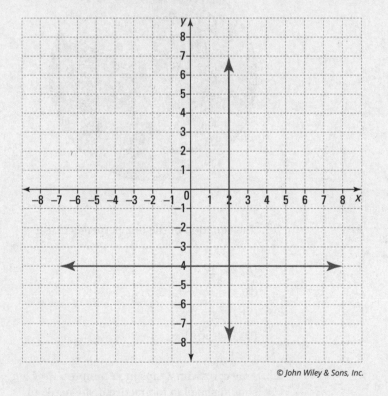
© John Wiley & Sons, Inc.

(A) $y = 2$, $x = -4$

(B) $y = 2x$, $y = -4x$

(C) $x = 2$, $y = -4$

(D) $y = -2x + 4$, $y = x$

37. Steve, Brooke, and Rachel are all avid readers. Based on the following bar graph, which statement is true?

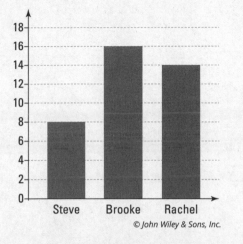

© John Wiley & Sons, Inc.

(A) Brooke read more books than both Steve and Rachel combined.

(B) Rachel read the least number of books out of all three.

(C) Brooke can read more words per minute than Steve or Rachel.

(D) The total books read by all three is 38.

38. Ms. Jones has 14 boys and 18 girls in her class. Which expression illustrates how she would calculate the probability of selecting two boys' names in a row if she doesn't want to select the same boy twice?

(A) $\frac{7}{16} \cdot \frac{13}{31}$

(B) $\frac{7}{16} \cdot \frac{18}{31}$

(C) $\frac{7}{16} \cdot \frac{9}{16}$

(D) $\frac{1}{14} \cdot \frac{1}{13}$

39. Which is equivalent to
$(3x^2 - 4x + 5) - (x^2 - 3x + 2)$?

(A) $2x^2 - 5x + 7$

(B) $2x^2 - x + 3$

(C) $2x^2 - 7x + 7$

(D) $4x^2 - x + 3$

40. What is the measure of $\angle M$?

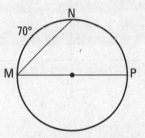

© John Wiley & Sons, Inc.

GO ON TO NEXT PAGE

41. What is the domain of the function illustrated in the following graph?

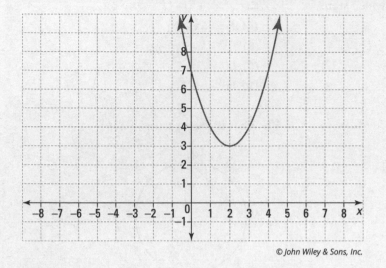

© John Wiley & Sons, Inc.

(A) $[2, \infty)$

(B) $(-\infty, \infty)$

(C) $[0, \infty)$

(D) $(-\infty, 2]$

42. If you know ABCD is a trapezoid, which of the following is true?

(A) Opposite sides are congruent.

(B) Opposite angles are congruent.

(C) The sum of all angles is 360°.

(D) Both diagonals are congruent.

43. Which value of x is not a solution to the equation $2x(x-3)(x+4) = 0$?

(A) 0

(B) 3

(C) −4

(D) −2

44. What is the next term in this sequence: 2, 2, 4, 6, 10, 16, . . .?

45. What type of number is the sum of $(3 + 2i) - (4 - 2i)$?

(A) irrational number

(B) complex number

(C) natural number

(D) integer

46. Which is equivalent to $(x^2)^{\frac{1}{3}}$?

(A) $x^{\frac{3}{2}}$

(B) x^6

(C) $x^{\frac{2}{3}}$

(D) x^8

47. How many outfits can Kelsey make if she has 4 shirts, 2 pairs of pants, and 3 pairs of shoes and is picking one from each category?

48. What 3-D figure is formed if the shaded region is rotated 360° about the *x*-axis?

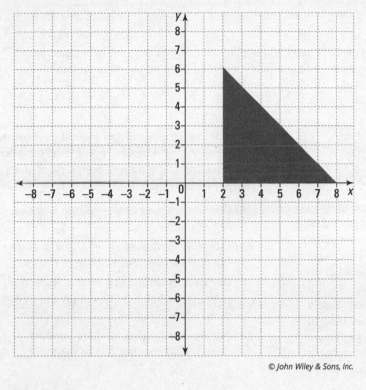

© John Wiley & Sons, Inc.

(A) cylinder

(B) cone

(C) rectangular prism

(D) sphere

49. What number must be added to the following data set in order to have a median of 23?

2   30   16   12   14   23   37

(A) 20

(B) 42

(C) 8

(D) 5

50. Suppose Charlie's house is located at $(2, 5)$ and the bank is at $(-6, 11)$. If the dry cleaner is located half-way between the two points, what would its coordinates be?

(A) $(-2, 8)$

(B) $(3, -3)$

(C) $(-3, 3)$

(D) $(8, -2)$

51. Given a cube whose face has an area of 9 in^2, what is its volume?

52. In a triangle, the sides have a ratio of 2:3:5. If the perimeter is 70 feet, what is the length of the shortest side?

DO NOT TURN THE PAGE UNTIL TOLD TO DO SO   **STOP**   DO NOT RETURN TO A PREVIOUS TEST

Section 4: Social Studies

TIME: 75 minutes for 47 questions

DIRECTIONS: This section tests your knowledge of social studies. Pick the best answer(s) for each question and then mark the space on your answer sheet that corresponds to the question number and the letter indicating your choice.

1. Read the following excerpt from Abraham Lincoln's Gettysburg Address (November 19, 1863).

   It is for us the living, rather, to be dedicated here to the unfinished work which they who fought here have thus far so nobly advanced. It is rather for us to be here dedicated to the great task remaining before us — that from these honored dead we take increased devotion to that cause for which they gave the last full measure of devotion — that we here highly resolve that these dead shall not have died in vain — that this nation, under God, shall have a new birth of freedom — and that government of the people, by the people, for the people, shall not perish from the earth.

   What is the purpose of the federal government as proposed by Lincoln in his address commemorating the national cemetery at Gettysburg, Pennsylvania?

   (A) Our work is now done — there is nothing left to do.

   (B) Our work is impossible — there is nothing that can be done to change things.

   (C) Our work is unfinished — it is up to the people to uphold and maintain the freedoms of this country.

   (D) Our work is limited — there are only certain changes that can be made.

2. Study the following immigration graph from 1900–2000. What trend do you notice about immigration to the U.S. after the quota system was abolished in 1964?

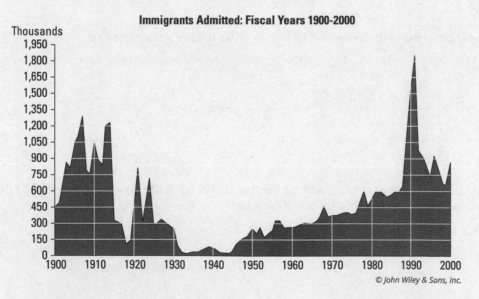

Immigrants Admitted: Fiscal Years 1900-2000

© John Wiley & Sons, Inc.

   (A) Immigration began to increase throughout the 60s, 70s, and 80s, and spiked to an all-time high in the 90s.

   (B) Immigration rates remained steady for the rest of the century.

   (C) It returned to rates similar in the early part of the 20th century.

   (D) It had no significant impact on immigration rates.

3. Read the following excerpt from the Seneca Falls Declaration of Sentiments (July 1848).

We hold these truths to be self-evident: that all men and women are created equal . . . the history of mankind is a history of repeated injuries and usurpations on the part of man toward woman, having in direct object the establishment of an absolute tyranny over her. To prove this, let facts be submitted to a candid world . . . he has never permitted her to exercise her inalienable right to the elective franchise . . . he has compelled her to submit to laws, in the formation of which she had no voice.

Elizabeth Cady Stanton and Susan B. Anthony modeled their document after the Declaration of Independence and meant to draw attention to

(A) the achievement of equal rights by women nearly 70 years after the signing of the Declaration of Independence.

(B) the need for women to gain their right to vote and to participate in making laws that they will be governed by.

(C) acknowledge that they soon will be equal with men.

(D) the fact that their fight for equality is baseless.

4. President FDR issued Executive Order 9066 on February 19, 1942, just over two months after the Japanese attack on Pearl Harbor on December 7, 1941. It was aimed at the nearly 120,000 Japanese in this country. Beginning with the first group of Japanese from Bainbridge Island in Washington State, the intent of this order was to

(A) force the 120,000 Japanese in America (two-thirds of this group were American citizens) to relocate to Japan.

(B) encourage the Japanese in America to take responsibility for the Japanese attack on Pearl Harbor by issuing an apology.

(C) relocate the 120,000 Japanese in America to ten different internment camps ("military areas") away from the coastlines of Washington, Oregon, and California for nearly the duration of the war.

(D) take away citizenship rights of all Japanese Americans.

5. By using vertical and horizontal integration business practices in his company of Standard Oil in the late 1800s, J. D. Rockefeller was able to

(A) compete with the competition with minimal success.

(B) control nearly 90% of the oil production in the U.S. by controlling land, drilling, transportation, manufacturing, and selling of petroleum products (creating a monopoly).

(C) open up the oil business for competition.

(D) prevent monopolies from forming.

GO ON TO NEXT PAGE ▶

6. Examine the following chart.

New Deal Legislation

AAA Agricultural Adjustment Act	Protected farmers by providing subsidies to reduce production, educational programs to prevent soil erosion
CCC Civilian Conservation Corps	Sent young men 18-25 years old to work on reforestation and conservation projects as well as sending money from paychecks back home to families
FDIC Glass-Steagall Act	Created a system of insuring bank deposits and securing banks from failures
Social Security Act	Provided old-age pension and unemployment insurance to those 65 and older as well as providing aid to blind, deaf, disabled, and dependent children
TVA Tennessee Valley Authority	Built a series of dams along the — river to prevent flooding and provide electricity through hydro-electric production
WPA Works Progress Administration	Employed well over 8 million people to work on government infrastructure projects as well as the arts, theater, and literary projects

According to various actions of FDR's New Deal legislation, a major component of these programs was:

(A) the federal government assuming more of an active role in responsibility to help the welfare and well–being of its citizens.

(B) the federal government encouraging the state government to do more in assisting in a variety of programs.

(C) to demonstrate the limits of assistance to the general public from the federal government.

(D) to demonstrate the cooperation between the states and federal government in providing programs of assistance to help those in need.

7. 1968 was a very significant year in U.S. history and is often referred to as a watershed year. All the following events happened in 1968 EXCEPT for

(A) the assassinations of Martin Luther King Jr. in April and Robert Kennedy in June.

(B) the turning point of the war in Vietnam with the Tet Offensive, which resulted in North Vietnam launching a surprise attack on U.S. forces in South Vietnam.

(C) the peaceful negotiation of the end of the conflict of the Vietnam War due in large part to war protests at home in the U.S.

(D) the election of Nixon as president with a campaign promise of "a secret plan" to end the war in Vietnam.

8. The repeal of the 18th Amendment in 1933, known as Prohibition, meant that alcohol could once again be legally bought and sold. What was the main economic reason why the federal government favored its repeal?

(A) freedom of individual choice

(B) so the government could gain revenue from the sales taxes on alcoholic beverages

(C) so the government could stop spending money investigating alcohol smuggling

(D) so the members of the government could get drunk once in a while

9. President Johnson gave this address to Congress on March 15, 1965, just one week after "Bloody Sunday" in Selma, Alabama, where African Americans were staging a march from Selma to Montgomery and were brutally attacked in their attempt to speak out for voting rights for African Americans.

I speak tonight for the dignity of man and the destiny of democracy. I urge every member of both parties, Americans of all religions and of all colors, from every section of this country, to join me in that cause. At times history and fate meet at a single time in a single place to shape a turning point in man's unending search for freedom. So it was at Lexington and Concord. So it was a century ago at Appomattox. So it was last week in Selma, Alabama. There, long-suffering men and women peacefully protested the denial of their rights as Americans. Many were brutally assaulted. One good man, a man of God, was killed.

There is no cause for pride in what has happened in Selma. There is no cause for self-satisfaction in the long denial of equal rights of millions of Americans. But there is cause for hope and for faith in our democracy in what is happening here tonight . . . the bill that I am presenting to you will be known as a civil rights bill. But, in a larger sense, most of the program I am recommending is a civil rights program. Its object is to open the city of hope to all people of all races. Because all Americans just must have the right to vote. And we are going to give them that right . . . their cause must be our cause too, because it is not just Negroes but really it is all of us, who must overcome the crippling legacy of bigotry and injustice. And we shall overcome. . . . "

The intent of this speech was to

(A) continue to ask for patience in African Americans achieving equality in voting rights.

(B) continue to urge Congress to wait for voting rights action and to pursue other portions of his Great Society legislation.

(C) urge Congress to act now in securing voting rights legislation for African Americans and also throwing his support as president behind this legislative action.

(D) urge states to step up their actions in doing away with barriers to African Americans being able to vote freely.

10. President Truman began to promote the policy of containment to stop the spread of communism in the Cold War between the U.S. and USSR. This policy was in response to all the following EXCEPT

(A) the detection of radiation in Siberia in late August 1949.

(B) the creation of a communist government in China in October 1949.

(C) the invasion of South Korea by communist North Korea in June 1950.

(D) free elections that began happening in the Soviet Bloc of countries in Eastern Europe after the end of World War II.

11. During the progressive era, many reformers sought to bring about needed changes in society. One of the tragedies that helped bring about change was the Triangle Shirtwaist Factory at the Asch Building in New York City on March 25, 1911. As a result of this tragedy, building reforms were made that included all the following EXCEPT:

(A) Sprinkler systems would be required to be installed in businesses.

(B) Immigrant workers would be limited as far as where they worked and how many hours they were allowed to work.

(C) Doorways would open outward instead of inward.

(D) Workers would practice fire drills in the workplace.

12. As a result of family life in the 1950s, which of the following can be closely related to the emphasis on family life at this time?

(A) Women who entered the workforce during World War II retained their jobs after the end of the war.

(B) Families chose to relocate to the inner cities in order to be closer to work.

(C) Television shows chose not to focus on family life and family values.

(D) A massive growth in population began to occur from 1946 to 1964, with what became known as the "baby boomer" generation.

13. The Founding Fathers realized a huge error of the balance of power (or lack of power) in the Articles of Confederation. So, when they designed the new government under the Constitution, they divided the power of the federal government into three distinct branches.

Three Branches of Government

Executive	Powers include the enforcer of the laws of the country
	Titles include commander in chief and chief executive
	Negotiates treaties and meets with foreign dignitaries
	Signs bills into law or vetoes the bill before becoming law
Legislative	Comprised of the House and Senate; their job is to create laws to run the country
	They can declare war
	They can override a presidential veto
	The Senate must ratify treaties and presidential appointments to the Supreme Court and cabinet
Judicial	Major job is to interpret the laws of the country; they can overturn legislation by declaring it unconstitutional
	Their rulings in court cases create public policy to be upheld

What does the structure of the three branches of government do about power in the federal government?

(A) It divides the power among the three branches so that one branch does not have authority over the other two branches — all three have distinctive roles.

(B) It gives the majority of the power to the president.

(C) It gives the majority of the power to Congress.

(D) It fails to recognize the power struggle among the three branches.

14. U.S. citizenship was not fully defined until the 14th amendment was ratified in July 1868 following the end of the Civil War in 1865 and the beginning of Reconstruction:

"All persons born or naturalized in the United States, and subject to the jurisdiction thereof, are citizens of the United States and of the State wherein they reside." (The Civil Rights Act of 1866 guaranteed citizenship without regard to race, color, or previous condition of slavery or involuntary servitude, thus granting citizenship to the 4 million former slaves.)

Citizenship then became defined as:

(A) Anyone born in the U.S. (and including the 4 million former slaves after the Civil War) is automatically a U.S. citizen.

(B) Citizenship would be denied to children born in the U.S. if either parent had illegal immigrant status.

(C) Citizenship was limited to blacks actually born in the U.S. after the Civil War.

(D) State and U.S. citizenship status remained separate.

15. The wording of the necessary and proper clause, or "clastic clause" (Article 1, Section 8, Clause 18) states:

"The Congress shall have Power . . . to make all Laws which shall be necessary and proper for carrying into Execution the foregoing Powers, and all other Powers vested by this Constitution in the Government of the United States, or in any Department or Officer thereof."

How does this give Congress legislative authority?

(A) It limits what Congress can consider for legislation — the states are given first priority.

(B) If Congress deems a law to be "necessary," it can craft legislation for a bill to become law if it benefits the people in the country.

(C) The power to craft legislation must be shared with the President and the Supreme Court.

(D) Congress must be careful not to overstep its reach in crafting legislation to create laws.

16. Examine the data in the following chart about the extension of voting rights.

Constitutional Amendments and Laws for Voting Rights

15th Amendment – 1870	Allowed all men to vote regardless of race or color
19th Amendment – 1920	Granted women the right to vote
24th Amendment – 1964	Banned the poll tax for voting privileges
Voting Rights Act – 1965	Prohibited racial discrimination in voting and banned literacy tests
26th Amendment – 1972	Lowered the voting age from 21 to 18

What outcome below can you speculate did NOT occur as a result of these actions?

(A) Women began to participate more in government by exercising their right to vote.

(B) Younger began to participate more in government by exercising their right to vote.

(C) Voting rights became more limited.

(D) African Americans began to participate more in government by exercising their right to vote.

17. A major focus in securing civil rights for various groups of Americans has been the right to vote. After the Civil War, all men regardless of color were granted the right to vote, which was ratified in the 15th Amendment in 1870. What reason might African-American women have for not being completely satisfied by the passing of the 15th Amendment?

(A) They wanted the voting age to be reduced to 18 years old.

(B) African Americans were restricted in elections that they could participate in.

(C) The 15th Amendment only applied to *men*. Women were still not allowed to vote until the passing of the 19th Amendment 50 years later.

(D) Only African Americans who had served in the military during the Civil War could exercise their right to vote.

18. The *Miranda v. Arizona* Supreme Court case in 1964 was significant for those under arrest because now, at the time of an arrest, police would be required to

(A) use anything that a defendant said at any time in his arrest.

(B) uphold 5th and 6th Amendment rights of defendants of no "self-incrimination" and the right of counsel by informing the person of his constitutional rights (now known as *Miranda Rights*).

(C) only apply the 6th Amendment to defendants, allowing them counsel from a lawyer as part of their "Miranda Rights."

(D) apply with certain limits the 5th Amendment to criminal defendants.

19. The power of a veto with legislation is a significant feature of the legislative process. Which of the following statements best expresses the power of a veto?

(A) Presidents have rarely used this power to prevent a legislative bill from becoming law.

(B) The Supreme Court has no authority in the legislative process of a bill becoming a law.

(C) Congress can overturn a presidential veto with a two-thirds majority vote in both the House of Representatives and the Senate.

(D) If the president vetoes a bill, thus preventing it from becoming law, there is nothing that Congress can do at that point.

20. Congress retains its right to establish public policy to benefit the public at large. One example of its use of public policy has been the legislation known as "No Child Left Behind" (2001), which is an extension of earlier legislation under the Elementary and Secondary Education Act. The overall intent of this new legislation was to

(A) extend the federal government's reach into education by providing more aid under Title I for disadvantaged schools, a focus on high standards for education, and increased testing to measure standards.

(B) place the education system fully under the authority of the federal government, taking that control away from local school boards.

(C) allow the federal government to use limited forms of school testing for standards.

(D) limit the government's actions in the field of education.

21. The Constitution has just four words to say about impeachment — "high crimes and misdemeanors." Two Democrat presidents (Andrew Johnson in 1867 and Bill Clinton in 1998) have been impeached, and one Republican president (Richard Nixon in 1974) faced impending impeachment proceedings before resigning from office. Which of the following scenarios do not fit with presidential impeachment?

(A) After a president is impeached, a trial takes place in the Senate, with the chief justice of the Supreme Court presiding over the trial.

(B) Perjury (lying under oath), obstruction of justice (using barriers to hinder a criminal investigation), and abuse of power (claiming that you are above the regular reach and intent of the law) are valid reasons for impeachment proceedings to take place.

(C) A president can face impeachment proceedings based on political reasons from the opposing powers in Congress.

(D) After a president is impeached, he is immediately removed from office.

22. Examine the following chart about term limits for the three branches of government.

Term Limits

President	According to the 22nd Amendment, he is now limited to serving two 4-year terms as president
Congress (House and Senate)	Representatives serve 2-year terms and can serve unlimited terms as they get elected to serve
	Senators serve 6-year terms with 1/3 of the Senate being up for reelection every 2 years; they can serve unlimited terms as they get elected to serve
Supreme Court	They are appointed by the president to serve lifetime appointments

Which of the following limitations would help a president build and secure a legacy after he is out of office?

(A) Congressional elections on various cycles would help a president build a lasting legacy.

(B) A president only serves eight years at the most and has insufficient time to build a lasting legacy.

(C) A president has an opportunity to extend his legacy with appointments to the Supreme Court, as the justices serve for life.

(D) The Supreme Court has a minimal role in helping establish a president's legacy after he leaves office.

23. The election of 1980 began what was called the "Reagan Revolution" in American politics.

Election Results – 1980

Reagan (R)	489 Electoral College votes; 43,901,812 popular votes
Carter (D)	49 Electoral College Votes; 35,483,820 popular votes

© John Wiley & Sons, Inc.

GO ON TO NEXT PAGE

All the following interpretations from the election results can be made EXCEPT

(A) Ronald Reagan won by a landslide in the Electoral College.

(B) Jimmy Carter was able to only take seven states in the Electoral College.

(C) Ronald Reagan failed to take any states in the South.

(D) Ronald Reagan won by a very large majority in the popular vote.

24. Civil liberties in the U.S. as they relate to protecting the freedom of expression is one of the mainstays of the rights of people in a democracy. Which of the following is one of the best examples of the freedom of speech in this country?

(A) The Supreme Court ruled in *Texas v. Johnson* in 1989, protecting the right to burn the U.S. flag as a symbol of symbolic speech.

(B) The Supreme Court ruled in *Tinker v. Des Moines* in 1969 that high school students could not wear black arm bands as a symbol of protest against the Vietnam War. Schools are learning environments, and the arm bands were seen as going too far in free speech.

(C) The 5th Amendment allows people accused of a crime to remain silent so as not to incriminate themselves.

(D) The *New York Times Co. v. United States* in 1971 prohibited the newspaper for one year from printing an article, the Pentagon Papers, containing damaging evidence about the government's actions in the Vietnam War (that the government had, in essence, been lying to the American public about war strategy).

25. Inflation generally occurs when the price of goods increases with a decline in purchasing power. Businesses depend on consumers to spend money on items so that an adequate demand for goods and services is in place. If inflation continues to rise over a 2- to 5-year span, use the chart to determine what impact a rising inflation rate might have on the spending power of consumers. All the following scenarios are true EXCEPT:

Consumer Goods

Food and drink items	Basics of milk, orange juice, cereals, meats, vegetables, fruits, and coffee prices increase
Restaurants	Price increases on certain menu items
Gasoline and transportation	Fuel prices increase; auto-related goods and services increase (tires, oil, and so on)
Clothing	Apparel and shoes increase
Housing	Rent, insurance, household items have price increases
Entertainment	Movie tickets, cable TV, music, newspapers, and magazines experience price increases
Education	Tuition rates increase at private schools and two-year and four-year state colleges, forcing families to make decisions about schooling

(A) There will be no overall big spending changes for most consumers.

(B) Certain consumers will need to make certain choices on what items to buy and possibly look for cheaper alternatives.

(C) As prices go up and consumer income is stagnant, certain items may experience price increases in order for a business to remain profitable, yet consumers may not always be able to afford the price increase.

(D) Consumers will decrease their spending on luxury goods and services.

26. Taxes at local, state, and federal levels allow all three levels of governments to provide goods and services for the general population. Infrastructure like bridges and highways, social programs, education funding, national defense, and local law enforcement are among some of the items funded by government taxation. All the following are true about taxation EXCEPT:

(A) Governments at all levels depend upon the collection of taxes (revenue) to fund programs.

(B) Federal taxes are the same in each state, but each state and local entity can set varying tax rates and situations for taxation.

(C) Sales taxes, property taxes, income taxes, and corporation or business taxes vary at different levels and have different purposes.

(D) After tax rates are in place, they can't be challenged or changed.

27. An improved standard of living in a country with a growing population depends on a growing economy, job growth, and increased income. In a country that uses a market economy model for growth, what is true of that model?

(A) The central government is solely in charge of all economic policy in running the country.

(B) Traditional ways of doing things control economic growth, with little or no areas for change or innovation, and are subject to an overall resistance to change.

(C) Production, trade, and a consumer-based economy are the mainstays of capitalism.

(D) A combination of government control and traditional and free enterprise systems tries to make the best environment for optimum economic growth.

28. The free enterprise system depends on entrepreneurship. As businesses are created, they realize that their goods and services are scarce, meaning that there are limits on resources to meet the various wants. As a result of this, all are true about various factors of production EXCEPT:

(A) Physical capital (buildings and tools) can help businesses increase their profit margin.

(B) Managing human capital (education, training, wages, hours worked) can help businesses increase profit margins.

(C) Natural resources (land, water, and things in the land) have no impact on the profit margin of a business, as these costs are fixed over time.

(D) An entrepreneur gathers data on various factors of production, competing businesses, and market trends to maximize profit.

29. Which of the following expressions best summarizes labor unions?

(A) strike while the iron is hot

(B) a bird in the hand is worth two in the bush

(C) all for one and one for all

(D) many hands make light work

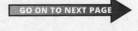
GO ON TO NEXT PAGE

30. Education level plays an important factor in a person's earnings and job possibilities over a lifetime of work. In considering the impact of education and levels of earning during a person's life, which of the following is not true based on the graph?

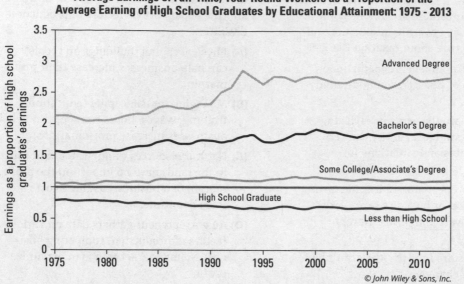

Average Earnings of Full-Time, Year-Round Workers as a Proportion of the Average Earning of High School Graduates by Educational Attainment: 1975 - 2013

© John Wiley & Sons, Inc.

(A) Earning a high school diploma diminishes a person's possibilities for increased income.

(B) An associate degree or a bachelor's degree greatly impacts the income possibility for a person.

(C) If a person does not complete high school, earnings potential is greatly diminished compared to those with a higher level of education.

(D) The higher level of education a person has, the higher his odds at having better earnings potential.

31. A personal budget is simply a plan for saving and spending. When establishing your budget, you need to consider such things as "wants" and "needs." What is one of the first steps a person needs to take when establishing a bud-get plan?

(A) Make a plan for spending on household items only.

(B) Track your spending for a two-week period and make a plan based on your spending habits during that time.

(C) Spend all your spare cash now because after you have a budget, your spending will be restricted.

(D) Money problems rarely cause stress or difficulties within relationships, and people often do not feel trapped by jobs that simply help them pay their monthly expenses.

32. The Silk Road trade route from around 144 AD to the mid-1450s, on land from China and India to the Mediterranean, and sea routes from East Asia to the Middle East and parts of Africa, connected this part of the world and allowed for cultural exchange and interactions. All the following are true about interactions EXCEPT:

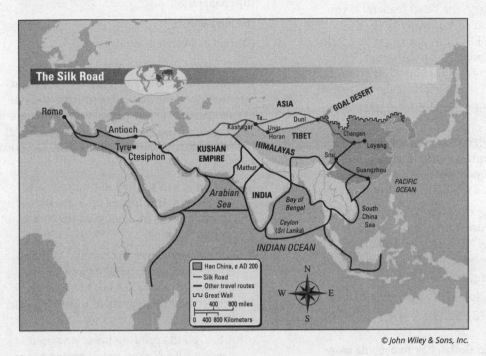

© John Wiley & Sons, Inc.

(A) Religious interactions along the routes were kept to a minimum while trade was encouraged.

(B) There was a great deal of cultural diffusion along the land and sea routes, which amounted to a great deal of cultural exchange between the regions.

(C) While Europe was experiencing the Middle Ages and challenges, the Silk Road was connecting the Mediterranean region to that of India and China.

(D) Goods, technologies, philosophies, and diseases were exchanged along the land and water routes of the Silk Road and connected various parts of the world as they engaged in exchanges.

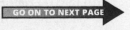
GO ON TO NEXT PAGE

33. The Berlin Wall (1961–1989) was a visible symbol of the Cold War divisions of Western and Eastern Europe. In June 1987, President Ronald Reagan visited Berlin and urged Mikhail Gorbachev, the USSR leader: "If you seek peace, if you seek prosperity for the Soviet Union and Eastern Europe, if you seek liberalization: Come here to this gate! Mr. Gorbachev, open this gate! Mr. Gorbachev, tear down this wall!" The historical significance of this speech is important for all these reasons EXCEPT:

(A) It was a challenge to Mikhail Gorbachev to continue his reform policies of *glasnost* (openness) and *perestroika* (restructuring).

(B) In just a little over two years, democratic reformers worked to tear down the wall, beginning on November 11, 1989 (this was part of democratic reforms that had been sweeping across Eastern Europe).

(C) Reagan and Gorbachev were able to start a series of negotiations to dismantle the Berlin Wall.

(D) Reagan asked Gorbachev to become more involved in European foreign affairs.

34. World War II had been ravaging countries since September of 1939. The war ended in Europe on V–E Day — May 8, 1945 — with the surrender of Germany. Yet, the war lingered on in the Pacific. After a successful U.S. test of a nuclear weapon at Trinity Site in the desert area near Alamogordo, New Mexico, President Truman made the decision to drop two atomic weapons on Hiroshima (August 6) and Nagasaki (August 9). As a result of dropping the bombs on Japan:

(A) Japan refused to surrender and continued to fight back against the United States for another year.

(B) the bombs did minimal damage to Japan and failed to work as designed.

(C) the bombs wrecked massive damage on the two cities, killing thousands instantly, forcing Japan to surrender, and ending the war on August 15 (V–J Day — victory over Japan) with the formal surrender on September 1 onboard the USS *Missouri*.

(D) the U.S. continued its policy of "island hopping" in the Pacific for another year.

35. Which of the following is likely to be highly valued in a free market economy?

(A) individualism

(B) cooperation

(C) job security

(D) redistribution of wealth

36. Johannes Gutenberg's invention of the printing press with movable type in 1455 was one of the major accomplishments of the Renaissance period. As a result of this invention, all the following are impacts of the printing press EXCEPT:

(A) The Bible was printed in multiple languages, and this helped spur a religious reform movement known as the *Protestant Reformation.*

(B) Books became more accessible to the masses and encouraged people learning to read, as millions of books were printed within 50 years of this invention taking hold.

(C) Although the printing press was used, people still relied on hand-copied books for accuracy.

(D) As more books were printed, an increase in education took place as people gained a broad range of ideas through reading books.

37. After the Treaty of Versailles was signed, formally ending World War I, the former allies retreated into a policy of appeasement. France, Britain, and the U.S. began to ignore political actions in Germany, Italy, the USSR, and Japan. As a result of the rise of powerful totalitarian leaders, how would this lead to the outbreak of World War II in September 1939?

Totalitarian Leaders

Hitler	Once in control in 1932, he began to consolidate government power using the Gestapo (secret police) to maintain loyalty and sought to use government power to purify German culture
Mussolini	Once in power in Italy in 1929 with "one party rule," he promised to bring stability and glory to the country of Italy; rights were restricted and rivals were suppressed
Stalin	After coming to power in 1924, he used extreme measures to consolidate his power to keep firm government control over the people in Russia
Hirohito	Emperor of Japan (1926), and people were taught absolute obedience to him and service to the country

(A) The League of Nations was able to keep the power of the totalitarian leaders in check.

(B) Leaders in the U.S., Britain, and France began to challenge the power of the totalitarian leaders.

(C) The totalitarian leaders began to expand their power and influence in their nations, and some had even made plans of expansion, and this was virtually unchecked until the outbreak of World War II in September 1939.

(D) The totalitarian leaders were unable to extend their power and influence and were soon replaced by other leaders within their countries.

38. World War I was a four-year-long conflict, ending with an armistice on November 11, 1918, with the surrender of the Germans to the Allied Powers. The Great War (as it was originally called), or the "war to end all wars," ended up with nearly 10 million military and nearly 7 million civilians dead. During the war, new weapons and strategies were employed.

Weapons of Warfare and Tactics in WW I

Tank	Introduced by the British and used by both sides during the war
Gas mask	Created to counter the attacks of poison gas, especially in the trenches
The machine gun	Used at first by the Germans, but by the end of the war, both sides were using them and they greatly increased the casualty count on both sides
Poison gas (mustard and chlorine)	Although in violation of previous treaties prior to the outbreak of WW I, Germany, along with other countries, began using this chemical weapon as a major weapon of destruction
Trench warfare	Used primarily along the border of France and Germany and consisted of a 600-mile-long series of trenches that led to a long stalemate in fighting and increased casualties

Based on the chart, what impact did the weapons and strategies have on the war?

(A) They greatly increased the casualty rate in the war in both military and civilian casualties.

(B) Despite the newness of weapons and plans, the casualty rate only saw modest increases from the previous battles on the European continent.

(C) Although new weapons were developed, each side failed to fully copy what the other side had begun to use.

(D) So much effort was used developing new weapons that it actually shortened the duration of the war.

GO ON TO NEXT PAGE

39. OPEC was formed in 1960 primarily to coordinate and stabilize oil prices for consumers and a good price return for producers. It has now expanded to 14 member nations and continues to influence prices and the production of petroleum for the global market today. Today, OPEC

(A) has decreased in importance because global supply of petroleum has declined.

(B) controls the supply and cost of petroleum in the global marketplace and influences economic trends around the world.

(C) is spiraling out of control, and it tries to keep up with demands for petroleum in China and India.

(D) has given up its control and influence to the United States.

40. China's one child policy was enacted in 1979 by Deng Xiaoping as a means of controlling China's spiraling population growth. China's current population is around 1.3 billion — roughly 20 percent of the entire population on planet Earth. All the following are results of China's policy EXCEPT:

(A) It has created an imbalance of boys to girls, as male babies are preferred by couples.

(B) China's population continues to spiral out of control.

(C) Urban families are limited to one child, and rural families may have more than one child.

(D) The population growth has stabilized, but as China's population ages, it risks not having enough people to replenish people in the workplace and not having enough people paying into government programs.

41. Location is one important aspect that plays a major role in the climate of a region. If the climate of a region is arid (hot and dry), has minimal annual rainfall, limited vegetation, and extreme temperature variations, where would you expect to find a climate description like this?

(A) the Sahara Desert in northern Africa, the Gobi Desert in Mongolia, and the Outback in Australia

(B) The Sahara Desert in northern Africa, the Amazon region in eastern Brazil, and the Outback in Australia

(C) The Empty Quarter in Saudi Arabia, the Sahara Desert in northern Africa, and the western region of the Amazon in Brazil

(D) The Empty Quarter in Saudi Arabia, the Outback in Australia, and the Nile Delta region in Egypt

42. Every four years, cities around the world aggressively bid against each other to host the Summer Olympic Games despite the high cost and effort associated with them. What is the main benefit a city expects to gain from hosting the Olympics?

(A) profits from the additional gold medals that the hosting country is expected to win

(B) new sporting facilities that can be used after the Olympics is over

(C) more new residents as people who come to visit the city for the Olympics decide to stay permanently

(D) an enhanced reputation as an international center of the arts and culture

43. Which of the following is most likely to be studied by a macroeconomist?

(A) what causes low unemployment

(B) how a company turns raw materials into a finished product

(C) how Apple prices its iPhone

(D) how much discretionary spending a teacher makes each month

44. The diversity and growth of the population today around the world has become increasingly intertwined. Because of the explosive growth of global connections in the past several years, how have people been impacted by the growth of computer technology (satellite communication, Internet, cell-phones, and so on)?

(A) Communication still remains a difficult challenge around the world.

(B) Communication and news items are now seemingly "instant" so that people are aware of what is happening in the world around them.

(C) The entire world's population now has access to this new technology.

(D) Only certain news items and messages are accessible to the majority of people.

45. *Culture* is simply a collection of elements that make up a unique people group. Based on the components in the following chart, how do these items work together to form a distinct culture?

Culture Components

Family patterns	Some societies are maternal-based, others paternal-based; nuclear families and extended families are typical family patterns in society.
Customs and traditions	Rules of behavior, food, dress, rules and laws, and traditions handed down by generations help shape and determine civility and forms of expression in society.
Language	Oral and written forms of expression shape a people group's identity. Societies can have more than one official language. Languages are used to preserve and express a society's ideals.
Arts and literature	The fine arts (music — instrumental and choral), art forms, and literary tales represent values in society.
Religion	Prayers, rituals, sacred texts, and answers for the meaning of life are significant in many societies. Buildings (churches and temples), music forms, and artistic representations also play a major role.

(A) Cultural items that make different people groups distinct are diminishing.

(B) Cultural items continue to make people groups unique from one another in the world today.

(C) Cultural items from one group to another do not influence other groups.

(D) Cultural items today are not impacted by changes in our world today.

46. The former Soviet Union exerted a great amount of political influence on Eastern Europe from World War II to the end of the Cold War. As a result of the end of the Cold War in Europe, many geographical changes occurred. Examine both maps — pre- and post-Cold War. What is one of the biggest political changes between the two maps?

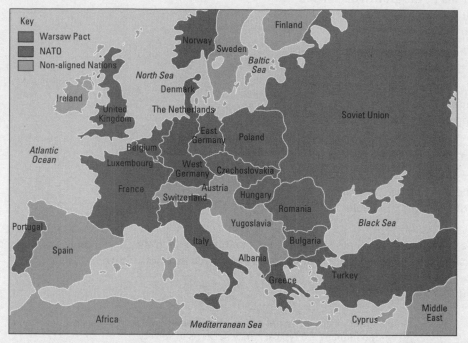

© John Wiley & Sons, Inc.

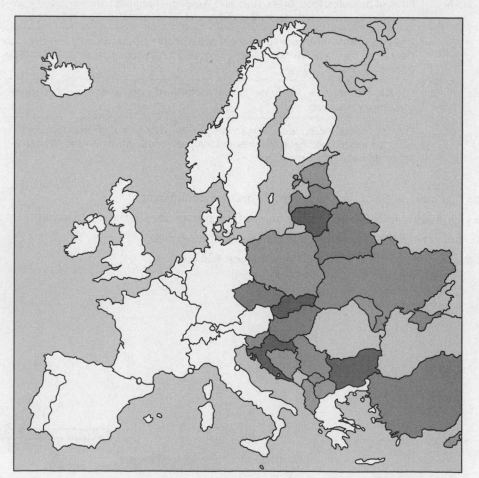

© John Wiley & Sons, Inc.

(A) Several countries were formed based on political and ethnic groups throughout the region, resulting in the creation of several new independent countries.

(B) Russia still retained some of its former territories.

(C) Some countries chose to unite together to form larger political entities.

(D) Ethnic groups had minimal impact on the creation of new countries after the end of the Cold War.

47. Immigration patterns and refugees fleeing their countries for political and social reasons remain challenges in many parts of the world today. All the following are complications as a result of this movement of people EXCEPT:

(A) People fleeing a region for political reasons in their home country may not be easily accepted in the country they migrate to.

(B) Countries that have experienced large numbers of illegal migrants entering their country may attempt to form new laws to restrict movement of people into their country.

(C) The new migrants and refugees often find acceptance in their new country of destination.

(D) News items today still show the struggles of migrants and refugees, but difficult circumstances have not deterred these people from seeking out a better life in a new country.

DO NOT TURN THE PAGE UNTIL TOLD TO DO SO **STOP** DO NOT RETURN TO A PREVIOUS TEST

Section 5: Science

TIME: 85 minutes for 47 questions

DIRECTIONS: This section tests your knowledge of science. Pick the best answer(s) for each question and then mark the space on your answer sheet that corresponds to the question number and the letter indicating your choice.

Use the following information to help answer Questions 1–3.

The conservation of energy states that the mechanical energy of an isolated system is always conserved. Energy cannot be created or destroyed; it can only be converted from one form to another. When a pendulum bob is released from its highest point, it swings down through the lowest position before swinging back up to the same height on the other side, as shown in the following diagram.

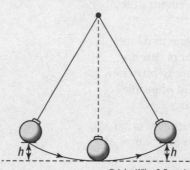

© John Wiley & Sons, Inc.

1. What happens to the potential energy stored in the bob when it swings down to its lowest point?

   (A) The potential energy is destroyed.

   (B) The potential energy is converted into light energy, which allows you to see the bob as it swings.

   (C) The potential energy is converted into kinetic energy.

   (D) The potential energy remains constant because energy is always conserved.

2. Choose the correct order of words to complete the following statement that describes the motion of the pendulum bob as it swings from its highest to the lowest position.

   When the pendulum bob is at the top of its swing, it has maximum_____ energy and _____ speed, whereas when the bob is at its lowest point, it has maximum _____ energy and _____ speed.

   (A) potential, maximum, kinetic, minimum

   (B) potential, minimum, kinetic, maximum

   (C) kinetic, maximum, potential, minimum

   (D) kinetic, minimum, potential, maximum

3. If the mass of the bob is 2 kg and the maximum height it reaches is 5 m, what is the speed of the bob as it swings through the lowest position?

   (A) 0 m/s²

   (B) 6 m/s²

   (C) 10 m/s²

   (D) 100 m/s²

4. What causes a solar eclipse?

   (A) the moon passing between the Earth and the sun

   (B) the sun passing between the Earth and the moon

   (C) the Earth passing between the sun and the moon

   (D) the rotation of the moon

5. Which of the following correctly fills in the blanks in the right order in the following statement?

The normal number of chromosomes in a human body cell is 46. When the sex cells (sperm and egg) are created during _____, the haploid number of chromosomes, _____, results.

(A) meiosis, 23

(B) meiosis, 46

(C) mitosis, 23

(D) mitosis, 46

Use the following information to help answer Questions 6–8.

The rock cycle describes the processes by which the Earth recycles rocks by transforming them from one type to another. The rock cycle is shown in the following diagram.

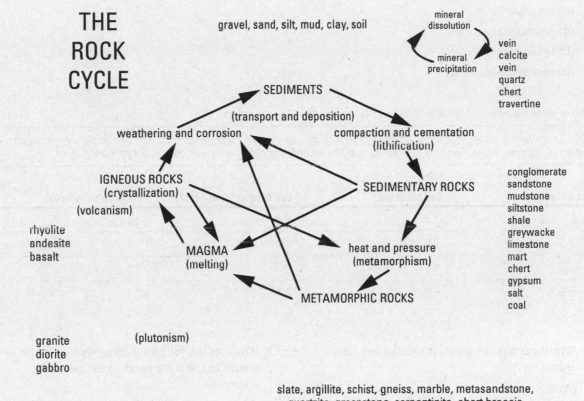

THE ROCK CYCLE

gravel, sand, silt, mud, clay, soil

mineral dissolution
mineral precipitation

vein calcite
vein quartz
chert
travertine

SEDIMENTS
(transport and deposition)

weathering and corrosion

compaction and cementation
(lithification)

IGNEOUS ROCKS
(crystallization)
(volcanism)

SEDIMENTARY ROCKS

conglomerate
sandstone
mudstone
siltstone
shale
greywacke
limestone
mart
chert
gypsum
salt
coal

rhyolite
andesite
basalt

MAGMA
(melting)

heat and pressure
(metamorphism)

METAMORPHIC ROCKS

granite
diorite
gabbro

(plutonism)

slate, argillite, schist, gneiss, marble, metasandstone, quartzite, greenstone, serpentinite, chert breccia

© *John Wiley & Sons, Inc.*

6. Which of the following statements does this figure support?

(A) Sediment forms only from the weathering and erosion of sedimentary rocks.

(B) Magma forms directly from all three types of rocks.

(C) Metamorphic rock is produced from sediment.

(D) Each type of rock is continuously transformed into the other types.

7. Fossils are produced when a plant or animal dies and its remains become buried in mud, silt, or sand, which then gets compacted and compressed into rock. Which of the following types of rock are most likely to contain fossils?

(A) magma

(B) sedimentary rock

(C) igneous rock

(D) metamorphic rock

8. Which of the following best describes magma?

(A) melted rock

(B) frozen rock

(C) evaporated rock

(D) weathered rock

9. A chameleon has special pigment cells that allows it to blend into its surroundings. This adaptation is best used for

(A) sexual reproduction.

(B) asexual reproduction.

(C) predation.

(D) respiration.

Use the following information to help answer Questions 10–13.

A physics student is testing out Newton's laws of motion by applying different forces for 2 seconds to different-colored toy cars of different mass. The cars started at rest. She records the data for the toy cars in the following chart.

Car Color	Car Mass (kg)	Car Acceleration (m/s^2)	Final Velocity (m/s)
Red	1.0	9.0	18
Blue	3.0	3.0	6
Green	9.0	0	0
Purple	6.0	2.0	4

10. Which car has the greatest unbalanced force acting on it?

(A) the red car

(B) the blue car

(C) the green car

(D) the purple car

11. Which of the following correctly fills in the blanks in the right order in the following statement?

The _____ has the smallest final momentum, and the _____ has the greatest inertia.

(A) red car, blue car

(B) green car, purple car

(C) purple car, red car

(D) green car, green car

12. Which two cars have the same unbalanced force acting on them and end up with the same momentum after the force has been applied to them for 2 seconds?

(A) red car, green car

(B) green car, purple car

(C) red car, blue car

(D) blue car, purple car

13. At the end of the 2-second period, the blue car collides with the green car, causing the blue car to stop suddenly. What speed does the green car move off at?

(A) 1 m/s²

(B) 2 m/s²

(C) 9 m/s²

(D) 18 m/s²

Use the following information to help answer Questions 14–17.

The electromagnetic spectrum consists of a continuous range of different types of electromagnetic waves. Visible light accounts for only a small part of the entire spectrum. The electromagnetic spectrum is shown in the following diagram.

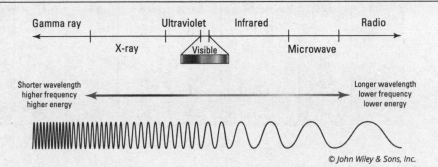

© John Wiley & Sons, Inc.

14. Which type of electromagnetic radiation is used during a CT scan at the hospital?

(A) gamma rays

(B) X-rays

(C) microwaves

(D) radio waves

15. Which of the following colors in the visible part of the spectrum has the highest energy?

(A) green light

(B) yellow light

(C) blue light

(D) red light

16. Which of the following best explains why we use radio waves for our communications applications?

(A) Radio waves have long wavelengths and are high energy waves.

(B) Radio waves have long wavelengths and are low energy waves.

(C) Radio waves have short wavelengths and are high energy waves.

(D) Radio waves have short wavelengths and are low energy waves.

17. Which of the following statements is supported by the figure of the electromagnetic spectrum figure?

(A) Some insects, such as butterflies, can see ultraviolet light.

(B) Gamma rays have longer wavelengths than visible light.

(C) The human eye can only see a small fraction of the electromagnetic spectrum.

(D) Microwaves can be used to cook food.

18. Select the chemical equation that is not correctly balanced.

(A) $2Na + Cl_2 \rightarrow 2NaCl$

(B) $CH_4 + O_2 \rightarrow 2CO_2 + 2H_2O$

(C) $3O_2 \rightarrow 2O_3$

(D) $2Mg + O_2 \rightarrow 2MgO$

19. The Earth's inner and outer core are similar in what respect?

(A) They are both mostly solid.

(B) They are both mostly liquid.

(C) They are both mostly gaseous.

(D) They are both mostly made of iron.

Use the following information to help answer Questions 20–24.

The periodic table organizes elements based on their atomic structure. As with any grid, the periodic table has rows (called periods) and columns (called groups). The group tells you how many valence electrons the element possesses, whereas the period tells you how many energy levels the atom has. Each row and column has specific characteristics. A simplified period table showing the first three periods of Group A elements is shown here.

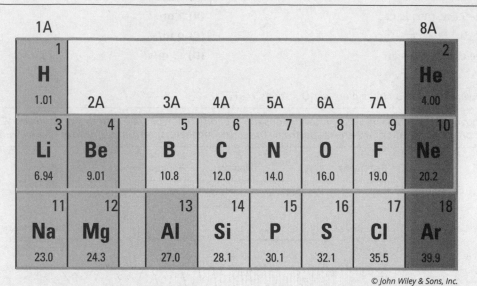

© John Wiley & Sons, Inc.

20. Which of the following elements is the most chemically reactive?

(A) Argon based on its Group 8 status.

(B) Sodium based on its 1 valence electron.

(C) Carbon based on its 4 valence electrons.

(D) Sulfur based on its 6 valence electrons.

21. How many valence electrons does an oxygen atom (symbol O) have?

(A) 2

(B) 6

(C) 8

(D) 16

22. All the following statements about carbon (symbol C) is true EXCEPT:

(A) Carbon has 6 electrons.

(B) Carbon's first energy shell can hold a maximum of 2 electrons.

(C) Carbon has 3 electron shells.

(D) Carbon contains 6 neutrons.

23. Which of the following is true about fluorine (symbol F)?

(A) Fluorine has 19 neutrons.

(B) Fluorine has more electron shells than chlorine (symbol Cl).

(C) Fluorine has 9 valence electrons.

(D) Fluorine needs to gain one more electron to have a full outer shell.

24. Which of the following statements is true?

(A) Sodium reacts with chlorine by sharing valence electrons to form a covalent bond.

(B) Magnesium reacts with argon to form ionic bonds.

(C) Carbon reacts with oxygen by sharing valence electrons to form covalent bonds.

(D) Hydrogen bonds to itself, forming ionic bonds.

25. Which of the following statements is true?

(A) Venus is the closest planet to the sun.

(B) Jupiter is a terrestrial planet.

(C) Saturn is a giant gas planet.

(D) Jupiter is about the same size as the sun.

26. All the following statements provide evidence supporting the Big Bang theory EXCEPT:

(A) spectral analysis of star light showing a relative abundance of hydrogen and helium

(B) sound waves left over from the Big Bang

(C) the discovery of cosmic microwave background radiation

(D) the Doppler effect showing that star light is redshifted

27. Select the correct order from smallest to largest:

(A) star, galaxy, universe, cluster, solar system

(B) star, solar system, galaxy, cluster, universe

(C) solar system, star, galaxy, cluster, universe

(D) universe, cluster, galaxy, solar system, star

28. What can you deduce about a star if the light from it has been blueshifted?

(A) The star is moving away from Earth.

(B) The star is moving toward Earth.

(C) The star is cooler than most other stars.

(D) The star is older than most other stars.

Use the following paragraph and diagram to help answer Questions 29–32.

Food chains are used to represent the flow of energy in an ecosystem. An expanded food chain is called a food web. The arrows in a food chain or food web go in the direction of the energy flow or rather to the organism that is doing the eating. An example of a food web is shown here.

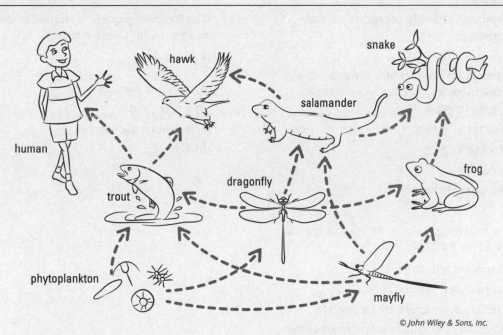

© John Wiley & Sons, Inc.

29. If a virus were to suddenly wipe out most of the dragonfly population, which species in the food web would increase in number?

(A) salamanders, frogs, and trout

(B) mayflies and snakes only

(C) phytoplankton only

(D) The population of each of the other species in the food web would remain unchanged.

30. Which of the following correctly fills in the blanks in the right order in the following statement?

The phytoplankton is a_____, the dragonfly is a_____, and the hawk is a _____.

(A) tertiary consumer, producer, primary consumer

(B) secondary consumer, primary consumer, tertiary consumer

(C) producer, tertiary consumer, secondary consumer

(D) producer, primary consumer, tertiary consumer

31. The maximum number of individuals of a particular species that the ecosystem can handle is known as

(A) natural selection.

(B) biodiversity.

(C) predation.

(D) the carrying capacity.

32. All the following statements regarding a food web are true EXCEPT:

(A) Plants are autotrophs.

(B) Animals are heterotrophs.

(C) Primary consumers are herbivores.

(D) When an organism is eaten, most of the energy stored in its body is transferred to the consumer.

33. What organelle is found only in plant cells and enables the plant to produce its own food?

(A) chloroplasts

(B) cell wall

(C) vacuoles

(D) mitochondria

34. All the following statements provide evidence supporting the common ancestry theory EXCEPT:

(A) All organisms on Earth have a large percentage of their DNA identical to that of other species.

(B) A lot of different animal species, including humans, start out looking the same as embryos.

(C) Scientists believe that of all the species on Earth that have ever existed, 99 percent of them are now extinct.

(D) Many different animals have similar anatomical structures.

35. Which type of particle is emitted in the nuclear decay reaction shown here?

$$^{238}_{92}U \rightarrow \,^{234}_{90}Th + \,^{4}_{2}\alpha$$

(A) an alpha particle

(B) a beta particle

(C) a gamma decay

(D) a proton

A gardener is interested in growing pea plants of a particular height. He draws a Punnett square to display all the possible combinations of alleles when two hybrid pea plants are crossed to help him determine the possible genotypes of the offspring. T represents the dominant allele for tall plants, and t represent the recessive allele for short plants. The genotype of one parent plant is shown on the top of the square, and the other parent's genotype is shown on the left of the square. The genotypes of the offspring are shown in the boxes. The Punnett square is shown here.

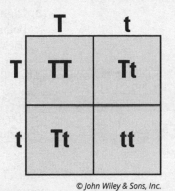

© John Wiley & Sons, Inc.

36. Which of the following statements is true regarding the phenotype of the parents?

(A) Both are short.

(B) Both are tall.

(C) Both are of medium height.

(D) One is short and the other is tall.

37. What is the probability an offspring will be tall?

(A) 0%

(B) 25%

(C) 75%

(D) 100%

38. If the gardener wants to grow only *short* plants from now on, what genotype should he select for the mother and father plants, respectively?

(A) tt, TT

(B) Tt, TT

(C) TT, tT

(D) tt, tt

39. Which of the following correctly fills in the blanks in the right order in the following statement?

The allele for short plant is _____, and trait is only expressed when the genotype is _____.

(A) dominant, homozygous

(B) recessive, heterozygous

(C) dominant, heterozygous

(D) recessive, homozygous

40. Why is there a greater level of genetic diversity for species that reproduce sexually compared to those that reproduce asexually?

(A) The offspring from parents that reproduce sexually inherit a mix of traits from both parents.

(B) Organisms that reproduce sexually tend to produce more offspring than those that reproduce asexually.

(C) The offspring from parents that reproduce sexually inherit brand new traits entirely unlike those of either parent.

(D) The offspring from parents that reproduce sexually inherit only the traits from the dominant parent.

41. Different locations on Earth experience regular climate changes at different times of the year. The year can be split into four seasons (spring, summer, autumn, and winter), which are marked by particular weather patterns and daylight hours. What is the main factor that causes the change in the seasons?

    (A) movement of tectonic plates

    (B) global warming

    (C) the tilt of the Earth

    (D) the distance of the Earth from the sun

42. Which *two* events listed here are highly predictable?

    (A) earthquakes

    (B) hurricanes

    (C) the position of the moon in the night sky

    (D) solar eclipses

43. According to the best scientific estimates, approximately how old is the Earth?

    (A) 6,000 years old

    (B) 5 million years old

    (C) 5 billion years old

    (D) 15 billion years old

44. Which of the following systems includes the solid surface of the Earth?

    (A) atmosphere

    (B) hydrosphere

    (C) biosphere

    (D) lithosphere

45. Which of the following did NOT play a major role in Darwin's explanation of evolution?

    (A) natural selection

    (B) adaption

    (C) survival of the fittest

    (D) DNA

46. Which of the following is an example of a positive feedback mechanism in the climate system of Earth?

    (A) Higher ocean temperatures lead to an increase in the numbers of tropical fish found off the coast of Great Britain.

    (B) Higher global temperatures cause the polar ice caps, which reflect sunlight back into space, to melt, leading to further global warming.

    (C) Higher global temperatures cause the sea levels to rise.

    (D) Global warming causes extreme weather, including severe thunderstorms.

47. Some of the stars you see in the night sky are so far away from Earth that the light from them has taken millions of years to reach you. So what you are really seeing is what those stars looked like millions of years ago. You are actually seeing into the past. To help us handle these huge distances, we use a special unit of measurement called a *light year* to describe them. As its name suggests, a light year is equal to the distance that light travels in one year. Light travels at 300,000 km per second in the vacuum of space.

    Proxima Centauri is the name of the star that is closest to Earth (not including the sun). It is approximately 40 trillion km (4 light years) away from the Earth. How long does the light from Proxima Centauri take to reach the Earth?

    (A) 300,000 seconds

    (B) 40 trillion seconds

    (C) 4 seconds

    (D) 4 years

Chapter 26

Answers and Explanations for Practice Test 2

After you finish the practice test in Chapter 25, take some time to go through the answers and explanations in this chapter to find out which questions you missed and why. Even if you answered the question correctly, the explanation may offer a useful strategy that helps you improve your performance.

Answers for Section 1: Language Arts – Reading

1. **B.** Passage 1 tells you that the mountains are covered in snow, so it makes sense that the thirsty travelers planned to use the snow on the mountaintops as a source of water, making Choice (B) correct. Choice (A) makes no sense when they could simply melt the snow they were standing on to get water. There is no indication that they had been there before or that there is a village in the mountains, so you can eliminate Choices (C) and (D).

2. **B.** Passage 1 tells you that they were afraid of overlooking a water source if they were all grouped together, so they split up to give themselves a better chance of finding water, making Choice (B) correct. Choices (A) and (C) are incorrect because they agreed to split up for the common good of the group.

3. **B.** *Providential* means "occurring at a favorable time" or lucky, making Choice (B) the best answer.

4. **D.** Passage 1 clearly states that the travelers were in danger of dying of thirst, making Choice (D) correct. The group was working together, so Choices (A) and (C) are wrong. They were not simply tired and thirsty; they were in danger of dying, so you can reject Choice (B).

5. A. The excerpt mentions how well desert plants can adapt to deal with the harsh changing conditions of the desert. The author hopes that humans will learn to adapt as well as plants have been able to, making Choice (A) the best answer. You can reject Choices (B) and (C) because they make no sense. She wants humans to be able to adapt like plants can (rather than to grow humans the same height as plants). The plants are doing fine without the humans' help, so Choice (D) is wrong.

6. B. The end of the first paragraph mentions Choices (A), (C), and (D) as methods that plants use to reduce water loss. Choice (B) would actually increase water loss and is not mentioned in the passage, making it the correct answer.

7. C. The tragedy lies in the fact that many of the deaths occur close to water but the travelers are unaware of nearby water sources lying inches below them, making Choice (C) correct. The author focuses on the tragedy of desert deaths, so eliminate Choice (A). Choice (B) may be true, but mummification is not the tragedy the author is referring to. Choice (D) is too extreme because not *all* deaths could be prevented, even if precautions were taken.

8. C. The last paragraph states, "It is related that the final break down of that hapless party that gave Death Valley its forbidding name occurred in a locality where shallow wells would have saved them." Hence, the name refers to a tragic event that involved a party of travelers who died of thirst while trying to cross the desert, making Choice (C) correct.

9. B. Passage 1 focuses on a survival story, while Passage 2 focuses more on the plants and fauna of the desert and mentions some of their scientific names. Hence, Passage 1 is less scientific than Passage 2, making Choice (B) correct.

10. C. The opening paragraph describes the filth, stench, and lack of water in the neighborhood, which suggests the inhabitants are poor. Hence, Choice (C) is correct.

11. B. The passage mentions Choices (A), (C), and (D) as little luxuries that Katie misses, hence you can eliminate these choices. Mrs. Hutchinson is a person (not a luxury), making Choice (B) the correct answer.

12. D. Charlotte asks Katie if she is better than Ma to make her sister feel bad about complaining all the time, making Choice (D) the best answer.

13. C. The passage mentions that Ma hesitated and answered carefully with concerns about how much Katie would have to learn to become a nurse, making Choice (C) the best answer. She is not delighted, making Choice (A) wrong. She is not scornful (Charlotte was) and does not dismiss the idea as ridiculous, so you can reject Choices (B) and (D).

14. D. The relationship between Charlotte and her sister can best be characterized as irritable because both sisters seem to annoy each other constantly, making Choice (D) correct.

15. C. The passage states that Ma takes Katie to see a "white doctor" because Katie needed real medicine beyond what her mother could do for her, hence, Choice (C) is correct. Katie is not white or racist, so you can reject Choices (A) and (B). There is no indication that Ma had exactly seven and sixpence on her, so Choice (D) is wrong.

16. B. The passage mentions that Katie misses the soft sea mist of Port Elizabeth, so it must be near the sea, so you can reject Choice (A). It also states that Katie knew she was not clever in her head like Charlotte. All her cleverness was in her hands. Hence, Choices (C) and (D) are true statements and can therefore be rejected. Although Charlotte calls Katie lazy, this is not true, making Choice (B) the best answer.

17. B. The overall tone of the passage is realistic because it describes some of the hard facts of life (like poverty) that Katie and her family have to deal with. Hence, Choice (B) is correct. Although Charlotte may have been argumentative, the tone of the passage is not, so Choice (A) is incorrect. The passage was not nostalgic (having fond memories) or angry, so Choices (C) and (D) are wrong.

18. C. The second paragraph of the passage states that the village was founded by some of the Dutch colonists; hence, Choice (C) is correct.

19. B. The second paragraph of the passage states that the wives look for "change in the magical hues and shapes of these mountains," and that these changes are as perfect as using a barometer. Hence, Choice (B) is correct.

20. C. The passage mentions that Rip's usual response to his wife's requests was to shrug his shoulders, Choice (A); shake his head, Choice (B); and cast up his eyes but say nothing, Choice (D). That makes Choice (C) correct.

21. A. The passage mentions that Rip's wife nags him constantly whenever he is home, so the only way he can get any peace is when he is outside the house, away from his nagging wife, making Choice (A) correct.

22. B. The passage mentions that the village wives took Rip's part in all family squabbles and that they blame his wife for his domestic fights, making Choice (B) correct.

23. B. The passage mentions that the village children would shout with joy whenever they see Rip approaching, making Choice (B) the correct answer.

24. C. According to the author, Rip's main character flaw is that he has a strong dislike of all kinds of profitable labor, making Choice (C) the correct answer. He is popular in the village and helps his neighbors, so Choices (A) and (B) are wrong. The passage also says that Rip's problems catching a fish were not from a lack of perseverance, so Choice (D) is wrong.

25. D. The passage states that Rip was popular, hated doing household chores, and that not a dog would bark at him throughout the neighborhood, so you can reject Choices (A), (B), and (C). That leaves you with Choice (D), which is a false statement because the passage states that his children were as ragged and wild as if they belonged to nobody, hence Choice (D) is the right answer.

26. C. In the opening part of the passage, Aunt Polly says, "if I get hold of you I'll . . ." so Tom does not answer his Aunt because he is hiding from her to avoid being punished, making Choice (C) correct.

27. C. When Aunt Polly catches Tom she says, "There! I might 'a' thought of that closet. What you been doing in there?" so Choice (C) is correct.

28. B. The passage hints that Aunt Polly is a religious woman, because she quotes from the Bible several times, making Choice (B) the correct answer.

29. A. When the author says that Aunt Polly's spectacles were built for "style not service," he means that she wears them to look good but they don't help her to see better, so the best answer is Choice (A).

30. B. In the last paragraph Aunt Polly says, "he's my own dead sister's boy," so Tom lives with his Aunt Polly because his mother is dead, making Choice (B) correct.

31. B. Because Tom is always up to mischief, Aunt Polly thinks he has a bit of the devil in him, so Old Scratch is the devil, making Choice (B) correct. There is no mention of a family dog, Choice (A), or Tom's good friend, Choice (D). Choice (C) doesn't make sense considering Tom's bad behavior.

32. D. Mark Twain intentionally made grammatical errors in Aunt Polly's speech to reflect her personality, making Choice (D) the best answer. Choice (A) is wrong because Mark Twain was an excellent writer and knew how to use grammar correctly. Choice (B) isn't bad but isn't the best answer. Choice (C) is not a true statement.

33. C. The opening paragraph states that Denning is the greatest authority on meteorites; hence Choice (C) is correct.

34. C. The opening paragraph states that the meteorite produced a line of flame high in the atmosphere, left a greenish streak behind it that glowed for several seconds, and first appeared at an altitude of approximately 100 miles above the Earth, so you can reject Choices (A), (B), and (D). The narrator did not see the meteorite fall, making Choice (C) the correct answer.

35. A. The author uses capital letters when describing the object as the Thing to emphasize that this was no ordinary object, making Choice (A) correct.

36. D. The physical appearance of the Thing that made it unusual compared to other meteorites includes its large size, its cylindrical shape, and its unusual color, so you can reject Choices (A), (B), and (C), making Choice (D) the correct answer.

37. D. What disturbed Ogilvy about the ash was that it was falling off the Thing only from the end of the cylinder, making Choice (D) correct.

38. B. Ogilvy initially assumed the stirring noise coming from the Thing was due to unequal cooling of its surface; hence Choice (B) is correct.

39. C. The movement of the black mark indicates that something within the cylinder was unscrewing the top; hence Choice (C) is correct.

40. D. In the closing paragraph, Ogilvy eventually makes the connection between the object and a recent flash he saw on Mars, so he realized the Thing is actually a spaceship from Mars, making Choice (D) correct.

41. B. The maid went to her bedroom around 11 p.m. and witnessed the murder shortly after that time, making Choice (B) correct. Choice (D) is when she woke up and told the police about the murder, so it should be rejected.

42. B. Later on in the passage it is revealed that the victim was a famous person; hence, the phrase "high position of the victim" means important person, making Choice (B) correct.

43. D. The victim is revealed to be Sir Danvers Carew, making Choice (D) the correct answer. Mr. Hyde was the murderer, not the victim, Choice (A). Mr. Utterson was the lawyer, Choice (C).

44. B. The fact that the victim's purse and gold watch were found at the scene of the crime makes it clear that the motive for the murder was probably not robbery; hence Choice (B) is correct.

45. **C.** The maid was able to recognize Mr. Hyde because she had seen him once before when he had come to visit her master and she had taken an instant dislike to him, so Choice (C) is correct.

46. **A.** The passage states that the maid initially paid more attention to the older gentleman in the alley because she thought he was handsome, so Choice (A) is correct. Choices (B), (C), and (D) all refer to Mr. Hyde (not the older gentleman), so you can reject them.

47. **A.** The passage describes the brutal attack in detail in which the victim was beaten with a cane and kicked to death, making Choice (A) the best answer.

48. **B.** The officer's eyes light up with professional ambition because he realizes that solving the murder of such an important person would be very good for his career, making Choice (B) the correct answer.

49. **B.** The passage states that the lawyer gave the murder weapon to Dr. Jekyll many years ago; hence Choice (B) is correct.

50. **D.** The passage describes Mr. Hyde as a person of small stature, wicked-looking, and ill-tempered, so you can reject Choices (A), (B), and (C). Choice (D) is a false statement because it was the victim (not Mr. Hyde) who had white hair, making Choice (D) the correct answer.

Answers for Section 2: Language Arts – Writing

Part 1: Language

1. **A.** There is an error in the punctuation of Choice (A), which includes an unnecessary comma after "including." The three other sentences are punctuated correctly.

2. **C.** The first sentence most often introduces the topic of the rest of the paragraph. Choice (D) is a bit broader than needed, as it is about "crafting" instead of cross-stitch, in particular. Choices (A) and (B) seem to be additional information but don't explain what the paragraph is about. Choice (C) does that the best, so it's the correct answer.

3. **B.** In Choice (B), "inconvenient" is spelled incorrectly.

4. **D.** The key here is to find the error in the original sentence: that is, the misused verb. It should be in the past tense, as it is in Choice (D), the best answer. Choice (A) fixes the wrong verb, while Choice (B) makes the sentence awkward (although correct). As for Choice (C), while the sentence is correct, it changes the meaning a bit.

5. **C.** The trick with this type of question is to choose the answer that keeps the meaning but presents the necessary information in the clearest way. Here, Choice (C) is best. Choice (A) doesn't make sense (how can Jessica be "around the lake"?), while Choice (B) is needlessly complicated. Choice (D) is similarly too convoluted to be best.

6. **B.** There's no need for "mashed potatoes" to have a hyphen, so Choice (B) is the answer. The other sentences are fine, as Choice (A) shows how to accurately write a time period, Choice (C) how to capitalize a holiday, and Choice (D) how to capitalize a type of cuisine.

7. A. An opening sentence should introduce the topic of the paragraph. Here, all four choices seem like they might work, but a closer inspection shows that there is one best answer. Choice (B) reads like a topic sentence but doesn't introduce the rest of the paragraph. Nor does Choice (C) or Choice (D). Choice (A) leads nicely into the paragraph and includes a mention of Hemingway, who comes up again in the paragraph. Choice (A) is the best choice.

8. B. Choice (B) is the best answer, as it transitions from the first paragraph into the information that is provided in the second paragraph. Choice (A) belongs in the first paragraph. Choices (C) and (D) are both interesting facts that could be included in the second paragraph but are not good topic sentences.

9. A. Choice (A) is the best combination provided. Choice (D) isn't even a complete sentence, so it can't be correct. Choices (B) and (C) both slightly change the meaning of the sentences, because Choice (B) implies that you can't swim and surf at the same beach and Choice (C) changes the focus of the sentence to the beaches instead of those enjoying them.

10. A. Choice (A) contains an error. The names of seasons don't need to be capitalized. Note that Choice (C) is correct because the sentence uses "east" as a direction instead of a location. If Choice (C) read "Traffic is not nearly so bad there as it is heading to the east," that would be incorrect.

11. B. Choice (B) is the best answer because "imperative" means "of highest importance," which is the idea that the sentence is trying to get across.

12. C. The trick here is to choose the sentence that keeps the general meaning of the example with better grammar. Choice (A) is out because the verb is dropped in the main clause. Choice (B), too, can't be correct, as "being returned" makes no sense. Choice (D) is a correctly written sentence but doesn't include enough information (what is Anita interested in?). That leaves Choice (C), the best choice.

13. D. Choice (D) contains a misspelling of "embarrassed."

14. C. The best option available is to change the comma to a colon and allow the remainder of the sentence to follow as a list. That's Choice (C).

15. C. The grammatical error is in Choice (C), which should use the verb "is" (to match "either," not "them"). The remaining three sentences are correct.

16. D. Choice (D) is the best revision, which manages to shorten the sentence while retaining the meaning. Choice (A) confuses the point of the sentence, as does Choice (B). They're awkward and change the ownership of the cat to "ours," which isn't clear in the original. Choice (C), meanwhile, gets the meaning right but is just as awkward as the original.

17. A. The last sentence should bring a sense of conclusion to the paragraph. Choice (A) does that by reporting on the outcome of the vote. The other answer choices simply add more facts to the paragraph's description of the meeting but don't complete it.

18. A. The word for the blank must indicate that Washington's plan was foiled by the battle's quick beginning. Choice (A) best does that. Choice (C) is almost correct but doesn't quite fit in the sentence as needed.

19. B. You need a sentence that justifies the "therefore" at the beginning of the next sentence. Here, the best option is Choice (B), which provides a fact that shows why the "therefore" is needed. Choice (A) is already implied, while Choices (C) and (D) are irrelevant.

20. **C.** The best answer is Choice (C), after the third sentence. The fourth sentence of the second paragraph is clearly about Fort Necessity today, whereas the beginning of the paragraph had been about the fort's past. Adding in a paragraph break makes the most sense there.

21. **C.** Choice (D) is gibberish, and Choices (A) and (B) don't solve the problem of the missing "to" in the original sentence. Choice (C) does that and thus is the best answer.

22. **A.** The word "maintenance" is misspelled in Choice (A).

23. **D.** There's an error in every sentence except Choice (D). Even if you're not sure that Choice (D) is correct, you should be able to spot the other errors. In Choice (A), no comma is needed after "where." In Choice (B), there should be at least one comma (after "there," and possibly two, with another after "cottages"). In Choice (C), the semicolon should be a colon.

24. **C.** This is a tricky set of sentences, but Choice (C) clearly contains an error. All adjective forms of country names — even when commonly used like "French fries" — should be capitalized.

25. **B.** Choice (B) is the best concluding sentence to this paragraph because it makes a general statement that concludes the topic of little penguins. It's easy to imagine this paragraph as part of a longer essay or list. Choice (A) simply offers another fact about little penguins, while Choices (C) and (D) turn to another topic, an odd thing to do at the end of a paragraph.

26. **A.** The best combination of the two sentences is Choice (A), which keeps the meaning but eliminates the fragment that was in the original. Choice (B) tries to fix the problem with a semicolon, but that is incorrect. Choices (C) and (D) make the sentence needlessly complicated. Remember to be wary of any answer that splits the prepositional phrases apart!

27. **B.** The best answer is Choice (B), which ties together the ideas of the prior two sentences into one closing thought. Choice (A) is off-topic (the paragraph is about the keytar, not the piano), and Choice (C) begins a new idea about the topic. Choice (D) seems like it could be correct, but the careful reader will note that it is an exact restatement of the provided paragraph's first sentence. That's repetition and can't be correct.

28. **C.** The best answer here is Choice (C), a more concise rewording of all the ideas in the original sentence. Choice (D) keeps the same meaning but is cumbersomely long. Choices (A) and (B) are both shorter sentences but drop some of the meaning of the original.

29. **D.** Remember to look for the sentence that introduces the topic — in this case, you want to find a sentence that introduces e-readers. Choice (A) does not because it's about reading, generally. Choice (B) does introduce e-readers, but negatively, which the rest of the paragraph does not support. Choice (C), meanwhile, would only work if the rest of the paragraph was about the author's personal experience, which it is not. That leaves Choice (D) as the best answer.

30. **B.** Remember to look for the sentence that is correct. Choice (B) is the only choice that is so here. Choice (A) has an error in title (only very important titles, such as President of the United States, get capitalized). Choice (C) includes "Catholic," which should be capitalized, and Choice (D) uses "the West" as a location, which also should be capitalized.

31. **D.** Choice (D) does the best job of rewriting the sentence so that it satisfies the request to emphasize the park's location. Choice (A) simply switches the order of the two phrases in the example. However, not only does this not satisfy the request to make the location more important, but it's also not really a sentence because it lacks a verb. Choice (B) is a better sentence but doesn't fully emphasize the location of the park, whereas Choice (C) emphasizes that the park is lovely in the fall.

32. A. Choice (A) contains a misspelling of the word "rhythm."

33. C. You need a transitional word that best makes it clear that while the Supreme Court can listen to every case, they are not required to do so. Choice (C) is the best answer because "however" shows that relationship. Choices (A) and (D) show a different relationship, one that clarifies, whereas Choice (B) doesn't belong in the middle of a paragraph (and is usually used in connection with words like "first" and "second").

34. A. Here, you need a sentence that introduces the information that follows, which is a very general overview of who comprises the Supreme Court. While Choices (B) and (D) are true statements, they're much more specific (and off-topic) than Choice (A). Choice (C) is a good guess, but Choice (A) is clearly more on-topic and thus, the best choice.

35. C. Choice (C) is the best answer because the last sentence in the paragraph appears to begin a new topic — about the specific court cases decided by the Supreme Court — which should begin its own paragraph.

36. D. Choice (D) is correct. All three of the remaining answer choices contain an error. Choice (A) should have "is" instead of "being," while Choice (B) should read, "After I have visited there. . . ." Choice (C) uses the wrong verb for the subject. "You" should always be followed by "are."

37. B. Choice (B) is the best revision. It changes the order of the sentence so that "Nadia and I" becomes the subject (changing "me" to "I" correctly) and eliminates wordiness. Choice (A) uses "me" as a subject, which is almost always incorrect, and Choice (C) keeps the strange word order. Choice (D) is close to being correct, but, of course, the last word is wrong.

38. A. The original is two independent clauses placed close together. Changing the comma to a period, as in Choice (D), would work if you could also capitalize "she." Removing the comma, as in Choice (B), or adding an unnecessary comma, as in Choice (C), doesn't fix the sentence. That leaves Choice (A), the correct choice.

39. B. Choice (B) is the clearest sentence. Choices (A) and (C) are unnecessarily long (as well as unclear), and Choice (D) confuses the meaning of the original sentence.

40. A. The sentence that best concludes this paragraph is Choice (A) because it takes the information thus far provided and uses it to draw a conclusion. Choices (B) and (C) are off-topic, and while Choice (D) could be relevant, it doesn't conclude the paragraph.

41. D. Choice (D) is the best answer. The problem in the original sentence is the helper verb — there isn't one! Choice (A) doesn't fix that problem, and Choice (B) changes the word "waiting" into the fancier "awaiting," but doesn't add in the helper verb. Choice (C) does add in "is" but without clarifying the meaning.

42. D. Choice (D) contains an error. When a direction is referred to as a location, it should be capitalized, as in "the West."

43. C. Choice (D) makes a great concluding sentence, but you're asked to find the best sentence to begin the paragraph. Because Choice (B) is too general, and Choice (A) not quite on-topic, that leaves Choice (C), the best answer.

44. A. Choice (A) contains a misspelling of the word "pronunciation."

45. D. The best answer here is Choice (D), to eliminate the semicolon. It is not needed in the sentence.

46. A. Choice (A) is punctuated incorrectly, as there is no need for the comma after "hiking."

47. B. The sentence contains the idea that the word "occupational" gives an impression. The best word to mean something similar is Choice (B), "implies." Choice (D) may be tempting, but the remainder of the sentence shows that "asserts" doesn't work well with "but."

48. C. The best answer is Choice (C), which shows the relationship between the two ideas the best by revealing the passage of time. Both Choices (B) and (D) imply that the second sentence discredits the information in the prior sentence, which is incorrect. And Choice (A) shows a transition that is not natural.

49. A. Choice (A) is the best answer because it introduces the information to come in the second paragraph. Choice (B) is extraneous information, and neither Choice (C) nor Choice (D) is relevant to the rest of the paragraph, although each of them is more on-topic.

50. C. Choice (C) best combines the two sentences in a way that reads clearly and makes the meaning comprehensible.

Part 2: Writing

The following is an example of an essay that would likely score a 4 on the TASC. It scores high because the author takes a clear stand on the opinion presented in the essay; in this case, it supports the author's logic. The essay includes solid details and facts from the text. Compare it to your own sample essay and note where you might improve.

I agree with Ron Boyer, the author of "Against Mining in Bristol Bay," that they should not mine in the Bristol Bay watershed. Bristol Bay is in Alaska, and is very remote. People who go there want to see the brown bears that live near there and fish for salmon in the river. It's important that the river and other bodies of water there stay pristine and clean, so I agree with Boyer that the mining should not happen.

Boyer points out that if people were to mine near Lake Clark National Park, many bad things would happen. Animals would lose their homes and food sources. They would have to build many roads that are not there now and also pipeline. And fewer people would go to visit Lake Clark National Park because it would look uglier and have fewer animals there. That is a terrible outcome if mining is allowed.

Boyer quotes the famous environmentalist Edward Abbey, who pointed out that we need wilderness even if we're not going to go to it. That's a good point. If we only think about things that we'll actually use, we might be in favor of the mine, which would give us copper and gold. But we also need to look after other people and creatures, and that means preserving the wilderness, even if we're not going to go to it ourselves. Everything on earth is connected; you can't take away wilderness in Alaska and not have it affect wherever you are. Boyer is smart to use a quote that reminds readers of this.

For all of the above reasons, I agree with the author Ron Boyer. We do need to protect Lake Clark National Park, and the Bristol Bay watershed, which it is in. Mining is important, but it's not important enough to destroy some of the last wilderness we have. The author convinced me of his argument.

Answers for Section 3: Mathematics

Part 1

1. **B.** To calculate the value of each carton, calculate the volume of each and divide by the appropriate price. So for the carton the volume is calculated by $V = lwh = 80$ in³; so the value is $\frac{80}{3.25} = 24.62$ cubic inches per dollar. The volume of the can is calculated by $V = \pi r^2 h = \pi(2)^2(10) = 40\pi \approx 125.664$ in³ so the value is $\frac{125.664}{2.4} = 52.3$ cubic inches per dollar. This means you're getting more for your dollar when you buy the can, so Choice (B) is correct.

2. **D.** First rewrite each of the numbers into the same form (decimal form is probably the easiest). $\frac{3}{100} = .03$, $5\% = .05$, $\sqrt{7} = 2.64$, and .7. Now you can order them in descending order, which means from largest to smallest: 2.64, .7, .05, .03 and then substitute your original numbers back in: $\sqrt{7}$, .7, 5%, $\frac{3}{100}$, thus Choice (D) is correct.

3. **4.17%.** Because these are all independent events, you calculate each probability and multiply them. So the probability for each coin landing on heads is $\frac{1}{2}$ because there is 1 way to get a head out of 2 possible outcomes. Similarly, the probability for rolling a 4 is $\frac{1}{6}$ because there is 1 way to get a 4 out of 6 possible outcomes. Now you multiply the individual probabilities: $\frac{1}{2} \times \frac{1}{2} \times \frac{1}{6} = \frac{1}{24} = .0417 = 4.17\%$, which is the correct answer.

4. **B.** To solve this type of problem, you can substitute each of the choices in for x and solve or you can rewrite the original problem to be in the same base. Because the right side of the equation is a fraction, you know that its exponent is going to be negative: $3^x = 27^{-1}$. Now you can rewrite 27 in base 3: $3^x = (3^3)^{-1} = 3^{-3}$. This means that $x = -3$, Choice (B).

5. **A.** Because the area you're looking for is a portion of the circle, you can construct a ratio of the part of the circle being used by the shaded region: $\frac{60°}{360°} = \frac{1}{6}$. Now set up a proportion with that ratio and the area of the circle: $\frac{1}{6} = \frac{x}{\pi(3)^2}$ and solve: $6x = 9\pi$, so $x = \frac{9\pi}{6} = \frac{3\pi}{2}$, Choice (A).

6. **B.** Because $\sqrt{127}$ is greater than $\sqrt{121} = 11$ but smaller than $\sqrt{144} = 12$, you know your answer must be greater than 11 but less than 12. Hence, Choice (B) is correct.

7. **C.** Because there's an average of 114 cups of coffee and each pot produces 8 cups, you can divide 114 by 8 and get 14.25 pots of coffee per hour. The store is open for 10 hours each day so it uses 14.25 x 10 = 142.5 pots of coffee on an average day. This means that the shop will need to brew 143 pots, Choice (C), to make sure there's enough coffee.

8. **A.** This a converting units problem, and it's important to remember how many feet are in a mile and how many minutes are in an hour. Setting up your ratios you get: $\frac{15 \text{ mi}}{1 \text{ hr}} \cdot \frac{5280 \text{ ft}}{1 \text{ mi}} \cdot \frac{1 \text{ hr}}{60 \text{ min}}$ (recall that it's important to place units in opposite places). Simplifying this conversion, you find that Cory travels at 1,320 ft/min, Choice (A). If you misplaced the converting ratios, then you would end up with Choices (B) and (D).

9. **A.** With rational exponents, recall that the denominator becomes the index of the radical so $\frac{1}{2} = \sqrt{\ }$. This means you take the square root of 64 first: $\sqrt{64} = 8$ and then cube it: $8^3 = 512$, which is Choice (A). Choice (C) is incorrect because you reversed the roles of the exponents. Choices (B) and (D) are incorrect because you took the radical or raised it to the power incorrectly.

10. **B.** Because the cost per hour can be associated to the slope of the graph, it is the ratio of the difference in cost divided by the difference in time. In this case, you can see that the ratio (slope) is $\frac{10}{1} = 10$ dollars/hour, Choice (B). If you selected Choice (C), you found the y-intercept or the initial fee for parking in the garage. If you selected Choice (D), you were not careful when reading the graph because the graph "starts" at 15, not 0.

11. **216.** The first step in solving this problem is to find the length of each side of the cube. The volume of the cube is $V = x^3$, so you can substitute in the known volume and then take the cubed root to find the length: $\sqrt[3]{216} = 6$. Now that you know the length equals 6, you can substitute it into the formula for surface area of a cube, which is $A = 6x^2$. This gives you the correct answer, which is 216 square inches.

12. **B.** Because the entire expression is to the zero power, the simplified form is 1, Choice (B). If you selected Choice (A) or (D), you remembered the zero exponent rule incorrectly.

13. **B.** It may be helpful to determine a formula or relationship between the two variables. In this case, you can see that the y-intercept is −1 because that is the y-value that occurs when $x = 0$. If you look for a constant rate of change, you can see that it is 2. This means a formula for the relationship is $y = 2x - 1$. Using the relationship, you can solve for the missing x-value: $3 = 2x - 1 \rightarrow 4 = 2x \rightarrow 2 = x$, Choice (B).

14. **A.** Because the direction of the shapes are different, you can rule out Choice (B) because a translation maintains the original orientation. Similarly, the objects aren't mirror images of each other over the x-axis or over the line $y = x$, so this rules out Choices (C) and (D). This leaves Choice (A), which is the correct answer because the top image can be twisted 90° to produce the lower image.

15. **85.** To calculate the mean of the scores, add up the given scores and divide by the number of scores: $\frac{510}{6} = 85$.

16. **A.** This first thing you must do is simplify both sides of the equation. Because this is a quadratic equation, you can solve this in multiple ways. One method is factoring, in which you set the equation equal to 0 by subtracting 6 and 6x from both sides. This results in a trinomial, where you can factor it.

$$x^2 - 10 = 6 + 6x$$
$$x^2 - 6x - 16 = 0$$
$$(x - 8)(x + 2) = 0$$

Solving this requires setting each factor equal to 0, and solving the resulting equations produces Choice (A). Another method to solve is by using the quadratic formula.

17. **D.** The probability of these two events are dependents because the probability of selecting the blue piece depends on what happens when the other piece is picked. For this reason, first calculate the probability of selecting a red piece and then the probability of selecting a blue piece assuming the first piece picked is red. Then multiply the resulting probabilities: $\frac{7}{21} \cdot \frac{5}{20} = \frac{1}{3} \cdot \frac{1}{4} = \frac{1}{12}$, Choice (D).

18. **D.** You can express .8 as both a percentage and a fraction. As a percent .8 = 80%, which rules out Choices (B) and (C). You can then check the supplied fraction options but rewriting them as decimals: $\frac{2}{25} = 0.08$ and $\frac{4}{5} = 0.8$, which shows that Choice (D) is your answer.

19. **A.** Drawing a picture may help you understand what's going on in this problem.

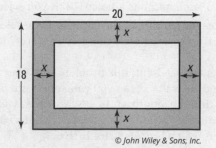

© John Wiley & Sons, Inc.

This image shows that the dimensions of the window part (the inner rectangle) can be found by subtracting the borders from the outer dimensions: width $= 20 - x - x = 20 - 2x$ and length $= 18 - x - x = 18 - 2x$. Calculating the area of the inner rectangle is found by multiplying the two resulting expressions: $(18 - 2x)(20 - 2x)$, Choice (A).

20. **C.** You're told that this is part of a right triangle, which means you can use trig ratios to solve for the indicated angle. Again, constructing a picture would be helpful to show which leg is the opposite and which is the adjacent (recall that the side and angle with the same letter are opposites). Setting up a trig ratio, notice that you don't have the hypotenuse, so you use tangent: $\tan A = \dfrac{\text{opp}}{\text{adj}} = \dfrac{5}{7}$. To solve for the angle, you must use the inverse trig function to isolate A: $\tan^{-1}(\tan A) = \tan^{-1}(\frac{5}{7}) \approx 35.5°$, Choice (C). If you used sine or cosine, you would have incorrectly selected either Choice (B) or (D).

21. **6.71.** To calculate the length of a segment between the two points, use the distance formula: $\sqrt{(-2-4)^2 + (5-2)^2}$ (be sure to substitute in the values correctly and in the same order). Simplifying what is underneath the radical results in $\sqrt{(-6)^2 + (3)^2} = \sqrt{36+9} = \sqrt{45} \approx 6.71$.

22. **C.** Because the logs have the same base, you can set "what's inside" equal: $2x = x + 3$. Solving this equation, you get Choice (C), $x = 3$.

23. **B.** Looking at the answer options, notice that they're looking for the prime factorization of 2,592. To do this, make a factor tree by dividing 2,592 by one its factors. Completing the factor tree, you get $2{,}592 = 2 \cdot 2 \cdot 2 \cdot 2 \cdot 2 \cdot 3 \cdot 3 \cdot 3 \cdot 3$, which is equivalent to $2^5 3^4$, Choice (B). Choice (C) is incorrect because you switched the exponents, and Choice (A) is incorrect because you flipped the role of the base and exponent. Similarly, Choice (D) is incorrect because you both switched the role of the base and exponent and switched the exponents.

24. **11.25.** Be careful when selecting the corresponding sides because the orientations of the two figures are different. Also, the question is supplying you with more information than you need — you don't need the 2 in this case because there's not a corresponding measure on the larger figure. To solve this problem, you can either find the scale factor or set up a proportion: $\dfrac{\text{Small}}{\text{Large}} : \dfrac{4}{15} = \dfrac{3}{x}$. To solve a proportion, cross multiply and solve the resulting equation: $x = 11.25$.

25. **24.** In this problem, you can construct a diagram to determine the number of different arrangements: $\overline{}, \overline{}, \overline{}, \overline{}$. This is asking, how many options does Sarah have for 1st, 2nd, 3rd, 4th the first book on the shelf? Because there are 4 books she has 4 options for the first place. Next you ask, how many options does she have for the second book on the shelf after the first book is placed? Because 1 book has been placed, that leaves her with 3 options for the second place. You can fill in the rest of the diagram in a similar fashion, $\dfrac{4}{1st}, \dfrac{3}{2nd}, \dfrac{2}{3rd}, \dfrac{1}{4th}$. To find the total number of different orders, multiply the numbers you filled in: $4 \cdot 3 \cdot 2 \cdot 1 = 24$.

If you wanted to use a formula to solve this problem, you'd use one of the counting principles: permutations or combinations. In permutations, order matters, while in combinations, order does not matter. Looking at the formula sheet, you can see both of these options. In this case, it would be a permutation. In the formula, n is the number of things given to arrange and r is the number of things you're choosing. $_4P_4 = \frac{4!}{(4-4)!} = \frac{4!}{0!}$. Recall that the "!" indicates a factorial where you multiply each integer down to 1: $4! = 4 \cdot 3 \cdot 2 \cdot 1 = 24$ and $0! = 1$.

26. **B.** Because you know she has the same number of 1s and 5s, you can let x represent this amount. Similarly, you know that she has twice as many 10s as 1s, so this amount would be $2x$. The sum of these three amounts equals 52 (don't forget to multiply by the value of each bill): $1x + 5x + 10(2x) = 52$. Solving this equation tells you that $x = 2$: $1x + 5x + 20x = 52 \rightarrow 26x = 52$. Recall that x is the number of 1s and 5s, not 10s as the question is asking. You need to double this amount, so Choice (B) is the correct answer.

Part 2

27. **D.** Because both of these events happen in a reliable pattern, you can either make a list or determine the lowest common denominator (LCM).

Week 1: H & N
Week 2:
Week 3:   N
Week 4: H
Week 5:   N
Week 6:
Week 7: H & N

LCM $(2, 3) = 6$. In both cases, you can see that there will be 6 weeks, Choice (D), until the two events occur in the same week again.

28. **C.** This question relies on your ability to interpret a graph and draw in prior knowledge about workout routines. Be sure to select the best answer for the situation in the problem. Because the heart rate is gradually getting lower during that time period, you can assume that Jason is not doing any labor-intensive activities, which rules out Choices (A) and (D). Similarly, you can assume that he is not stretching because that usually occurs prior to a workout, so Choice (B) does not explain what is going on either. This means that Jason is probably finished with his workout and is doing a cool down after the 40-minute mark, so Choice (C) is correct.

29. **D.** Rearranging an equation involves performing the opposite operations surrounding the wanted variable. The first thing to do is multiply both sides by d: $ad = bc^2$. Then divide both sides by b: $c^2 = \frac{ad}{b}$. If you stopped here you would have selected Choice (A). However, this is incorrect because c is not completely isolated yet — you need to take the square root of both sides: $c = \sqrt{\frac{ad}{b}}$, so Choice (D) is correct.

30. **C.** To find the inverse of a function, start by substituting y in for $f(x)$, then switch x and y. Now solve for y:

$$y = \sqrt{x-4}$$
$$x = \sqrt{y-4}$$
$$x^2 = y - 4$$
$$x^2 + 4 = y$$

This means the correct answer is Choice (C).

31. 18. Because there are 100 students and percentages are out of 100, the number of students who selected pink as their favorite color is 18.

32. A. Because you're looking for a line *perpendicular* to the given line, the new equation would have a negative reciprocal of the given slope: $m = -\frac{1}{2}$ so the new slope is $m = 2$. Because Choice (A) is the only equation with that slope, it is the correct answer. Choice (C) represents a line parallel to the given line, while Choices (B) and (D) have slopes that have no specific relationship with the given slope.

33. 21. The first thing to do is figure out how long it takes Amy to swim one lap: $12 \div 4 = 3$ minutes per lap. Because she needs to swim 7 laps, multiply 7 by 3: $7 \times 3 = 21$ minutes.

34. A. Simplify by subtracting 4 from each part of the inequality. The solution to this inequality is now $-3 < x \leq 1$, which means there should be an open circle at -3 and a closed circle at 1 with shading in between. This corresponds to Choice (A).

35. 2. The first step to solve this problem is to calculate the volume of the rectangular prism on the right: $V_{right} = lwh = 4 \cdot 4 \cdot 4 = 64$. Now look at what dimensions you're given for the rectangular prism on the left: $V_{left} = lwh = 16 \cdot 2 \cdot x = 32x$. Because the two volumes are equal: $32x = 64 \rightarrow x = 2$. This means the missing dimension is 2.

36. C. For this problem it's important to recall that a vertical line occurs when x equals a constant. Similarly, a horizontal line occurs when y equals a constant. For the vertical line, you find its value based on where it crosses the x-axis, which is 2. This means the vertical line has the equation $x = 2$. In the same way you find that the horizontal line has an equation of $y = -4$. The solution is Choice (C). If you selected Choice (A), you switched the rule of vertical and horizontal lines.

37. D. When reading the possible answers, you can eliminate Choices (A) and (B) because they're false. Now you have to choose between Choices (C) and (D). While Choice (C) is plausible, you don't have any information about the rate at which they can read, only the number of books. Checking whether Choice (D) is true, you add how many books each of them has read: $8 + 16 + 14 = 38$, which is true. Thus Choice (D) is your answer.

38. A. The first step to solving this problem is to find the total number of students in Ms. Jones's class, which is 32. Now you have to decide whether selecting two boys' names in a row without calling on the same student is dependent or independent. Because selecting the second student is influenced by whom you call on first, these events are dependent. Calculating the probability results in: $\frac{14}{32} \cdot \frac{13}{31} = \frac{7}{16} \cdot \frac{13}{31}$, which is Choice (A).

39. B. When simplifying a subtraction problem, be careful to distribute the minus sign through the entire second polynomial. This means the resulting expression is $3x^2 - 4x + 5 - x^2 + 3x - 2 = 2x^2 - x + 3$, which corresponds to Choice (B).

40. 55. Because $\overline{MP}$ is a diameter arc, MP is a semicircle which totals 180°. This means that arc NP measures 110°. Looking at the types of angle M is, you see that it's an inscribed angle. The measure of an inscribed angle equals half the measure of its intercepted arc. $\angle M = \frac{110}{2} = 55°$.

41. B. This graph most likely corresponds to a quadratic function, which is a domain of all real numbers, Choice (B). If you selected Choice (A), you found the range of the function.

42. C. The only statement that holds true for a trapezoid is Choice (C). If opposite sides and angles were congruent, you'd be looking at a parallelogram, so that eliminates Choices (A) and (B). Similarly, Choice (D) is only true for rectangles.

43. **D.** To answer this question, you can approach it two ways. You can substitute in the given values and see which one makes a false statement, or you can solve the given equation using the zero product property. Using the second method means you set each part equal to 0: $2x = 0$ $x - 3 = 0$ $x + 4 = 0$. Solving these three equations shows you that $x = 0$, $x = 3$, or $x = -4$. This means that Choice (D) is the answer because it's not part of the solution to the equation.

44. **26.** The pattern appears to be that you find the next term by adding the two previous terms in the sequence. For example, 6 was found by adding 2+4. Thus the next term in the pattern is 26.

45. **B.** First simplify the expression given to you: $(3 + 2i) - (4 - 2i) = 3 + 2i - 4 + 2i = -1 + 4i$. Because there's an "$i$" in the answer it's a complex number, so Choice (B) is correct.

46. **C.** Using the power rule for exponents you multiply the inside/outside exponents. Multiplying the exponents results in $2 \cdot \frac{1}{3} = \frac{2}{3}$, which means the answer is Choice (C), $x^{\frac{2}{3}}$.

47. **24.** Because each part of the outfit doesn't depend on another and because you're selecting one of each, you can multiply $4 \cdot 2 \cdot 3 = 24$ outfits.

48. **B.** Rotating the shaded region around the x-axis would result in a cone, Choice (B).

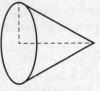

© John Wiley & Sons, Inc.

To form a cylinder, you'd need to have started with a rectangle of some kind.

49. **B.** To find the median of a data set, first put the given values in order from least to greatest: 2, 12, 14, 16, 23, 30, 37. This reveals that you had to have a number greater than 23 to have 23 as the median. Thus the answer is 42, Choice (B).

50. **A.** Because you're looking for a point halfway between the two points, you can use the midpoint formula: $(\frac{x_1 + x_2}{2}, \frac{y_1 + y_2}{2})$. Substituting in the values from the two given order pairs, you see that the dry cleaner is located at Choice (A), $(-2, 8)$. If you flipped the location of the x and y coordinates, you would have selected Choice (D). If you mistakenly subtracted the x and y values instead of adding them, you would have incorrectly selected Choice (B). Similarly, if you both flipped the x and y coordinates *and* subtracted instead of adding, you would have selected Choice (C).

51. **27 in³.** You're told that the figure is a cube, which means all its dimensions are equal: $l = w = h$. Because you're told its face has an area of 9 you can find the dimensions of the cube: $lw = 9 \rightarrow l = w = 3$. This means the volume of the cube is $V = lwh = 3 \cdot 3 \cdot 3 = 27$ in³.

52. **14.** The relationship between the sides means you can multiply each side by the same number and the relationship will hold true. In this case you can multiply all by x and add them together because that is how to calculate the perimeter: $2x + 3x + 5x = 70$. Solving the resulting equation gives you $x = 7$. However, this is not the length of the shortest side; this is the amount you multiply by 2 to get the length of the shortest side: 14.

Answers for Section 4: **Social Studies**

1. **C.** The challenge was that it's up to the people to uphold and maintain the freedoms of this country. Key words from the document include "unfinished work," "dedicated," "devotion," "highly resolve," and "government of the people, by the people, for the people."

2. **A.** After the immigration law was changed to abolish the quota system that began in 1924, immigration rates by decade grew dramatically, with a huge spike of immigration in the 1990s.

3. **B.** That women needed to take up the fight for equality and voting rights (that would not be accomplished until the 19th amendment in 1920).

4. **C.** Executive Order 9066 forced the relocation of 120,000 Japanese in America (two-thirds were U.S. citizens) to ten different military internment camps. This lasted until nearly the end of World War II.

5. **B.** Rockefeller was able to create a huge monopoly with Standard Oil, controlling 90 percent of the petroleum production and sales in the U.S. He forced out competition and managed price controls with production, transportation, and sale of his product.

6. **A.** As a result of FDR's New Deal plan, the federal government began to take an increasing role in the economy and establish government programs to benefit people.

7. **C.** 1968 was a tumultuous year for the U.S. with the ongoing conflict in Vietnam, the assassination of two leaders (MLK and RFK), and Nixon's campaign pledge of a "secret plan to end the war on Vietnam." After the Tet Offensive in February of 1968, the public's perception of the Vietnam War began to plummet.

8. **B.** By making the sale of alcohol legal again the government could gain revenue from the sales taxes on alcoholic beverages, which is the main economic reason that the federal government was in favor of repealing the Eighteenth Amendment. Choice (A) is true but is not an *economic* reason so it must be rejected. Choice (C) is also true but is not the *main* economic reason. Choice (D) is hilarious (and probably true!) but should be rejected.

9. **C.** President LBJ's speech was intended to urge Congress to move on legislation securing voting rights for blacks.

10. **D.** Free elections didn't happen in the Eastern Bloc countries in Europe — they became controlled by the communist government of the USSR. Other challenges around the world escalated tensions between the U.S. and communist actions in Europe and Asia.

11. **B.** Although many laws began to be in place for buildings in the workplace, no changes were made about immigrant workers and working conditions. Worker abuses and working conditions continued to be major targets of union activity.

12. **D.** The baby boomer generation was born between 1946 and 1964, resulting in a massive population bubble in society and a big emphasis on families and family values.

13. **A.** Government power in the Constitution is divided into three distinct branches, each with distinctive roles to divide power.

14. **A.** U.S. citizenship is defined as anyone born in the U.S. is an automatic citizen.

15. **B.** This is often known as the "necessary and proper" clause that if Congress deems a law to be necessary, it can craft legislation for a bill to become a law.

16. **C.** Voting rights were expanded by these amendments not restricted. Choice (D) is a true statement since African-American men were able to vote with the passing of the 15th Amendment; hence you can reject this answer. Choice (A) can be rejected since women could now vote due to the passing of the 19th Amendment (women). Choice (B) can also be rejected since younger people could now vote due to the 26th Amendment.

17. **C.** The 15th Amendment only applied to *men*. Women of all races were still not allowed to vote until the passing of the 19th Amendment 50 years later.

18. **B.** Miranda Rights include protection from self-incrimination and allow for counsel to be provided.

19. **C.** To overturn a presidential veto, a two-thirds vote is needed in both houses of Congress.

20. **A.** The NCLB legislation aims for higher standards in schools, increased testing, and more aid for education programs.

21. **D.** Being impeached simply means an accusation of a crime that may have been committed — a person is not removed from office until a trial is held.

22. **C.** By making lifetime appointments to the Supreme Court, the president has an opportunity to extend his legacy once out of office at the end of his term.

23. **B.** Reagan took 45 states and Carter took 5 states and the District of Columbia with electoral votes.

24. **A.** Flag burning was deemed to be "protected speech" despite how people feel about the actual burning of an American flag.

25. **A.** Depending on the severity of inflation, most consumers will be making some choices on spending, which may mean buying less, switching to alternatives, and so on.

26. **D.** Government at all three levels — federal, state, and local — can set tax rates and make changes to those rates.

27. **C.** Capitalism depends on production and trade with a consumer-based market economy.

28. **C.** The free enterprise system depends on physical capital, natural resources, human capital, and trends in the marketplace. These capital resources and trends change over time. An entrepreneur needs to track these items and changes to make the business successful.

29. **C.** Labor unions are involved in collective bargaining to get better working conditions for all their members.

30. **A.** Just having a high school diploma is simply not enough to increase your earning potential over a lifetime. You must consider some form of education or training beyond high school to increase your earning potential.

31. **B.** In beginning to establish a budget, you need to track your spending over a two-week period so that you can begin to analyze spending habits to create a budget that works for you.

32. **A.** Religious beliefs were one of the major things exchanged along the Silk Road. Christianity, Buddhism, Hinduism, and other religious beliefs were shared from India to other regions, which helped spread those religious beliefs to other regions. This trade route was significant for the exchange of goods and ideas along the route.

33. **D.** Reagan took the opportunity at the Brandenburg Gate in 1987 to encourage democratic reform in Eastern Europe, and within a little over two years, major democratic reform swept across the region, including the collapse of the Berlin Wall in November 1989.

34. **C.** The two bombs that hit Hiroshima and Nagasaki on August 6 and 9 in 1945 brought an end to the war in the Pacific by August 15 and finally ended the overall conflict of World War II.

35. **A.** A free market economy values individualism, which encourages people to become entrepreneurs.

36. **C.** The printing press allowed for millions of books to be printed and shared with the masses. This decreased dramatically the reliance on hand-written texts.

37. **C.** The increased actions of the totalitarian leaders and the lack of a response to stop their actions led to the eventual outbreak of World War II, with three of the four totalitarian leaders (Germany, Italy, and Japan) forming an alliance in the war.

38. **A.** The new weapons of warfare and military strategies greatly added to the increased casualty rates of World War I, both in military and civilian casualty rates.

39. **B.** OPEC continues to control production and the output of petroleum and greatly influences economic trends around the world.

40. **B.** China's problem is no longer spiraling out of control because of the one child policy, but it has created a major population imbalance of the ratio of boys-girls, along with the need to replace workers as older workers retire.

41. **B.** The arid regions are desert regions in Asia, the Middle East, Australia, and Northern Africa. Brazil is in a tropical zone.

42. **D.** Cities fight for the honor of hosting the Olympics to enhance their reputation as international centers of the arts and culture. The question stem tells you that hosting the Olympics is costly, so Choice (A) is incorrect. Although the sporting facilities may be used after the Games are over, this is not the main benefit to the city, so Choice (B) is not the best answer. Most cities are not looking for additional residents, so Choice (C) can be rejected.

43. **A.** A macroeconomist focuses on the large picture of the economy, including causes of unemployment.

44. **B.** Despite where a majority of people are located in the world today, communication of news items is seemingly becoming more "instant" so that not only in large urban centers but also in remote parts of the world people are finding connections to communication to get their message out and connect with others.

45. **B.** Cultural items still make people groups around the world today distinct from one another and are important in preserving the history and culture of people groups.

46. **A.** When the USSR dissolved in 1991 and formed a confederation for a brief time, it eventually resulted in the creation of several independent countries in the region largely based on ethnic groups.

47. **C.** New immigrants and refugees around the world today are still facing discrimination and hardship in their new countries. Immigration and refugee rates are still on the rise and are evident in many news items being reported online, in print, and on television news programs today.

Answers for Section 5: **Science**

1. **C.** When the pendulum bob is released from its highest point, its potential energy is converted into kinetic energy, making Choice (C) the right answer. The conservation of energy tells you that energy can't be created or destroyed, so Choice (A) is incorrect. The potential energy isn't converted into light energy in this case, so Choice (B) is wrong. Because potential energy depends on height, the bob will lose potential energy as it swings downward, making Choice (D) incorrect. Only mechanical energy is conserved (not potential energy).

2. **B.** The correct order is **potential, minimum, kinetic, maximum.** When the pendulum bob is at the top of its swing, it has maximum **potential** energy and **minimum** speed, whereas when the pendulum bob is at its lowest point, it has maximum **kinetic** energy and **maximum** speed.

3. **C.** The mass of the bob is 2 kg, and the maximum height is 5 m, and gravity = 10 m/s/s, so the PE = 100J. The potential energy gets converted into KE, so you can calculate the speed of the bob at the lowest position as shown here:

   loss In PE = gain in KE
   $$mgh = \frac{1}{2}mv^2$$
   $$(2)(10)(5) = \frac{1}{2}(2)(v^2)$$
   $$100 = v^2$$
   $$v = 10$$

4. **A.** Solar eclipses are caused by the moon passing between the Earth and the sun, which casts a shadow on the Earth, so Choice (A) is correct. The sun is much farther away than the moon and therefore can't pass between the Earth and the moon, eliminating Choice (B). The Earth does pass between the sun and the moon, but this would not cast a shadow on the Earth, so Choice (C) is wrong. The moon does not rotate, making Choice (D) a false statement.

5. **A.** All regular cells divide in the process called *mitosis,* but only sex cells are produced by the process called *meiosis.* So the correct answer must include meiosis and hence, should be either Choice (A) or (B). Because the sex cells contain only half of the parent's genetic material (haploid) and the question tells you the parent cells have 46 chromosomes, half of 46 is 23. Choice (A) is correct.

6. **D.** The rock cycle describes the processes by which the Earth recycles rocks by transforming them from one type to another, making Choice (D) the correct answer.

7. **B.** Fossils are produced when a plant or animal dies and its remains become buried in mud, silt, or sand, which forms sedimentary rock as the former plant or animal becomes compacted, making Choice (B) correct.

8. A. According to the diagram, magma forms when either igneous rock or metamorphic rock melts to form molten rock beneath the Earth's surface, making Choice (A) the correct answer.

9. C. The pigment helps the lizard to blend into its surroundings, making it very difficult for the lizard's prey to see the lizard. Then suddenly, SMACK! The lizard takes the prey with its tongue, which is an example of predation (predators hunting prey), making Choice (C) the correct answer. Lizards reproduce sexually so Choice (B) asexual reproduction is incorrect. Blending into their surrounding doesn't help them find a mate, so the answer is not Choice (A). Respiration, Choice (D), doesn't have anything to do with the color of the lizard.

10. D. You can calculate the unbalanced force acting on each car by multiplying the mass by the acceleration (using $F = ma$). The red and blue cars have the same unbalanced force of 9N, so you can eliminate Choices (A) and (B). The green car is not accelerating, so there's no unbalanced force acting on it, which eliminates Choice (C). That leaves the purple car, which has an unbalanced force of 12N acting on it, making Choice (D) the correct answer.

11. D. The green car has the smallest final momentum, and the green car has the greatest inertia. The momentum of an object is given by the mass multiplied by the velocity ($p = mv$). The green car has a final velocity of zero, which means it has zero momentum, making it the correct answer to the first blank. The inertia of an object tells you how easy or difficult it is to change the object's state of motion. Linear inertia depends only upon the mass of the object, so you're looking for the car with the largest mass (the green car again); hence the correct answer is Choice (D).

12. C. The red and the blue car both have an unbalanced force of 9 N acting on them ($F = ma$). Their final momentum is also the same, 18 kg/m/s ($p = mv$), making Choice (C) the correct answer.

13. B. The conservation of momentum states that the total momentum before the collision is equal to the total momentum after the collision. In this case, before the collision the blue car has a momentum of 18 kg/m/s ($p = mv$), whereas the green car has zero momentum. After the collision, the blue car has transferred all its momentum to the green car, so the green car now has a momentum of 18 kg/m/s. Because the green car has a mass of 9 kg, that means its velocity must be 2 m/s ($p = mv$), making Choice (B) the right answer.

14. B. X-rays can penetrate matter, so they're used during a CT scan at the hospital, making Choice (B) correct. Although gamma rays can also penetrate matter, they have higher energy, which makes them too dangerous to use on humans, so Choice (A) is wrong. Microwaves would start to cook the person being scanned, so you must reject Choice (C).

15. C. According to the diagram, the energy of the waves increases as you go from right to left. Out of the answer choices given, blue light is the farthest to the left, making it the highest energy wave of the four. Hence, Choice (C) is correct.

16. B. Electromagnetic waves all travel at the same speed, but what makes them different is the length of their wavelengths. A short wavelength makes for a high energy wave, and this makes them more dangerous. So Choices (C) and (D) are not correct. If a wave of the EMS has a long wavelength, it's unlikely to have high energy, so that makes Choice (A) incorrect and Choice (B) correct.

17. C. Although Choices (A) and (D) contain true statements, there's no support for these statements in the diagram. Gamma rays have shorter wavelengths than visible light, so Choice (B) is not true. Humans are only able to see the electromagnetic waves that are in the visible light region, which is only a small fraction of the overall spectrum; hence Choice (C) is correct.

18. **B.** The conservation of mass tells you that the number of atoms of each element must remain the same on both sides of the equation. Choices (A), (C), and (D) follow this rule, so they're correct. Choice (B) is the correct answer because it has only one carbon atom before but two carbon atoms after the reaction.

19. **D.** The Earth's inner and outer cores are both made mostly of iron. The inner core is mostly solid, whereas the outer core is mainly liquid.

20. **B.** Group 1 metals are highly reactive because it's easier to lose just one electron to gain a full outer shell; hence sodium is the most reactive out of the four answer choices.

21. **B.** The number of valence electrons is given by the group number. Oxygen is in Group 6 and therefore has 6 valence electrons.

22. **C.** Carbon is in the second row (Period 2), so it has 2 electron shells, making Choice (C) a false statement and the correct answer. Choices (A), (B), and (D) are all true statements and therefore can be rejected.

23. **D.** Fluorine is in Group 7, so it has 7 valence electrons, making Choice (C) incorrect. It is in the second row, so it has 2 energy shells, which is less that the 3 energy shells that chlorine has (Row 3), so Choice (B) is incorrect. Fluorine must have 10 neutrons because its atomic mass number (the sum of the protons and neutrons) is 19 and fluorine has 9 protons, making Choice (A) incorrect. Because fluorine already has 7 valence electrons, it only needs to gain one more electron to have a full outer shell of 8 electrons, making Choice (D) the right answer.

24. **C.** Sodium reacts with chlorine, but because sodium is a metal, it forms ionic bonds (not covalent bonds), making Choice (A) false. Magnesium won't react with argon because argon is in Group 8 and therefore already has a full outer shell (making it nonreactive), so you can reject Choice (B). Because hydrogen is nonmetallic, its atoms join together via covalent bonds, not ionic bonds, making Choice (D) a false statement. Carbon reacts with oxygen by sharing valence electrons to form covalent bonds, so Choice (C) is a true statement and the correct answer.

25. **C.** Mercury (not Venus) is the closest planet to the sun, making Choice (A) false. Jupiter is a giant gas planet, not a terrestrial planet, making Choice (B) false. The sun is much bigger than any of the planets (more than a million Earths could fit inside the sun!), so Choice (D) is a false statement. Saturn is a giant gas planet, so Choice (C) is correct.

26. **B.** Choices (A), (C), and (D) all provide evidence supporting the Big Bang theory and can therefore be rejected. Spectral analysis of star light showing a relative abundance of hydrogen and helium supports the Big Bang theory, which predicts that the first elements to be created would be the lightest ones (hydrogen and helium). This makes Choice (A) a true statement. The discovery of cosmic microwave background radiation is predicted by the Big Bang theory, so Choice (C) is true. The Doppler effect showing that starlight is redshifted supports the idea that the galaxies are all moving away from each other after the Big Bang occurred, so Choice (D) is true. Sound waves can't travel through the vacuum of space, so Choice (B) is a false statement and therefore the correct answer.

27. **B.** A solar system consists of at least one star and the planets that orbit around it, so stars are smaller than solar systems. This makes Choices (C) and (D) incorrect. A galaxy contains millions of stars and is therefore bigger than a solar system. Millions of galaxies form a cluster, so clusters are bigger than galaxies. The universe contains all the clusters (and everything else), so the universe is the largest and must come last in the list, making Choice (B) correct.

28. **B.** According to the Doppler effect, the frequency of the light emitted from moving objects will shift toward either the red end of the spectrum or the blue end (depending on the direction of motion). Objects that are moving away from Earth are redshifted. Objects that are traveling toward Earth are blueshifted, making Choice (B) the correct answer. Blueshifted light doesn't tell you how old or how hot the star is, so you can reject Choices (C) and (D).

29. **C.** If a virus were to suddenly wipe out most of the dragonfly population, more phytoplankton would survive because fewer grasshoppers would be around to eat them, making Choice (C) correct. Salamanders, frogs, and trout all eat grasshoppers, so the number of these animals would decline because one of their sources of food (the grasshopper) would be less abundant. This means that Choices (A), (B), and (D) are all incorrect.

30. **D.** Because phytoplankton are autotrophs, they produce their own food and are therefore called *producers*. Dragonflies eat the plants and are therefore *primary consumers*. The hawk is higher in the food chain and eats several other consumers, making it a *tertiary consumer*. Therefore, the phytoplankton is a producer, the dragonfly is a primary consumer, and the hawk is a tertiary consumer, making Choice (D) the correct answer.

31. **D.** The maximum number of individuals of a particular species that the ecosystem can handle is known as the *carrying capacity*, so Choice (D) is correct. Natural selection explains how species adapt and evolve to produce a greater biodiversity (variations of animals), but this doesn't answer the question stem, so you can reject Choices (A) and (B). *Predation* refers to the relationship between hunters and prey, so Choice (C) is incorrect.

32. **D.** Plants produce their own food and are therefore autotrophs, making Choice (A) a true statement and therefore not the right answer. Animals can't make their own food and must consume the energy stored in plants or other animals, so they're heterotrophs. Hence you can reject Choice (B). Primary consumers eat plants and are therefore classified as herbivores, so you can reject Choice (C). When an organism is eaten, only 10 percent of the energy stored in its body is transferred to the consumer. The rest is wasted as heat, making Choice (D) a false statement and therefore the correct answer.

33. **A.** Chloroplasts are found only in plant cells and enable the plant to produce its own food via photosynthesis, making Choice (A) correct. Only plant cells have cell walls, but these organelles are used to provide a protective outer support for the cell (not to produce food), making Choice (B) incorrect. Similarly, only plant cells have vacuoles, but these organelles are used to store nutrients (not to produce food), making Choice (C) incorrect. Both plant and animal cells have mitochondria, which are used to produce energy via cellular respiration by burning food (nor producing food), so you can reject Choice (D).

34. **C.** Because all organisms on Earth have a large percentage of their DNA identical to that of other species, this suggests that they all evolved from a single species, which supports the common ancestry theorem. Hence, Choice (A) is not the right answer. If we all have a common ancestor, it's not surprising that a lot of different animal species start out looking the same as embryos or that many different animals have similar anatomical structures. Hence, you can reject Choices (B) and (D). Although scientists believe that 99 percent of all species that have ever lived on Earth are now extinct, this doesn't give any support to the common ancestry theory, making Choice (C) the correct answer.

35. **A.** The question stem shows an alpha particle (containing 2 protons and 2 neutrons) being emitted in the nuclear reaction, making Choice (A) correct.

36. **B.** The information in the passage and the Punnett square shows that both parents have the same genotype (Tt). This means that they are both tall because they each contain the dominant allele (T), which represents tall plants. Hence, Choice (B) is correct. Choice (A) is wrong because the parent genotype would have to be (tt) to be short plants. Choice (C) is wrong because the allele for tall plants is dominant, which means that the genotype (Tt) would still result in tall plants (not medium plants). Both parents have the same genotype, so Choice (D) must be wrong.

37. **C.** Because the allele for tall plants (T) is dominant, any genotype that contains it (Tt) or (TT) will result in tall plants. The Punnett square shows that 3 out of 4 (or 75 percent) of the offspring have genotypes containing the dominant allele, making Choice (C) correct.

38. **D.** You're told in the supporting information that the allele for short plants is recessive, which mean that the offspring will only be short if its genotype is homozygous (tt). Because the offspring gets one gene from each parent, both the mother and father should have the same genotype (tt) to rule out the possibility of a dominant gene (T) being passed on to the offspring. All the answer choices except Choice (D) contain parents with at least one dominant T gene that could be passed on to the offspring making it tall.

39. **D.** You're told in the supporting information that the allele for short plants is recessive, which mean that the plant will only be short if its genotype is homozygous for the recessive gene (tt). Hence, the correct phrase should be: The allele for short plant is *recessive*, and trait is only expressed when the genotype is *homozygous*, making Choice (D) the correct answer.

40. **A.** The offspring from parents that reproduce sexually inherits a mix of traits from both parents. This leads to a greater level of genetic diversity for the species because the genes of the offspring are no longer identical to either of the parents; hence, Choice (A) is correct. In contrast, the offspring from asexual reproduction inherits genes that are identical to its parent. This does not lead to increased genetic diversity. You can eliminate Choice (B) because the number of offspring doesn't have anything to do with their genetic diversity. You can reject Choice (C) because the offspring from parents that reproduce sexually does *not* inherit brand new traits entirely unlike those of either parent (it inherits a mix of traits). Choice (D) is false because the offspring from parents that reproduce sexually inherits traits from both parents.

41. **C.** The movement of tectonic plates causes changes to the surface of the Earth but does not cause the change in seasons, so you can eliminate Choice (A). Global warming can make each season hotter than before but it doesn't cause the seasons to *change* from one to another, so Choice (B) is wrong. Many people mistakenly believe that the distance of the Earth from the sun, Choice (D), is the main factor in seasonal changes, but this is actually not as important as the tilt in the Earth, Choice (C). The earth tilt is responsible for the sun shining more on one hemisphere in summer and then shining more on the other hemisphere in winter, which results in the seasonal changes in temperature. Hence, Choice (C) is correct.

42. **C and D.** The motion of the moon and the planets is highly predictable because they have cyclic orbits that repeat themselves, so solar eclipses and the position of the moon can be predicted with great accuracy. All the other choices represent events that are unpredictable because they don't take place at regular intervals.

43. **C.** There's a lot of evidence that supports the theory that the Big Bang created the universe approximately 15 billion years ago. The Earth was created about 10 billion years after the Big Bang, making it about 5 billion years old, so Choice (C) is the correct answer. Choice (A) is the estimate given by some religious leaders, but you can reject this because the question stem asks for a scientific estimate. Also, the 6,000 years old estimate makes little sense considering the overwhelming evidence from fossils and carbon dating, which suggest the Earth is billions of years old, not thousands of years old. Choice (B) mistakes millions for billions and can therefore be rejected. Choice (D) is the estimate for the age of the universe (not the age of the Earth).

44. **D.** The lithosphere includes the upper part of the mantle and the tectonic plates that make up the surface of the Earth. The atmosphere is the layer of gas surrounding the planet but does not include the surface itself, making Choice (A) incorrect. The hydrosphere includes all the water vapor, water, and ice present on the Earth (including the oceans, rivers, and polar ice caps) but not the surface of the Earth itself, making Choice (B) incorrect. The biosphere contains all life forms on Earth (not the surface of the Earth), so Choice (C) is wrong.

45. **D.** Although all the answer choices are useful in explaining evolution, DNA had not been discovered during Darwin's time, so it could not have been part of his explanation, making Choice (D) the correct answer.

46. **B.** Positive feedback mechanism occurs when an initial change in one system leads to responses from other systems that amplify the initial change in the first system. Only Choice (B) is an example of this and hence is the correct answer.

47. **D.** Since Proxima Centauri is 4 light years away from Earth, the light from the star takes 4 years to reach the Earth.

Answer Key

Section 1: Language Arts – Reading

1. B	11. B	21. A	31. B	41. B
2. B	12. D	22. B	32. D	42. B
3. B	13. C	23. B	33. C	43. D
4. D	14. D	24. C	34. C	44. B
5. A	15. C	25. D	35. A	45. C
6. B	16. B	26. C	36. D	46. A
7. C	17. B	27. C	37. D	47. A
8. C	18. C	28. B	38. B	48. B
9. B	19. B	29. A	39. C	49. B
10. C	20. C	30. B	40. D	50. D

Section 2: Language Arts – Writing

1. A	11. B	21. C	31. D	41. D
2. C	12. C	22. A	32. A	42. D
3. B	13. D	23. D	33. C	43. C
4. D	14. C	24. C	34. A	44. A
5. C	15. C	25. B	35. C	45. D
6. B	16. D	26. A	36. D	46. A
7. A	17. A	27. B	37. B	47. B
8. B	18. A	28. C	38. A	48. C
9. A	19. B	29. D	39. B	49. A
10. A	20. C	30. B	40. A	50. C

Section 3: Mathematics

1. B	12. B	23. B	34. A	45. B
2. D	13. B	24. **11.25**	35. **2**	46. C
3. **4.17%**	14. A	25. **24**	36. C	47. **24**
4. B	15. **85**	26. B	37. D	48. B
5. A	16. A	27. D	38. A	49. B
6. B	17. D	28. C	39. B	50. A
7. C	18. D	29. D	40. **55**	51. **27 in^3**
8. A	19. A	30. C	41. B	52. **14**
9. A	20. C	31. **18**	42. C	
10. B	21. **6.71**	32. A	43. D	
11. **216**	22. C	33. **21**	44. **26**	

Section 4: Social Studies

1. C	11. B	21. D	31. B	41. B
2. A	12. D	22. C	32. A	42. D
3. B	13. A	23. B	33. D	43. A
4. C	14. A	24. A	34. C	44. B
5. B	15. B	25. A	35. A	45. B
6. A	16. C	26. D	36. C	46. A
7. C	17. C	27. C	37. C	47. C
8. B	18. B	28. C	38. A	
9. C	19. C	29. C	39. B	
10. D	20. A	30. A	40. B	

Section 5: Science

1. C	11. D	21. B	31. D	41. C
2. B	12. C	22. C	32. D	42. C and D
3. C	13. B	23. D	33. A	43. C
4. A	14. B	24. C	34. C	44. D
5. A	15. C	25. C	35. A	45. D
6. D	16. B	26. B	36. B	46. B
7. B	17. C	27. B	37. C	47. D
8. A	18. B	28. B	38. D	
9. C	19. D	29. C	39. D	
10. D	20. B	30. D	40. A	

The Part of Tens

IN THIS CHAPTER

Following some tips and strategies to study for the TASC

Pacing yourself on the test and double-checking your answers

Avoiding mistakes that can sink your TASC score

Chapter 27

Ten Ways to Maximize Your Score

I f you consider yourself to be a poor test-taker, then this chapter is for you. Passing the TASC exam requires more than just knowing the content of each subject well. You also need to know how to take the test itself. You've probably heard the phrases "book smart" and "street smart"; well, achieving a high score on the TASC requires you to be "test smart."

In this chapter, we cover the strategies that strong test-takers adopt to maximize their chances of success. I also point out how to avoid the common mistakes that poor test-takers often make that sink their scores. The ten tips listed here will go a long way toward sharpening your skills and helping you to achieve the score you deserve on the TASC.

Stick to a Regular Study Plan

If you're serious about getting your TASC diploma, then you need to get serious about studying. So in the weeks before your scheduled test date, plan out a reasonable, achievable study schedule and stick to it. Take a practice test to determine which subjects or topics are your weak points and assign enough time in your schedule to cover them thoroughly. Make sure that your study goals are realistic — if you try to do too much too soon, you may fall so far behind that you end up abandoning your schedule altogether. So plan to take one day off per week from studying; it will help you to relax and give you something to look forward to at the end of the week.

Focus! Focus! Focus!

Set aside blocks of study time during which you won't be disturbed by friends or family members. Avoid distractions when studying; turn off your cellphone, ignore your email, and avoid browsing the web (which will suck away your precious study time faster than a black hole!). Don't skip any planned study sessions to accept invitations to hang out with friends. Skipping a session or two may not seem like a big deal at first, but it's the start of a slippery slope. So make studying your top priority and stick to your schedule. This may sound like hard work (and it is!), but it will all be worth it in the end when you proudly hang that TASC diploma on your wall.

Take a Mock Exam (or Two, or Three!)

Strong test-takers know exactly what to expect when they enter the testing room, and they're never surprised by the structure of the questions or the content of the exam. Test day should not be the moment when you "discover" that the TASC contains a science section or that you're expected to write essays, for example. The best way to become familiar with the layout and content of the TASC is to take practice tests. Familiarize yourself with the types of questions (multiple choice, gridded response, constructed response, essays, and so on) that appear in each section of the test and practice answering them within the allotted time. Practice makes perfect, so the more mock exams you take, the better your final score will be.

Don't Forget Your Name

WARNING

By "don't forget your name," I don't mean to imply that you may literally forget who you are. I mean don't forget to put your name on your answer booklet. You would be horrified to learn how many students, in the past, have handed in their answers without writing their names on them. (No points for guessing how well those geniuses did!) Listen carefully to the directions that the proctor gives you before the exam begins, and don't be afraid to ask questions if you're unsure how to fill in the identification page of your answer booklet (or the identification screen for the online version of the test). Always follow the proctor's instructions; if you don't, you run the risk of being disqualified and sent home, scoreless and miserable.

Make Time Your Friend

Keep an eye on the clock and make sure that you pace yourself accordingly so you don't start to fall behind on any section. Set yourself reasonable targets and stick to them. For example, when you've used up half of the available time for a particular section, you should have completed approximately half of that section's questions. Try to save a few minutes at the end of the test to check your answers; make sure that you've selected the correct bubble in your answer booklet that corresponds to your intended answer to each question.

Give Them What They Want

No matter how well you understand each topic, if you don't give the TASC-writers what they ask for, you won't score any points for your answer. Always double-check to make sure you've answered the question being asked. This is particularly important for the essay section. If you stray off topic or misunderstand the main point of the essay prompt, you'll end up with a zero score, no matter how well written your essay may be.

Don't Leave Any Questions Blank

REMEMBER

Because there's no penalty for wrong answers on the TASC, you would have to be crazy to leave any questions unanswered. Although guessing should always be the last resort, it's a whole lot better than throwing points away by leaving a question blank. Even if you have no idea what the right answer may be, try to eliminate one or two unlikely answers and then make an educated guess and move on to the next question. Let me repeat this one more time just to be clear — there's simply no excuse for leaving any question unanswered on the TASC exam.

Write Legibly

If you're taking the paper version of the TASC exam, make sure that your handwriting for the essay section is legible. No one is expecting you to be the next J. K. Rowling, but if your handwriting looks like a drunken spider fell into an inkwell and then staggered home across your page, you may be in trouble. Keep in mind that the people marking your essay have to read hundreds of pages per day, so they're probably not going to spend extra time trying to decipher a page full of unintelligible scrawl (unless they're interested in hieroglyphics!). If the markers can't read what you've written, your essay will receive a zero score, so make sure that your handwriting doesn't let you down. If your handwriting is truly awful, consider taking the computerized version of the test instead (hopefully, your typing is legible!).

Don't Leave Early

TIP

Want to know a secret that separates strong test-takers from poor test-takers? Strong test-takers never leave the exam early. Instead, they use every single minute of the allowed time to check their answers to make sure that they haven't missed anything important. The TASC is a long exam, and it's understandable that, after weeks of studying, you're probably itching to get back to your real life, but try to be patient just a little longer. Make the most of the time available and go back to any questions that you may have skipped or guessed the answers to. Reread the questions carefully to make sure that you didn't miss any crucial information (or accidentally miss an entire page of the test!). This simple strategy can make all the difference between achieving a passing grade and having to do the whole thing again.

Keep Calm and Carry On

If you come across a question that you can't answer, don't panic. Simply do what the British did during World War II — keep calm and carry on. Don't spend too much time on any question, particularly one that you probably don't know the answer to. Instead, take a deep breath and make your best educated guess, and then move on to the next question. You can always come back and check it later if you have time.

Chapter 28

Ten Ways to Work through Test Jitters

Have you ever had this common nightmare? It's test day, but your alarm didn't go off. You wake up with a headache (from overdoing it at last night's TASC Stinks party) and now you're running late, so you have to skip breakfast. You put on the only clean T-shirt you have left (the one with the itchy label that drives you crazy) and begin searching for your car keys and photo ID. You eventually find them buried beneath a mountain of dirty clothes, along with your calculator (whose batteries died last summer). You set off toward the test center but you've never been there before, so you get lost several times along the way. You finally arrive, in full panic mode. You have no idea which room you're supposed to be in so you end up trying every door in the entire building before finding the right one. You enter the testing room just in time to hear the proctor announce that the exam has ended. You howl in dismay, and everyone turns around to stare at you. People are sniggering and pointing. You look down and discover that you're not wearing any pants!

Okay, this amusing example may be a little exaggerated, but it serves to illustrate some of the common mistakes that can throw you off your game and ruin your chances of success, even before putting pen to paper. The ten tips in this chapter show you how to avoid these pitfalls and get into the right frame of mind to help test day go as smoothly as possible.

Prepare Your Bag the Night Before

I may not be a Boy Scout, but their motto, "Be prepared," still comes in pretty handy when trying to reduce those pre-test jitters. Prepare your bag the night before and make sure that you have everything — admission ticket, photo ID, car keys, pens, pencils, good eraser, calculator (with fresh batteries), watch, snacks, and anything else you may need for the test. Knowing that you have everything packed and ready to go will allow you to relax and may even help you get a good night's sleep since your mind won't be working overtime worrying if you've forgotten something important.

Set Your Alarm(s)

It may seem a bit obvious to advise you to set your alarm clock, but you'd be surprised how many students fail their TASC exam simply because they slept in late. "My alarm didn't go off" has to rank up there with "The dog ate my homework" as one of the lamest excuses ever, so why leave things to chance? Why not set your alarm clock as well as the alarm on your phone? And maybe even set the alarm on your computer or tablet as well. That way, you can go to bed safe in the knowledge that if one alarm fails to go off, at least you'll still have the others there to wake you. Don't you just love simple solutions?

Relax and Get Plenty of ZZZZ's

A good night's sleep can make all the difference to your performance on test day, so make sure that you go to bed at a reasonable time and get plenty of rest the night before. Spend the evening doing something relaxing — go to the movies, head to the gym for a workout, or get your yoga on — anything that will help take your mind off tomorrow's exam. On the other hand, don't relax *too* much — you don't want to be out partying until 2 a.m., for example. You'll have plenty of time to catch up on your social life after you get your TASC diploma.

Don't Cram the Night Before

WARNING

Try not to fall into the trap of staying up late the night before for a last-minute cramming session. Pulling an all-nighter just before the test won't improve your score; it will only confuse you and leave you feeling exhausted the next morning, unable to focus properly or perform at your best. Besides, if you've followed your study plan, you can sit back, take a well-earned rest, and wake up on test day feeling as fresh as a daisy, ready to take on the world (or at least the TASC exam!).

Eat a Healthy Breakfast

Your brain needs food to function properly, so it's essential to eat a healthy breakfast on test day. Choose foods that are rich in proteins and carbohydrates to help maintain your stamina. Avoid sugary foods or fried foods that may give you a quick burst of energy initially but leave you feeling sleepy afterward.

TIP

The TASC is a long exam, so bring snacks to nibble on throughout the test. Note that some foods tend to increase anxiety; these include artificial sweeteners, soda, candy, coffee, and chocolate. So rather than reaching for your favorite candy bar and soda, it may be better to bring fresh fruits and vegetables, which are not only tasty and nutritious but also help to relieve stress. Also, try to avoid caffeinated drinks — you don't want to be running to the bathroom every ten minutes!

Wear Comfortable Clothing

When you prepare your bag the night before, pick out the outfit you plan to wear the next day. Dress comfortably, preferably in layers, so you can adjust to the temperature of the testing room if it happens to be too cold or too hot. Remember, test day isn't the right time to try out your new skin-tight jeans or that waist training corset you just bought. Uncomfortable clothing can be a real distraction, so don't wear scratchy materials or anything so tight that it could cut off your circulation. After all, you'll be sitting in the same position behind a desk for several hours — not strutting your stuff on the catwalk!

Visit the Test Center Beforehand

If you're unfamiliar with the location of the test center, consider doing a trial run there a few days before your scheduled exam. This will help you determine the best route to take and the exact location of the testing room. Then, when the big day comes, you'll already know exactly where to go and how long it takes to get there so you can arrive relaxed, with plenty of time to spare. After all, there's only a limited amount of time allocated for each section of the TASC, so you don't want to waste any of it running around like a headless chicken trying to find the right testing room (or even the right building!).

Arrive Early

Taking a standardized test can be pretty intimidating, even at the best of times, so the last thing you want to do is stress yourself out by arriving late. Luckily, this rookie mistake can be easily avoided. If you follow the other tips in this chapter, then your test day should go something like this: You wake up feeling refreshed from a good night's sleep and switch off your three alarm clocks. After eating a healthy breakfast and putting on your most comfortable clothes, you grab your bag (which contains everything you need) and head off toward the test center. Because you already know exactly where to go, you arrive at the testing room with plenty of time to spare. After mentally picking out your seat for the exam, you relax, knowing that you already have a big advantage over all the newbies who will arrive late in various states of panic.

Avoid Distractions

Avoiding distractions is the key to being able to focus during the exam, so when you enter the testing room, select a desk that's away from the windows or doors, and preferably away from your friends. In fact, it's a good idea to let your friends know that you plan to ignore them for the duration of the test. Tell them it's nothing personal but that you simply want to collect your thoughts and prepare mentally for the task ahead. Panic is contagious, so if people around you are beginning to freak out, move away from them — they won't do you any favors. Stay focused and stay positive.

Have Confidence in Yourself

Everyone feels a little anxious when taking standardized tests, but the tips in this chapter should help you stay positive and keep that anxiety at bay. There's simply nothing better at calming test jitters than knowing that you're well prepared for the exam. You've studied hard over the past few weeks, so think of this as an opportunity to show how much you really know. Have confidence in yourself — you can do this!

Index

Constitutional Convention, 174

constructed response question format, 10

consumer goods, 224

consumers (in ecosystem), 253

consumers (in marketplace), 225

continental drift, 271

convection, 247

convection currents, 270

convergent boundaries, 271

Copernicus, 191

correlation, 159

cosine (cos), 152

cosmic microwave background (CMB) radiation, 268

cosmological distances, 262

cost-benefit analysis, 223

counting (natural) numbers, 86, 88

covalent bonds, 239

crashes (economic), 180, 228

credit scores, 226

Crick, Francis, 255

Crusades, 189

crust, 270

cups, 162

cylinders, volume of, 149

cytoplasm, 250

D

da Gama, Vasco, 191

da Vinci, Leonardo, 190

dams, 219

Dark Ages (Medieval period), 188

Darwin, Charles, 260

Davis, Jefferson, 176

D-Day invasion, 181, 194

debt, 226

decimals

converting fractions to, 90

converting percentages to, 91

converting to fractions, 90–91

Declaration of Independence, 173, 200–201

decomposers, 253

decreasing functions, 127–128

deficits, 228

Democratic Party, 210–211

dependent (subordinate) clauses, 51–52

dependent events, 167

dependent solutions, 108

depressions (economic), 228

descending order, 91

descriptive word placement, 60

diameter, 146

digestive system, 251

Digital History website, 172

dilations, 152

dimensional analysis (units of measure), 91–93

diploid cells, 256

distribution method, 112

distribution rules, 84

distributive property, 96–97

divergent boundaries, 271–272

DNA, 255–256

domains, 123, 128–129

domain-specific words, 36–37

dominant traits, 257

Doppler effect, 267

drag and drop question format, 10

Dred Scott v. Sandford case, 176, 207

Dust Bowl, 180

dwarf planets, 264

dynamic systems, 275–276

E

early civilizations, 185–188

Earth science

carbon cycle, 273–274

dynamic systems, 275–276

human interactions with environment, 278–279

plate tectonics, 270–272

rock cycle, 274–275

spheres, 271

structure of Earth, 269–270

water cycle, 272–273

weather and climate, 276–279

economics

defined, 222

foreign policy, 230–231

international trade, 230–231

macroeconomics, 226–228

market types, 225

microeconomics, 225–226

Gulf of Tonkin Resolution, 182
Gulf War, 184, 197
Gutenberg, Johann, 190

H

Hamlet (Shakespeare), 33
Hancock, John, 200
haploid cells, 256
Harper's Ferry, 176
Hart, Russell, 24–25
heat transfer, 246–247
Hebrew (Israelite) civilization, 186–187
Henry VIII, 191
herbivores, 253
heterogeneous, 257–258
heterotrophs, 252
Hinduism, 186
Hirohito, 194
Hiroshima, 181, 195
histograms, 155–157
historical maps, 216
Hitler, Adolph, 181, 194
Hobbes, Thomas, 191
Holocaust, 194, 220
Holy Roman Empire, 189
homogeneous, 257–258
homographs, 72
homonyms, 72
homophones, 74–75
Hoover, Herbert, 180
horizontal method, 111
House of Representatives, 203–204
human body systems, 251
Hundred Years War, 190
Hurricane Katrina, 184, 220
Hussein, Saddam, 184, 197
hydrosphere, 271–272
hyperbole, 36
hypotenuse, 152

I

"i" before "e" except after "c," 67
"I Have a Dream" speech (King), 183
igneous rocks, 274–275
immigration, 178–179, 220
immune system, 251

imperialism, 193
income tax, 229
inconsistent solutions, 108
increasing functions, 127
independent clauses, 51
independent events, 166–167
index, 85
India
  ancient civilization, 185–186
  caste system, 187
indulgences, 190
Industrial Revolution, 192
inequalities
  does not equal, 103–104
  graphing, 119–121
  linear, 103
  quadratic, 104–105
  rational, 105–106
  symbols for, 102
inertia, 243
inflation, 226, 228
informative (explanatory) essays, 77, 79
inheritance, 257–258
inscribed angle, 147
insulators, 248
integers, 87–88
integumentary system, 251
intercepts, 129–130
interest, 226
interjections, 34, 46
International Space Station, 218
intersection of sets, 163–164
intersects, 142
ionic bonds, 239
ions, 239
Iranian hostage crisis, 184
Iraq War, 184, 197
iron age, 187
iron curtain, 195
irony, 32–33
irrational numbers, 85, 87–88
ISIS, 197, 222
Islam, 188
isosceles triangles, 144
isotopes, 236
Israeli-Palestinian conflict, 196
Israelite (Hebrew) civilization, 186–187

J

Japanese-American internment camps, 181
Jefferson, Thomas, 173, 199–200
Jim Crow laws, 178, 209
Johnson, Andrew, 177
Johnson, Lyndon B., 182–184
judicial branch, 202, 204

K

Kennedy, John F., 182–183, 208, 212
Kim Il Sung, 182, 196
kinetic energy (KE), 245
King, Martin Luther, 21, 183–184
KKK, 178, 209
Korean War, 182, 196
Kublai Khan, 189

L

labor, 227–228
labor unions, 228
laissez-faire economics, 192, 227
Language Arts-Reading test
  academic words, 36–37
  analyzing two or more texts, 37–38
  argument, 27–28
  domain-specific words, 36–37
  figurative language, 35–36
  interpreting words and phrases in context, 34, 37
  key supporting details and ideas, 23–25
  literary devices, 32–33
  number of questions, 9, 11, 283, 371
  overview, 9
  parts of speech, 34–35
  passing scores, 12
  practice test answers and explanations, 345–349, 369, 435–439, 459
  practice test questions, 287–300, 375–387
  purpose, 33
  structure, 28–31
  themes and main ideas, 19–23
  time limit, 9, 11, 283, 371
  topics included in, 9, 11
  types of questions, 9
Language Arts-Writing test
  avoiding grammatical errors, 53–64
  capitalization, 65–66
  essays, 77–80
  number of questions, 9, 11, 283, 371
  overview, 9
  parts of speech, 41–46
  passing scores, 12
  practice test answers and explanations, 350–355, 369, 439–443, 459
  practice test questions, 301–311, 388–398
  punctuation, 66–67
  sentence construction, 46–52
  spelling, 67–69
  time limit, 9, 11, 283, 371
  topics included in, 9, 11
  types of questions, 9
  word usage, 72–76
large-print version of TASC, 7
latitude, 216–217
League of Nations, 179
least common denominators (LCDs), 90
Lee, Robert E., 177
legislative branch, 202–204
Lenin, Vladimir, 194
Lewinsky, Monica, 184
Lewis and Clark expedition, 175
life science
  cell structure, 249–250
  ecosystems, 252–254
  evolution, 258–260
  human body systems, 251
  photosynthesis, 251–252
  reproduction, 255–257
  respiration, 252
  traits and inheritance, 257–258
light years, 262
like terms, 96
Lincoln, Abraham, 175–177
linear equations, 99
linear functions
  defined, 131
  graphing, 114–117
  identifying from graphs or tables, 131–134
linear inequalities, 103
lines
  in circles, 146
  defined, 141
  parallel, 142–143
  perpendicular, 143

metals, 219

metamorphic rocks, 274–275

metaphors, 35

Michelangelo, 190

microeconomics
  bankruptcy, 226
  budgeting, 225–226
  debt, 226
  defined, 225

Middle Ages, 188–190

middlemen, 225

mid-ocean ridges, 271

militarism, 192

Milky Way, 264

Mill, John Stuart, 200

minerals, 219

minor arc, 146

Miranda v. Arizona case, 208

Missouri Compromise, 174–175

mitochondria, 250

mitosis, 255

mode, 160–161

momentum, 244–245

monomials
  box method of multiplying, 113
  classification of, 111
  defined, 110
  distribution method of multiplying, 112

monopolies, 225

Montesquieu, 191, 200

Montgomery Bus Boycott, 183

Moon landing, 182

Morgan, J. P., 178

Mott, Lucretia, 175

Mount St. Helens, 221

Muhammad, 188

multicellular organisms, 249

multiple-select response question format, 10–11

multiplicative identity, 96

multiplicative inverse, 96

multistep equations, 97–99

muscular system, 251

Mussolini, Benito, 194

mutually exclusive events, 166

N

NAFTA (North American Free Trade Agreement), 231

Nagasaki, 181, 195

Napoleon, 192

National Federation of Independent Businesses v. Sebelius case, 208

nationalism, 192

nation-states, 189

Native Americans, 220

NATO (North Atlantic Treaty Organization), 195

natural (counting) numbers, 86, 88

natural gas, 219

natural logs, 138

natural resources, 218–219

natural selection, 260

negative exponent rules, 84

nervous system, 251

neutral substances, 241

neutrons, 236

New Deal, 180

New York Times Co. v. United States case, 208

Newton, Isaac, 191

Newton's laws of motion, 243–244

Nixon, Richard, 183–184, 196, 208, 212

non-rigid transformations, 152

normal reaction force, 244

North American Free Trade Agreement (NAFTA), 231

North Atlantic Treaty Organization (NATO), 195

nouns
  defined, 34, 41–42
  plural, 56–57
  proper, 42
  as subject/object of sentence, 42, 47–48

nuclear fission, 237

nuclear fusion, 237, 262

nuclear weapons, 181–182, 195, 237

nucleus (atomic), 236

nucleus (cellular), 250

O

Obama, Barack, 184, 197, 213

object of sentence, 47–48, 64

About the Authors

Dr. Stuart Donnelly has prepared students for the TASC and GED, both academically and emotionally, for the past two decades. After he was awarded his PhD in mathematics from Oxford University at the age of 25, Dr. Donnelly moved to Hong Kong, where he established the territory's most successful tutoring service. Upon his return to the United States in 1998, he founded *Tutors of Oxford NYC* and *Doctor MCAT*, which specialize in providing the finest quality one-on-one tutoring available in New York City. With over 20 years of private tutoring and teaching experience at all levels, including teaching at both George Washington University and Western Connecticut University, Dr. Donnelly is considered by many leading educators to be one of the most experienced and qualified private tutors in the country. Many of his students have been admitted to some of the world's leading schools and universities. Stuart lives on the Upper East Side of Manhattan with his wife and young son.

Nicole Hersey is a Lecturer of Mathematics and Education at the University of Rhode Island. She currently holds a Master's degree in Secondary Education from the University of Rhode Island. Her scholarship focuses on the learning of mathematics, mathematical thinking, and pedagogical content knowledge.

Ron Olson is a high school teacher with over 33 years of teaching experience. He is a National Board Certified Social Studies Teacher (2007) and holds a MA degree in Secondary Education from Adams State University in Alamosa, Colorado (1993) and a BS degree in Education with a History Major and English Minor from New Mexico State University in Las Cruces, New Mexico (1981). He has experience teaching Advanced Placement U.S. History and Advanced Placement U.S. Government in addition to working as a workshop consultant for The College Board. He is currently working at Clover Park High School in Lakewood, Washington teaching Advanced Placement Government, Civics, and Contemporary World Problems and is the National Honor Society advisor. He lives in Bonney Lake, Washington with his two cocker spaniels and enjoys cooking and photography in his free time.

Kathy Peno, PhD, is Professor of Adult Education at the University of Rhode Island where she coordinates the Adult Education Master's Program and prepares adult educators in the military, health care fields (including nursing, pharmacy, and dentistry), and in corporate and higher education organizations. She also teaches and advises doctoral students in the Adult and Higher Education specialization for the joint PhD program between Rhode Island College and the University of Rhode Island. She holds a Master's Degree and a PhD in Adult Learning and Human Resource Development from the University of Connecticut. Her scholarship focuses on professional learning and skill development from novice to expert with an emphasis on the role of mentoring. She has written, consulted, and presented extensively on workforce development, professional development, and mentoring as a vehicle for continuous performance improvement in organizations.

Shannon Reed is an essayist, humorist, and novelist. She taught secondary English in New York City for eight years and is currently a professor at the University of Pittsburgh. Shannon holds a BFA in Theatre with a minor in writing from Otterbein College; an M.A. in Educational Theatre/Secondary English from NYU; and an M.F.A in Creative Writing: Fiction from the University of Pittsburgh. She also holds a New York state teaching certificate in English: 7–12.

Connie Sergent, MEd, earned a BS in Geology/Geophysics from the University of Arkansas at Fayetteville. She completed requirements for a Science Composite Teaching Certificate while pursuing a MS in Science Education in Biology at Texas Woman's University in Denton. She completed graduate school at Our Lady of the Lake University in San Antonio, receiving a MEd in Curriculum and Instruction in Science Integration. Connie presently has over 25 years of high school science teaching experience teaching everything from Biology, Chemistry, Geology, Meteorology, and Oceanography to Advanced Placement Environmental Science. Along with being a classroom teacher, Connie is also a Consultant for the College Board and National Math and Science Initiative where she helps train numerous new teachers every year. In addition to this publication, she has contributing author credits for a number of science products and Environmental Science textbook products.

Publisher's Acknowledgments

Executive Editor: Lindsay Sandman Lefevere
Project Editor: Tim Gallan
Copy Editor: Todd Lothery
Art Coordinator: Alicia B. South

Production Editor: Antony Sami
Cover Image: © vstock / Getty Images, Inc.